CHURCH TRANSFORMATION THROUGH TURBULENCE

PROPELLED ORCHESTRATION OF CHURCH AND NATIONAL CONCERNS

DR. DAVID M. GITHII

AUTOBIOGRAPHY

Moderator's Tenure in Office

PROPELLED ORCHESTRATION OF
CHURCH AND NATIONAL CONCERNS

Dr. David M. Githii

First published in Kenya in 2025

Cover designed by Winstone Sharrad

Photo Credits: Pixabay.com

Manuscript typing- Tabitha Njeri

Book edited by Winstone Sharrad

Printed by DPL

For any book order or inquiries, the author can be reached through Email: dgithii@yahoo.com.

Local Phone contact (Kenya) 0722-659-252.

International contact +254-722-659-252 as well as WhatsApp number.
ISBN: 978-1-968966-69-0

DISCLAIMER

This book is a firsthand account with illustrations aimed at shedding light on previously unknown facts based on the author's actual experiences. The intention is to provide clarity and understanding without any harm or ill intent to any individuals, places, facts, institutions or persons. While every effort has been made to present the information accurately, the author regrets any unintended omissions or commissions that may occur in perspectives and interpretations.

Table of Contents

THE AUTHOR

Dr. David M. Githii, former fiery and reformist PCEA Moderator of the General Assembly, is the son of a world war II and Mau Mau warrior, Benson Githii Muhia. He describes his life as one not only baptized by fire but one whose sojourn is through '*the burning bush*' as well. Dr. David Githii is credited for championing change from the traditional Scottish Missionary style of worship in the PCEA Church to a more vibrant Holy Spirit-led worship that now embraces praise in worship, among other lasting changes in the denomination. He viciously fought corruption not only in the PCEA Church but also in Church-affiliated institutions like in hospitals and schools. An outspoken cleric on national issues in the country, more so in the area of idolatry and governance. He soldiers on as a stalwart, with his path blazed by God.

He was raised at Gikambura village, next to the PCEA Mother Church, the Church of the Torch, located at Thogoto in Kiambu County, not far from both Alliance Girls High School and Alliance Boys High School. He would become a staunch PCEA member until 2014. He was saved on the 31st of October, 1976, the date and month of '**Reformation Day**' when Martin Luther, a key figure in the Reformation, is said to have nailed his '**95 Theses**' to the door of the Wittenberg Castle Church in 1517. It is no wonder Dr. Githii has the spirit of a reformer.

He studied at Gikambura Primary School and then proceeded to Kirangari High School for his secondary education. He would later join Thogoto Teachers Training College attaining P1 grade. He then taught in various schools in Nakuru County as a Head Master before joining the Holy ministry in 1980. He therefore took theological studies at the then St. Paul's United Theological College, presently St. Paul's University, graduating in 1983 with a Bachelor of Divinity Degree (BD). He was ordained on December 30th. 1984 and labored at Dr. Arthur, Rongai and Loresho Parishes.

Dr. David Githii pursued post graduate studies at the University of Dubuque, Iowa, in the USA, where he attained a Master's Degree in Religion (MAR). He then proceeded to Fuller Theological Seminary in California, USA, where he attained a Master's Degree in Theology (THM) and a Doctorate Degree in Missiology (DMIS) in 1993. He also undertook extensive leadership studies and research in Scotland.

He has taught in various institutions of higher learning, such as;

Presbyterian University of East Africa (PUEA), Daystar University, St. Paul's University, Presbyterian College and PCEA Lay Training, among others.

Dr. David M. Githii has held other senior administrative and leadership positions in the Presbyterian Church of East Africa (PCEA), both as presbytery Moderator and presbytery clerk at different times and in different places in Kenya. He was also the Director of Lay Training in the Presbyterian denomination.

He is an author of a number of books such as; 'Kenya Repent or Perish', 'The Progressive Infiltration of Idolatry into the Universal Church and Nations: A chronological Perspective', 'How to Grow a Healthy and Vibrant Church Through Small Church Groups', 'Tithing: Principles and Practices' and 'Phases of The Church'. He is also the founder of both Cheptoroi Secondary School in Nakuru County and El Gibbor Altar Ministries. He pioneered the establishment of PUEA, where he became its 1st. Chancellor.

Dr. David M. Githii is widely traveled worldwide. He is married to Lucy Wanjiku, and God has blessed them with six children and a number of grandchildren. The six children are Benson Githii, Sammy Gichuki, Amos Ndicu/Thuku, Nicholas Githang'a, Mary Wangari, and Terry Njoki.

DEDICATION

This book is dedicated to the Very Rev. Dr. George Ernest Wanjau, former PCEA Moderator of the General Assembly, whom God used to inspire and support me in various ways in my ministry and in particular:

I. While I was undergoing some practical training at Thogoto Parish, which was part of the South Kiambu Presbytery, there came a time when the presbytery had to be summoned to pass a minute declaring that I should never be ordained as a PCEA clergyman. The reasons given for this were;
    a. That I had traits of the charismatic spirit as I was using 'Nyimbo cia kiroho' (Holy Spirit-inspired songs in preaching and teaching.
    b. That I was initiating what I referred to as 'Elder Districts'. To them, this was not only a very divisive spirit but also a very foreign idea as far as the PCEA traditions were concerned.

This being the case, Dr. Wanjau summoned South Kiambu Presbytery officials into his office raising his concerns over the prolonged time for my ordination. And having heard the reasons behind it, he negotiated with them and they came up with a memorandum of understanding whose content is covered elsewhere in this book. Otherwise, the scheduled Presbytery meeting was called off.

II. During my tenure of office as GA Moderator, there had been several occasions that the church courts and business committees had met with an agenda either to impeach or block me from being re-elected. At such crucial moments, it's Dr. Wanjau who chaired the meeting and diffused the tension.
III. Dr. G.E. Wanjau played a big role in the formation of the Elder Districts in the PCEA church by supporting its agenda in various meetings in which, by virtue of being Moderator of the General Assembly, he was Chairman of the courts and business committees through which the agendas were being floated.

Dr. Wanjau died on the 10th of April, 2024 and was celebrated as a hero of faith by both the church and nation. He died while the PCEA General Assembly meeting was being inaugurated. He, therefore, died a few days before this book was printed.

I remain so indebted to him, hence the reason behind my dedicating the book to him as my spiritual mentor.

ABBREVIATIONS

1. AEO- Area Education Officer
2. BOT- Board of Trustees
3. CHAK-Christian Health Association of Kenya
4. CHE- Commission of Higher Education
5. CMS- Church Missionary Society (Anglicans)
6. CSM- Church of Scotland Mission (Presbyterians)
7. CUE- Commission of University Education
8. ECHO- Evangelical Covenant Order of Presbyterians
9. EPC- Evangelical Presbyterian Church
10. GA- General Assembly
11. GAC- General Administrative Committee
12. ICT- Information Technology
13. KCPF- Kenya Christian Professionals Forum
14. LEGCO- Legislative Council
15. OCPD- Officer Commanding Police Division
16. PC(USA)- Presbyterian Church of USA
17. PCA- Presbyterian Church in America
18. PCEA- Presbyterian Church of East Africa
19. PEFA- Pentecostal Evangelical Fellowship of East Africa
20. SDA- Seventh Day Adventist
21. TEE- Theological Education by Extension
22. TSC- Teachers Service Commission

ACKNOWLEDGEMENTS

My gratitude first goes to the Lord God Almighty(El Gibor) for giving me life, a calling and the gift of discerning and writing. I also wish to make special mention of my wife, Lucy Wanjiku, and my daughter, Terry Njoki, for their unquantifiable sacrifice in kind and psychologically standing with me as I braved the countless hours in the day and night writing what is now a book. Thank you for the companionship and great dedication to ensure that there existed a peaceful environment in which I not only remained well-fed but in which I was in great shape to write. Without your support this book may have never been a reality.

I am also very grateful to all my children and their spouses for their patience and interest that inspired me. Thank you for the material support, prayers and inspiration that helped me engage my mind and to immerse myself in the spirit. It was invaluable in enabling me to accurately piece together the facts and information in this book.

I cannot forget to offer my heartfelt and special accolades as well to Tabitha James (Tabitha Njeri) of Kigoco FM Radio Station, who spent so much of her time and energy scrutinizing and aligning research material. In the process of doing this, she had to peruse through volumes of notes and diaries to type and produce the manuscript. Her great encouragement, selfless determination and offer of her services revitalized me when I got exhausted from the overwhelming research and intense writing.

Tabitha was of great inspiration, especially when I had to grope back to past events and occurrences over the years to come up with accurate information. I am greatly indebted to her.

Lastly, to Winstone Sharrad, kudos for editing the manuscript, fine-tuning, formatting and arranging the book. No words or any amount of reward can compensate for the many sleepless nights that he endured.

FOREWORD

Sorrow and tears teach us not only the way to cultivate but also to curve out the destiny of our lives. This is a wise saying that Dr. Githii would not only grasp but also embrace in his fiery journey into great victory despite vicious attacks and stiff opposition against his efforts to bring phenomenal transformation in the PCEA Church. These included changes from the comfort of beguiling traditional Scottish missionary ways.

In his quest to bring restoration in both physical and spiritual perspectives of the PCEA Church, Dr. Githii would be guided by a transformational philosophy that beckoned him to stay on course in the very rugged terrain of Scottish Missionary traditions. After all, a philosophy that was to abandon everything immediately after things became unpleasant is a shallow, mistaken and distorted view of life. Simply put, tribulation has always marked the trail of the true reformer. In fact, it can be easily said every great book has been written with the author's blood, tears a spirit of agony and anxiety. Yes, every great breakthrough has always been preceded by tribulation and in the form of persecution, opposition and resistance. It is no surprise then that Dr. Githii got saved on the 31st. October, which is Reformation Day. Indeed, God had put in him the spirit of reformation. Incidentally, some people who are aware of his accomplishments as he fought the occultic agenda, corruption, idolatry and superficial Christianity call him **'Githii the Reformer.'**

How could he let the Liberals continue arm-twisting the congregations as they pursued their covert occultic agenda? Dr. David Githii felt called to overcome the tight evil grip of the arm twisters that were suffocating the church. For him, to allow beliefs and practices that become a vehicle for indoctrination into the occult or subservience is denying his calling. It was with this in mind that he left no stone unturned until he fully exposed occultic symbols, symbolisms and traditions that held the church captive from inception. The repercussions were so dire, and some were life-threatening. Not once or thrice did he escape assassination. In fact, at one point, he says he had to stop at a police roadblock to escape from some people who were trailing him. In another incident, he had to take a drastic detour to Kikuyu to avoid harm. But despite all these, the great message that kept him going was, "*For each of us, if God sends us over rocky paths, he will provide us with strong shoes. He will never send us on any mission without equipping us well.*" God affirms this when he says, "*Thy shoes shall be iron and brass.*" Duet.33:25. No wonder Dr. Githii rubbed shoulders the wrong way with the traditionalists. He knew that it is also through the most difficult trials that God often brings the sweetest discoveries of Himself.

Indeed, the resilience displayed by Dr. Githii in the face of immense brimstone and fire from those opposed to the message of truth and doing right could not overwhelm his effort to fight widespread corruption, occultism, symbolism, devil worship, lesbianism, gayism and other evils. Yes, they crucified him, protested against him, and rejected his reforms, but he patiently pressed on, looking unto God in submission for guidance.

Dr. Githii would anchor his endurance on the fact that if we are patient and submissive, most certainly, that will be a greater blessing to the world around us during our suffering and pain than when we thought we were doing our greatest work. Otherwise, the glory of tomorrow is rooted in the drudgery of today's suffering. Many people want the glory without the cross and the shining light without burning fire, but the crucifixion comes before the coronation. An unlit candle does not shine. Burning must come before the light. We can be of little use to others without a cost to ourselves. His burning came, his crucifixion came, his pain came, and his suffering came, but look at the great gains already manifesting in the PCEA Church from vibrant praise in worship, elder districts, subdivisions, intercessory, decentralization, revitalized minister's lives among others. In the ensuing melee and onslaught, indeed, the candle was lit; it melted through the burning, and so it radiates the light throughout the denomination and many generations to come.

This is a testament that tribulations imprint on every great accomplishment; it is the door to triumph. It marks footprints. In fact, no one wins the greatest victory until he or she has walked the winepress of woe. The footprints are visible everywhere. The steps that lead to thrones are stained with splattered blood, and scars are the price for scepters. When PCEA engages freely in intercessory and verbalized individual prayers and praise in worship these are the marks of footprints from the immense suffering by Dr. Githii.

When I asked him what inspired him, the words of St. Paul's in Phil. 4: 13-14 are what he echoed, *"But one thing I do: Forgetting what is behind and straining toward what is ahead, I press on toward the goal to win the prize for which God has called me heavenward in Christ Jesus."*

Winstone Sharrad

Editor, Writer & Author

"Then I heard the voice of the Lord saying, 'Whom shall I send? And who will go for us?' And I said, "Here I am, send me." (Isaiah 6:8)

"Ignorance of truth keeps us in bondage. Did you know that truth is not altered by our ignorance of it nor changed one iota by our denial or rejection of it?

Nor does the truth change when it is cloaked by a veil of deception.

Truth needs no defense, and the opinion of man cannot alter it."

(Ron G. Campbell- Author of *'Free from Freemasonry'*)

1 THE SPRING BOARD

This book is part of my autobiography, exclusively based on my tenure as PCEA Moderator of the General Assembly. But one may wonder where I come from. I will start by first highlighting a bit of my background in life: I went through my **basic education at** Gikambura Primary school and thereafter proceeded to Kirangari High School for my secondary education. I then joined Thogoto Teachers Training College, from where I graduated as a P1 teacher. I was then posted in Nakuru in 1972, where I taught in various schools as a headmaster before I felt the call to join the Holy Ministry in 1980. I, therefore, joined St. Paul's United Theological College from September 1980 to May 1983. Here I did research on the history of this institution covering the period from 1930-1982. I graduated with a Bachelor's Degree in Divinity.

I thereafter proceeded to Thogoto Parish for parochial training from May 1983 to 1984, after which I was ordained on Sunday, December 30th. 1984, ready and equipped for ministry. The following year, I was posted to Nakuru Parish headquarters in 1985 to serve in Nakuru town. I would serve here till I was posted to Rongai Parish, serving from 1986 to 1987. I would later be posted to Loresho Parish in 1988, from where I would proceed to the University of Dubuque in Iowa, USA, for further studies in 1989. Here, I researched; **The History of the East Africa Revival Movement** from **1937-1993.** I then graduated with a Masters of Arts in Religion (MAR) Degree. I would later join Fuller Theological Seminary in California from 1990- 1993. I completed my studies, attaining a Masters and a Doctorate Degree. For my doctoral dissertation at Fuller Theological Seminary in California, USA, I researched **The History and Development of Western Education by The Presbyterian Church from 1900-1993.** In order to come up with a comprehensive research work, I made visits to: Edinburgh University and also the National Library, both in Scotland. Actually, this was where most of the communication between the pioneer missionaries in Kenya was archived. I also carried out some other research work from places like the Kenya National Archives. I also used questionnaires to interview the elderly who had some memories about the coming of missionaries to Kenya.

These are old people who had deep roots in the PCEA. I also undertook extensive leadership studies in Scotland. This then makes me the person with the deepest historical foundation of the Presbyterian Church in the whole denomination. I am an archive as far as all the denomination's roots are concerned.

After completing my studies in 1993, I labored in parochial ministry at Muguga Parish; then, I got seconded as a clergy to Daystar University to teach as a Senior Lecturer, where I taught from 1995 to 1999.

At one point, while I was at Daystar, the Business Committee had decided to recall back the clergy seconded to other institutions as their services were required in the church. It was for this reason that I received a letter from the Secretary-General advising me to go back to the church.

This was quite some food for thought! My colleagues, on the other hand, would not approve of this and tried all they could to discourage me from accepting this move. They had argued that this was the strategy of the Church to humiliate me by plunging me into a financial crisis. They held the view that I was already comfortable in the university, where I enjoyed a *"huge"* salary as well as many other good benefits for myself and my family by then at Daystar. These included travel reimbursement and health insurance for the family and myself. My colleagues had asked me why I should go back to the Church to earn a meager salary, which was nothing close to what I had been used to.

Nevertheless, the weight of the call in my heart outweighed the prestigious benefits. I, therefore, wrote a letter to the Church indicating that I would exit from Daystar University and submit to that humble calling by going back to the Church. This radical decision had come despite the pressure from my staff and others who had earlier endeavored to dissuade me from going back to the Church.

In my acceptance letter, I had requested that I be posted as a lecturer in one of the theological schools at either St. Paul's United Theological College (present-day St. Paul's University) or the PCEA

Presbyterian College (present-day Presbyterian University of East Africa (PUEA).

However, to my surprise, I was posted to Mathare Parish and having clang to my divine call, I therefore decided to do my own research on the historical background of Mathare, and my findings indicated the following:

Mathare Parish comprised the second largest slum area in Kenya, after Kibra commonly known as Kibera. Due to poverty, this parish lagged behind in many ways: Spiritually, the dwellers seemed to have lost hope and seemingly wondered how a good God could lead and leave them in such a desperate situation. No wonder the parishioners were a depressed lot who needed information in order to come out of their poverty mindset.

Economically, the parish was the second poorest after Kibra. The money accessed/quota to this parish by the Head Office had accumulated over the years because they were unable to pay. As a result, very few pastors would have wanted to be posted to this parish. It is unfortunate that the appointment committee placed pastors here as a form of punishment rather than in good faith. As a result, the pastors did not feel motivated to work with devotion.

This parish had lagged behind in every aspect of its life, be it financial, spiritual or development. It could even hardly complete its accessed money by Head Office. It was spiritually handicapped in the old Scottish traditions.

MINISTRY AT MATHARE PARISH

No sooner had I reported at Mathare Parish than I got immediately engaged in ministry in a very aggressive way. I adopted a door-to-door evangelism approach and reached out to people in marketplaces, schools and even bus terminuses.

I came up with a raft of intensive plans, measures and endeavors that included activating the Elder District fellowships, Bible Studies and many seminars to teach people on many Christian life-oriented topics. No wonder, then, the parish experienced a lot of awakening

3

in all aspects of life, including both spiritual and physical, such as economic, among others. As a result of these teachings, financial giving increased so much that before long, we were able to clear all Head Office arrears. We also started some viable projects and the climax of the above new developments was to have the parish subdivided into two, that is, Mathare Parish and Eastleigh Parish. The former parish comprised six congregations. By the year 2000, I was now the parish minister of Eastleigh Parish, while another pastor was assigned to Mathare Parish.

THE GENERAL ASSEMBLY ELECTIONS

At the time, the Mathare Parish was experiencing positive growth. We were making great progress. I had worked hard and there were many breakthroughs in Mathare. The Parish now attained a name not only in the Presbytery but also at the Headquarters. My focus was indeed on turning around the Parish, and that's where all my energies and focus were. But then the Kirksession transferred two elders from one congregation to another for the obvious reasons that they were inciting the congregation against fully cooperating on some aspects the Kirksession had been given the mandate to carry out. I was aware that a few leaders in the congregation were not happy with that transfer but I had underestimated the magnitude of their concerns.

It therefore happened that, one evening on a Sunday, I missed attending the Church service. While I rested as I watched the news on TV, I noticed that members of the affected congregation had been involved in a demonstration and were waving placards with writings: *'Githii must go!'* This came as a surprise to me because I had always known the leaders of that congregation to be very supportive and understanding in all the major decisions made, including the transfer of the two elders. I made a phone call to the Session Clerk to find out the reason behind all this turmoil. He responded that there were rumors that I would be one of the candidates in the forthcoming GA Moderators elections and that some leaders from the Headquarters wanted to block me from appearing on the list. Therefore, the strife was being fueled by some of these top hierarchy officials in the PCEA at the Head Office. They included a past

4

Moderator known for endorsing GA candidates. It was during the time of elections of the SG and GA Moderator that talk about the pattern of endorsement by the fathers surfaced. The church's situation was so dire that the traditional path of elections was fast shifting. In the past, the presbyteries mainly depended on one of the previous Moderators who acted under the guise of being the image of the church Fathers and consultants. This had been the trend during the past elections.

By now, the church was suffocating spiritually, physically and economically, with young people leaving at an alarming rate. The question of who from the entire PCEA fraternity would be elected to redeem the church loomed. There was a sense of urgency to turn things around and bring sanity to the church.

Whatever the case, I felt fully occupied in my current ministry at Mathare Parish. I could not have imagined my name being on the list of those being earmarked as potential candidates for the much-coveted seat. I had considered myself as being among the least known in Church circles.

My understanding of the election matter from previous experience was that only previous high office holders would qualify as candidates. These were people who previously held important positions in the denomination or were in such positions as Secretary General, Deputy Secretary General, Heads of Departments and so on. Furthermore, it was a well-known fact that one of the past Moderators traditionally dictated and determined the outcomes of the election through his endorsements. Anyone not approved by him would definitely not win the election.

This past Moderator was an ardent defender of the PCEA Traditions, as evidenced by his clinging to Scottish Missionary traditions. Rev. Gatu, who was the denomination's Secretary General for 18 years and the GA Moderator for 6 years, carried the day most of the time. He was perceived as the custodian and archive of PCEA traditions. He was a great contributor to the '**Practice and Procedure**' (PCEA Constitution), including all matters relating to PCEA; after all, he was the mastermind behind this PCEA constitution. Therefore, his word was taken as divine. This so-called Senior Church father was deeply aligned and rooted in the cultural structures of the Church of

Scotland missionaries from where he drew his strength and power. So naturally, such a traditionalist would hardly recommend a seemingly little-known uncompromising and charismatic person like me, whom they called radical and rebellious. By the way, it was Rev. Gatu who ordained me. He, therefore, knew me very well, especially on my stand regarding elder districts and my call to do away with Scottish traditions. He knew my leaning toward the truth of the gospel. After all, whoever was to be elected was to be known as a very partisan and a true defender of 'Church Traditions.'

Consequently, by inciting my parishioners to rebel against me, they expected that I would be disqualified from the race by falsely alleging that I had 'failed' to run a parish. This would imply that I was not fit to be an administrator of the denomination. Unfortunately, the strategy by the perpetrators of the mayhem in the parish was short-lived and long forgotten by the time the final list of candidates was released.

To my surprise and the surprise of those who wanted to block me, my name appeared on the list of the six top candidates whom the vetting committee had filtered. I wasn't excited because I assumed that my being on the list was just a, by the way. To many, it seemed I had the slightest chance as a candidate to be elected from the list of 5 top giants contesting with some having endorsement of the 'church fathers.' And who was I in the first place to contest against such incredible forces with all the backing from the past Moderators? The news of my inclusion in the GA elections did not excite me at all since I assumed that it didn't make any difference, especially since the other five candidates were highly known in the Church circles. Two of them had served as Secretary General of the Church for six years each and as Deputy Secretary General for four years each. Thus, each had served a total of ten years and was well-known in every parish and presbytery of the denomination. The other two had served as Deputy Secretary Generals four years each while the fifth one was the head of the youth department in the entire denomination. I was just an underdog. I was a nobody!

These five embarked on fierce and protracted campaigns. Backed by known heavy financiers, they traversed the whole of East Africa, especially Kenya and Tanzania, which were part of the denomination's territory. It is for this reason the denomination is known as the *Presbyterian Church of East Africa*.

Despite my having no ambition to be a Moderator, I did harbor a desire in my heart. And I desired that if God, in his miraculous ways, would open a door for me to be the GA Moderator, then I would do everything focused on glorifying his name. Whatever the case, I remained calm, concentrating on my work, not even considering what could be going on around me. I never made any phone call anywhere to any person to discuss any issue concerning elections.

But why were the candidates engaged in aggressive campaigns? For one to be elected to the position of Moderator of the General Assembly, one must attain 2/3rds of the number of presbyteries that comprise the entire number of denominations at the time of election. There were 28 presbyteries then, which meant that the winner had to acquire at least eighteen presbyteries.

The campaign mood in the whole denomination was very loud and messy. There were all kinds of manipulation, including bribery. In some areas, convoys of campaign vehicles could be seen coiling along the roads leading to the various presbyteries. Many resorted to flights to reach out to far-flung areas or remote countries and places like Mombasa, Tanzania and Uganda. Behind all these heavyweights were very wealthy rich people sponsoring the very expensive campaigns, with the main agenda being that their candidate wins to pave the way for open doors for corruption in the Church in favour of the sponsors.

They would be tendering masters engaging in bid rigging during procurement. This featured quoting skyrocketing prices to the benefit of a clique. The tendering masters would also have a say in other matters concerning Church life, including influencing the transfers of pastors who were especially considered traitors for not toeing the line in their respective parishes and presbyteries. Many of these were Freemasons/ Illuminati and devil worshippers, both clergy and laity alike, some of whom supposedly owned pistols that they could come with dangling in their pockets to Presbytery meetings and other church meetings. Most of these, including some clergy among them, had never confessed to being born again as Christians. Yet they were full of pretense and often saluted you,

"*Praise God,*" while in their hearts, they were clinging to ungodliness. Their agenda was to sabotage any leader who seemed deeply rooted in the word of God. They had money, so they used it to compromise Gospel-based leaders. The victims of these '*liberals*'' machinations were pastors who did not dance to the paymaster's tune.

This position was very strategic because the moderator happens to be the chairman of key Church committees, including the General Administrative Committee (GAC), the General Assembly (GA), the Business Committee and the Appointment Committee. With their candidate winning, the campaign funders would have an opportunity to push their sponsored agenda through. The other reason, which is diabolic, is that since some of these funders would be initiated members of Freemasons and New Age Movement, they would have a leeway to infiltrate Satanism into the Church, including homosexuality and devil worship. Remember, my competitors were people with money, having served in the Church for many years. They had accumulated a lot of wealth. This was especially true of those who had held high ranks in the Church both as secretary general and deputy secretary general. They had extensive connections with affluent individuals, both locally and internationally, who could easily sponsor them.

It would surprise the reader to learn that, in the midst of all these campaigns, competition and hullabaloo, as indicated earlier, I never spoke a word to anyone to indicate any interest in being elected as the Moderator. My silent slogan was, '*Let the will of God be done.*' I felt that if God was to qualify me, He would call me like David, who did not campaign for kingship. It was Samuel who was directed by God to anoint him as King. The biblical verse that sustained me was Psalms 46:10; "*Be still and know that I am God; I will be exalted among the nations, I will be exalted in the earth.*" I had learnt that there were many people in the church who were praying for a David, who would bring reformation and restoration as well as lead the church to both physical and green pastures.

THE ELECTION DAY

Then came the Election Day. And the process was completed without any incident. The results were announced on the 25th of December, 2002. On this Christmas morning, I was awakened by a call from someone who asked whether I had read that day's Newspaper. But I told him I had not since I was still in bed. He told me that the unexpected happened. I had been elected by more than eighteen presbyteries as the 17th. Moderator of the General Assembly. I wanted to quench my curiosity, so I sent someone for the day's Newspaper and to my surprise, it was true. I was voted in by 19 presbyteries, which was more than the constitutional requirement of 2/3rds of the number of existing presbyteries. Afterwards there were numerous congratulatory calls both locally and internationally. It was indeed a surprise Christmas gift. The Daily Nation of 25th December 2003 carried this heading: '**Githii Picked to Head Presbyterian Church.**' It went on to further elaborate:

"The Presbyterian Church of East Africa has elected a new Moderator. The Rev Dr. David Githii, previously the Moderator of Nairobi Presbytery, replaces the long-serving spiritual leader, the Rev Dr. Jesse Kamau, who has been Moderator for two terms. The Rev Githii, who is also in charge of the Eastleigh Parish, will be enthroned during the Church's 17th. General Assembly in April. The Rev Githii got 19 votes out of 28 in the elections held on Monday at the Church's head office in Nairobi. He is credited with having initiated several development projects in the Church. He also initiated Elder District prayers, where worshippers gather on a weekly basis for prayers. The young Githii joined standard one at a much-advanced age, at 12, due to financial problems. In school, He participated in long-distance races and in soccer, too, but it was in academics that he excelled. And as he himself put it, he was always "among the best pupils". For his secondary school education, he was at Kirangari High school. He then studied for a P1 teacher's certificate at Thogoto Teachers College."

THE INSTALLATION TO MODERATORSHIP.

Having been successfully elected, the next move was to have me installed as the Moderator of the 17th General Assembly in a colorful ceremony where all presbyteries were represented in a General Assembly held at St. Andrews Church, Nairobi, on the 14th of April, 2003. It was in my speech that I spelt out my vision and mission for the Church. In doing this and according to the tradition of the Church, I had to give a biblical verse that would act as a pointer to my vision. My predecessor had, in the past six years, used Revelation 21:5, "*I am making everything new!*" I saw this as a prophetic voice indicating that the making of '*new things*' was to happen after him. By then, the situation of the Church spiritually, economically, politically and even socially was pathetic. A letter had already circulated in all the presbyteries and parishes calling upon the clergy and the entire Church leadership and lay people to act urgently to redeem the Church especially from its financial handicap. In fact, one of the tele-evangelists based in Nairobi City, in one of her TV deliveries and having seen the letter that had been written to the PCEA Church leadership, mocked PCEA Church, saying she could buy it with her financially stable mega Church. The truth of the matter is that the majority of PCEA clergy were living from hand to mouth as there was no money generated from their parishes to meet their salaries. It was for this reason that I felt that, to realize redemption of the Church, there had to be a total revolution in the spiritual and physical arenas of the Church. I therefore picked as my theme Luke 13:8b, "*leave it alone for one year, and I will dig around it and fertilize it.*" My understanding was that, for the Church to come back to its feet, there had to be both a great spiritual and physical awakening – there was, therefore, to be both spiritual and physical cultivation and fertilization. One thing I knew was that this kind of revolution would definitely encounter very severe opposition from the various interested '*liberal*' parties whose main agenda was always to suppress the Church physically and spiritually. This scenario is expected when new wine is put into old wineskins.

In my acceptance speech, I told the delegates that a time has come when we have to disown some of the traits of the Scottish culture that are intertwined with the gospel of God's kingdom, which was supposedly introduced by the missionaries. I told the delegates that our persistent connection with the Church of Scotland in spiritual matters was like a tick persistently biting the skin of a dying cow. When the cow finally dies, the tick will likewise die. This church was in the intensive care unit (ICU). I told the delegates that the Western side of the church is dwindling at a very fast rate because they have opened doors to ungodly ventures.

I also raised an alarm over the infiltration of idolatry, including homosexuality and lesbianism in Western Countries and Europe at large, plus an open door to other ungodly evils like abortion and the spirit of unbelief.

Thanks be to God; I had already researched the Scottish culture in relation to the gospel the pioneer missionaries had planted in Kenya through the Church of Scotland Mission in the late 20th. Century. I carried out this research for the documentation of my doctoral Dissertation entitled: *'The introduction and Development of Western Education in Kenya by the Presbyterian, 1891-1991.'* This project became an eye-opener to the spiritually poor foundation upon which the PCEA Church was established. In fact, I came to realize that not all the missionaries were deeply Christian. Most of them were grounded in Freemasonry or Illuminati.

Remember, it was the Scottish Church minister, Anderson, who wrote the Masonic constitution that was launched in 1723. It is a fact that the Freemasonry fraternity originated in Scotland in 1307 when the Knight Templars were outlawed in Europe and were greatly persecuted, many of them settling in Scotland. Thus, by the time the missionaries arrived in Kenya in 1898, Freemasonry had been in existence for 500 years in Scotland. And since Freemasonry was the sole builder of the sanctuaries, no wonder then the Church buildings in Scotland were loaded with occultic symbols that were meant to spiritually pollute the Church environment. Likewise, the missionaries from Europe installed numerous Masonic symbols in the Churches they built in Kenya and, of course, elsewhere that they evangelized worldwide.

It was also in this speech that I promised, among other things, that I was to reclaim all the Church institutions that were seemingly grabbed by some individuals. These, among others, included the hospitals and schools.

I also promised to change the style of worship by introducing musical instruments like key boards and drum sets. I was at the same time to pave the way for the Holy Spirit to be involved in worship by introducing Praise in Worship. I was also to fight the seemingly deeply entrenched corruption and immorality in the Church, including homosexuality, lesbianism and devil worship.

I was also to fight the spirit of materialism which was invading the Church. My inauguration was covered by many of the Kenyan media houses. One article in the Lifestyle of Sunday Nation, May 18th, written by Anthony Njagi of Daily Nation Newspaper, carried the heading: '**Former teacher wants to make PCEA more appealing to the young.**' In describing the manner in which I delivered my speech, Anthony Njagi said:

"He was in high spirits. On the pulpit, he swayed and turned, moved forward and backward, talking, cajoling and really working up the audience. His clenched fist pumped the air as he hammered his point across to the charged assembly that had gathered at St Andrew's Church, Nairobi, recently. And that is how he loves to do and convey the message in a forceful manner to the congregation. Oratory is one of his hallmarks, and no doubt when he handed over the microphone to the chief guest, Vice – President Michael Wamalwa, who represented President Kibaki at the PCEA's 17th. General Assembly, the audience was left yearning for more."

Anthony further says:

"On April 22nd, this year, the St Andrews Church hosted one of the largest crowds ever in the history of the Church in East Africa. And motorists and other people using the busy Uhuru Highway that day must have wondered what was happening at St. Andrews Church. It was a colourful ceremony with plenty of activity. A carnival mood enveloped the Church and its environs. Songs, dances, and recitations could be heard hundreds of metres away. This was, indeed, a special day- the installation of its new Moderator of the PCEA. He had won the Moderator's election by 19 votes out of 28 to beat other five contestants. And with this achievement, Dr. Githii has joined an elite league of the top African leaders of this Church since independence 40 years ago" (Lifestyle, Sunday Nation, May 18, 2003, pg. 2).

Anthony continues to give even further highlights by saying:

"This humble man of cloth, who is now at the helm of his Church, has come from very far, having started out as a primary school teacher. Determined to succeed in that noble career, he worked hard and, at the initial stage of his teaching career, was appointed the head teacher of Olmanyatta primary school in Subukia, Nakuru, in 1972. Then, nobody would have ever guessed that Githii would later earn himself a doctorate in theology and rise through the ranks to become the PCEA Moderator. This is the highest title in the PCEA church which has three million plus followers."

The question that was in people's minds was: *"How on earth did Githii manage to sail through wrestling the Church out of Gatu's tight grip?"* The answer as to why this Moderator failed to block me from being the GA Moderator is that God had already predestined me for this kind of position. And for this reason, God had designed a way to have His agenda delivered.

Thus, for the first time in the history of the Church, the majority of the people agreed to elect a person who had shown good qualities of leadership and, more so, someone who had some visible contribution to the entire denomination, one with an uncorrupted mind. I then happened to top the five other candidates who, in spite of having held top positions as either the Deputy Secretary General or Secretary General or both, had not left anything tangible in the life of the Church. It was business as usual. They upheld the same Scottish Church traditions; the same vicious circle of doing things: The same *'worship lifestyle'* through the Practice and Procedure of the Scottish.

Since the five candidates had been in top leadership before, chances of maintaining the status quo were highly likely had they been elected. The routine would have been, *"Well, we have always done it this way."*

When it came to me, the Church had recognized my contribution to the life of the Church despite not having been at the Head Office. Actually, they talked of pillars that I had established in the Church. These, then, are the contributions that betrothed me to the Church; contributions that overpowered the most powerful past Moderator in the history of the Church and that paved the way for me to take this most revered and highly esteemed position in the Church-the Moderator of General Assembly.

These contributions included the following:

Teaching: I contributed to the teaching/ training of many pastors at both PCEA Lay Training Institute and St. Paul's United Theological College. One thing to note is that I had started teaching before I got ordained. The teaching I provided in the church went against the traditions of the PCEA church. According to these traditions, only ordained individuals were permitted to teach theological students, as they were believed to have more experience in church life. And yet, there were certain practical areas of the church that only an ordained minister could explore. Unfortunately, at the time of my graduation from St. Paul's Theological College, the Church lacked an ordained person to teach Church History or Mission. So, the Church had no alternative but to place me to teach these two courses in spite of my not being ordained. Noteworthy is the fact that it was necessary for me to undergo some practical training under an experienced Church minister while, at the same time, teaching the theological students! In order to achieve this twin mission, it was therefore necessary that I be posted to a parish near the PCEA pastoral Institute so that I could teach as well. It was for this reason that I was posted to Thogoto parish which was in the same jurisdiction of south Kiambu Presbytery. This posting gave me an early opportunity to interact with the future Church clergy. Besides, teaching was my original career of choice. My relationship with the students was, therefore, naturally very amicable. Even after I was ordained, I continued to teach. As the parish minister at Rongai, I hosted students and interacted with them for many years. The more I taught the students, the better our relationship became. Later, after my post-graduate studies, I also taught as a part-time lecturer at St. Paul's Theological College, where PCEA students had been studying over the years. It then followed that at the time of elections in 2003, many of my former students were manning parishes. Some of these students had responsibilities in crucial sectors of the Church including holding positions of Presbytery Moderators and Clerks. These pastors became easy catalysts for my campaigns and indeed, they gave their all on my behalf. In fact, it is these students who advised their pairing elders, who were voting members in the presbyteries, to vote for me.

Elder Districts: This is another area that led to my being rated high among other candidates. God used me to birth the Elder District Movement in PCEA Church. I can say for sure if I never became a PCEA pastor, there would be a 99% chance of not having this noble movement in the PCEA Church. I borrowed the idea of Elder Districts from my former career as a headmaster in primary schools and as a secondary school administrator.

Refer to chapter 3 for more details on this. But on the whole, this time round and unlike other elections where a past Moderator dictated who should be elected, presbyteries, in vetting the candidates, also looked at one's record of achievement outside the Church Arena. I had also excelled in other administrative areas in my life, particularly as headmaster, in the areas of sportsmanship, uplifting of buildings, the birthing of Cheptoroi Secondary School, as well as uplifting of both spiritual and physical aspects of life in all the places I had responsibilities. These included institutions in presbyteries and parishes. I had also demonstrated great leadership skills. My leadership as both Presbytery Clerk and Presbytery Moderator in a number of presbyteries, including Nairobi Presbytery, were also on score cards. I was also highly rated when it came to matters concerning the oppressed and needy people. My relations with people, including the church ministers and their needs, were also rated high.

As soon as I got installed and at the end of the GA Meeting, I got straight into work. I organized seminars for all categories of church groups, parishes, presbyteries and regions. My main agenda was to educate the people on the importance of having the mind to own the church and the need for each person to feel called to take the church from one glory to another. It was a way of bringing morale to the people since the way things were then, many people had lost hope because of the pathetic state of the church. As earlier established, the church was financially, spiritually and socially demoralized and in doldrums. I was on the run the whole of the first year, mobilizing people to a kind of new awakening. This was despite my being engaged in other physical and spiritual development projects and responsibilities in the church. One of the things that I called people to embrace was the spiritual awakening through the renewal of worship. In this new look worship, the worshipers would get out of the seemingly frozen way of worship to a vibrant one, which at the same time would be accompanied by musical instruments such as keyboards, drum sets, well-set public-address systems and African rhythmical ways of worship. This liberal way of doing things would give allowance to the move of the Holy Spirit. This liberty would allow the worshippers to lift up their hands and perform all kinds of movements as led by the Spirit.

Unfortunately, this was not taken easily by many church leaders. It was regarded as radical and a total deviation from the traditional ways of worship as framed and designed by the pioneer missionaries. It is to this tradition that the clergy and elders were custodians and under oath to defend. No wonder, in one of the church meetings, one senior past Moderator furiously addressed me by saying,

"You are behaving as the worst enemy of this church. This church has its traditions of doing things and particularly in regard to worship. There is no way you can bring such changes. And if they ever happen, it will be under my dead body. Take that and assimilate it. This is total madness."

In response, I said:

"You are wrong! I am not only the best friend of this church but also its best redeemer with God's help. You people have acted like moles eating up the church through some disguised manipulations claiming to defend the foundations laid out by the church's founding missionaries. With God's help, I aim to bring new wine into the life of the church. The old wine skins are going to be torn out. You come to me like Goliath, but I come to you in the name of the Lord whose house you have turned into a den of robbers."

At this juncture, the said past Moderator stood vibrating in anger and said,

"We will see who is in charge and if you are not going to change, I will leave no stone unturned until you vacate that seat. You can't bring unsacredness into that seat. I have always complained of the danger of some people having elected, deviating from our traditional ways. I am always consulted on the best person to take the position of the Moderator." And with that vitriol

and like Judas the betrayer in protest, he left the room. Not before long, the first GAC at Kihumbu-ini took place.

I now wanted to make this meeting my springboard to introduce vibrant worship into the church and even bring about other key changes.

2 HOLY SPIRIT INSPIRED WORSHIP

GAC AT KIHUMBUI-INI PRESBYTERY

The GAC held at Kihumbui-ini Presbytery was held from April 13th - 18th in the year 2004, turned out to be the key eye opener for the worship revolution in the PCEA. The first agenda in any GA/GAC is the roll call to ensure that all presbyteries and Church groups are well represented. This is followed by the welcoming of the invited guests, who also deliver greetings from their various Churches/organizations.

Usually, this covers most of the morning session. Then lunch follows and then the first item on the agenda in the afternoon is the Moderator's speech. Generally, in every General Assembly (GA) and General Administrative Committee meeting (GAC), the Moderator is always allocated some time to give his/her speech as a way of elaborating his/her past year's achievement, as well as his/her agenda. This acts as a pointer to the direction he/she would be piloting the Church.

My speech here was very crucial because there was already planned impeachment against me immediately after I delivered my speech. The reasons for the impeachment were to be based on the content of my speech. One of the reasons that the liberals had aggressively wanted to have me voted out was because they had already read the contents of my report.

Days before the scheduled meetings, the delegates receive a docket that contains the compiled speech of the Moderator and other important reports. This ensures that the delegates are well-informed and prepared to not only engage in meaningful discussions during the meetings but that they are also privy to the content. This, therefore, means that they had read and fully analyzed my speech. The delegates were well-prepared for the GAC meeting, with guns ablaze, having analyzed and discussed the key points of my speech in their parishes, presbyteries and even in hotels. This meant that they were ready to execute their heinous plot against me through a very informed strategy. In the afternoon, when I took to the floor to read my speech, I covered and highlighted the following areas:

I brought to light the fact that for 1,236 years, the Church of Christ had been enslaved by the Roman Catholic Church, which had become a substitute for the authority of the Church instead of the Bible. A closed door existed between the worshiper and God. The repentant sinner did not confess his/her sins to God but to the priest. It is this enslavement that John Calvin, the founder of the Presbyterian Church, had addressed. He was born on July 10th. 1509 and died on July 27th. 1564.

Calvin wanted a Church that could emulate the Apostolic Church, and I gave some of its characteristics. Calvin insisted that the Church should open its doors to the Holy Spirit, among other things. I encouraged the church to embrace a form of worship that allowed people to worship in spirit and in truth. This included the use of various musical instruments, which could enhance the worship experience and help people connect with their faith. Indeed, the use of various musical instruments has been a significant part of African cultural traditions and has played an essential role in worship songs. By embracing this form of worship, the church could connect with its roots and create a more inclusive and diverse community.

I challenged the Church to come out of its self-imposed cocoon of Scottish heritage, which I likened to a **tick clinging** to a **dying cow**. I also likened the Church of Scotland to a sick person in an intensive care unit. I, therefore, called upon the Church to plunge more and more into the scriptures than in foreign cultural influences. I challenged the delegates to emulate the principals and theology of the denomination's founder, John Calvin. I reminded them of great Church pillars like Martin Luther the Reformer and other biblical reformers like Hezekiah, David, Nehemiah and Ezra.

It seemed that my description of the church of Scotland was communicated to every church in Scotland. I had lost touch with all the ten churches I had connections with while studying there. The churches in Scotland disowned me, accusing me of disrespecting their denomination by claiming that it had become so weak that it would cease to exist in the next 50 years unless something was done. Despite this, a retired church minister in Scotland supported me. Part of the letter he wrote said the following: "*You mention worship, and you say; "It is time we disown the Presbyterian Church from the Scottish inherited style of worship. Let me say at once I agree with you 100%. You have mentioned the decline of the Presbyterian Church in Scotland. Here again, I agree with you because the statistics of the Church decline are somewhat alarming and justify your use of the phrase intensive care unit.*"

In one area of my speech in this GAC, I categorically stated the need for change in the style of worship from the Scottish entrenched traditions to what would be in line with the Apostolic Church. I was set in my mind to do whatever it would take to bring about revival in the Church worship. I found it unfortunate that the Scottish pioneer missionaries had their culture of worship entrenched in the Churches they planted. In fact, they valued their culture over the Apostolic Church's scriptural ways of worship.

It is for this reason that I implored the delegates to bring about some changes in the style of worship in the PCEA. I called upon them to embrace the ways of the Apostolic Church in worship with the real study of the Scriptures. I besought them to embrace the Holy Spirit and adopt praise accompanied by musical instruments, just as David has advocated for in Psalm 150.

I requested the delegates to create an opportunity where Church music would be set to present the African cultural perspective in the application of musical instruments. This would include rhythmical movements accompanied by praise. In this case, every congregation would have a team called '**Praise in Worship**,' a team that would be leading the service instead of the customary one led through a sluggish drum beat by an individual whose only qualification was being advanced in age.

I warned the church leaders that they would be likened to the tick-sucking blood of the dying cow if they continued associating themselves with the Scottish culture as their mode of worship. The matter would further be exacerbated if they continued emulating other activities that leaned on the Scottish culture and traditions. This continuity would eventually lead to both the cow and the tick dying. I also encouraged the church to recognize the role of the Holy Spirit in the church. I warned them that when the Church shuts out the Holy Spirit, it means, the church service will be dull and more of a formality. This had been the mood that existed in PCEA for over one hundred years.

It was this resistance to the move of the Holy Spirit in the PCEA that the Lord would lead me to challenge the church leaders and delegates in the GA and GAC meetings. For instance, in a GAC held at Chogoria, I would ask the church to embrace the Holy Spirit. I said: *"In order to open up the Church for the Holy Spirit to move in, we have, like Gideon, to smash the Scottish traditions that over the years have held the Church in bondage. It is an idol to be smashed out and its dust thrown into the 'Forgotten dust – bin.'*

I took the opportunity to remind the delegates of some of the characteristics of the Apostolic Church-the pioneer Christian Church:

• They spent their time **learning** from apostles – it was a Church that read the scriptures with much eagerness. They mined spiritual gold from the scriptures.

• They were like **family** to each other; they loved one another – the spirit of forgiveness and tolerance was in their midst.

• They **broke bread together** – they shared meals and also shared in various biblical based discussions in different homes as well.

• They **prayed together**.

Through the Holy Spirit, they had known the value of prayers as the best bridge to connect with God and the source of power to overcome the enemy. They even had time for intercessory prayers where they opened their mouths and talked to God in unison.

I reminded the delegates that for the first 300 years since the ascent of Christ, the New Testament Church had no buildings. Believers worshiped in House Churches. It was only when Constantine became the Roman Emperor in AD 312 that big cathedrals were built and replaced the House Churches, which clearly reflected the priesthood of all believers, unlike the Constantine Churches in which the priest was the sole actor in almost everything- '*the know-it-all*' and '*jack of all trades*' mentality. I therefore called upon the delegates to fully utilize the elder districts, which acted as House Churches, in order to experience enriched and vibrant worship.

Scripture tells us that in the early home church, there was great growth. Each day the Lord added into their group others who were being saved (**Acts 2:47**). This happened when the Holy Spirit was in control. The members of this early Church had taken the word very seriously. They were people with a zeal to teach others the word of God. Their faith was not in a closet; neither was it coated with obscure traditions. It was a church that knew no boundaries.

I reminded the delegates that this was the very endeavor that John Calvin was insisting Presbyterians should possess to aggressively spread the word of God. I said: *"This GAC should come up with modalities through which PCEA will aggressively carry out mission work. It is because of our being so much localized in Eastern and central Kenya and a few places in Rift Valley area that we are poorly represented nationally."*

It is also important to note that the New Testament Church used secret ballots in their election for Church officials. This method was initiated by the Apostles to replace Judas (who hanged himself after betraying Jesus). In Acts 1:26, it is clearly stated that the Apostles cast lots between Justus and Matthias.

The Church was never formed until the Holy Spirit took charge. When the Holy Spirit took control that day, about *"three thousand believed… and were baptized"* (**Acts 2: 41**). Note that the 120 got directly connected with the *'current'* of the Holy Spirit – they immediately turned into a spirit-led worshipping Church, which was a translation of the words that Jesus had told the Samaritan Woman: *"Yet a time is coming and has now come when the true worshipers will worship the Father in Spirit and in truth, for they are the kind of worshipers the Father seeketh… His worshipers must worship in Spirit and truth."* (John 4:23-24).

At this juncture, my speech had changed many aggrieved spirits. The Holy Spirit was at work, shedding a new light of understanding in their hearts and minds. When the opportunity came for the delegates to have an input in my speech, the liberal delegates, led by one of the past Moderators, vehemently opposed this idea of spiritualizing the

Church worship. He had already set the battle-lines within the delegates. He had written a note that was already circulating among some liberal delegates. The note which finally landed on my hands read:

"This Church has operated well over all these years; why should we have changes that divert it from the path it has taken over the years? This is why I have voiced all the way that this man was not qualified to be a Moderator. He is too immature for this seat. In fact, this is why I was in the forefront to have him impeached in this GAC. How does he think he can change the style of worship that all other Moderators have so wonderfully protected for over one hundred years plus? Let him be told that any such changes would happen over my dead body. How dare he provoke me, one who has been known as the custodian of PCEA Church traditions? -An individual who has been schooled and tutored more in the Scottish Church's traditions when I was a student there? Githii is bringing his learning from the very conservative School of World Mission, which is part of Fuller Theological Seminary in America, where they advocate more on Scriptural traditions over the cultural values as spelt out in our Church constitution. How on earth can he so much demean the wonderful work carried out by the pioneer missionaries, many of whom died laboring in mission fields?"

There were several attempts by the liberals to inject the delegates with the motion of my impeachment, but they got intercepted by the conservative group. I also devised a tactic of fronting or giving more opportunities to positive-minded speakers on the floor. Therefore, the more the debate progressed, the more people came to my side. The spirit of resistance to any changes was very high. Campaigns were already ongoing to block the passing of any worship-related resolutions.

Finally, the matter was left in the hands of those already selected to evaluate the Moderator's speech and present their findings to the delegates for adoption or rejection.

This was in line with the traditions of PCEA. It was customary that after the Moderator had read his/her speech, a group of about ten delegates selected by the Moderator would have a seating and come out with resolutions related to the speech. Such resolutions would be brought to the GAC delegates for adoption or rejection.

I had already selected the ten delegates, and having read the speech on a Tuesday, they were expected to present their findings on Thursday. My only dilemma was that, as long as one of the past Moderators who was the chief opposer to these changes was present, it would be very hard for such resolutions to see the light of day. This retired Moderator was regarded by the delegates as the ardent curator of PCEA traditions.

Given the slim chances for the worship resolution to pass, I resorted to praying for God's wisdom. I even set aside some intercessors to pray over the issue. God finally gave me some wisdom. I found a way to escape. I convinced the delegates to continue with the meeting till late in the evening, hoping that the former Moderator would be overtaken by sleep and then leave to proceed to his rest room. It would be then, at that time in his absence, that I would call for the resolutions on the Moderator's speech. I was almost sure that the furthest he would remain awake especially having taken dinner, would not be beyond 9 pm.

It then happened that before the delegates adjourned for the evening meal, I raised a motion stating: *"Noting the heavy agenda before the GAC and the limited time we have, I propose that we take some time this evening to clear some of the agendas which will lessen the burden so that we will be done by lunch time on Saturday because some delegates will be travelling to far places. Otherwise, as you can all note, we are getting behind schedule yet we have a lengthy and weighty agenda to handle."*

This motion was seconded and adopted. No sooner had the delegates taken their dinner than they all came back for more deliberations. As we proceeded with the business, I constantly kept a watchful eye on the opposing past Moderator until around 8:30 pm when he started to doze. One Thing I very well knew was that, without his presence, the other liberals were powerless. I then called one of the clergymen and whispered to him:

"The past Moderator is having a hard time as he is dozing; please approach him and request that you take him to bed. This will give me an opportunity to call for the deliberation on the Moderator's speech. I am sure you know what I am up to." Simon responded, *"It is true he is being overtaken by sleep. I will do that now."* It worked! The past Moderator accepted the offer. As soon as he got into the car, I said: *"It is important we adjourn*

the meeting at 9 pm, and therefore, we can only work on an agenda that will not demand a lot of time. In this case, let us now look at the Moderator's speech resolutions."

I immediately called upon the people who had been working on the Moderator's report to take the floor and present it to the delegates. Already, some of the delegates were dozing, and I knew they would work it fast so that they could proceed to their beds. It was as I had predicted. All the resolutions were passed without much pressure.

The resolution to have an overhaul in the style of the PCEA worship was passed and a committee to work on it was put in place. A letter was to be written to all congregations, letting them know of the changes in the style of worship, which was to start with immediate effect. The traditional one-man manned drum was to be discarded and replaced with key-boards, drum sets and other musical instruments that the congregation and especially the young people, desired to have.

Every congregation was given the green light to recruit praise in worship teams and groups of intercessors. Physical movements during congregational worship were now allowed according to the beats and rhythms of the tunes and songs sung. Raising of hands in worship was also allowed. People would even speak out their prayers audibly. It was also decided that presbyteries and Kirksessions were to deal with any minister or elder who would try to block any of the resolutions pertaining to worship.

The following day, when the custodian past Moderator learned about the passing of the resolutions, he was burning with fiery rage. He was overheard saying, *"This cannot be! This cannot be! The system of the Church cannot be distorted while some of us are alive."* It then happened that, after the morning session of the meeting, and having said a prayer over food, I asked the members of the Business Committee to remain behind as I had something to communicate to them. (The Business Committee is the Church organ that takes care of Church matters between the GAC and GA). Having communicated to them what I had in mind, I was on the verge of dismissing them when the agitated past Moderator, his eyes red and glowing with fiery anger, stood up and said:

"*Moderator, I understand that there are the so-called resolutions that were passed regarding some changes in the Church worship. I am fully opposed to this, and as I said earlier, these are the Church traditions that the leaders of this Church have safeguarded over the years. It, therefore, cannot be that a single person like you can reverse this system. I am therefore declaring such resolutions as null and void.*"

Even as he was speaking, there were a number of hands raised with echoes of "*Point of order! Observation! Point of Information!*" I, therefore, pointed to one of them to speak. He said, "*Moderator, the speaker is confusing the delegates. He boasts of being a custodian of the Church traditions. One tradition says when an agenda has been debated in a Church court and it is adopted, it cannot be revisited, for it has already entered into the Church by- laws. In this case, the speaker is out of order and I am proposing we don't waste any more time in debating this. After all, we are just a section of the whole house. The others have already left for lunch. Moreover, we are already getting late for our lunch.*"

More hands were raised. I pointed to another person to speak. He said, "*Moderator, I am supporting the person who has just spoken. I am urging you, Moderator to dismiss us so that we can take our lunch and come back for the other agenda meant for today. After all, the past Moderator is the author of the Church constitution. In this case, he should know better what the constitution says. When an agenda on any matter has been deliberated upon, and a resolution concluded, such matters cannot be revisited.*"

I then asked, "*Is that the opinion of the majority.*" The air was torn apart by the shouting that followed where the members in one accord said: "*Yes! Yes!*" The matter ended there, and I immediately declared the meeting over.

It is no wonder the PCEA Church has enjoyed a changed pattern of worship, including keyboards, drum sets, a lively worship with clapping and raising of hands. There is also an allocated time for each person to speak out personal prayers. In my humble opinion, this is one of the lasting beacons that through God's help, I planted into the PCEA. If this never happened, then the PCEA as we know it today would be quite different with only a handful of young people, not to mention of the many people who would have left the Church. I am always thankful to God for using me despite the scars of opposition that I encountered.

I am always thankful to God for the boldness that He bestowed upon me through the power of the Holy Spirit. One of the distinguishing marks of the Holy Spirit in the New Testament Church was the spirit of boldness. One of the greatest qualities of faith is to attempt great things for God and expect great things from Him through holy boldness and daring steps. When we are dealing with a supernatural being and taking instructions from Him that are humanly impossible, it is actually easier for us to take a lot than it is to take a little. And it is easier to stand in a place of bold trust than in a place where we cautiously and timidly cling to the shore.

This is the kind of understanding and trust in Him who according to John 15:16, He chose me rather than me choosing Him: He set me apart and commissioned me to go and bear fruit that will last. Looking back, I am thankful to Him for He used me to bear lasting fruits in PCEA.

People called me all sorts of names, they scandalized me, and many times planned to eliminate me, but God remained my Rock. I took refuge in Him: He was my Fortress, my Shield, the Horn of my salvation, my Deliverer and my Stronghold.

After this meeting and the subsequent great achievements, I felt energized to boldly and uncompromisingly leave no stone unturned until PCEA was swimming in the Apostolic Church model. I went about teaching and calling upon the church to adopt everything to do with spiritualizing the denomination.

Some of these included:

1. THE ROLE OF THE HOLY SPIRIT

The place of the Holy Spirit in the PCEA was of great concern to me, especially the notion and belief the Church held for many years that this denomination had nothing to do with the Holy Spirit. They emphasized that PCEA is not a 'Kiroho Church.' (Not a church filled with the Holy Spirit). Karoo is a Gikuyu word meaning spirit-filled; hence, PCEA had no association with the Holy Spirit. They instead emphasized '*Mutaratara*', which is another Gikuyu word meaning, a church addicted to a special orderliness in church matters.

This is a concept congenital to the Church of Scotland, where traditions take precedence over the Holy Spirit. Like them, the PCEA upheld what Jesus referred to as the '*Traditions of the Elders*.' In the PCEA church, this spirit is enshrined in a precious document which holds the Church guiding principles referred to as, '*Practice and Procedure*.' This, in reality, is the Church **Constitution**. It is ideally a replica of Scottish traditions, practices and procedures, which, in essence, override the totality of the scriptures. This then dehydrates the Church spiritually.

Cognizant of this appalling situation, I felt it my duty to call upon the Church to embrace the gifts of the Holy Spirit. This is the main foundation of the Church. Remember, Jesus had cautioned the disciples against leaving Jerusalem until they got imparted with the power of the Holy Spirit. The impartation took place much later on the Day of Pentecost, which apparently happens to be the Birth-Day of the Universal Church.

This is why, in spite of much opposition, I felt the need to go the extra mile to summon the Church to embrace this catalyst of Church empowerment. I kept on emphasizing the fact that the Holy Spirit is the heartbeat of the Church. Hence, without this heart-beat, the Church is rendered lifeless. It is the Holy Spirit that inspires the congregations into prayerfulness, praising and reading of the Word as contained in the scriptures. My joy has always been based on the fact that, by the time I finished my terms as the Moderator of the General Assembly, the Church had fully embraced the role of the Holy Spirit in its body. People could at least worship God in Spirit and in truth.

Unfortunately, as soon as I got out of office, much of my charisma was suppressed by those who came into office after me. In fact, a lot of their energy was used in trying to erase all that I had instilled into the life of the Church, both physically and spiritually. Fortunately, the charismatic trend had already become so entrenched in Church life so much such that they could not totally erase the movement. But one thing they somehow managed to eradicate is the movement I had already started in raising an army of intercessors in the entire denomination.

Some of these include Elder Districts, decentralization, motivation of sub-divisions of presbyteries and parishes, something that was suffocated before I took the reins of leadership. Many projects are still serving their intended purpose despite other vital ones having been sold to quench the spirit of corruption, which crept in back and fast after my departure.

In my endeavor to convey the role of the Holy Spirit, I made reference to Authors who matter in this field. For example, John Calvin, the Founder of the Presbyterian Church. I told the leaders that, according to John Calvin, as indicated by T.H.L Parker in the book, *'John Calvin,'* the Holy Spirit is the one who matters most as far as the spirituality of a person is concerned. Parker, in quoting Calvin, says: "*The Lord teaches us in His word, then He confirms it in Sacrament, but He shines in our minds by the light of His Holy Spirit and opens a way into our hearts for His Word and Sacrament.*" (Page 50).

Further, the importance of the Holy Spirit in the life of the Church is pointed out by Thomas B. White in his book; '**The Believers Guide to Spiritual Warfare**,' where he says, "*When we do not yield to the control of the Holy Spirit, we become potential targets of evil spirits.*" I further pointed out that the Holy Spirit is the driving force for the Church. This was even revealed on the Day of Pentecost, where a crowd of Jews under the conviction of the Holy Spirit cried out: "*Brethren, what shall we do?*" and Peter said to them, "*Repent and be baptized every one of you in the name of Jesus Christ and you shall receive the gift of the Holy Spirit*" (Acts 2: 37-38).

The Holy Spirit is within the god-head. This is why Jesus told His disciples, "*I will ask the Father, and He will give you another counselor to be with you forever – the spirit of truth…Holy Spirit… will teach you all things*" (John 14: 15, 25). The Holy Spirit should be part of the worship of God. Thus, as Jesus put it, "*A time is coming… when the true worshippers will worship the Father in Truth and in Spirit... God is Spirit, and His worshippers must worship in Spirit and in Truth*" (John 4:23 – 24).

Simply put, there is no true worship where the Holy Spirit is not totally involved. It is unfortunate that the pioneer missionaries that planted the Word of God in Africa and elsewhere chose not to portray the Holy Spirit as a vital aspect of the Christian life. But rather, they could only give what they possessed. They lacked the zeal to embrace the Holy Spirit in totality. Many were leaning towards Freemasonry.

2. THE IMPACT OF PRAYER IN THE CHURCH

I spent quite some time and energy to emphasize the subject of prayer - the importance of prayer to the life of the Church. Even before I had become the GA Moderator, I was known as a person who had great concern over the way the PCEA seemed to demean the role of prayers in the Church. Prayers had been the preserve of one person with what was referred to as the long prayer verbalized by an individual. This particular 'long' prayer had to be short and precise and in a common sequence that included mandatory prayers for the government, the church, the sick, as well as the weather among other things. The conclusion of the prayer was marked by the Lord's Prayer.

In my endeavor to push this message to the Church, I used to refer my listeners to the authors Doug and Brand in their Book, 'Prayer that Shapes the Future', in which the two authors remind us of the role of prayers during the time of reformation. In the book, they say: *"If you go back to the beginning of most of our denominations and mission works today, you will find that they were founded on the basis of dynamic prayers. This was true, for example, not only of the Lutheran Reformation but of the Scottish Reformation as well. It was said of John Knox that Mary Queen of Scots, feared his prayers more than all armies of Scotland. Thus, as we expose the roots of the Presbyterian movements in sixteenth-century Scotland, we find there evidence of dynamic prayer. The Presbyterian denomination, like so many others, have sprung up from prayer"*.

It was in that regard that I persistently called upon the Church to give room to the ministry of intercession. While doing this, I pointed out the fact that the missionaries blocked this important '*artery*' for the Church's empowerment. I, therefore, encouraged the Church leaders to pave the way for the intercessory ministry where those gifted as intercessors and prayer warriors could enrich the Church by standing in the gap.

I further reminded the Church that God has called the Church to seek Him in prayers and intercession so as to attain the power to subdue the enemy and take dominion over the Church and the land. In doing this, the Church will have to move to higher spiritual realms illegally held by Satan and take it by force (Matthew 11:12). It will also create an atmosphere where the Holy Spirit can transform the Church and the families of that particular Church (John 14:26).

Prayers **liberate** communities from idolatry and all kinds of evil. Prayers lay new **foundations** that can sustain the goodness of God (John 4:39-42) and stand out against iniquity (Deut. 30:19-20). Through prayer, **God speaks** to the Church prophetically. Prayers also help people to **listen and hear God** when they pray for the church, the families and the nation, among others, as portrayed in Luke 11:2, was my message.

One thing I was aware of was the fact that the PCEA leadership had, over the years, been opposed to people praying loudly. Wherever I found an opportunity, I reminded my listeners about the fact that the reformers were also known for praying loudly. For example, a friend of Martin Luther the Reformer, in telling how Luther prayed aloud, said, "*Not a day passes in which he does not employ in at least three of his very best hours.*" He then continues to review how Luther prayed loudly by stating: "*Once I happened to hear him at prayer. Gracious God! What spirit and what faith is there in his expressions! He petitions God with as much reverence as if he were in the divine presence, and yet with as firm hope and confidence as he would address a father or a friend*". Calvin advocated that "*if the spirit of God so moves you that, you feel, you simply must give utterance to what is in your heart, then do not hesitate.*" John Wesley spent two hours daily in prayer. He began at 4 a.m. in the morning. In most cases, he prayed as if he was talking with God. Yet, it is this version of prayers that PCEA and some other denominations have earnestly resisted.

My main concern as the GA Moderator was the **prayerlessness in the Church**. It was one of the areas that I had to point out during any of the meetings and seminars. In a GAC held at Chogoria, I took the

31

opportunity to remind the delegates that the prayer system in PCEA had its Foundation set in the traditional Scottish manner that only allowed the one praying the monopoly to pray in the set sequence. The congregants were supposed to remain completely silent and not even respond with an *"Amen"* as the speaker continued to pray. If anyone happened to interject, such an individual would be marked by the elders and rebuked in the church vestry after the service. This was when the elders and deacons did a postmortem of the service in the vestry. The victim would normally be warned against such behavior since it portrayed one as being possessed by the Holy Spirit, something that was totally against PCEA culture. To reverse this, I had called upon the Church leadership to allow members, including the leaders, to pray for themselves in the Church.

I emphasized that praying in church should be a communal activity, not a one-man show. It's worth noting that the missionaries never prayed in their own words; instead, they relied on pre-written prayers. As a result, their prayers often lacked a spiritual appetizer.

To encourage communal prayer, I reminded people of the events that took place in the upper room on the day of Pentecost. This event established the model of prayer in the church, which was the Lord's Prayer as taught by Jesus. In the upper room, everyone present participated in prayer. This communal prayer system was what led to the birth of the church of Christ. I told the delegates at Chogoria, *"I am always convinced that a prayerless Church is a half-dead Church. It could be likened to Lazarus who, though resurrected, could not do anything because he was tied up until Jesus said, 'Take off the grave clothes and let him go'"* John 11 verse 44.

I went on to say, *"In fact, spoken-out prayer is important. This is why before Jesus called out to Lazarus from death, he first prayed loudly, as verses 41 and 42 indicate. A prayer spoken out between an individual and God is quite powerful. This is why John Calvin, Martin Luther and John Wesley had to pray quite often through verbally spoken prayers. Jesus was not enjoined by the congregation when he spoke out a prayer that could lead to Lazarus' resurrection. His prayer was a direct communication to God."*

In my endeavour to hammer this message home, I persistently reached out to the parishes, presbyteries and various Church groups to always instill the spirit of prayer into the Church. I would tell them to "*Take off the grave clothes and let it go!*"

In the Chogoria GAC, I took the opportunity to remind the delegates of the pioneer Presbyterian Missionary Dr. Irvine, who evangelized that part of Kenya and established the Presbyterian Church. Among all the Scottish missionaries who came to Kenya, none surpassed Irvine in terms of his prayer life. Irvine was very much submerged in prayer in his entire Christian life.

This evidence is captured by John Wilkinson in his book, '*The Story of Chogoria'*, in which he says, "*One of the most significant activities in the daily life of Chogoria was Prayer*". Dr. Irvine is quoted to have written back to Scotland saying that there was much labour in planting the mission work, "*but the far harder work of winning souls is done by the far harder work of praying.*" Dr. Irvine became well known for his practice and belief in prayer as a natural expression of the Christian life. He talked of prayer as a '*telephone to heaven.*' Dr. Irvine arrived in Chogoria in October 1922 and had his first church dedicated in June 1923. I, therefore, called upon them to emulate Irvine and stimulate the church into in-depth prayers, just like the Apostolic Church did.

In my endeavour to win over the Church in the aspect of prayer, I also argued that Jesus treated prayers as the force behind every achievement in a Christian's life. His disciples had come to realize the same and hence, the reason behind their well-known plea to their master, '*Teach us how to pray.*' This plea by the disciples to Jesus spells out the outstanding importance of prayer in the Church.

It is important to note that the disciples had already realized that it was customary for Jesus to leave them at particular hours to be on his own in prayer. The disciples were inspired by this habit and desired it as a heritage from the master himself. They did not ask for knowledge in preaching, nor for wealth, fame, power or for the ability to extract money from the mouth of a fish. They just wanted to know "*how to pray.*" In saying this, they were asking Jesus to teach them how to ask, knock and seek the kingdom of God first. Just as Jesus had emphasized by saying, "*Ask and it will be given to you; seek and you will find; knock and the door will be opened to you*" (Mt.7:7).

William Beckham, in his book, '*The Second Reformation*', echoes the importance of prayer when he says:

"*Prayer must take on a comprehensive meaning. It must happen at all levels of the Church, including in the cell meetings, in leadership meetings, in the weekly body life of the cells, in the whole Church and in families as individuals. The largest Churches in the world do not just have a cell system where everyone can have community life; they are also known for their prayer.*"

In my seminars on prayer and other related meetings, such as on the 24th of January, 2004 at St. Andrews, March 19th, Nairobi Region, 25th March, Central Region, June 22nd at Elburgon, January 6th, 2005 in Murang'a Presbytery, January 27th, Limuru, March 19th, 2005 Eastern Presbyteries, July 8th. 2005, Nakuru West Church, 2nd September, 2005 at Tumutumu Presbytery, 3rd September 2005 at Nyeri Hill Presbytery, 9th September 2005 at Former Nyandarua Presbytery, among others, I made it clear to the participants that the truth of the matter was that the heartbeat of the Church life was prayer – it is the Church booster – without which the Church loses spiritual network. I used to direct the Church to what E.M. Bounds says in his book, '*The Weapon of Prayer,*' "*When the Church is in the condition of prayer, God's cause always flourishes, and His Kingdom on earth always triumphs. But when the Church fails to pray, God's cause decays, and evil of every kind prevails.*" In other words, God works through the prayers of His people, and when they fail Him at this point by not praying, decline and deadness ensue. It is according to the divine plans that Spiritual prosperity comes through the prayer – channel.

I did, in many speaking engagements, emphasize the fact that a praying Church creates a spiritual atmosphere most favorable to preaching. The Spirit of prayer in a congregation begets an atmosphere surcharged with the Holy Spirit. In this way, God removes obstacles and gives the Word of the Lord the right of way. People in the church seats given to praying for the Church are the poles, which hold up the wires along which the electric current runs. But they hold up the wires along which the divine power runs to the hearts of people. They make conditions favorable for the preaching of the Gospel and for the people to worship and receive God's blessings.

No man will pray long and continue in sin. Praying breaks up bad living. Prayer makes the word of the Lord go forward strongly and rapidly. Unbelief and prayerlessness go together. It is written of our Lord in Matthew's Gospel that when He entered into His own Country, "*He did not do many mighty works there because of their unbelief.*" Their unbelief was anchored on their prayerlessness. Prayerlessness in the Church seats is a serious hindrance to the learning of the Word of the Lord. It also creates a hindrance to the praise in worship breakthrough.

The preaching of the Word to a prayer-less congregation falls at the feet of the preacher. It has no traveling force; it stops because the atmosphere is cold, unsympathetic, and unfavorable to it getting to the hearts of men and women. It takes prayers in the pulpit and prayers in the pews to make preaching captivating, life-giving and soul-saving. I always kept on telling the Church that the origin of the PCEA Church's prayerlessness goes back to the times of the missionaries. Only a few, like Dr. Irvine, had the breakthrough in prayer. Incidentally, Irvine did not come from Scotland. He was sent by the Gospel Missionary Society from America. He designed the Chogoria Church pews in a way that enabled one to kneel in prayer. Irvine wondered how the Church could try or expect to fulfill its mission/ mandate or to be a pleasing organ to God without anchoring its total commitment in prayer.

It is no wonder that the Scottish missionaries hated Irvine due to his prayer life. They called it non-procedural and non-Presbyterian as it did not align with the mode of worship life practiced by the Church of Scotland. This was despite the founder of this Church, John Knox, being a very prayerful person. Knox was what we could refer to today as a prayer warrior, and after his death, the prayer life of the Church was distorted by the Freemasons who had greatly infiltrated the Church.

Unfortunately, many of such Masonic adherents came to Kenya and other countries as missionaries where they planted the same spirit of unbelief. As a result, the Church has never marveled at the dwarfed past of prayer life. I remember saying the following at a seminar held in the Central Region:

*"The pioneer converts were babies who had to take spiritual milk, but we are not. We have spiritually matured and don't have to depend on outsiders to lead us in the path of spiritual life. Our guiding tool is scripture, which we can now read for ourselves under the influence of the Holy Spirit. We no longer need **'brokers'** in order to know the truth contained in the Word of God. And having known the truth, we need to go to the Western countries to evangelize them because they brought us a half-baked message on the assumption that they knew the truth. Little did they know that they knew not. They had a gospel that was mixed with the Masonic spirit of anti-Christ. They even defiled the sanctuaries by embedding pagan gods in them. But all in all, we thank God for the little they gave us, for by God's grace, it acted like yeast and led us to the true revelation of God's Word."*

In another seminar I held in Nairobi Presbytery, I conclusively and affirmatively said:

"Let us not again willfully grieve the Holy Spirit by declining, neglecting or hesitating to seek to have Jesus in full as He is willing to give Himself to us. If we believe that prayer is the greatest need in our work and in the Church, if we truly desire to pray more, then let us turn to the very source of power and blessing. Let us believe that the Spirit of prayer, in His fullness, is for us.

I further said:

Let even the Ministers and elders enroll themselves as intercessors in big numbers. Let us also be encouraged as the household of PCEA to be spending more time in prayers, more often as we possibly can. We should even feel compelled by the Holy Spirit to sacrifice our sleep at night for spiritual connectivity with our creator. Unless we do this, this Church will continue to be spiritually dwarfed. Prayer is the fountain that waters God's way of life in any fruitful Church. If neglected, the Church will continually exist like a big but hollow bread."

I emphasized the fact that without prayer, the Church is robbed of its sweetness, and its beauty becomes cold, formal and dead. But when rooted in the secret place where God meets and walks and talks with His own, the church will grow into such a testimony of divine power that all men will feel its influence and be touched by the warmth of its love. Thus, resembling our Lord and Master, the Church will be used for the glory of God and the salvation of our fellow men. This is true because prayer gives wheels to the Church under God's Word and gives wings to the Church's growth under the influence of the Holy Spirit.

The life, power, and glory of the Church are in prayer. The life of its members is dependent on prayer. The presence of God is secured and retained by prayer. The very place of the church is made sacred by its prayer ministry. Without it, the Church is lifeless and powerless. Without it, even the sanctuary itself is nothing more than just another structure altogether. Prayer gives a peculiar sacredness to the sanctuary; it sanctifies it, sets it apart for God, and conserves it from all common and mundane affairs. It is for this reason that Jesus called the Church building the *"House of Prayer."* The only thing that hinders this flow in the Church is the presence of occult symbols in the sanctuary.

The Church should train intercessors and prayer warriors on how to spiritually demolish these strongholds and, at the same time, raise up godly altars.

Looking at the present prayer life in the PCEA, I am always thankful to God through whose hand, this denomination got totally dressed up in expressive prayer life. The old resistant spirit of unbelief lost its grip and now the denomination is no longer tightly tied to the old system, though there still is a big room for improvement. But the reader should be aware that this was not easily done without stiff opposition and the calls for my imminent impeachment were the price I had to pay ultimately. The time was a real psychological torture, with numerous meetings held in different presbyteries to hinder the new wave of change. The liberals, the ungodly cartels, only seemed to bark, but God had made them toothless and could, therefore, not bite. But worth noting is that, I would not have achieved much without birthing the movement on intercessory prayers.

INTERCESSORY PRAYERS

I used to tell the Church that our prayer lifestyle could be likened to a ship sailing close to the shore. This is anyway risky for the ship and results in very slow movement if any. I, therefore called upon the

Church to launch out into the sea and then have no fear of stormy winds. In my seminars on this topic, I used to talk of an old Englishman who used to pray;

"O Lord, send us into the deep waters of the sea, for we are so close to shore that even a small breeze from the Devil could break our ship to pieces on the rocks. Again, Lord, send us into the deep waters of the sea, where there will be plenty of room to win a glorious victory." Otherwise, sailing close to the shore is like fair-weather faith, which is not faith at all. We want to sail near the shore just because we can see the land and, therefore, feel safe. But how important is it for God to keep us focused on things that are unseen, for we are so easily snared by the things we can see?

If Peter wanted to walk on water, he had to walk. However, if he wanted to swim to Jesus, he had to swim. He couldn't do both. Similarly, for a bird to fly, it must stay away from fences and trees and trust the buoyancy of its wings. If it tries to stay within easy reach of the ground, it won't fly well. It could also be easily hit from the ground. I used to tell my audience that we must move out of our comfort zones and dive into the great sea of prayer. This is intercessory prayers! And we, therefore, become **intercessors.**

This call was greatly resisted by the traditionalist defenders of **Scottish Traditional Culture**.

Nevertheless, spiritually, I was convinced that this was from the Lord. I believe that a person who hasn't learned to use the power of the Holy Spirit to guide him or her toward heaven hasn't yet mastered the art of sailing and is still an apprentice.

It is in recognition of the significance of prayer in an individual's life, as well as in the **life of the Church**, in mind, that I called for the creation of the intercessory ministry. This ministry equips the Church to engage in all kinds of spiritual warfare and is the Church's primary spiritual weapon. It comprises the helmet of salvation, the breastplate of righteousness, the belt of truth, the shield of faith and the Sword of the Spirit, which is the Word of God. Intercession then becomes the Christian's main avenue to bring about breakthroughs in all sectors of the Church life. It is only comparable to the stone that David used in knocking down Goliath. It is in this regard that I challenged the Church to facilitate the establishment of a PCEA

Prayer Centre, where the members of the denomination could go to seek the face of the Lord. Unfortunately, this idea of building a prayer centre was embraced by very few Church leaders, and therefore it never materialized. But the truth of the matter is that if what I was asking for was a money-generating institution, it would have easily sailed through because of the existence of the money-thirsty spirit among many of the Church leaders. Income generating institutions are treated as a good source of money but not an institution that would help the Church in generating spiritual life in the Church!

I would say with finality that by God's grace, I raised a host of intercessors. I could not have fully succeeded in the area of activating prayers and overcoming the evil strongholds that were dwarfing PCEA both spiritually and physically without placing gatekeepers in the Church. These gatekeepers were the intercessors and prayer warriors. Such were the people whom God had given the gift of intercessory and they became the driving force of the Church. Biblical examples of intercessors include King Jehoshaphat, as indicated in 2Chr 20, Esther (Esther 4:15-17), and Anna (Luke 2:36-37), among many others.

I would liken intercessors/prayer warriors with Gideon's three hundred soldiers who, just by the use of trumpets and firebrands, defeated the Midianites, the Amalekites and all the other Eastern peoples, *"thick as Locusts.... Their camels could no more be counted than the sand on the seashore"* (Judges 7:12). How did the three hundred defeat those people? *"They blew their trumpets and broke the jars that were in their hands...the Lord caused the men throughout the camp to turn on each other with their swords"* (Judges 7:12, 22).

The intercessors have spiritual fire placed in their hearts (jars) and the swords of the spirit. And for the intercessors to be spiritually empowered with authority to do that, I had to commission them. It is for this course that I had an intensive program of commissioning intercessors as one part of my Moderator's duties. I remember in the first three months, I commissioned intercessors, therefore, creating pockets of intercessors in the entire PCEA. No Spiritual battles would be won without commissioned intercessors.

In the various seminars I organized, I reminded the participants that it's the Lord's desire that more and more intercessors be raised in the Churches for the sake of the nations, churches, families and institutions. Intensified prayers and fasting are the best weapons to use during times of crisis. From the 15th till the 21st of September, I met ministers of the National Fraternal at Pwani PCEA, where we talked about many things, including the need and power for intercession, homosexuality, symbols and so on. The country was then facing a lot of issues. This was why having sensed the dark cloud that was to envelope Kenya in 2007, on February 2nd. I met all intercessors in the Nairobi region on Feb 6th. I extended the same to the Tanzanian Presbyteries. On February 10th, I had another meeting with the intercessors in the Nakuru region, followed by the Mt. Kenya region on the 24th of February the same year. On March 15th and 28th, 2007, I would continue with impactful meetings with the intercessors in the Mt. Kenya region and adjoining areas. I then summoned PCEA to pray and fast for 40 days (Oct. 21st – Nov 30th) before the 2007 elections. They further prayed and fasted the last 7 days before the elections (20th Dec to 26th). The election day was held on Dec 27th.

In my efforts to further intensify the issue of intercessory prayers, on November 9th, we had an intercessory Kesha in the Nairobi Presbytery. Later, on 23rd November, there was a meeting of the intercessors in Eldoret. We continued with intercessory prayers long after the elections. For instance, on March 7th. - 17th. in 2008, I was part of the Mombasa Pentecostal Msafara that engaged in praying for Kenya from Mombasa to Kisumu.

On August 11th, there was a National Intercessors Conference organized by the Pentecostal churches in Eldoret to which I was invited and participated for the good of the nation. On October 31st, the same year, in Nakuru, at the Nakuru West Presbyterian Church, we held National intercessory prayers. The Murang'a National Intercessory prayers followed on the 1st and 2nd of November the following month, in 2008, at Muranga Presbytery.

God had already prepared the ground for this as already the Church was vibrant with intercessors. All the Church was praying. I believe that kind of intensified prayers and fasting had a great impact on the nation of Kenya. That election was followed by hostility, where over 1,200 people perished. I believe the situation would have been comparable to what had taken place in Rwanda if it were not for the many believers and Churches that were engaged in prayers.

Thank God, there is a worldwide reawakening in the area of intercessory prayers. One just needs to look around the globe and see that the Holy Spirit is at work. And this was my message to PCEA. I drew their attention to renowned advocates of intercessory prayers like Robert Raines who speaks on the awareness of the coming universal church revival. In this regard, he calls upon the church to watch for its tide rolling in, and then to catch it, and to seek to ride with it and to make new channels for these rivers of grace. He says, *"We are to be instruments for the Holy Spirit who is awakening us and breathing power into our sleeping Churches to create the conditions of conversion."*

Robert further says: *"The Holy Spirit is at work in power in our time. The dry bones are beginning to live again. The hand of God, still small on the horizon, is becoming big with judgment."*

He further says, *"The Holy Spirit is loose again in the world; lives are changing; the Church is being reborn and renewed in place after place.... Persons are becoming apostles. There is hope for the recovery of the mission. Now is the day of salvation. Now are Christ's people summoned to prepare for his coming."*

USE OF ANOINTING OIL

I called upon the Church to make use of anointing oil. The church then considered it as heresy. Anointing oil could neither be used nor mentioned in PCEA. Yet, the use of anointing oil is biblical. The Apostles used it. Apostle James calls upon Church leaders to use it when he says, *"Is any one of you sick? He should call the elders of the Church to pray over him and anoint him with oil in the name of the Lord"* (James 5:14). James says that this kind of anointing by an elder or pastor will have immediate spiritual results. Its immediate consequence, as James says, is an impact on the one being anointed because *"The prayer offered.... Will make the sick person well, the Lord* will raise him up. If he has sinned, he will be forgiven" (James 5:15). Now what is wrong with the use of anointing oil if it has such a positive spiritual impact? I kept on insisting that the Church had to search for the truth hidden in the scriptures. I told them that God's truth is not found in manmade traditions and constitutions.

I even quoted David J. Schwartz, who, in his book, '*The Magic of Thinking Big*', says, "*Don't let traditions paralyze your mind. Be receptive to new ideas. Be experimental. Try new approaches. Be progressive in everything you do.*" I kept reminding the people of the fact that the Church's path is marked by the devil's strategic attacks, which we call spiritual warfare. It is for this reason that Apostle Paul called upon Ephesian Christians to:

"*Take the whole armor of God that you may be able to withstand in the evil day, and having done all, to stand. Stand therefore, having girded your loin with truth, and having put on the breastplate of righteousness, and having shod your feet with the equipment of the gospel of peace; above all taking the shield of faith, with which you can quench all the flaming darts of the evil one. And take the helmet of salvation and the sword of the Spirit, which is the word of God. Pray all the times in the Spirit, with all prayer and supplication*" (Eph. 6:12 – 18).

Those who are Church leaders should especially remain alert to satanic attacks. Again, quoting Thomas White in his book, '*Spiritual Warfare,*' where he says,

"*Any servant of Jesus Christ who poses a serious threat to the power of hell will be targeted and will encounter resistance, especially at times of strategic ministry. The anointed agent of Christ's kingdom must be equipped to discern and deal with the efforts of the enemy's kingdom.*"

In his book, '*Prayer that Shapes the Future,*' Brad agrees with Thomas when he says: "*Only by dynamic prayer can we move against '**the gates of hell.'** ..the demonic, the occult, and the false spiritualties that are gaining strength all around us. There are times we will need to overcome the demonic strongholds through anointing.*"

This book is part of the books that cover Dr. David M. Githii's autobiography. The others include; 'Life through the Burning Bush' and 'Called to serve relentlessly.'

Other books written by the author include; 'Progressive Infiltration of Idolatry into the Universal Church and Nations: A Chronological Perspective,' 'Kenya Repent or Perish,' 'How to Grow a Healthy' and 'Vibrant Church Through Small Church Groups,' 'Tithing: Principles and Practices,' 'Phases of The Church,' 'Exposing and Conquering Satanic Forces over Kenya." Unfortunately, apart from the 'Progressive Infiltration of Idolatry in the Universal Church and Nations' (a must-read book), all others are out of print.

3 THE ESTABLISHMENT OF ELDERS' DISTRICTS IN PCEA

Elder Districts could qualify as one of the key pillars that God led me to establish. No one looking at the PCEA today and noting the great role played through the Elder Districts would wonder how the Church ever existed without this channel through which both physical and spiritual aspects of the Church needs are met.

But to be what it is today, this concept has a history behind it. This is a history not many people in the PCEA Church know about- its birth and development. If there is one thing that I will ever be remembered for by the PCEA's future generations, it is the establishment of Elder Districts. The conception of the concept of the Elders' Districts into the PCEA was through my two personal experiences.

During my leadership as a headmaster of various schools between 1972 and 1980, I had successful teams in soccer and athletic competitions. My school teams used to go all the way from Zonal level to district and even provincial level. Therefore, my schools were widely known, especially in the Nakuru District, for excelling.

This excellence was achieved through the mechanism of subdividing the whole school community into Small groups called 'Houses' with each named after mountains found in East Africa, such as Mt Kenya, Mt Kilimanjaro, Mt Longonot, regardless of their orientation, that is, whether soccer, athletic or class in nature used to work in a competitive Spirit. For Example, in sports, groups competed among themselves (two at a time) on different days and then I could finally set a time I called Inter-house competitions where all the houses were to compete in athletics. I could then invite an education officer as a guest of honour, together with the parents and other guests.

A blackboard would be placed in the middle of the field with slots for each house. Therefore, as the students progressed in the competition, the marks each person gained were placed in one's house slot. The feeling that one was being watched by the other students, guests of honour, parents and other local dwellers made the child perform to their best ability. After the competition there were gifts for the best performers. Certificates were also issued for those who attained positions 1 to 3 in each event. There were also trophies for the overall House winners from positions 1 to 3.

These groups would become more visible in sports. Under the government public schools' curriculum, there were two seasons for schools' competitive games: The second term (May to August) was scheduled for athletics, with soccer slated for the third- term (September to October). The competing schools were organized in groups, the smallest ones being the 'Zones.' A number of zones formed a division, and a number of divisions formed a district. Again, a number of districts formed a province while the provinces were national.

The schools competed from the zonal level, with the winning teams advancing to district levels. Those who qualified at the district level could advance to the provincial level. The winners in the provincials met other qualifiers from the other provinces for the national levels. The schools I headed were known for their sporting prowess right from the zonal to national level. What was the secret? The secret lay in the fact that my students began the spirit of competition from the 'Houses' at school.

For example, in athletics, the students first competed among themselves in their houses. The competitions would include field events - throwing shot-put, javelin and discus. The track events were both short and long races, including relays. In this way, each house identified the gifted students per event. Then, the houses would compete in groups of 2, 3 and 4, with each house getting its best performer in each given event.

Finally, there was a special day set, referred to as the 'Inter-Houses Competition', which was a full Sports- Day complete with invited guests, including parents and guardians.

For every race, each house was expected to present their best for the competition. For instance, in the 100-meter race, every house gave out their best person for 100 metres. From every event, I took numbers one to three to represent schools in the zonal competition. Most of these would then end up as winners in the other levels- with a number of them going to the national level. This model enabled me to put up a well-trained, refined and coordinated team. It is no wonder then that this always resulted in my schools always dominating in almost all events with many of my contestants making it to the national schools' championships.

The same would apply to soccer (football) with houses competing among themselves first. Then, combined teams would play against each other. In the course of these knock-outs, we could identify the best players and the best positions they could play in the school team, such as the goalkeeper, center-forward, wing or full-back, among others. These then would form the school team. Through this model and the metrics, the school came out with some of the best performers who could go up to the National Levels. This model was applied in the academic field as well and had a catalytic effect, resulting in excellent academic performance in National exams. The school was placed in positions one to three out of 258 schools that comprised the then Nakuru District.

It was when I was a student doing my practicals at Thogoto Parish that the idea of this unique model loomed in my mind. I wondered whether it would be possible to break the church into small groups as had been practically applicable in the Church environment. I then decided to make an attempt by approaching the parish minister under whom I was being tutored. I explained the idea to him, but to my surprise, he responded by saying, "*That idea doesn't sound good, not even godly. It is a divisive idea which will not only portray you as one with a divisive spirit. It is likely to delay your ordination since the presbytery will look at this negatively.*" With this kind of discouragement, I declined to make any further move for fear of being intimidated. But this did not last long. I could not resist the urge to pursue the idea of introducing a 'small Church groups' movement, which I then interpreted as the Lord's calling, to launch such a movement in the denomination.

I crafted another strategy, yes, another move, to approach the elders of a congregation known as Musa Gitau Memorial Church.

The parish in which I was posted for my practicals as a student-Thogoto Parish, then comprised seven congregations. I cast and explained my vision to the elders of this congregation. To my delight and surprise, they 'bought' the idea. But there was yet another hurdle: the parish minister, who would be a stumbling block to the birthing of the idea.

The elders strongly felt it was such a wonderful idea just to be dismissed like that. So, they sought ways to convince the parish minister, whom they thought could easily yield to the idea as he would have needed their support because of some strife in the parish.

Unfortunately for them, the parish minister was bitterly opposed to the idea, and he said that such a divisive move would not be allowed by the presbytery in which he was the chairman. But the said elders of Musa Gitau congregation defiantly vowed to do whatever it took to support me.

Later on, there was a seminar organized for the congregation which I was to facilitate. I thought this was a perfect opportunity to launch into the deep. It was during the seminar that we managed to pave the way for starting the Elder Districts.

With the help of elders like Lawrence Kiruku (who was my former teacher in primary school), GT, and Michobo among others, I had the Elders Districts program implemented. I had the entire congregation of Musa Gitau Memorial Church subdivided among the eight elders. I then had these small groups meet every Wednesday for at least two hours for fellowship, which included praises, sharing the Word (a kind of Bible study) and prayers.

I then moved a step further to give the districts a number of biblical verses to memorize and recite for at least a month. I could then look for adjudicators to assess the districts at the time set for the competitions. I had certificates issued to the best performers. The whole idea here was to bring people together as the only viable way to cement some lasting cohesiveness within the group. The zeal to win made them work in harmony with a spirit that built unity and oneness. At other times, I could give the groups a selected song from the hymnal and ask them to practice singing in some set-up patterns. This also ended up in competition. Musa Gitau Memorial Church could also be considered the 'labour ward' of Elder Districts in the entire PCEA Church.

The Elder District Movement then became the driving force for the Church's growth in all its aspects: spiritually, economically, politically, and socially or in any other area of the denomination's life. The movement is there to stay over many generations. No wonder, then, the creation of the Elder Districts became one of the key considerations and a catalyst to my being elected as the GA Moderator of the General Assembly, among others.

Secondly, I borrowed a leaf from the apostolic church on the issue of Elder Districts. The New Testament – model of 'House Churches' inspired me. For example, Paul, writing to the Christians in Rome, tells them, "*Greet Priscilla and Aquila.... greet also the Church that meets at their house*" (Rom. 16:4-5). The Apostolic Church existed in pockets of House Churches. In Acts 2:46, Paul says this about such groups, "*They broke bread in their homes and ate together with glad and sincere hearts.*"

Again, take the case of Paul's letter to the Churches in Colossae, where he writes, "*Give my greetings to the brothers at Laodicea, and to Nymphas and the Church in her house*" (Col. 4:15- 16). It then means that, the House Churches became a catalyst for the rapid growth of the Apostolic Church. It paved the way for easier sharing of the scriptures advanced unity and harmony in the believers' lives.

Having realized this, a question came into my mind as to how this House Church model could be applied in a given congregation, with each operating in small groups.

By this time, I was a student doing my practicals at Thogoto Parish in the South Kiambu South Presbytery. I had just finished my theological studies at St. Paul's United Theological College, which is now St. Paul's University.

In the PCEA, after graduating from a theological school, one is placed under an ordained minister for further parochial practical training. Thogoto parish comprised five congregations: Kimuri, Ondiri, Musa Gitau, Lusigiti and Renguti.

I was, therefore, a student under an ordained clergy. My role was, therefore, to learn and follow instructions but not to suggest or come up with any input. That being the case, there was no way I would have floated my idea on the church's small groups, which I have given the name; **'Elder District.'**

Thus, as a student under supervision, it was very risky to come up with anything new and unheard of in PCEA. I knew that if a call to do something for God's purpose did not carry any risk, then it wasn't a call from God. Think of those twelve elders who were given the mandate to take the Ark of Covenant into the waters of River Jordan when the river itself was **'at flood stage?'** as stated in Joshua 3:15. Today, most of the so-called holy men of God would have not dared do such a thing. They would have said, "*You will never see me taking that kind of risk. They will be swept away together with the Ark.*" Yet, "*the priests.... stood firm on dry ground.*" (verse 17).

I felt a divine boldness from heaven. I knew that it was God's obligation for me to have faith and not overlook the fact that I am His vessel to carry out His plans. I was certain that God honours faith - a stubborn faith that solely focuses on His purpose. Faith can assist God in shutting the mouths of lions and quenching the most destructive fire. When we have this kind of stubborn faith that honours God, He is pleased. I believe that all things are possible with God, and this has been the foundation of my faith.

With the faith I possessed, I resolved to float the idea of birthing Elder Districts throughout the PCEA community with God's guidance. I discussed my plan of subdivision with my mentor, the parish minister, and explained to him what was in my mind. This was the subdivision of each congregation into small groups that would be placed under the management of an elder for fellowships and Bible studies. I had asked for an appointment with him. After a prayer, I went into his office and said:
"*I have this idea of having the congregation subdivided among the elders in each church. Based on my experience as a Headmaster, I came up with the idea of creating small groups named after mountains and encouraged them to participate in sports competitions, including soccer and athletics. I found success with this approach in my schools and thought of applying the same concept to the church, but I will need your support to make it happen*".

In response, the parish minister said:
"*I really don't understand the kind of myth you are talking about. denomination has been doing quite well in its current strategic*

49

administration over the years. I warn you that such an idea would not only put you in problems with the Kirk session of this parish but also with the presbytery and even the General Assembly. That is a very misplaced ambition," he concluded.

In response, I said,
"I will see what I can do about it, but I also like listening to God for His word in Isaiah 30:21 says, 'Whether you turn to the right or to the left, your ears will hear a voice behind you, saying, this is the way; walk in it.' And in this case, if this is from the Lord, He will show the way forward. Ours is only to be sensitive to His voice and then act in obedience."

When I later shared my vision with a few elders, they also really discouraged me, especially when I told them about the parish minister's response. They tried to show me that this sort of move would jeopardize my being licensed and my ordination. But then, the more I tried to put this idea out of my mind, the more the will to put it into practice puffed up in my mind. When those thoughts persisted, sometimes making me lose sleep, I discerned that as a hint from God to act.

I became aware that my path towards ordination would be rough, but on the other hand, I realized that the burden of suffering was like a tombstone hung around our necks. Yet, in reality, it was simply the weight necessary to hold the diver down while he was searching for pearls. I also realized that my boat could be tossed by the waves while He *'continues to sleep'*, but incidentally, we are told He never slumbers nor sleeps; neither is He ever too late.

I strongly felt that this was a mandated mission for me to accomplish. I decided to sell this noble idea to the elders of the Musa Gitau congregation. This congregation was named after Reverend Musa Gitau, one of the pioneer African clergy, ordained in 1926. It so happened that those elders were eagerly searching for ways that could enrich their congregation spiritually. They had a positive attitude towards the spiritual feeding of their congregation.

I decided to secretly introduce the idea of Elder Districts to them because I knew at least three of the elders would have opposed the idea. Worse still, those three were in the parish minister's inner circle. I proposed to those elders the need to improve the spirituality in

Musa Gitau Church. I argued that in order for that to happen, we needed to have at least a two-day seminar for the elders and deacons. I assured them that I had some good teachings to offer.

When those elders embraced the idea, I further requested them to propose the same to the parish minister. They should craft a seminar termed **"the spiritual re-awakening of Musa Gitau Memorial Church leadership"** and, at the same time, request that I be the speaker at the seminar. I further advised them that, in urging that I be the speaker, they should argue that, having graduated with a Bachelor of Divinity degree and having listened to my sermons, they felt that I could give some good teachings on this topic. Thank God, my idea sailed through quite well, and the Kirk session allocated a day for the seminar. They also emphasized that the seminar was mandatory for every leader. Lunch would be provided and there would be certificates of attendance issued to the participants.

On the material day, the seminar had a hundred per cent attendance. The topic in my teaching was; *'Congregation's Spiritual Awakening Through Small Church Groups'*. In my teaching, I focused on the Apostolic Church and its rapid growth through emphasis on House Churches. At the same time, I said, *"Rather than calling these pockets of fellowships or House Churches, I propose we call them **'Elder Districts'** simply because they are under the supervision of an elder."*

I explained the fact that the early Church's small group model had several benefits, which if embraced by the parish leaders, would propel Church growth not only spiritually but also physically. The Church in the home provided the most dynamic setting for the distinctively unique Christian fellowship and worship. I gave the following as the benefits of the small church groups, which I called **'Elder Districts'**:

1. The household structure provided a **natural setting** and enabled **Christians to gather together** for **worship** and **fellowship** from the earliest days (see Acts 2:46-47). It was the hospitality found in these House Churches that made it possible for the Christian worship to have common meals and unity, which then acted as a catalyst in sustaining fellowship in each group.

2. The House Church **contributed to the experiential understanding of the Church's essence**. The family household basis must have had an overwhelming effect on the early believers' understanding of the Church as a family-the very household of God (Ephesians 2:18-19; 3:14-15; 5:1; 6:23).

3. The House Church was **a culturally relevant model**. House Churches provided decentralized freedom for breaking bread together and creative expression within the varying cultural settings.

4. The house Churches **nurtured a healthy social integration** of the early Christians. The Apostolic Church was, thus, evidently a healthy cross-section of society reflecting a broad social mixture, from wealthy land – owners to the common slave.

5. The House Church **positively influenced the development of the Church's leaders**. The hosting elders of the small groups became the natural leaders of the Church rather than inheriting leadership. Its structure imparted, through the hosts, actual leadership, which in turn determined the form of Church life (1Corinthians 16:16).

6. The household Church **strengthened the concept of corporate solidarity in the Christian life**. Consequently, conversion in the New Testament was not an exclusively individualistic experience; but often the whole household undertook this experience, resulting in whole household conversions. **Examples include** Cornelius (Acts 10:1-2), Lydia (Acts 16:15-15), and the Philippians jailer (Acts 16:31-34).

In my teaching, I further narrated the benefits of Small Church Groups/Elder Districts, stating that:

•Every Church member receives **equipping for the work of the ministry**.

•**Full – time leaders** are set aside for prayers and to seek God's face for the body of Christ.

• At the small group level, members **take off their masks** and receive **edification** and **healing**. Real New Testament fellowship takes place.

• **Leaders and Pastors provide oversight**, vision and accountability for members of the groups who are also **accountable** to each other in a more understanding and responsible manner.

• Members' **lives overflow with the life-giving experiences** that occur during the group's fellowships, which is reflected in the celebratory worship on Sundays.

• **Multiplication of groups** of converts, disciples and leaders constantly occurs. The small group lives like a cell that continues to sub-divide, forming other cells.

• Operating Small Church Groups has a **radical** and **dramatic impact on society**.

• **Primary care** for individual members is provided **at the group level** instead of the congregation (Ephesians 4:12), and at the same time, leaders equip the members for the work of ministry.

• The '*one another*' passages found in the New Testament have a context in which real spiritual warmth can be experienced.

• The **administration** of the Church is **simplified** around the basic group unit. This significantly reduces the multiple programs necessary to run a traditional Church because the spirit created in a small Church group enhances this basic unit of the Church.

• The Church centered in home groups is designed to **survive persecution** and **pull down the spiritual strongholds** through combined efforts to wage spiritual warfare against the powers of darkness.

• The community of Small Church Groups is **a place of healing for the individual and the family**. One can easily share his or her concerns in such a setting.
• The group **produces** large numbers of **servant leaders** who enable the work of ministry to take place at the basic group level.

• The growth of the Church **doesn't depend on how much square footage can be financed and provided**. The building formula of the Small Church Group is to grow and then split and build.

• The **lost are reached** through the group's friendship evangelism because small groups touch the hearts and needs of the world around them through neighborhood associations.

• The small groups of Christians meet outside the Church building premises and become **basic units of the Church**. There is more freedom of association, sharing of ideas, and eating together in this kind of setting. It is a better forum for the expression of people's gifts. It is a place where one can **share joys** and **sorrows**.

• The small groups can easily advance the congregation's evangelism as the groups take turns to promote such activities as door-to-door evangelism, crusades and open-air meetings. This boosts the delivery of the gospel to the world, thus **enhancing the multiplication** of disciples by equipping them with the work of the ministry.

• The **welfare of the needy** is easily carried out since there exists a spirit to touch the heart and the needs of the world, for example, orphans, widows and widowers.

• The small groups create an **environment for individual** members to **grow** in faith, and one is able to express this faith verbally and practically.

• In a small Church group, individual members are helped to **nurture and activate their spiritual gifts and talents** for the benefit of the kingdom of God. This is essential for edification, equipping and so on in the natural setting of groups in an unhurried environment.

• Members experience both **physical and spiritual healing** as individuals and as families.

• Through the combined unity and effort in the small Church groups, **resources** for the ministries are **available**. The sacrificial spirit is enhanced, especially when the groups meet with the intention of raising funds.

• There is a **corporate endeavor in seeking the face of God** and in cultivating a spirit of intercession through a conducive fellowship, hence more praises and intercession and relaxation in the delivery of the Word. It acts as a training camp for the slow learners, and members become **spiritually connected naturally. The spirit that exists** takes individual masks off, as life **becomes a reality through the relaxed interaction; hence, the worship is more inclusive.**

• The **outgrown groups can easily give birth to other congregations** which finally lead to new parishes and even presbyteries.

That seminar became a great eye-opener to the Musa Gitau Church leadership, and before we totally wound up the seminar, the leaders unanimously agreed to the subdivision of the congregation among the elders. Three elders were given the mandate to formulate the boundaries and give the report to the elders and deacons after three days. True to their word, the report came out after three days.

This move was equally welcomed by the congregation. We then proceeded to subdivide the congregation among the elders. Thus, for the first time in the history of PCEA, the Elder Districts were birthed. Every member of the congregation was attached to an individual elder and deacon. This was in 1984.

I then came up with a program on Elder District visitations, which gave birth to the tradition in PCEA where pastors have to visit the homesteads in every Elder District in each parish. In fact, as soon as a pastor reports in a new parish, the first thing is to visit the districts to acquaint oneself with the individual members.

At first, the elders were hesitant because they had never known of a pastor visiting individual homes of the parish members, but nevertheless, I managed to convince them.

Meanwhile, my Parish Minister was monitoring me with a lot of apprehension. One day the parish messenger brought me a note from the minister which stated that I was required urgently in his office. I discerned that he was already angry with my overlooking his advice and coming up with what I called Elder Districts. When I got into his office, his mood, body language, and facial expression showed open hostility to me. I took a seat and said: "*I got your letter indicating that I came here.*"

He replied;
"*Yes, I felt that I needed you to clarify what I have heard from an elder from the Musa Gitau Church. From what he told me, you have already initiated a program through which you have created smaller Churches within the congregation, and if I recall well, I did caution you from doing anything that is contrary to our Church constitution and traditions. I also warned you that doing such a thing would greatly affect not only your ordination but also your future ministry in this denomination. Just tell me whether you have done something like that?*"

I then said:
"*Before I respond, I feel that it is important we say a word of prayer as we ask God for some guidance in this discussion.*" He said curtly: "*If you feel like praying, you can go ahead.*" I said a short prayer asking for God's presence to guide us through the deliberations, and then I continued to say,
"*Whatever that elder told you is true. Possibly, what he never told you is the fact that everything cropped out after my teaching in that seminar that you had given me blessings to teach. In my teaching and among other topics, I did touch on how the Apostles uplifted the spirituality of the early Church through the small Church groups that they named '***House Churches***.' It was after my teaching that the elders and deacons got excited about that move, and they, in one accord, recommended the launching of what is referred to as the '***Elder Districts***'.*"

I continued to say,
"*They argued that, because the small group is to be manned by an elder, they, therefore, recommended the group's name to be known as an '***Elder District***' rather than call them House Churches or cell groups. In my teaching, I never went outside the Bible, and I believe the Church treats the Bible as the primary guide in matters of spirituality rather than the constitution, which should take a secondary perspective.*"

At that juncture, the minister conclusively said,
"*I am sure your action will not be taken lightly by the presbytery, and whatever outcome this will have in your life, you will have to carry the cross*

alone. Meanwhile, you can leave now. I just wanted to make sure that you were involved in this and if you were the prime mover in this 'divisive church mentality.' "

I left his office. I did not falter in creatively carrying out the advancement of the Elder District activities. Together with the mobilized Elder District visitations, I organized for all the individual district members to meet every Wednesday in homes for fellowship. They would study the Bible and do some praises and prayers. Each district would also present a song on some allotted Sundays.

I went ahead to formulate what I called *'Elder District Competitions,'* where, at one time, I gave a common scripture text to be rehearsed by each group and on an agreed day, they would all come together in competition. During other times, I could give the groups a song that they could practice singing in accordance with the set rules after which the groups came together for competition. I used to outsource some adjudicators from other congregations from Musa Gitau.

The adjudication focused on the following criteria to award marks:
1. Entry   = 5 Marks
2. Arrangement   = 5 Marks
3. Accompaniments   = 10 Marks
4. Rhythm/ Actions   = 40 Marks
5. Flow of music   = 5 Marks
6. Costumes/Dressing   = 10 Marks
7. Sound Production   = 5 Marks
8. Age/Gender   = 15 Marks
9. Impression on the adjudicators   = 5 Marks

Suffice it to say, the more I progressed in bringing out the lifestyle of Elder District activities, the more my Parish Minister became angry and more especially because other congregations in Thogoto Parish had started adopting the same. At one time, he confronted me and said,

"This Church has existed under the current undivided congregation over the years, and it has been doing well. I am taking your introduction of Elder Districts as a divisive way, which is totally opposed to the traditions and constitution of this Church. It is even detrimental to the body of Christ. This

will not go well with you and now especially that you are a minister in the making."

UNPRECEDENTED ANIMOSITY

I really could not understand why the priest could not see the logic behind what I had introduced into the Church. The elders from Musa Gitau persistently tried to convince him about the essence of the Elder Districts but the more they did this, the more they got into loggerheads with him. There was another unexpressed reason for my being persecuted. Thogoto, being the area where the pioneer missionaries first settled, was predominantly Presbyterian. Therefore, the Church here was very loyal to the British colonialists or imperialists. The dwellers here were known as '*Athomi*,' literary meaning the educated ones, the Christianized and hence, the civilized lot.

I had come from a place known as Gikambura widely referred to as Ndeiya, neighbouring Thogoto to the Western side. It somehow leaned towards the remote areas where people were predominantly Maasai in orientation. In this case, the Thogoto people regarded the Gikambura/Ndeiya people as gentiles- uncivilized, uneducated and therefore qualified to be considered pagans. No wonder Thogoto people referred to the Ndeiya area as Ndeiya Ng'ombe. Ng'ombe, in the Gikuyu language, means a cow.

The cow is regarded as a dormant animal; hence, Ndeiya people were seen as dormant people in all aspects of life, including their lifestyle. This area was anti-colonialist, and it was considered the breeding ground for the Mau Mau Movement. Thus, during the struggle by Africans for independence to be free from colonial rule, the dwellers of Gikambura Ndeiya, among others, aggressively demanded the land they regarded had been grabbed by the British. A big percentage of men in this area ended up in guerilla warfare. They had to hide in forests and caves. Many others ended up in prisons, with scores being killed.

This was unlike Thogoto, where a substantial number of the staunch Christian men enjoyed their freedom and were referred to as '*Home Guards*' these acted as informers to the missionaries who then would pass on the information to the imperialists. Even at Gikambura

Ndeiya, there were fewer Home Guards compared to Thogoto. It is also correct to say that there were many men around Thogoto and its surroundings who were Mau Mau fighters. In fact, one of the most wanted senior chiefs by the Mau Mau fighters, Chief Waruhiu wa Kung'u, was shot around the Thogoto area. Thogoto was under the protection of the missionaries.

Thus, by virtue of hailing from Gikambura Ndeiya, I was seen as a child of pagans, uncivilized, with a poor Christian background and tainted by Mau Mau activities. This was worsened by the fact that my father was one of the most noted Mau Mau fighters who, when arrested, was jailed for seven years with hard labour. Gikambura people were not seen or considered as believers. For many years, the only PCEA building available in the area was the Church of the Torch, located in the middle of Thogoto. It is no wonder Thogoto people treated Ndeiya people as gentiles. This is the lense through which Thogoto Church elders and priests viewed non-Thogoto residents. At that time this included my family and I. Families could hardly invite me in their homes.

That being my background, it was felt that I had no mandate to minister to them. What if I got ordained and then I happened to be posted there by the PCEA Appointment Committee? That could have been the worst-case scenario which they dreaded. They could not fathom how to handle it should it have occurred. They hated being ministered to by a; *'pagan oriented'* person, the *'son of a cow spirited'* person. Therefore, in order to prevent such an occurrence, they had to strategize on how to frustrate me as well as block me from being ordained.

One of the ways of frustrating me was to deny me housing or any other kind of support. It is the PCEA tradition that the parish provides decent housing for the student during their practicals, as well as other kinds of support. This includes scheduled visits by parish groups such as the Women's Guild, the Kirk Session, and the youth, among others, to the pastor/student to offer provisions. This is especially for the pastor/students with families.

The Kirk session insisted that if I needed a house, I had to rent one from my own resources, yet I had no other source of income. To make matters worse, they never provided me with any house allowance.

Thank God my parents lived in the same parish, and I was forced to live with them. They lived in a three-roomed house, one of the rooms serving as the 'Sitting Room.' The house was made of timber off-cuts and set with an earthen floor. Some water had to be sprinkled on the floor before sweeping so as to calm down the dust!

The fully furnished and habitable house is traditionally provided before a student trainee is received by the presbytery after being posted. It is the duty of the presbytery to ensure this happens. There has to be good bedding, a gas cooker, running water, electricity – a self- contained house. In contrast, where I lived in my parent's home, there was no electricity and no gas cooker. For light, I depended on a Jerri can with some paraffin set with a wick.

In cooking, my mother used firewood, which, in most cases, was not dry and therefore produced a lot of smoke. The parish minister remained adamant about my accommodation and could not listen to the many pleas over my plight to offer more appropriate housing. He and the Kirk session chose to turn a deaf ear to this. One or two elders and a few Church members wanted to pay for my house rent, but they feared there could be negative reprisals against them from a section of the elders. It was claimed that having been brought up in abject poverty, that was the kind of environment that suited me. But much of the bitterness had to do with my endeavors to establish Elder Districts.

During my entire stay at my parent's home, not a single person from the Church membership, elders, deacons or Woman's Guild ever visited me. Some would have loved to, but they could not do it for fear of being excommunicated from the Lord's Table or facing other forms of intimidation. By treating me this way, the parish minister and his Kirksession had deviated from the traditional and constitutional way of handling people who come to minister to them especially those from outside Thogoto. The alternative was to be given some house allowance if one lived in an owner-occupied home. But still, I did not get anything. In fact, for the whole period of almost two years that I was at Thogoto Parish, I experienced high levels of hostility from the people I would have considered my mentors, teachers, parents and neighbours. Some reports given in the presbytery meetings portrayed me as '*dangerous to the whole denomination for my endeavor to establish Elder Districts and for openly interpreting the scriptures in-depth, something the elders did not want.'*

One time, in a presbytery meeting, one senior clergyman described me as *'unworthy material for ordination and as one possessed with a divisive and a non-Presbyterian spirit.'*

He went further to say, *"I really dislike his charismatic spirit. He even uses* **'Nyimbo cia kiroho'** *to appetize his sermons and teachings. One very serious mistake the presbytery can make is to ordain him."*

Every time my name surfaced in the presbytery meetings for the purpose of deliberating on my licensing followed by the ordination, such motions were down played by some elders. They had the leeway to do so because the presbytery Moderator was the Thogoto Parish minister, and hence, he gave them the opportunity to do so. No wonder my ordination dragged on for a long time. I remember at one time, a concerned elder approached me and, with great concern, advised me thus;

"Why don't you change or abandon the creation of elder districts? Or abandon altogether, exposing your charismatic spirit? This would make things easier for you. I really sympathize with your situation. You had a prime job as a headmaster in various schools. You have attained high status in education, and here you are being treated as garbage by people who seem not to regard even God, though they claim to be His servants. As an elder and being one of those close to the parish minister and a member of the Kirksession, I can assure you that, the path to your ordination is getting narrower every day. Already, the parish minister, including most of the elders, is not with you, and it might take a long time for you to be ordained if ever it will take place."

I remained in that situation from June 1983 to the end of December 1984. Usually, a student is licensed within the first 6 months, which is immediately followed by ordination. Remember, they also hated me because I hailed from a *'non-athomi community'* as well as from *'non-athomi parents'* who were also Mau radicals.

There were no plates and cups to fit the Christian 'civilized *status'*. Christianity, as they emphasized it, was the assimilation of Scottish culture: It meant one being Europeanized. As for me and my parents, we were typically *'Kikuyunized.'* The whole agenda was to leave no stone unturned to deny me ordination. No wonder my parish minister had surrounded himself with a cartel, which advocated for my never being ordained as a PCEA minister.

At one time, a presbytery meeting was organized with only one agenda - to declare me as a non-PCEA material for ordination. The meeting intended to pass a resolution declaring that I be disowned by the presbytery, meaning I should go home. The matter reached the ears of the Moderator of the General Assembly, Dr. George Wanjau. He then wisely called the officials of the Kiambu South Presbytery. One of those who attended briefed me on what transpired during the meeting.

Upon their arrival in Dr. Wanjau's office and after some casual deliberations on the life of the Presbytery, both physical and spiritual, the Moderator asked them: *"What has become of this student under training in your presbytery by the name David Githii? I have some concern because all the other students who graduated with him have all undergone ordination through their presbyteries including some who even graduated after him?"*

It is then that the presbytery officials accused me of being; arrogant, unteachable, charismatic, one with the spirit of divisiveness, having no regard for the Church constitution and Church traditions. They informed Dr. Wanjau that a presbytery meeting was already scheduled to send me home because I was a dangerous, revolutionary minded person who should not be given leeway to be part of the PCEA clergy. They further accused me of having a spirit that discerned spiritual things very differently from the PCEA spirit of looking at things with a constitutional and traditional eye.

They expressed their fears that it was the same spirit that I had used in dividing the Musa Gitau congregation into Elder Districts. They claimed the same spirit could also be used to divide the whole Church congregations in the future. They described me as one with a very high degree of contagious spiritual influence. They also accused me of constantly promoting the role of the Holy Spirit in the Church through my sermons and songs, something that PCEA was not accustomed to.

They argued that the role of the Holy Spirit in the Church was not a context that the Scottish Presbyterian missionaries introduced into the Church. They further accused me of teaching what they called 'Nyimbo cia Kiroho' (Songs oriented to the Holy Spirit), which had nothing to do with the traditions of the Presbyterian Church. Such spiritual-based songs were not part of the recommended PCEA hymnals, which in the Gikuyu language are known as 'Nyimbo cia kuinira Ngai' (Songs in Praise of God).

They argued that the Holy Spirit oriented songs were purely for the Pentecostal Churches because they are the ones who claim to be connected to the Holy Spirit. They also accused me of allowing individuals to sing during the Sunday services, songs that were outside 'Nyimbo Cia Kuinira Ngai.' But worse still, they accused me of inviting non-Presbyterian musicians to make presentations in the Church, something that was contrary to the Church traditions.

Dr. Wanjau was not moved by their claims. He said:
*"I would request you to understand the background Githii has come from. He comes from Rift Valley, where the East African Revival Movement is very strong, and they are known for advancing the singing of praise songs, which are known as '**Kiroho Songs**' and, of course, the presbytery that recommended him to go for theological training knew all about this, but they found something potential in him that would be an asset for this Church and especially in the area of teaching and training."*

He continued to say,
"The training committee noticed some of the things you are accusing him of but still qualified him to go for training. In fact, out of sixty-four candidates who had been invited for the interview, he emerged number one, and he was, therefore, one of the nine who qualified to proceed for training at St. Paul's Theological College to pursue Diploma studies, but when his Curriculum vitae was studied by the admission Committee at St. Paul's Theological College, and having qualified him as a very intelligent person, plus the fact that he had all academic qualification for the degree work they offered him the opportunity to pursue Bachelor of Divinity degree work. In view of this, I am requesting that you go ahead and ordain him and I will then transfer him immediately to another presbytery."

The officials from the South Kiambu Presbytery were not satisfied with Dr. Wanjau's argument. One of them said,

"*But Moderator, we have to take into account the fact that wherever he will be posted after ordination will still be PCEA, and he will take the same Church-defiling stuff there. This being the case, I am proposing that we come up with a memorandum of understanding to have him ordained, but then you post him under a very senior clergy who can discipline and drill him into the policies and doctrines of PCEA, including its traditions. This means he will not be posted to man a parish. He will be under disciplinary action. We have agreed to ordain him just because of the respect we have for you. Otherwise, he is a good material for the Pentecostal Churches.*"

Another person said, "*It is important that we agree on the clergy under whom he will be posted.*" To this, the Moderator responded by telling the delegates that he was in agreement that I be posted under a very senior minister, one who was reputed for being a disciplinarian. Such a clergy was to observe me until such a time that the presbytery under whose jurisdiction I was to be posted would recommend that I be released to work on my own. Such a time was indefinite. The officials agreed with this arrangement, though they were not completely satisfied, only because they respected Dr. Wanjau in his capacity as the Moderator of the General Assembly.

I kept on waiting upon the Lord. Once we learn to wait upon the Lord to lead us in everything, we feel His strength, and our walk becomes steady. The whole truth is that God gives us complete power for every task He calls us to perform. And anything that does not align with obedience to Him is a waste of time and energy. It requires much more courage to stand and wait and still not lose hope.

Waiting is great work. One has to bear in mind that there is never a majestic mountain without a deep valley, and there is no birth without pain. Also, we must be willing to let go, surrendering completely to Him, and we must cease to rely on our own wisdom, strength and righteousness. The heavenly bound path is always rough, straight and narrow. We have much to learn from Pilgrim's Progress.

I was eventually ordained on 30th December 1984. As per the memorandum, the Appointment Committee posted me to Dr. Arthur Parish in Nakuru Presbytery, Nakuru County, under Rev. Kirathi, a former community chief. Many referred to him as the archive, architect and protector of Presbyterianism. The secretary to the Appointment Committee had attached a note to my posting letter stipulating that I be critically observed and fully aligned with the Presbyterian spiritual lifestyle.

The letter also indicated that there was a need to '*peel off*' that non-Presbyterian, charismatic Spiritism in me. He was also to deal with that divisive spirit in me, which was leading me to come up with what I called '**Elder Districts,**' which, according to them, was a very dangerous move for the Church because it created other smaller Churches within a given congregation with the elder as its priest. With that kind of chieftain background, Kirathi was found fit to straighten me and have me totally aligned with the '*traditional blood system of Presbyterianism,*' where things to do with kiroho songs and other hymnals were out of bounds.

FURTHER ACTIVATION OF ELDER DISTRICTS

I reported to Dr. Arthur Parish on 2nd January 1985. Rev. Kirathi looked at me suspiciously with ridiculing eyes. He did not even greet me; instead, he said:
"*So, you are the Presbyterian priest who doesn't know the way the Presbyterian Denomination operates? You have fallen in good hands; I will straighten you up. Welcome!*" It seemed I had come from a frying pan into the fire. Honestly, I did not discern anything spiritual in this minister. He spoke so authoritatively that I was left astounded. I stayed under Kirathi for three months, but those were really very difficult months for me.

Things were even made worse by the elders, some of whom were also under instruction to straighten me because, according to them, '*I had no knowledge of how the Church should operate.*' Thus, rather than me serving them, they were supposed to serve me by creating hedges in everything I did or said. This had even leaked to the Church members. Everywhere I went, I was treated as that '*Unschooled pastor in Presbyterianism.*'

In a strange twist of fate, after only three months, Rev. Kirathi was transferred to Eldoret, 70 miles away. Another senior minister reputed as a zealous protector of Presbyterianism, Rev. Stephen Kariuki, was transferred from Eldoret to Western Kenya Presbytery. He, too, was under instruction to keep a close eye on me.

He had been cautioned that I possessed a spirit that could easily revolutionize the Church in the wrong spiritual direction. Nevertheless, unlike Kirathi, Stephen was somewhat reasonable. He spoke to me with some concern. He seemed a good mentor. But then, no sooner had he reported that he informed the presbytery that his former presbytery, where he was the presbytery Moderator, had a partnership with a presbytery in Germany, which they intended to maintain in the form of exchange programs. He, therefore, requested Nakuru Presbytery to grant him leave for some time, which the Presbytery did.

That being the case, there had to be a minister in charge during Rev. Kariuki's absence. The presbytery found itself in a dilemma because they could not have me taking over the responsibility of the parish because according to the letter they had received from the Appointment Committee, I could not be trusted as I was still under observation. It was recommended that Rev. Nyutu Muhia, who was the presiding parish minister at Gilgil Parish, 50 miles away, be the minister in charge.

Some elders tried to block Rev. Nyutu from taking over, arguing that he had a very wide parish comprising more than 20 congregations. Moreover, he had to commute 50 miles, which meant extra expenses to be met by Dr. Arthur Parish. Rev. Kariuki seemed to share the same sentiments, but he was overruled by a majority of the elders. One of them said,
"To say that we have Githii in charge is very illogical. We all know that this man, David Githii was placed under us for some training and the flushing out of some negative spiritual stuff that can be destructive to the body of Christ. How can anybody in his right senses come up with such an outrageous idea that we have him in such a parish like Dr. Arthur where, not only elders and deacons but the Church members are very mature and well versed with Presbyterianism? This can't happen!"

Thus, Rev. Nyutu was given this added load to manage the Dr. Arthur Parish, which comprised 32 congregations. He was now expected to manage the 52 congregations. Rev. Nyutu had unsuccessfully tried to argue against his being given that big responsibility, but the presbytery dictated that he take it because he was the presbytery clerk. After the Presbytery meeting and as we were having lunch, Rev. Nyutu whispered to me:

"You are the one to run the Dr. Arthur parish until Kariuki comes back. These people have no regard for the shepherding of Church members; they only think about protecting their powers and the Scottish traditions. You might not know it but there are many in this presbytery and the entire Church who understand the validity of your spiritual stand, I being one of them. This Church has blocked the role of the Holy Spirit in the Church over the years, yet without the Day of Pentecost, the birthing of the Church could not have occurred. I also understand the role that small Church groups, which you are calling Elder Districts, can play in this Church. It is my prayer that you succeed in this endeavor. As the Presbytery Clerk, I will use my office to back you, but silently."

Rev. Nyutu lamented the fact that there were so many people in PCEA who were spiritually empty. They did not understand the potential of my ideas. He wished that they could give me time and added: *"I mean what I have told you. You are the one in charge of this parish whatever the duration the parish minister will be away. But this is between me and you."* He would promise to convene a session meeting but, on the eve of that meeting, would call the Session Clerk that morning and inform him that he had been caught up by an urgent issue in his parish and since the session meeting could not be postponed, he would instruct the Session Clerk that I chair the meeting: *"As the presbytery clerk there is nothing, they can do to me,"* he would say.

This is exactly what he did on this particular Dr. Arthur parish Session Clerk, and he informed him of his inability to turn up for the meeting and dictated that I chair the meeting. When the session convened, the session clerk informed the session that Rev. Nyutu would not be available and being the presbytery clerk, he had authorized Githii to chair the meeting. Although some of the elders reflected a spirit of disapproval, there was no argument about it. I gave the opening devotion, went through the matters arising from the previous meeting and finally came to the day's agenda.

The sequence of the agenda list was read out, and I added another of my agenda that read; *'The establishment of Elder Districts.'* The debate over the agenda went quite smoothly. When we finally came to the agenda on the Elder Districts, I explained what it all pertained to. I gave the background of my experience with schools' houses and how I was convinced the same idea of small groups in the Church could be productive both from the physical and spiritual perspectives. At that juncture, there were many raised hands from people who wanted to speak.

The first speaker said,
*"I am reminding the session members about what we heard the first time that Githii reported in this parish. He was described as **a divisive spirit,** and this was what was being referred to. I am now cautioning this session not to continue with this agenda; otherwise, the presbytery will be on our case for allowing such a divisive spirit to prevail in our parish. Also, don't forget that Githii is under some kind of discipline."*

Another elder manifesting some anger said,
"I am supporting that speaker. We cannot allow any subdivisions of our congregations. This Church has lived harmoniously over the years. How then can someone come with the mind of dismantling that harmonious lifestyle of the Church?"

It seemed I was treading on a tightrope. But then, there was this elder, Kinyanjui, who agitatedly rose on a point of order and said:
"First of all, I want to congratulate Rev. Githii for the way he has handled the agenda in this Kirksession. I apologize for what I heard in regard to his lack of experience and ignorance of the Church constitution. I am impressed by the way he has made very appropriate references to our constitution. In fact, he has done far, much better than many ministers I have known."

He went on to say:
*"In regard to what he refers to as **Elder Districts**, let me remind this session that this very idea was once introduced in this parish by Rev. Jacob Mugo, who, as we all know, was a very able and loved parish minister here. But then, we sidelined this idea which he had borrowed from his stay in America when he was pursuing his studies. Now that the same agenda has resurfaced and this time from a different person who has very well explained how it helped him to come up with excellent sportsmen and women, teams to reckon with, let us then take this as a confirmation of the same and hence, embrace the idea and put it into practice. Who knows, such a move could, at*

the end of it all, be beneficial to the whole Church and who knows to be Githii has come into the Church for a time like this."

He further said, "I have always felt that our Church needs some re-examination of how we take the shepherding of the members. Elders live a very isolated life from the members. Elder Districts could be the answer to draw elders closer to members. It is only in this way we can come to know the joys and sorrows of the members."

Another elder, Wagaituri, who seemed to carry a lot of respect from the elders, spoke his mind thus:
"I am amazed about the way Rev. Githii has handled this meeting. I cannot comprehend why some people decided to taint him as a weak minister who knew nothing about PCEA. To me, he has demonstrated that he is above many ministers I have met. He is a person that God has blessed with great wisdom and understanding. This is a wonderful minister to shepherd a parish. In fact, putting him under another minister is a great waste of talent. I also admire his idea of Elder Districts. I have always wondered how one elder and the Church members can share the same forum. I therefore propose that we adopt the birthing of Elder Districts in this parish."

A number of other elders spoke, and apart from a few, all others spoke in favour of establishing Elder Districts and my ability to handle the meeting. One of the elders conclusively said:
"I have come to the same conclusion, and I am calling upon this session to rise to the occasion to protect this minister. This is a gift that God has given to this denomination. I can prophesy that the so-called Elder Districts will be one of the best things that Githii will have instilled in this denomination. It will give deep roots to this Church. Let us do as Rev. Jacob had suggested some years back. At the same time, let us embrace Rev. Githii in his endeavor to establish Elder Districts, as he calls them and even pave the way for him to visit homes through this avenue of Elder Districts. Let us, from now on, be positive about his ministry and, at the same time, talk positively about him to the members. Remember, Githii is our child because it is this presbytery that recommended him for theological training. So, we cannot recommend and then discard him."

At one point, I called for a vote, and surprisingly, over 90% of the elders voted for the inauguration of the Elder Districts. In the final analysis, the elders decided that elders in every congregation meet on an agreed day to mark boundaries for every elder's Elder District, each with a name. All the names of districts were to be forwarded to the session clerk, and copies of the same were given to me.

After this, I gave a conclusive comment thus:
"I thank God who has given me an understanding heart. God has given me some favour in discerning things to do to expand His kingdom, but there are many who do not believe in those discerned things." This is why Apostle Paul called upon Colossian believers to: *"Pray also for me, that whenever I open my mouth, words may be given me so that I will fearlessly make known the mystery of the gospel…Pray that I may declare it fearlessly, as I should."*

I went on to say,
"Paul is saying that God uses him in the propagation of the gospel, but people fail to grasp his message. Instead, they think of him as a crazy person. They did the same to Jesus when they said that He performed miracles through the power of Beelzebub. I have loved all your comments. Please keep me in your prayers because, through dreams, God has revealed to me that He has things He wants me to accomplish in this Church and in doing so, I will meet a lot of opposition. In fact, I feel like the words in Jeremiah 1:19 refer to me when he says; 'They will fight against you but will not overcome you, for I am with you and will rescue you,' declares the Lord," has become the pointer of the path that I will travel. But I have walked on the same path in the past in some of the schools where I was headmaster and as God helped me to overcome. The same God will help me overcome these at this time.

Having said this, one elder raised up his hand to speak and said: *"Rev Githii, I just want to encourage you with Paul's words to the Romans in Romans 10:11, where he says, 'Anyone who trusts in him will never be disappointed.'"*

Things moved very fast in the formation of Elder Districts. Before long, the term Elder District was a household name. Elders had already mobilized their districts for fellowship meetings. While some elders earmarked at least one day within the week for their Elder District fellowships, others whose districts had more employed people earmarked Sunday after the usual service as the time for their fellowship in some households. I also embarked on visiting the congregations and carrying out some teaching on the benefits of Elder Districts. By the time Rev. Kariuki, the parish minister came back, he found a well-established system of the Elder Districts, something that he embraced and gave it a further push. He could not do otherwise, for the Kirksession owned it by a minute.

In my endeavour to persistently push my agenda, I was very convinced that it was through the most difficult trials that God often brought the sweetest discoveries of Himself. Otherwise, the best things in life are the result of being wounded. Wheat must be crushed before becoming bread, and incense must be broken by fire before its fragrance is set free. The earth must be broken with a sharp plow before being ready to receive the seed. And it is the broken heart that pleases God. Our God may drench us with grief, but he will refresh us with His mercy.

I was convinced that God's love letters often come to us in dark envelopes. Isn't it glorious to know that no matter how unjust something may be, even when it seems to have come from Satan himself, by the time it reaches us, it is God's will for us and will ultimately work for our good? Romans 8:28 affirms this when it says, *"And we know that all things work together for the good of those who love God, to those who are called according to His purpose."* The word purpose, as reflected here, suggests a deliberate plan, a proposition, an advance plan, or a design.

The truth of the matter is that; we live fascinating lives if we are living in the center of God's will. All the attacks that Satan hurls at us through the sins of others are not only powerless to harm us but are transformed into blessings along the way. God's will is the most hopeful, pleasant, and glorious thing in the world. It is the continuous working of His omnipotent power for our benefit, with nothing to prevent it if only we remain surrendered and believe that all things are possible with Him. In accordance with Luke 10:19, we have been given the power to *"trample on serpents and scorpions, and over all the power of the enemy and nothing by any means shall hurt us."*

FURTHER ELDER DISTRICT COHESIVENESS

In order to further create more cohesiveness in the Church through the **Elder Districts** just as I had done at Musa Gitau Church, I introduced some form of competition among the Elder Districts. For instance, I initiated a 15-minute drama based on the parable of the Ten Virgins as narrated in the book of Matthew 25:1-13. This went hand in hand with hymn 311 from "*Nyimbo cia Kiroho*" (Holy Spirit-based hymns), which carried the same scriptural message at the same time and comprised six stanzas.

For three months, all the districts aggressively practiced these items. The districts were to first compete within their congregations, and the winners would meet some others at the zonal level, with the winners then meeting at the parish level. On this material day, I invited the Deputy Secretary General, Rev. Patrick Rukenya, as the guest of honour. This memorable day was marked by a lot of activities as each team made its presentations. We started with music and then the drama. Rev. Rukenya was very impressed by what he saw. As he issued certificates to the winners, he commended the effort and said:

"*This idea of the Elder Districts could be a catalyst for both spiritual and physical development in the whole denomination. I will share this idea with the other GA Officials and map out a way through which this system can be embedded into the whole Church fabric. Mine is to congratulate Rev. Githii for coming up with this kind of revelation. Let us all give him total support even as we embrace the Elder District Movement.*

He advised;
I also congratulate the elders for having taken the initiative to understand Githii. It seems God wants to use him mightily in the life of this Church. Otherwise, the establishment of Elder Districts would never have taken place in PCEA if Githii had never become a minister in this Church. This is a lasting beacon in this Church. All glory be to God, who reveals the hidden things to his chosen servants. Otherwise, I will push other GA officials to back Githii in the establishment of this fruitful innovation in the PCEA denomination."

THE GENERAL ASSEMBLY EMBRACES ELDER DISTRICTS

Soon after the hosting of the Elder Districts competition at Dr. Arthur Church, the dedication of the PCEA Ruguru Church, Bahati, Nakuru, took place. The officials of the GA conducted the function. But shortly before this function took place, Rev. Rukenya called and asked me to have the winners of both the drama and songs performed on the PCEA Ruguru Church dedication day. It was easy for me to do this because I was the Presbytery Clerk.

When the winners of both the drama and the songs performed, it left most the people shedding tears because the performance portrayed a real picture of what would take place on the final judgment day in heaven. Just as the five virgins who had oil were allowed into the wedding, so shall those who are able to overcome the world get to heaven. Conversely, like those without oil who got blocked from entering the wedding ceremony so will those without oil be locked out in heaven.

These two symbolisms were represented in both the drama and the song. It is no wonder, then, in the course of the presentations, many within the congregation had tears streaming down their faces, including the GA officials. It was then that the GA Moderator asked Rev. Kariuki, the presbytery Moderator;

"How did all this take place?" In response, Kariuki said: *"All this is the work of Rev. Githii. He has come up with a mechanism where the congregations are subdivided among the existing elders. Such groups meet in their own locations on an agreed day for fellowship within the week. They carry out praises and prayers, and at times, they do Bible Studies. In the beginning, I really hated the idea, simply because I did not comprehend what it was all about, but I have come to recognize it as a real catalyst for Church growth in many dimensions. These competitions have greatly helped in creating strong unity among the Church members. It is also creating a sense of belonging in the members to the body of Christ."*

At this point, the Deputy Secretary General interjected and told the GA Moderator;

"This is what I told you about what I witnessed in the groups' competition at Dr. Arthur Church, and I remember telling you of this new movement that Githii has started called Elder Districts. It is something that we need to embrace and have permeated every presbytery, parish and congregation in our entire Church. We need to have time with Githii so that he may explain the intricacies involved for us to pave the way for its forward progression."

After the Church dedication ceremony, the GA Moderator, the Secretary-General, and Deputy Secretary General had a session with me. We talked at length about how I came up with this idea and my vision and mission for this revelation. I told them how I had first started this project at Rev. Musa Gitau Church and how it has also found fertile ground in Dr. Arthur Parish.

The GA Moderator, while addressing me, said,
"Please, let me understand. Is this the idea you were trying to promote when South Kiambu Presbytery leaders wanted to block you from being ordained?" In response, I said, *"Yes, this is the Church model I was trying to establish and thank you for having saved my day."* Then he said, *"Then, I am so delighted that I managed to save the situation."* After further deliberations, the three officials then promised to do all it took to ensure they helped me have the noble movement fully established in all the presbyteries. They promised to keep in touch with me. Unfortunately, I never heard from them again thereafter.

Meanwhile, Dr. Arthur Parish Kirksession floated an agenda to have another competition for the Elder Districts. They insisted that it would act as another catalyst to bind the whole parish membership into a lasting harmony. It would also move the parish spiritually to a higher level. The session then mandated me to work out the set pieces in both drama and folk songs. This really excited me. This time around, I asked the districts to work on the book, *'Pilgrims Progress.'* They were to read that book and come up with a 15-minute play.

Each of the Elder District was to come up with their own six-stanza song composition and a tune based on an African folk song. This picked up quite well in the whole parish. As usual, the congregations held their competitions internally then they proceeded to the zones, after which I organized for the day the parish-level competitions were to take place. This turned out to be a very spiritually moving experience. If only you, the reader, were familiar with the contents of the book; 'Pilgrims Progress', then you can imagine how it would challenge the Christians if it was well set, what the main character in the book encountered on his journey before standing at the gate of heaven can be turned into a very moving episode.

That is why, as the play and songs progressed, many people shed tears. They had been moved by the spiritual fragrance of the songs and drama displaying the trying Christian pilgrim's sojourn. As usual, the winners were issued with certificates. This was in November 1985.

In the month of October 1985, the Nakuru Presbytery met and unanimously decreed that I be given my own parish to manage and lead. They had written to the Appointment Committee stating that I should never have been placed under a minister because, from the word go, they had found me fit to run a parish on my own. They stated: *"His posting is overdue. We have found him far, much better than many of the ministers who in the past have served in this presbytery."* In January 1986, I got posted to Rongai Parish which borders Dr. Arthur Parish. By then, I had a concern that the officials at the Head Office had not talked to me in regard to further pursuit in the establishment of the Elder Districts, and I was figuring out how I would not only get in touch with them but also have a session with them. I had to formulate a way to have them in my new appointment.

AN ORGANIZED CRUSADE

As soon as I reported to Rongai Parish, I organized a three-day crusade. I then invited the Head Office officials as speakers in this crusade. To my joy, and with much gratitude to our Lord, they accepted to be guest speakers. I then got in touch with the minister at Dr. Arthur Parish and requested him to allow the two Elder District winners in '**Pilgrims Progress**', both drama and song, to come and perform the same in our parish crusade, to which he accepted.

The two teams, one with the folk song and the other with the drama, came and performed in the presence of the GA officials. When the GA Officials saw the two group's sterling performance, they were so impressed. They then remembered a similar performance at the dedication of Ruguru Church, where two groups had presented a drama and a song on the Ten Virgins. With their eyes wide open and wet with tears, the GA officials watched in awe as the Elder Districts performed at the conclusion of the presentations. The GA Moderator addressed both the Secretary-General and I. He said:
"This is wonderful. We can no longer wait to have the Elder District Movement totally implemented into the Church." It was then that the GA

Moderator said; *"David, I am sorry that we never came back to you as per our earlier promise. When we go back to the office, we will have a meeting in which we will look for ways and means to fast-track and have this **Elder District** model rooted into the entire Church."*

As we had our lunch, the Secretary-General, revealed the fact that the more they had watched the Elder District activities taking place, the more they had come to like the move. He told me that while they were seated and watching, they had been exploring more broadly the role the Elder District could play in the whole Church. They had, therefore, reviewed the whole objective of the Elder District and had come to the conclusion that it is high time ways and means were developed to pave the way for the infusion of the movement into the whole Church. At one point, the two got into a whispering conversation, after which the GA Moderator said,

"You know, David, we were amazed by the way you could make people come up with such so well-dramatized messages. The previous dramatized message from the Ten Virgins drama, including their own composed songs and now this performance from the Pilgrims Progress book, leaves me so amazed. Both the song and the drama were so well harmonized, with such a convincing message.

He further said,

"We have quietly deliberated on this and have decided this being February; we only have almost a month to go before the General Administrative Committee (GAC) in April. The venue will be in Elburgon Presbytery, which is a half-hour drive from here. We have already earmarked the two groups in both the drama and the song to avail themselves in that meeting so that they may showcase their performance. They will present what they did today, and we can include their previous performance based on the Ten Virgins. As you know, this meeting taps into all the key PCEA leadership from East Africa. This will be the best forum for you to introduce the Elder Districts Movement to the whole Church."

He further said,

"In this case, you will be given 25 minutes to explain what is meant by an Elder District. I would also recommend that you come up with a write-up explaining the same in detail regarding an Elder District. That document will be photocopied and given to all the delegates so that they can use it to introduce this wonderful channel of Church Growth and Evangelism into their parishes and presbyteries. I am sure you are capable of doing all this. I

discern that God has bestowed upon you very specialized talents and wisdom."

The Secretary-General said, *"In fact, I have already itemized it as one of our key agenda in that GAC. So, David, do all that you can to help us install this noble ministry into the church."*

GAC HELD AT ELBURGON

The GAC took place as scheduled. At the appointed time, the four teams presented their special items. After their performance, there was great excitement with the delegates wanting to know more about the origin of such refined presentations. It was then that the Secretary-General told them that all they had witnessed was the product of Rev. Githii through what he called "Elder Districts." He went on to say, *"At this time, I want to give this opportunity to him so that within the next few minutes, he educates us on what an elder district is, how it functions and in which ways it can be beneficial to the Church. Welcome, David."* I took that opportunity to talk about the establishment and development of small Church groups in the Church. I then narrated how this idea came to me through my teaching profession and how I had already experimented with it at both Musa Gitau Memorial Church and now at Dr. Arthur Parish.

In my presentation and to illustrate my point and in an endeavour to convince the delegates, I carried a huge and long sweet potato vine with long offshoots (branches). I told the delegates that this huge and long leafy vine had not met its productive mandate because, rather than being buried in the soil, it was left to grow unattended on top of the ground. For maximum productivity, both the stem and the offshoots should have been buried. I likened that vine to the church. The PCEA church carried a big name and covered a big ground (East Africa), but it had not created the ways its member's hearts would be buried with real shepherding. The way to do this is to create branches within the congregations and attend to them by feeding them spiritually.

To further drive my teaching home, I gave a presentation on a tree in the form of PCEA. In doing this, I was trying to equate the small Church groups with the branches of a tree. I presented the sample of a tree which I called, *'The PCEA Tree'*.

In comparing PCEA to a tree, I likened the fruits to the General Assembly: The branches to the Presbyteries, The trunk to the parishes, The tap root to the congregation, The primary roots to the Elder Districts and the hair roots to the members.

In conclusion, I said:
"It is important that we develop the Small Church groups as a natural part of the Congregation. It cultivates, nourishes and fertilizes the "Church Tree", causing it to be more productive in many ways. The Church is a working community in witness and service. The Church is God's working represented on earth, with each member as His ambassador. Each is, therefore, charged with the responsibility to be in contact with the Lord through spiritual worship, to be in harmony with the other members and to be in contact with the world, which is the sphere of his or her ambassadorial duties. This is what 2 Cor. 5:17-21 advocates.

I continued to say,
There is no better way to accomplish this than in small group gatherings where there is a contagious spirit. In other words, the Small Church group is like an electric conductor. When the group is in contact with her heavenly source of power, its members become effective spiritual witnesses and are useful to the unconverted world. Each has a gift that the Spirit distributes according to His will (1 Cor.12). Although some of these gifts are for the internal functioning of the Church, many are for the effective witness and service outside the Church. Some have a dual role with gifts of healing, working of miracles, discerning the spirits, helping the needy, visiting the sick, and so on."

I then handed the written document containing the information on how the Elder District is established and how it is run, including its benefits, to the Secretary-General. This document was photocopied and distributed to all the delegates. They were required to photocopy these further and then distribute them to the leaders in their various parishes and presbyteries.

The delegates also recommended that I make the Elder District Movement part of my teaching to the students who were undergoing training for ministry at PCEA Lay Training Centre, where I taught Church History every Wednesday.

Besides teaching, I also invited pastoral Institute students to the Rongai parish for at least two weeks during their holidays. I posted those students to individual elder districts within the parish congregations. The students really enjoyed this because of the experience they gained as well as the gifts and finances they received when they left the Elder Districts for home. This was quite helpful because many of them had families.

This is how God paved the way for the final establishment of Elder Districts in PCEA Church. Nevertheless, it was an endeavor that left me with a lot of scars because of the so much opposition, frustration and persecution I went through to make such gains. All said and done; the Elder District Movement became the prime mover of the PCEA Church in many dimensions. For example, it has become an avenue of financial contribution, fellowships, Bible studies, reaching out to the needy, evangelism, engaging in mission work, planting of new Churches, clergy support, and many other things. I later wrote a book based on the Elder Districts concept but instead used another title, "*Small Church Groups*", for the sake of other Churches who use such names as Cell Group, Fellowship Group, etc. The book's title is, '*How to Grow a Health & Vibrant Church Through Small Church Groups.*' I remain convinced that the secret behind rapid spiritual Church growth is to run the Church through smaller and smaller groups. And this is what Robert Raines affirms in his book, '*Life in the Church,*' in which he says, "*The influence of the people in the 'koinonia' groups is truly like leaven – often hidden, usually quiet and gradual, but permeating the total membership.*"

I went the academic way by referring to some authors who have embraced the small church group's idea. I quoted William Beckham, who, in his book, '*The Second Reformation,*' says, "*Small groups are beneficial as a social unit. Small groups furnish a framework for emotional therapy, support systems, social interaction, fellowship, task accomplishments and even religious experiences.*"

William further observes, "*In a cell Church, every member is a minister. Therefore, personal and group ministries touch the lives of hurting people because basic Christians can identify and react to real needs. Cells are healing units at the cutting edge of hurts.*"

To William, the small Church groups are the heart of the functioning of the Church, and he therefore emphasizes this importance by saying,

"The Koinonia groups provide the context in which the institutional Church may begin to become the Body of Christ and in which nominal Church members may become Disciples of Christ. Within such groups, Christians are being equipped for the work of ministry, first in the Church and then in the world."

Emphasizing the importance of increasing the small groups by ordaining more and more elders to handle smaller groups, I referred to Rick Warren's book, *'The Purpose Driven Church,'* where he says,

"One of the sayings I quote to our staff and lay leaders repeatedly is, 'Our Church must always be growing larger and smaller at the same time…. You can't share personal prayer requests in the crowd. Small affinity groups…are perfect for creating a sense of intimacy and close fellowship. It's there that everybody knows your name. When you are absent, people notice."

Rick Warren further says,

"A cell Church will not function without a way to develop every member into a productive disciple. Evangelism must begin to overflow from cell life through natural relationships. New believers are brought into meaningful cell life to be nurtured into productive disciples. During the test cycles, cells learn friendship evangelism as a natural part of cell life. Cells welcome and incorporate non-believers who come seeking Christ and community. Cell members contact hardcore unbelievers by meeting their needs."

Robert Raines is another author I referred to. Raines says;

"The Church must foster and sustain the conditions in which Koinonia (fellowship) can be known. This cannot be done for most people simply through morning worship. Worship is indispensable in the weekly meetings of the Christian Community. There cannot be firsthand Koinonia among hundreds of people. The best evidence of this is the fact that hundreds of people in a given local Church can worship faithfully for years without any noticeable change in the quality of commitment or direction of life. The Church needs to lead its people into small–group fellowship where the conditions for Koinonia prevail. This is especially important in this age where the spirit of individualism is fast prevailing."

I carried this kind of message to all presbyteries, parishes, regions and Church groups. I am always thankful to God because the message was finding a place in peoples' hearts. It's no wonder the ministry of Elder Districts in the entire denomination has found a fertile ground. All glory be to God who so wonderfully and by His grace empowered me to birth this movement that has become the main artery of the church, giving spiritual nourishment to all its organs.

THANKSGIVING DAY

It was also during my time in office as the Moderator of the General Assembly that the introduction of a Church Thanks Giving Day on every first Sunday of April was established. I felt that the denomination had to have a day per year to materially give to the church. I also emphasized that when a parish ordained elders without having them adequately trained, it was tantamount to weakening the Church leadership, especially in PCEA, where an elder is ordained for life.

I challenged the church leadership to resist by all means ordaining half-baked leadership. I insisted and convincingly carried this message throughout the denomination that elders should not be ordained in a hurry. Sometimes, it happened because a Minister was being transferred or because he or she wanted to beat a certain deadline or in cases where a minister wanted to reward some people for having supported him or her in the parochial work or through some physical and personal support with material things like money.

It is unfortunate that, worldwide, and in many cases, the Church leadership is held by some corrupt and uncaring people, some of whom are devil worshippers and even homosexuals. Such kinds of people today hold positions in Church leadership, including the top echelons in denominations, parishes and congregations. Quite a number of church leaders worldwide who hold the offices of archbishops, bishops, archdeacons, lay readers, Moderators, deacons, prophets, and apostles, including the offices of chairpersons, secretaries and treasurers, just to name a few, are unfit for those offices. It is unfortunate that this trend is spreading like wildfire.

CHURCH ELECTIONS

I also called upon the Church leaders to be vigilant while appointing the laity (lay people) in Church leadership and administrative positions. More especially those being recruited to church eldership. The system then involved a few people grooming those they preferred to be placed in certain leadership positions in the Church despite some of those candidates being known to be spiritually polluted in character.

Hence, I initiated a transparent way of electing elders. Surprisingly, it was one the most resisted movements by the PCEA 'watchdog cartel.' These cartels were hell-bent on causing malnutrition in the church in both the physical and spiritual. They would argue, "*We have always done it this way*," which in itself was misleading and was the devil's manipulative way of weakening the status of the Church. This cartel could care less about the spiritual status of the proposed elders for ordination. This also applies to leadership positions. It did not matter whether one was a well-known thief, a corrupt man, a drunkard, a brutal fellow, one who kept concubines or anyone who harbored other wickedness.

The opinion of members of the church did not matter either. This was even if they shouted the loudest in rejecting such a dubious person whom the Kirk session was forwarding for eldership ordination.

The voices of members would be buried with threats from the elders that they would be blocked from taking Holy Communion.

Undaunted, I pushed on and pointed out, "*This Way of selecting Church leadership is wrong. It is a manipulative way that denies the Church members their democratic right to elect credible leaders.*" I believed that it was a corrupt system meant to hinder Church members from participating in the election of their leaders. Those who advocated for such a system were spiritually empty, and their work was to cause strife in the body of Christ, not to mention their defiling the Church. It is not unusual to find such leaders thriving through corruption, manipulation of power, all kinds of wickedness, nepotism, and attaining power through bribery, among other schemes.

Another reason that contributed to the election of the wrong people was that the proposer of the candidate was often in their circles. It was a neighbor, former classmate, schoolmate, relative, or spouse who had benefited from economic support from the candidate who desired a church leadership position in return for the favour. Some were elected as a reward. Such favors included getting a job, training or fees for one's children or immensely supporting the Church in finances and other material gains. There were also instances of a rich person sponsoring Church leaders in goat eating (roast meat) or, in Swahili, what is referred to as 'nyama choma.' A potential leader would also be one who helped in an individual's fundraising activity, sponsors elders in dowry contributions, or tribesmen or classmates.

In saying all this, I was calling upon an overhaul in Church leadership. I was advocating for reorganization in the way leaders were elected. I was pushing for members to be allowed to own the people who led them. I maintained;
"There ought to be no more imposition of Church elders and other leaders. The best way was to hold elections through the secret ballot, which is also biblical." In fact, the Bible says: "In those days Peter stood up among the believers (a group numbering about a hundred and twenty) and said," ... "Concerning Judas... it is necessary to choose one of the new men who have been with us... So they proposed two men... then they prayed, 'Lord, You know everyone's heart. Show us which of these two you have chosen,'...Then they cast lots..." (Acts 1: 15-26, Life Application Bible).

I insisted that in any church elections, the members ought to have a say on who was to be the Chairman of the Church, the Treasurer and the Clerk, and this should also apply to departmental leaders. At one point, I said: "PCEA qualifies to be in the category of mainstream Churches and unlike Pentecostal Churches where the senior minister usually had a leeway in the choice of the leaders, mainstream churches had a semblance of "governmental" structure in its administration."

I was advocating for the fact that a Church was supposed to lead the way in dealing with corruption, nepotism, sectionalism and tribalism. "All Church elections ought to reflect total transparency," I asserted. I, therefore, called upon the Church to have all elections carried out through secret ballots. I aggressively followed this matter until I got a breakthrough on the congregations' participation in electing Church leaders as well as voting through the secret ballot.

While I had a big success in having that door opened, I must admit that it was a head-scratcher. I bore a lot of spiritual scars. I had to overcome a lot of harassment and even death threats. It is no surprise that soon after the end of my two terms as the GA Moderator, this cartel managed to expel me from PCEA. In all these challenges, God was ever with me, even as affirmed in His words in Isaiah 9:7: "*It is the zeal of the Lord God Almighty (El Gibbor) who did it and for His own glory.*" This is why I named my newly founded ministry El Gibbor Ministries.

DEACON ZONES

As already indicated, the Lord used me to establish Elder Districts in PCEA. Simply put, if I never became an ordained pastor in this denomination, chances are 99% that there would never have been such a term as Elder District in PCEA, where an elder has his/her administration powers vested in an Elder District. In pursuit of further subdivisions of the Elder Districts, I called upon the Church leadership to come up with a resolution that there be further subdivisions of the elder districts into what I called "*Deacon Zones.*" In a leaders' seminar held at Tumutumu Presbytery, I remember asking;
"*Why do we have a loaf of bread wrapped up but in sliced pieces? It is to make it easier for the bread to be easily taken rather than one person taking the whole bread.*" This is true of the Elder Districts. They need to be sliced among the deacons. The smaller the group, the better the services.

In one of the GACs and in my pursuit to establish Deacon Zones, through the support of the GAC delegates, I remember saying,
"*With this in mind, I am calling upon this GA to instruct all Presbyteries to see to it that all elder districts are subdivided into 'Deacon Zones,' which some people call 'Cell Groups.' Also, to see to it that the deacons are set free to organize their zones for Bible studies, prayers, worship, giving and other pastoral works. In this case, the elder will act as the 'Managing Director', and he or she would be visiting Deacon Zones on a rotational basis to fellowship with the members. A schedule where all the Deacon Zones will be meeting together for fellowship on a monthly basis as per the agreement*

between the elder and the deacons involved would be prepared. Deacons are not supposed to be spectators, as the Church has always treated them. They need to be doers as well. After all, this is the best way to prepare and train future Church leaders."

But it is also good to point out that some elders and Kirksessions were reluctant to formulate Deacon Zones because they saw them as avenues to erode their power. These would hate to share their power and self-appraisal with deacons. They would love to maintain, *'The traditions of the Elders,'* something that Jesus himself rebuked when he told the Pharisees: *"You have a fine way of setting aside the commandments of God in order to observe your own traditions"* (Mark 7:9). It's shocking that even as I write this, there is a possibility that there are congregations and parishes that might not have totally embraced the role of Deacon Zones. But I am glad that I played my role in that endeavor, and there is fruitfulness in this branch of the church. All glory be to God!

The same concept of Deacon Zones is what I had used in subdividing the previous 28 presbyteries such that, by the end of my tenure as the GA Moderator, the number of presbyteries was 47 compared with the 28 that existed at the time of my taking over as the GA Moderator. It was for that reason that there was a remarkably great increase in parishes and elder districts. Otherwise, prior to my becoming the GA Moderator, both parishes and presbyteries had existed as large areas, with some parishes comprising as many as thirty congregations!

For instance, Rift Valley Presbytery extended from Mai Mahiu all the way to Kisumu. Nairobi Presbytery extended from Nairobi all the way to Mombasa with the responsibility to oversee Tanzania. In carrying out the subdivisions, I based my reason for doing that on the fact that it was easier to serve people within smaller groups.

In all this, I was striving to ensure that the Church had taken spiritual food to church members whom I had compared to *'hair roots.'* I remember telling a regional meeting of leaders at Kikuyu Township, in Rungiri Presbytery that:
"I believe it is God's agenda that people be fed even in further smaller groups. This is the same idea that Jesus had when He advised His disciples to have people 'sit down in groups on the green grass' as recorded in the book of Mark 6:39. Jethro had the same idea when he advised Moses to

appoint officials who then would take responsibility over smaller groups of people in hundreds, fifties and tens as found in Exodus 18:21" I made the Church leadership understand that it was the same principles I was advocating for in further sub-divisions was biblical.

TRAINING OF ELDERSHIP CANDIDATES

Another knot that I untied in spite of much opposition was the training of the eldership candidates. Prior to my becoming the Moderator of GA, those earmarked for eldership positions were never given any serious training. They were just assembled in one day given a short lecture including how one was to be accompanied by one's spouse on the ordination day and how to prepare and handle the Holy Communion service. They were also drilled on how the Sunday worship service ought to flow. Emphasis was laid on the fact that they should understand they were Teaching Elders. That is, their decisions and not those of the parish ministers carried the day. After this brief lecture, they were released to go and prepare for the following day's ordination.

There were those who felt that the Church had existed over many years without elders undergoing intensive training, an argument that had by now become a cliché: '**We have always done it this way**!' This lot felt that even without the intensive training, the elders were doing a great job. They also claimed that training could be very costly for the parishes in terms of logistics transport expenses, food costs, and the facilitators' fees.

My experience revealed that unless elders got thorough training to equip them before being ordained, they always ended up being blind leaders or '**half-baked leaders**.' It was for this reason that I initiated **a one-week residential training'** for all those people elected to be ordained as elders. In this regard, the parishes had to send all their potential candidates for eldership to the PCEA Training and Conference Centre for thorough training before they were released for ordination. This was to happen on specific dates each year.

The curriculum was set to cover a wide scope of leadership as taught by teachers well-versed in each area they lectured on. At the end of the training, certificates tabulating the courses one had taken were issued. This turned out to be a great achievement for the Church. But, like all other changes I had initiated, I faced a big opposition, which I finally subdued. The torrential opposition came from some past Moderators and senior clergy and elders. One of the key biblical verses that really inspired my desire to have a breakthrough in this venture was **Psalm 11:3,** which says, *"When the foundations are destroyed, what can the righteous do?"* It was my feeling that all the wrong foundations all over PCEA had to be addressed, *"Not by might nor by power, but by my spirit says the Lord Almighty."* (Zechariah 4:6).

I was very much aware that such spiritual battles could not be won by organizing physical battle fronts. They were to be won by letting Jehovah Sabaoth be in charge. In my case, in order to have a breakthrough, I had to spend a lot of time meeting Church leaders within presbyteries and regions. I even had to meet Business Committees, convincing the leaders of the importance of such a move like the training for the elders.

In one of the meetings, I remember one person asking me;
"Why on earth are you planning to revolutionize every sector of this Church? Does it mean that there was nothing worthy existing in this denomination before you became the Moderator? I think you are becoming too dangerous in the life of this Church, and it's not shocking that there are ongoing meetings plotting on how the presbyteries will have you impeached."

In response, I used the words found in Acts 4:36; 38-39. I said:
"Those who are meeting to plot my being impeached are like the Jewish Sanhedrin. They should remember Gamaliel's advice to the Sanhedrin when he said: 'Consider carefully what you intend to do…leave these men alone! Let them go! For if their purpose or activity is of human origin, it will fail. But if it is from God, you will not be able to stop these men; you will only find yourselves fighting against God.' I continued, *"In this case, let the so-called PCEA Sanhedrin think carefully for they will not succeed as this is God's divine path to bring restoration into the PCEA. And if this were not true, they would have impeached me by now. This is because they are using the physical approach, and I am using the spiritual perspective. I am depending on God's guidance."*

In other words, like the initiation of the elder districts, the movement to train elders before ordination had, over time, become a force to reckon with in the Church's spiritual and physical solidarity. It had become a great leadership asset to the entire Church. This proved the fact that God's most beautiful jewels are often delivered in rough packages by very courageous people, but within the package, we will find the very treasures that are worthy of being kept in the king's palace.

But it is also true to say that I got so much harassed and humiliated in my endeavor to have this noble venture established. Besides the impeachment plots, there were scandals created against me. What really kept me standing firm was the knowledge that, at times, God chooses opposition as a catalyst to our faith and holy service. In this case, I was reminded of the fact that the most prominent characters in the Bible were broken, threshed, and ground into bread for the hungry.

Jacob, like wheat, suffered severe threshing and grinding. Joseph was bruised and beaten and was forced to endure Potiphar's anger, having been manipulated by the latter's wife. Because of her framing, Joseph ended up in prison. But he also rose to be the Prime Minister of Egypt. David was for a long time hunted by Saul like an animal of prey through the mountains. He was bruised and ground into bread for a kingdom. What about Paul? He could not have become bread for Caesar's household had he not endured the bruising through whipping and stoning. It was for the same cause that he had to be ground for the Roman royal family. We find Jephthah in Judges 11, undergoing a harsh rejection by his family where he is chased out of his own family. But later, the same family went for him to become their ruler.

What I learnt from such experiences was that when you are fighting from every side for the sake of God's kingdom, totally submit your own judgment to that of the Spirit of God, asking Him to shut every door except the right one. Meanwhile, keep moving ahead, and as you continue down the road, you will find that He has gone before you, locking outdoors you otherwise would have been inclined to enter. Yet you can be sure that somewhere beyond the locked doors is one He has left unlocked, and when you enter through it, you find yourself face to face with a river of opportunity.

I have this experience to share: When God called me into the ministry, I was in a very prosperous teaching profession. I say prosperous because, as a headmaster, my school was either number one or two in Nakuru District out of 258 schools in national examinations. I was on the verge of being appointed an Area Education Officer (**AEO**). At the same time, and was promoted from **P1** to **S1** status. But then, I left the Ministry of Education to the Holy Ministry. My inspiration to join the Holy Ministry came from the PCEA Njoro Parish whose minister owned a very old bicycle and was always in a torn shirt collar with dusty clothing.

He used to come to my school for what was referred to as the Pastoral Program, where he talked to the PCEA-affiliated pupils. He used to leave his very old bicycle leaning against the school fence as if he did not want people to see it. I also had a bicycle but of very high quality and chances were, sooner or later, I was to drive as I was then being groomed for the position of AEO.

It is not surprising that many people talked of my being out of mind by this paradigm shift. But as things later stood out, by responding to what the human eyes interpreted as a downtrend, it became a great river of opportunities, not only for me but also for my family. Many other families, including the PCEA fraternity, where the Lord used me greatly not only in running Parishes / Presbyteries but also in getting a prominent position as the General Assembly Moderator, benefited as well.

BREAKING THE CONGREGATIONS ON SUNDAYS

Another area that I persistently pursued to transform was the breaking of congregations on some Sundays. This was at least once a month so that individual Elder Districts members could fellowship outside the Church, away from their usual Church sanctuary. This meant that the congregations would have the districts fellowship in homes or in certain designated places. This would bring people together, making them interact and share their joys, sorrows and a common Word. They would even carry out some Bible study.

In one of the GACs and in my pursuit to establish the breaking from congregations on appointed Sundays, I continued enlightening the delegates on the importance of this initiative. The meeting went well with very positive engagements. While seeking a resolution from the delegates, I Conclusively said:

"I am now calling upon this GA to make it appropriate for all our congregations to be breaking away from regular Sunday Services in order to be led in worship by Elder Districts at least every 3 months or even on a shorter time basis depending on the way the Holy Spirit leads the parish leaders."

After the GA passed this resolution, I felt it my duty to caution the delegates that the breaking of the congregations was meant to assemble the congregations purposely for fellowship and should not be an avenue for money collection. I said this because I had come to learn that most of the PCEA leaders tend to emphasize on money more than on the spiritual nourishment of the flock. I made this statement:

"Let these not be times to emphasize on money collection. I might be wrong, but I discern that some Church leaders will be calling for the breaking of the congregations to create ways to fundraise. This is wrong, and the spirit of God does not dwell in such gatherings. Let the people meet and seek God's kingdom, and he will make the financial provision. That is why he bears the name Jehovah Jireh. When the Districts first seek God's face, then money will automatically come."

Having said this, one of the delegates stood up and said:
"The problem is that every year, the Church and especially from the presbytery level, increases the accessed money allocation in huge percentages, and because of this, you find that every year there is a balance carried forward in unpaid arrears, yet it is the elder who is put to task when this money is not paid. This is very stressful for the elder. The Elder Districts then become an open forum for the elders to fall into the temptation to push the members to give because this kind of forum is very conducive for the elders not only to encourage members to give but for him to remind them of the importance of giving. In this case, the elder will take this opportunity to tell the members about the Church's needs and also give them a report on their progress on the accessed money payment as compared to other congregation Elder Districts."

He further said:

"We understand the logic you have in trying to push for the birthing of this system of breaking the congregation once in a while, but I am sure elders will find themselves in a dilemma. You will be surprised to learn that already there are people who are declining to be elected as elders because of the stress elders are encountering in trying to raise the money the Church has access to an elder. There seems to be no criteria put in place for carrying out the assessment. Unfortunately, this kind of stress is affecting the elders' families as one is forced to divert money meant for family use to paying the accessed money."

All said and done; I insisted that there had to be days the congregation would be breaking, and elders and ministers were to see to it that the appointed day was specifically reserved for spiritual growth. But as it turned out, this was easier said than done. Due to the spirit of materialism in the church, those gatherings were turned into fundraising ventures. They hardly focused on the Word of God. They also came to be treated as times of feasting with little to do with spiritual feeding. Spirituality was measured by how much money the district raised and how luxurious the meals were. But all the same, it has retained some fruitfulness.

ELDERS' DISTRICT ROTATION

I initiated yet another move. I proposed that once an elder had shepherded one Elder District for 3 years, they had to move to shepherd another district for a duration of another 3 years. When one moved out, another elder from another District would replace him or her. I referred to this movement as *'Elder District Rotation.'* I moved widely throughout the denominations, explaining to the congregations the importance of that kind of shepherding. In reality, it was another way of distributing the elders' gifts. In one main church court meeting, I gave the opportunity to the delegates to debate this concept. I remember one person who, in opposing the motion, said:

"Moderator, your idea is great, but I see that we will encounter some problems where elders are supposed to rotate within the districts within a given congregation. I foresee elders becoming reluctant to rotate within the districts of a congregation, especially when they have completed their

allotted 'assessed money' or had a smaller amount, and now a time comes when they are forced to move to another district that has accumulated the accessed money over the years. Already, I am aware of cases in our presbytery where elders are opting to resign or asking for early retirement because the payment of the accessed money is becoming a heavy burden on them. I am also aware of cases where people are turning down the request to be ordained as elders because they realize the financial implication involved."

As the debate continued, another person said,
"We cannot stop doing what is good for the Church for fear of the unknown. After all, the presbyteries are there to see that there is a good flow in the rationing of the accessed money as per the strength of a district. The problem we are likely to encounter here is that I have seen some congregations who do not care about the poor. In this case, it is not uncommon to witness a congregation subdividing the money equally to all districts, yet some of the districts comprise very poor people who live from hand to mouth. There are those whose districts are comprised of well to do members, yet they are made to give the same amounts as those in an Elder District comprising of poor people. Such rich people write cheques and have their accessed money paid within the first month, while the poor ones will have carried forward unpaid money year after year."

He continued to say,
"This is why an elder will be reluctant to move while being aware of such inequity. It becomes stressful, therefore, to move to a poor congregation. Moderator, this GA should give some guidance on this very traumatizing trend. If not, then there is no need to initiate the so-called 'Elder District Rotation,' though, according to me, it is a wonderful way to enrich the members spiritually as it creates an avenue for unity and oneness in the group. It also creates an opportunity for the distribution of the elders' gifts. The Elder will also learn from different kinds of people."

After a lengthy time debating on this issue, I finally said:
"Now that we've heard everyone's views on this motion, and while we still have other items on the agenda to address, I recognize that Elder District rotations are essential in empowering church members and in distributing the talents of the elders. This, in turn, will nourish the spiritual roots of our congregation. I move that the GA pass the resolution on Elder District rotations and instruct the Presbyteries to subdivide the 'assessed money' to match each district's financial ability. The GA will also empower the

presbyteries to take the appropriate measures against any elders who resist the resolution on Elder District Rotation."

I then called for the vote, and the motion carried the day. It easily became normal for an elder to move from one Elder District to another every three years. Further, most of the congregations shared the accessed money in accordance with the people's ability and if there was a congregation that had not mastered the move, it was the presbytery to blame.

Another aspect that I also introduced was the collection of offertories through the Elder Districts during the Sunday service. It is safe to say that my administration's initiative has aligned most of the church activities today.

I am always thankful to God for these achievements; otherwise, many of these changes took God's hand. I had to wrestle with very powerful forces of opposition. In most of these deliberations, I had to speak out of my written speech in order to convince those who meant good for the Church.

While effecting all those changes, I wholly depended on prayers. Most of the time, I was on my knees. I am fully convinced that every prayer a Christian makes in faith according to the will of God and His promises, offered in the name of the Trinity and under the influence of God's throne, whether for temporal or spiritual guidance, will be fully answered. No prayer made in Him will be in vain. The answer to prayer might not surface immediately, but in accordance with God's will and timing.

The seed that lies underground in winter is taking root in order to see a spring harvest, though it appears not above ground and seems dead and lost. This is true of the winter wheat. These seeds are, in most cases, overlaid by some inches of snow. Likewise, delayed answers to prayer are not only trials of faith, but they give us opportunities to honouring God by our steadfast confidence in Him under apparent repulses. Just dare to trust Him! And discover that the very force which barred your progress and threatened your life, at His bidding, becomes the materials of which an avenue is made at liberty.

I can imagine the excitement of the children of Israel as they moved along that highway, running in the midst of the piled walls of waters on both sides of the avenue, but ashamed or confounded that they had mistrusted God or murmured against Moses, even as they watched those mighty walls of water that piled by the outstretched hand of the Eternal, in response to the faith of a single man. It is with such thoughts in mind that I decided never to surrender but to hold tightly to my faith in God and trust that, with God, all things are possible. I had practiced a lot of patience and persistence before I could see the flowering of the tree and its fruitfulness. I had to overcome a lot of made-up scandals and evil plotting.

1. THE FIVE-FOLD MINISTRY

Another issue I turned my attention to was the inclusion of the Five-Fold Ministry into the Church. This is one area the pioneer Scottish missionaries neglected simply because they never embraced the Holy Spirit and the gift of prophecy. I found it unfortunate that the PCEA does not recognize what is referred to as 'The Five-Fold Ministry.' They tend to sideline the office of a prophet and the role of the Holy Spirit. In addressing this issue, I said,

"As a Church, we cannot expect to know the same power of the Holy Spirit that the early believers experienced unless we have wineskins similar to theirs. Moreover, there can be no mighty spiritual awakening in our day without a great shaking of our Church in worship, leadership, the review of the constitution, prayer and fasting and embracing the Five-Fold Ministry. It is by doing this that the Church will experience the fullness of the awesome power of Christ."

I went on to say: *"These are analyzed in Ephesians 4:11 where it says, 'It was Him who gave some to be apostles, some to be prophets, some to be evangelists, and some to be pastors and teachers.'"* This is again echoed in 1Cor 12:28, Where Paul says, *"And in the Church, God has appointed first of all apostles, second prophets, third teachers, then workers of miracles, also those having gifts of healing... those with gifts of administration, and those speaking in different kinds of tongues."*

This shows the Five -Fold ministry is the foundation of the Church ministries. The problem is that, over the years, the PCEA suppressed these gifts in the name of safeguarding the Scottish traditions.

I reminded the church leadership that the Five-Fold Ministry was the pillar of any God-oriented ministry. While I had some penetration in the recognition of the Holy Spirit, I did not achieve much in the area of prophecy and the gift of healing. The argument was that those gifts were only functional during the Apostolic Church. Unlike, their times, we now have many hospitals which are equipped with modern technology.

On prophesies, they claimed we have the gift of discernment through Christ. Unfortunately, this argument is weak because, cases are known where people have been healed through prayers and the laying of hands. Also, there is a worldwide witness of things that have been prophesied which have come to happen. The Bible does not refute the gift of prophecy; it only warns us to be aware of those called *'False prophets.'*

2. STANDING FOR THE WORD

For many years, I was concerned that the congregation did not give much honour to the Word when it was being read. I had the feeling that one of the ways to honour the Word was for the congregation to stand up during the readings as the service was taking place. People go to Church mainly because of the Word. In the PCEA traditions, it is the Bible (Word) that leads the Church procession from the vestry, and with respect to this Word, the congregation stands, indicating that the Word is the most honorable commodity for the service. Jesus himself is the Word. John reveals this when he says, *"In the beginning was the Word, and the Word was with God, and the Word was God"* (John 1:1).

It was in this regard that I called upon the Shimo La Tewa GAC delegates' attention by saying:
"I am requesting this GAC to recommend that the Congregation be standing as the two readings were being read during the Church service. If standing for a person one respects can be meaningful in human reasoning, how much then is it worth standing in honour of the Word being read? It is another way for the congregation to show their readiness to receive the Word from which the preacher will feed them." Unfortunately for me, this idea never went through, though I had some support, but these turned out to be the minority.

3. READING CULTURE

Noting the great decline in the reading culture among Christians, I made an awakening call to the Church to revive the culture of reading. I reminded the delegates and participants of the Shimo La Tewa GAC of the fact that the Presbyterian Church worldwide was founded on reading culture. It was meant to be a body thirsting for the search of knowledge. It was for that reason that John Calvin, the founder of the Presbyterian Church, came up with the first-ever academy during the Reformation. Calvin himself was a man of books, reading and writing despite his heavy reformation duties.

Without reading, even the Reformation by Martin Luther would not have picked up. It was unfortunate that, the reading culture had been declining pretty fast due to the upcoming technology. This was also true in regard to the Kenyan society. Many read for exams or promotional and work-related studies. Many people lose touch with books after school. It is my understanding that if people are not readers, their minds will continue to be condensed. People will then get detached from the great knowledge which is buried in books including the spiritual world.

Hosea says: "*My people are destroyed for lack of knowledge*" (Hos. 4:6). Hosea seemed to be inferring that God wouldn't appreciate being served by ignorant people. Hence, he says, "*Because you have rejected knowledge, I reject you from being a priest to me*" (Hos. 4:6). God says that His words are not twisted or crooked, "*They are faultless to those who find knowledge...for wisdom is more precious than rubies...choose knowledge rather than gold...and nothing you desire can compare with it."* (Proverbs 8:9-11).

Knowledge is life, and it has to be sought diligently. This was the agenda of the New Testament Church as "*they devoted themselves to the apostles' teaching*" (Acts 2:42). I therefore persistently called upon the Church to reawaken the spirit of reading from the Elder District, parishes and presbyteries. Another area I greatly lobbied for promotion into the church was the Theological Education by Extension (T.E.E). We had its curriculum highly enriched, especially at the Diploma level. This was made possible by my being the chancellor of the PUEA. My spirit of becoming an author was an added avenue of encouraging readership.

4. ALTAR WINE

During my tenure as GA's Moderator, I had always voiced the importance of using non-alcoholic beverages and non-yeasted bread in serving Holy Communion. I called upon the Church to use the grape juice. In my advocacy on this, some elders and ministers disliked me because they felt that I was distorting the Church practice held over the years. There were even those who were bitter with me because they were used to that alcoholic taste because they were once alcoholics, with some even secretly drinking alcohol.

These groups of people ensured that more than enough altar wine was prepared so that there would be more left over which then they drank after the service. Their argument was that Jesus blessed wine at Cana in Galilee and that there is nowhere in the Bible where it is pointed that the guests at the wedding got drunk, nor does it point out that the disciples got drunk during the Last Supper. But because some Church leaders distort the scriptures to fit what they want to give a green light to, the drinking of the Altar wine has remained.

It is, therefore, not unexpected that quite a number of clergy and lay people are addicted to alcohol due to their taking off the altar wine. In fact, some end up in rehabilitation centers. I knew of such a case in PCEA.

When I became the GA Moderator, I raised money to have the said pastor rehabilitated, but unfortunately, after three months, he took some wine, which then activated the whole process again. His life got totally distorted. He got disconnected from his family. He has since died.

That was one case, but there are several of them in the Church worldwide. That is the reason why, in a GAC, I called upon the delegates to discard the altar wine and embrace non-alcoholic drinks like grape juice, apple juice, and other amicable drinks. There is nothing so special about the Altar Wine. This is a creation by human beings. Otherwise, any kind of food or drink can be used in serving Holy Communion so long as it is liturgically set apart.

Jesus just used what was on the table. It is not necessarily that both bread and wine were purposely selected to be used as the elements in carrying out His Last Supper celebration. It just happened that the common drink in Palestine at that time was grape juice, just as our common drink is tea or coffee.

This is my thinking: In calling the Church to abandon the use of Altar Wine, I called upon the Church leaders to critically look at the issue and discard the use of Altar Wine and, hence, endorse the use of non-alcoholic drinks. The idea was never picked up. But as days go by, my discernment is that the idea will materialize because the Holy Spirit is at work bringing new revelations to the body of Christ.

THE IMPACT OF THE ABOVE CHANGES

As a result of the changes, there emerged both a great spiritual and physical impact on the Church life: The church became a beehive of activities. There was revived Spirit-led worship. We introduced the drum sets, keyboards and other musical instruments. People got so warmed up spiritually, and they no longer worshipped in a static position. They could lift up their hands, clap and even make bodily movements rhythmically in the African way like was, prior to the coming of the missionaries.' African traditional songs involved a lot of mobility.

The word also became sweeter and more convincing through the influence of the Holy Spirit- a sharp contrast to what used to take place in the times of worship – in other words, the service became lively.

It was as a result of those changes that there was a revival in the entire denomination. The Church was newly empowered. The stronghold of chronic resistance to Godliness got diluted and we enjoyed a lot of breakthroughs. We also managed to have many of the presbyteries and parishes subdivided. This made it easier for the Church ministers to have smaller areas of operation for ease of feeding the flock spiritually.

There also emerged the construction of numerous permanent Church buildings, hence the mushrooming of the dedication of new projects in the entire Church. Such projects were school-related, farming, hospitals, polytechnics, and business premises like hotels – in other words, income-generating projects cropped up.

Key among those were the three-star hotels, one in Mombasa (Milele Beach Hotel), another in the city of Nairobi (Milele Hotel), and yet another in Nakuru. Other already established institutions that were dormant in status had their progress renewed, such as the many stalled projects in the parishes and presbyteries. The Woman's Guild project (WOGET) in Mombasa had a total renewal in its outlook and status.

Another important move was the revival of the educational system. Schools that were poorly run for years breathed life again with the climax of starting the Presbyterian University of East Africa, whose idea had dragged for twenty years until I took over the reins of leadership as the GA Moderator. There was also the expansion of theological education to accommodate an added training of more ministers to cater to the increased parochial work due to the subdivision of parishes and presbyteries. The training of Lay people was also expanded with an introduction of a one-week training course prior to the ordination of new elders. The central part of this kind of training was designated at the PCEA Lay Training and Conference Centre located in Kiambu County, Zambezi, next to my home.

As the work of the Holy Spirit continued, and as it will be elaborated later, the exposure of occult symbols in the Church buildings was enhanced. In particular, the sanctuaries built by the missionaries were flooded with occult symbolisms like St. Andrews Church in Nairobi County, the Church of the Torch in Kiambu County and St. Margaret Church in Mombasa County, among others. Addressing these strongholds sparked a big controversy that not only caused uproar in the PCEA but also from the Western Mother Church, the Church of Scotland.

Suffice it to say the liberals progressively opposed me in all areas of my administration. They had vowed to leave no stone unturned until they voted me out of the Church. They could use all the means they could think of, including bribing the members of the key Church committees and Church courts to have me ejected from the General Assembly seat. As much as they tried, the Lord kept His Word that He had communicated to me when He paved the way for me to become the Moderator. Like Jeremiah, He had told me:

"Get yourself ready! Stand up and say to them whatever I command you.... They will fight against you but will not overcome you, for I am with you," declares the Lord"* (Jer. 1:17-19). God had further told me: *"See today I appoint you...to uproot and tear down, to destroy and overthrow, to build and plant"* (Jer. 1:10).

4 INSTITUTIONAL LIBERATION

The day I got consecrated, I told the General Assembly that, among the areas of Church life that I would focus on was putting the Church on a higher spiritual level, especially by dealing with the satanic strongholds that were deeply entrenched within the entire Church life. But most important was the reclaiming of the Church institutions like hospitals and schools, among others that were under siege.

I emphasized the fact that there was a great need for the Church to safeguard her institutions. I reiterated that the church must aggressively protect the Church's institutions, including schools, colleges, and hospitals, as well as instill Godliness in them. I had noticed that there were some cliques of institutional leaders who had grabbed some of the Church's institutions which they had turned into their own private properties.

Worse still, the government had on several occasions grabbed Church lands and administrative positions in institutions, especially in the schools. I recommended the formation of a committee that included some educational experts to research the needs of our schools. This included the question of land ownership which was becoming a contentious issue between the Church and schools. There were cases where the Church or schoolland had not been well demarcated. In some cases, the Church seemed to oppress the school by taking too much of the land, leaving the schools squeezed into small portions with little room for expansion.

Already, there were many cases of invasion in Church institutions by non-PCEA members. I personally knew a school under the sponsorship of PCEA whose head teacher was not a member of the Church. In some institutions, the senior leadership positions were not held by PCEA members. In such cases it was difficult to discipline such a person in accordance with the laid down Church procedures when there was indiscipline.

It was with this understanding that I urged the Church leadership to instruct the Presbyteries, Parishes and those in positions of authority to make sure that the senior positions in our institutions were in the hands of the PCEA members. Such leaders would have their accountability and transparency scrutinized where necessary. In cases where these leaders were not available, advice could be sought from the Head office.

I gave an example of Alliance Girls High School, whose administration had been in the hands of the PCEA all the years since its establishment, but the government had removed the PCEA-based head teachers and tried to install a non-PCEA head teacher. The hospitals were run down by cartels who threatened whoever would dare interfere with the operation of these institutions. Let me highlight some of the opposition I faced while trying to redeem the church-sponsored institutions, especially the hospitals:

1.KIKUYU HOSPITAL LIBERATION

This is among the first missionary founded hospitals in Kenya. Dr. William Arthur was its first doctor. Presently, it is nationally known for its orthopedic and eye-sight treatment. Unfortunately, its welfare had been eroded by long-existing high levels of corruption. It was for that reason that, as the GA Moderator, I decided to redeem the institution not only from poor management but also to bring it back to its former glory and sound financial status.

I decided to act during the ground-breaking ceremony on the 1st. July 2003 at the dental department. Upon arrival, I asked the hospital's administrator to assemble everyone in the chapel, doctors and workers because we were to start with a devotion which I was to lead. We carried on with the worship until I came to deliver the sermon. At the conclusion of the sermon, I said:
"During my installation as the GA Moderator, I communicated that one of the things I would investigate was the running and the productivity of our institutions, Kikuyu Hospital being one of them. As such, some members of the Business Committee and I would soon be visiting the hospital to inspect how things were on the ground."

Looking directly at the management, I said: *"Please, make sure you cooperate on this crucial endeavor."* After this, I commissioned some intercessors, and then we all went out to carry out the groundbreaking. This was climaxed with some refreshment. I then went back to the Head Office.

I then asked the Secretary-General to write a letter to the Kikuyu Hospital Management Board to officially inform them of our going there on the 29th. July, 2003. The letter explained that we would need to meet separately, the members of the board, the doctors/nurses and the subordinate staff.

To strengthen my grasp, I met the Business Committee, to whom I explained my intention to liberate the hospitals, beginning with Kikuyu Hospital. The Committee gave me the green light.

On the agreed day, I went to the hospital with six members of the Business Committee. We first met the board members. Having sat down to start the meeting, I said, *"Thank you for turning up for this meeting and now..."* The chairman of the hospital board interjected and said: *"Moderator, it is important for you to understand that as the chairman of this hospital, I am the one to chair this meeting. You cannot just come and hijack the meeting, yet we are the people on the ground and we understand the situation better than any of you people. You have a better understanding of the Head Office where you operate from."*

In my response, I said: *"Please understand that this is not a board meeting. This is a Business Committee meeting working under the mandate of the General Assembly."* The board chairman again interjected: *"There is no way you can chair this meeting. I totally object to this. No way! No way!"* Another member of the Business Committee addressed him: *"Chairman, we will have no quarrel with you. Ours is to do what the Business Committee authorizes us to do. We will just go back and take the report that the chairman of the board blocked us from carrying out any business, and I am sure being an experienced clergyman and well versed with our Church constitution, you do understand the consequences of this upon your life and ministry."*

Then I said,
"It is now upon you to give your final word because immediately I rise up, things will take the course which the Business Committee member has just

communicated to you." In response, another hospital board member said, "*I beg you, Moderator, to give us time to walk out and do some consultation before you decide to go.*" I said, "*That is a good idea; just don't take long.*" The board members went out, and before long, they came back.

A member of the board said,
"*Thank you, Moderator, for giving us that time. We have made consultations and have decided that the chairman of the board is out of order as far as the Church constitution is concerned. We have decided that you go ahead by engaging us with some deliberations, hoping that you will not demand to speak with any other group*". From that point, we engaged the board in some deliberations. From the talks, we discovered that most of the board members had no idea of what went on. It was a cartel of four people who were running the hospital affairs. We learned of many discrepancies that were wrecking the hospital.

Having finished with the board, I said:
"*Of course, even your body language tells us that you are not together in the running of the hospital. Most of you have no clue about what takes place in the running of the hospital. Meanwhile, can we have the doctors and nurses?*" On this, the chairman of the board said, "*Moderator, with all due respect, don't pressure us any further. In our consultation outside and as the board of this institution, we are totally opposed to such a move. I believe we have given you all the information you needed, and therefore, there is no need to meet any other group.*"

I chipped in:
"*I believe you have a letter from the Secretary-General stipulating that we are meeting three groups in this hospital. We have already finished with you so we still have two more groups to interview on matters of this hospital. But I repeat what we had earlier said, that we will just go back and then report your resistance in paving the way for us to talk to the other groups. Please be advised that we cannot come here to waste time. It is now either you call the people I am asking you to summon, or we leave.*"

Some members of the board did some communication through eye gestures, and one of them said,
"*We really never expected you and your group to expand this meeting to other groups. Most of us had no idea that there was a letter from your office indicating the people you would want to meet. This being the case, we are*

bound by the Church constitution which gives you the upper hand in this case." It was then that the doctors and nurses were called in.

I encouraged them not to fear as no one would be intimidated or followed up by the hospital's administration. One only needed to imagine the institution being his or hers as well as think of the many souls that found rest in their health status because of the hospital. I urged the team on by telling them, *"It is only when you have pain over the mess that is going on here that you will hear God whispering to your ears to come out and save this hospital, which has catered for God's creation over the years."* This group was very open. They narrated to us all the hurdles they were facing, which were all creations of both the administration and the board. As one of them put it:

"For many years, the Church has had no ownership over this hospital. It is never in the hands of a cartel that comprises a few people. They hire and fire. They promote and demote. They share the money generated from the hospital to the extent that we are now on the verge of missing our salaries. There is also a lot of money that comes from overseas for 'supporting the hospital', and even this money ends in the cartels' pockets. Surely, something has to be done, and your intervention Moderator is very timely. But one of the key reasons that has dwarfed this hospital is the way the cartels employ people with no regard to the money consumed in meeting the salaries."

He went on to say:

"They have employed many of their relatives and friends without any consideration of the financial status of the hospital. Worse still, most of these people have been promoted haphazardly -some from being cleaners to ward attendants. Yet those who have been workers in the hospital for many years end up being the lowest paid without any promotions simply because they have no godfathers."

After those people had spoken at length, I called upon one of the Business Committee members to thank them and also give them a final word of encouragement, after which they left.

We then asked the board to come in. Their faces had suddenly aged and were marked with lines of anger. Their laboured breathing said it all. I said:

"We have learnt a lot from these groups, and this will help the Business Committee in formulating ways to straighten some of the things we have heard. But of course, not everything is negative; there are some positive

things we have heard from them. Meanwhile, we want to listen to the general workers and the administrator can call them for us even as you leave the room."

It was then that the chairman of the board shot up and, vibrating with anger, said, "Enough is enough, Moderator! We have softened as far as the other groups are concerned, but this time, we are united in stopping you from talking to the workers. This time, it is a big No!" One of the Business Committee members, in response, said:

"Moderator, these people know that the general workers are the ones who have deeply suffered under the current administration of this hospital, and this is why they are now offering this intense resistance. However, we need not waste our time arguing with them. I propose that we go with the evidence we have gathered and let the Business Committee be aware of what is taking place here, but at the same time, tell them of the arrogance we have found within this board and the fact that we were blocked from listening to the general workers. I can see the reaction from that Committee. These people not only dread losing their membership in this board, but at the same time, I also see them losing their priesthood and eldership as well. This attitude has to be crushed by the Business Committee."

I then said, "We came here to ratify things in this hospital and that is a job we have to accomplish." At that juncture, one of the board members stood up and said: "Moderator, I really appreciate the initiative you have taken to redeem this hospital. Let me bring to your attention the fact that there are three of us on this board who have a big concern about the way this hospital has been slowly moving towards the cliff. In fact, our hearts are puffed up with joy when we witness the Business Committee move to redeem this hospital, which of course is long overdue, but as they say, 'It is better late than never.'"

He continued to say, "I therefore move that you continue with your work on unearthing what has been eating up this hospital for a long time. Something would have happened but many of those who had the power to intervene are always compromised through some bribes. I believe that it is God who has sent you as our Moses to bring about the deliverance of this hospital. Your decision to collect views from the employees is very commendable. Please, don't leave any stone unturned until you get to the core of the truth."

In response, I then said, "*Is there anybody else who wants to add anything besides what that board member has just said?*" Another member of the board stood up and said:

"*Moderator, that member has spoken on behalf of many in this board. The only thing he should have said is that quite a number of us would even have come to your office, for we have come to know that you are one person who can hardly be corrupted. Our leaders here thrive on corrupting those leaders who would question them on the running of the hospital. We always hesitated in pursuing this matter because one of the key leaders, who is a clergy in this board, owns a gun, and we really fear for our lives. That is the way to go unless they have a change of mind. I find this as the highest level of highhandedness by a group of people collaborating to sabotage the Church. Now, Moderator, why waste more time? Send your Secretary-General to summon the workers.*"

I then enquired from other hospital board members by asking the question; "*Are the other members of the board of the same opinion?*" And to my surprise, 70% of the members present were in favour. It was then that I called upon the hospital finance officer to summon the workers. Actually, they were eagerly waiting for that moment. They had all assembled in a nearby open space, waiting to be summoned. The finance officer only waved at them, and they all came in. Meanwhile, the members of the board went out.

I started by encouraging the workers to stand out and be counted in giving out the whole truth on what had caused the destabilization of the hospital in all its faculties. To further convince them, I quoted John 8:32, "*The truth will set you free.*" I then reminded them that the hospital carried their livelihood and it was important that they give us the right things that could help us in bringing about the restoration of positive life in the hospital. Here, we were talking about a group of sixty people who were aggrieved by the kind of frustrations they were encountering in the institution. When I called for their contributions, almost all of them raised their hands. For a whole hour, they poured out their hearts and disclosed to us the following:

- Many staff were employed without the correct papers.
- Many staff were at first employed as casual workers but ended up in very prime positions and earned far much higher salaries than the people they had found there.

- There were many ghost workers. Some employees had lost their jobs over the years, but they continued to be reflected as still working in the hospital. Their salaries ended up in the pockets of leaders of the hospital.
- There were several names of people who had already died, but their names still remained on the payroll.
- There were some who, upon employment, were placed in higher job groups that did not match their papers or experience.
- There were those who, upon employment, were paid double or more over those who had been in the same department for more than ten years. As soon as they were hired, they were given promotions immediately, yet there were those who had never been promoted yet had served for over fifteen years.
- There were incidents where money was said to have been stolen on its way to the bank, yet those were inside jobs in which some of those in the leadership ended up being beneficiaries.
- There were some who were on the hospital's payroll, yet they only technically reported for work as they were employed elsewhere. They had colluded with some leaders in the hospital who were beneficiaries of the salary paid to those absentees.
- Some in the hospital administration abused the workers in many ways, including demanding sexual favours from women. Some male employees were also sodomized. (*Soon after this meeting, one person had his job terminated due to his homosexual tendencies.*)
- ☐There was misuse of hospital vehicles by the leaders. Some treated the hospital vehicles as their own property.
- Any time a key member of the board got into the hospital premises, they would be entitled to some allowance, even if one was just passing by. Thus, these key members of the board regularly presented themselves to the hospital with the sole aim of collecting a stuffed envelope.
- Many times, the patients were underfed. This was deliberately done so that some money could be saved, which ultimately ended up in the leader's pockets.
- All payments for procurements were inflated so that the leaders would benefit from any of the sales.
- All procurements and tenders were awarded through corruption. It was not a question of who had the right skills; rather, it was who gave the most in terms of buying out the tender.

- A lot of hospital supplies were taken home by the leaders, some for home consumption and others were used to increase the stocks in their businesses while medicine was sold out to outside chemists.
- The medicine recommended for the patients by the doctors had their prices inflated so that some money could end up in the pockets of the leaders.
- All those seeking treatment were charged exorbitantly. Emergency surgeries were also charged exorbitantly, and the money was paid upfront before treatment or admission. This was unlike what happened in other Church hospitals like Kijabe Hospital, which is affiliated with the African Inland Church, and Nazareth Hospital, which is affiliated with the Roman Catholic Church. The way these Churches were running their hospitals and other institutions was very commendable.

All monthly cash collections were just enough for the salaries with no development being carried out. Any development was through the overseas supporters, but these had their own people on the ground to monitor and ensure proper use of that money. It was through this avenue that both the orthopedic and dental facilities were constructed. Unfortunately, there were some expatriates who were also compromised in corruption.

Having collected all the necessary information, and after thanking all the workers for their transparency in giving the information, we headed to the Head Office.

I asked the Secretary-General to write a letter to all Business Committee members inviting them to an urgent meeting. I also decided to hold that meeting at night. The meeting's venue was the Presbyterian University, just next to Kikuyu Hospital. I deliberately did this so that early the following morning, the Business Committee would visit the hospital and witness some of the things voiced out by the doctors, nurses and other workers. It was also important that whatever was to be decided by the committee would be carried out immediately and without any delay.

The Business Committee met as scheduled. There were other items on the agenda concerning the Church, but the hospital issue was the main agenda. The report on the visit to the hospital was tabled and deliberated on at length. It was decided that three top officials were to be sacked. These were the hospital administrator, the matron and the finance officer. The hospital board was also to be replaced with nine members of the Business Committee to act on an interim basis for one year, after which a new board could be put in place. It was already morning when we then headed for the hospital.

We summoned the three top officials. The Committee's final decision to relieve them of their duties was read to them. They were instructed to collect their belongings and leave. Each was served with a letter to that effect. The letter also stipulated things to do with their terms and conditions of service and in regard to their benefits. I then commissioned the Interim Board, and after this, we all left.

The interim board embarked on its work. They harmonized the status of employment. They first pruned out all those who were illegally employed. These were people who had no documents that would have qualified them for employment and those who, in some ways, had been undermining the hospital's welfare. Some had even committed serious crimes but were always given cover by their cronies in high positions. They sought out ghost workers, those who were unfairly promoted those who were paid more than what they were supposed to, among many other things.

As the one year of the interim board's recommended term of operation was drawing to a close, the hospital's status had greatly improved, giving the institution a good pointer to its bright future. After one year, a new board was installed, and they did a marvelous job. They even streamlined the condition, requiring patients to pay upfront before admission or treatment. One could now be attended to and pay later if they were not able to pay immediately. The hospital stabilized and it offered its mission services in the way it was meant to do- to glorify God's name. At least at that time!

It was very unfortunate that the cartel that had always been fighting my administration created a scandal painting me as the one who had demanded the removal of all the employees who had their services terminated. This is something that created some animosity between me and those employees. Some of them came from Gikambura, my home place. Those people tried to tarnish my name in the

110

community. But the truth of the matter is that according to the PCEA constitution, the GA Moderator has no power to avert or veto any decisions passed by the Business Committee or the decisions of the board so made by the Business Committee. Nevertheless, the board chair was unhappy with everything and kept haunting my life. But God protected me by fighting for His kingdom.

Those workers should have blamed the people who had corruptly created the employment for them, something that made them lose their jobs. The good thing was that all that was unearthed from the hospital's mismanagement was common knowledge within the Kikuyu locality. The community knew about the biased employment, financial mismanagement and the demand for high deposits before one got treatment or was admitted. In fact, I received a lot of phone calls from the surrounding communities, congratulating me for having intervened and for restoring the hospital to its former glory.

2. CHOGORIA HOSPITAL LIBERATION

Chogoria Hospital is located in Meru County, possibly 190 kilometers north of Nairobi. This PCEA-affiliated hospital could be referred to as a Mission Hospital because it was founded by pioneer missionaries. For many years, it has medically attended to a wide variety of people around Mount Kenya. Over the years, it had been vandalized by a few members of its administration such that by the time I took over the PCEA leadership, the hospital had become a den of corrupt robbers in all its sectors.

In fact, one missionary doctor had colluded with the hospital administrator, and together, they had siphoned millions of shillings from the patients' treatment fees as well as from other overseas donations. Like in the case of the Kikuyu Hospital, I felt it was my duty to intervene and save the hospital from imminent collapse. Incidentally, the same hostility I faced at Kikuyu Hospital recurred here. The cartel at Chogoria had vowed to finish me if I ever dared venture there.

The first day of my visit to the hospital was marked by a very high-level spirit of resistance. Rev. Mwamba, who served as both the Moderator of Chogoria Presbytery and the chairman of the Eastern Region, had teamed up with some other clergymen who had already sensed danger and had taken a stand to protect me. The hardline stance that the administrator at Chogoria Hospital had taken spoke volumes. Consequently, my security was beefed up to protect me from harm, especially because the hospital administrator had vowed to eliminate me. When I got to Chuka, we stopped at Chuka Police Station to pick up some police officers. I had one police vehicle behind me and another in front for the 15-minute drive.

I was to first meet with the hospital's board members, but they never showed up, although they had the information that the GA Officials were to visit the hospital and were to meet them first. When I asked for the doctors to meet us in the hall, they also never showed up. I later learned that all these people I was trying to reach out to were under very strict instructions from the administrator never to show up, failure to which they would face the administrator's wrath. I had no option but to meet with the administrator first.

I was in the company of the Chogoria Presbytery leaders, two members of the board who had turned up at the last minute. Both the Secretary-General and his deputy had also joined us. I led in interrogating the administrator on the general welfare of the hospital. Then, we had a tour of the hospital and visited all the departments, after which we held a second meeting.

We had found the hospital in a deplorable state. Worse, as we interacted and interviewed the workers and nurses while we moved around, some were courageous enough to whisper to us how the hospital had been run down. One worker whispered to me: "*The hospital is totally run down, and we are all stressed up.*" A nurse told me that the good medicine was sold to outside chemists, and patients were sometimes treated on expired medicine with very low healing effects. Another nurse confessed:
"The administrator practices a lot of nepotism. He is very oppressive to the workers, especially those he found already working in the hospital before he got into his position of administrator. Most of the workers are very depressed

apart from those who have some connection with the administrator or the doctor from America who seems the second in command."

One doctor took courage to tell me:
"The situation is very bad. Now that our GA Moderator is here, you need to declare this hospital closed or you come up with a new modality of running this institution. I am telling you, this hospital is just on the edge of the cliff and can collapse at any time. We have been approaching the Eastern Region branch of the Church on this matter, but the force exerted on this hospital is so strong for them because there have been death threats. The cartel that is running this hospital is using hospital money to buy out people who strongly question them, and those who cannot be bribed have been threatened with death. There are those who have lost their jobs for enquiring about the mess that has gripped every sector of the hospital. So far, there has been no force strong enough to face this manipulative system where people are forced to work for very low wages as the big fish in the hospital continue to enjoy unchecked salaries and allowances. It seems in every department, there is a cartel that pretends to advance the course of institutions but in the real sense, they are busy eating up the institutions' resources both externally and internally."

One of the senior doctors looking at me said agitatedly:
"We are tired of witnessing people initially employed as casual workers but they end up being in the well-paying departments having gone through hastened promotions. Others are recent employees and because they are relatives or they are able to bribe their way around, are paid far much higher salaries than those who have been in the same department for over ten years. What we have here is an institution that has no semblance of Christian values. Please, let your team do something."

He went on to say:
"I am confident that some changes will occur especially when this issue has been taken by you, our able GA Moderator. We have come to know you as a very transparent leader. I just wish you had come to take that position several years back. Both the Church and its institutions could have been very productive. We are very excited about your presence. You can almost feel the excitement that invaded this institution as soon as you became the GA Moderator. Let me just say conclusively that what we have here, Moderator, is a puzzle, and we have to work on it until this hospital regains its old glory and good reputation. On behalf of the other government administration, including the chief, let me assure you that we are totally

113

behind you. I also note that the clergy is as well behind you. They often talk nicely about you especially in regard to the fact that you are fighting for their rights as they have been leading a very oppressed life through most of the elders and a few of the senior clergy."

We then felt we had a good reason to act immediately; we ordered the administrator to step aside from his duties to pave the way for investigations. But he became adamant and refused to cooperate. At first, when we asked the police to help us in forcing him out of the office, they seemed reluctant and I remember one member of the board whispering to me: *"He has bribed them. They are on his side. We have to look for help from elsewhere. I know of an officer holding quite a high rank in Nairobi; I suggest we call him for some guidance."* I then said, *"That sounds quite a good idea."*

I then shared the idea with Rev. Mwamba and the other members of the region or presbytery, and together, we decided to contact that senior Police Officer at Nairobi Police Headquarters. Upon calling him, the said police officer responded quite positively. Incidentally, he hailed from the same area, and he was also concerned about the declining welfare of the hospital. He called the Officer Commanding Police Division (OCPD) at Chuka and instructed him to do the necessary as soon as possible.

This OCPD, who was stationed at Chuka, called the police officers who had accompanied us to the hospital and instructed them to force the administrator out of his office. Before long, the administrator was out of the office, and his deputy immediately replaced him in an acting capacity. As soon as this episode was over, both the Secretary-General and his deputy left in any case. They seemed to treat this as my duty and an impossible endeavour and, hence, showed no interest at all in what was going on.

They left for Nairobi with Rev Murigu driving and Rev Gathanju being the co-driver. I would have loved it if they had remained behind with me so that we could reconcile the opposing groups. I did not leave Chuka as I feared the two opposing groups would have turned the hospital into a battleground. The atmosphere was already polluted with anger and divisions among the workers.

There was the minority who sided with the administration because of the benefits they were enjoying as the loyalists, and I felt that, unless those two groups were reconciled, there could be no peace, and the working environment could be polluted. I, therefore, decided to spend the night there so that I could take time with the workers the following morning to reconcile the groups. The following morning, as I was just about to move out of the house, someone knocked at the door. He turned out to be an agitated clergyman. He said:

"You know what, the administrator is already in his office, and he says that he cannot leave, and if he has to, then someone will have to die, and of course, that is you. So, my suggestion is that you leave this matter alone. It would be very unwise for you to come and die here or be maimed. This man is burning with rage. I also believe he is distorting some data in the computers."

I responded:

"My friend, have you forgotten St. Peter's words to that mighty Sanhedrin Court when he said, 'Judge for yourselves whether it is right in God's sight to obey you rather than God. For we cannot help speaking about what we have seen and heard." (Acts 4:19). I further told the clergyman that we ought to be ready to fight for God's best with the knowledge that the best things are always achieved through difficult paths. It calls for readiness to endure climbing steep mountains, dense forests, and the enemy's chariot of iron since hardship is the price of the victor's coronation. Further, I reminded the clergyman that arches of triumph are made not of rose blossoms and strands of silk but of hard blows and bloody scars. The very hardship we were facing had been given to us by the Master for the express purpose of enabling us to glorify His name. I drew the attention of the minister to David. I explained the fact that the Lord had to force David, through the discipline of many long and painful years, to learn of the mighty power and faithfulness of His God. Through those difficult years, he also grew in principles for his glorious career as the king of Israel. Sometimes, God allows us to wrestle with painful experiences so that we become well-tested leaders. We then left for the office. As we walked, I recited the Lord's Prayer three times. From afar, I could see Rev. Mwamba and a group of other ministers standing in an open ground not far from the office.

When we got to this group, Rev. Mwamba briefed me on what was going on and told me that the administrator was already in the office. And he looked very charged, and it seemed he could easily strike to kill. I then took the opportunity to encourage this group. I reminded my comrades that difficulties and obstacles were God's challenges to our faith. When we are confronted with hindrances that block our path of service, we are to recognize them as vessels for faith and then fill them with the fullness of complete sufficiency of Christ. And that, as we move forward in faith, simply and fully trusting in Him, we are tested. It is for this reason that many times, believers find the stone being rolled away.

I further told them the beauty of our heavenly mansions so much depends on the scars we will incur while in God's service. I asked Rev. Mwamba to summon the clergy in the presbytery office. Soon, we were configuring the steps to take. We called the OCPD at Chuka. We explained the situation. He then sent a police officer with the message that the administrator, two other clergymen and I be transported to his office. We boarded the police vehicle and soon were in the OCPD's Office.

He grilled the administrator. At one point, he asked him: "*Is the Moderator your employer?*" In his response, the administrator said: "*He is not. My employer is a Church affiliated body known as CHAK.*" The OCPD further inquired: "*And who commissions the Church members that represent the PCEA in what you are calling the CHAK?*" He responded, "*It is the GA Moderator.*" The officer pressed on: "*Then, in this case, who is above the other, CHAK or the Moderator?*" The administrator kept quiet.

At that juncture, I noticed the police officers in the room were preparing themselves for some kind of action. It seemed the administrator had also noticed their body language and suspected that he was going to be arrested, for he quickly changed the tone of his words:
"*Your honour, sir, I will now go with your decision. It is true the Moderator is the overall, and I have sidelined him in my duties,*" he confessed. Then the OCPD said: "*I was just about to order your arrest, but I am giving you the last warning. You should have honoured and obeyed the Moderator because he is your employer, and for that reason, I am ordering you never*

116

to step at Chogoria Hospital or its premises, and if you do, I will order the police to arrest you immediately, and I am sure you can imagine what will follow."

The stubborn administrator left. Then the OCPD addressed me:
"*Thank you, Moderator, for the initiative to redeem this hospital. I receive complaints about it almost every day, and because it is a Church-related institution, I find my powers limited. Otherwise, I am now in a position to make a follow-up, and where I will require your help, I will call you. This situation includes even the Church sponsored schools. You can rest assured that I will be in charge and will also work hand in hand with the Chogoria Presbytery Officials. But most importantly, I have liked your non-compromising spirit. Thank you for not accepting bribes. This administrator and his cartel have survived through bribes.*"

He went on to say:
"*I am sorry to tell you that some of your Church officials have fallen into that trap. And for that reason, I am not surprised that some of your other Head Office Officials are not with you. I just wish we could have administrators of your caliber in r every sector of our administration, including the national government. It is unfortunate that corruption has invaded the lives of many leaders in both the political and Church realms. And how I wish God, in his miraculous ways, could provide this nation with God-fearing leaders like you. The problem we have is that the government leaders operate only from the physical aspect but do not apply the spiritual perspective.*"

We were ferried back to the hospital by the police vehicle. We entered the administrator's office, summoned the deputy administrator and confirmed him as the acting administrator. We told him to be ready to work with a temporary board that the Church Business Committee would put in place for a short period before another hospital board was commissioned, its chairman being Rev. Njue. They did a wonderful job.

I then directed him to assemble all the workers in the hall, where, by God's grace, I had the workers reconciled. I even commissioned some intercessors to continue standing in the gap for the spiritual and physical advancement of the hospital. After this, I left for Nairobi. Surprisingly, even when I went back to the Head Office, neither the Secretary-General nor his deputy ever enquired about what had transpired after they had disappeared.

Through this experience, it was as if God was teaching me that at the very heart and foundation of all His dealings with me, no matter how dark and mysterious they could be, I must dare to believe in and affirm His infinite, unmerited, and unchanging love. Yet love permits pain to occur. It also emerged from my mind that, sometimes, God causes severe winds of trial to blow upon His servants as a way of developing their gifts. Just as a torch burns more brightly when waved back and forth, and just as a juniper plant smells sweetest when thrown into flames of fire, so the richest qualities of God's truly called servants often arise under the strong winds of suffering and adversity.

Bruised hearts often emit the fragrance that God loves to smell. In this case, the former stinking hospital attained a good fragrance because soon, people were flocking to the hospital due to the change of guard in administration. The news of the renovation and transformation had spread far and wide. The hospital's good smell became the talk of the day. In the minds of many people, this was nothing but a miracle. But the truth of the matter is that miracles are performed through spiritual power, and our spiritual power is always in proportion to our faith.

I always find it unfortunate that some people always avoid things that are costly or things that require self-denial, self-restraint, and self-sacrifice. Yet, it is hard work, and difficulties that ultimately lead us to greatness, for greatness is not found by walking on a carpeted path. Rather, it is found by being sent to carve out one's own path with one's own faith and positivity of mind. Otherwise, when one is unsure which way to face life's challenges, it is important then to submit one's own judgment to that of the spirit of God, asking Him to shut every door except the right one.

Meanwhile, one will keep on moving ahead and consider the absence of a direct indication from God to be evidence of His will that one is on His path. And as one continues down the long road, he or she will find that, God has gone before him or her, locking doors one would otherwise have been inclined to enter. Yet, one can be sure that somewhere beyond the locked doors, is one He has left unlocked-one that is broader than anything one would have dared to imagine, even in one's wildest dreams, for it leads to far much greener fields of life. Many times, we have to learn of God's innovation and activation of His power in us through some hard ways.

3. TUMUTUMU HOSPITAL

This hospital was not as run-down as both Kikuyu Hospital and Chogoria Hospital. With the help of some members of the Business Committee, we interviewed the doctors, nurses and general workers, and the results were far much better than what we had encountered at both Kikuyu and Chogoria Hospitals. There were, however, a few cases of nepotism, especially in employment, but we were able to iron that out. Again, unlike the other two hospitals, I did not encounter any resistance in accessing whatever information I needed. That was the only hospital I felt welcome and we were even offered tea on our arrival and later were given a sumptuous lunch. Like in the other hospitals, I also commissioned some intercessors.

4. ALLIANCE GIRLS HIGH SCHOOL

Another instance of my encounter with the cartel that was misusing the Church institutions was at Alliance Girls High School, located a 5-minute drive from Kikuyu Town. There existed a cartel that not only sucked the financial resources in this institution but, at the same time, that was also frustrating the headmistress. The leader of the cartel was a very senior clergyman who was also the Chairman of the Kikuyu Hospital Board, which had resisted my interventions at the Hospital. This clergyman was aggressively leading this evil campaign against me. He had a tight grip on this institution. He and his cartel had orchestrated the transfer of the headmistress, with him being the mastermind. He was on the verge of replacing her with someone he could easily manipulate. Their maxim was, "*Take control of the top leadership of any institution, and the goodies will be landing on your table like manna from heaven.*" His aim was to have unhindered access to financial resources and other kinds of manipulations for his gain in this very able school. In fact, his intentions did not include the well-being of the school academically, physically and spiritually but to bring down the school's good name in matters of physical, spiritual and academic performance. I was really pained by their evil intentions, and I took it as my mission to protect the school at all costs.

This time, however, I did not seek help from the police. I turned to the school board of management for support. I brought to the attention of board members the looming dangers of allowing the Church cartel to have a say in the decisions on who should become the headmistress. Thank God the board comprised of very able and mature people led by the board chairman, Mr. Njoroge who at that time was the Permanent Secretary in the Ministry of Energy.

We sought and got help from Gabriel Lengoibon, the Secretary to the Teachers Service Commission (TSC). Through the board chairman's influence, we managed to visit Lengoibon in his office on the 24th. February, 2009. He warmly welcomed us and keenly listened to our concerns. He gave us another appointment and told us:
"Just go and get me three names of headmistresses of your choice, and I shall pick one of them. You have two weeks to work on that, and I am sure there will be a good outcome. I will do my best. We have to fight the cartels not only in regard to education-related institutions but the same war has to be declared in all government sectors. Otherwise, corruption will take a domineering position in this country. It is also very unfortunate if the Church that is supposed to fight corruption is also imbibing it." We requested him to give us one week instead of two weeks after which we would present him with the three names.

Meanwhile, the clergyman who never wanted to lose the grip of this nationally known school came to my office angrily, wagging a finger at me:
"I know that any time I am at loggerheads with you, my wife falls sick, but even though this is the consequence, this time round, you have either to do away with any interference at Alliance Girls High School or I deal with you accordingly." What he meant was that I either keep off from influencing the choice of the new Headmistress at Alliance Girls High School or I get eliminated.

I knew very well that this clergyman owned a gun. Nevertheless, I told him:
"It's good you have given me two choices; I will choose the latter. Go ahead; I know you own a gun. Use it on me. But let me be very clear with you; I will not allow you to continue eating the Church institutions like a mole.

You have already siphoned a lot of money from Church institutions, including Kikuyu Hospital." The man left, but not before he cursed, wagging the same finger at me:

"You think you are a saint, eh....eh.... I will deal with you. You are not the first. You cannot keep on blocking my ways of advancement. No other person has ever dared to challenge me. How dare you! You will know that PCEA has mighty pillars. You cannot fail to enrich yourself when placed in green pastures and then block others from feeding from it."

To many, this kind of threat would have led them into submission in fear of a bullet piercing through their bodies, but I did not. I was convinced that I could not help others who had suffered under greedy hearts without paying a price for it. I understood that afflictions are the costs we pay for our ability to sympathize with the oppressed. Those who wish to liberate others must first suffer. If I was indebted to rescuing others, I had to carry the Cross; otherwise, to experience the greatest happiness in God's service and ministering to others cannot be possible without drinking from the cup Jesus drank from and without submitting to the baptism He endured.

Graduates from the 'School of Suffering' are exceptional scholars. I decided not to focus on what may happen to me the next minute for the simple reason that the same everlasting Father who took care of me each and every day would either shield me or He would give me His unwavering strength, thus relieving me from all thoughts of cowardice. I also knew that one of my channels of survival was through my knees. I was constantly on my knees, asking God for protection because this was not just about me, but it was in obedience to His call. Is He, not the God who was with Daniel in the den of lions and the three young men inside the furnace that had been heated seven times above the usual?

Luke 4:18 reminded me of the fact that God has sent me as well to heal the brokenhearted, to proclaim liberty to the captives...to set at liberty those who are oppressed, which was also the focus of my ministry while here on earth. The fact that this clergyman's wife fell sick any time he confronted me, as per his testimony, was an indication that God was fighting for me. Hence, I relaxed and fought on.

It did not take long before the board chairman summoned the board, and we went through the names of the proposed good headmistresses. We finally came out with three names. After one week, we went back to the TSC offices and met our mutual friend, Gabriel Lengoibon. We submitted the three names that we had selected, and he picked the name Dorothy Kamweru, who also happened to be our favourite choice. Our research revealed that Dorothy was a hard-working, non-compromising and transparent leader. At one time, she had served as an education attaché at the Kenyan Embassy in London.

With that move, we triumphed in the appointment of the right person for our outstanding national school. Having grown up at Gikambura which is within the vicinity of this school, I had developed a great love and affinity for the school over the years. It was for this reason that I could not watch as the school fell into the hands of "Terrorists." I was ready to redeem it with my flesh and blood if that was the only way. The words that hung on my office door boosted me in my everyday endeavours. These words read: "If God sends us over rocky paths, He will provide us with strong shoes." Meaning that He will never send us on any mission without equipping us well.

God himself affirms this in Deuteronomy 33:25, where He says, "Thy bars shall be iron and brass; and as thy days, so shall thy strength be" (ASV). I also had this conviction that the imprints of tribulations are on every great accomplishment. It is the door to triumph. Otherwise, no one wins the greatest victory until he or she has walked the winepress of woe. The footprints are visible everywhere. Those called into the path of liberating people under oppression should be aware that the steps that lead to thrones are stained with spattered blood and that scars are the price for scepters. That we will wrestle our crowns from the giants we conquer and that every breakthrough has always been preceded by tribulations of persecution, opposition and resistance!

5. PRESBYTERIAN UNIVERSITY OF EAST AFRICA (PUEA)

PCEA stands unrivalled by any other denomination when it comes to the establishment of education-related institutions in Kenya. Sadly, pioneer missionaries from other denominations were not in favour of Africans getting Western education. They feared that if Africans received a good education, they would later question the legality of British occupation in Kenya. But the Scottish missionaries felt different. They needed messengers in their offices and in other sectors of life. Thus, as soon as they started evangelizing the Africans, they started to educate the converts.

Dougall, in his book; '*Christians in the African Revolution,*' says;
"*In the pioneer stages, of course, there was little or no distinction between the Church and school. The same building served both purposes. It's no wonder, then, that the PCEA, under the very minimal lease, released the land where Alliance schools, both boys and girls, stand today. It was only later that the other missionary bodies adopted the idea of schooling the Africans.*"

But, over the years, PCEA did not have a university to its name. For many years, it was part of St. Paul's United Theological College and was co-owned by the PCEA, Anglican Church, Methodist Church and the Reformed Church of Kenya. It was not until twenty years before I became the Moderator of the General Assembly that the idea to start a university under the sole ownership of PCEA surfaced. The agenda for the establishment of a university was in the Church deliberations for twenty years. In fact, it is said that the birthing of the Methodist University of Kenya was an idea stolen from the PCEA.

The presiding Bishop of the Methodist Church had attended one of the PCEA General Assembly meetings as one of the invited guests. He then heard the agenda of the Presbyterian University being deliberated upon. He ran away with the idea and revealed it to his denomination, and before long, the Methodist University was established.

I decided that the establishment of a PCEA University would be one of my key missions to accomplish as a GA Moderator. It finally took off the ground as a result of my persistent calls for its birthing through the several motions I raised about it at both the General Administrative Committees and Business Committees. But it was during the 2007 GAC held in Mombasa that the university was finally birthed opening its doors in August of the same year. This turned out to be one of those great miracles that God has bestowed upon this Church.

I became the first Chancellor; Prof. Ribu became the first chairman of the University Council, while a temporary person was put in place to act as Vice-Chancellor (VC) until such time a permanent VC would be recruited competitively. The news of its establishment spread fast, and more and more students applied for admission, more so because it was a Christian institution. There were other advantages like it's being strategically located in the central part of Kenya within Kikuyu Township, not far from Nairobi. Also, it was in the neighbourhood of pioneer missionaries' location, which accommodated both Alliance schools, Kikuyu Hospital, Church of the Torch and the University of Nairobi's Faculty of Education.

On Wednesday 28th. March 2008, in the company of six others, I met the Commission for Higher Education (CHE) Secretariat to negotiate the university's future plans, including issues related to the issuance of a charter. The (CHE) members were excited about the progress the university was making within such a short span of time. Their excitement was even more stirred when we showed them the long list of the already admitted students, including the list of all other applicants. The commission advised us to polish the curriculum of the Core Courses and submit it to them for approval.

But unknown to me, there was a cartel with a hidden agenda whose intentions were to loot the university's resources. I came to learn about it when they started to keep me in the dark. They held secret meetings where key issues were discussed. They were keen to keep me out of the picture of what was going on in the life of the university. It was only when CHE had made a visit to this university and demanded to see all the documents that I was able to see for the first time most of the vital documents that those running the University had concealed from me. They had started to treat the University as their own private property.

I will forever remain grateful to the Chairman of the University Council, Prof. Ribu, who, after this meeting, became quite close to me. He always kept me informed on what was going on at the University; though the said cartel did its best to also sideline him. This was the same cartel that was constantly fighting my administration. It was unfortunate that some of those in the inner circle of the university's administration had also become part of this cartel.

They wanted to make sure that, as the chancellor, I was not involved in anything regarding the University. They were determined to sideline me as they tightened their grip on the university affairs. At one time, they even blocked me from planting a tree at a function that took place on the university grounds, yet I was the founding chancellor. Thank God, He gave me the wisdom to wrestle with this corrupt cartel.

According to the university by-laws, the Moderator of GA, the Secretary-General and the Honorary Treasurer are members of the Board of Trustees (BOT), yet this cartel ignored this and failed to invite me to some of the crucial meetings. However, I always managed to learn about some of the cartel's resolutions from people who were members of both the board and the staff. Most of the resolutions were only meant to loot the university's donations from overseas, but I was quick to block them. I was able to connect with the donors who communicated to me any time they sent the funds and I was able to follow up on how the money got used.

In their evil plans, they had coined a slogan, *'Please Collect Everything Available'* (PCEA), from the initials of the Presbyterian Church of East Africa. This was why they were sidelining me because they knew I would intervene to block them from the misappropriation of the university money. In many instances, I managed to block the ways they had invented to be misusing the university finances, especially the numerous seating allowances amounting to thousands of shillings.

When at one time the CHE visited the university, they were not amused by the fact that the hiring of staff was being done through the back door. That was contrary to the CHE's regulations that all vacant positions had to be advertised. For example, a parish minister had been hired as the Director of Education, yet this minister had failed even to teach at the former Presbyterian College and had been taken to a Parish where he did not deliver either. Most of the hiring was done through bribery. Most of those hired were close relatives.

Notable also were cases of forcefully ejecting some PCEA ministers who were already teaching at the University and had been assessed and found qualified to teach at the University. Their only crime was leaking out information on the misappropriation of funds which the cartel leaders wished to remain secret. They insisted that the ministers be posted by the Appointment Committee elsewhere.

But as the Moderator and the chairman of the Appointment Committee I never gave in to their demands. Another reason why the ministers were getting kicked out of the university was because they were teaching the real truth from the scriptures. The cartel was opposed to this as they were after making the institution liberal so that they could derail the students from the core truth as presented in the Bible. In fact, this was even encouraged by some of the Western donors who regarded the university as a fertile breeding ground for **Pluralism**, **Relativism** and the **New World Oder**. This is the kind of teaching that has '*killed*' the biblical truth in most of the Western countries' seminaries and universities.

Another controversial issue was the appointment of the Vice-Chancellor. The cartel was reluctant to appoint a **substantial holder** to this office because they regarded the position as one area where they made a lot of money in the form of bribery from potential candidates. They were also after a person whom they could easily manipulate to be part of their devious schemes. The cartel sought to fill the position through the back door, yet the letter of **Interim Authority** from CHE issued in August 2007 clearly stated that the position of Vice Chancellor had to be advertised. I had been persistently asking the Board of Trustees (BOT) to advertise the position but they had all along refused to do so.

Finally, the BOT installed a new vice-chancellor without even bothering to consult me as Chancellor. As far as I was concerned, his installation was null and void, and whatever emoluments he received were illegal. Worse, he was at the same time working on part time basis at Kenyatta University. The same cartel designed a fee structure that was far beyond that of the established University's tuition fees. They even demanded Ksh. 10,000 from Presbyteries for any student who hailed from any presbytery. This soliciting of funds from the Presbyteries was done without even contacting the Business Committee or the Head Office officials.

I was getting very concerned that the university was drifting in a direction that would, sooner rather than later, bring it down, especially on the misuse of funds and the corrupt ways of hiring personnel, including the employment of unqualified faculty staff, bribing in the tendering process, quoting exaggerated prices of supplies and which most times they awarded their friends and relatives. In an effort to salvage the institution, I raised those issues in GAC meetings, calling upon the delegates to seriously look into the issues that were hindering the development of the university. I recall telling the delegates the following:

"In view of the current situation at the university and bearing in mind that it is going very fast towards the wrong direction, I call upon this GAC to take steps in renewing both the Board of Trustees and the University Council of the Presbyterian University of East Africa. This new blood will pilot the University in achieving what I promised the **CHE** *officials. This included the University doing things as per the* **CHE** *regulations. This will also make it easier to fundraise and establish other connections with other bodies both locally and overseas. For example, while in the USA, I contacted two Universities- one in the State of Iowa and another one in Virginia who wanted to partner with our university, but this kind of development cannot take place without a commendable Vice Chancellor, board of trustees and the university council. The cartel that is running the university has vowed that they will do whatever it takes to create a scandal about me so that a way will be created to pass a vote of no confidence in me. They regard me as the main stumbling block in their misguided efforts to loot the university to the maximum,"*

I submitted. I further said: *"In view of the current situation at the university, it is important that this GAC instructs the Chancellor in consultation with the new BOT and the University Council to be immediately involved in the search for a substantial Vice-Chancellor. Further, the new university leaders should streamline the University's employment policy and nullify all the recent employments and the positions be advertised through the media and Church forums like presbyteries and parishes and any other avenues that could be thought of."*

It was after the intervention of the GAC that a new path for the university was opened. This was a great relief to me because prior to this, I was lonely as I engaged the university cartel in a good fight to redeem the running of the institution. The situation was made difficult because a lot of money was being dished out in bribery to those who would otherwise have come on my side. The cartel had labeled the university as an income generating project for their personal gains. They were greedy for the money that came through tuition fees and overseas donations.

It was even a struggle to get the right kind of vice-chancellor because, as we have noted, the cartel wanted someone they could easily arm-twist for their own selfish gain. But I insisted on having a well-qualified VC- with good credentials, a person of integrity, devoted to his/her work and one who could protect the institutional finances from those whom I referred to as scavengers. It is not surprising; they secretly bribed some of the members of the Business Committee and encouraged them to pass a vote of no confidence in me so that I could be kicked out as the Moderator of the General Assembly. One member of the committee confessed and told me: "*The cartel believes that for as long as you are the GA Moderator, they have no way of getting a free hand in enriching themselves from the money flowing into the university kitty. It is for that reason that they have promised their supporters in the Business Committee a lot of money after they ensure you have been dethroned. I am therefore encouraging you to keep on fighting the good fight. Let them do whatever they want to do after you leave the office if the Moderator who takes after you will not be protective of the university's welfare.*"

In that struggle, what I found shocking was the fact that some of the key officials were not giving me full support. It seemed they were compromised. In most cases, I fought such battles alone. Remember, I faced a similar situation in rescuing the other Church institutions from the grip of individuals who were financial suckers of institutions such as Chogoria Hospital, Kikuyu Hospital and schools like the Alliance Girls.

The good thing was that God had blessed me with a group of very devoted members of the Business Committee who clung to my side, and with their help, I finally succeeded in having the rightful vice-chancellor, Prof. Peter Thairu, installed. Unfortunately, this very intelligent, dedicated and very able administrator was fought from all sides because of blocking the cartel from scooping money from the university kitty. But by using my position as both the Chancellor and General Assembly Moderator, I managed to have him stick to that position.

Through his efforts, the university picked up, and before long, it received great recognition and became a reputable institution-wide and far. Prof Thairu championed the cause of the university such that the student population rose to two thousand even though he was under much pressure to accommodate corruption. He stood his ground, though he could only hold it as long as I was the GA Moderator. No sooner had I left office, having successfully completed my two terms (six years), than he was put under a lot of humiliation and finally got kicked out of the university.

With Rev. David Ritho Gathanju as the new GA Moderator, things took a nosedive. The new Board of Trustees and the University Council were compromised. The university reverted to being a gold mine from where many enriched themselves. No wonder the university started to decline rapidly. The report presented by the Nation Newspaper on Thursday, 26th January 2018, portrays the crumbling down of the university. In part, this report said:

"The government yesterday ordered the closure of the Presbyterian University of East Africa for failing to meet the financial and academic standards required of its license of operation. Acting Education Cabinet Secretary Fred Matiang'i revoked the license in a letter dated 23rd January addressed to the Commission for University Education (CUE). He said, "In view of the above, I authorize you to initiate the process of winding up the university."

The report went on to indicate that an audit report submitted to the CS by **CUE** dated 22nd. January had recommended the letter of interim authority awarded to the university on the 10th. August 2007 be revoked. The report further said that staff at the university were on salary arrears spanning two years, and the institution had unpaid arrears on salaries and allowances amounting to Ksh. 611 million. The university had also defaulted on the remittance of staff salaries and deductions for repayments to financial institutions, leading to some staff members being listed at credit reference bureaus. The report also noted that the university lacked adequate resources to meet its obligations, given the deficit realized in the four years under review.

The collapse of the university was a result of greed by some of the Head Office officials who took office after me and who, at the same time, colluded with the university administration in dehydrating the institution financially. Due to this looting, the suppliers went unpaid for long periods of time, including the lecturers and the subordinate staff. Many of these cases ended in the courts of law. The looters did not even want to promote the university academically since it could mean hiring highly qualified staff who would have attracted high salaries and minimized the chances of their fattening from its kitty.

It is for the same reason that they kicked out the very able Vice-chancellor Prof. Thairu, and also one of the reasons that I was always at loggerheads with the PCEA leaders at the Head Quarters because of my aggressiveness and persistence in calling out on the denominational leadership to address the wickedness that had engulfed the denomination and its institutions. This was especially because of the prevailing overwhelming spirit of corruption, devil worship and the fast-invading spirit of homosexuality.

During my tenure in office as the GA Moderator, I defrocked six pastors for practicing homosexuality. Unfortunately, these things were not announced to the denomination members as they would have taken the initiative to vote out the Church leaders who were creating avenues for this kind of spirit to creep into the denomination. I am sure the Church membership did not even realize the kind of pressure I was undergoing in trying to redeem PCEA from the grip of cartels of Freemasons/Illuminati and New Age Movements. It took God's hand for me to bring a turnaround in the crumbling of the so-called *"Tradition of the Elders,"* where many changes took place, including the Praise in Worship, the establishment of Elder Districts and the subdivisions of presbyteries and parishes as well as decentralization.

Let me re-emphasize that one of the reasons that made the university prosper during my administration as the Moderator of the General Assembly was the *'big wall'* that Prof. Thairu and I had formed around the university's finances and resources. As I have already stated, I was always under pressure from those who wanted to help themselves with the money that came through the student fees and the donations from overseas and especially from the USA, from the Greater Atlanta Presbytery in the state of Georgia, whose unsurpassed contribution heavily boosted the founding of this university.

Of course, there were many other channels through which money came to the university, including from companies, PCEA presbyteries, parishes and individual Church members who gave very generously, especially because they were told such contributions were meant to be shared through which they could benefit in dividends as the institution continued to mature. But the reality was that the cartel was only using that as bait to reach the depth of individual pockets.

No doubt those at the Head Office hated me so much that having finished my term of office as the GA Moderator, I requested that I be posted to teach at the PUEA as a lecturer, but my request was turned down. They feared that I could not only expose the manipulation that was going on at the institution, including sexual abuse of female students, but I could also stand in their way and prevent them from scooping the money from the university's kitty.

It is unfortunate that the Church, which is biblically mandated to fight such wickedness as corruption, is in itself swimming in a strong current of corruption. It seems Isaiah's words are relevant to these Church leaders when he tells God's people:
"When you spread out your hands in prayer, I will hide my eyes from you; even if you offer many prayers, I will not listen...Your rulers are rebels, companions of thieves; they all love bribes and chase after gifts." (Isaiah 1:15, 23).

Another thing that really helped me in fighting for the establishment of PUEA was practicing calmness in spirit and trusting that what I was doing was part of God's agenda. One thing that God's Spirit had led me to discern was that a quiet spirit is priceless in value when performing outward activities. Nothing so greatly hinders the work of God's unseen spiritual forces, upon which our success in everything truly depends, as the spirit of unrest and anxiety. There is tremendous power in stillness. A great believer once said, *"All things come to him who knows how to trust and to be silent."*

This saying is rich in meaning, and a true understanding of it would greatly change our ways of working. Instead of continuing our restless striving, we would *'sit down'* inwardly before the Lord, allowing the divine forces of His Spirit to silently work out the means to accomplish our goals and aspirations. And it will work if only we attain that quietness in spirit enough to be carried along by the current of its power. It is like the work of a refiner. It calls for God's wisdom and guidance, persistent time in prayers and, at times, fasting.

Our Father, who is Jehovah Sabaoth, is a non-comparable refiner as he is the creator of the other so-called refiners. He seeks to perfect his saints in holiness. He knows the value of the refiner's fire. It is with the most precious metals that a metallurgist will take the greatest care. He subjects the metal to a hot fire, for only the refiner's fire will melt the metal, release the dross, and allow the remaining pure metal to take a new and perfect shape in the mold.

A good refiner never leaves the crucible so that the fire will not become even one degree too hot and possibly harm the metal. As soon as he skims the last bit of dross from the surface and sees his face reflected in the pure metal, he extinguishes the fire. And so is the working of the Lord in our lives. He had to refine Isaiah, who, due to his sinful filth, could not accept to be in the Lord's service. In this regard, he said,
"Woe to me! I am ruined! For I am a man of unclean lips... Then one of the seraphs flew to me with a live coal in his hand.... with it he touched my mouth and said, 'See, this has touched your lips, your guilt is taken away, and your sins atoned for.'"-Isaiah 6:5-7. He was then mandated to go and be the refiner of the Israelites' life of idolatry.

Our capacity for knowing God is enlarged when we are brought by him into circumstances that cause us to exercise our faith. So, when difficulties block our path, may we thank God that he is taking time to deal with us, and then we lean heavily on Him. The more I have been exposed to afflictions in my endeavor to promote the kingdom of God, the more I have come to be trained in the area of spiritual warfare, and the more I have been drawn to God.

In all these battles, I was aware that masonic cartels that existed for many years were tapping their power from satanic symbols entrenched in the church and its institutions, including the university, on two fronts- physical and spiritual. These symbols were both inside and outside the buildings. These evil activities were thus activated through the symbols. But I used my spiritual authority to suppress and oppress these. I had raised up intercessors that were helping me in this warfare. But unfortunately, those who took over from me did not know how to handle this.

THE ASPECT OF CHURCH SUBDIVISIONS

There was a cartel in the PCEA whose target was to make sure that this noble denomination remained stranded/stagnant in all its sectors of life. A case in point is where they held the church in bondage by disallowing any subdivisions that enabled fewer people to be catered for in smaller groups. It was when the church existed in huge masses that they were able to suffocate it. Hence, they resisted any way that could make the church members spiritually nurtured and nourished. Therefore, subdivisions are one area I decided to venture into, especially the subdivision of presbyteries and parishes.

Subdivision of Parishes

As things were prior to my becoming the GA Moderator, no Parish could be subdivided unless there was a dedicated stone-built Church, and the parish must have cleared all the assessed money (Cess as it is known in Church circles) by the head office, among many other requirements. Unfortunately, the assessed money was allocated in a greedy manner because, in most cases, it was far beyond what members could afford. Thus, the accumulation of unforwarded money to the Head Office kept on accruing over the years.

It then happened that in all the Church meetings, whether in the Local Church Committees, Kirksessions, Presbytery, Business Committees or departmental committees, the main agenda, which could be deliberated for hours on end, was that on unpaid money to the parish, to the presbytery and to the Head Office. There were hardly any issues to do with development or spiritual perspectives included because, after all, there was no money to be allocated for such. And for this reason, subdivisions of the parishes rarely took place. Apart from the mother Church, the burden on the access/quota made it impossible for parishes to put up other stone-built Churches. No wonder many parishes existed with many congregations, some with as many as thirty congregations all under one parish minister with one stone-built church which also served as the Headquarters for the Parish.

With God's help, I managed to influence the other Church courts (Kirksessions, presbyteries, General Administrative Committee, General Assembly and Business Committee) to pass resolutions that paved the way for the subdivision of parishes and decentralized matters concerning the transfer of personnel and other administrative issues.

Previously, before the subdivisions, a congregation could stay for several weeks before they saw a minister on a Sunday, yet Sunday was the day of celebration of Holy Communion, baptisms, confirmations and other ecclesiastical duties. Unfortunately, the minister had the tendency to give more attention to the congregations that were financially endowed or the able people! Their focus was on forwarding the parish accessed/quota money demanded by the head office, without which the minister could earn their monthly salary. In fact, most of the sermons by ministers were about giving.

Nevertheless, in spite of much opposition and threats, I persistently anchored my trust in God, for He was the one who, upon positioning me as the GA Moderator, guided me through the words in Jeremiah 1: 17-19; 2:5, 13, by saying;
"Get yourself ready! Stand up and say to them whatever I command you. Do not be terrified by them, or I will terrify you before them....They will fight against you but will not overcome, for I am with you and will rescue you....They followed worthless gods and became worthless themselves....They have forsaken me, the spring of living water and have dug their own cisterns, broken cisterns that cannot hold water." No wonder God helped me such that as I came to the end of my tenure, numerous parishes had been sub-divided, creating other parishes.

Subdivision of The Presbyteries

Subdivisions of the presbytery were yet another obstacle in the life of the Church. The Church tradition advocated for no subdivision of the presbyteries until and only after the presbytery had cleared the allocated access/quota to the head office. There also had to be a permanent Church building for the new presbytery(s). Having noted the financial burden on the parishes, with a number of them forming a presbytery, it was obvious that the presbytery could not clear the head office cess/quota or even put up a permanent structure for a new presbytery.

That is why many of the so-called presbyteries comprised a few parishes which formed several congregations. For example, Nakuru Presbytery comprised three parishes -Nakuru (32 congregations), Njoro (30 congregations), Rongai (20 congregations) and Gilgil Parish (26 congregations); such examples were reflected in all denominations. You can imagine the magnitude of work each parish minister had on their heads. There was no way a minister manning such a number of congregations could be effective. To add insult to injury, the ministers had no means of transport. Some had only bicycles, but many depended on public transport, and some places had none; worse still, some parishes covered a large mass of land.

As indicated earlier, there were only 28 presbyteries in the entire denomination by the time I became the GA Moderator. Remember, this is a denomination that covers three countries: Kenya, Uganda and Tanzania. Apart from Kenya where a number of presbyteries existed, the other two countries existed as individual presbyteries. It was through passing resolutions in the Church committees and courts that I was able to penetrate and have resolutions passed that enabled the subdivision of the presbyteries irrespective of whether they had paid the money accessed to them by the head office or not.

At one time, what we now know as Nakuru Presbytery covered Gilgil, Nakuru, Eldoret and Kitale.

Notable also is what we call Nairobi Presbytery which at one time covered Thika, Nairobi, all the way to Mombasa.

Then, there was what is called Meru Presbytery, which covered the entire Meru region, including Embu.

Some presbyteries had accumulated thousands of shillings in the course of their existence. It was not until God used me to defuse this hindrance that the financial and spiritual dormancy within the presbyteries got broken through the subsequent presbytery subdivision. The subdivision created smaller and more manageable presbyteries. For example, what used to be *'three'* presbyteries in the Eastern Region (Meru) got further subdivided, making a total of eight presbyteries. What used to be the South Kiambu Presbytery was subdivided into seven presbyteries. By the time I finished my term of six years as the Moderator of the General Assembly, the number of presbyteries in the entire denomination had increased to 47 with more others already identified for subdivisions.

Such subdivisions helped maximize the financial status of a presbytery since there was no longer much money used in reaching out to the presbyteries' Church functions and presbytery meetings. Such traveling has also been causing a lot of fatigue in the ministers who got worn out looking for venues for the meetings or functions. This made them arrive home late in the evening. Subdivision also made it easy for people to bring resources together.

Finally, I had a breakthrough in this area of subdivision. Parishes and presbyteries could undergo subdivisions irrespective of whether they had paid all the cess or had a permanent church building. This greatly eased the burden of shepherding a huge parish. For example, between the years 1986-1987, I was the Parish Minister of Rongai Parish, which comprised twenty congregations. Since then, this parish has been subdivided into four parishes. Dr. Arthur Parish in Nakuru, which in 1984 comprised thirty-two congregations, now comprises seventeen parishes at the time of writing this book.

Another fitting example is what was formerly Chogoria Parish in Meru County, which comprised several congregations. By the time I completed my six years as Moderator of the General Assembly, the parish had undergone major subdivisions, paving the way for over ten parishes. My argument was that, by creating smaller parishes, the minister was then in a vantage position to reach out even to individual families and, hence, adequately feed them spiritually. It also made it possible for the parish minister to be available to congregations beyond the customary Sundays.

The impact of these subdivisions made the denomination experience a renewal both spiritually and physically. There was a great spiritual awakening.

This is the time that physically, the Church managed to come up with many income-generating projects like the Milele hotels in Mombasa, Nairobi and Nakuru. The Church was also set up PUEA. Consequently, the dormant PCEA institutions like the Hospitals and many other PCEA oriented schools were revitalized.

These changes did not come easily. The cartels had been benefiting when the presbyteries, parishes and institutions were in that pathetic situation. There were others who felt that I had undermined the Church traditions and therefore advocated for non-subdivisions of the parishes and presbyteries. It was for that reason they earnestly worked hard to pave the way for my downfall. That is why they organized meetings to plot for their mission in every presbytery and even in some parishes. Their plots included my being eliminated altogether because of my circumventing their evil ways to access the money from the Church and all its related institutions.

As we saw before, my ascent to the position of GA Moderator, millions of shillings given in Sunday offerings, tithes, overseas donations and from other sources were being pocketed by individuals who manned the various church facilities. Corruption had been rampant in the church since most of the top creams in church leadership had been compromised since they were alibis thriving through the corrupt systems and all kinds of manipulations.

But there was the other thing that concerned the occultists in the denomination. They were bitter with me because of my aggression in addressing their evil altars that had been raised in the Church buildings and other church-related institutions, particularly **PUEA** and the Church logo. In confronting all these evils, I risked my life in order to glorify God by bringing sanity to the denomination. Many times, God directed my steps to protect me from being eliminated. Remember, we are not talking of worldly criminals, but some clergy, elders and well-placed people in the Church!

For example, there are three specific instances where I had to flee as I was being pursued by hired killers. In one of these, I had to stop at a police roadblock where I sought refuge and cover from the police manning the roadblock.

THE UPGRADING OF MINISTERS LIVES

Prior to my becoming the Moderator, the traditions of the Church dictated that pastors were not to receive any financial support from the members of the Church.

Pastors were seen as a cursed lot who, by virtue of their calling, had seemingly taken a vow to live in poverty. But the worst enemies of the ministers were some of the Moderators of the General Assembly. They claimed to adhere to the Church traditions that treated the minister as an enemy. They advocated for ministers to depend entirely on their salaries. In fact, there was one notorious Moderator, Rev. Muindi, who, in collaboration with past Moderator Rev. Gatu, had written letters to all Kirksessions and presbyteries insisting that pastors should not get any other financial support apart from their salaries, which in itself was meager and was received in trickles. In fact, most pastors lived from hand to mouth. They were a miserable lot.

Some Moderators even held seminars with lay Church leaders to educate them on this. This meant that members could not financially extend favours to pastors even at the time of induction, licensing, ordination or during times of farewell. This applied to logistical or any support towards sustaining the minister's transportation, like helping them buy a vehicle through a funds drive. I remember when I got inducted in Mathare parish in Nairobi in 1999; there was no opportunity for members to extend a handshake to me as a welcome gesture.

This was to ensure that I did not receive any goodies or gifts from members. To make matters worse, at the end of that service, I was told to join in the procession back to the vestry. I was held captive in the vestry, where the presbytery Moderator introduced some discussions that went on for a long time. Meanwhile, the Church members and the guests I had invited were waiting outside the church, expecting at least to shake my hand. When the time of my stay in the vestry got so much prolonged, they could not bear it any more. By the time I left the vestry, many of them had left. They had no opportunity to congratulate me and pass on any gifts they had for me. That was the whole intention of the presbytery leaders. The delay was deliberate, so that I could not benefit from the church members. It was all anchored on church traditions and the teaching of some of the GA Moderators and some well-placed senior clergymen. This was the same scenario I witnessed in my other church inductions, including the ones that took place at PCEA's Dr. Arthur in Nakuru, Rongai Parish, Loresho Parish and Muguga Parish. It was the same trend even during my licensing and ordination.

There was a spirit, as stated earlier, mostly promoted by some of the GA Moderators that aimed at impoverishing the pastors by every possible means. They ensured that no appreciation or tokens would be given during somber events like funerals to joyful occasions like conducting wedding ceremonies, including elder district visitations. Any member who dared break this rule would be ruthlessly dealt with and labeled rebellious by the elders. The hostility against the clergy was always fueled by the GA Moderators and the senior clergy, who were themselves well-established materially and financially. Many of them owned personal cars.

I always felt pained that the Church leaders blocked not only the blessing of the pastor through members and invited guests, but they also blocked the blessings that the church members would have experienced in supporting servants of God. It is not surprising then that out of ten ministers at the time, only one or two owned vehicles were weighed down by mechanical problems.

Likewise, out of fifty ministers, only an average of one owned a home. Ministers lived in well-furnished parish mansions, something that blinded them from knowing the benefits of owning a home or a farm. This was ideal in making a family experience some settlement rather than a minister's family being like a rolling stone that gathers no moss. This was an aspect that gave me a lot of concern. It is for this reason that when I became the GA Moderator, I never moved to what was referred to as the GA Moderator's 'palace'. I instead opted to live in my home in Zambezi.

I felt it my duty not to leave any stone unturned until I had unblocked all the blocked avenues that hindered the ministers from enjoying the fruits of their labour. This cut across all their personal and ecclesiastical functions, including times of induction, ordination, licensing, farewells and supportive fundraisings, among others. In doing this, I faced a lot of opposition from the past Moderators and the very senior clergy who felt it was only their sole prerogative or right to own property and to dominate others even in all sectors of denominational leadership.

1. DECENTRALIZATION

Before I became Moderator of the General Assembly, all concerns of the clergy were handled at the head office in Nairobi South C. This meant that clergy from any place in Kenya, Tanzania or Uganda with a concern regarding the salary, a loan, or any parochial and presbytery issue would travel to Nairobi. The officials at the head office considered themselves the protectors of both the church and Scottish traditions, traditions that were not only oppressive to the spiritual life of the church but even more oppressive to the life of church ministers and workers.

It is for this reason that I focused on a move to bring about decentralization. This meant, making the Presbyteries handle all the ministers' welfare, including salaries. But I already knew that this was not going to be easy.

In order to have a breakthrough in both decentralization and upgrading the lives of the ministers, I used a lot of physical and spiritual energy as well as God-led strategies. I organized seminars for elders and other church leaders. I moved from one region to another and even to individual presbyteries. I also utilized every opportunity to educate church members whenever I had a function such as ordaining ministers, subdivision of parishes and presbyteries and during church fundraisings. There were some very rusty knots to be untied, and I engaged the power of the Holy Spirit in making a difference. I did a lot of praying and fasting so that I could have a breakthrough over those issues. The degree of opposition to such a move was very high. I could not win such battles without an army of intercessors.

I, therefore, embarked on commissioning of intercessors wherever I had a church function. There was no other way to combat the spirit of opposition against this move which was at higher gear. The words that kept razing in my mind are those found in the book of Zechariah 4:6: "*Not by might nor by power but my Spirit.*" I felt the need to prove to the ministers' oppressors that working in the Lord's vineyard as a minister did not represent a curse or slavery. Rather, it represents an avenue of blessings both spiritually and physically.

Many of the church ministers and workers were already sick and weak. I did not believe that God would let me carry the GA Moderator's position, which is a banner of his victory and then calmly withdraw to see myself captured or beaten back by the enemy. Never! I always believed that God, who had chosen me in accordance with John 15:16, would not abandon me. If anything, He could be deliberately passing me through this kind of pressure so that I could be well refined for His kingdom, just like the sweetest perfumes are obtained only through tremendous pressure or, better still, the fairest flowers that grow on the most isolated and snowy peaks, or the most beautiful gems that naturally have suffered the longest at the jeweler's wheel.

Likewise, the most magnificent statues have endured the most blows from the chisel. But all these have no shortcuts to be what they stand for. They are subject to God's law. Nothing happens that has not been appointed with consummate care and God's foresight, and with this in mind, I decided never to compromise. In spite of the threats, and like Esther, I decided to override all the opposition, '*If I die, I die.*' Surprisingly, rather than decline in faith, I became more and more puffed up with the zeal to face the confrontations head-on.

Many times, I felt lonely but at the same time, felt some angelic power embracing me. One lesson I learnt is that it is in these places of severe testing, with no human way out of our difficulty, that our faith grows and is strengthened. And to my surprise, doors started opening with most of the Business Committee members coming to know the truth which eventually set the ministers free. Ministers began experiencing a newfound love from their parishes, leading to a movement. I remember one minister telling me:

"We are praying that God will continually bless you for having become a blessing to us. There is a totally new understanding among the parishioners as far as their relationship and the renewed support for the ministers is concerned. For sure, the ministers have been treated as enemies before, especially by most of the elders and some of the past Moderators. We feel so relieved. But we also know that this has left you with a lot of scars, but it is the same with Jesus, he was left with a lot of scars. It seems that is the only path to take in bringing about some liberation or, call it, bearing fruit-fruit that will last."

In response, I said:

"At His own timing, God brings about some Martin Luther's, John Calvin's, Nelson Mandela's and other spiritual warriors when He wants to accomplish a mission. Any meaningful liberation cannot happen without having God's hand in it. I am glad that God is using me through his zeal, just as he did through the likes of Elijah and Gideon."

For sure, the opposition was stiff. I remember one time I called for a meeting of all the Eastern Region elders. I challenged them to allow fundraising to support ministers in buying vehicles. I remember asking them;

"How do you feel when only one minister owns a vehicle out of all the ministers that labour among you, yet you expect good service from them?"
One very senior clergy responded by saying: *"Moderator, you have engaged yourself in rolling a stone that you have no strength to push. The elders have heard a different gospel preached to them over the years, mostly by the senior clergy, including some past Moderators. The message has always been that ministers ought to emulate the missionaries who established the gospel without ever owning a vehicle. They used to walk, and the richest owned a bicycle. This is the foundation, and the path the Presbyterian Ministers of the gospel are supposed to trek. Service offered to God calls for denial. It is Jesus who commanded His determined followers to walk through this avenue when He called upon His followers to carry one's cross and follow Him."*

The speaker went on to say:

"So, my advice to you, Moderator, is that you deviate from that topic and teach us how to be productive in God's kingdom without having to drive. Otherwise, it is the spiritual drive in our hearts that will motivate our legs

to carry us. Anything out of this will not go along with the gospel that we inherited from those poor missionaries. It will be just a waste of time. After all, roads in Meru are very slippery when it rains and also very dusty in times of dry weather. These roads are very rough and bumpy. This could mean incurring other expenditure to the parish in maintaining the vehicles."

This speaker was one in the class of a few ministers, who had an opportunity to study overseas. He had succeeded in owning vehicles as well as personal housing. All said and done, by the time my full tenure of six years as GA Moderator ended, quite a significant number of ministers were driving their own vehicles. Today, almost every minister located in Meru and the entire PCEA owns a vehicle, apart from the newly ordained ones.

I am always grateful to God that in spite of much frustration and persistent opposition and persecution, this door opened. My endeavor was rewarded. All glory be to Him who has called these servants of God to labor with Him in His vineyard.

Now, looking back, I am thankful to God because he guided me in achieving my two themes: *"Leave it alone for one more year, and I will dig around it and fertilize it"* from Luke 13:8b and: *"You did not choose me, but I chose you and appointed you to go and bear fruit -fruit that will last"* (John 15:16).

I also see that most of the ministers' problems were sorted. The tradition of receiving gifts and blessings during ministerial events, such as inductions, ordinations, receptions, and home visits, had now been deeply rooted in church culture. This also extended to students under practicals before being ordained. I recalled during my college days when I was a student doing my practicals at Thogoto Parish for almost two years; I never saw anyone visit our home – no elders, no deacons, no church members because they were under threat never to visit me and it was against church traditions. None of the church leaders, elders, women's guild or parish ministers knew my home.

2. INTIATION OF OWNER-OCCUPIED HOMES

Prior to my becoming the GA Moderator, one could easily identify the ministers who owned homes. Almost all Parish Ministers lived in Parish mansions or houses. I therefore took it as my challenge to encourage pastors to own their own homes. Over 99% of the clergy had previously lived in parish houses, most of which were built next to the church (usually the parish headquarters). Before a pastor occupied the house, the presbytery would ensure that the house was well furnished with good furniture such as sofa sets, a dining table, bedding, a refrigerator, a gas cooker, electricity and water, among other things. This had brainwashed the ministers from thinking of owning their homes.

Ministers were required to roam about with their families on transfer, with some being subjected to frequent shifting, especially if they were not on good terms with some head office officials.

The ministers' children were a confused lot as they persistently experienced new environments following their parent's transfers. Their learning was unstable as they kept on changing schools. It is no wonder that many pastors were going through severe stress/depression. Worse still was that retired ministers became even more depressed because they found themselves in the wilderness, without their own homes.

The Church had not even strategized in any way to help them after their retirement. They somehow became beggars and paupers because, financially, they had no savings. They had in all their working life depended on their meager salaries. These salaries never reached some of them because their parishes could not manage to meet the parish-assessed money required by the Head Office through the presbytery. The results were many succumbing to depression, poor health, and, at times, unstable marriages. Their wives would keep wondering how the employer could claim to be the Church of Christ and yet it could not take care of its own workers.

Ministers had no option but to watch their families suffer. Every day, throngs of ministers jammed the head office corridors, each trying his/her lack to present their *"woes"* to different offices, which, in most cases, ironically made them *"cry even more bitterly"* as they could not get any help. They were told to go back to their very financially crippled parishes to mobilize the parishioners to give money assessed to them so that out of that, the minister could get his/her salary. This is the situation I found when I took the reins of power as the GA Moderator. It was a very hopeless and disturbing situation.

The first thing I did was to increase pastors' salaries, including opening other avenues for the ministers to get extra allowances through extra responsibilities. I also educated the pastors on the importance of saving so that, with time, one could own a piece of land and then put up a house. At first, it didn't have to be a fancy home, but where God would give some favour into opening a door for a good-looking house, the better. I advised them to save more through SACCOS and other banking institutions so that, with time, it could be easy to acquire a loan.

I aggressively visited presbyteries and the regions, encouraging ministers to take the challenge. In many instances, I did the encouragement on a one-to-one basis. I even encouraged them to venture into creating income-generating projects like keeping cows, chickens, or any other project and, where possible, encourage their spouses to busy themselves with something that would be an asset to the family and their livelihood. I used myself as an example because I lived in my home, and I even refused to vacate my house to stay in the GA Moderator's Palace, which was in a luxurious location in Nairobi.

Quite a number of clergy condemned me for opting to live in the countryside rather than occupying the flashy church house, which gave the GA Moderator the dignity he deserved. For them, it was a letdown to the church. They hated me for demeaning the status of the *"Presbyterian Church of East Africa."* They could not even understand how I could accept to take the church position without a new car model but instead opted to use the old and wrecked vehicle that the head office gave me initially.

It's true the church was in such bad financial shape that there was hardly any money to buy a vehicle for the incoming GA Moderator. I remember one time on the 3rd. In May 2003, the vehicle broke down around Gilgil on my way to Nakuru, where the presbytery leaders were waiting for me to conduct a seminar for Elders and Ministers at Nakuru West Church. I opted to go by Matatu, but Gitonga, the Secretary-General and Kinyanjui, the Deputy Secretary General, then blocked me from boarding a matatu that I had already waved to stop. They urgently called for a vehicle from Nakuru. My official vehicle used to have constant punctures as the tyres were quite worn out. It required constant repairs.

The vehicle broke down again when I was on official duties in Nyeri, as well as while I was on my way to Meru and in the midst of a traffic jam. In the latter incident, a member of the PCEA, driving a very luxurious car, stopped and asked: *"Do you need any help?"*
"We are almost done. Thank you." I responded.
"Moderator, is that vehicle meant for the GA Moderator?" he asked. *"Is this the best the Church can afford?"* he asked, wondering. He opened his mouth wide and said: *"What a shame to a church with such a big name to give junk to their Moderator of the GA Assembly?"* Then he drove away in anger. He never even gave any financial support.

But I asked God never to allow such a situation to ever occur to any other incoming not only Moderator of the General Assembly but also any other GA official. I personally declared that I would lay a financial foundation in the church so that, never again would an incoming official of GA ever suffer like me.

I then vowed to work so hard for the Church to ensure it got and sustained financial stability. God blessed the work of my hands such that, by the time my tenure of office was over, two new models of Prado vehicles for the incoming GA Officials were in the head office premises even before the officials assumed office. I prayed that never again would an incoming church official suffer the way I suffered, though I did it without bitterness. Meanwhile, I organized meetings to reach out to the ministers, telling them the importance of improving their lives in every sector. Most importantly, I assured them of my zeal in supporting them to combat the negative ministers and elders. I even used my personal resources to support individual needy cases.

It was my joy to see that, by the time my six-year term came to an end, there was a great paradigm shift among the pastors in buying

146

parcels of land and putting up owner-occupied houses. And to further facilitate the pastors to have more money for personal development. I emphasized the provision of owner-occupied house allowances as an incentive package for the pastor's financial growth.

By the time my tenure of office was drawing to an end, the spirit of wanting to own a home was already contagious, such that by the time of writing this book, slightly over ten years after, quite a high percentage of PCEA pastors were living in their own homes. What a better ministry than this, where pastors are no longer beggars but lenders and a source of bread for the hungry! Let me re-emphasize the fact that the reason the pastors easily embraced my advice was mainly because I had opted to live in my house rather than the Church's GA Moderator's designated housing in Nairobi, which the past PCEA Moderators had previously treated as their State House. This became a real catalyst for the contagious spirit to put up minister's personal houses. I also spent time with the individual ministers, sharing with them their joy and sorrow. I was easily available for them.

As already stated, my endeavours in encouraging and promoting the betterment of the ministers' lives were not without resistance. The cartel in the church, comprising some rich clergy, elders, and past Moderators, had vowed to ensure that the clergy remained poor so that they could easily be manipulated. Sometimes, the struggle was quite intensive. One of the things that encouraged me never to give up were the very words that I had hung on my office door that read, *"When God sends us on a stony path, he provides strong shoes."* While I also did a lot of praying with the help of intercessors I had widely commissioned in the church, I was at the same time encouraged by the following biblical references: Philippians 4:13, *"I can do all things through Christ who strengthens me."* 2nd Cor. 10:3-4, *"The weapons we fight with are not the weapons of the world. On the contrary, they have divine power to demolish strongholds."* The strongholds, in this case, were the PCEA Scottish traditions, which were occultly formulated to suffocate the pastors and their families who were placed under the church elders and clergy as the custodians. These were enforced by several by-laws formed by the church leadership over the years.

Isaiah 41:10-11 was of great encouragement to me:

"So do not fear for I am with you; do not be dismayed, for I am your God; I will uphold you with my righteous right hand. All who rage against you will surely be ashamed and disgraced; those who oppose you will be as nothing and perish."

Also, Jeremiah 15: 20-21, gave me some solace:
"I will make you a wall to this people, a fortified wall of bronze; they will fight against you but will not overcome you, for I am with you to rescue and save you, declares the Lord. I will save you from the hands of the wicked and redeem you from the grasp of the cruel."

In carrying out this thankless work, I was not only focusing on those who were clergy by that time, but I was at the same time focusing on future generations of both the young people and the ministers in the PCEA. This is one legacy I wanted to leave: to see that ministers did not live like slaves - a frustrated lot in the so-called Lord's Vineyard. I felt called to remove all the *'stiff-necked traditions'* that could as well entangle the future crop of church members.

Most of the decisions favouring the clergy passed through my influence in the church courts and committees- Business Committee, GAC and GA. Bear in mind that before such meetings, I would persistently have gone around across the denomination educating and convincing the presbytery and regional leaders, both clergy and lay people, on the importance of uplifting the lives of clergymen/women.

In doing all this, I was aware that I was jeopardizing my life in the church and that this could have some negative effects both on my life and ministry. But I felt the worth of being a sacrificial lamb rather than keep on watching the church, the young people and the clergy struggling in their lives when I could do something while I was in office. There was no need to say, *"I wish I attempted to rectify the situation."* That would have made me live a life full of guilt. It is for this reason that I felt encouraged in spite of the threats I received. Some of the threats were connected to the Government, especially by one of the Moderators who boasted of being the custodian of Presbyterianism.

A case in point is the way Rev. Dr. Timothy Njoya got frustrated for having preached on what was considered anti-government sermons.

He was aggressively calling upon the government to stop oppressing people and instead act like a lift in uplifting their lives. For that reason, he was transferred from St. Andrews Church in Nairobi to Tumutumu, though this happened prior to my being made a GA Moderator.

Looking back, I am always thankful to God because although my efforts left me with a lot of scars, including being disowned as a PCEA clergy, it always pleases me to note that, in many ways, I managed to pull the clergy and the church out of a very deep pit. At the same time, it reminds me when Jeremiah was pulled out of that pit he had been thrown by his enemies as recorded in Jeremiah 38.

All the same, I cautioned the pastors and warned them that, as much as God was continually expanding the boundaries of their lives, that should not make them forget God and start worshiping money. I cautioned them against being possessed by the spirit of financial greed or to preoccupy themselves with the ambition of accumulation of wealth. But rather, they should be filled with the desire and zeal to advance the kingdom of God in the hearts of people. I did realize that, as people progress in material favour from God, it is easy to drift into the spirit of competition and comparisons. There is a danger of evaluating and comparing what one owns with what another pastor owns - the kind of car one drives, the kind of house one has built, its location, and the personal utilities, among others. This is what leads to the spirit of greed and corruption. To emphasize this point, I referred to the book of Deuteronomy, where God cautioned the children of Israel thus:
"When you eat and are satisfied, when you build fine houses and settle down... then your heart will become proud, and you will forget the Lord your God, who brought you out of the land of slavery... you may say to yourself, 'My power and the strength of my hands have produced this wealth for me'" (Duet. 8:12, 14, 17).

Through these words, I warned the clergy to love God and labour more in His vineyard for God's given riches. I say 'God-given' because recently, there have been many pastors universally whose source of wealth is through some crooked ways.

3. THE ASPECT OF TITHING

In order to deal with the state of the financial backlog in PCEA, I had to drive the church membership to own the spirit of giving towards the work of God, including being supportive of the ministers. To achieve meaningful success, I decided to carry extensive teaching on tithing from parishes to the presbyteries and regions. I did this by holding seminars and also hammering this theme in my Sunday service sermons and during any other opportunities that came my way. While, in fact, they were opening avenues to introduce liberalism in these institutions. I also encouraged the ministers to carry out this crusade down to the Elder Districts.

To create an effective move, I wrote a book titled; '**Tithing**: *Principles and Practices*.' This book was widely read within the Church. I also used my other book, '**How to Grow a Healthy and Vibrant Church Through Small Church Groups**,' in the promotion of Elder Districts. Despite the opposition, many ministers supported me, and as a result, we had a big breakthrough in church giving. This resulted in the mushrooming of church projects from parishes, presbyteries as well as the Head Office.

4. TRAINING OF MINISTERS

The training of ministers was the other great concern. I had learnt that most of the liberals in Western countries were infiltrating the so-called '3rd World countries.' Theological institutions pretend to give support in the form of training, infrastructure and teaching material. In a number of key PCEA leaders' meetings, I used to float this issue of training ministers. In raising this issue, I was concerned about the way the liberals had invaded theological institutions. What used to be spiritually refined theological teachings had been distorted by the liberals. One of the ways they had done this was through charitable manipulation. They had come up with promises to support the institution in financial matters and in infrastructure. This meant helping to put up new buildings expanding the libraries by bringing in new books and such items like computers. They had also promised to help turn the Theological Schools/Bible Schools into Universities. Here, I am referring to all Theological Schools/Bible Schools being converted into universities.

This last approach was very crucial because it brought in secular subjects, which opened the door for many non-theological students including non-Christians. Non-Christian lecturers also found an opening to come and teach. The aim here was to defile the influence of Christianity in the institution and then, finally, have the theological school swallowed up by secularism. Further, they brought in their teachers, claiming that they were supporting the teaching. They justified this since they were able to pay the salaries of this lot as well as meet their other necessities. Those teachers were liberals, and they taught not only liberal theology but also liberal subjects to the non-theologian students.

Yet another way the Western Liberals are diverting the spiritual aspects of the theological students is to sponsor some of these denominations' students to study overseas. They take such students into the already Liberalized Theological Schools. There are known cases of some students who had to terminate their studies because of refused to compromise their faith as demanded by the liberal teachers. As a student, you either have to support the spirit of liberalism, or you will get marked for failure in your exams. It was in that connection that I constantly called upon the **PCEA** church leaders to consider putting up a separate theological school completely detached from the university's influence. I said:

"This Church needs to be very selective in the institutions of learning that ministers go to for studies overseas because a majority of these institutions are promoting the kingdom of the devil by recruiting the students into Satanism. Believe it or not, already many theological institutions in Western countries are in full gear in the promotion of Satanism, including homosexuality and lesbianism. Over 70% of the lecturers are pro-gay. Ironically, all these theological schools started as well-grounded Christian seminaries. They are now like salt that has lost its taste. They qualify as breeding grounds for Satanism. This is true of schools like **Yale** *and* **Stanford**. *I therefore call upon the Church to start a well-equipped Theological School, one not attached to a university that includes secularized subjects."*

On the same note, I reminded the church leaders of the importance of terminating the partnership with the Presbyterian Denomination in America: *"The area of partnership with the Western Church needs to be dropped. It calls for quite some alertness."* I kept on reminding the church leaders of how, in their General Assembly of 2004, the Presbyterian Church in the USA, commonly known as PC(USA), mistreated me when they withdrew the opportunities and privileges they had promised in my invitation letter while attending the GA. Such benefits included a full board and an opportunity to give my Church's greetings to the GA. I was to be one of the delegates they called an 'Advisory Delegate.' This meant that I was to participate in the GA debates, implying that I could raise up my hand and, when given the opportunity I had the freedom to speak my mind. I was also to be provided with substantial pocket money.

Suffice it to say that all those benefits were withdrawn soon after my arrival. Reason? Because I refused to support the agenda that was being proposed in the General Assembly calling for the ordination of homosexuals and the endorsement of same-sex marriages. That was my only crime. But there was also another crime that they accused me of having committed - that as a General Assembly Moderator and the one who had chaired the General Administrative Committee held at Kihumbuini from 21st to 26th April in the year 2004, I influenced the committee to terminate the partnership between the PC (USA) National Capital Presbytery with PCEA Elburgon Presbytery.

The termination of this partnership was reached because we had come to the sad realization that the National Capital Presbytery embraced homosexuality, lesbianism and same-sex marriages. We also learned that they were trying to recruit our members when they interacted during our exchange programs. In fact, we came to the realization that their partnership was not meant for spiritual well-being but that it was an avenue for them to reach out to Africans for evil recruitment.

This, coupled with my lack of supporting their agenda, made them very angry, since a word of support from me would have boosted their votes. In fact, they lost the motion by a very small margin. Nevertheless, not long afterwards, the pro-gay group won. At the time of writing this book, a war is raging within the PC (USA) because the biblical-based churches are pulling out of the PC(USA).

In an effort to discourage churches from pulling out of PC (USA), their head office and presbyteries insist that the dissenting factions must surrender their facilities back to the church or buy them at market value. Those who are able to pull out are joining the newly formed denominations such as the Evangelical Covenant Order of the Presbyterians (ECHO), Evangelical Presbyterian Church (EPC) and the Presbyterian Church in America (PCA).

The liberals in PC (USA) and other similarly minded denominations distort the Word of God by arguing that the Bible is no longer recognized as the Word of God; it is a composition of traditional stories told by people in their own times. To them, the Bible is an irrelevant book. Only immature and misguided people can believe in the Bible. And true to their word, when the PC (USA) GA Moderator was interviewed by the media on why she allowed the mistreatment of a key church leader from Africa (this author), she is quoted to have said:

"The Church in Kenya, including the entire Africa, is spiritually at its immature stage. They are in the adolescent stage as far as the understanding of scripture is concerned. They still anchor their faith on the old understanding of the scripture, which is already overtaken by time."

I informed the church leaders that the best thing the Church in Kenya and the entire Africa could do was to mobilize missionaries from Africa to go and evangelize in Western countries and, at the same time, pray vehemently for this fast-declining church both in membership and spiritually. For instance, the 2022 statistics from Wikipedia placed the population of active members of the Presbyterian Church in the USA at only 1,140,665, which works to a dismal 0.341% in the country's total population compared to about 3.1m active members in the denomination 40 years ago. The issue of decline is affirmed by the PC (USA) website in a heading: **PC(USA) 2021 statistics continue to show declining membership**; featured by Rick Jones/Office of the General Assembly- April 25, 2022. (pcusa.org). This missionary-oriented agenda should go hand in hand with the planting of new churches in those parts of the world. This is why we need a **'Theological School'** to train such missionaries or a school whose curriculum would include a course on missionaries to evangelize overseas.

I also called upon the church to scrutinize the formation of all partnerships with churches overseas; otherwise, they would continue using such avenues to recruit church members into all kinds of demonic and evil things. Further, I called upon the Church to empower the Business Committee to vet and give the green light to new partnerships that were being launched. They should put in place a committee to work out the modalities for such unions.

Unfortunately, the USA is aware that the church in Africa is gullible and, hence, easily susceptible to manipulation. The African church then, as it is now, had a general tendency and weakness for valuing money more than Christ's Gospel with its biblical principles. It was in that connection that I called upon the PCEA to take a giant step of faith. I said:

"A time has come when PCEA should value the true gospel over and above the dollars. The Western devil worshippers know this weakness, and they 'bribe' their way to pollute the Church. They are even using money to plant their people in the churches." I further said: *"It is high time that we terminated the partnership with PC (USA) and instead affiliate our partnership with the churches that uphold the true biblical principles such as the Evangelical Covenant Order of the Presbyterians (ECHO), Evangelical Presbyterian Church (EPC) and Presbyterian Church in America (PCA). These new denominations have also decided to go out for missions globally rather than give their money to the PC(USA), a denomination they accuse of having drifted from the Word of God to embrace the unbiblical stuff, yet the Bible makes it clear that one cannot serve God and mammon."*

I always took the opportunity, whenever I had it, to remind the PCEA leaders of the fact that there were three ways through which the church in America was infusing their rebellious spirit into Bible-believing churches:

Relativism: This view suggests that truth is not absolute but experienced. This means that what is truth and reality for one person is not necessarily the same for another. According to this school of thought, the Bible is a record of what its authors experienced as truth at their time and, therefore, not necessarily a valuable resource for those seeking the will of God today. Therefore, a person, as such, is a god and, therefore, has a choice to do what he/she decides to do as led by their conscience.

New Age: This is a system of thought which understands that truth is not universally self- revealing (transcendent) in a uniform manner. In this case, some people experience God through the life and teaching of Jesus Christ, while others experience reality through creation and others through the unveiling of wisdom (Sophia). It argues that we are out of the old age with its old revelations. We are now in a new dispensation, a new millennium with more advanced technology, which in itself is dictating the path the New Age ought to take.

Pluralism: This is a conviction that truth is found in a multitude of religious experiences through which there is fellowship with God and salvation. Thus, for Christians to say that Jesus Christ is the only way to get to the Kingdom of God is not only erroneous but also an expression of intolerance. The mission of the Church is not to convert people to Christianity but to enhance all elements of humanism, including education and health, among others, which anchor on charity as one of the other ways to get to God's kingdom.

Symbolism: This is the belief that there is no one way to God. Therefore, this opens ways a way of worshipping idols- idolatry. These gods are, therefore, entrenched in the form of symbols in **'Theological Schools'** and **'Church Buildings.'** These dedicated symbols create an evil environment within their surroundings to manipulate people's minds.

5. THE CALL TO REPENTANCE

I often pointed to the fact that the body of Christ had done things that would not be pleasing to God. The Church had, in many ways, drifted from its role of caring for the poor, orphans and widows and acted as an oppressor in many ways. Rather than reaching out to the needy, many were quick to enrich themselves and create a spirit of strife for power. Again, the church leaders were very oppressive to those who had been born again through the East African Revival Movement.

Many of the church leaders had participated in the 1969 oath-taking in which many innocent Christians were killed. Many got maimed for life for refusing to take the oath. This was because it involved a lot of witchcraft, including the shedding of animal blood. This oath

155

was mainly taken by the Agikuyu, the majority of who were Christians. The oath was aimed at discriminating against other ethnic communities. On the other hand, the Agikuyu were taking vows that no other tribe in Kenya would ever take the presidency of the nation.

They vowed that the presidency would forever be in Kikuyu/Meru/Embu's hands. It is as a result of such wickedness that I called upon the PCEA leadership to embrace the spirit of repentance on behalf of other tribes in Kenya, Christians and non-Christians. I was also calling upon them to repent for the sons of British Missionaries and Colonialists. Otherwise, God could not in any way bless the Church and nation unless the church came up with a move that portrayed a meaningful repentance of the past evil deeds.

In particular, the church will need to repent on behalf of the nation's iniquities, such as:

✓ Sins of our forefathers before colonization
✓ Sins of the colonisers and missionaries
✓ Sins of both Mau Mau and the atrocities of home guards
✓ Sins of Mount Kenya over the 1969 Oath-taking
✓ Sins over the pioneers of the prevailing corruption in Kenya
✓ Sins over the political violence, including bloodshed
✓ Sins over the spirit of manipulation in the elections
✓ Sins over land grabbing and the pain so inflicted
✓ Sins over oppressive and treaties made between Kenya and foreign governments
✓ Sins over selfishness of both political and religious leaders
✓ Sins over operative gangs and bandits in Kenya over the years
✓ Sins over loss of life through abortion and other means
✓ Sins over widespread immorality, including LGBTQ
✓ Sins over the transport sector
✓ Sins over widespread idolatry in the nation
✓ Sins over tribalism, nepotism, favouritism

The benefits of repentance include;
▪ Repentance is God's second chance.
▪ Repentance paves the way for God's kingdom.
▪ Repentance opens doors of grace.

- Repentance touches the heart of God and favourably causes Him to relent from His anger or judgment.
- Through repentance, the church gains a God-given mandate to operate in the spiritual realm.
- Repentance gives us a platform to have a conversation with our Creator and carry out spiritual warfare against the forces of evil.
- Repentance displaces the power of Satan, rendering his basis of accusations and control powerless before God.
- Repentance unites us with the Holy Spirit, who spiritually equips and empowers us to effectively handle spiritual warfare.

However, the act of repentance should always be done in sincerity and never in hypocrisy.

6. THE ACT OF LAYING HANDS IN ORDAINING A CANDIDATE

Having noted the fact that there was rapid mushrooming of homosexuals among the pastors, I felt the need to protect the person being ordained from being impacted by evil spirits at the time of ordination. It is for this reason that in one of the GAC meetings, I called upon the church leadership to pass a resolution deterring other people from laying hands upon the person being ordained. I made this move because I had already realized that there were some devil worshipers among the clergy, as well as practicing homosexuals. It is a tradition in the PCEA that at the time of ordination, all the present clergy directly lay their hands on the candidate being ordained. As I have already said, I felt this could impact the candidate with some negative spiritual influence. It is in this connection that I felt compelled to move this motion:

"In view of the presence of ministers and elders in the universal Church who practice devil worship and also practice homosexuality and lesbianism, and in view of the fact that such ministers lay hands upon the candidates at the time of their ordination, I am therefore calling upon this G.A.C to make it a rule that only the person ordaining the candidate will be laying hands on him/her."

It was unfortunate that the liberals fervently fought this motion, which never saw the light of day. But though this turned out to be the case, I was happy to see quite a number who aggressively argued for the motion only that they were in the minority. I still believe that kind of motion will one day go through, for God will instil the truth in the minds of church leaders in the near future. They will come to adopt what I had advocated for some years back. This is true because the issue of the increase of pastors/elders and members who will be engaging in these dirty practices will keep on increasing until it comes to be likened to a pregnant woman who denies her pregnancy, yet her belly has fully bulged. There will also come a time when these evil/homosexual practicing people will raise a motion in the General Assembly that they be recognized as a genuine group and never be discriminated against.

In a GAC held at St. Andrews Church in Nairobi, I took the opportunity to remind the delegates of the importance of striving to seek God's holiness and the spirit of discernment. In this regard, I said,

"Please, allow me to remind you of Paul's words in the book of Romans 12:2, who called upon Christians not to 'conform to the pattern of this world' but to be transformed by the renewing of your mind then you will be able to test and approve what God's will is." I foresee a time when the church, like the prodigal son, will come to its senses.

To further drive this message home, I narrated to them what Billy Graham once told a group of Christians in North Korea about a group of worshippers in their Church who were invaded by armed soldiers. The soldiers pulled out a picture of Jesus Christ off the wall and forced all the worshippers to line up. Each one of them was ordered to spit on this picture and step on it, and whoever would resist would be killed. One young girl watched as the pastors, elderly members, church elders, and deacons went forward in great fear and spat stepped on the picture and walked to the other side.

But when her turn came, she stood next to the picture and looked at it with great love to the one who had died for her. Tears started flowing out of her eyes. She then picked up the picture, wiped off the spit and boldly said, *"Go ahead, kill me. I can't deny the one who died for me, neither can I step upon his image"*. She was then directed to a nearby house where it was assumed she was to be executed. No sooner had she entered the house than there was a loud bang of a gunshot.

Her action activated the courage of the others and a good number of them opted to die for the love of Christ was anchored into their hearts. Whenever a person resisted, he/she was directed into the house, and there followed a sound of gunshots, and for this reason, many decided to save their lives. The soldiers loaded all those who had denied Christ into trucks and took them to be executed. The ones who could not compromise their faith in Jesus were all released, and they went home. Meaning, the gunshots that were coming from the house were not real gunshots. They were only meant to scare the ones who had not yet confessed to believing that, for sure, those who had resisted got killed.

While invading the church, the soldiers wanted to find out who among the Christians could not compromise or betray the new regime of North Korea! They argued that if people could stand for the one they believed in, they could as well stand firm for the country they loved- their motherland. They could not betray the nation to their enemies. Those people who did not deny Jesus were not only allowed to live but they were as well allowed to continue worshiping Jesus Christ and were greatly honoured by the government.

The government even supported them in their needs, both spiritual and physical. I then told the delegates;
"In our mortality, we often forget to keep our eyes on Jesus in the midst of the storms of life. We often lose our perspective and become fearful and anxious. We need to be reminded each day that it is Jesus who gives us stability and urges us to find strength and help in looking up. Instead of focusing on materialism, we better be guided by Paul's words in Philippians 4:19, 'And my God will meet all your needs according to His glorious riches in Christ Jesus.'"

7. ACADEMIC ACHIEVEMENTS

Another way that I tried to encourage the pastors was in their academic advancement. Being a scholar, I greatly encouraged pastors to take the challenge of advancing their academic status. My concern was that the church members were greatly getting advanced in education, especially in this digital age. Those pastors who were still lagging behind academically would quickly be out of touch with their parishioners. I warned them that in the near future, a member of the clergy without a minimum of a Master's degree would be considered inferior in serving people. This is true in other fields, including primary school teachers. I also advised the clergy to desist from eyeing the overseas colleges as the only way to acquire education as had been the case over the years.

The Westerners had brainwashed the clergy from Africa to believe that only those who had taken their studies overseas, especially in Europe or America, had the necessary academic qualifications. Knowing very well that there was no truth in such a mentality and it was outright deception, I took the initiative to convince pastors to take their academic advancement locally. And it worked.

Many PCEA pastors have aggressively engaged themselves in academic advancement locally. It is always joyous for me to see one of my cherished dreams getting some fulfilment. It was also through that vision that I pushed for further upgrading of the Theological Education by Extension (TEE) to diploma level with learners being attached to the Presbyterian University of East Africa (PUEA), an institution I helped in its establishment becoming its first chancellor as indicated earlier.

8. CLERGY REFRESHER COURSES

I also persistently called upon the church leadership to recommend ways that the ministers could attend refresher courses as most of them had their last training when they were in a Theological School. A machine will need constant oiling and greasing if all its parts are to continually function. It is for that reason that I called upon the church to come up with a mechanism for the clergy to attend refresher courses for at least three months after a determined period of service. This is important, especially now that there is rapid growth in technology, bringing in a lot of challenges to the church globally. The churches should sponsor especially the ministers for training in Information and Communication Technology (ICT).

I, at the same time, called upon the church to churn the cropping out of some previously unheard-of wickedness like homosexuality, devil worship and corruption in the church, especially by some of the church leaders. I also alerted the church on the emerging spirit of materialism that was engulfing the church leaders as well as the prosperity gospel. My calls and teachings through seminars and writings were not in vain. I created enough awareness, and changes were noticeable.

9. RETIRED CHURCH MINISTERS

Prior to my becoming the GA Moderator, while I served at Muguga Parish, I accompanied a group of ministers to have prayers with the late Rev. Waiyaki who was seriously sick. He looked worn out physically and appeared to be undergoing a lot of stress. One of the things he told us was never to bank on the church for any help after retirement. He regretted that the church likened a retired minister with a piece of sugarcane, which, after being chewed and its juice squeezed out, the fibre that held the juice is thrown away, not even caring where it lands. In most cases, it is thrown into the dustbin or fed to animals or in some cases, it becomes part of firewood. It is treated as a useless material despite it having produced juice.

Likewise, the church, having squeezed the spiritual juice out of the minister, dumps them. This is despite some of these ministers having spent all their energy in promoting the life of the church both physically and spiritually over the years. They are sadly and finally treated disrespectfully and rendered useless, never to be remembered on retirement. It's like one being removed from the church records. They are very poorly paid if there is anything in the first place. He said;

"Now that I have retired, I have been going through a lot of poverty, and the church has always turned a deaf ear even when I cry out for help. Now, it seems I have come to the end of the road in life. I plead with you to be mindful of the retired ministers, for many have succumbed to death due to the neglect of those who should be carrying the burden. Their families even come to hate the church, wondering whether it is a godly-oriented institution."

As he spoke, tears were freely flowing uncontrollably out of his seemingly dying eyes. Finally, he said: *"I just pray for blessings upon each one of you for having come to bid goodbye to one of the dying soldiers of Christ. Goodbye, we will converge in heaven."*

We were all tongue-tied and in tears for the words he said about the negligence of ministers and, specifically, the words of farewell he had uttered. Having said those words, he got into bed and covered his head even as we said our final prayers for departure. He never spoke to us again. He seemingly went to his final meditation inside the blankets. That emotional encounter with the late Rev Waiyaki awakened my realization of the fate of the retired ministers. Shortly before he passed on, I started to research the condition of the life the retired ministers led. I discovered that many of the retired ministers were undergoing a lot of suffering, with some having their money retained through manipulation in the guise of 'unpaid money accumulated in the form of arrears over many years.'

It pained my heart when I came to realize how much those ministers were suffering together with their households. The church had totally neglected them. The presbyteries they were attached to had nothing to do with them. Most of them lived from hand to mouth.

It is for that reason that as soon as I occupied the GA Moderator's seat, I immediately embarked on straightening the lives of retired ministers. I had this issue addressed in all the church courts and committees, including the Business Committee.

At one time, a committee was formed to work out the modalities on these issues. Thank God this Committee acted as per my request, and the anomalies were rectified. From that time, the presbyteries took the burden of the retired ministers and money was allocated for them each month.

In the past, retired ministers had no voice in the presbyteries. I persistently addressed this anomaly, and retired ministers' presence in the presbytery meetings was embraced. Their contributions to church meetings were respected. Shortly thereafter, a process was set to continuously update ministers' pension schemes, including medical cover, with the aim of improving it.

One thing the reader should be aware of is the fact that to pave the way for the recognition of the retired ministers and the improvement of their pensions was not a carpeted path. I had to wrestle through very tight opposition, especially from those leaders who had already established themselves and had accumulated a lot of wealth. Those ministers were in a class of their own, with a good number of them driving Mercedes Benz vehicles, which were the most expensive vehicles by then.

These were the same vehicles that some of the former Moderators, secretary generals and even deputies drove. They did not want other ministers to get into their class of elites and to lead the so-perceived

'Westernized lifestyle' or, better still, the Scottish ways of life. They were well connected with the government, from where they also got a surplus of their wealth. In fact, one of the key past Moderators had a direct line to the president's office, both during the Jomo Kenyatta and Moi regimes.

Quite a number of them were well connected to the powerful provincial commissioners and district commissioners which was another source of their wealth. They had tried to woo me into their class with promises to introduce me to some of these paths to quick wealth, but they found me impervious to their greedy and wayward ways.

I likened those opposing church leaders who also used some prominent elders to the government leaders who manipulated the poor in society so that the poor would never rise. They fear that if the poor (**Wanjiku**) got economically enlightened, they would lose the grip they have on them come election time. Wanjiku would not have that hunger for money, which would weaken the influence of the money dished out at such times to make people vote for them.

They, therefore, made laws and by-laws that would suit them by oppressing the poor. In the same way, some of those church leaders manipulate the constitution (Practice and Procedure) to gain power to spiritually and physically oppress the church members, ministers and workers. As a result of my encroachment in the territories of the 'elite,' there were calls at different times for my impeachment, but the clergy and other church leaders came to my rescue by supporting me. The ground, therefore, became too hard for them to dethrone me. One thing those leaders opposed to me did not understand was that God had clearly revealed to me that His servants must be taught the value of the hidden side of life. The person who is to serve in a lofty place before others must also assume a lowly place before his/her God. Such a servant should not be surprised if God occasionally ill-bulldozed the changes and amendments to the Constitution.

The PCEA leaders should listen to the voice of God telling them, *"Dear child, you've had enough of this hurried pace of accumulating wealth, power, publicity and prestige. Be still and take time to listen to me."* He/she must be like Elijah and hide themselves at Kerith Ravine-a restored heart to Christ, one yearning to serve the person irrespective of his/ her status. They should refrain from seeing people through the eyes of class, power and wealth. They should feel more called to use that wealth to promote the lives of people rather than use it to oppress them. They should always be aware that God could as well make their brooks of wealth dwindle leaving only the trace of a ground that once hosted a river.

This was and still is the heartbeat of my desire: '*Serving others because in serving them, I am serving God through his image.*' Otherwise, there are many blessings we will never receive until we are ready to pay the price of pain that we endure through striving to stand in the gap of the oppressed. Yet, the path of opposition and persecution is the only way to reach the said blessings.

In my endeavor to help the clergy, I encountered some very severe opposition, which was also marked by all kinds of threats, humiliation, frustrations, character assassination, and even scandalized. I remember this day when two of the PCEA tycoons met me as I bade farewell to the presbytery leaders after carrying out a teaching session at PCEA Nyamachaki, Nyeri. One of them, with a clenched fist, came near my car and said:

"*Moderator, the only thing you have to be very careful about is to avoid jeopardizing your position by advancing your advocacy in making changes in this denomination. We have our stand and the way we do things over the years. Your utterances, especially when they touch on the lives of the clergy, are very disturbing. We have, over the years catered for them; we even encourage church groups like Woman's Guild to visit them. After all, the clergy are employed people. You cannot keep on insisting that we go the extra mile on them. In any case, we follow the voice of the past Moderators who know better about this church. We feel that by advocating for what you are crusading for, you are abusing these not-very-learned people but people of great experience. You cannot claim to be liberating the clergy while, in fact, you are putting the whole denomination in a distorted and confused state.*"

I replied:
"*As for me, I am doing what the Spirit of God is leading me to do. I am not the only one fighting for the truth. I count myself in the line of those whom God has assigned the role of a reformer. And for your information, tribulation has always marked the trail of the true reformer. This is the story behind the likes of Paul, John Knox, Wesley and all the rest of the mighty*

army of the Lord. I can also bring to your notice others like Nelson Mandela of South Africa, the Kenyans who dared challenge British occupation in Kenya, such as Koitalel arap Samoei, who was a Kalenjin imperialist challenger, Jaramogi Oginga Odinga, Waiyaki wa Hinga, Dedan Kimathi, Jomo Kenyatta. We can also recognize Mahatma Gandhi of India, Kwame Nkrumah of Ghana, and Julius Nyerere of Tanzania. Other examples include Rev Dr. Timothy Njoya, Ndingi Mwana Wa Nzeki, and Bishop Alexander Muge, among others."

My response made the man really hot under the collar. Vibrating with anger, he furiously said,

"You see, now you are talking politics, something our church has always condemned. Our church has nothing to do with politics. None of the past Moderators has ever involved himself in politics." To this, I responded:

"That is the dilemma of our denomination and other churches at large. They were brainwashed by the missionaries to look only up into heaven and not be mindful of the earthly happenings, which in itself is utopian. The missionaries corroborated with the imperialists to take away the land from Africans. The first duty of the church is to make the earth a habitable place. Otherwise, how can the person serve God if his/her spirit is agonizing? The eminent duty of Adam was to take care of the earth. I will do my best to erase this foreign mentality from the minds of our members."

In my struggle with the liberals /PCEA Watchdogs, I was encouraged by the words I had hung on the wall in my office that read: "Wherever God's finger points, His hand will clear a way."

One thing I have learned through the challenges that I encountered in my endeavor to glorify God through PCEA ministry is that our lives are very mysterious. In fact, it would be totally inexplicable unless we believed that God was preparing us for events and ministries that lie unseen beyond the veil of the eternal world like tempered steel; we will be required for special service. We are like the craftsman's knife – 'the sharper the craftsman's knives, the finer and more beautiful his work of sharpening us for future engagement in the expansion of His kingdom. He put us through tough testing, and where his finger points, his hand will clear the way.

God started to sharpen me when in my early teaching profession; he paved the way for me to be appointed the headmaster of Olmanyatta Primary School in the fifth month of my teaching career. This was quite unique. Otherwise, people got appointed to such positions after working for quite some time. God did not want any time to be wasted before he got me into that training school of leadership.

That is why God's ways of doing things are quite mysterious. His Word confirms this when it says,
"For my thoughts are not your thoughts, neither are your ways my ways.... As the heavens are higher than the earth, so are my ways higher than your ways and my thoughts than your thoughts." (Isaiah 55:8). I also clung to Psalms 37:39-40, *"The salvation of the righteous comes from the Lord; He is their stronghold in time of trouble. The LORD helps them and delivers them; He delivers them from the wicked and saves them because they take refuge in him."*

Also of great encouragement were the words found in Romans 8:31, 33, 37, *"If God is for us, who can be against us? Who will bring any charge against those whom God has chosen... Who shall separate us from the love of Christ...No, in all these things, we are more than conquerors through Him who loved us."*

10. PRACTICE AND PROCEDURE

Practice and Procedure is the documented manual that contains all the laws and by-laws that govern PCEA life both spiritually and physically. This document was prepared under the influence of the Church of Scotland. It was rather written to ensure that the PCEA would forever align and be held under the captivity of this foreign denomination and its Christian cultural setup. It is not shocking that the document is oriented to the Western culture. It embraces the scriptures in a Westernized and culturally disguised way that distorts Christianity. This is the document that I was calling upon the Church to revisit and come out with a more scriptural and more African cultural-oriented one. It is for this reason that through my guidance, a committee was formed to carry out some amendments that could not only align with the scriptures but also that would be conducive and relevant to African culture. This idea was not well received by the liberals who used this document to drag behind the Church both physically and spiritually. But there were, at the same time, many among the Church leaders and the laity who supported this idea of coming up with another version of the Church constitution. The laity in the church was especially thirsting for a constitution that could open the door for some revival in the denomination. In this regard, a committee was formed to work out the modalities and come up with a new modified document.

The committee did quite well, but unfortunately, I finished my term as the GA Moderator before the committee was through in coming up with a new Church constitution. The liberals took this opportunity and brought to a standstill the progress so formerly initiated. No sooner had I left the office than my name was removed from the working committee. The reason for doing that was to avoid any influence I would bring that could lead to the authorship of a more spiritually oriented document and also my would-be persistence in calling for continuity in changing the constitution.

They feared that my being on the committee would hasten the writing of the document, something that they dreaded. They wanted to slow it down to a point where it would never materialize. But the worst part is the fact that the old document overshadows the scriptures. Incidentally, the liberals would rather have a decision that is totally not in line with scriptures to carry the day just because that is the line the Constitution takes. It is the measuring rod rather than the Word of God. The church constitution is more valued than the scripture.

My observation was that until the so-called Practice and Procedure document is revised, PCEA would be mark-timing in many ways and for many years. That is why I was so persistent in calling upon the Church leadership to rewrite the Church constitution, for it is a carrier of spiritual corruption by putting the denomination in the custody of some kind of bondage. It was by God's grace that I was able to bulldoze my way through overlooking the constitution that I managed to bring about some changes in the Church and especially the faculty of praise in worship, the enormous subdivisions of parishes and presbyteries, the decentralization and the improvement of the lives of ministers among others.

As already stated, the above accomplishments sound easily done, but in reality, they almost cost me my life. But God still wanted me to produce not only fruits but fruits that would last. This is in line with his having chosen me with a mission to be accomplished. This is in accordance with his Word that says, "*You did not choose me, but I chose you and appointed you to go and bear fruit -fruit that will last"* (John 15:16). Also, through the book of Jeremiah 45:5, he affirms this when he says: *"Wherever you go I will let you escape with your life."*

5 CONFRONTATIONS WITH HOMOSEXUALITY "VIRUS"

My opposition to homosexuality went a notch higher in 2004 when I attended the PC (USA) General Assembly as a representative of the PCEA. This GA took place in Richmond, Virginia, in the United States of America. I arrived on the 25th of June. The officials of the PC (USA) GA, led by their GA, cunningly and with sweet words approached and asked me to reciprocate their invitation and the obvious promised generosity by supporting the agenda to be floated in the GA regarding the ordination of homosexuals and allowing same-sex marriages.

The PC (USA) Moderator said this to me: *"Since you come from Africa, where we hear the Church is growing in leaps and bounds, and also having come from one of the biggest Presbyterian denominations in Africa, your support will give us many votes. Remember, we have paid for your return ticket and already prepared a good gift for you in the form of dollars. We have also placed you in the special category of 'Advisory Delegates.' This gives you not only the opportunity to sit with our delegates but also to vote. The advisory delegates vote first on a given motion. This is meant to gauge and guide the mandated delegates to finally vote based on what other people are thinking."*

She went on to say: *"While this kind of motion might not find its way in your Church's GA, here we are quite advanced, noting that our denomination has been in existence for over two hundred years. Thus, compared with your denomination, we are quite mature. I am sure at one time in the future, this same agenda will surface in your Church. We have come to a time when we have to understand that God created people so differently that some are born with the traits of homosexuality and lesbianism. Such people have no option but to live in obedience to how they were created. They have, therefore, to fall in love with people of the same sex and even marry such. It is for this reason we have earmarked you to be a delegate so that, when we get to this motion, you will raise up your hand and say, 'On behalf of my Church back in Kenya and the church of Africa, I am in support of this motion. It carries a 'meaningful purpose.' Also, remember we have paid full board accommodation for you."*

In my response I said: *"My concern here is the fact that the Bible has clearly pointed out how a true believer should conduct his/her life. But of most importance, the book of 2 Timothy 3: 16 makes it clear that 'All scripture is God-breathed.' After all, was Sodom and Gomorrah not set ablaze due to the dominant practice of homosexuality? Also, the book of Leviticus rejects this menace, calling it an abomination in the eyes of God as indicated in Leviticus 20:13, "If a man lies with a male as he would do with a woman both of them have committed an abomination, they shall surely be put to death."* I continued to say, *"In this case, as much as you qualify that people are born differently, the Word of God explains how true believers should live. It very clearly indicates that God has categorically forbidden homosexuality, lesbianism and same-sex marriages, and it is for this same truth that I will not support you in this agenda."*

Then one of the officials said, *"David, why don't you appreciate that we have met your two-way air ticket? We are providing you with full accommodation, and we are at the same time giving you substantial pocket money and many other goodies, as the letter we sent you states. Then why let us down? Come on, David. Having taken your studies here in American colleges, you should understand what we are talking about. After all, we are thinking of increasing what we had affirmed to give you in terms of dollars as a way of saying a very big thank you. We shall as well sponsor any of the projects you will propose to us whether for the church or personal. David, how can you lose such an opportunity coming to you like manna in the wilderness?"*

In spite of this eloquent talk that mainly capitalized on goodies, I stood my ground and said: *"There is no way I can compromise my faith with earthly gifts. Here I am, you can do with me whatever you want. The fact is that I do not know anybody in this GA, but one thing I am sure of is that if you decide to abandon me, my redeemer will uphold me with His right hand, and even if he will not, I will not compromise on such high level of wickedness. That is what made Sodom to be rained on with fire from heaven."* Conclusively, one of them sarcastically said, *"Okay, David, we will see, and of course, what we plant is what we harvest, for every venture in life has its consequences."*

That evening, as I was having my dinner in the hotel I was booked in, the waiter handed the bill to me. My immediate response was: *"Thank you, but I am not supposed to pay. I am a guest of PC (USA), and they are meeting all my expenses."* The waiter said, *"We have been instructed to tell you to pay for your meal and that the denomination here has nothing to do with you. In fact, the words the person used were 'He is on his own.'* He then asked me, *"What part of Africa do you come from?"* Then I said, *"I come from Kenya."* Then he responded, *"That is far from here. How did you come to know these people?"*

I then handed him the letter I had received from the Stated Clerk of PC (USA), to which he responded, *"Then why mistreat you in this way? Doesn't the Bible say the church is the light of the world? Why this darkness?"* He wondered. In response, I said, *"It is unfortunate that this denomination has reversed the truth of the gospel they advocated when they brought to us the gospel as missionaries.*

Then, this waiter-turned-friend said, *"I really understand your predicament, but as things stand, I have no help to offer. I wish I was in a position to offer you any help, but I trust God will intervene at this time of great need in your life."*

He then left to serve other people. This came to me as a shock, for I had no idea that people so seasoned in Christianity could display such a high degree of hatred. After all, they had written a letter to me even before I had left Kenya indicating all the benefits awaiting me including full accommodation.

My dilemma was that the only money I had was $80 which I had intended to spend on snacks during a stop-over at the airport in Europe. Fortunately, I did not spend it as the stop-over duration turned out to be very short. I proceeded to my room, took the $80 dollars, and paid for the food. I am not even sure whether it was enough. I just handed it to the waiter, telling him that was the only money I had. I was, therefore, left penniless.

I really could not comprehend why the Church could put me into that kind of suffering, yet it is this Church, PC (USA), among other Western denominations that had brought the gospel to Africa, which was then known as *'The Dark Continent'* and whose missionaries told Africans that there was no other truth nor any other Bible/gospel apart from the one they preached to our people. It was the main pointer to the heavenly way. Yet, now they had reversed the real gospel to embrace paganism.

The next day, on the 26th of June 2004, there was an ecumenical breakfast. This meant that all the people who had come from outside the USA were to have breakfast together. After the breakfast, some announcements would follow. Names of all those who were to collect pocket money were called out and my name was not among them. It had been removed. There were then those who were to be among the delegates and my name had also been removed. My name was also missing from the list of those who were to be given an opportunity to greet the delegates on behalf of their denominations. It was also deleted from the roll of those who would be issued food coupons.

Simply put, I had been stripped of everything and totally disowned by the PC (USA) officials. I felt so lonely, disoriented and an outcast among the so-called 'Brethren' in Richmond, Virginia. I was left stranded and traumatized, but I consoled myself through the truth that this was one of those avenues through which one was meant to carry the real cross and not follow anyone. That same day, as I sat somewhere on the grass at around 11 a.m., a white American approached and came where I was.

He warmly greeted me and then said, "You look lonely. Are you a black American, or do you come from Africa?" I introduced myself;
"My name is David Githii, and I come from Kenya, Africa." He responded; "How nice to meet you! You might not have known it but the GA we are having is a very evil Assembly. They are advocating for very wicked things that they want to pass as resolutions, including the ordination of homosexuals and same-sex marriages. A group of us are meeting this evening to pray over this evil general assembly, and now that we hear that people from Africa are very prayerful, why don't you join us? Your presence will be seen as a way God has decided to boost our prayers." In response, I said; "I will be very willing to avail myself for prayers." He then pointed to the room where I was to join them at 8 pm.

As per my word, at 8 pm in the evening, I joined this group of about twenty people. They first introduced themselves. When my turn came, there was a lot of clapping. A few people hugged me. After this, the prayer session started, some choruses were sung, and before long, the whole group was on fire. After praying for quite a while, a time came when people were to give individual prayer request items.

172

Some requested prayers regarding their congregations, others, and individual families, among others.

It was at this juncture that I stood up and explained my predicament. I told them how the officials of PC (USA) had written me a letter promising all sweet things, including money full board, as one of the delegates and how they had discarded me when I refused to uphold their agenda on the ordination of homosexuals/same-sex marriages. I then gave them the letter, which was read to the group. I told them how I explained to the PC (USA) officials that the scriptures were the breath of God.

No sooner had I come to an end than all these people stood up and accorded me an astounding standing ovation. When they finally calmed down, one of the leaders asked:
"How can we have such spiritual warriors here in America? This is the kind of people God is seeking. People who can stand for the kingdom in season and out of season. I just wish we had at least ten such people in this General Assembly. Thank you, our brother, in Christ. Now, brothers and sisters, they refused to feed him; we are going to overfeed him. They refused to give him pocket money, we are going to give good money. Get into your pockets and take out your chequebooks and write out cheques in my name. I will cash them out and give him the money." After this, the leader went ahead and said, *"This man has nothing in his pockets and has to have money in his pocket- in this case, take out money from your pockets and place it on the table."* The cheques were put in a big envelope, and the cash was handed over to me. This far exceeded whatever GA officials would have given me. The leader then said, *"Let our brother David grasp Paul's words in Philippians 4:19, that, 'and my God will meet all your needs according to His glorious riches in Christ Jesus.'"*

I could not believe my eyes while I watched people as they walked to place money and cheques on the table. They were then asked to volunteer themselves so that two people would keep me company each day during the four-day duration of the GA, which would end on 3rd July 2004.

They organized themselves in such a way that, at least, there would be two people with me each day, the whole day. They would pick me up from my room around 7 a.m. and take me for breakfast, which they paid from their pockets. We could attend the morning GA sessions together until lunchtime when they took me for lunch and likewise paid for the lunch.

After GA sessions, my friends could take me around Richmond to visit museums, national parks and other attractive sceneries. Finally, they took me for dinner, which they paid for from their pockets. They then took me back to my room to retire for the night. Then, another set of people would pick me the next day and follow the same pattern for each day.

At this juncture, a pastor by the name of Dean Weaver asked me, *"David, how long are you in America?"* I said; *"I am here for a month."* Then the pastor said, *"In this case, I would like you to accompany me to my church back in Pittsburg. I would like you to give this testimony to my congregation. I will book the flight and include you in my flight back home."*

Then, another person by the name of Elder Edward said to him, *"After you are done with him, please put him on another flight so that he can also share his testimony in our congregation, East Minister Church in Kansas."*

Yet another Minister, Doug Brown, made the same request that after Edward was through with me, he put me on another flight to our congregation to give the same testimony. For sure, the arrangements went well, and I managed to testify in all these congregations.

Worth noting is that I was given some money in appreciation for the deliberations. I find these experiences matching with Isaiah 41:10-11 where the word of God says, *"So do not fear, for I am with you; do not be dismayed, for I am your God. I will strengthen you and help you; I will uphold you with my righteous right hand. All who rage against you will surely be ashamed and disgraced; those who oppose you will be as nothing and perish."* It also reminds us that we don't labour in vain. And that we should never compromise for material gain in accordance with Matthew 6:33; *"But seek first his kingdom and his righteousness, and all these things will be given to you as well."*

After going through the day's schedule, I was asked to kneel down for an intensive prayer over my life, ministry and family. We then continued in prayers, testimonies and singing and parted company after midnight. We then continued the following day. Two people picked me up from my room, and we headed for the GA morning devotion in which the Moderator of the General Assembly, Susan Andrews, preached. Her sermon really angered me so much. She spoke of a 'family' as also consisting of two homosexuals who were rearing children. She commended this as a very good thing to do when two people of the same sex can decide to marry and adopt children.

The fact that she equated same-sex relationships with heterosexual families infuriated me. This was the focus of her sermon- '*to promote homosexuality*.' She was indirectly telling the assembly, '*Let us go for it in full swing and support it*.' Hers was not a sermon. A sermon comes from the Scriptures. She did not preach God's Word. It was rather a promotion and campaign on homosexuality that she was conducting. Surprisingly, she was being applauded.

THE HARASSMENT GAINS GROUND

The story of my mistreatment by the PC (USA) ran like wildfire, reaching many churches in America. This happened through the interviews that were conducted by some local newspapers. There was also a popular news magazine known as, '**Layman**' edited by Park Williamson. This man had interviewed me on my predicament and had it all covered in the Layman magazine. The magazine was then distributed to all Presbyterian Churches in America. Most of the delegates also had the opportunity to possess a copy.

The news was also transmitted through the internet. When the PC (USA) Moderator, Susan Andrews, was interviewed by the local newspapers as to why the Church officials had mistreated a Church leader from Africa, she is reported to have described African Christians as being in the '*adolescence/young-adult stage*' in their faith and somehow moving out into their own independence, and yet still figuring out how to be in a relationship with God and PC (USA).

By saying this, she was inferring that the Church in Africa was very young in its spiritual growth and was yet to mature. Andrews' statement was reminiscent of comments made by Bishop John Spong after African Anglicans overwhelmingly condemned homosexual behavior in Spong's Episcopal Church, USA. Spong told the press

175

that the African bishops were *"Limited to their experience, susceptible to superstition, and had only recently moved out of animism."* When Park Williamson asked me to respond to what Susan Andrews had said on the immaturity of the African Church, I said the following: *"The statement that the Kenyan Presbyterian Church is not mature and is in the 'adolescent stage' in its growth is a big insult to us from the African perspective. It just reminds us of the colonial mentality that enslaved us for 70 years. Under the colonial rule, even in the Church, we Africans were not given a chance to take leadership positions because we were regarded as 'not yet mature Christians.'"*

I was really moved by one of the candidates of the slated clerk election, Rus Howard, who, when he took to the podium to support his candidacy, pointed at me and said, *"See the hypocrisy of our leaders; they have openly mistreated this godly man for not supporting their agenda on ordaining gays and the solemnization of their marriages. They have even denied him food among other things they had promised him. That is why we need God-fearing leaders in this denomination; otherwise, the Church is heading to the cliff."*

He then looked me in the eyes and said, *"Please, on behalf of our not-so-godly denomination, I am advancing our apology to you and your Church and, of course, the entire Church in Africa. I am doing this on behalf of the many Presbyterians who have been moved by your stand on not compromising the gospel truth."* Howard then moved out of the podium, shook my hand and said, *"Take courage, my brother; there are many here who share your views."*

As Howard spoke, many of the delegates had already read about my predicament both in the local media and in the LayMan Magazine. A wave of applause rolled across the hall with many standing up as they loudly clapped their hands. Nevertheless, there were many who never rose in appreciation because they were for the agenda of promoting gayism.

In spite of this mistreatment by a Church that claimed to stand for justice in the world and having hailed from the super-power nation itself – the USA, I had, through their media and other forums, declared in no uncertain terms that I believed in the sanctity of the scriptures and no amount of pressure or bundles of dollars could alter my stand. As long as I was the Moderator of the General

176

Assembly, there was no way I could condone the PCEA bowing to abomination due to the enticement through the power of dollars! This is the path PC(USA) had taken to mislead denominations and Churches from the 'Third World' countries into wickedness.

One other thing that angered the leaders of this American denomination is the fact that before my travelling to the PC(USA) General Assembly, under my chairmanship of the General Administrative Committee held at Kihumbui-ini Presbytery; we had severed the partnership between Elburgon Presbytery (PCEA) in Kenya and National Capital Presbytery, located in Maryland, USA. This was after we had learned that the National Capital Presbytery was recruiting the Kenyan Church into homosexuality through their exchange programs. I remember one member of the Kihumbui-ini GAC meeting crying: *"How can they bless what God has called sin? The Bible does not allow this. This is a great abomination in God's kingdom. This is quite unnatural. Such is not even traceable in the animal kingdom. We don't even have a word for homosexuality in my mother tongue"*. One other person contributing to this debate posed the question: *"When their missionaries came to our land, they brought us God's Word and told us it was the whole truth, why do they now reverse that very truth? Have they forgotten what the Holy Spirit revealed to them in the first place? I liken them to a pig that, after being washed, goes back to roll itself in the mud again."*

Having realized that so many people blamed her for having mistreated me, as reported by the media and the Layman Magazine, Susan Andrews approached me during recess to offer her personal apology, but I would not listen to any of it. I told her on the face: *"You have not only offended me; you have offended the membership of PCEA and Kenya as a nation. The best thing you can do is to write a letter of repentance to the Presbyterian Church of East Africa. You have to understand the difference between an apology and repentance. You have acted in a rebellious way, which the Bible equates to witchcraft. You are placing your denomination under God's judgment through your endorsement of gayism into the body of Christ. I hear the words that John wrote to the Church in Ephesus echoing, 'You have forsaken your first love. Remember the height from which you have fallen! Repent and do the things you did at first. If you do not repent, I will come to you and remove your lampstand from its place (Rev. 2:4-5). It is very unfortunate that the Church here in America has spiritually misled this superpower nation whose foundation was laid in the*

Word of God by the American founding fathers and whose constitution is grazed in the Word of God. No wonder the American dollar carried the word, 'In God we trust.'"

Susan tried all the more that I accept her apology, and when I persistently turned a deaf ear, she opted to send a diplomatic person to further press me into accepting the apology. This was none other than Jon Chapman, who was the coordinator of Southern and East Africa in the Division of World-Wide Ministries. He not only wanted me to forgive Susan for her racist words, but he also wanted to reconcile me with the National Capital Presbytery. He, therefore, called together a group of National Capital Presbytery representatives to 'dialogue' with me as to how we could have some reconciliation and agree on a continued partnership between Elburgon Presbytery in Kenya and the American National Capital Presbytery which the PCEA had terminated through the GAC held at Kihumbui-ini Presbytery. In this issue, this is what Layman magazine wrote: *"But Githii was no more intimidated by their numbers than he has been with the dollars his Church might lose for its unwillingness to play games with Louisville. When representatives from the National Capital Presbytery met him for some dialogue, he spoke forcefully to them, charging that they had attempted to divide his Church back in Kenya. Githii said his executive council is furious with the National Capital. Apparently, a delegation from East Africa to the National Capital was in the planning stage when the Presbyterian Church of East Africa severed relations with the National Capital. The East Africa Council declared that because of the partnership termination, the trip was canceled as well. 'We said we will not allow a trip planned by the gay Presbyterians that exposes our people to gay couples and deviant living, Githii told The Layman.'"*

The Presbyterian Church of America was and remains the prominent donor to the PCEA Church. According to the Presbyterians News Service, as reported by Layman, *"almost $300,000 (Ksh30,000,000) was flowing from the Presbyterian Church (USA) to the Presbyterian Church of East Africa."* In regard to this, William Parker, the author of Layman, commented, *"This kind of money was such a substantial amount of cash for the Africans to forfeit, but Githii says he is willing to push his denomination to pay that price if the denomination's integrity is at stake. Otherwise, it would be inappropriate to compromise with evil because of money. It is Jesus who said that one cannot serve God and mammon."*

The news of this matter spread among evangelical commissioners who gathered in Richmond. Several Church representatives began to discuss ways to counter-attack the pressure that the PC (USA) officials were putting on their African brothers and sisters. Noting that sessions in the Presbyterian Church (USA) were free to distribute the financial contributions of their people wherever the Lord led them, some commissioners suggested that they might be forced to redirect their General Assembly per- capita contributions toward mission projects in the less privileged countries.

These were the first signs of the PC(USA) splitting into two other denominations, namely, the Evangelical Presbyterian Church (EPC) and the Covenantal Order of Evangelical Presbyterians (ECO). Another name for these newly formed denominations is '*Confessing Churches*' because they stand with the truth of the scriptures.

Speaking on the issue of redirecting the mission funds, one Confessing Church Leader told The Layman paper: "*This may be exactly what the Confessing Churches have been seeking. We're Presbyterians, and we don't want to withhold money from Presbyterian causes, but we must know the ministries we support are faithful to the Gospel. Redirecting our contributions to ecumenical needy Churches would meet both criteria. That's a positive thing that Confessing Churches can do.*"

My nasty experience in the hands of the officials of PC (USA) was as well reported by the Kenyan newspapers. For example, according to the Standard Newspaper volume 37, number 3/July 2004, with the topic: **Shunned prominent African Church leader offended by PC(USA)**, RICHMOND, VA, reported that "*Rev. Dr. David M. Githii, Moderator of the 4.2 million members Presbyterian Church of East Africa had traveled 6,000 miles to address the General Assembly of the Presbyterian Church (USA). But when he arrived in Richmond, he became persona non grata, and although 'other ecumenical delegates' were welcomed to the podium to bring greetings from their people, Githii was told that there would be no time for him.*"

In highlighting the same predicament, the Standard Newspaper of early mid-2004, in an article titled, "**Cleric Takes Anti–Gay War To The US,**" went on to say, "*A Kenyan clergyman has taken the war against homosexuality to the doorsteps of Americans. PCEA Moderator Rev David*

Githii is warning Americans practicing homosexuality that they are 'doomed for hell.'"

The paper went on to further elaborate on the fact that: "*The US has the greatest number of self-confessed homosexuals and lesbians in the world. A press statement from the Church's head office says Githii, who is on a visit to that country, issued the warning to the citizens. He warned that just as God refused to spare Sodom and Gomorrah from fire in the Bible, He would also not spare homosexuals and those defending the act. The clergyman urged the Presbyterian Church in the US to uphold Bible teachings, saying they were inspired by God.* It continued to quote him thus; "*I also challenge you to stand against those teaching that the Bible is just a collection of stories,*" *says the statement attributed to Githii. He urged G-8 to write off debts owed by Kenya and poor countries as a way to embrace God's love for humankind.*"

COMING BACK TO KENYA

It was unfortunate that upon my return to Kenya from Richmond, I was confronted by some in the PCEA leadership that I had left behind. They accused me of having jeopardized the main source of their donations from overseas.

As a result of this highly publicized stand, I had thought that coming back to my Church in Kenya would lead to my being received as a hero and a defender of faith. Unfortunately, and to my surprise, when I came back, some Church leaders treated me like an enemy. These were the liberals who were collaborating with PC (USA) leaders in carrying out the recruitment of homosexuality within the PCEA. They were a mixture of both clergy and elders and other prominent masonic people. I was accused of having jeopardized/betrayed the PCEA on their financial support from PC (USA) by not supporting that denomination's officials in their unbiblical agenda. It was, therefore, not shocking that the leaders who were also liberals came up with formidable opposition as well as called upon other leaders, especially those at the level of presbyteries, to come up with modalities to have a vote of no confidence on me as the Moderator of General Assembly. They were also experiencing pressure from the leaders of PC (USA), who threatened to cut off the financial support unless action was taken against me. Thank God, their plotting did not bear fruit, which reminded me of God's Word, which says, "*For the Lord Almighty has purposed, and who can thwart him? His hand is stretched out, and who can turn it back?*"(Isaiah 14:27). But all said and done, this issue became a big springboard for my harassment in the PCEA. This was especially because I was blocking donations from America and elsewhere from being misappropriated by these *'leaders.* In fact, that had been the fulcrum of the grudge and the agitation to have me impeached. I remember one of the leaders telling me: "*You should have verbally supported our colleagues in PC (USA) while you didn't mean it in your heart. What was easier? To support that or to cause the Church to lose all those massive donations we have been receiving over the years? This needed a second thought before you reacted the way you did. I tend to think that it was unwise to even try to reform a denomination that is in the midst of a superpower.*"

I recall telling this person: "*God is not a respecter of human distorted minds. God gave us the freedom to make choices and expects us to choose what is right. However, Adam and Eve thought that eating the forbidden fruit was a small matter that would not bother God, but this decision resulted in eternal judgment for humanity. We toil so much because of that 'small thing' by Adam and Eve,*" I responded and continued, "*And by telling me that I should have verbalized the support while not meaning it in my heart, that is to mock God, which by itself is sin.*"

I continued to say, "*There is no need to sell my faith and trust in God with dollars. After all, the Word of God says in Philippians 4:19, 'God will meet all your needs according to His glorious riches in Christ Jesus.' He also owns silver and gold. The whole world belongs to him.*"

I told these people by all means to resist any temptation to enrich themselves with this cursed money because its source does not align with the scriptures. I gave them the Anglican Church as an example. In this regard, I said: "*Think of the Anglican Church in Kenya. This denomination has openly dissociated itself from those Churches in Western countries that are after allowing the ordination of homosexuals and gay marriages in their Churches. This denomination is at the same time discouraging educating their ministers in foreign universities and seminaries, especially those well-known institutions that are pro-gay. We need to be alert! Be reminded of Jesus' words, '..when you see a cloud rising in the west, immediately you say it's going to rain. How is it that you don't know how to interpret this present time?'*" (Luke 12:54-56).

CONTENTIOUS PARTNERSHIPS

The other bone of contention that even stirred the anger of the church leadership more was the issue of the two presbyteries - Elburgon and Thika. Elburgon had already partnered with the National Capital Presbytery of Maryland, USA, while Thika had partnered with Detroit Presbytery, also located in the USA. These two PCEA presbyteries had a long-standing partnership. But we had come to discover that during the exchange programs, the Americans were recruiting Africans into homosexuality, as we stated earlier. It happened that when the Americans visited the Elburgon Presbytery, their main agenda was to recruit Church leaders into gayism. Unfortunately, when they visited, they were not allowed to sleep in one place. They were accommodated into various homes by Church members despite their insisting that they be allowed to sleep together in one place. The presbytery leadership stuck to their guns on their being housed separately by individual Church members. Thus, when they went back to Maryland, they wrote emails to their friends sharing with them the positive things they had enjoyed in Kenya but they were quick to talk of one negative thing that they had encountered. They were not allowed to sleep together, so they missed practicing their homosexuality. They were also informed that the African culture forbade same-sex kissing, be it among males or females.

Some of these people forwarded these emails to some of the Kenyan people in America, who transmitted the same to us. This is how we came to learn of their obsession with homosexuality. We also learned that when the Kenyan delegates visited the National Capital Presbytery, every endeavor was made to recruit them into gayism. The act of terminating this partnership had, therefore, greatly angered the leaders of PC (USA). It then followed that when I visited the 2004 PC(USA) General Assembly, where I was harassed and humiliated, the leaders of the National Capital Presbytery had tried to convince me to revive the partnership, which I had declined, citing the scriptures as totally opposed to anything to do with homosexuality and same-sex marriages. One of them had argued, *"But you have to understand. Here, we are talking of people born with these hormones that crave this kind of sexual orientation. How can you question God's mode of creation? You and your so-called PCEA are being very unrealistic. We do trust that when you get back to Kenya, you will think over this issue from a deeper perspective. Our aim is to give support to that presbytery in all its ways of life. Please, think about it. The beneficiaries are your people."*

In response, I said: *"I do understand your concern over the many needs our people have, but you seem to have strings attached to your perceived partnership. You want to support materially, but you also want to pass an evil gospel to these people. Homosexuality is evil, and it is a grievous sin. We cannot entertain that kind of behaviour. This is a concluded matter. Don't expect anything better than what I have already told you. At least not when I am still in office!"*

Another incidence that had also irked both Detroit Presbytery and Thika Presbytery was when the Detroit Presbytery officials made a visit to Kenya and consequently visited my office. They were accompanied by the officials of Thika Presbytery. Their agenda had been to convince me to revive their partnership. The reasons they gave were exactly those shared with me by the National Capital Presbytery. Their argument was that they had a lot of wealth, which they wanted to share with the impoverished people within the Thika Presbytery.

To this, I said, *"There is no way we can exchange our spiritual gains with material things. I believe in the Word of God in Matthew 6:33, '... seek ye first the kingdom of God and other things will be given to us.' Remember the Rich man who boasted of his wealth, but Lazarus lived in poverty? But then, who inherited the eternal life? It was Lazarus! We want to lead our people to that Everlasting Life rather than settle them in the temporary material gains. After all, the Word of God in Philippians 4:19 has pointed to us the fact that 'God will always supply all our needs according to the riches of his glory in Jesus Christ.' Please expect no other decision on this matter. It is a closed case."* It was then I said a word of prayer, and my guests left.

I could tell that the Thika Presbytery officials were not happy with me. They would have loved this partnership to continue as it had given them an open door to visit America. There was also the financial gain through the dollars one would acquire during such a visit. After all, some would go there and refuse to come back and instead choose to settle in America. I said to them, *"I do understand* your mentality of having homosexual-oriented Americans as your friends. People who are even advocating same-sex marriages. I would rather you let our focus be on God, who, in accordance with John 15:16, 'chose us to be his co-workers in his vineyard.' Trust in God, and he will do great things in your life. Just be obedient to His word."

I alerted these leaders on the diabolical mission of the Americans through the partnership. It was all about propagating their gay and lesbian agenda as well as fronting devil worship. I also reminded them of God's words that he spoke through prophet Isaiah; "*I am the Lord; that is my name! I will not give My glory to another or My praise to idols*" (Isa.42:8). I emphasized the fact that the accommodation of homosexuality and same-sex marriages into the Church lifestyle was not only idolatrous but rebellion against the Kingdom of God.

This tells you of the pressure I was experiencing as I tried by all means to block any loophole that would permit the infiltration of homosexualism into the church. I had no idea that the evil had already found its way into the church. That is why I had to defrock the six pastors for participating not only in homosexuality but also in devil worship. That was why, during the General Assembly of April 2009, I had called upon the church to form a commission to go around all PCEA churches to find out the extent to which the homosexual virus had penetrated their domains and then advice the church on how to arrest the covertly thriving twin evils. Unfortunately, instead of seeking the cure, some of those in leadership, including some past moderators, turned up to be my greatest persecutors.

Their focus was more on the money donated from America and not the sinful and evil source. Below is a more detailed account of the heightened opposition.

THE DECISIVE AND HEIGHTENED OPPOSITION

The struggle between me and PCEA leadership climaxed during the Church's 20th General Assembly that took place at St. Andrew's Church, Nairobi, from April 16th to April 21st, 2012. I raised a motion calling upon the PCEA to terminate its partnership with the entire PC (USA) denomination because of their continued advocacy for the ordination of homosexuals and the promotion of same-sex marriages. The motion was rejected. They categorically stated that there was no way the PCEA could forfeit those *'fat'* donations in dollars. Someone even said, *"We shall be cleansing that money through praying over it."*

Having noted the rapid recruitment of homosexuals and devil worshipers, as well as the rampant immorality in the Church, I raised yet another motion in connection with this menace. I called upon the Church to form a commission to investigate the reasons behind this recruitment and the surging spirit of immorality and corruption. This commission would then advice the Church on the way to arrest such evils from polluting the Church. I realized that this evil menace had already grown deep roots, for none of the past Moderators had enough courage to confront it head-on. For instance, at a past GAC held at Mombasa, the then Moderator was not bold enough to expose the culprits. He said he was aware and had some names of the culprits. On being challenged to unmask them, he became reluctant to do so. Instead, he literary whispered that we leave the building where the meeting was and instead go to discuss the issue outside beside the beach. For he said, *"Walls have ears."* And even at the beach, he did not disclose them.

My motion to form a commission was rejected. The liberals felt threatened as it would have ended a thriving ground through which they carried out the recruitment. It was also argued that such a move would have publicly exposed the mushrooming vice whose outcome would have definitely paraded homosexuals and devil worshipers in the Church. Such a report would then leak to the media and thus expose the denomination's nakedness.

Unrelenting, I moved yet another motion in the same General Assembly voicing the need to change the type of bread the Church used in celebrating the Holy Communion and instead use any other form of home-made bread because the wafers that the Church used was occultic bread, rife with New Age Movement and Freemasonry/Illuminati symbols. To further emphasize my concern, I said, *"It is for this reason that I did not participate in the Holy Communion that the Moderator celebrated this morning because my faith/conscience cannot allow me to take what I know is a representation of an idolatry."*

Upon moving these three *'sensitive and contradictory'* motions, I was accused of having a wrong attitude with the intention of misleading the Church. The Moderator secretly formed a committee with only one agenda - to discuss me and come out with a lasting solution on how to silence me. This committee, which was purely comprised of liberals, came out with a decision to have me given an early compulsory retirement with immediate effect. By then, I was an active minister at Baraka Parish, which was part of the Kajiado Presbytery.

Retirement thoughts were far from my mind. And true to their word, the GA ended on Saturday, 21st April and on 24th April, I received a letter which in part said, "*Due to your persistent spirit of misleading the Church, and noting your contradictory motions in the just ended GA, the Church has recommended that you proceed on for early retirement with immediate effect. Note that you are not supposed to carry out any duties within the entire PCEA Church.* "This matter was never communicated to the church fraternity because it was the work of the Liberal cartel.

This was a total psychological torture. Worse still, no plans had been in place to mentally prepare me. There was neither any form of counseling forthcoming. I was left with no salary; neither was I assigned any pension. My services were terminated without notice. I was rendered inactive, and I was blocked from all the Church facilities according to the dismissal letter.

This was unlike the previous Moderators who were thoroughly prepared psychologically at the time of their retirement. Why was I being treated in such a negative manner? The aim of the GA Moderator and his liberal counterparts was to make me suffer so that I could compromise and stop exposing corruption and other wickedness within the denomination. Placing me into retirement was seen as the best way to silence me as it put me in a voiceless environment, something I had refused to do for the sake of the gospel and my faith. But in doing so, the PCEA leadership was at the same time being pushed by both the PC(USA) in America and the Church of Scotland.

The leaders of the Church of Scotland were unhappy that I had challenged their Christianized culture with which they had manipulated the African converts to believe that the Scottish culture was the gospel truth and the centrality of the scriptures. They were also concerned that I had pointed an accusing finger at what they referred to as the artifacts that were entrenched in the Church buildings, which I referred to as occultic symbols similar to the ones Freemasonry had engraved in their sanctuaries.

The PC (USA) had been at war with me because, as they claimed, I had exposed the infiltration of the virus of homosexuality and same-sex marriages in PCEA through them. They were vexed because I had refused to support the PC (USA) motion on the ordination of homosexuals as church Ministers and church Elders in the 2004 GA held at Richmond, Virginia. There was also the issue of the fact that I had influenced the termination of the PC(USA) partnerships with PCEA Presbyteries and PC(USA) Presbyteries.

It is unfortunate that some of the Western denominations are taking advantage of the financial constraints of the Churches in Africa to manipulate the leadership into accepting Satanism in exchange for Dollars, Pounds and Euros. Unfortunately, this is rapidly dehydrating the spirituality and physical growth of the African Church. In this regard, God has already detached Himself from these Churches that are evil carriers. His word affirms this when it says, *"Those who cling to worthless idols forfeit the grace that could be theirs"* (Jonah 2:8).

What greatly disturbed me was the way some denominations in the USA and Europe had become aggressively involved in further distorting the very gospel that the Africans received from them. This is a continent they had referred to as the *'Dark Continent.'* This darkness was apparently in reference to the absence of Christianity prior to the coming of missionaries. Most African communities by then are believed to have worshiped their ancestors, all kinds of physical features like mountains, rivers, animals, trees and even their community heroes and heroines. But then one wonders what the scriptural passage they so often quoted emphatically to their converts from Galatians 1:8-9 which says: *"Let God's curse fall on anyone, including us or even an angel from heaven, who preaches a different kind of Good News than the one we preached to you… I say again what we have said before: If anyone preaches any other Good News than the one you welcomed, let that person be cursed"* (NLT Life Application Study Bible).

So, the funding today by foreign donors to some African Churches/governments is aimed at manipulating them to accept all kinds of Satanism. Unfortunately, because of the prevailing poverty in Africa, many, including the clergy/ government leaders, are yielding very fast to this bait, thus ending up being victims of these foreign machinations. It is also important to note that, like some Western denominations, some Western countries are using economic power to entice African nations. But it is also important to say, on the other hand, that as much as Satanism has infiltrated the western Churches, there are still many Churches/ countries and denominations that are striving to seek righteousness in their endeavor to promote the Kingdom of God. And, of course, there are other Western countries that are against the practice of wickedness. Here, I am thinking of churches founded by the diaspora, the newly formed denominations that are splinters from the already compromised old denominations, such as EPC and ECO, both in America. God will use these to bring revival.

Some of these Churches were the ones founded by the Diaspora members. The newly formed denominations are splinters from the already compromised old denominations, such as the Evangelical Covenant Order of the Presbyterians (ECHO) and Evangelical Presbyterian Church (EPC), both in America. God will use these to bring revival in Western countries.

One of the things that took place at the GAC held at Kihumbui-ini was the termination of the partnership between some Presbyteries in America and those in the PCEA Church. Such included PC (USA) National Capital for solemnizing same-sex marriages. This, they claimed, had jeopardized their financial support. Even worse still was my defrocking the ministers whom they had recruited during their studies in America and whom they had trained on how to carry out massive recruitments within PCEA Church.

As expected, some in the PCEA leadership had sympathized with these carriers of evil lending credence to the fact that they may have also been involved in the evil practices. Otherwise, why did they not fight these evils, including the heavy cloud of corruption? Personally, I was aware of quite a number of ministers in this Church who were involved in homosexuality both at the Presbytery levels and at the PCEA General Assembly.

To show the American Church's grip on homosexuality, I voiced out this, "*Recently, a minister in America wrote to me seeking some advice because the Presbytery was forcing him to celebrate Holy Communion with a minister who openly advocated homosexuality so that he could refuse and consequently get defrocked. Another minister wrote to me enquiring whether he could be affiliated to PCEA because his Church wanted to defrock him because of his being opposed to homosexualism.*" It is in this regard that I told the delegates: "*The universal church, including the PCEA, should first strive to spiritualize the Church rather than forming partnerships with denominations that are no longer toeing the line of Godliness. It is only then that God will open avenues for wealth. God has the key, as gold and silver belong to him. If anything, the Church should feel called to be part of those who will redeem the nations by condemning and fighting all kinds of wickedness, including sexual diversions and corruption. This is what the South Koreans did and now their country has been moving from one glory to another.*"

Further, I told the delegates:
"*I am now calling upon this GA to strengthen the Kihumbu-ini resolution so much that there will be no room left for this Church to exchange her birthright with the American dollars. To accept this is detrimental and akin to defiling our Church, and we will soon be an empty vessel. Thanks to God, there are many, even in PC (USA), who are fighting for the survival of the Church there. These are people who are struggling for the renewal of the Church, people who are struggling for the Church to be placed into new wineskins. Ours is to pray with and for such people who will not surrender the faith to the powers of evil.*"

EXPOSITION OF HOMOSEXUALITY "VIRUS" IN PCEA

In January 2012, I was posted to a new parish known as Baraka Parish within the Kajiado Presbytery. It had been curved out from the Rongai Parish. However, just as it had happened at Sigona at the time of my entry, some of those at Head Office cunningly incited some pastors and elders both at Baraka Parish and Kajiado Presbytery to block me from landing there.

There was quite some resistance in trying to block me, but like Sigona, God worked it out through some understanding elders like Mr. Karanja, Mrs. Githuka, and Mrs. Mbuthia. They worked very hard to create a door for me to get into Baraka Parish. I was finally inducted as the first parish minister of Baraka Parish, which comprised three congregations, with Macedonia being the headquarters.

It was while I was manning this parish that I attended the General Assembly meeting that took place on the 16th. April – 22nd. April 2012 at St. Andrews Church in Nairobi. At break time on the second day of the GA deliberations, I approached one of the key GA leaders and explained to him the importance of raising the issue of mushrooming homosexuality and devil worship in the church. I told him, "*I am ready to raise this motion and, at the same time, substantiate it by giving some very concrete evidence.*" This church leader responded by saying, "*I am not sure that such a motion should be raised at this time that the new office is just getting started.*"

I said, "*I am sorry; I feel so obliged to raise this matter such that if you and the other GA leaders will not include it in the agenda, then I will go ahead and do it. I feel bound by the words in Psalm 11:3, which states, 'When the foundations are being destroyed, what can the righteous do?' I also feel held captive by the words found in Isaiah 51:7-8, 'Hear me you who have my law in your hearts. Do not fear the reproach of men or be terrified by their insults.' As this leader was standing up to go, he said, "I will talk with some leaders, and we will let you know what we think about your request.*"

On the third day, I approached the same GA leader and inquired whether he had talked to the other GA leaders in regard to my request. He told me that some people would talk to me that afternoon.

When the afternoon business started, I was summoned into a separate room where I found seven people. One of them, whom I assumed was the chairman, said,
"*Past Moderator, we have been instructed to have seating with you as you have an agenda that you want to be floated in this GA. What is it about?*" I

said, *"I would have expected whoever sent you to meet me to have elaborated to you the theme of my motion."* One other person said, *"Of course, he has hinted to us what is in your mind, but it is always good to hear from the horse's mouth."* It was then that I told them about the mushrooming homosexual virus in the church, and I said it was high time it got arrested before its pregnancy polluted the church to the chore. Then one of them said, *"Can you share with us some of what you refer to as evidence."* I then pointed to the rampant wickedness and corruption (including misapplication of Church funds), the mushrooming recruitment of both lay people and clergy into homosexuality and lesbianism and the partnership with PC(USA), a denomination that was already ordaining homosexuals and lesbians as well as practicing same-sex marriages; trends that were already eating up the Church in all its faculties of life. I cautioned that unless the PCEA changed its tactics in dealing with those issues, the Church would continue to swim in the current of God's curse and judgment in which it was already hooked.

I explained the fact that I had come to that conclusion because I had noted with great concern the rapid recruitment that was going on in the PCEA as far as homosexuality and devil worship were concerned. I reminded them of the six pastors I had defrocked for homosexuality and devil worshipping during my tenure in office as Moderator of the GA Assembly.

I reminded them of the first PCEA minister who got defrocked in 1998 because of being a homosexual and a devil worshiper and that the question he posed to the church was, *"Because you have expelled me, what are you to do with all the other PCEA pastors and elders who practice the same, as we are many?"* Yes, *"all the others?"* meaning, by 1998, the number of homosexuals and devil worshipers in the PCEA Church was already swelling.

The same statement was echoed between 2003 and 2009 by the six PCEA ministers I defrocked. They said, *"What are you going to do with all the other homosexuals and devil worshipers in PCEA?"* One of them is quoted to have said, *"This behaviour is already too deeply rooted for the Church to uproot. Its roots are not here, it is deeply rooted in Western countries from where it is financially sponsored."*

I explained to them the fact that I found it quite unfortunate that among other reasons, why the practice was fast mushrooming in PCEA, was because of the Church's partnership with PC (USA). I further explained that while I was the GA Moderator, I had by all means tried to push the Church to severe the partnership. For example, the 2004 GAC I chaired to terminate the partnership between the Presbytery of National Capital in the state of Maryland in America and PCEA Elburgon Presbytery.

This had been because of the leaked information that the National Capital Presbytery was already recruiting Elburgon Presbytery members into homosexuality during their exchange programs. I also noted that the homosexuals in the PCEA were already positioning themselves for leadership positions in all Church sectors and especially in Presbyteries' and Kirksessions.

This was the same strategy that the Western countries were employing. After they had occupied most of the leadership positions, they would then bring a motion to have an acknowledgement or recognition within the Church life. In fact, in the near future, the struggle at the time of elections in the PCEA will be more between the scriptural-based Church leaders and the pro-gay and devil worshippers. Already, this is the main struggle within the churches in Western countries.

I also explained to them one incident that had happened when I was the GA Moderator at a seminar for intercessors in one of the churches in Kambui, Kenya. When I took the break, a woman came and said to me, "*I was wondering whether you can help my daughter to get into a school because after accepting Jesus Christ as her Lord and Saviour. She was chased away by the school because, in her confession, she revealed that she had been a devil worshipper.*" I had the mother call the girl so that I could pray for her. I had her first give her testimony to the group of the intercessors. In her testimony, she said:
"*I had been a Devil worshiper for some time. The people who recruited me and some other young people are elders in this church. They had been taking us to some buildings in Nairobi where they had us take satanic rituals and forced us to do filthy things, including all kinds of sexual perversion. These acts were oriented toward worshiping the devil. These elders had threatened to kill us if we could ever tell anybody. When the Word touched my heart, I decided to confess my sins, including the sins of the devil. Worship, and if I*

die, I die and go to live with Jesus. You cannot believe it, but the people who had recruited me and many others are elders of this church. They include." But before she could pronounce the names, Rev. Gituiria, standing next to her, quickly covered her mouth with her hand; thus, she never mentioned the other names. This is proof that the operation and devilish activities are going on in the church through the promotion of church leaders.

Another incidence is a time I held a Presbytery-based seminar in one of the PCEA churches in Kikuyu town. In my speech, I did touch on the mushrooming Devil worship in the church and nation, something that had made the government set up a commission in 1994 to carry out an investigation on that. After the service, a woman approached me and said,
"Moderator, there are so many people who could not understand you when you said something about the devil worshippers in the church. I could be one of them some months back, but this time around, I could understand you quite well. Until a few months ago, my husband and I used to talk, read the Word of God, and even pray together, but not so now. He has so much changed that he even doesn't tell me where he goes at night. He has become very hostile and secretive. He seems to do things secretly."

The woman went on to say,
"Recently, I discovered that he has been recruited into devil worship and homosexuality by some elders in this church. I will not tell you their names because they are people you know, people who in all ways pretend to be not only Christians but born again – people who are supposed to be models to the flock, but they are wolves in sheep skins. What many Christians don't know is that there is a big recruitment of Christians into devil worship and homosexuality that is going on in the PCEA Church. Please, continue to pray for me because I am now living between two Kingdoms, one godly, that is me and the other Satanic, that is my husband. I also need your advice on how to live in these two worlds."

There is this other incident where a young man, a gospel singer, told me how a group of pastors invited him to sing in an overnight gathering they had organized at Njabiini. When the young man arrived around 5.00 pm, he met some pastors, and others kept on coming. He noticed that as pastors kept on coming and settling down, they were caressing one another and even kissing. When the time for introduction came, he could hear peculiar introductions. For example, someone would say:

"My name is Kigethia …..(he had the name of a pastor Kigethi). I pastor in such and such a place. I am married, but my partner in this fellowship is this man sitting next to me whose name is James" - meaning his homosexual partner. What followed after supper was all hell. The gospel singer had to escape secretly from the scene. A few days later, this young man came to my office and shared the story with me. I then inquired from him whether, by chance, he had shared telephone contact with any of them. Luckily, he had the contact of one of the pastors whose original home is in Rungiri in Kiambu County. I then told him to call that pastor and pretend that he wanted to be recruited the soonest as possible. I asked him to set the phone on loud speaker. I also realized from his talk that their leader was a pastor we had sometimes defrocked back for being a homosexual. I told him to say something like: What of the person who acted as the leader and seems he was once a pastor? It was then that he made the call. The pastor was very excited upon hearing the gospel singer. He first posed a question, 'How is it that you left us without a word of bye?' The gospel singer said, *"I found myself at odds as I did not have a partner; in fact, this is why I am calling you because I would like to be recruited as soon as possible."*

In his response, the pastor said:

"Thank you, in fact that is why we were inviting you. It's one of those ways we are reaching out in our recruitment. We are reaching out to all classes of Church leaders, youth, women's Guild and others. In fact, soon, we will be a power to reckon with. We are rapidly but secretly building up the number. Anyway, we need to meet soon so that I can give you some guidance in being recruited as a member."

The gospel singer said, *"I live in Ongata Rongai"*. The pastor said, *"Let us meet the day after tomorrow. I will give you a call and advice you on the venue. Meanwhile, make sure you do not tell anybody."*

Then, the young man asked him, *"Who was that man who was referred to as "chairman." The pastor said, "This is Kinothia; he hails from Thogoto. He was a PCEA minister who got defrocked because he acted foolishly and exposed himself. One should be very careful not to expose himself. We like behaving like moles in our lifestyles and recruitment. Many of us are sponsored locally and overseas."*

The next thing I did was to instruct my secretary to call that pastor to my office on a particular day because him being the presbytery clerk, I needed some information. It also happened that I was leaving office since my two terms in office had come to an end. So, I was in the process of handing over to the incoming officials. Thus, when the pastor came, I called two of the incoming officials, the Moderator Rev. Gathanju and the Secretary General Re. Gitonga who were already familiarizing themselves with the new offices. I narrated the story on how the pastor spoke with the gospel singer over the phone as I listened. The pastor never denied instead he remained quiet though he was shivering a lot, his mouth dry. He was speechless with great knee knocking fear.

After he had left the office, I told my colleagues, "*If only I had another month in office, I could make sure this minister is defrocked.*" My colleagues did not comment. They were somehow reserved. No wonder even at the time of writing this, fifteen years, this minister (and many others who are known by the church leaders) are still enjoying "*ministry*" in the same denomination. I am sure together with his comrades they are still busy recruiting, even as they continue preaching, serving Holy Communion, baptising and laying hands on the flock. It is no surprise then that when I insisted on forming a committee to investigate this mess in the church, I was first given a mandatory premature retirement and to add injury to insult, I was finally expelled. Such cases are numerous in the universal Church.

What does all this evidence tell us? It just reveals the filth in the body of Christ. It reveals that, there are many in the churches that are there just to defile the church. They use money, power and influence to carry out the recruitment. They are attached to or are agents of the New Age Movement, Illuminati and Freemasonry. They have even taken prime positions in the churches and their related institutions by financially corrupting the system. But take note, no one denomination is immune. Lesbianism, homosexuality and abortion are predominant in the church. No wonder, much of church life is marked by strife, jealousy, struggle for power, corruption, immorality, gossip and so on.

While I was the PCEA moderator of General Assembly, I received a phone call from a vice-chancellor of a seminary in USA. He was concerned that one of our student pastors was openly worshipping the Devil and practicing homosexuality. He told me that, that was not a unique case, they have foreign students portraying the same and there were several from the American based churches. He said, *"it is becoming a thorn in the flesh in the American based seminaries and I am surprised that it has already found its way into the Third world countries."* Nevertheless, he had the student deported.

I have another incident where a minister revealed to me how another minister had come to recruit him but he warned him never to try again. I persuaded this minister to open up and expose him so that I could have him defrocked but he declined because they hailed from the same neighbourhood in Meru. He feared that this minister would mobilize neighbours to fight him because he looked so innocent to everyone. He even contributes a lot in the community affairs, possibly through the donations he receives from overseas to propagate and promote the recruitment of homosexuals and devil worshippers. I had several of such cases.

Another incidence is when an Anglican clergy brought a young man to me because the young man was undergoing some depression. This young man revealed to me the fact that the root cause of his depression was as a result of the sexual abuse he had undergone over a time for four years from a PCEA church clergyman who was supporting him in paying school fees. This man regularly sodomised him, and anytime he resisted, the said clergyman would threaten him that he could withhold the Payment of school fees. This boy had come from a very poor family and he had a high desire for education. Thus, he always gave in. This young man told me:

"I have been seeking to let PCEA church leadership know my predicament, but they have never accepted to meet me because they did not want to open wounds as they were aware that there are many such people in the church. Then, I met this Anglican pastor who told me that you would not only be interested in listening to me but you will at the same time take steps. I also realized that by sharing my story with you, it will start a process of my healing and restoration. Please help me to meet this man. I need to tell him

the pain he inflicted on me. I am sick…" At this time, he was sobbing and crying bitterly.

I then asked the young man to write down his complaints and concerns and hand in those notes to me. I thereafter called the officials of the presbytery from which the immoral clergy had hailed from and asked them to investigate the truth behind the boy's complaints and hand in the report to me after two weeks. Surprisingly, when the clergyman was summoned by the Kambui Presbytery leaders and where he was given the letter to read, was questioned as to what he thought about the boy's complaints, he responded by saying, *"it is the whole truth. I started practicing homosexuality from the time I was a teenager."* He even went on further to say, *"I am not alone. We are many in the church. We have a fellowship for such."* The church then had then the minister defrocked. The said clergyman at that time was the head of the PCEA Communications Department.

There is this other incident where a watchman asked the parish Kirk Session to help him recover the debt he was owed by the Parish Minister who, upon carrying out acts of homosexuality, had refused to pay him as per agreement. The watchman said, *"I am in great pain and can hardly sit down, as the pastor used to sodomise most of the night."* When the minister was questioned about this, he accepted that he regularly sodomised that watchman. I will call him Ndeba (not his real name)

These are but a few cases among others, for rumours have it that there are many clergymen who sodomise watchmen. I had him finally defrocked, upon which he said,
"What are you to do with all the others? We are soon becoming and army and our roots are worldwide."

What does this tell you? It tells you and me that, there is a big movement of devil worship recruitment which is at the same time going hand in hand with homosexuality and lesbianism. The recruitment involves especially among others, the **Elders, Pastors, Evangelists, Youth, Women's Guild** and all categories of Church leadership and membership.

One thing I was already discerning was that the incoming officials would not deal with the gay pastor because one of them was at the forefront in opposing me for defrocking pastors. He had argued that such pastors should be exposed as it will tarnish the name of the church. He and others in the Church had the slogan; *'Let the wheat and weeds grow together until the End Time.'* From this I discerned that no more defrocking of such ministers would take place in future. And by the way, it is good for the reader to know that by the time of publishing this book in 2023, none has ever been defrocked, yet the mushrooming of the same continues. I felt that homosexuality and devil worship weeds were so much polluting the Church and should not be allowed to remain in the Body of Christ.

No wonder, the said minister I had summoned in the office is still very active in the Church, still manning one parish after another. No doubt he and many others are busy carrying out recruitments, baptizing, commissioning leaders, ordaining, laying hands on believers and serving Holy Communion. Remember what the pastor said over the phone; *"We are… reaching out to all classes of people… we are already becoming a force which in the near future will be a power to reckon with."* And this is the whole truth.

I further informed this group of seven that the recruited people turned occultic and carried out their duties so cunningly and in Christian pretense such that one could hardly suspect them. The bottom line was that; they have a strategy, an evil strategy to defile not only the Church buildings but the Christians as well. They are the highest proprietors of wickedness in the church including immorality and greed for wealth and even swap up wives.

But the saddest part of the story was that no sooner had I vacated the GA Moderator's position than the process of re-admitting those pastors who were defrocked in the tenure of my office started. One who was re-admitted at Mai-Ihii-Parish did not survive for long for he got re-defrocked after he was brought before the Kirksession with evidence on how he was wooing young people into the acts of homosexuality.

I told my listeners that the devil had given those homosexuals and devil worshipers a very sweet tongue. They are very eloquent in the delivery of their sermons and this was why the common Church members and leadership could not easily detect them. In many instances, they even came to the defense of these gays when they were confronted for their actions. This then opens a wider door for the increase of this occultic cartel in the Churches. And since most of them occupy the higher positions in the presbyteries and dioceses, they are able to protect each other. It is for the same reason that the homosexuals have finally hijacked the Church in the Western countries.

I further informed the group that in the course of my leadership as the Moderator of the General Assembly, on several occasions, a number of pastors came and shared with me how some of their pastor colleagues had approached them in an attempt to recruit them. It was unfortunate that when I asked such pastors to bear witness so that I could influence the church to defrock those homosexual pastors, many did not want to come out openly for fear of being victimized by the members of that group. They actually went to the extent of issuing death threats to any *'loud mouths*. It was for those reasons that at one time I had called upon the General Assembly to come up with a commission to carry out thorough investigation and advice the Church on the way forward.

In conclusion, I told the group about an elder from Rift Valley Region who had called me with a lot of concern over what he referred to as, *"The deteriorating of morals and the upsurge of filth in the PCEA:* He said, *"Reverend Moderator Githii, what is happening to the Church because every pastor who has been brought to our parish is ending up being a very immoral person? We have a number of children who are the products of different pastors who had been posted to minister in our parish. Why is it that immorality has permeated so much in the PCEA?"*

He went on, *"I even know of some Church elders who have been taking Church women to lodgings and yet they participate in the Sunday services including being celebrants in the Holy Communion, baptisms and in laying of hands-on people. Aren't these the evils you are pointing out? Do you have an idea as to what should be done?*

In response, I said,
"I have blown the trumpet severally but the Church turns a deaf ear. I can only advise that you and others commit yourselves into prayer and fasting. Otherwise, the roots have gone too deep. But the obvious reason why it

becomes so difficult to deal with these people is that, quite a number of top church leadership are already well initiated into some of these Masonic Movements and practices."

I also shared with my listeners about a time when I talked about these issues with a group of pastors in a seminar and as I voiced out these evidences, I could tell from the facial expressions that most of the listeners were in agreement with what I was saying. I gave this message in the morning session which means later on the participants went for lunch. It was during lunch time that some very concerned people approached me wondering what could be done to safeguard PCEA from the evils that I had pointed out.

My response was that, this could only happen if the Church would take Paul's words as recorded in the book of Ephesians 6:12 that; *"Our struggle is not against flesh and blood but against the rulers...against authorities, against powers of this dark world, against the spiritual forces of evil."* I further explained to those concerned PCEA Pastors that what was eating up God's people was the spirit of fear and greed for money, power and maintaining of the status quo.

I emphasized the fact that what God wanted the Church to understand was the fact that the Word of God cautioned against fear when it says; *"For God has not given us a spirit of fear, but of power and love and of sound mind"* (2Tim 1:7). The Word of God further affirms that; *"Though we live in this world, we do not wage war as the world does. The weapons we fight with are not the weapons of this world. On the contrary, they have divine power to demolish strongholds"* (2Cor. 10:3-4).

I told the group of seven how I had pointed out to the pastors in the seminar how the spirit of paganism had already infiltrated the Church. Already and like the time of Constantine, the universal Church is undergoing paganization rather than amending the broken altars and feeding the people with the Word. This evil spirit is turning Christians into hearers of the word only and not doers, as written in the book of James 1:22. I reminded the group of how I had persistently continued to expose the idolatry that was eating up the church and the nation.

I further told the 7 that the more I continued to champion this revelation on the occult, the more my struggle with the liberals increased. This is because they felt that I was encroaching into their territories and space by exposing their strongholds. I made it clear to them the fact that all the persecutions I had faced were a result of my pointing at the evils such as occultic symbols, sexual perversion including homosexuality, same-sex marriages, the widely-spreading devil worship in the Church and the mushrooming idolatry as well as rampant immorality. There was also the worship of money rather than the worship of God, the owner and giver of silver and gold. Yet it is God who meets the desires of those who love and honour him. It is this spirit that had given birth to this rampant wickedness.

This is what I have been striving to remind the Church by seemingly taking the role of a prophet. I said, *"In doing this, I am acting in obedience to God's Word, 'Stand up and say to them whatever I command you. Do not be terrified by them, or I will terrify you before them'"* (Jer. 1:17). I always feel the urge to keep letting the Church know that in the area of dealing with some of the grey areas on church wickedness, the church was wrongly representing the kingdom of God. The leaders are off the mark.

When one of the seven asked me how I felt about facing so much opposition while continuing my endeavor to oppose sexual-related wickedness, I explained that when it came to fighting for God's kingdom, I knew that when God commanded me to speak out, the seeds I planted were not to bear fruit immediately. I visualized it as winter wheat, which remains buried in the ground waiting for the spring. I am sure this wickedness unless checked will one time overwhelm the church.

This is true of every prophetic message. In many cases it takes years for the truth to be birthed. It is only then that people will testify that: *"This was said by so and so."* It is important to note that this prophetic culture is not only for the PCEA church but also upon the universal church and at the same time is true on worldwide governments. If only people had listened to Noah, so many people would not have perished. What if people had listened to prophets like Jeremiah? Israelites would not have ended up in Babylon. I had all the way realized that God's timing was not ours to command. If we do not start the fire with the first strike of our match, we must try again. God does hear our prayers, but He may not answer them at the precise time we have appointed in our own minds. Instead, he reveals himself to our seeking hearts, though not necessarily when and where we expect. Therefore, we need to persevere and be steadfast in our life of prayers. We must remain focused, never compromise or lose hope. We must continue emulating the examples from the old days of flint, the steel, and brimstone matches where one had to strike the match again and again and again. Perhaps they had to strike dozens of times before they could get a spark to light their fire. They were very thankful when they finally succeeded. It is this kind of reasoning that I will never give up in spite of the strong opposition and intimidation I face.

Like in the Flint and Steel old days, I feel the need to exercise the same kind of perseverance and hope regarding heavenly things. This is one thing the believers should be aware of. Believers should realize that when it comes to faith, we have more certainty of success than we could ever have had with flint and steel, for we have promised as a condition. It is Theodore L. Cuyler who said, "*I do not believe that there is such a thing in the history of God's eternal kingdom as a right prayer offered in the right spirit that remains forever unanswered.*"

I believe that the Lord knows what is best for me, and that my surroundings are determined by him. And wherever he places me, he does so to strengthen my faith and power and to draw me into closer communion with Himself. Even if I am confined to a dungeon, my soul will prosper. I know that when I endure temptations to bow down to the powers of darkness, God's grace is magnified, leading me to a higher degree in spiritual maturity. I believed that, once I arrive at my heavenly home, I will look back at the turns and trials along my path and will sing the praises of my Guide, Jehovah Sabaoth. Simply put, no matter how many twists and turns the road has had, there is always one smooth and straight portion. So, whatever comes my way, I will always welcome God's will and refuse to be deviated from aggressively advancing the kingdom of God, in spite of the resistance. I refuse to be threatened or to be compromised in a manipulative way from loving and serving the Lord who according to John 15:16 chose and commissioned me to go and bear fruits-fruits that would last. For me, these are the fruits for the future generations as well the current generation.

After I shared my thoughts with the seven, the chairman said,
"Past Moderator, we thank you for sharing your inner thoughts with us. We are also aware of your persistent call upon the church to expose some of those grey areas in the church, nevertheless, not everyone agrees with you. Many people feel that you should also think of the people you are calling homosexuals and devil worshipers. These people need to be sympathized with. As I have learned, the problem is not them, the problem lies in the fact that they have inborn genes which at one time in one's life, surface in the blood stream and such people end up being in bondage. I am concerned that I did not hear anywhere where you sounded sympathetic to these people. You have never even said a prayer for them. That being the case, we want to release you now. We will take a bit of time as we digest all that we have heard from you, after which we shall take our recommendation to those who sent us with an agenda to find out what the church should do with you. Please, note that, it is not about what to do with the homosexuals and devil worshipers but about what to do with you as an individual."

Meanwhile, six of them left the room, and one was left behind and came to me, he said;
"Moderator I wanted to let you know that the issues you are raising were privately discussed and I happened to be among those delegates picked to discuss the same. It was found that your agenda may have negative repercussions on the GA floor. It will be so divisive to the Church and it would demoralize the so-called homosexuals. Just between you and me, some of us are very sympathetic to the homosexuals and devil worshipers. I will not be surprised that they are birds of a feather."

This is the time I was given the information on my unexpected retirement. This man then embraced me and he was already shedding tears as he tapped on my back. Finally, he said; *"Moderator the Lord is with you, He will not abandon you as you soldier on to protect His kingdom. You will be constantly in my prayers. God is faithful."* Having said so, while wiping some tears in his eyes, the man left.

Shortly thereafter, I headed for the GA meeting. The deliberations of the day went on and at one point, I raised my hand and by God's grace, the Moderator gave me the opportunity to speak. It was then I raised three issues but not without interruptions from the chair in line with the raised hands from the floor on points of order and points of information.

I asked the church to terminate their partnership with PC (USA) because of their biblical diversion from the truth as they were ordaining and solemnizing the same sex marriages. I told the delegates that such kind of spirit was very dangerous in the spiritual realm as far as our church was concerned.

On 19th April 2012, I called upon the church to form a commission to investigate the rampant spread of homosexuality in the church and reminded the delegates of the fact that during my tenure in the GA office, I had defrocked six pastors for the same evil actions.

I asked the delegates to form another commission to investigate the reasons behind the rampant corruption in the church. The misuse of church money was smelly in the eyes of God. The same commission would also look into the issue of immorality in the church which was defiling the denomination especially when it involved the church leaders.

Having voiced out my feelings in the midst of murmuring and insults, one of the delegates said, *"Moderator, we should not dwell on Githii's call because it is not part of the agenda we have."* That statement was supported and seconded and the matter ended there.

After the meeting, quite a number of people congratulated me for the courageous move but regretted the fact that they could not come to my support for fear of being victimized by the GA officials and, more so, by the homosexuals. These liberals kept on threatening anybody who would dare expose them. But there were those sympathetic to the homosexuals who also talked to me. One of them said,

"PC (USA) is our main donor and there is no way we can surrender that money. After all, we do pray over that money. And as for the commission, such a move would definitely have a report as an outcome and that kind of report would leak to the media, something that would strip the nakedness of the church. Your observation is true but the path of your approach is not acceptable. No wonder, as I hear, they have prematurely retired you. I hope you have a copy of that."

I told this man,
"My joy is that I have cleared my conscientiousness. Like Pilate, I have washed my hands. But what I know is that this denomination is under God's

judgment. I find it unfortunate that PCEA has decided to accommodate it. It is no wonder this denomination will experience a lot of turmoil on its spiritual journey. You cannot hide a leopard and it fails to eat you or your children. There is no well that can produce both salty and clean water at the same time."

The GA ended on a Saturday, and I received the letter barring me from the PCEA the following week on Tuesday.

I realized that the issue of homosexuality in the church needed further action. I therefore persistently called upon the PCEA Church to form a commission to investigate the extent of homosexuality and devil worship in the Church and to advice on the way forward.

FORMATION OF A COMMISSION

In calling upon the Church leadership to set up a commission to investigate the mushrooming of homosexuality and devil worship, I had in mind such a commission that the then President of Kenya, Daniel Toroitich arap Moi had formed. This was after he realized the rampant spread of homosexuality and devil worship spirit in Kenya. In other words, the President appointed a 9-man commission in July 1994 headed by the late Catholic Bishop Nicodemus Kirima.

Exactly a year later, the Kirima Commission prepared a bulky report, which was privately handed to Moi at State House, Nairobi. A widely read newspaper, 'The People', had this to review, *"We can now disclose that Moi's kitchen cabinet advised against the release of the report because it may have triggered disclosure of big names involved in the vice 'including one or two members of the very committee that investigated the same.'"*

The President had ordered the probe in the wake of a series of ritual killings, claims of demonic attacks in schools and mysterious road accidents in the country. The report of the Kirima Commission concluded that, *"Devil worshipping had penetrated into the roots of the political, economic and religious powers in the country through Freemasonry."*

So highly placed and connected were the Freemasons that the commission reported and admitted its inability to fully penetrate and expose it. Conclusively, they said, *"In view of the conflicting information regarding the activities of Freemasons, and given the secretive nature of the society both to its members and to the general public, the commission strongly recommends that the government institutes appropriate machinery to further investigate its activities"*, said the Kirima Commission.

Students in high school and colleges told the commission how they had been recruited by other students or teachers into the cult and the details of the rituals they went through to become members. Students showed the commission incisions on their bodies that had been used to draw blood. One student from a Kisii SDA Teachers College told the commission that he had participated in eating human flesh and blood.

Another student from Kiambu led the commission to the house where he was initiated into the cult at Gigiri area of Nairobi. In the report the commission found that the cult existed in Kenya and attracted a substantial following among the wealthy and powerful. This was specifically through being members of Freemasons Society. According to the report, the Freemasons have temples (lodges) in all the major towns in Kenya like Nairobi, Nakuru, Kisumu, Eldoret, Kitale, Nyeri and Mombasa.

On the strength of the allegations, the commission summoned top leaders of the society. The society denied the accusations. *"They impressed upon the commission that most of their members are people holding responsible positions in both public and private sectors and are men of high integrity who could not be involved in activities they had been accused of."* Nevertheless, the masons, as they are also called, conceded that they were a secret society arguing that, *"Like any other societies, we have our own secrets."* They said that Freemasonry was not a religion but had a religious basis in that, the prime qualification for entry was a belief in a Supreme Being.

They also informed the Commission that; *"they were involved in many charitable activities and that signified their concern for other people's welfare,"* says the report of the commission. The Commission subsequently requested for a site visit to one of the lodges to verify some of the statements by the masons. Thus, *"A visit was made to their lodge along Nyerere road in Nairobi. The Commission was taken on a guided tour by senior officials led by the Grand Secretary, in full view of members of the press and was also shown a video tape on a Freemasons function in England presided over by the Duke of Kent,"* says the report.

I therefore raised a motion to this effect in this GA. I pleaded with the Church to form a commission like the one the Kenya government had formed some years back aimed at investigating the rapid mushrooming of Devil worship in Kenya. In calling upon the Church to do Likewise, my aim was to make it go to the root cause of this menace which was deeply dehumanizing the spiritual and physical welfare of PCEA.

I was concerned that this *"virus"* could as well contaminate the Church just as it had done to the PC (USA) from whom PCEA had adopted this spiritually destructive element into the Body of Christ. My argument was that the Commission could find out the extent to which this virus of homosexuality and devil worship and the consequent rampant immorality, had penetrated into the Church. The commission would then have come out with some recommendations on how to have it eradicated. This is what happened with the government commission, the so called *"Nyayo Commission of Inquiry."*

Though this commission withheld most of its finding because it turned out that many of the key government dignitaries were involved, it did caution *'Wananchi'* (public). For example, in the East African Standard of 20th September 1996, President Moi is quoted to have warned that, *"Wananchi and students to be on the lookout for devil worshippers as this form of perverted idolatry was very real in Kenya."* He said that it was a very strong movement carrying out rapid recruitment in all the sectors of the society and was being carried out by evil people. According to The Finance Magazine, this Commission had come to a conclusion that, *"The practice of the Devil Worship was rampant, finding its way to individuals, institutions and society in general."* The reference to institutions here includes the Church as well.

6 IDOLATRY IN CHURCH BUILDINGS THROUGH SYMBOLISMS

OCCULTIC POWER INFLUENCE

It is unfortunate that the Church worldwide has embraced evil symbols almost in totality. No wonder the universal Church is marching in accordance with worldly orders. Consequently, it has become so weak that it seemingly appears not to have enough spiritual energy to counterattack the powers of darkness. I can, without fear of contradiction, say that at least 60% of the church sanctuaries have been defiled in one way or another. This is mainly through the way the money for church construction was sourced out, the entrenchment of evil symbols and how the churches acquired their names. A name carries a blessing or a curse.

The occultic powers not only affect the Church, the immediate environment of the building but also extend their tentacles to a huge area of its surroundings. It is no surprise that the precincts and vicinities where the pioneer missionaries first settled, (where the so-called Mother Church is located), are chronically impoverished and also appear to suffer curses and seem to be dominated by oppressive spirits.

This is true of mother Churches established by the mainstream Churches including: Presbyterians, Anglicans, Methodists, African Inland Church and the Roman Catholic Church. One would expect the early missionary settlements to be the most developed areas, but they are by far the most backward compared to other recently initiated settlements in terms of physical and spiritual developments.

Unlike these recent developments, the so-called pioneer missionary settlements have taken years to develop. And even this development is promoted by new-comers who are buying land in those locations. The reason for this lack of development is that the missionaries gave a half-baked gospel, with an eye in taking over the land in Kenya. Again, the Church buildings of those mother Churches had some occultic foundations. Church buildings were filled with all kinds of evil and satanic symbols characterized by tall steeples, tainted window glasses, as well as on the walls, windows, floors, pulpits, seats and roofs. Church buildings on the other hand were designed in the shape of Masonic symbols.

In my endeavor to educate the church masses, I did point out the fact that in the occultic world, steeples are a representation of obelisks (which are meant to represent the male organ)'*phallus*'- which symbolizes fertility, virility and masculine power- procreation, strength, and creative forces of life. (*You can Google, Obelisk- Wilkinson, R.H (2003)*).

Jeremiah refers to Obelisk in Jeremiah 43:13. Hepropolis, the '**City of the Sun**,' was a centre for Sun-God worship and was recognized for these sacred pillars. You have probably seen obelisks and may not have known what they represent. An obelisk is a rectangular monolithic column diminishing upward with the sides gently inclined but not so as to terminate in a pointed apex, but to form at the top, a flattish pyramid figure by which the whole is finished off and brought to a point (Ron G. Campbell).

It is comparable to the end point of a pencil, only that the one for an obelisk is triangular in formation. Campbell gives a classic example of an obelisk to the centre of the cross axis of the federal district of the United States, in Washington, D.C. He says, "*There you will see the Washington Monument, a 555-foot representation of the original obelisks of Egypt*" p.78) –Obelisk picture p78.

It is no coincidence to find obelisks raised in public places especially in big cities and busy road junctions. In church buildings they are disguised as 'steeples' but in reality they are obelisks, a represenation of the sun-god.

People elect Masons in all fields of life because they blind people through their manipulative charitable hypothesis; as Campbell puts it, "*They are men of charity and good works. They remain unchallenged as 'the world's greatest philanthropy…' These services to mankind represent an unparallelled example of the human fraternal commitment and concern of this unique and honourable fraternity.*" (P.23).

No wonder,many of them end up being elected in positions in governments, organisations and institutions including faith based institutions and organisations and NGO's. They also find their place as bankers, lawyers, judges and so on. Unfortunately, such have nothing to do with God,Christians and other faith based institutions (the God of Abraham, Jacob and Isaac and Jesus Christ) they worship the Great Architect of the Universe whose representative symmbol is capital **G** and whom they as well worship through the representation of numerous symbols. Hence, their philanthropic spirit has strings attached. It is a bridge to entrench their satanic symbolisms in the communities, institutions, including church buildings, schools, hospitals, business premises and transportation (roads), vehicles and all kinds of public means of transport and so on. In this way, the recipients are hooked in the bondage of the dark world.

In fact, all the instructions in Freemasonry's myseries are communicated in the form of symbols. The square and compass is the most widely used and known symbol of Freemasonry. In one way, this symbol is a kind of trademark for the Freemasonry....The symbols of the first three degrees of Freemasonry are drawn from the medievial stonemasons' guilds, the profession which it **'spiritualizes.'**

The grand lodges claim that they are simply the custodians of these ancient symbols, that is, they protect them from change. Yet do not seek to intepret them.

Other references to this include; **'The Complete Gods and Goddesses of Ancient Egypt'**, Budge, E.A.W. (1902). **'The Gods of Egyptians: Studies in Egyptian Mythology,'** Hornung, E. (1999). **'The Ancient Egyptian Books of the afterlife.'** This is true in all sanctuaries built by the ancient empires including- Egyptians (*Osiris, Isis and Horus*); Greeks (*Zeus, Hermes, Diana/Artemis*); Romans (*Zeus, Jupiter, Venus*); Israel (*Baal, Asherah/Astarte and Tammuz*); Babylonians (*Nimrod as Baal or Sun god, Semiramis as Queen of Heaven symbolically represented by the Moon, Tammuz represented by the stars*).

This is why we have the representation of the sun, moon and the stars entrenched in various Church buildings as in the case of the churches that were built by the missionaries. But it is also good to say that this entrenchment of evil oriented symbols in the sanctuaries by secret societies has taken even a higher application in most of the modern Church buildings among all the denominations. I estimate that 70% of Church buildings worldwide are victim to this.

It is unfortunate that the genuine Church leaders and their followers are ignorant of this hidden stumbling block to the real gospel truth or call it, satanic spiritual manipulation. Paul pointed to such satanic representations entrenched in temple buildings when he said, "*As I walked around and looked carefully at your objects of worship, I even found an altar with this inscription*: **To Unknown God**" (Acts 17:23).

What Paul refers to as objects of worship were the entrenched satanic representations of Greeks, Romans, Egyptians and Babylonian gods in various forms including, symbols, images, statues of human, animals and various physical features. Ezekiel talks of the same where in the book of Ezekiel we find him talk of the temple thus; "*So I went in and looked, and I saw portrayed over the walls all animals and all the idols of the house of Israel*" (Ezek. 8:10- emphasis mine).

Note that these were various representations of idols entrenched on the walls of the Temple which was referred to as the House of God. In modern language, the House of God is the sanctuary. Jeremiah laments on the same thing when he says, "*The people of Judah have done evil in my eyes, declares the Lord. They have set up their detestable idols in the house that bears my name and have defiled it*" (Jer. 7:30). Note the negative effect of the idols; *they have '**defiled**' it*. And this is the main agenda of the occultists; to defile the sanctuaries and likewise, defile the worship that is carried out in that supposedly House of God. Unfortunately, they do it in a disguised and manipulatively manner such that, the undiscerning believer cannot realize the presence of evil in the sanctuary. Instead, they see them as decorations.

Their minds have been so compromised to an extent that some will even fight with what I am exposing here. They think that these are crazy thoughts. But the Bible affirmatively confirms this kind of unyielding spirituality when it says, "*The man without the Spirit does not accept the things that come from the Spirit of God, for they are foolishness to him, and he cannot understand them, because they are spiritually discerned*" (2 Cor. 2:14).

What then happens when the sanctuary gets defiled? Again, Ezekiel has an answer when God tells him to tell the Israelites, "*Therefore as surely as I live, declares the sovereign Lord, because you have defiled my sanctuary with all your vile images and detestable practices, I myself will withdraw my favor; I will not look at you with pity or spare you*" (Ezek. 5:11). This is exactly what happens when a sanctuary or any other building for that matter accommodates idols.

God withdraws His grace; He abandons the house that is called by His name. This, he further affirms in Isaiah 42; 8 when he says, "*I am the Lord; that is my name! I will not give My glory to another or my praise to idols.*" Yes, Jehovah Shammah, the Omnipresent withdraws His presence and what do the people experience? Jonah has an answer on this for he says, "*Those who cling to worthless idols forfeit the grace that could be theirs*" (Jonah 2:8).

The presence of idols in the church buildings has a huge presence in the Bible. We can regrettably observe that church leaders are involved in serving these idols knowingly and unknowingly. That is why Ezekiel is instructed by God to go into the temple and witness the flooding idols within its walls and laments when he says: "*So I went in and looked, and I saw portrayed all over the walls all kinds of crawling things and detestable animals and all the idols of the house of Israel….were twenty-five men with their backs toward the temple of the Lord and their faces toward the east, they were bowing down to the sun in the east*" (Ezek. 8:10, 16). The same is true of the present church buildings. These 25 men could as well be a representation of even church leaders.

JOHN CALVIN: CHURCH BUILDINGS IDOLATRY

When John Calvin founded the Presbyterian Church in Geneva, Switzerland, in 1559, his main focus on Church reformation was the revival of Apostolic Church worship, the Church government and the destruction of images and idols in the then, Roman Catholic Church buildings. According to Christopher Elwood in his book, '**Calvin**: Armchair Theologians', "*Religious practice has the tendency to equate God's power with material things.*"

Accordingly, Calvin aggressively attacked the presence of images and idols in the sanctuary because to him they violated the first two of the Ten Commandments; "*you shall have no other gods... and you shall not make for yourself an idol...*" Calvin insisted that having images in the sanctuary was "*a false distinction, given human psychology and our tendency to worship what is tangible and visible as opposed to the spiritual worship we owe to the invisible God.*" Calvin claimed that painted or colored windows tapped the sunlight blowing out the environment occultly. He was totally opposed to the installation of coloured/ tainted windows in the sanctuaries.

Calvin further observed that "*A human mind is a perpetual factory of idols that makes us prefer... to worship our fabricated and domesticated gods to respond to the living God.*" Accordingly, Calvin insisted that;
"*No images, drawings or sculptures of any kind would be in the sanctuary because once you have looked at the image, the damage has been done in your mind. This is especially because the worshippers' mind having been set into a worshipping environment the moment one entered the Church building, the mind is already set to grasp any image, sound or words as part of worship and spirituality.*"

It was with that in mind that;
"*Calvin criticized freely the religious ideas and practices of his day. And he did so in order to distinguish truth from error. Error had become confused with truth simply because they carried with them the weight of* '**Custom and tradition**.' Calvin advocated that, "*Presbyterian Church should put efforts to expose error and distinguish the living God from false and idolatrous depictions which became a hallmark of Calvinism*" (emphasis mine). Ironically, it is in doing this that the liberals in PCEA were ever at war with me – a move that finally made them kick me out of the denomination.

Thus, when I decided to expose the presence of entrenched idolatry in church buildings, I was practicing the real Calvinistic spirit. John Calvin would have applauded me, and he possibly did it from the heavenly perspective. For Calvin, the applauding would have been especially when he noted that most of those symbols were related to Freemasonry symbols. Important to note is the fact that I felt so empowered by the Holy Spirit to carry on this mission, pointing to the direction the Church should follow.

One thing that confirmed that I was on the right track was the way the Freemasonry fraternity got disturbed. For example, one doesn't need to be a scholar in psychology to smell a rat when two prominent politicians who were non-PCEA members rushed to the Church of the Torch, Kikuyu, to protect the symbols when a local newspaper came up with propaganda that I was visiting that church with a demolition squad.

It made me realize even more the fact that there was something fishy and especially when the said politicians were suspected to have some attachment to Freemasonry. (This will be elaborated in detail later in the book). It is important to note that churches like the Church of the Torch, St. Andrews Church, Nairobi and Watson Memorial Church, Kikuyu, among others were built by Scottish missionaries who essentially carried the spirit of Freemasonry.

It is important to note that among the pioneer missionaries who came to Kenya, most of them were influential Masonries in Scotland and elsewhere in Europe. They also claimed to have founded Christianity in the so-called, 'third world countries.' They planted the so-called churches, but in reality, they planted Masonic lodges.

It is worth mentioning that Freemasonry is not foreign to the Scottish Church. A good pointer to this case is the Sunday Standard Newspaper of the 25th January 2004, that had highlighted some key people worldwide who had been or were known to be Freemasons. On page seven, it read in part, "*A Church of Scotland minister is credited with rewriting the Masonic constitution. Also, Dr. Steel, a former Moderator of the Church of Scotland, is an already confessed Freemason.*" Important to note is the fact that Dr. Steel was at one time the minister of St. Andrews Church, Nairobi.

This then tells us that Dr. Steel was not only a 'church minister' but also a representation of Masonic Lodges with St. Andrews Church as one of them. No wonder the Scottish missionaries introduced a superficial gospel wrapped in a spirit of deception. That is why they had to suppress not only the role of the Holy Spirit in the Church but even the mention of the name, 'Holy Spirit.' This is true of all denominations that are referred to as Mainstream Churches. Such include the Presbyterian Church of East Africa, Anglican Church of Kenya, Methodist Church and African Inland Church, among others.

Their Church buildings were put up by the missionaries and flooded with occultic representations. This is also true of some of the Pentecostal Churches. They unknowingly inherited these occultic spirits from their mainline mother Churches. The saying is true, '*Like mother, like son.*' This is even more visible in the wide use of tainted glass windows. Why are they tainted? Windows are meant to let light into the building. The tainted glasses block the light. It makes no sense.

FOCUS ON SYMBOLS IN CHURCH BUILDINGS

The entrenchment of evil symbols in Church buildings was of great concern to me. This is why in my Moderator's Report of the 19th GA, which was held on 14th April – 18th April 2009, I earnestly called upon the Church to spiritually and prophetically denounce all that was putting the church in the bondage of the devil. This included the occultism upheld in church buildings. This was the time Rev. Gathanju was being installed as the incoming GA Moderator after the moderator's consecration on December 3rd. 2008.

As an incoming Moderator, Rev. Gathanju had written a speech in which he unknowingly seemed to support my calling upon the Church to have her spiritual ears and eyes open to discern the evil concealed in the symbols. The theme of his speech was: **My people are destroyed for lack of knowledge** (Hosea 4:6a). He hit the nail on the head and exposed the fact that there were things that were causing both spiritual and physical retardation in the life of the Church which people needed to be educated on to bring about a breakthrough in the entire life of the Church.

The theme went hand in hand with Jesus' words, "*You shall know the truth, and the truth shall set you free*" (John 8:32). In fact, the theme emphasized what I had strived to instill in PCEA Church. Thus, Gathanju's 19th GA theme was a result of his assessment of the Church's spiritual bondage. He realized that something was 'eating' up the Church over the years. But he did not seem to know it, yet he was not ready to go by my exposition of the idolatry and wickedness, including homosexuality and devil worship, that was prevalent in the denomination.

Simply put, Rev. Gathanju's theme looked somehow ironical. On one hand, he had all times resisted my advocacy in calling upon the church to negate the evil that was infiltrating the church through foreign traditions imported into the church through evil overseas influence. This included the entrenchment of pagan symbols in the church buildings. On the other hand, like other '*good*' Presbyterians, Rev. Gathanju was advocating for the sustainability of the spiritually dry Scottish traditions including a drum that was used to lead songs in the church. Of course, the drummer was an old man in every church, which I had already done away with. Rev. Gathanju could not see anything wrong with the church logo though in this, he was not alone. Almost all the people in the church were misled by that very enticing Kiswahili word JiteGemea, meaning self-reliance, which was a Masonic manipulation with Capital **G,** a representation of the Masonic god, GAOTU.

His campaigners used the kikuyu slogan, "*gucokia rui mukaro*," which means restoring the old course of a river that had drifted. The meaning of this was that during my Moderatorship, I had changed the old church traditions from the reformed ones to the apostolic ones.

In other words, the incoming Moderator was among the people who fought me because of my continued aggression to expose paganism and wickedness that was polluting the Church. In fact, since my speech in that GA was literally based on the exposition of evil symbolism entrenched in the Church buildings, the Masonic and New Age Movement-oriented symbols in the sanctuaries, Rev. Gathanju, who had already assumed the Moderator's Chair tried through all means to block me from reading my speech.

He gave the liberals a lot of time to champion the debate and block me from reading my speech. That attitude was fueled by the fact that I had slides and power points to portray some of the symbols appearing in some Church buildings, especially those at the Watson Memorial Church, Church of the Torch, and those earlier removed from St. Andrews Church in Nairobi. All the symbols were to appear on the screen as I progressively read the report. That was what the liberals feared most. In fact, were it not for the courage exhibited by Rev. Dr. Alphonse Kanga, I could not have read my speech. Dr.

Kanga finally opened the door for me to read the report when he challenged the seating Moderator by asking,

"*Moderator, I don't understand why the reading of this report is being blocked. It is as if we have already had the report read, and since we haven't read it here in the GA, how do we even know the content of the report? It is not until the report is read that we will then have the comments and questions fronted. In this case, we should stop behaving as if we already heard the report being read. I am aware that we have individually read the report but that is not authoritative until it is first read on the floor of the GA. And for this reason, I am proposing that we let Dr. Githii go ahead with the reading of the report. This is what our constitution stipulates.*"

Alphonse's sentiments were supported by a group of people which then paved the way for me to read the speech. But I was barred from portraying the slides. I then embarked on reading my report. But then the Moderator harassed me so much that I could not read the report harmoniously. I was cut short now and then by people from the audience, still insisting that I should be stopped from going on with the reading. But there were those who called out that I be allowed to have the slides exposed progressively as I read the report. But the Moderator categorically directed that there was no way he could have those slides exposed as it could lead to the splitting of the church, and that would have consumed a lot of time. The Moderator said: "*We cannot have the whole report read because we had already individually read the report as we had those dockets for some time. Also, in regard to the displaying of the so-called evil-influenced symbols that are portrayed in the Church buildings, we cannot have such exposure to the delegates. Such will create turmoil and division among the delegates. I would hate to start this GA in a bad spirit.*"

He went on to say,

"*As you can see, the theme I have floated to the Church indicates that I am aware of some not-so-good spirits that have blinded our Church leaders and members. My aim is to have the Church plunged into some teachings so that they will come to know the truth, as Hosea had called Israelites to give an ear to the prophet's utterances in the book of Hosea 4:6. We have also had to adhere to the minutes and resolutions of our courts and committees. I concur on the fact that Dr. Githii had embarked on teaching the Church on some of these things but it is his approach that has brought him into collision with our Church Practice and Procedure and also the traditions. I totally disagree with the exposing of the slides.*"

In spite of the interrupted reading on my report to this GA, I managed to pass the message on the fact that those were some of the things that were eating up the Church among others. It was and will always be that the presence of satanic symbols, which act as objects of evil contact in the Church buildings, will continually weaken the church both physically and spiritually. One common characteristic of these symbols, whether on the windows, walls, on the floor, on the roof, on the pulpit, altar area or in the pews, is that they all look beautiful and attractive to the eyes. In fact, they appear as decorations or what we would call '*Artifacts.*'

But we should be warned that all that glitters is not gold. The Bible affirms this when it says, "*And no wonder for Satan himself masquerades as an angel of light…. his servants masquerade as servants of righteousness*" (2 Cor. 11:14-15). One question worth posing is: "*Where did all this evil beautification of the Church come from?*" One thing that I was much aware of was the fact that very few among the church leaders, or the membership for that matter, knew the source of the satanic symbolism. The devil had robbed them even the reasoning capacity to ask- Why have tainted window glasses that would rather do their duty to allow light into the building. These instead block the light from entering the sanctuary. And, what is the real representation of the so common colors of green, blue and orange/yellow?

In the midst of the murmuring and with some people shouting "*point of order*" and "*point of information*", God gave me the courage and the stamina to bulldoze through the speech.

I took the opportunity to explain to the delegates the background behind the evil symbols. I explained the fact that the origin of the idolatrous symbolisms and images, which were satanic presentations, went back many years. With many of the delegates paying attention to what I was saying, I quickly and wisely developed the story behind the Masonic movement, as highlighted in the next few pages.

I explained the fact that the Freemasonry Movement had its birth in the two countries that represent the "*early civilization*" –that is Egypt and Babylon. It all started in Babylon under the leadership of

Nimrod, who was a grandson of Noah. All the buildings in Babylon, especially the temples, were flooded with all kinds of idols, sculptors, images and statues, among others.

It is this Babylonian idol symbolism that spread far and wide, particularly through trade. These were then embraced by the Egyptians, Hindus, Greeks, Romans, Israelites, Phoenicians, and other races. Consequently, in the course of centuries, this evil religion spread all over the world. I told the delegates that the pagan gods had their temples flooded with all kinds of symbols that represented various gods and goddesses. For example, Lorna and Lucia, in their book Ancient Egypt, tell us that the Egyptian religion included: *"Hundreds of deities: many as local gods who became the focus of important cults, while some were borrowed from other cultures. Some deities were merged or 'syncretized' with each other, blending their attributes, sometimes allowing a lesser god to take on the distinction and importance of a greater one. Most of the major, or universal deities represented cosmic forces, such as the sun or the flood, or were associated with the mysteries of human life, such as birth or death"* (pg. 280).

As Lorna and Lucia further put it, *"The deity would be represented by a cult statue placed in the innermost part of the temple- in the sanctuary, which was the most secret and sacred area. Although the deities were often thought to possess creative powers.... They were also seen in human terms...the god's need for a house and family"* (pg. 148).

The temples had not only priests but also both male and female prostitutes. This was because the main pattern of worship of those gods was mainly through sex. This prostitution was not only physical but also mental. The channel of all this was through meditation and visualization. Through this avenue, the prostitutes were able to prostitute with the figures of people and even animals that were entrenched in every segment of the entire temple and mainly on the walls of the temple.

There were images of mating figures in the form of homosexuals, lesbians, men and women. There were those of people mating with animals, gods to gods and goddesses. All these figures had their actions and sexual organs greatly exaggerated to cause psychological and mental emotions and hence release the symbolisms in their minds to create some sexual arousal, leading them into the world of sexualism.

This is the kind of worship that the Israelites embraced while in bondage in Egypt. This is something that led to their confrontation with God because the first commandment forbade them from worshiping idols. Many of their kings got entangled in this worship. But there were those who embraced the true worship and were arms ups against idol worship, which they endeavored to destroy. For example, when Jehu took over power, "*He sent word throughout Israel and all the ministers of Baal came... They crowded into the temple of Baal until it was full from one end to another... Now Jehu had posted eighty men outside – he ordered... go in and kill them. So, they cut them down with a sword... they brought the sacred stone out of the temple of Baal and burned it. They demolished the sacred stone of Baal and tore down the temple of Baal*" (2 Kings 10:21, 24-27).

Using the biblical approach and trying in all ways to convince the delegates, I brought in this illustration of the Israelites, showing how idolatry distorted God's relationship with them to the extent that God said to Israelites, "*I hate, I despise your religious feasts; I cannot stand your assemblies. Even though you bring me burnt offerings and grain offerings, I will not accept them; though you bring choice fellowship offerings, I will have no regard for them...I will not listen to the music of your harps*" (Amos 5: 21-23).

It was in that regard that God saw the Israelites' worship as a mockery of Him because they were also worshipping the very idols in the temple, which made Him withdraw His presence from the sanctuary. As God put it, "*things that will drive me far from my sanctuary*" (Ezekiel 8:6). It is this idol worship that God revealed to Ezekiel when he told him to get into the temple "*and see detestable things they are doing here*". So, Ezekiel "*went in and looked, and I saw portrayed all over the walls all kinds of crawling things and detestable animals... all idols... in front of them stood ... Elders...Each had a censor in hand, and a fragrant cloud of incense was rinsing*" (Ezekiel 8:10-11).

Then God asked Ezekiel, "*Have you seen what the elders of Israel are doing in the darkness each at the shrine of his own idol?*" (V12). Ezekiel was even further surprised, for he says, "*I saw women sitting there, mourning for Tammuz.*" (Tammuz was the son of Nimrod and his wife

Semiramis). Upon further entry into the temple, Ezekiel witnessed that "*between the portico and the altar, were about twenty – five men. With their backs toward the temple of the Lord and their faces toward the East, they were bowing to the sun in the East*" (Ezekiel 8:16).

Note that these men were worshiping the sun, as the sun's orange colour is more noticeable at sunrise. It's no wonder, then, that God says, "*Because of all your detestable idols, I will do to you what I have never done… because you have defiled my sanctuary with all your vile images and detestable practices. I myself will withdraw my favour. I will not look at you with pity or spare you*" (Ezekiel 5:9). God was so angered by Israel's worship of the Sun, Stars, the Moon and all kinds of symbols, and He said, "*They will be exposed to the sun and the moon and all the stars of the heavens which they have loved and served and which they have followed and consulted and worshipped*" (Jer. 8:2).

In addition to this, I said: "*In fact, the first Freemason Centre outside the Holy Land was built on the St. Claire Estate in Scotland. This Masonic movement, in the course of the years, came to be embraced by all churches in Europe, including Kings and the Church Ministers. We should not forget that a Presbyterian Church minister by the name of James Anderson (1678 – 1739) was not only the person who formulated the codification of Masonic rituals but was also the author of the First ever Constitution of the Freemasons, which was published in 1723. Anderson ministered in the French Protestant Chapel in Swallow Street, London, where together with the 'gospel,' he was immensely involved in the Ministry of Freemasonry.*"

Scotland diluted the truth in the gospel. Most of the pastors turned into dry bones and, therefore, lost the aspect of the Holy Spirit, the Church's prime mover. Thus, though such pastors used the Bible, they, on the other hand, clung more to the Masonic interpretation of the scriptures as contained in the Masonic constitution. In most cases, the Bishops/Moderators acted as the heads of the Masonic lodges, holding the highest positions of "**Grand Masters.**"

In this regard, I likened the gospel received from the missionaries to '*an egg*' from which much of the yoke had been sucked out through a very small hole. Only a small portion of the yoke remained inside the egg. It is that small portion of the yoke that I compared with the small portion of the gospel message that the missionaries gave us. The missionaries, in this case, brought a gospel wrapped up with

Scottish culture and Masonic '*Religion*' with very little Christianity. This gospel then lacked the most important biblical content - the Holy Spirit and salvation. They brought us a dehydrated gospel. I could liken it to small yeast introduced and which percolated into the whole dough with time. It is by God's grace that this Gospel, like the yeast, infiltrated the whole world.

I further told the delegates that the Church was and still is, in many ways, operating under Masonic spirits and the Scottish culture. This is just as it was in the times of the Dark Ages of Roman Catholicism. That was why the PCEA and some other mainstream Churches were facing a lot of spiritual and physical challenges. It is important to note that Scotland was under Roman Catholicism for 922 years, from AD 637 to AD 1559, when John Knox founded Presbyterianism in Scotland. The history of the Roman Catholic Church during that time was full of malice. In conclusion, I said: *"It is unfortunate that the Church of Scotland lost the deep spirituality which John Knox infused it with. John Knox was so prayerful that the Queen of England was quoted to have said that she feared Knox's prayers more than a combination of many armies."*

I further told the delegates that Freemasons were the sole Church building architects. This fact is also voiced by Yvonne in his book, **'Freemasonry: Death in the Family,'** page 79, where he says: *"Architecture is a huge idol with Freemasonry. There is even the office of the Great Architect. The architecture of Egyptian pyramids forms the idolatry and witchcraft at the base of Freemasonry. To study, to learn, to develop and to think are also the idols for a person to be able to become a Master Architect."* Yvonne further tells us, *"The things built to Freemasonry are also protected by Masonic Guards in the spiritual realm. These Guards are very similar, if not identical, to the sphinxes of Egypt who guarded the pyramids. Spiritually, the false apostolic anointing of Freemasonry is determined to keep the Church a Masonic Temple"* (Page 80).

I went on to emphasize the fact that most of the Churches in Scotland had lost the spiritual worship focused on Jehovah God but turned the focus to the Masonic god, The Great Architect of The Universe. This god was symbolized by The All-Seeing Eye, which was also known as **Horus,** which was the guardian of Masonic Orders: *"The time is ripe for the Church to trace its footsteps back to the Apostolic Church.*

In any case, this is the Church that Jesus commissioned His disciples to launch."

Some people clapped while others stood up to affirm the truth that I had revealed. In fact, one person, in response to my message, wrote a note and had it passed to me. It read;

"That is a great revelation, and I am sure, like me, there are many people who have heard this truth for the first time. This then reveals the inspiration behind my successor, Moderator of General Assembly Rev. Gathunju's theme that my people perish for lack of knowledge. I just wish this message could be documented and distributed to all members of this Church." But the truth of the matter was that the message was not well received by all the delegates for even as I was speaking, I could hear further murmuring indicating that the message was a bitter pill for the liberals to swallow.

At that juncture, I said: *"Moderator, with all humility, I do request you to yield your heart and let me show the delegates a few of the symbols as a way to verify what I am talking about. As the delegates will see, these are some of the symbols found in some of the churches that were originally built by the pioneer missionaries, so that in reality the delegates can grasp what I am talking of and...."*

I was interrupted by one of the past Moderators who stopped me from presenting the slides, arguing that they would not add any value to what I had already said and that what I was saying was irrelevant to the strengthening and adherence to the practice and procedure and the long cherished Scottish traditions.

Unfortunately for me, that statement was supported by a number of other liberals, and I was finally blocked from displaying the slides. I knew that they became aggressive in blocking that display because they realized that their hypocrisy/manipulation would be exposed. But some insisted that I continue reading. And so, I did.

In conclusion, I told the delegates that unless the PCEA removes all Masonic idols from the churches and institutional buildings, their relationship with God will continue to be distorted. I had told them that God would not watch as people worshipped Him together with Mammon. God has categorically spoken through prophet Isaiah when he said, *"I am the Lord that is my name! I will not give My glory to another or my praise to idols."* I, therefore, called upon the delegates to look for ways to dissociate the Church from the Freemasonry/Illuminati influence.

Having delivered my speech/report in which I forcefully echoed all that the Lord had revealed to me, I retired from the Moderator's Chair. From that point, I was referred to as the Past Moderator, and I sat in the area reserved for the past Moderators. It was important that I used a bit of force in reading my report as it was biblical, for the Bible says: *"From the days of John Baptist until now, the kingdom of heaven has been forcefully advancing and forceful men lay hold on it"* (Mt. 11:12). After all, as Timothy puts it, *"For God did not give us a spirit of fear, but a spirit of power, of love and self-discipline"* (1 Tim. 1:7).

Nevertheless, I was greatly encouraged by the many people who came to me at lunchtime congratulating me for what they called an eye-opening message that I had incorporated in my report. A number of people even thanked me for my endeavor to fight the evils in the Church, including Idolatry, devil worship, corruption, and misappropriation of Church funds, among others. I remember one of the delegates telling me: *"I just wish you had another term as the GA Moderator; you could have brought every negative aspect of this church to an end. All could have turned into history. I fear what will happen now that you are not the Moderator. People fear that some of the things you had dealt with will crop up especially the corruption and the misappropriation of funds, which was so prominent before you had taken the reigns as the GA Moderator."*

He went on to say: *"I am afraid the present leadership might be compromised and become part of the corrupt system. The good thing is that, since you are courageous and God uses you, and as a past moderator, you will still be putting bumps so that, at least, things will not explode especially things to do with corruption. I consider you as a strong voice in this church, but I also know that the liberals would manipulate things in all ways to block you from carrying out your God-given mandate- the non-compromising spirit."*

In response, I said, *"Let us leave everything to God. It is His church, and He will know the best ways to shepherd it. Otherwise, thank you so much for your positive observation in regard to my tenure as the GA Moderator."*

The slides they rejected include those symbols entrenched in Watson Memorial church, the Church of the Torch and another Church located at Ng'enda in Gatundu, Kiambu County. It does not matter how much the human mind will try to suppress the truth; God will always reveal it in His own timing. Following is the elaboration of the same. I will now highlight the ones at Watson Memorial church as an example:

I. WATSON MEMORIAL CHURCH

Watson Memorial Church was the first Church building constructed by the Scottish Missionaries in Kenya. It, therefore, marks the birthing of the Presbyterian Church of East Africa, which comprises Kenya, Uganda and Tanzania. This pioneer Church building is located at Thogoto next to both Alliance Girls and Alliance Boys high schools. It is also adjacent to Kikuyu Hospital and was dedicated in 1911. It was named after the pioneer missionary, Watson, hence, 'Watson Memorial Church.' He belonged to the Church of Scotland Mission (CSM), which in 1955 changed its name to the denomination we now call the Presbyterian Church of East Africa. Watson died in 1907, leaving behind his wife, Minnie Watson, who endeavored to carry on the mission work.

Watson Memorial Church is an outstanding example that reveals the fact that, just like the other mainstream Churches, the Scottish missionaries brought the distorted 'gospel' of Christ. Instead, they were propagating a gospel that was intertwined with pagan religion with its attachment to the Masonic/Illuminati and New Age Movement. They subscribed to their beliefs and practices - products of the ancient occult mysteries and traditions that originated from Babylon. This fact is well demonstrated by the representations found on the tainted glass windows at Watson memorial church walls. It is a Church building loaded with occult symbols. Some of the symbols are hereby explained as follows:

The steeple with an attached Cross with all sides equal. A Cross with all sides equal is not a representation of the Christian Cross as we know it.

These are the symbols installed inside the building:

The horned symbol in the upper arched window.

WATER SPIRITS
REPRESENTATION(BLUE)

SUN GOD

MASONIC SIGN

STAR

MOON GOD

LAZY 8

1. "Jesus'" Masonic sign

One obvious observation while looking at the tainted window in Watson Memorial Church is the Masonic sign that the crucified 'Jesus' is portrayed as having made. One will note that there is the manipulation of the said representation of a crucified Jesus. The representation is all Masonic. The occultist is aware that the manipulated picture of Jesus will not be noticed by an ordinary eye. It will appear enticing through the decorations and the beauty portrayed in this tainted window picture.

Why portray the Masonic sign as indicated in 'Jesus' right hand? This is because what you call Jesus here is a Masonic god, the Great Architect of the Universe (GAOTU), and whose representation is the Sun god.

2. The sun god

To the right side of Jesus' head, there is the picture of the sun-a god with a human face and the head of this god is encircled by the radiation of the sun (the glow). This is the worldwide recognized representation of the Sun-god. The worship of the sun originated in Babylon. (Just Google "*The origin of sun god worship.*")

3. The moon god

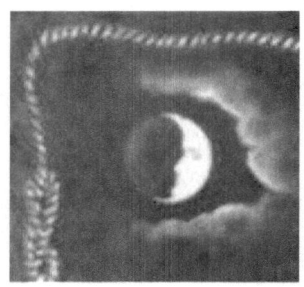

To the left of 'Jesus' head is the moon god. In the Masonic world, the Moon is treated as a goddess and is always represented with half human face. Its origin is the wife of Nimrod, known as Semiramis, whom the Babylonians worshipped as the moon goddess or Queen of Heaven. (You can Google "*Moon as a goddess.*")

4. The star

Somewhere at the bottom of the stained window is the star, which is a representation of the god Venus – the Roman goddess of love. Valentine's Day is based on this goddess of love, which is Lucifer in spirit. The Oxford English Dictionary refers to the planet Venus as Lucifer. Hence, this star is a representation of Lucifer. It occultly activates the spirit of immorality, poverty, violence, unbelief, hatred, homosexuality, and lesbianism, among others. This star is a representation of the Pentagram. (You can Google *Occultism attached to pentagram*) as a way of getting to deeper understanding of what this star represents.

Also notable are the decorations marked all around the frame of this stained-glass window. These decorations in the occult world are referred to as Lazy 8, which is a representation of various gods all originating from:

The Egyptians – *Osiris, Isis and Horus*
The Babylonians – *Nimrod, Semiramis and Tammuz*
The Israelites – *Baal, Asherah, Ashtoreth and the spirit of Jezebel*
The Romans – *Saturn, Jupiter and Venus.*
The Greeks – *Zeus, Hermes and Diana/Artemis.*

(The reader can Google all these gods for more information.)

5. The upside-down cross

This is another very common Masonic symbol that is meant to ridicule and demean the Cross of Jesus. This symbol is hung on the wall. In the Masonic First-Degree vows, the first thing the candidate performs is to break the Cross, which is meant to dissociate oneself from Jesus Christ of Nazareth and the entire Christian fraternity. This symbol appeared in the Kenyan newspaper, the Daily Nation, on Sunday, June 13, 2010, when a story was written in connection with the historical background of the Church of the Torch. From the notes that were compiled by the task force set up by H.E. DT Moi, the then President of Kenya, to investigate devil worship activities in Kenya, the upside-down cross was found to bear another name, southern cross, which was also found in the Masonic lodges and it is intended to ridicule the Christian cross and religion. This cross is used widely, including being engraved on some jewelry, clothes and tattoos.

6. Picture of chalice/grail and upside down cross.

On one of the walls at Watson Memorial Church is a cloth hanging on the wall bearing two images, one showing the chalice / Holy Grail and its shape is that of a Holy Communion cup. The Freemasons hold this cup in high esteem. They believe that it is their duty to look after this magical cup containing the blood of Jesus which they also call 'The Philosopher's stone.' It is therefore a very vital symbol to Freemasons who originally formed a secret society and came up with propaganda that when Jesus died, Joseph of Arimathea brought a chalice and harvested the blood of Jesus and hid it. They believe they are the offspring of Mary and Jesus and therefore take it as their responsibility to take care of this magical cup which contains Jesus' blood which they also call 'The priory decisions.' The Chalice is their principal symbol. It is also associated with the legendary King Arthur. (The reader can Google names like, chalice, Holy Grail, upside down cross, king Arthur, etc.)

Also noticeable on the Watson Memorial Church wall is the cloth hanging on the wall with two images on it, one being an **Ankh** or Egyptian cross or **Crux** as **Anta** and the other being the pagan god known as **Dagon** in the form of a **fish**.

Ankh is an ancient occult symbol associated with immorality, fertility cult -a symbol holistically used in numerous occult rituals. In both the Babylonian and Egyptian mythology, it is identified with the worship of sun god called "*Ra*" where the worshipper seeks power from this '*supernatural*' god. Commonly, the Ankh is attached to a chain and then worn around the neck as a necklace sometimes in the form of a horn-shaped bone. It is Texe Marrs who in his book: 'Mystery Mark of the New Age', says that: "*The New Age claims that the wearer of ankh jewelry will be the beneficiary of wisdom, peace, prosperity and long and healthy life. The circle or the oval at the top the cross is a sign of fertility. In truth, the ankh is a defiling example of a satanic circle surmounting the cross...it attempts to depict Satan as supreme over the sacrifice of Jesus*" (Pg. 112).

From the book: '**The origin, practices and traditions of Halloween,**' **Ankh** is described as the ancient symbol of immortality and fertility - a satanic rite symbol. It is an emblem to identify the wearer as; a worshiper of the sun god '**Ra**,' a seeker of satanic beliefs and who practices worship to the unknown gods of the supernatural. The wearer acknowledges the sun god '*Ra*,' works the voodoo of the unseen world through this idol. This idol is very common in women's necklaces. It has over the centuries been used as a good luck charm by occultists and the superstitious people.

Dagon, a god resembling a fish is one of the dominant gods in the occult world. It is a common feature among the Freemasonry, Illuminati and New Age. This was the chief Philistine's god. The fish is a representative of this god, '**Dagon**.' (*For further understanding, the readers can Google*). It is the same god mentioned in Judges 16:23 and 1Sam. 5:2. This god is also entrenched around the main entrance to the Presbyterian University of East Africa. Also found at the main entrance of this university is the entrenched Cross on the floor in form of a logo. As one enters, he or she is made to demean the Cross by stepping on it. No wonder the university has been in a lot of turmoil and at times threatened with closure. (Google *'Ankh' and 'Dagon.'*)

Notable around the altar area at Watson Memorial Church is the doomed metal cover fixed on the ground and slightly protruding above the ground. This is where the ashes of Watson's cremated body were buried. It is therefore Watson's grave. This makes the Church building a representation of a grave. From this grave, a wide crack runs along the floor heading to the center of the main door. This crack is joined by another crack that originates from the altar in the northern side where an occultic pot is placed and from its bottom on the ground- at the center is where this crack originates which also leads towards the main door then joins the one from the grave and the two cracks merge into one proceeding towards the main door entrance passing through its center (dividing the door in the ground way into two) before it extends outside.

This is an indication of the strong occultic powers attached to the occultic points of contact. Is it by coincidence that wide and big cracks would start at the grave and another from the center of the occultic pot and then the two join to form one big crack dividing the Church floor into equal parts and going through the very center of the door? The answer is no! This reveals the presence of evil powers. That explains the fact that the building is nothing else but a Masonic Lodge disguised as a *'Christian Church.'* For your information, this building was fabricated in Scotland and brought as pieces of structure by sea. It is no wonder, it carries Masonic symbols.

It is the Masonic altar that has been in control of the entire denomination over the years. It is an altar intertwined with the Scottish Culture and the Traditions of the Elders. This Church will never be at peace as long as this satanic altar is speaking over the denomination. It is the mother altar of Satanism. It represents many of the physical and spiritually premature deals. Trying to expose this altar put me at loggerheads with the PCEA leadership. No wonder they stopped me from displaying it the GA.

Other things the reader should not lose sight of are the three outstanding colours that are noticeable on the tainted glass window at Watson Memorial Church. These outstanding colours include **Orange, Blue** and **Green**. These colours represent the Sun – god,

Water Spirits and Mother Earth goddess or Moon – god or Queen of Heaven. We can learn what such colours represent through Elizabeth Chare, who, in her book, '*Corona Class Lessons pg. 53*,' tells us that in the occult world: "*Colours have a peculiar fascination for New Agers. Evidently, as part of the initiation rites, aspirants have their visual sense overwhelmed by a colourful, vibrating explosion of lights, hypnotizing people... New Age leaders preach about the seven rays of the initiation, referring to the colours of the rainbow... the seven colours of the rainbow are said to be "qualities of the godhead to which a person can aspire.*"

In the world of Freemasons, Illuminati and the New Age Movement, each of the three colours have specific representation; the **green** colour represents the **Mother Earth goddess**, green being the colour of the vegetation that covers the earth. The occultists worship the earth likening it to a mother who feeds her children just as the earth feeds people. The **blue** represents the **water spirits**. The waters are the residential places for powerful demonic spirits. The occultic world worships these spirits, blue being the colour of the waters. Have you ever wondered why the witchdoctors like operating around the waters?

The **orange/yellow** colours represent the **Sun god**, the colour of the sun being orange. The sun is the most widely worshiped object in the occultic world. It is no wonder then that these three colours are the most outstanding ones in all the tainted Church glass windows worldwide. The reader should be aware that the freemasons dedicate these images, colours by chanting evil over them at the same time chanting evil rituals thus turning them into satanic altars. They actually take what is good and turn it to breed evil influence even around their surroundings. Along the road or contact objects, they act as black spots.

In most cases, the occultists will present these colours in Christian oriented images (pictures] that appeal to the human eyes. For example, they would portray them on the windows as those of saints, Jesus, Apostles or any other biblical oriented images and designs, yet their main aim is to camouflage the representation of evil powers ingrained in the image. To the innocent Christians, the colouring looks wonderful but they do not realize the defilement being caused by such evil bent colours in the sanctuary environment.

Christians, as I have always maintained, should ponder and ask, if windows are meant to bring light into the sanctuary, why then block the light through the coloring or tainting of windows? Colours are the most widely used symbols by the occults to defile the Church buildings. This defiling also happens during the praise and worship sessions, where in most cases the flooding of various colours flash about. These hypnotize the worshipers with demonic powers taking control. Worshippers shout thinking that they are worshiping the Living God but in reality, they have been conformed to worshiping Baal, the Masonic god. These are the same floodlights and stroboscopes dedicated to evil that throng discotheques, entertainment joints, and even some churches today including in matatu's.

These colours tap the energy of the sun and create frequencies cum vibrations that defile the church environment thus distorting people's minds and creating emotions. It is no wonder therefore that many of the main church windows or altars are built or designed facing the East, where the sun rises from.

This was happening to Israelites when God said, "When you spread out your hands in prayers, I will hide my eyes from you; even if you offer many prayers, I will not listen...Take your evil deeds out of my sight." (Isaiah 1:15-16).

Another demonic representation in the Watson Memorial Church's tainted glass windows is the hidden shapes of triangles. Occultists make use of dedicated triangles just as they will do with a dot in a circle or a pentagram. It is **Texe Marrs** who, in his book, '**Mystery Mark of The New Age**', highlights the fact that: "*The triangle represents the combined energies of Satan, his false New Age 'Christ', the demonic angels of hell and mankind. In this way, in the spiritual realm, the environment in the Church building gets into turmoil through the energies of Satan that raise vibrations in the Church environment. And the word of God preached loses the power, and the worship in many cases, does not ascend to a higher level. Though it may seem to be high, it could go even higher... There are certain evil powers in operation, which are a creation of Illuminati/ Masonic strategies that have been 'eating up' the Church like a mole over the years. Remember, the devil's desire is to have the pathway to God sealed forever.*"

Texe Marrs further educates us on the fact that; "*New Age and Illuminati and Freemasons followers are told that the following idols or symbols are very important for their spiritual uplifting into the occultic world: The Lotus, the triangle, the cube, the point in a circle, the ley lines, certain signs of the Zodiac, and the Holy Grail. Also mentioned are the following animal forms- the goat, the bull, the dragon, the lion, the dog and the bear*" (Pg. 165 -166).

The reader will only need to have a strong spirit of discernment and then take a glance inside the Church buildings. It will be quick to notice at once, the many triangles and other occultist representations that are deep-seated in the sanctuary whether on the floors, roofs, windows, doors or walls. In most cases, there is a symbol fixed on the floor just outside or inside at the main entrance door. It is strategically placed such that one has to step on it as they enter the sanctuary to switch off the spiritual aspect in the Christian and reconnect that person to the evil influence already browsing in the sanctuary environment. It is no wonder that David Ickes, in his book: **'The Biggest Secret'**, wonders why the Church continues to uphold occult symbols yet: "*The triangle and other New Age symbols.... are almost always chosen for their occult value and significance. For example, the triangle is the most popular of all occult symbols and I find no justification for its use by Christians... We must contend with the fact that overwhelmingly, the New Age... views the triangle as a mystical and anti – Christian symbol at its best. Why should we stubbornly insist on making the triangle into a sign of positive value if its use can be misconstrued and is subject to so much detriment?*" (pg. 1290).

Another occult representation at the Watson Memorial Church tainted glass windows is the **heavenly constellation** which is in form of collective stars. In the occult world, the stars are a representation of Tammuz or Horus, the son of both Nimrod and his wife Semiramis, the founders of Babylon and its accompanying worldwide Satanism. This representation releases negative energy over the environment within its location. Occultists greatly focus on the heavenly bodies in their worship.

This is why God is so concerned with those who would promote this kind of evil. Job speaks of this when he says; "*If I have observed the sun when it shines, or the moon moving in brightness, so that my heart has been secretly enticed, And my mouth has kissed my hand; This also would be an iniquity deserving of judgment, for I would have denied God who is above"* (Job 31:26-28). Duet.4:19 offers the same argument when it says; *"And take heed, lest you lift your eyes to heaven, and when you see the sun, the moon, and the stars, all the hosts of heaven, you feel driven to worship them and serve them, which the LORD your God has given to all the peoples under the whole heaven as a heritage"* Jeremiah says, such, *"will be exposed to the sun and all the stars of the heavens, which they have loved and served and which they have followed and consulted and worshipped"* (Jer. 8:2).

Suffice it to say that all these occultic symbols that were entrenched in Watson's Memorial Church including those ones portraying a 'Jesus' showing a Masonic sign, the sun–god, moon- god, Tammuz (Venus), the cracks on the floor, chalice, the Lazy 8 and the upside-down cross, tell it all regarding the missionaries' association with the Illuminati or Masonic spirit.

Remember Watson's Memorial Church building was construction in Scotland and then shipped to Kenya in sections. It was therefore made in form of a Masonic Temple hence saturated with dedicated Masonic symbols. The Christian converts were brainwashed to embrace it as a true representation of a Christian Church building while in reality it was and still is a Freemasonry temple (lodge). The god worshipped inside the building was none other than and still no other than the Masonic god known as, Great Architect of the Universe. This is also the sun–god (Nimrod), hence, the reason for the presence of the sun - god, Moon god and Tammuz in the Watson Memorial Church tainted glass windows.

It all points to the fact that the missionaries were bound by the spirit of paganism and hence, esteemed the worship of the moon (Queen of Heaven), the earth as Mother Earth goddess and the Sun as the male god. It is even ironic in that, over the years, Watson Memorial Church has as well acted as the habitation of children's Sunday school where they assemble for Sunday school classes. Thus, over the years, the children have been exposed to pagan spirits right from childhood and they grow up bound by the spirit of unbelief. It is until recently that it is no longer put into this use.

II. THE CHURCH OF THE TORCH

Another example I can highlight on a church flooded with masonic symbols is the church of the Torch. This church reflects the truth that the missionaries founded Masonic temples which they disguised as Church buildings. This is a gigantic Church that took five years to build (1928-1933).

In its neighbourhood is Kikuyu Hospital, both Alliance Girls and Alliance Boys High Schools, Thogoto Teachers College, the Nairobi University College of Education and next to it is the Presbyterian University of East Africa (PUEA).

This Church is another classical example of the occultic Church foundation raised by the missionaries in their Kenyan mission field. This Church is a den of occultic symbols. One will only need to look at the windows and their tainted glass and all those pictures/images of people portrayed on the walls. One will even note a picture of a person stepping on a snake. Don't be deceived by the *'Jesus'* holding a lamb, pretending to declare, *'I am the good shepherd.'* The so-called good shepherd is the Masonic god, the Great Architect of the Universe. Otherwise, this picture and statement have a hidden Masonic interpretation. The staff that *'Jesus'* is holding has its tip ending in form of a snake's mouth. In the Masonic understanding, the whole staff is a snake. The colours; blue, orange and green are visible as part of the tainted glass windows. Remember the saying, *'All that glitters is not gold'* or what Paul told the Corinthians, *"For Satan himself masquerades as an angel of light"* (2 Cor. 11:13–14).

The **All-Seeing Eye** at the top of the upper front wall of the church and in fact the whole wall is an occult representation. The arched shape of the windows marked with 3 vertical bars and one horizontal bar – making three attached **distorted crosses**. It has a big steeple, visible from far. A **steeple** is treated as a male sexual organ by the secret societies. Until recently, all sanctuaries in Western countries had to have a steeple running high above all other buildings in a specified area. It was an occultly domineering edifice. Another name used for the steeple is **Obelisk**. An obelisk is a tall four-sided monument with a pyramid like shape at the top. Typically, it has a pointed tip, a *'pyramidio.'* It from ancient Egyptian and is associated

235

with the **sun god 'Ra'** believed to serve as a connection between the earthly and divine realms.

Notable also is the fact as we have seen that the tainted glass windows are strategically placed facing the Eastern side so that they can easily **tap the rays** of **sunlight** and especially in the morning when the worship service is going on. The **rays activate witchcraft** and cause occultic vibrations that would then pollute the environment of the sanctuary as explained earlier. One other thing one is likely to experience in the church of 'The **Church of the Torch'** building is the **spirit of fear**. There is a feeling of **mysterious fear** that embodies a person and especially if one is alone and the worst would be if one is inside the building alone at night. The environment is saturated with dread. Rather than that feeling of God's presence, one is invaded by a spirit of fear. As I grew up, this is the Church we used to go to. By then, there were **several owls** that had made their habitation on the ceiling at the base of the steeple.

Most of the things that make part of the Church of the Torch building include the shape of the lamps that have a connotation of Masonic influence. The pulpit is also adulterated including the embedded cross in a circle. This cross is designed in form of an X which has a negative connotation. It's center acts as a representation of a dot in the circle. The evil represented in this cross is concealed by referring to it as, '*St Andrews Cross*' Why St. Andrew's? Did St. Andrews die for humankind?

It was John Calvin the founder of the Presbyterian Church who argued that, "*The only one viable cross is the undistorted cross of Jesus. All other crosses are meant to demean the Holy Cross which is a symbolic representation of the source of our salvation. And because the Cross of Jesus is the source of salvation, the devil will do whatever it takes to distort it including altering its shape and representing it as + sign with all sides equal.*"

By engraining the distorted cross at the pulpit, the occults manipulate the preached Word making the message fall at the preachers' feet. Thus, any proclamation of the Word from that pulpit is nullified and instead of promoting the kingdom of God the Almighty, it glorifies the occults' god, the sovereign Satan – the

"Great architect of the universe." When we talk of occults we are talking about the Illuminati, Freemasonry and New Age Movement who also acted as pioneer missionaries.

Notable also, high up in front of the altar wall are these words written in Gikuyu language: *'Ninii Utheri Wa Thi'* (I am the light of the world). People will be deceived thinking these words refer to God the Almighty. Remember the Freemasons believe that their god is the creator, and also the light of the world – that is the creator and Architect of the universe. So, they knew too well that Christians would take those words to represent their God or even Jesus for that matter. To the secret societies, Lucifer is the bearer of light.

This truth is even revealed by one of the architects and pioneers of the Freemasonry Movement, whose name is Albert Pike and who is also the author of; **'Morals and Dogmas.'** On page 321 of this book, Albert Pike says the following about the Masonic god: *"Lucifer, the light–bearer! Lucifer, the son of the morning star! It is he who bears the light and, with its splendor's intolerable, blinds feeble, sensual, or selfish souls? Doubt it not."*

Over the years, and unlike in other Presbyterian Church buildings, there has never been a symbol of Jesus' Cross on the front wall of the Church of the Torch. Instead, where such a cross could be placed, are the words: *'Ninii Utheri Wa Thi.'* One time while speaking to some Church leaders in this Church as the Moderator of GA, I remember telling them, *"My call to the leadership of this Church is to install a wooden cross at the front wall"* but my advice went unheeded for a long time.

On the tainted windows at the Church of the Torch, are representations of snakes, the knight Templars, and many occultic symbols. What they call in Gikuyu language, *'Kanitha wa Irima'* (underground Church) and which acts as the boardroom for meetings, Church offices and the vestry. It is nothing else but an underground Sub–Masonic lodge. Equally, the entire Church building is a Masonic lodge - the mother of all Masonic Temples in Kenya, if not East and central Africa.

On the walls of this sub-lodge hang pictures of dead people, many among them who had not even confessed Jesus Christ as their Lord and Saviour. Some are honored for having held powerful positions in the government. Many, though labeled Christians, led a life of a high level of nominalism or a very secularized lifestyle, some being addicted to alcohol and immorality and others obsessed by the oppressive spirit that afflicts the poor. I happen to know the backgrounds of many of these people.

Just imagine, since its inauguration in 1933, this parish had never set apart a building that would be called an office until only recently after 88 years! What they had been referring to as an office is one corner of the sub-lodge. This is unlike the PCEA administration's way of life because today every parish in this denomination has well designed offices which in most cases are completely detached from the Church building. It is enough to say that no Church can be dedicated without an office.

For many years, the ministers at the Church of the Torch had been using the presbytery premises as their offices which are far from the Church building. But then, the Presbytery took what used to be the Church office and therefore had left the Church without an office. They then reverted to 'Kanitha wa Irima' as the Church's office. At one time the parish minister, Rev. Kabuba had attempted to start an office construction but it was blocked at its initial stages. Who would block such a viable project if not the people associated with the secret societies' influence? They want every activity to take place inside the Masonic temple, which in this case is the Church of the Torch and the inclusive basement sub-lodge.

CHURCH DESIGN

One thing that the reader should note is that, the Church of the Torch was built in the design of the occultic **ankh** symbol. The circular front part of the wall forms the loop (circular in shape) of an **ankh** and the winged sides make sidewise shape of the ankh. Also looking from the front, the Church's construction is in form of an upside-down cross Facing East.

Notable also is the symbol of the Cross entrenched on the floor in the altar area. One will also note that peculiar long distance between the leaders' seats at the altar and the pews where the congregation is seated which is at an abnormal distance-far from the people. This is common with most of the pioneer missionary churches. Is not the shepherd supposed to be close to the sheep? This distance evokes fear rather than respect and alienates the leaders from the led.

There is no way the 'shepherds' and the flock can interact in the Sunday worship in this kind of setting. When the pastor comes nearer to people, he is so elevated high in the pulpit, an indication that, he is not at the same level with the congregation. This is unlike PCEA Thirime Church which is a daughter Church of the Church of Torch. The Thirime Church in reality is far more vibrant in every way compared to the mother Church.

This was my constant message to PCEA, pleading especially with leaders to denounce those idols clinging in the houses of God. But my case was just as the Israelites resisted Jeremiah's message and accused him to the king saying, "*This man should be put to death. He is discouraging the soldiers…as well as all people, by the things he is saying to them. This man is not seeking for the good of these people but rather their ruin,*" And true to their words, "*They lowered Jeremiah by ropes into the cistern; which had no water in it but, only mud. And Jeremiah sank down into the mud*" and they left him there to die" (Jer. 38:4,6).

Did not Joseph's brothers do the same thing to him? "*They took him and threw him into a cistern.*" (Gen. 37:24). And by God's providence, Joseph was saved by his brother Reuben who advised the rest to have Joseph sold to the Ishmaelite's and he ended up in Egypt where at one time he became the prime minister.

Jeremiah, on the other hand, was saved by an Eunuch who reported Jeremiah's fate to the King. The king then authorized him to go and pull Jeremiah out of the cistern. Likewise, the PCEA liberals thirsted for my blood.

OCCULTISM BY DEFILEMENT OF THE CROSS

 There is also the defilement of the church of the Torch through the distortion of the Cross referred to as the **St. Andrews Cross** which in actual fact is a masonic symbol (More about it later). The cross shown above is imbedded at the pulpit of the Church of the Torch. A true Cross representing the **Cross on which Jesus was crucified** should not be presented or illustrated through a cancellation sign. Neither can it be placed in a slanting angle. As an enchanted symbol; it is aimed at rendering null and void all that is uttered from the pulpit. The occult disguises their presence by incorporating such symbols as a form of church decoration in the sanctuary. Satanic leaning crosses are painted or ingrained on the floor of the Church buildings.

Generally, it is not uncommon to find a cross entrenched from the main entrance door to the altar area or where people kneel during the time of baptism or weddings.

Please, Understand me. I am not saying that all sanctuaries be demolished. Mine is only to bring out the enlightenment/revelation as God has revealed to me. I am sure that the many others, whom I have made references to, can substantiate my findings. It is for the Church leadership to cleanse the sanctuaries and where a new sanctuary is to be built, the Church leaders should be sensitive and keen to ensure that no Satan related symbolism is included in the Church building. Neither should there be money raised through use of evil entrenched names like Harambee whose meaning we shall unravel later.

Unfortunately, there some of the top Church leaders belonging to the secret or underground evil fraternity of Freemasons, Illuminati or New Age Movement who will block any move to cleanse or remove the occult symbols from the sanctuaries. You will know them by their fruits. There are some symbolisms imbedded inside the walls and foundations including under the altar and on the roof tops. This is usually done at the time of construction of the church.

It was during a GAC meeting held at the Milimani Presbytery that I aggressively addressed the issue of symbolism in the Church buildings. I went on to impart this knowledge to the delegates. I informed them that occultists strive for ways to communicate with the evil world through the dedicated symbols. This they especially apply while the Church worship is going on. While the innocent members in the congregation are focused on the worship, the occultists - the Freemasonry/Illuminati and New Age Movement are busy activating the evil energy through the evil symbols fixed on the walls, the floor, windows and elsewhere in the Church building.

In doing this they apply what they refer to as meditation and visualization. In the book, '**Spiritual Growth in Youth Ministry**', the author, J. David Stone, talks about the methods used in meditation and visualization by the occultists in activating the powers of darkness. He says this is through symbols that act as contact objects just as we use power point to activate images on the screen. They use the power of meditation and visualization, just as the ancient pagans used to do. In most cases, they utilize a breathing technique during their meditation practice. They concentrate their thoughts on specific objects strategically placed throughout the church buildings. Thus, meditation and visualization are the two main avenues through which occultists advance evil into the world. According to David Stone, in carrying out meditation and visualization, the occultists are instructed: "*Repeat this breathing exercise several times. Next, try to imagine God; keep searching in your mind (for however long it takes) to form an image of God. When the image is there, you will know it. Do not worry if this first exercise takes a long time. After the image is clear, focus on it for as long as you can. You may have to fine-tune it by focusing on each part of the image and visualizing yourself with that image. Eventually it will speak*" (P70).

I continued to hammer this hidden knowledge to the delegates though I could tell from some facial expressions that not all were in agreement with what I was saying, yet I could at the same time see many jovial faces that seemed to say; "*Go on, and expose more of this stuff.*" I explained that within a church congregation, individuals

241

with titles like; elders, lay readers, Bishops, overseers, founders or apostles strategically seat themselves, some among the congregation and others at the front, to maximize the impact of activating evil powers through the various techniques they had been trained on. They do it so quietly and in disguise such that the unsuspecting congregation will not notice it. They pretend to be part of the worship but in reality, they are worshiping their god, the Great Architect of the Universe.

The ability of an image or symbol to spring to life, to move and speak within the receptacles of people's mind comes about through the technique of *"spiritual exercises"* which is an open satanic channel like an open field, in a hall or in a house and it is as effective as the method of manipulating the mind though images. The occultists study mythology to learn how to exercise the imagination so as to create living images and then guide them in the path of life. They thus become living objects of worship. Whenever people enter such a sanctuary, they become hypnotized and Satan's demons manipulate their minds like their own property.

It is therefore easy to realize why there is such widespread or mushrooming of evil symbols in the public transport vehicles like buses and matatus. Such occultic symbols dominate most of the business premises including many commercial and rental houses. It is not unusual to find dedicated symbols disguised in form of decorations set on the floor of such premises. This is more especially in the big shopping malls/supermarkets. Most of these evil symbols have their origins from Hinduism, Babylonians, Egyptology, Greeks and Romans. Many of these will be represented as chequered floors, many set at the point of entrance.

The Satanists believe that after having an image well entrenched into the mind through visualization, breathing exercises, positive imaging and other techniques, they can then summon their symbols that have been transformed into deities, to come forth and serve them. Indeed, they believe these dedicated symbols are alive, and can act and speak. According to Foster Bailey, in the book, 'The Spirit of Masonry', *"A symbol is a precipitation or appearance on earth which is rooted in an inner cause. It is an outer effect of inner livingness"* (pg. 59).

At that point, I cautioned the Church to guard the Church buildings from being adulterated by the Satanists and reminded them of Texe Marrs' concern, as reflected in his book, '**Mark of the Beast**', where he says: "*Of course, if a group or Church uses a symbol that is clearly occultic in nature, there is no reason to take this lightly. The pentagon, the horns, the Egyptian ankh, the crescent moon with an accompanying star, the Swastika, the triangle within a circle, the circle within a triangle, and the pyramid are virtually always a sign of satanic influence... we don't have to play into the hands of the Devil, foolishly excusing, explaining away, or too quickly dismissing such use*" (pg. 129).

THE PULPIT

The Pulpit remains the key and central part in a sanctuary. People purposely go to Church to adore God, but most importantly to hear the word of God as preached from the pulpit. It's no wonder then; the Pulpit becomes one of the targets of the devil worshippers. The occultists are always after distorting and diluting the preached word. That is why for many years, the PCEA traditions of the elders and the church lifestyle deems it antichristian to deviate from the tradition of remaining at the pulpit while preaching. Traditions have it that, any words uttered outside the Pulpit are rendered powerless and therefore, non-effective. Is this really true?

A Pulpit does not add any spiritual value to the preached Word. It is all the manipulation of the Scottish missionaries, most of whom were Illuminati or Freemasons and who came disguised as ambassadors of Christ but in reality, they were occultists. It is no wonder most of the Pulpits built by the missionaries were already adulterated through use of occult symbols. Some of these were buried under the pulpit walls and in other strategic places within the sanctuary.

Examples of Church buildings where occultic symbols were found buried in the Pulpit include; PCEA **Nyamachaki** Church in Nyeri and PCEA ya **Mumbi** Church located in Eldoret town. The satanic representations were discovered when those pulpits were being renovated. Things like human hair, bones and other questionable items were found buried under the very place the preacher stepped as he/she preached the word.

The same satanic symbols within the pulpit were found at St Andrews Church in Nairobi, St Margret's PCEA Mombasa, and the Church of the Torch, Thogoto, Kiambu County. Did you know that there are several pulpits that are constructed in the shape of certain symbols representing certain Masonic gods? Any sermon delivered from such a pulpit with dedicated satanic symbols embedded in them undergoes immediate spiritual nullification. In this case, the congregations just listen but the word does not touch their hearts because the preacher is under the control of evil powers. Such symbols were removed from the St. Andrews Church and some people who worshiped those idols in form of symbols left the church.

These days, one can even see some images fixed in the portable glass pulpits. What many Christians do not know is that, most of these images engrained in the glass pulpits are occultic in nature. It is therefore important that if one does not know the meaning behind an image entrenched in such glass pulpits, it is advisable to avoid using it. This is the same message I communicated to the PCEA leadership. Some images of the cross on glass pulpits are distorted. I asked them to caution their congregations to be conscious of the kind of pulpits they used.

I also, persistently emphasized that the leaders refrain from restricting the preacher to be bound in the pulpit area as they preached. This was seemingly a difficult thing to do. In one Business Committee meeting, one of the past Moderators accused me of, at times, moving out of the pulpit while preaching. He was so agitated that another past Moderator had to go and calm him down. He was widely supported by some clergy and elders who threatened to impeach me if I continued with the same pattern of moving out of the pulpit as I preached. One senior elder said: "*I have spent all my life being a faithful member of this Church, but I have never seen such a daring leader like our current Moderator who dares to get out of the pulpit, something that defiles our treasured traditions. This Business Committee should force him to stop this unbecoming behavior. The last time he preached in our Church, I walked out of the Church building the moment he got out of the pulpit, and many of the elders and deacons followed me. I could not continue sitting and watching him distort the image of the Church.*"

The meeting turned into a battleground, with at least 60% of the delegates rising in tempers. Some wanted to come and get me out of the seat so that another past Moderator could take up the seat as they deliberated the way forward in handling me. But surprisingly, there were at least 40% who aggressively supported me and who blocked them from coming to my seat. Since I am not the type to easily give up on what I believe, I convincingly said: "*There is no time I will ever give in to the pressure of people who want this Church to remain in the satanic domain. I will fight the good fight, believing and trusting that the one I am fighting for will never surrender me to the enemies of His kingdom. I am aware that I am saying very mysterious things to you just because you were fully brainwashed in these traditions since your childhood. But God does not want the future generations to spiritually walk the spiritual path that their ancestors walked through. This is why God is using me. And let me make this clear: this is a battle you will never win. I have a dream that, sooner or later, we will be swimming in some spiritual currents in this denomination. Our people have been spiritually living in the Westernized culture, which had been whitewashed as 'Christianity', which in reality is focused on occultism. It will not be long before God shames you as you watch preachers coming out of the pulpit. This will happen within your lifetime.*"

As I write this, my heart is filled with joy as I have witnessed the replacement of the enclosed pulpits with more portable ones, with most of them bearing the image of the Church logo. This trend has continued and before long, the stone built enclosed pulpits will be history. In this case, I did not labour for nothing. Furthermore, the trend in limiting the preacher inside the pulpit has continually faded away. Whenever I witnessed God's miraculous happenings, the thing that has always impressed me was the absolute quietness in which it was done. I was also impressed by the absence of anything sensational and dramatic from the mighty power of Freemasons and devil worshipers that had placed the Church under their bondage. Nevertheless, as I stood lonely in the midst of severe oppositions and confrontations but in the presence of the Almighty God, I realized how easy all this was for him to do without even the faintest effort on His part or any meaningful help from me.

I constantly heard God's inner words encouraging me through prophet Isaiah thus; "*See, I will make you into a threshing sledge, new and sharp, with many teeth. You will thresh the mountains and crush them and reduce the hills to chaff... I, the Lord, have called you in righteousness. I will take hold of your hand. I will keep you and will make you be a covenant for the people... See the former things have taken place and new things I*

245

declare; before they spring into being I announce them to you" (Isaiah 41:15; 42:6,9).

These same words were affirmed by Apostle John in the book of Revelation 21:5, *"He who was seated on the throne said, 'I am making everything new! 'Then he said, 'Write this down, for these words are trustworthy and true."* The words, *"**I am making everything new**"* was the 16th General Assembly theme, as directed by my predecessor, Moderator Jesse Kamau, which in reality was a prophetic utterance as the 17th General Assembly made things new under the guidance of my 17th General Assembly theme as found in Luke 13:8, stating, *"Leave it alone...and I will dig around it and fertilize it."* And speaking of mountains and hills, as stated above by Isaiah, the spiritual life of PCEA was marked by negative spiritual mountains.

But by God's grace, I managed to act in the spirits of both King Josiah and King Hezekiah. As recorded in 2nd Kings 18:4, King Hezekiah, removed the high places, smashed the sacred stones and cut down the Asherah poles. He broke into pieces the bronze snake Moses had made, for up to that time the Israelites had been burning incense to it. Likewise, as recorded in 2nd Chronicles 34:4, under the direction of King Josiah, the altar of Baal was torn down, he cut into pieces the incense altars... and smashed the Asherah poles.

Thanks to God who so miraculously used me to have the said mountains and hills leveled. It does not matter what people think about me; the fact remains that God used me to bring restoration into the Church. And all glory lands on His throne. The word of God points to the fact that when an individual or an institution is spiritually weak, such operates in line with the spirit of the world, yet *"We have not received the spirit of the world but the spirit from God, that we may understand what God has freely given us."* Otherwise, *"The man without the spirit does not accept the things that come from the spirit of God, for they are foolishness to him, and he cannot understand them, because they are spiritually discerned. The spiritual man makes judgments about all things, but He himself is not subject to any man's judgment"* (1 Cor. 2:12-14).

However, there is a dilemma in that God gives a revelation to a person but does not extend the same revelation to other people. Thus, the tendency is that when the person tells people what the Lord has revealed, they refute the revelation. This was true with Joseph when he told his dream to his brothers. They had even plotted to kill him in their denial of his dream. The same was true with Miriam. She led the way to question Moses' revelations from God. She and Aaron took it as a human creation/manipulation. They posed the question, *"Has the Lord spoken only through Moses? Hasn't he also spoken through us?"* (Num.12:2). And because of this, *"there stood Miriam-leprous, like snow."* (Num. 12:9). The same question was severally asked by PCEA leaders. They could not heed what I was telling them as the Lord revealed the truth about the crooked ways through which Satan was spiritually weakening the Church. Instead, and like Jeremiah, they were always seeking opportunities to stone me. But as God's word says in Psalms 18:2, the Lord remained the Rock in whom I took refuge; He was my Fortress, my deliverer, my Shield, my Horn of Salvation and my Stronghold.

In my humble acceptance of all the humiliation and frustration I encountered, I retained my focus on the power of God and the mysterious way of working out the puzzles we could not solve. I knew that straining and striving would not accomplish the work God gave us to do. Only God Himself works without stress and strain and never overworks. He can do the work He assigns to those who love him and whom he has called with a mission to accomplish. I realized that when we restfully trust Him to do it, the work will be completed and will be done well. And the only way to let Him do His work through us is to fully abide in Christ through the faith that He fills us and equips us to the maximum, enabling us to trample upon snakes, scorpions and all the schemes of the devil.

MODERATOR'S CHAIR AT THE CHURCH OF THE TORCH

Inside the Church of the Torch Underground Church (*'Kanitha wa irima'*) is the Moderator's Chair, which, in fact, is the Freemasonry Grand Master's chair. It was deliberately and purposely installed there to serve as a throne of Freemasonry / Illuminati. The Grand Master also carried the title of Moderator – hence, the seat is referred to as the Moderator's Chair. This Moderators Chair is a representation of a throne found in every PCEA congregation.

In fact, no other person is allowed to sit on the Moderator's chair apart from the parish minister and, to a certain extent, an ordained minister. Not even an elder and lay person can sit on it.

The shapes and decorations could differ, but there has to be a seat referred to as the Moderator's/Bishop's Chair. It is always a huge chair predominantly reserved for the senior pastor. Most of the mainstream Churches are also victims of the Freemason's spiritual imprisonment. This is especially because most of their missionaries were carriers of ungodly spirits of the secret societies. It is no wonder that there exist occultists in some of the top leadership positions in Churches. Thank God there are many good and faithful Church leaders who have not compromised with the powers of darkness. Such can be found in every denomination represented globally. But it is also important to say that, among those who qualify as occultists, there are many who do not know whether they have been recruited into occultism because, as we have established, most just find these people with a good charitable spirit. These are people who are so mindful of their comrades. They have no idea that they have been recruited into the world of darkness. Unfortunately, once recruited, it is next to impossible to withdraw because of the vows never to leave or to reveal the secrets of the secret society. At times, they are forced to sacrifice their relatives.

The Moderator's or Bishop's Chair was Emperor Constantine's invention, which was also called *'Ex-cathedra'*, which means the *'throne'* and was used by the judges in the Roman courts. This was adopted into the Freemasonry as a seat of high rank in the lodges and later introduced into the churches.

Regarding the Moderator's chair, I persistently pointed to the Church the fact that the origin of this chair was from the Freemasons. It was the seat for the Grand Master, the leader of the Masonry Movement that started in Scotland around 1307. This was the chair that was later introduced into the Church as the Moderator's/Archbishop/Bishopric seat. The Roman Catholic Church was the first to use it, but at the time of reformation, the same was adopted by both the pioneer leaders of the Church of Scotland and the Anglican Church. This was because most of the Church leaders, including clergy, were already initiated into Freemasonry. Such chairs were saturated with occultic symbols.

I gave as an example the moderator's chair found at Church of the Torch's underground lodge. I pondered: *"Would Jesus have chosen such a chair to sit on?"* One time, while speaking to the Church leaders in Meru, I said: *"The Missionaries failed to imitate Christ as the model of humility. They were bossy in many ways – a spirit that contradicted Jesus' call to take both the towel and the cross. If there was the spirit of humility, there could not be such a huge Moderator's Chair fraught with all kinds of symbolism in decorations. They lacked the spirit of servanthood. They were not after washing peoples' feet. Symbolically, it is hard for one to bend down from that Chair to reach people's feet and wash them. In fact, the position of the seat dictates that the minister be washed his/her feet. The Moderator's seat acts as an altar of power in view of the fact that the Moderator's Chair has its origin in the Masonic spirit of power and enthronement. I called upon the presbyteries to consider doing away with the Moderator's Chair from our sanctuaries. It only portrayed some sort of spirit of kingship, yet Jesus calls for the spirit of humility/servanthood."*

Regrettably, that was one area in which I never had a breakthrough. This is because people love power and recognition; hence, this message never found a landing point. The trend to use the Moderator's Chair has never changed in spite of the fact that most of these seats are rooted with all kinds of symbols including some distorted crosses. Some have their sizes so exaggerated that whenever a short person sits on them, his or her legs hang up in the air unless something else is provided for the legs to rest on!

Why all this trouble? Some Pentecostal Churches have adopted these high-powered, enthroned seats – a display of a highly elevated, powerful person. Do you think Jesus would have elevated himself in such a chair? Didn't he castigate the Pharisees for taking the seats of honor when he said, *"What sorrow awaits you Pharisees? For you love to sit on the seats of honor in the synagogues and receive respectful greetings..."* (Luke 11:43-NLT).

249

IDOLATRY INTERTWINED WITH THE PCEA LOGO

Aware that the PCEA logo had some spiritual undertones intertwined with occultic spirits, which were, therefore, a hindrance to both spiritual and physical growth, I had to take the bull by the horns to have these removed. It is for this reason that I had to go around to disseminate knowledge on the same.

In instilling the knowledge of idolatry entrenched in the logo to the church fraternity, I first carried out some teachings explaining how the Church logo was the property of Freemasons. I aggressively reached out to presbyteries, parishes, congregations and even Church committees, including the Business Committee members. I explained that the capital **G**, as entrenched on the logo, was a representation of the masonic god whom they referred to as the Great Architect of the Universe (GAOTU). However, many in the Church leadership were angered by my persistent teachings to disseminate that knowledge. Their fear was my getting support to eradicate this occultic logo that had for long spiritually suffocated the Church. Those who persistently opposed me kept on referring to me as a crazy reformist. In spite of this resistance and by God's grace, I kept on with the teaching to those who were willing. Congregants were spiritually blind to the occultists' evil operations through the entrenchment of occultly dedicated symbols. I remember one time, while teaching a group of Church leaders in one of the presbyteries, someone dared to ask me:

"*By the way, how did you come to learn about these seemingly mysterious findings?*" In answering this question, I said: "*I was also in the same boat of ignorance until I learned this truth while I was working on my doctorate degree at Fuller Theological Seminary in Pasadena, California, USA.*

I further said: "*Through my studies and research, I had come to learn how Freemasonry or Illuminati and the New Age Movement had the practice of entrenching their evil-oriented symbols on things to do with Churches, utensils, clothing, tools and all kinds of things that a human being would be associated with. For my doctoral dissertation research on the History of the PCEA, I went to Scotland a number of times and carried out intensive research at Edinburgh University and in the National Library. It was important that I include Scotland because all communication between the*

250

pioneer missionaries and the Church of Scotland are all archived at these two institutions- Edinburgh University and the National Library."

I went on to say: *"It was out of that research that I came to know about the infiltration of Freemasonry in the Scottish Church. Anderson, a Scottish Presbyterian minister, was the one who wrote the Freemasonry Constitution, which was published in 1723. No wonder most of the pioneer missionaries had Masonic affiliation. It was for those reasons that the Church buildings that were constructed by the missionaries were flooded with Masonic symbols, and it was good that the missionaries came because they introduced us to Christianity in whatever opaque form it reached us."*

I explained that it was through learning and researching that I came to discover that the capital 'G' as found in the PCEA logo was disguisedly a representation of the Illuminati god (**GAOTU**), who is simply Lucifer. To support my argument, I even quoted some of the people who were renowned architects of the Freemasonry Movement. For example, Albert Pike, in his book Morals and Dogmas, says, *"All prayers in Mason lodges should be directed to one deity whom all Masons refer to as **GAOTU**. He is addressed as the Heavenly Father, Eternal God, or Almighty Living God."*

I also referred to J.S.M. Ward, a Masonic authority who has written several important books on Masonry. In his book, '**Freemasonry**: *Its Aims and Ideals*,' he says, *"I consider Freemasonry as a sufficient organized school of mysticism to be entitled to be called religion."* It is this kind of teaching that I aggressively championed and which, at the same time, made me an enemy of many who leaned towards Masonic teachings. Mostly those who had entrenched themselves in the Church and higher learning institutions.

In My teaching engagements in parishes and presbyteries, I used to tell my listeners that 70% of the universal logos had some attachment with occultism. This is true of the logos in various institutions, which in reality defile those institutions such as schools, churches, companies, hospitals, colleges, universities, and local and global organizations. This was mainly the work of the Freemasonry, the Illuminati and the New Age Movement, who had a great global influence over the buildings. I advised my listeners especially those not well versed with these secret societies, should learn more through the internet.

251

As was the case with the PCEA, these demonic influences can be cunningly and discreetly fixed in church logos. The whole theme in the logo, in this case, had nothing to do with the Church's spirit of self-reliance; it was a cunning way to have the capital **G** centrally placed at the heart of the Cross meaning empowering the Masonic. Thus, wherever this logo is put, it is the Masonic god who is in control, be it on signboards, letterheads, vehicles, dressings and buildings, among other places.

As already hinted, the cross was placed inside the circle, indicating that its power was suppressed. It is Texe Mars, in his book, '**Mystery Mark of the New Age** page 110', who says that the Cross in a circle is; "*the most diabolical and heinous of all symbols...indicates...that, Jesus Christ is contained, or restrained, within the circle of Satan. Its suggestion is that a sovereign Satan holds authority over God.*" He further says, "*An especially powerful occult symbol is formed wherever the circle is used to contain another occult symbol within; for example, the pentagram is formed by enclosing the five-pointed star within the circle.*"

I brought to the realization of many listeners the fact that many schools that teach symbology in their curriculum have all agreed that this symbol (*cross in the circle*) carries powerful occultic powers. They are powerful satanic strongholds.

In a GAC held in 2005, I raised concern over the Church logo. I alerted the delegates that the logo had a Cross enclosed in a circle, which in the occultic world meant that the power of the Cross, which is the symbol of Christianity, was rendered powerless. There was also the Word 'JiteGemea' (*self-reliance*), whose symbol of representation is the capital 'G'. The capital **G** was inserted at the heart of the cross, with the word 'JiteGemea' running horizontally inside the cross's horizontal bar and the **G** centered in the cross. Thus, 'Jite' was in smaller letters, and so was 'emea.' But the capital G was so much enlarged that it occupied the central part of the cross-section of both the vertical and horizontal bars. I, therefore alerted the delegates to the fact that unless this symbol was removed from the Church logo, the PCEA would be held hostage by the powers of darkness.

This took many delegates by surprise, and they unanimously voted to have a new logo. I emphasized that the **G** represented the initial of the Masonic god- GAOTU. I, therefore, called upon the delegates to give a green light to come up with a new Church logo. A committee was formed to undertake that task, and it was not long before a new Church logo came into place.

Old Logo

New Logo

Note the position of the capital 'G' in the old logo. It is always advisable that when an evil altar is destroyed, a positive altar has to take its place. Thus, upon the destruction of the PCEA JiteGemea cross, it had to be replaced with one conducive and in alignment with the Holy Spirit of God. Thus, through my initiative and through the Business Committee, a new Church logo was introduced with an undistorted cross. The logo also carries an image of a dove, symbolically representing the Holy Spirit. This, I thought, was important as the denomination had rejected the involvement of the Holy Spirit in its entire life prior to my becoming GA Moderator.

The new Logo had a symbol of the 'Burning Bush,' an indication that the Church is ever at war with the kingdom of the devil, but it will never be consumed. This is the symbolism of the Burning Bush that Moses saw and which, though burning never got consumed. The logo has a representation of the Bible, including some key Biblical words: Faith, Love and Hope.

As indicated elsewhere, with the old demonic logo gone, the PCEA did undergo a real rejuvenation in its life. The only dilemma is that those officials who took over after my term of office was over as the

Moderator of the General Assembly did not have the same zeal to uphold the suppression of the occultic strongholds that continue to 'suck' the spiritual energy of the Church. They downplayed this move to have the Church totally freed from the occultic attachment.

I reminded them of Robert Raines, who, in his book, 'New Life in the Church' (1980), says, "Some structures in our Churches have to die in order for new structures to come into being by the leading of the spirit." This is not an easy thing because of the desire to cling to the old ways of doing things. Incidentally, the so-called new ways were what the early church flourished on.

I also re-echoed Michael Brown's affirmation of Robert's views in his book, 'Revolution in the Church: Challenging the Religious Systems, with a 'Call for Radical Change' (2002) (pge20) says, "Who wants that kind of revolution in the Church-a revolution that challenges our traditional styles and structures; questions our traditional methods and models; confronts our traditions forms and fetishes."

This truth was revealed to the PCEA after the Jitegemea Cross was removed. Many good things took place after that. The once regarded as impossible became possible. For example, Praise and worship flourished. The relationship with God took a new turn and rapid new births of prosperous projects, including the buying of the former Giriama Hotel, a five-star hotel at Mombasa that was renamed Milele Beach Hotel next to the Indian Ocean.

The Milele Hotel located at the PCEA Head Office also had its construction completed, and I dedicated it. Another Milele Hotel located in Nakuru town emerged. There was also decentralization, subdivision of parishes and presbyteries and improved ministers' lifestyles.

There were several other projects that emerged, including the launching of the Presbyterian University of East Africa (PUEA), where I became the first chancellor. Prior to my becoming the GA Moderator, the agenda to start a university by that name had been debated in the denomination's main committees and Church courts for twenty years.

7 IDOLATRY IN GOVERNMENT BUILDINGS THROUGH SYMBOLISMS

The genesis of the journey of my encounter with the presence of occultism through symbolism outside the church and other places oriented with power in the country was when I was invited together with other mainstream church leaders to parliament for the customary national opening session of Parliament. The details of this expose of strongholds and the aftermath are dealt with in detail in a subsequent chapter on controversies. However, it is important to understand that dealing with evil is no mean task. It is a highly dangerous and risky endeavour that cannot be accomplished without the power of God, who is able to do all things. It needs persistence and holy stubbornness that is risk-oriented. People who truly believe in God without reservation have learned to have stubborn courage to confront the powers of darkness without first considering possible harmful consequences or outcomes.

Scripture encourages through Luke 10:19, which says, *"I have given you authority to trample on snakes and scorpions and to overcome all the power of the enemy; nothing will harm you."* God's will becomes their will, and they desire to do for Him whatever He desires and commands. They strip themselves of everything and, in their nakedness, find everything restored a hundredfold. This is the move of the Spirit that embraced me when I was called by God to address the occultism that is flooded in the Kenyan Parliament buildings.

In my book, '**The Progressive Infiltration of Idolatry In The Universal Church- A Chronological Perspective,**' I have explained the negative impact of the occultists -the Freemasons, Illuminati, New Age Movement, and Humanists, among others. These groups come out with all kinds of manipulation to defile the universal Church or the body of Christ and even some national buildings that carry national duties, for example, the Kenyan Parliament. Two ways in which they carry out their defilement are to create paganism in a disguised way and, at the same time, entrench satanic symbolisms in the related buildings. I have also dealt with the same stuff in my book, '**Exposing and Conquering Satanic Forces over Kenya.**'

It is as a result of these revelations that one time, when I was invited to pray during the opening session of the Kenyan Parliament, I took the opportunity to point and pray over the occultic symbols that are so conspicuous and that overly flooded the Kenyan parliament building both inside and outside. God revealed these evil strongholds to me as soon as I got into parliament. I felt a very strong presence of anti-God spirits. I also felt like it was the cooking pot of all Kenyan misery. A cooking pot because all that regards Kenya in matters of national governance is brewed there. Thus, all that promotes or demotes Kenya in all its sectors of life originates from Parliament.

A handshake from President Mwai Kibaki

In this revelation, I felt called upon to curse all the satanic symbols in the 'K*enyan kitchen*,' I recognized it as a God-given opportunity. In any case, God had severally made it clear in my mind through the words found in the book of Jeremiah 1:10 that God had made me understand that my appointed ministry, among others, was to uproot, tear down, and destroy all evil-oriented strongholds. I recognized these strongholds in the presence of big snakes on the grills in some parts of parliament. As I was entering the parliament premises, I also noticed the Blazing Star positioned at the main entrance of the parliament gate. But it was when I got inside the parliament that I came face to face with all kinds of occultic symbols disguised as decorations. There were also symbols of croaking frogs, both charging bulls and rhinos with long horns. There was also some representation of witchcraft on the walls.

IDOLS ENTRENCHED IN PARLIAMENT

The idols that God led me to expose and with the help of the media, which were entrenched in parliament buildings, include:

SNAKES:

The snake-related symbols or images are representative of the serpent (*Lucifer*) who tempted Eve in the Garden of Eden. It represents a great source of lies and all kinds of manipulation. Thus, the snakes are satanically dedicated symbols in parliament. They are raised in order to influence the environment in parliament buildings with the spirit of lies and all kinds of manipulations, including the spirit of greed. Who will not marvel at the ease with which most **politicians** will say something today only to negate it the next day without blinking an eyelid?

Or take the greed for money that influences the **politicians,** for example. Has it not birthed the highest level of corruption in the nation? It would not surprise me if some politicians had snakes as pets in their homes, offices, and vehicles.

FROGS

These are mainly found at the front entrance of the Old Chambers of Parliament above the main door facing the High Court. While on both sides of the stairs leading to the Speaker's Gallery is the mural of frogs and crocodiles. Whereas these are the representation of water spirits, the frogs' croaking stands for the fruitless noise. No wonder legislators make a lot of noise all year round, but nothing productive comes out of it. Their debating leaves a lot to be desired as far as the advocating of the well-being of '*Wanjiku*' is concerned. Nothing comes out of their heated debates. All debates are for self-benefits. These are debates that lean towards the oppression of the poor and are aimed at milking the poor of hard earnings through a very strenuous hard life. This includes heavy taxation to the common citizen to finance their spendthrift culture in unnecessary foreign trips and lavish lifestyles characterized by ownership of 4WD guzzlers and massive properties, among others. They increase the prices of basics such as fuel, electricity, and foodstuffs, which touch the common citizen. Yet these legislators keep on increasing their salaries and allowances and constantly fight **political** battles. However, none of these battles are aimed at helping the common man. It is all about their greed and desire for selfish gain in political mileage. They play psychological games on the minds of '**Wanjiku**.' They **dramatize their ambitions,** including making **well-calculated** and **convenient changes** to the law as enshrined in the constitution to suit their selfish interests. And where need be, they use the law to **forcefully bend the same law** to achieve their **manipulative motives**.

THE CROCODILE

Crocodiles are known for having strong teeth, jaws, tough, scaly skin, and a powerful whip-type tail. They use these physical weapons(characteristics) to crash their prey. These leaders use their power to eat up the nation with their mouths filled with **sharp teeth** like those of a crocodile. They **mercilessly crush** and **tear down** all that comes their way to fill up their stomachs. Ezekiel 34:2, 4 describes such a scenario thus: "*Son of man, prophesy and say to them: 'This is what the Sovereign Lord says: Woe to you shepherds of Israel who only take care of yourselves! Should not the shepherds take care of the flock? You have not strengthened the weak, healed the sick, or bound up the injured. You have not brought back the strays or searched for the lost. You have ruled them harshly and brutally.'"*

The leaders' accumulation of wealth has no end. Like the crocodile's wide jaws, with its massive razor-sharp teeth, these **leaders ferociously attack and maul each other** during debates to the extent of **trading accusations back and forth**. At the same time, they symbolically whip each other in the same way as a crocodile would with its massive tail. Just as crocodiles have hardened scaled skin, they also cover one another, such that when they get involved in corruption scandals, none of the cases will ever be prosecuted. Also, remember that the majority of the legislators are initiated into occultism.

TORTOISE

This is another symbol expressly entrenched in parliament buildings. This carries the spirit of laziness. Legislators pass so many motions, but they do not bring them to fruition, especially those meant to help the common person (Mwananchi), commonly referred to as '**Wanjiku**.' The legislators' hearts are as hardened as the tortoise's impervious shell. Many are spiritually blind. Many of them practice witchcraft. Don't be cheated; these symbols are demonically dedicated through acts of chanting evil and evil rituals towards them.

WITCHDOCTOR MURALS
Such murals are entrenched in Parliament and symbolize witchcraft. Hence, the influence in the practice of witchcraft by many members of parliament, which also ties with the presence of the horn-like symbols in parliament- some of the paraphernalia used by witchdoctors.

CHARGING BULL

There are paintings of bulls in the charging position, and to the right is a charging rhino. These two symbols occultly symbolize sexual strength, agility, and the spirit of turmoil. These two spirits are very destructive to legislators in every aspect of life, including the breeding of immorality, sexual abuse, corruption, and family disintegration, with quite a number of them being divorced or having concubines. Most of them are sponsors of those looking for sponsors and leaning toward sexuality.

This bull is the same that was worshiped by the Babylonians and the Egyptians. The very god that Aaron, with the help of the people, molded to be worshipped when Moses was delayed in coming down Mount Sinai. This is the god known as Baal or the Apis Bull. It is the key god worshiped by many ancient people, including the Greeks, Egyptians, and Canaanites, among others. In Egyptian mythology, it is known as the bull-headed god worshiped in Memphis and elsewhere.

BAPHOMET
Encyclopedia Britannica refers to a Baphomet as an invented pagan or Gnostic idol or deity that Templars were accused of worshipping, and that was later embraced by various occult and mystical writers. A view adduced by Wikipedia and Anne Kamiya of study.com

(updated on 02/22/2023) affirms this position by saying, "*Baphomet is an occult, pagan, and religious icon and an anthropomorphic figure with the head and legs of a goat and the human body.*"

The Baphomet is an upside-down pentagram; the two upward points symbolize the devil's horns. The three downward points declare a denial of the Trinity. Satan's spirits are supposedly invoked by the downward position of the center point. This is also a symbol found in the Kenyan parliament building.

Source:www.bigstock.com

HARAMBEE AND THE GODESS 'AMBE'

People called me a reformist. One of the things that paved the way for me to be labeled a reformist was the ways in which I ventured into pointing to the occultism or idolatry that had been so entrenched in the country. For example, I renounced the use of the word '**Harambee,'** which is affiliated with a Hindu goddess, *'Ambe,'* believed to be a provider of energy.

The word Harambee, used widely in Kenya, has its roots in the **Coolies** (Indians) who were imported by the British to build the Mombasa – Uganda railway. Unlike other cultures, the Indians have millions of gods, each credited with having the ability to affect human life in a particular and specific direction.

The construction work was so strenuous and involved handling heavy metal and other fabricating materials. It is for this reason that Indians believed that they needed divine strength. They, therefore, found comfort in 'Ambe,' a goddess, as the source of their energy for carrying out this heavy manual work of constructing the railway. This goddess would be handy as they handled the heavy equipment, tools, and debris to clear the way for the railway line. After all, 'Ambe' represents feminine energy and is often associated with motherhood. Nurturing and protection. She is considered the primal energy, or 'Shakti,' in Hinduism and is worshipped for her strength, compassion, and guidance. The laborious work in putting up the railway included the excavation of rocks and logs and the carrying of the heavy rails. To be effective in their work, they called for teamwork in a cooperative way to lift together. As a way of getting ready to do so, they had to invoke the name of their goddess, 'Ambe,' to release the energy to enable them to lift the loads.

They chanted in the spirit of worshiping her. As they chanted in hailing their Goddess 'Ambe' in the Gujarati language in the hearing of the Africans, it sounded like 'Harambee' or rather, the Africans could not pronounce it the Gujarati way, which was not unusual. There are many other English words as well that the indigenous Kenyan people mispronounced, such as; 'Kimbo' for cables; 'Thogoto' for Scotland; 'Rumuruti" for Remote Route; 'Kirigiti' for cricket; 'Dagoreti Corner' for the great corner and so on. 'Harambee' was thus also picked up by the politicians and popularized as a pulling-together slogan by the pioneer politicians of the nation, especially when Kenya gained independence. The phrase 'Harambee' is therefore derived from the praise or hail to the Hindu goddess 'Ambe.' In effect, when one says 'Harambee,' they unknowingly honour a **Hindu** Goddess, '**Ambe**.' The name became a very popular political slogan and was especially used by politicians when calling their audience's attention before he/she started addressing a big crowd. It has dominated the Kenyan environment since then.

As a way of getting people's attention, the politician would shout, "*Harambee!*" He/she could repeat this between three to five times as the crowd would each time respond by shouting "*Hiiii!*" meaning, "*Let us lift the goddess higher and higher.*" Rather than giving the honor to God through whose help the British Colonialists were overthrown, the politicians led people to give that glory to this goddess, '*Ambe.*' It was this kind of idol worship that I was denouncing. To me, that

261

kind of idolatry was demonically *'sucking'* the nation of Kenya; economically, religiously, politically, and socially.

Much of the Kenyan media was following me very closely as I persistently continued to expose this occultic disguised evil. For example, Moses Njagi reported in the Standard Newspaper of 3rd January 2005, said: *"Presbyterian Church of East Africa Moderator Rev. Dr. David Githii yesterday took issue with the use of the word Harambee, saying it is satanic. Githii said Harambee is an Indian god, and its assimilation into local languages was tantamount to praising the Hindu goddess 'Ambe.' Githii said the word was only borrowed from the Indians, who were building the Mombasa – Kisumu railway line."*

He went on to say: *"This word Harambee, which got adopted by the Kenyan politicians and incorporated into Kiswahili language to mean,* **"Pulling together,"** *has since been turned into a unifying spirit for the country. Accordingly, Githii says, this word carries evil and therefore goes against the doctrines of Christianity."* The paper went on to say, *"Githii persistently denounces any use of symbols that are linked with Satanism and Freemason society. According to Githii, the word Harambee is therefore used in glorifying a Hindu goddess called Ambe and, in Gujarat, the first three letters 'Jai' or 'Jay' mean victory or hail in Gujarati; they are used interchangeably to express enthusiasm, support, or celebration in my thinking perhaps the Kenyans interpreted the Jai or Jay Ambe in their own way as sounding Harambee. In the formation of this word, Harambee means 'hail or praise.' Thus, this word in its original state is written (praise Ambe), but in the Kenyan way, the two words are combined to form a Swahili word, 'Harambee.'"*

He continues to say: *"Githii adds, 'I felt it a duty calling for me to urgently let the Kenyans know the truth behind this word, Harambee, for it is only through knowing the truth that people can be liberated from the schemes and manipulation of the powers of darkness.'"*

One of the things I had persistently been calling for change is the name of the Kenyan soccer team, **Harambee Stars**. My concern has always been the fact that this team is named after the goddess **'Ambe.'** It is, therefore, not a surprise to me that this team has for many years never qualified to participate in All African Cup of Nations, and if they ever did, as in 2019, they did not go far because they lost in the preliminary stage when it got eliminated by Senegal by three goals to zero. Why does this team keep on playing dwarfing soccer? The scripture in Isaiah 42:8 gives us the answer when it indicates that God cannot participate in giving victory to those who cling to idols instead of clinging to Jehovah himself. It is Him who is worth all glory. He declares, *"I am the Lord; that is my name! I will not give my glory to another or my praise to idols."* Jonah 2:8 affirms this by saying, *"Those who cling to worthless idols forfeit the grace that could be theirs."*

I took a lot of time going around the Churches countrywide, educating people to create awareness in regard to the influence attached to the word **Harambee,** which at the same time is the spirit of Jezebel/Queen of Heaven, which was causing havoc to the body of Christ and the nation at large. I also made it clear that the spirit was causing havoc not only in the church but also in the nation, more so because of the raised altars in its name. The goddess is entrenched in the Kenya currency, the Court of Arms, with raised altars in the name of **Harambee Avenue** and **Harambee House.**

In my seriousness in exposing this spirit, I had written about it in my book, '**Exposing and Conquering Satanic Forces over Kenya**.' I have exposed this spirit as the greatest defiler of the Kenyan population, the Church, and the government.

Let me re-emphasize the fact that knowingly or unknowingly, and unfortunately, upon the attainment of independence in Kenya in 1963, the political leaders led by the founding Father President Jomo Kenyatta in their endeavor to call upon the nation to act or pull in one accord in building the nation, acquired or coined the slogan '**Harambee**' which denied the foundation of Kenya from being based on the spirit of God but on the pagan spirit of **Ambe (Harambee)**. This spirit became the spiritual foundation of the nation.

It is quite unfortunate that the Church also embraced this spirit of the goddess **Ambe**. Almost all sanctuaries in Kenya have been constructed by fund-raising in the spirit of '**Harambee**' which then declares the pagan god, **Ambe** as the sole owner of the money so raised in this spirit. The money thus has some attachment to this spirit of goddess **Ambe**. This, in the spiritual realm causes some defilement to the House of God.

263

It is not uncommon for someone to hand you a **Harambee** invitation card and at the same time tell you, "*I am inviting you to a harambee taking place in our Church.*" These kinds of invitations are so widespread and include money raised for the Church pews, building a pastor's house, buying musical instruments, buying a Church land, buying of ministers' vehicles, meeting hospital bills, raising funds for supporting education and even in raising money for Church groups such as the youth, Woman's Guild and Mothers Unions among others.

As a **PCEA** minister, I witnessed a lot of such harambees constantly taking place in the entire life of the denomination. Similarly, other denominations have been birthed unknowingly in the same spirit. This is not to say that fundraisings are bad, No! The only bad aspect is the use of that word "*Harambee*", which is intertwined with a goddess spirit, meaning, the money so collected is credited to the goddess, just because the fundraising was done in her name and favour. The spirit of God gets peeled off when a Church building becomes defiled as it loses the divine anointing. It is not uncommon after a fundraising to hear people ask: "*How much did you raise in your 'harambee'?*"

This is what the book of Isaiah 42: 8 highlights when it says, "*I am the Lord; that is my name! I will not give my glory to another or praise to idols.*" The Church ought to take heed to Ezekiel's call to the Israelites when he called upon them to clean up the temple by saying, "*As surely as I live, declares the Sovereign Lord, because you have defiled my sanctuary with all your vile images and detestable practices, I myself will withdraw my favor, I will not look on you with pity or spare you*" (Ezekiel 5:11).

The presence of dedicated symbols, whether by Freemasons, Illuminati, New Age Movement witchdoctors, diviners, sorcerers, and all the kingdom of the devil, releases occultic bound energies that pollute targeted surroundings. This is what Kurt Koch, in his book, 'How to Deal with Occult,' refers to when he says, "*The vibrational spiritual energy released is transmitted from the shrine (altar) to their destination.*" Destination, in this case, is the minds of people so long as they are within reach and their minds are spiritually weak, hence venerable to satanic influences.

This happens in all kinds of buildings, as long as there are some satanic symbols embedded. But where there are God fearing people in authority, such people will go for complete removal of these symbols. That was and still remains my message to all who could listen to me. That is why I always emphasize the fact that the redemption of Kenya as a nation from these evil powers which are in all sorts of forms planted in the National Assembly, the Senate and the County Assemblies, will require a majority of genuine and unhypocritical God-fearing people within these pillars of power. Doesn't the Bible say, *"When the righteous are in authority, the people rejoice, but when a wicked man rules, the people groan"* (Proverbs 29:2). Again, in Proverbs 28:28, it says, *"...When the wicked arise to power, people go into hiding; but when the wicked perish, the righteous thrive."*

Time is ripe for Kenyans to address the Kenyan problems not from the physical human or tribal eyes. Our enemy is the devil whose main target is to disorient the lives of Kenyans through occultic manipulations. Let Kenyans arise and confront the evils that are eating up the nation. It is time to commit the country totally in God's hands. Kenyans did it when they confronted the government on the snake image on the fifty-shilling note. It was removed. This is the time people stood up against the satanic symbols entrenched in public transport vehicles. But most importantly, Kenyans can decide to elect genuine leaders that have the welfare of the nation and its people at heart irrespective of their party, tribe or religious affiliations or financial cum economic status.

God has destined Kenya as a place of worship. Zephaniah 3:10-12 says: *"From beyond the rivers of Cush, my worshippers, my scattered people, will bring me offerings."* Kush, in this case, refers to Ethiopia and the two rivers, The Blue Nile and White Nile. This prophetic statement is in reference to Kenya because it is south of Ethiopia and also south of the two rivers.

Kenya's destiny is thus indicated as a special place for God where other nations will come to worship. It will be the springboard of end time revival. It is no surprise therefore, that many nations are seeking association with Kenya. But idols will hinder such revival and blessings because God cannot share his glory as well stipulated in Isaiah 42:8: *"I am the Lord; that is my name! I will not yield (share) my glory to another or my praise to idols."* For this to happen, Kenya has to surrender from all involvement in all forms of idolatry, something that is totally involving. They must then embrace godliness. It is after this that Zephaniah's prophetic utterance will come true as he says: *"On that day you will not be put to shame, because I will remove from this city those who rejoice in their pride, never again will you be haughty on my holy hill.' Zephaniah 3:11.* The holy hill mentioned here is Mt. Kenya. Zephaniah at the same time assures preservation to those who trust in the true God: *"But I will leave within you the meek and humble, who trust in the* name *of the LORD"* Zephaniah 3:12.

The truth of the matter is that when people turn to or support idolatry and place their trust in idols, they, as individuals, families, tribes, and nations, not only lose their destiny and heritage as a people of God and children of the kingdom, but they also lose their place in God as well, and this is true of Kenya's destiny.

This is because idolatry ensnares its followers into bondage that persists for generations, especially if those practicing idolatry never fully confess and deal with the stumbling blocks attached to idolatry.

It is not until this idolatry is removed that peace prevails. I know this is true because when I had these symbols removed from St. Andrews Church and changed the PCEA logo, the positive changes in the Church environment were quite visible. Like the Church altars, the national altars will call for deeply and spiritually determined officials in government who can map out ways of dealing with these evil powers. This is because such satanic altars can only be dealt with from a spiritual approach. That is why the Bible says, *"For though we live in the world, we do not wage war as the world does. The weapons we fight with are not the weapons of the world. On the contrary, they have divine power to demolish strongholds."* (Emphasis mine) Whoever will decide to confront such powers of darkness must be in total agreement with the Spirit of God. Otherwise, he/she will be overpowered by the evil powers entrenched in the strongholds.

The problem we have in Kenya is the fact that the electorate elect individuals who can only govern from the physical or temporal perspectives, neglecting the spiritual aspects. Governance is like a two-edged sword. For the sword to do a commendable work, it has to be sharpened both sides. The same is true on successful governance. We don't have to sharpen one side of the government (physical/temporal), we have to also sharpen the other side representing spirituality as well. Remember, when the head of state takes the oath, he/she is given the sword (a representation of the physical/temporal) but he/she takes the vows by holding the Bible which is a representation of the *'Sword of the Spirit'*-the spiritual side of the sword.

Unfortunately, many of the past presidents in Kenya seem to lack that spiritual aspect that upholds the sword of the spirit. The application of the physical aspect alone breeds oppression, poverty, corruption, misappropriation of the national wealth and strife of all kinds in almost all sectors of the country's life. One would expect the king to involve the people and especially the church and other religious bodies including intercessors and prayer warriors, prophets and apostles, in national prayers. Such should at times include fasting and national repentance which should involve both the church and government. If things have to work well, God has to be practically involved.

That was the secret of Kings like David, Hezekiah, Josiah and Jehoshaphat used and it is no surprise they are remembered as some of the outstanding kings in Israel. These Kings used both sides of the sword. It is in this connection that the word of God affirms this when it says: *"The man without the Spirit does not accept the things that come from the Spirit of God, for they are foolishness to him, and he cannot understand them, because they are spiritually discerned"* (1 Cor. 2:14). Thus, the spiritually discerning people are able to penetrate into the spiritual realm because they, *"have not received the spirit of the world but the spirit who is from God that (they) may understand what God has freely given us."*

Such would confidently say, *"This is what we speak, not in words taught to us by human wisdom but in words taught by the Spirit, expressing spiritual truths in spiritual words"* (1 Cor. 2:12). It is only when most of the national evil strongholds are dealt with that the sun will shine upon the national liberation and showers of blessings will fall more abundantly than ever before. But for this to happen, those in power should be God's trained soldiers. Here, I do not mean worldly training, which is more physical than spiritual. The Lord always trains His soldiers by not allowing them to lie on beds of ease but by calling them to difficult marches and service. He makes them wade through streams, swim across rivers, climb steep mountains, and walk many long miles carrying heavy backpacks of sorrow through persecutions and oppositions.

That is how He develops soldiers, not by dressing them up in fine uniforms to strut at the gates of the barracks or by appearing as handsome gentlemen to those who are strolling through the park. No, God knows that soldiers can only be made in battle and are not developed in times of peace. We may grow the raw materials that soldiers are made from, but turning them into true warriors requires the education brought about by the smell of gunpowder and by fighting in the midst of flying bullets and exploding bombs, not by living through pleasant and peaceful times.

Think of David: When Saul dressed David with the physical war garments, he refused to use them because he was used to the one with the divine power. The Bible states that, *"Then Saul dressed David in his own tunic. He put a coat of armor on him and a bronze helmet on his head. David fastened it on his sword over the tunic and tried walking around, because he was not used to them."* As a result, David said to Saul, *"I cannot go in these because I am not used to them. So, he took them off. Then he took his staff in his hand, chose five smooth stones and with his sling in his hand, approached the Philistine .... So, David triumphed over the Philistine with a sling and a stone"* (1 Sam. 17:38-40, 50). In the human eyes, compared with Goliath, David had nothing of the so-called battle armory. Goliath was physically dressed for war. He had a big sword, spear, javelin and a shield. David had both the physical and spiritual, with the latter carrying more weight.

The God-fearing kings of Israel and Judah never trusted their good armory in fighting their physical or spiritual battles. Instead, they strategized out on spiritual warfare. Good examples in this case include kings like: Josiah (2nd Chronicles 34), Hezekiah (2 Kings 18), Asa (2Chronicles 15), Manasseh (2 Chronicles 33), and Jehoshaphat 2nd Chronicles 20). Even in demolishing the occult related strongholds that had suffocated the lives of Israelites, they involved their battalions and people in strategic spiritual warfare. This called for the repentance of their sins and that of their forefathers. There was fasting, praises and other spiritual methods employed. It was only through that kind of approach that they triumphed over their enemies. No nation or institution can win any battles whether physical or spiritual without involving God in every of their endeavor. This includes the fight against corruption, drugs and insecurity among others.

No battle can be won by a nation or an institution that fails to address idolatry intertwined within its body. Jonah 2:8 reveals the negative impact that embraces an institution when it plunges itself into idolatry for it says, "*Those who cling to worthless idols forfeit the grace that could be theirs.*" Grace here also means blessings. In other words, such a nation or institution, blocks itself from enjoying God's blessings. The same message is echoed in Isaiah 42:8 where God has made his declaration thus, "*I am the Lord; that is my name! I will not give my glory to or my praise to idols.*"

No wonder then that many institutions, including schools, companies, government organizations, NGO's, and churches, are operating in ungodly environments because many of them are clinging to ungodly altars. Many of the institutions, including governments, are in the hands of drunkards with selfish ambitions and greed with little or no concern for the needy. The leaders are grabbers, immoral idolaters, with other unrighteous behaviours. Therefore, they would be unwilling to confront the idolatry in nations or institutions that have evil altars or strongholds entrenched in them.

For example, think of very important landmarks like Harambee House or those along Harambee Avenue both found in the city of Nairobi. Such landmarks are there in honour of a Hindu goddess called 'Ambe,' which is part of the name 'Harambee' in this context meaning that; all the activities that take place in this building related to the government of Kenya, are in honour of a goddess and not the God of Abraham, Isaac and Jacob, our redeemer, Rock, Shield, our horn of Salvation and stronghold.

Harambee House is therefore the headquarters of satanic governance in Kenya with **Harambee Avenue** being the satanic economic headquarters and will remain so unless something spiritual is done about it regarding the name.

To change such names would call for a seasoned man or woman greatly inclined to godliness. The nation cannot fare well while tied up in the knots of idolatry. This was the case with PCEA but when I led the crusade to change the occultic logo, the church flourished economically, spiritually and socially. The church also stopped using the word harambee in fund raising. This worked well during my tenure. But those who led after me, deviated.

The occultic powers have entrenched occultic strongholds which have given the devil a strong legal foothold in Kenya. No wonder the nation has over the years been swimming in the current of corruption, and all kinds of occultic manipulation. That is why it is very important for Kenyans and other nations to have a change of mentality when it comes to the election of national leaders. The same is true of other institutions including the Church. This is the message I kept on hammering to the PCEA leaders. The message was never received easily. Instead, it caused even more animosity between me and the Church and the government of the day. Despite this, I kept on encouraging my heart to trust the Lord through the darkness. I encouraged my soul to honour Him with unwavering confidence even in the midst of difficult situations. I believe that storms bring blessings and fruits are harvested much later after the dark rainy clouds have released the heavy rain storms. It is important to note that, exposing idolatry in the church and in Kenya was not an easy venture.

There was significant opposition and persecution during the changes, both from church circles and secular authorities. In all this, I kept on reminding myself that in spite of the humiliation and frustration, I should take it as my great privilege to enter into the fellowship of sharing in Christ's suffering as indicated in Philippians 3:10. At the same time, I understood that I was in great company.

I also inferred that all the suffering was designed to make me a vessel suitable for His use. The Holy Spirit kept on reminding me that Christ's Calvary blossomed into abundant fruitfulness and so would mine someday. I had come to understand that pain leads to plenty and death to life which is the law of the Kingdom of God. Otherwise, we do not call it dying when a bud blossoms into a flower. This is true even on my being expelled from PCEA where much of what was happening in the Church was what God had used me to plant and watch its budding and blossoming.

More often than not, when God lets us pass through pain, His target is to train us in attaining tested faith. Otherwise, if any gift escapes untested, it certainly will not be our faith. Like an arrow piercing the marrow, there is nothing that tests faith more than the feeling of being deserted, revealing its true foundation. Only genuine faith will escape unharmed from the midst of the battle after having been stripped of its armor of earthly enjoyment and after having endured the circumstances coming against it that the powerful hand of God has allowed.

I felt urged by the Holy Spirit to imitate Paul, who fought a good fight, finished the race and kept the faith. One would then pose the question; Why aren't many religious oriented people as loyal to the truth as Paul? Perhaps it's because our calculations differ from his. Paul had a unique perspective. What we count as gain, they counted as loss. In fact, there are many blessings we will never receive until we are ready to pay the price of pain, for the path of suffering is the only way to gain such blessings. This is true of the likes of Martin Luther the reformer, Martin Luther King Junior, Mother Teresa, Mahatma Gandhi, Nelson Mandela, Kwame Nkrumah, Steve Biko, Bishop Desmond Tutu, and Rev. Timothy Njoya.

In this case, the genuine believers will never compromise the truth for fear of being deserted, persecuted or even scandalized as long as the end product will have human beings liberated from the secularized and spiritualized oppression. Such, must trust the Lord through darkness and honour Him with unwavering confidence even in the midst of difficult situations. The reward of this kind of faith will be like that of an eagle shedding its feathers to receive a renewed sense of youth and strength. This is what the Bible affirms when it says, "*Those who hope in the Lord will renew their strength. They will soar on wings like eagles; they will run and not grow weary; they will walk and not be faint.* (Isaiah 40:31).

FURTHER ENLIGHTENMENT ON SYMBOLISM IN THE CHURCH

It is my prayer that in future, God's will be done that some Church leaders, are convicted by the Holy Spirit to have a concern over some of these symbols by secret societies in the sanctuaries. I pray that they will also address the issues of homosexuality, devil worship and corruption among other wickedness existing in the churches. But for them to venture into this spiritual warfare, they will have to have the Gideonic spirit. Gideon had to dress himself with courage in order to destroy the community altar whose high priest was his father. This story is narrated in the book of Judges 6. Those who will dare have these symbols removed or those who will block any entrenchment of symbols in the sanctuaries and other buildings will need not fear the retaliation exerted from the ambassadors of these idols. This is because it is through such symbols that the occultists control the minds of the Church members as well as pollute the spiritual aspect of the Church building.

Fortunately, with time, many of the Christians will have the real revelation on the evil powers endowed in these symbols and will be convicted against stepping on these symbols or even having them on the church buildings. They will rise up and demand for their removal. Fear will have evaporated from their hearts because the Holy Spirit would be working through them. They will not fear the consequences that would result from their actions.

They will be moved by the command of God just as Paul wrote to the believers in Corinth reminding them that, God had empowered them to fight over the evil but not to allow its influence spread like uncontrollable wild fire. In his encouragement to the believers, Paul said, "*For though we live in this world, we do not wage war as the world does. The weapons we fight with are not the weapons of the world. On the contrary, they have divine power to demolish strongholds*" (2 Cor. 10:3-4). During my tenure of office as the GA Moderator, I felt it was a God given mandate for me to aggressively continue to enlighten PCEA leadership/membership and the national leaders, on the encroachment of evil influence on the buildings through Masonic symbols.

As I soldiered on with my campaign to educate both the Church and the nation on the negative consequences of idols, I emphasized that the occultists chant evil over these symbols, which then become the foundation of the spiritual realm. They become contact objects that could be likened to black spots that are found in some sections of roads. Black spots are a common phenomenon in Kenya as well as in other countries. For example, the Kenya government had to rework the road around Sachangwan- Nakuru-Mau Summit Road as it was a very strong black spot that had claimed the lives of scores of people through road accidents.

These are often sacrificial deaths. Such a place has a very strong satanic altar planted there in the form of symbol (s) or had some satanic rituals carried out that involved human or animal blood. Unfortunately, there are some foreign people who, after winning tenders for road construction, plant altars as a representation of their gods, like Baal, the Great Architect of the Universe, the Dragon, and Dagon, among others.

That is why some parts of these roads are marked, '*Black Spots*' due to the persistent deadly accidents. It is not uncommon for pastors from different denominations assembling in such places in an attempt to defuse the contact objects or the evil chanted altars raised and to make prophetic declarations in defusing those powers. They anoint such sections of the roads and the government rarely gives them support, lending credence to the fact that it could also be privy to the evil powers installed in such blood thirsty places.

The reason why some in the PCEA leadership were in constant fight with me was because of the brainwashing of the Africans at the inception of the denomination from the missionaries to adopt Scottish culture rather than the biblical teachings in the scriptures. Many of these missionaries were Freemasons and acted with double standards in planting the Word. Their cultural influence was a way of '*civilizing*' the Africans through entrenching symbols in church buildings.

Africans were treated as 'barbarians'; people who needed to be rescued from the darkness that overshadowed the "*Dark Continent.*" This was sadly the foundation of the Church in Kenya and elsewhere in the world, whether Presbyterian, Anglican, Methodists or the

Roman Catholic Church. It is unfortunate that the people won over by the pioneer missionaries cherished the western culture above the biblical message.

Regrettably, even after over 100 years from the onset of Missionary influence, the struggles then seem to be the same today. More than anything else, the Church is held captive by the idolatry that the Masonic missionaries fortified in the life of the church that exists in form of symbolisms. Instead of being the custodians of the Word of God, the occultists who mainly exist as Freemasonry, Illuminati and the New Age Movement have become the custodians and depository of evil influences. This custodian spirit is spelt out by one of the Freemasonry pillars whose name is Albert Pike, who in his book, **'Morals and Dogmas'***(Pg.219)'*, describes Freemasonry as: *"The custodian and depository of the great philosophical and religious truths, unknown to the world at large, and handed down from age to age by an unbroken current of tradition, embodied in symbols, emblems and allegories."* (Emphasis mine).

Suffice it then to say that the Church's foundation was built on *'sand'* and not on *'rock,'* which has weakened the universal Church over the years. Yet, these are some of the things the PCEA leadership persecuted me for exposing. It finally led to my expulsion from the denomination in April 2014; from that point, I would be looked at by some as psychiatric material! No wonder, then, there were pockets of celebration in the denomination.

I can imagine the same kind of celebrations taking place when John Calvin was expelled from Geneva where they denounced his reforms and especially on the destruction of occultic symbols found in the sanctuaries, but only later to recall him to continue with his reformation. They had to come to understand his reforms were divinely inspired. Calvin also addressed the immorality that had become so rampant even among the priests. He had also questioned the continued drifting from Godliness to ungodliness, the corruption that existed in the church including the selling of indulgencies and compromising with the world, among others.

Church buildings solidified with satanic symbolisms, as Richard Ing puts it in his book, **'Spiritual Warfare'**; *"The fighters in the spiritual warfare are experiencing heavy opposition as the occultists discord or* *decantation may be controlled by the spirit of pride, witchcraft, Jezebel or rebellion. In this case, unless God's kingdom fighters know how to conduct spiritual warfare and bind up the strongman, they will be neutralized by the fighting going on within the ranks."*

In this regard, at one time, I called upon the delegates in a GAC meeting to pass a resolution. I said: *"In view of the occultic adulteration of the Church buildings and in view of the fact that this defiles the Church, I am of the view that this GAC instructs the Presbyteries to see to it that the Church buildings are cleansed from the satanic representations. Also, a committee be appointed to be overseeing the Church building development before it is dedicated in every presbytery."*

This call created a hot debate, and the pro-occults made such a huge outcry that the ones who would have supported the motion feared the threats that were being issued by the occultists. Unfortunately, as pointed out earlier, not many within the clergy and lay people understood what I was talking about. It was a myth to many. What they did not know was the fact that symbolic occultism had been in operation but very secretly under the influence of the Freemasons, Illuminati, and the New Age Movement.

In fact, these groups of people are known as *'Secret Societies'* because they operate under much-disguised underground movements. They have a strong representation in every human sector worldwide. They hate being exposed. They like eating up institutions. They cause human oppression and suffering both physically and spiritually, and many times, they cause great suffering to those who dare to expose them. But suffering is the carpet for the believers whose call is real. Believers should borrow a leaf from a Roman soldier who, when told by his guide not to take a certain journey because it would probably be fatal, answered, *"If it is necessary for me to go, it is not necessary for me to live."*

The truth of the matter is that there is a divine mystery in suffering – there is a strange and supernatural power in it. There is no known great saintliness of soul which did not pass through great suffering. When the suffering soul reaches a state of serene acceptance, where it can find a bittersweet beauty in its own pain and no longer pleads with God to be freed from suffering, then it has embraced its blessed purpose and ministry. Patience has its perfect work; then, the crucifixion weaves itself into a crown. The great thing about God's call is that real suffering is for the sake of both humankind and the kingdom of God. Thus, the truly called will pursue without being discouraged or complaining because suffering in quietness has a positive destiny. For example, Joseph's dungeon became his road to the throne in Egypt. Jesus' suffering became the redemption destiny. And how about Nelson Mandela, Indira Gandhi of India, Martin Luther the reformer, and John Calvin?

God's blessings to those who will cling to Him have no boundaries. Martin Luther the Reformer courageously resisted both the Roman Government and the Roman Catholic Church of the time. He faced the Pope in spite of the latter's hunting him like a wild beast. But God hid him and gave him the opportunity to translate the scriptures from Latin to German language which was then later translated into many other languages. Martin Luther lived a peaceful life and died at an advanced age.

God is graciously looking for today's Martin Luther, the Jehus, Gideon, and Josephs, who will face the uprising powers of darkness/occultism that are mushrooming and domineering through the avenues of Freemasonry, Illuminati, and the New Age Movement. These are also the authors of all the sinfulness flooding the world, including homosexuality, lesbianism, and abortions, among others. Could this be the result of God's wrath, which has led him to torment the world with Coronavirus, earthquakes, famines, droughts, floods, wildfires, and various other calamities? Is it possible that this is just the start, with more severe consequences to come from God? But the pathetic part is the lack of knowledge of symbolism idolatry in the church. The church has already embraced some of this wickedness, including idolatry in the form of images and symbols in the House of God. This is the same situation that faced the Church of Corinth. It is no wonder Paul posed the same question when he asked the Corinthians, "*What harmony is there between Christ and Belial? What agreement is there between the temple of God and idols?*" (2Cor 6:15-16). The Church should emulate David's spirit when he says, "*I hate those who cling to worthless idols; I trust in the Lord*" (Psalm 31:6). Here, I am talking of tangible idols, but the universal Church has numerous idols that are oppressive and have even been embedded in their constitutions and by-laws.

Many believers are unaware that occultists aim to establish a global government and a malevolent religion through their scheme known as the 'New World Order.'

More than ever, this evil movement is currently in total war with the kingdom of God. The battle line is drawn, but only those in God's Spirit can discern it. The Illuminati have arm-twisting God's word. For instance, when God showed Ezekiel, a man clothed in linen and whom God said, "*Go throughout the city…and put a mark on the forehead of those who grieve and lament over all the detestable things that are done in it…. but do not touch anyone who has a mark. Begin at my sanctuary*" (Ezek. 9:4, 6). The Illuminati have taken this to mean putting a mark on the forehead of all those who will abide by being members of the evil religion and evil government, with its icon, the number 666. In their defilement ambition, they target to defile the universal church to such a point that the church membership will keep on decreasing year after year. It is the occultist's joy at those times when the church remains closed for long periods, as happened during the coronavirus pandemic. As a result of this, there was a rapid decrease in in-person church attendance in the western countries.

These must be fought viciously in the spirit of God for liberation to occur from these covert dark forces.

8 CONTROVERSIES OVER SYMBOLISM

In this chapter, I highlight some of the opposition I faced as a result of exposing some of the characteristics of Freemasonry, Illuminati, and the New Age Movement. As we have seen, the symbols had already solidified in the Church buildings, a trend that was initiated by the pioneer missionaries, most of whom were agents of these occultic groups. St. Andrews Church, located in Nairobi, was one of these Church buildings that was flooded by this satanic influence.

ST. ANDREWS CONTROVERSY

The source of this controversy can be traced way back to 1994. That time, a group of people from this Church had made a visit to Scotland under the invitation of some Churches. While there, they noticed some queer symbols on the walls, floors, windows, pews, altar areas, and the pulpit, among other areas. They were also surprised that most of the symbols they saw were also visible in their Church building back in Kenya.

When they inquired as to what purpose those symbols stood for, they not only had their questions answered, but they were also given the history behind the symbolism found in the Church buildings. They were told that those symbols represented pagan gods that were being worshiped in their temples before the coming of Christianity in Scotland in AD 637.

But as a matter of fact, some of the Scottish Church members said that the idols had a negative spiritual effect upon the Churches. They were also told that most of the symbols were installed by Freemasons who were the sole builders of Churches in Europe with Scotland as their base. They were told the history of Freemasons. It goes back to 1095 when Pope Urban 11 sent the so-called Soldiers of Christ to redeem the **Holy Land**/Palestine from the Turkish Moslems who had invaded it. He would organise a crusade in which he called for the recruitment for those that would go and redeem the Holy Land from the Muslims. The so-called recruits were named, '**Soldiers of Christ**.' A number of crusades were then held. But finally, these

'**Soldiers of Christ**' settled in Palestine and would permanently control the area. In the course of their stay here, they acquired a lot of wealth until their final defeat in by Turkish Muslims in 1270. They would then retreat back in Europe- settling mostly in France and becoming dominant because of their wealth and arrogance. They would then question the pope's authority.

Later, these soldiers renamed themselves Knight Templar's. **Knight** indicates that they were militant in spirit and **Templar** is from temple because they had established their temple where '**Solomon's Temple**' had been. But they rebelled from Christianity and became '**devil worshipers**' their chief god being referred to as the Great Architect of The Universe (**GAOTU**) - and which is presented in the capital letter **G**. There are a multitude of other gods whose images they secured in the temples of their gods which are referred to as Lodges where they have entrenched occultic images, sculptors, statues, pictures, and other numerous kinds of symbolism.

In 1307, the pope and the king of France embarked on a severe persecution on the Freemasons with many being burned at the stake. As a result of this, many of them escaped to Scotland where they founded a new settlement.

While at Scotland, they highlighted their connection with the Holy Land as they claimed to have tapped that '**holiness or anointing,**' which they could pass to the buildings they constructed. They were therefore mandated to be the sole builders of both churches and government buildings in Scotland and elsewhere in Europe. But as masons they had to have a memorandum of understanding between them and the state. The memorandum indicated that, because they were people with special anointing, they had to have freedom in making the Church designs and also dictate the cost of the buildings.

Consequently because of this freedom, they came to be known as the **Free-Masons**. They embarked on an aggressive recruitment of as many people as possible to join Freemasonry. Later, the boundaries opened for them and before long, they were recruiting all over Europe. They targeted mostly the rich people, professionals and the clergy between 1307 and the time Scottish missionaries came to Kenya around 1898-a duration of almost 600 years, almost all clergy and government officials in the entire Europe had already been initiated into Freemasonry.

In fact, the author of the Freemasonry constitution was a Presbyterian Clergyman, James Anderson (1679-1739). He was ordained as a minister in the Church of Scotland in 1707. The constitution that he wrote was published in 1723 and mainly focused on the propagation of evil including the entrenchment of symbols of idols in the church buildings. No wonder the Churches that were built by the missionaries in the mission fields had the installation of the demonic symbolisms. It is these very occultic oriented missionaries from Europe who built the pioneer buildings of the mainstream churches in Kenya. This is the information that visiting groups to Scotland received.

As it turned out, when this group returned to Kenya, they alerted St. Andrews Church leadership on what they had learned about the flooding symbolism at St. Andrews Church and especially on the tainted glass windows. These colours are a representation of Masonic pagan gods which carried an evil influence in the Church buildings, that is, they had a negative impact upon the spiritual life of the Church.

They especially emphasized the fact that those images and symbols carried curses rather than blessings. They also expressed their concern over the spirit of unbelief they found in the Churches of Scotland and the fact that the once packed big cathedrals were empty and many had been turned into rental apartments, shops, theatres, and recreational halls. Upon hearing this, the Kirksession of St Andrews Church voted to have those symbols removed. Remember, this was happening in 1994.

As per the protocols of the Church, the St. Andrews Kirksession wrote to Milimani presbytery to inform them of the same. The presbytery through a minute gave the Kirksession permission to remove what they termed as idols or satanic contact objects within the sanctuary. But when they attempted to remove them, the real Masonic guards of those symbols in the congregation came from hiding. They aggressively resisted the removal of the symbols and the Kirksession retreated. They realized the opposing forces were very strong and more so because they had the backing of the then

Moderator of General Assembly. Those other leaders in the PCEA were filled with a similar spirit.

This issue never came back again until I came in office as the Moderator of the General Assembly in 2003. I came in denouncing the Scottish traditions and the Masonic symbolisms that flooded the Church buildings and had spiritually dwarfed PCEA for years. I called upon the Church to open the door for the Holy Spirit to give life to the Scottish culturally founded denomination. I called upon the Church leadership to study the symbolisms that acted as an obstacle to the Church's growth both spiritually and physically. It was then that some leaders of St Andrews Church revisited the issue of removing the *satanic symbols* engraved in the sanctuary.

Some of the church members who had gone to Scotland in 1994 had enumerated the history they had been given behind these. When they shared the same with St. Andrews Kirksession, the latter consulted with the presbytery for permission to remove them, which was granted. But when they attempted to remove them, all hell broke loose as the symbols were under the protection of the Freemasons/Illuminati and the New Agers. They said to me:
"Now that you have come in breathing fire and brimstone upon the satanic symbolism and Scottish representation in worship and culture in the church sanctuary, we thought of requesting you to come to our defense. In fact, if we had the support from the GA Moderator in office by 1994, we would have removed those symbols. Unfortunately, the Moderators who came after him was no better. They never spoke openly about this evil like the way you have come out openly. This is why we feel that, this is God's timing."

I said; *"You just go ahead. You have my whole support. But make sure you have time to arm yourself spiritually for this is a very high-level spiritual warfare. You have to take some days in prayer and fasting and you have also to keep it a secret."* After this I prayed for them and had time to cover them especially with The Armor of God, as portrayed in Ephesians chapter 6:13- 17.

A group of elders, deacons and Church members went for seven days of prayer and fasting. They then strategized how to have the symbols removed on the seventh day which was on a Saturday. They worked on the symbol's removal throughout the night. They removed those fixed on the pews, grilled on windows, doors, smashed most of the tainted-glass windows, and at the same time replacing them with colourless ones.

When the owners of these 'gods' came for the service in the morning, they looked so gloomy when they discovered that most of their gods were no more. One of them, a clergyman stood in front of the congregation and said: "*I cannot understand how you people could be in a jovial mood when the whole sanctuary is bleeding. Don't you see how much destruction has been carried out in this Church building? Some misguided people did all this last night. These people should carry the highest condemnation both here and in heaven.*"

It was then that people started to look around for some blood but there was none. Then one of the key leaders asked the clergyman, "*I don't see any blood.*" The clergyman responded to him, "*Your spiritual eyes cannot see this bloody environment not unless your eyes have the connection.*" The man asked him, "*What other connection yet I am already connected with Jesus Christ?*" The clergyman said, "*You sound like one of those bastards who have generated this evil at night. The symbols have life, hence, the cause of bleeding.*"

What ensued was a fierce controversy. The supporters of the symbols mobilized themselves and vowed to have the symbols re-installed and even threatened to take those who championed the course of the Symbols' removal to a court of law. But they encountered a dilemma because the other leaders told them to dare to go to the court and they would then be relieved of their leadership responsibilities. The PCEA constitution stipulates that, if a leader decides to take another Christian to a court of law, he/she has to first surrender any responsibility in Church including eldership.

When they encountered this dilemma, they came to my office to seek for support. They asked me to help them have the symbols restored and especially the tainted glass windows. I responded by telling them that the easiest help they could get was through the presbytery because, constitutionally, any sanctuary belonged to the presbytery in whose jurisdiction the building is located. They insisted that I had the overall power and that I was in a position to help them, failure to which they would take it that I was supporting those who had removed the symbols.

When I adamantly stood my ground, one of them said, *"Be assured that we have taken it that you are the one totally behind the removal of those artifacts and we will now deal with you."* And with that they left my office. They went to the media where they came up with some false propaganda. One morning, I was awoken by a pastor whose voice indicated a deep concern: *"Moderator, are you yet out of bed?"* he asked. *"I am just preparing to get out, is there a problem?"* I replied.

"You better get today's Nation Newspaper. It has very disturbing news about you. I and others will plunge into deep prayers for you and your ministry. In fact, the whole Church should be summoned for a corporate high-level spiritual warfare that should at the same time involve intensive prayer and fasting."

Without further delay, I got out of the bed and sent one of my workers to go and buy the newspaper. To my amazement, the paper carried a story indicating that I had formed a demolition squad to demolish all the Churches that were built by the pioneer missionaries. It even gave some specific dates as to when I was to demolish the Churches starting with the Church of the Torch. As I was reading the paper, another call came. It was from BBC: *"I am calling from BBC offices here in Nairobi. The BBC Head Office in London wants to speak to you in regard to your move to demolish all the Churches that were constructed by the British missionaries. This being the case and as a matter of urgency, you need to give us the direction to your home and we will speed up to pick you and bring you to our offices because this place is the only one you can have a private talk with our officials in London."*

I asked the contact person to direct me to where their offices were and my driver would take me there. Upon my arrival, I was placed inside a sound-proof room. I was connected to BBC office in London. The person on the other end questioned the authority and integrity that I was using in demolishing their missionary founded Churches. He was acting on the false propaganda that had been highlighted in the newspaper. The speaker was very harsh even as I tried to convince him that what was in the papers was not true.

But I admitted that I had no problem in having them removed as they were a representation of evil. He claimed to defend history while I defended the gospel. I told him that what he called historical artifacts were evil representations that did not deserve to be part of a Church building. I told him that what is historically satanic cannot be married with what is genuinely Christian. The only one outstanding symbol and that ought to be rightly placed in the Church building is the Cross which marks the biblical historical Truth.

Furthermore, I told him that was not the first time the controversy over the Church symbolism had occurred. I reminded him of the destruction of religious sculptures that happened in Europe in the 16th century where Catholic art and many other forms of Church fittings and decorations were destroyed in mob actions as part of the Protestants' Reformation in what came to be known as the Iconoclastic Fury. The wave of disorderly attacks reportedly occurred in Switzerland, Copenhagen, Denmark, Scotland, France and the then Roman Empires between 1522 and 1566.

I also drew his attention to the fact that one of the main activities of Church reformation by the reformers involved the destruction of sculptures, pictures, images and symbols in the former Roman Catholic Church buildings. John Calvin, the founder of Presbyterian denomination was known for his zeal to demolish the ungodly symbols in the former Roman Catholic Church. He claimed that satanic altars as entrenched in the Church building had destructive psychological and spiritual powers. It was all witchcraft targeting the mind. Before hanging up, the speaker said, "*All what you are saying does not make any sense to me. Meanwhile, it is important you stop this menace.*" With that he hung up and I left room.

That conversation alone was proof enough that I was fighting with the whole world and the mighty ones. The more the controversy heightened, the more the spirit of the Lord came upon me. The good news is that, in spite of the heightened controversy, most of the symbols were removed from St. Andrews Church. Nonetheless, many other methods were used by the liberals to silence me but by God's grace, I kept the fire burning. I was being encouraged by the word of the Lord. For example, Exodus 14:14 says, "*The Lord will fight for you, and you have only to be silent.*" Also, 2nd Chr. 20:17, "*You will not have to fight in this battle. Take up your position; stand firm and see the deliverance that the Lord will give you.*"

This is exactly what I did. The more the battle raged, the more I held my ground. But many times, I felt so lonely, yet the battle raged even more when I ventured into the Kenyan parliament and condemned the satanic altars that flooded the House. One of the questions that the reader is likely to ask is: *"What were those symbols that were removed from St. Andrews Church that caused the worldwide heated controversy?"* I highlight these in the next few pages:

THE SYMBOL IS REMOVED FROM ST. ANDREWS CHURCH
Entrenchment of symbols in St. Andrews Church created an environment of sorrow rather than praise in the church. The spirits were depicted in form of **coffins** and especially the Third-Degree Tracing Board that carried spirits represented by; **Spring of Acacia**, Skull, Urn, Chisel, Plumb line, Pentagram, Point within a Circle, Spirit level, Boaz, Grave Stone Marker.

SQUARE AND COMPASS.
Freemasons hold building tools in high esteem. Among these, the most valued are the square and compass, as illustrated in the pictures below:

These were superimposed in the design of the burning bush. They were conspicuously fixed above the altar on the right-hand side. These items are known to be the main identification signs of Freemasonry. The compass and square are the two *'Greater Lights'* of Freemasonry. Note the strategic positioning of these symbols, that is, at the altar. To radiate the powers of darkness and the defilement of the altar which can be termed as the *'kitchen'* of the sanctuary, it has everything that pertains to the worship: That is the readings, preaching, announcements, celebration of the Holy communion, the announcement of hymns to be sang, the beginning and the end of giving the offertory (*offertory prayers are offered at the altar*), the serving and distribution of Holy Communion elements begins at the altar, the main Bible is placed at the altar, Baptisms, the Commissioning of leaders, marriage solemnization, Eucharist Confirmations are all held around the altar. The Altar is the most polluted area of many sanctuaries-including its checkered floor. It's all witchcraft! The importance and use of symbols by Freemasonry is highlighted by Ron G. Campbell in his book: '**Free From Masonry**,' (Page 91/92) where he says: "*Masons today still use strange symbols, including the mysterious skull and crossbones. In fact, all the instructions in Freemasonry's mysteries are communicated in the form of symbols. These symbols help us to identify what Masonry is and provide us with possible keys to this organization's ancient past. The Square and Compass is the most widely used and known symbol of Masonry. In one way, this symbol is a kind of trademark for the fraternity, as the golden arches are for McDonald's.*"

CHECKERED FLOOR

This is one of the symbols found at St. Andrews. It is a dominant thing among the Freemasonry. It is their central form of defilement of the floors in buildings including those of sanctuaries, residential premises, commercial buildings and government buildings. All Masonic lodges have brightly coloured patterns with the dominant colours being black and white. These checkered pavements were common in the temples of the ancients; the Egyptians, the Greeks and especially the Romans ingeniously decorated the floors of their temples in this manner.

One of the Freemasonry pillars, Albert Pike, whom Ron G. Campbell quotes in his book, '**Free from Freemasonry**' (Pg.97), says, "*the pavements, alternately black and white, symbolize intended or not, the good and evil principle of the Egyptian and Persian creed.*" (Pg.863)

Here is an example of a checkered floor:

Source: (*https://www.google.com /search?q=checkered+floor*).

Checkered floors in most cases are mainly found around the altar area and at times at the main entrance door. Today the checkered floor is one of Freemasonry's recognizable symbols and is the ritualistic floors of all masonic lodges. The pavement is the area on which the initiations occur and is "*emblematic of human life, checkered with good and evil:*" The Mosaic pavement is an old symbol of the Masonic order. The reader can Google (*https://www.hamiltondisrictcmasons.org*) *They can exist in any other pattern of a decorated floor and not necessarily in black and white.*

It is a Masonic symbol of witchcraft used in controlling people's minds. It paves the way for the incantations and witchcraft to be easily cast against the congregation so that they don't comprehend the gospel. It creates a spirit of unbelief. Checkered floors are also common in the business premises. Such are aimed at controlling customers mind or the mind of the staff. Those squared black and white patterns which the eyes interpret as decorations are nothing else other than witchcraft. In the Church they are aimed at blindfolding the believers. The negative spirits so created lead to activation of Church wickedness including; power struggles, financial misappropriation, immorality, jealousy, strife and all kinds of manipulation including devil worship and homosexuality.

SYMBOLS IN THE CLOISTERS
The satanic symbols were on the plaque in the cloisters. This was a representation of the dragon cleverly designed to look like a Lion with a long tail and special legs. In the occultic world, the dragon stands for false impressions revolving around; sunrise, spring, fertility, happiness and prosperity. As the god of the rivers, lakes and oceans, the dragon is said to represent wisdom and strength. Strategically placed, the dragon at St. Andrews was a source of these elements but from the evil point of view. For example, wisdom would mean, the satanic manipulative spirit, sunrise would stand for sun-god (Sun) and fertility stands for the spirit of immorality accompanied by happiness. These spirits emanate from the dark world. It is for this reason Paul says, *"We have not received the spirit of the world, but the spirit who is from God"* (2 Cor. 2:12).

Window Panels (Facing the upper car park)

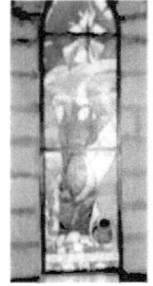  These window panels had pictures or designs showing Freemason symbols mainly of Waterford, a viper, symbols of worship of sun gods in the form of haloes and Ishtar (Queen of heaven or a Babylonian goddess). These windows with pictures of Saints like Abraham and

others bore symbols of the sun god. Two of them had a concealed frame of a Freemason coffin, with the saints cleverly concealed in those coffins. This coffin is usually used during initiation into Freemasonry. The initiate lies therein and is made to rise symbolically to indicate death and resurrection.

MAIN ENTRANCE GRILL

The design of the grill was very similar to that of the burning bush, and when closed formed the compass and square design (common feature of Freemason symbols). The grill locks were designed such that they reproduced heads which are used to represent the serpent in higher degrees of Freemasonry. The copper pots that formed at the intersection of grill meshwork are used to indicate the containers for the ashes of (*Hiram Abiff*), a legendary hero of Freemasonry, the builder of Jerusalem temple (Solomon's) and murdered in this temple.

The Masonic Broken Cross of St. Andrews

The origin of St. Andrews Cross is traced from an old heathen and Latin tradition (800AD) long before the Reformation. According to the legend, a Greek ship shipwrecked on the East Coast of Scotland carrying the bones of St. Andrews. This coincided with another legend, which was that Saint Andrew was martyred in Greece on a multiplication cross. One of the Scottish tribal chiefs claimed to have seen a cross made of the bones of Saint Andrews in the sky. He capitalized on this appearance and won battles over the Scottish chiefdoms. That is how the Saint Andrews cross became the official symbol in the Scottish national flag.

The Church of Scotland also adorned this cross. It is no wonder that today's logo of the Church of Scotland has Saint Andrew's Cross in the background and the burning bush in the foreground. PCEA embraced the adoration of this cross. It is embedded in many items and walls of the Church buildings, especially at the pulpit. This is true of the Church of the Torch and St. Andrews Church, which was removed. These crosses are mainly entrenched in the pulpit side that faces the congregation but may also be seen in other parts of the church buildings.

The cross is the most hated Christian symbol by the Freemasons. One area in which this hatred is exposed is the 29th degree, which is called by the Masonic as the **Knight of St. Andrews**. Saint Andrews was said to have a vision of a cross that gave faith, courage, and victory to the armies of Scotland. In the Masonic vow in regard to the 29th degree, one is expected to break the cross as a denial that Jesus was crucified. The candidate, in addition, makes a covenant and statement thus, "*Salah-Eddin must die,*" meaning Christianity must die.

Note also the shape of the St. Andrews Cross, which is X, the sign used to cancel or mark things wrong. Note also the fact that it is placed in a circle. Christ's kingship has been cancelled or nullified. Texe Marrs, in his book, '**Mystery Mark of the New Age,**' (Page. 119, says, "*The most diabolical and heinous of all symbols is the Cross within a circle. This indicates... Jesus Christ is contained or restrained within the circle of Satan." Otherwise, it is worth noting that St Andrew's Cross is the main symbol in many of the minister's scarves,* with the cross captivating the upper part of the cross. Many such scarfs also have the square and compass but are disguised as Alpha and Omega.

At St. Andrews Church, St. Andrews Cross was placed high at the front wall behind the altar area. Here, it represented the fact that Jesus was still on the cross and was not resurrected as taught by Christians. There were even women crying under the cross. This was symbolically the mourning over Tammuz. Satanists and other occults, including Freemasons and New Agers, delight in depicting Jesus on the cross and teach that Satan defeated Him on the Cross. Otherwise, traditionally, reformed Churches are supposed to use an empty cross. Worth noting in this case of the cross at St. Andrews

Church is the fact that above the head of 'Jesus,' there was a symbol of the sun-god, symbolized in the form of a halo.

Windows Facing Paved Area

These windows with pictures of saints like Abraham and others bore symbols of the sun god. Two of them had a concealed frame of a Freemason coffin, with the saints cleverly concealed in those coffins. This coffin as we have stated is usually used during initiation into Freemasonry where the initiate lies and is made to rise symbolically to indicate death and resurrection.

 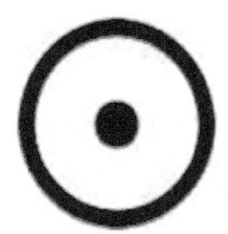

Symbols with a dot in the circle

This is a very satanic symbol that was fortified both at the pulpit and the altar table. The symbol alludes to the Sun-god (Sun worship) and is also associated with sexual orgies. The circle represents the female sexual organ, and the dot the male organ. The cross in the circle was distorted, and the dot placed at its heart indicates that the male organ is penetrating into the female organ at the heart of the cross. The cross is made to be the center of the sexual union. This symbol was placed at the pulpit to cause evil vibrations upon activation, which then rendered preaching useless as the power of the Word was defused through the evil vibrations in the spiritual realm.

Thus, the Sun-god was in charge of the pulpit. This same symbol was entrenched in the Lord's Table. Thus, the breaking of bread and the lifting of the cup was as well rendered meaningless. The Holy Communion was being dedicated to the 'Sun-god' who had taken control of the altar table. It formed a stronghold or a territory for the devil. It is no wonder then, upon its removal, some people left St. Andrews Church because their god had no more influence in that Church building. He had been overthrown.

SNAKE TAILS

These were entrenched on the curtain rails that terminated in snake representation. The rails comprised satanic worship symbols that were engraved on windows, window grills, and tainted windows with a variety of pagan and occultic representations. These ranged from snakes, reptiles, coffins, and worship of the sun gods, among others. See pictures numbered 1, 2, and 3.

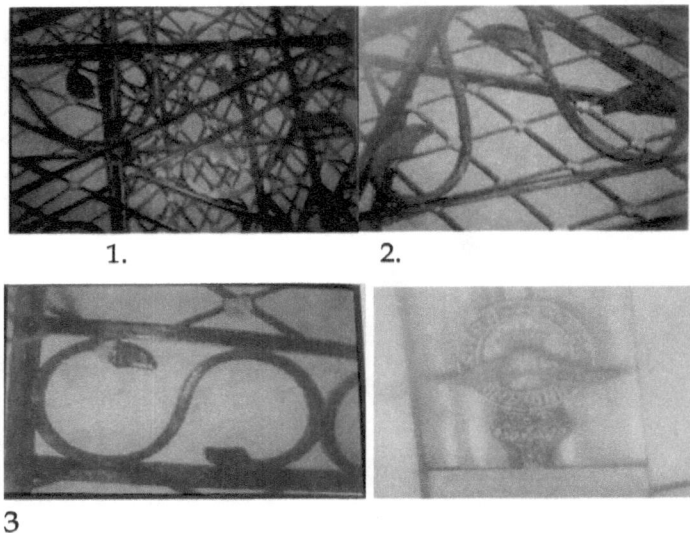

1.　　　　　　　　2.

3

Commemorative Plaques

Commemorative plaques for the dead were fixed in most places, including the pews. They were placed inside of what is known as the *'Tracing board.'* Memorial plaques represent the spirit of the dead- the spirit of the grave. They are strong sources of a Black Watch Commemorative Panel.

These commemorate British soldiers, complete with guns, that fought and killed Kenyans between 1950-54.

What has the Church got to do with the commemoration of British soldiers who killed Kenyans between 1950-1954, as the Black Watch Commemorative panel indicates? This is repugnant to Christians and symbolically promotes the culture of violence, death, and pride.

Occultic Tree of Life

There is also another picture of a tree with the snake deceiving Eve to eat the fruit of this particular tree. The accompanying snake heads or snakes are supposed to have given *'wisdom'* to the mother of human beings- Eve, when she ate the fruit. This is the Masonic pervasion of the word of God in Genesis 3. The snake is another major symbol used by the occultists to promote all kinds of manipulation through witchcraft and divination, among others.

Tree Near Old Church

It has been proved that Pioneer Freemasons, who were members of St. Andrews Church, carried out a pagan ceremony at this site. This involved the slaughtering of a goat. The bones were ceremonially buried there, and a tree was planted. This represents a pagan altar. Certain trees are esteemed by the occultists as sacred places to carry out their rituals.

JACOB'S LADDER

Jacob's ladder is a result of Jacob's encounter with an angel, as told in Genesis 28:12, where Jacob *"Had a dream in which he saw a stairway*

resting on earth, with its top reaching to heaven." Stairway here is the synonym of a ladder. This biblical symbol has undergone some manipulation by the Freemasons and the New Age Movement. In this case, the ladder is made to represent the Masonic journey of life and death.

When one gets to the top of the ladder as one progresses within the Masonic royal arch, one enters into the next world; death, upon which one sees the demonic light to which these occultists refer to as, *'There shall ye find light.'* There are also other satanic symbols that accompany Jacob's ladder. These include: Triangle in the circle, compass and square, cross in the circle, the Masonic tools, and sun - god in the Order of Knights Templar. Each step in the ladder has a representative symbol. Remember,

Freemasons were birthed out of Knight Templers, sometimes also spelt or expressed as *'Templar's.'* The above-named are just a few of the engrained symbols at St. Andrews Church that were removed.

IMPACT OF REMOVING SYMBOLS- ST. ANDREWS

The removal of most of the symbolisms at St. Andrews Church resulted in a lot of changes in its environment. The spiritual mood went up a notch higher, with many breakthroughs witnessed in worship. This paved the way for a more harmonized relationship between the congregation and the leaders. The physical developments were perceptible with a flourishing spirit of evangelism both within the parish environment and beyond. The spirit of giving and reaching out to the needy also increased. The ministry to the deaf also moved to a higher level.

There was remarkable growth in church membership that necessitated an additional third service. Who says that those evil branded symbols had no negative impact in whatever place they were secured? The truth is that those evil-oriented symbols spiritually polluted their surroundings but were disguised as artifacts by occultists. And since they looked attractive in the eyes of non-occultists, they were considered just as good art. But remember, all that glitter is not gold. The devil and his agents also behave like angels of light who are constantly on the move, looking for someone to devour. All said and done, there are still some elements of masonic symbols that have not yet been removed from St. Andrews Church. Unfortunately, because of these remaining symbols, together with the presence of Freemasons, frequent strife, power struggles, and economic pride will ever persist.

CONTROVERSY OVER UNIVERSITY SYMBOLISM

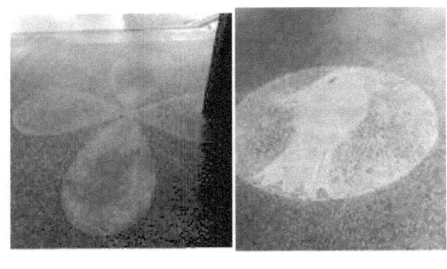

My persistence in pointing out the ills and wickedness in PCEA angered some of the leaders. This was especially their involvement in idolatry, corruption, and misappropriation of funds. There was also the mushrooming of devil worship and homosexuality that rubbed the wrong way. But what hurt them most was when I further pointed at the evil altars that were entrenched at the Presbyterian University of East Africa (PUEA) buildings.

These occultic symbols that people step on as they enter through the main door are a representation of the highest level of witchcraft in the occult. The cross symbols are engrained on the floor in the form of the PCEA Church Logo, which contains the Cross. Stepping on the cross demeans the authority of the cross as the representation of our salvation. Stepping on the logo also demeans the authority of PCEA, as the logo acts as its seal. Notable also are the other occultic symbols on the floor found next to the reception office, which include the Babylonian god, Dagon, in the form of a fish, and the Hindu occultic lotus flower that is also contained in a circle.

All these symbols are strategically placed so that whoever walks into any part of the University's administration building block has to step on them. This is the work of the New Age Movement and the Freemasonry/Illuminati. This is all witchcraft that has placed the university under the bondage of occultic powers. It is unfortunate that the Church has no idea of the covert agenda of the occultists when they display a passion for philanthropy. These secret societies thrive on charitable acts, and that is how they entrap institutions to get the upper hand in running them and secularizing them. This includes theological schools and Churches.

They also sponsor the construction and building of libraries and stock them with books from Western countries. Some of the material from these books is meant to brainwash the students or to drain them spiritually. This is true of the Presbyterian University of East Africa (PUEA). They also bring expatriates to teach the students. Most of these will focus their minds on distorting the scriptures. At the same time, they will manipulate the students into the spirit of homosexuality, lesbianism, and devil worship.

The recipient of the support fails to recognize the motive behind this passionate drive to give generously. It is in this connection that Loren Davis, in his book when he says: **'The Paganization of Christianity,'** unwraps the truth behind these moves: *"Many denomination colleges no longer require on their entrance application that their students are born again or that they believe in the Bible...Christian colleges want to be accepted by the world standards...Most ministers coming out of seminaries and bible schools are brainwashed, and their faith in the Bible and Christ has been spoilt... Many of them are silver-tongued orators who can change the Bible to mean anything they want to."*

It is of great importance to note that not everybody or organization that has a charitable spirit leans towards evil motivation. There are millions of charitable-minded people who do it from a humanitarian point of view. The recipients of the donations should study the history, vision, and mission of the givers. For the church, we will need not only to discern but also research the spirituality of the giver. This should be accompanied by prayers for the Holy Spirit to reveal the real motive of the donor.

This is the dilemma I find in PCEA. They are aware that the PC (USA) denomination has already adopted the ordination of gays and even solemnized their marriages, yet they have continued to partner with them despite my persistent calls to terminate the partnership. This is something that stirred up anger in the church leadership against me. In fact, this is the main reason they expelled me from the denomination. Notable is the fact that, apart from the symbols I singled out in parliament and the **'Harambee' idol**, I mainly concentrated on the spiritually orientated institutions, mainly the church. It is my understanding that if the Church can address the idolatry in its body, the secular idolatry will be defused. Spiritual things are contagious - the church should lead, then secularism will follow. Unfortunately, the way things are, the church seems to bow to the world.

As a result of my persistent call for the PUEA administration to remove those altars, the Church leadership authorized me to be blocked from teaching at that university. This was despite my being the founder of the institution and also its first Chancellor. The other reason behind my being blocked from teaching at this University was because it was feared that I could easily influence the students to have the symbols *'removed.'* It was even dreaded that if allowed to continue teaching there, I would eventually take over the university leadership, which some felt would hinder opportunities to carry out their corruption both externally and internally. It would also lead to the removal of the said satanic symbols or altars.

But the truth of the matter was that most of the people who ran the Churches and other institutions may not even be aware of the existence of such secret societies as the New Age Movement and Freemasonry/Illuminati. They might not even know their agenda because, outwardly, they look quite innocent. They come to them like angels or saviors of the institutions. Everything is done in disguise. They portray concern for human issues that the Church or the institution needs, and at that level, they appear like partners with the Church or institution.

No wonder the Presbyterian University of East Africa (and, of course, many others) is in constant turmoil. One would be shocked to learn of the heavy debts and monies that this Presbyterian university owes individuals, banks, and other institutions. Remember, the installation of most of these occultic symbols was the work of the many foreign and local donors, some of whom had Masonic Spirits. They claimed they had an agenda in promoting the institutions in the form of partnerships. In the fulfillment of their partnership, they install occultic symbols in the buildings they claim to support in constructing.

That way, they are able to spiritually pollute the environment and take control of the minds of the congregation or the students and staff through the occultic vibrations caused by the entrenched satanic symbols. Jomo Kenyatta, Kenya's first president, affirms these vibration powers in his book, '**Facing Mount Kenya**'; He says that such evil powers are *'transmitted by means of vibrations to the brain.'* If the functions and methods applied by the occultists through the vibrations of symbolism are carefully studied, it will be proved that, indeed, the evil vibrations manipulate the stability of the mind.

It's no wonder that even the issuing of a charter to this university took a long time. In my forceful combat against these evil powers entrenched in the symbols and through the intercessors, this

296

university was almost given a charter at one time when I was the Moderator, but this withered away as soon as I finished my six-year term as the Moderator. The university's low enrollment turned out to be one of the greatest struggles and headaches for the PCEA. This was also true when it came to the teaching staff, suppliers, and the lives of the students in general. It seemed like a fulfillment of the biblical statement, *"Those who cling to worthless idols forfeit the blessings that could be theirs"* (Jonah 2:8). This truth is also voiced by Ron Campbell in his book, '**Free from Masonry,**' where he explains: *"For anyone to engage in any form of idolatry is spiritually dangerous, if not deadly because it involves broken covenants and fractured relationships at the highest level." It is blatant disobedience to the first two commandments found in Exodus 20, which states: "You shall have no other gods before me" and "You shall not make for yourself an idol." In the end, the Church or the institution loses the blessings and instead earns God's judgments and curses. This is what God confirms when He says, 'I am the Lord that is my name! I will not give my glory to another or my praise to idols"* (Isaiah 42:8).

True to these words, the university has terribly forfeited its blessings. This is well shown by the Standard Newspaper of Monday, June 17th. 2013, which exposed the pathetic state the university was in:

1. *"The university faces several court cases relating to the hiring and firing of staff while the university is defending suits by suppliers and contractors over claims running into hundreds of millions of shillings."*

2. *"Students are granted degrees with cooked-up results wherever unpaid lecturers withhold results. Students, therefore, graduate with forged results."*

3. *"A member of staff at the university revealed that marks are given to students at random where the unpaid lecturers withhold the exams until they are paid. To their surprise, students still graduate." A lecturer Confirmed that the forgery of results has been going on at the institution. The batch that graduated in September 2012 was being given transcripts every semester, yet we were holding their results."*

4. *"The university has been hit by a series of financial management and academic scandals."*

5. *"Part-time lecturers are owed over 50 million shillings. Money they have worked for but have never been paid, even when they hold the exam results in protest. The university has virtually broken all the guidelines of running an institution of higher learning. At the same time, it is facing suits/ claims*

for unlawful cancellation of a number of supplier/contractor contracts. The mismanagement of the university has led to many students exiting the college. Enrollment has dropped from over 2000 two years ago to about 500 currently. This has pushed the university to financial collapse. It has also been unable to develop degree programs on its own. About eight of the courses that the university is teaching are done in collaboration with Kenyatta University."

The Standard Newspaper of 18th. June 2013 reported that: *"The Presbyterian University of EAST Africa (PUEA), which is at the center of academic, management and financial scandals, has less than six months to comply with requirements of getting a charter or have its license revoked."* This paper further revealed that, *"the university refused to pay a contractor 226 million and the High Court ordered PUEA to settle the 226 million it owes."*

The Standard Newspaper of 19th June reported that: *"The Presbyterian University of East Africa admitted about 180 students in its Kisii campus to pursue seven unaccredited degree programs deepening the academic problems at the Church-run institution...the students had paid Sh1.2 million... students... told of the suffering they have to endure."*

It is not surprising that the Nation Newspaper of Saturday, March 23rd, 2019, was updated on 28th June 2020, also carried the following heading: **'PCEA turns to members in a bid to save its Sh1.7bn hotel from auction, '**by Kipchumba Some. Some of the key highlights in the report included the following:" Church *aims to raise Sh13 million from parishioners every month for two years to clear the debt."* The main report stated thus: *"On Tuesday, March 5th. 2019 Rev Peter Kaniah, the secretary-general of the Presbyterian Church of East Africa (PCEA), dispatched letters to the 56 presbyteries across the country calling on them to come to the aid of one of their real estate projects- the Sh1.7 billion Milele Beach Hotel in Mombasa" from being auctioned.'"*

The sting of truth started biting after I left the seat of the Moderator of General Assembly. As if that is not enough, as I was writing this book on Friday, September 22nd, 2023 the Nation Newspaper carried the following headline by Stanley Ngotho: *"Court orders PCEA to vacate Kitengela premises after it loses land case to EPZ."* In the highlights the following were included: *"The Lands court has ordered the*

Presbyterian Church of East Africa to vacate its Kenya Shs. 650 million premises in Kitengela town within 60 days after it lost a land case to the Export Processing Zone (EPZ)."

Let me re-emphasize that as long as these occultic symbols have dominion over the university, there will never be peaceful progress in all its faculties. The Bible asserts this when it says, "*How can there be peace…as long as all the idolatry and witchcraft… abound*" (2Kings 9:22). Instead, the university will continue to impoverish the Church by draining its financial resources from parishes and Presbyteries. It will never stand out as a locally and internationally recognized institution. The student enrollment will ever be at low ebb as compared to other universities nationally. There is a possibility that the institution will finally be sold out to other developers. In fact, the strife has been to a higher level such that part of the university land has been sold. At one time, the University got deregistered and hence closed but under the interference of one of the top government officials re-opened it but this did not stop the strenuous life of this Christian based institution. This is a situation the university will go through-seasonal instabilities in different sectors of its life. The corrupt environment is likely to persist. And the demand for money from the church to support the university is likely to persist over the coming year including meeting non accrued debts and non-paid staff salaries.

As already stated, I was blocked from teaching at this university because I would have acted as a catalyst to expose the misappropriation of money and academic defilement through mismanagement. As if that was not bad enough, I was also blocked from teaching at the PCEA Lay Training and Conference Center, where a variety of training Church leaders takes place. This includes the training of the eldership candidates who undergo one-week training before they qualify to be ordained as elders. Ironically, that was a curriculum I had introduced during my tenure as the GA Moderator through a lot of opposition from the liberals whose agenda was always to suppress any move that would deepen the Church spiritually.

The liberals who are also members of the secret societies hate this kind of training that would equip the lay people spiritually. They feel that the trained elders would easily transmit the same to the Church members. Thus, blocking me from teaching the trainees was seen as a way to curtail increased spiritual understanding among the elders. There is also an advanced training for the evangelists. As it turned out, it was easier for me to teach at Daystar University as a senior lecturer and also at St. Paul's University and not teach at PUEA. What a manipulation of truth and justice!

CONTROVERSIAL MASONIC SYMBOLS AT SIGONA

Upon finishing my six-year tenure as the GA Moderator, I was posted to a one congregation Parish -Sigona Church where I reported my acceptance on 6th. October, 2009. This was unlike the tradition of posting the Moderator on the eve of his leaving the office. I had all along been accused of having caused quite some revolution in the old system of the spiritual lifestyle of the denomination. I had already done away with that **'one man drummer'** set up which was foundational in the music, providing structure, groove, and driving the overall sound as the congregation sung. I had instead introduced, key boards and other music accompaniments like drum sets. Worse still, I had brought a revival in the way people danced and raised their hands. To add insult to injury, I had paved way for individuals to verbalize prayers and praises during worship. This created an inclusive and participatory worship environment unlike the previous led or guided prayers. But I had also asked the church to stop partnership with PC (USA) and do away with evils existing in some sanctuaries and institutions.

In this case, my posting was to act as a punishment. Being posted to a small one parish congregation was so that stress and depression could engulf my life. They wanted to create the feeling of rejection in me. But what they did not know was that I was well grounded in the promises of God whenever I got into difficult situations. I had especially mastered God's Word as found in Philippians 4:13, "*I can do everything through him who gives me strength.*" And also, Romans 8:28, "*And we know that in all things God works for the good of those who love him, who have been called according to His purpose.*" The book of Joshua, 1:9 was of great encouragement, "*Have I not commanded you? Be strong and courageous. Do not be terrified; do not be discouraged, for the Lord your God will be with you wherever you go.*"

When I finally got settled at Sigona Church, we had a very productive time for the first six months. All the members came to like me, and I liked them as well. All was quite well until the Easter Sunday of 2010. While preaching on that Sunday, I pointed to the masonic symbols that were entrenched on the floor of the church building, the walls, and window panes, especially in the form of distorted crosses. I even pointed at the coffin-shaped cross engraved on the upper part of the front wall where the elders sat. I then posed this question to the congregation:

"Now that today is Easter Sunday, whose central theme is the Cross, which in reality commemorates the death of Jesus Christ and his saving power, I was then wondering whether you have ever felt some guilt or had a troubled conscience because of these crosses that are lined up on the Church floor. And that you walk comfortably on them. Worse still, there is this timber cross hanging on this front wall, with the cross itself being a formation of two coffins, one vertical and the other running horizontally.

I went on to further ask: *"Has not God categorically stated in Isaiah 42:8 that He will never share His glory or praise with any other god? Furthermore, don't you know that, in the occult world, a coffin represents both the spirit of death, unbelief and strife? And that these are the very spirits the symbols of a coffin activate in their environment, including in this sanctuary? This is the work of Freemasons, Illuminati and New Age Movement. You might not have heard of these groups but if you Google them, you will be surprised by how demonic these people are."*

My questions created a stir and some murmuring within the congregation and from the look in their faces and gestures; I could tell that the congregation took my challenge very positively. I overheard one person say, *"And how is it that we have never seen or thought of that and most importantly, how is it that none of our elders has ever had this kind of revelation or could it be that some if not all are Freemasons and they have the agenda to defile our Church building?"*

Soon the service came to an end and I joined the elders' procession back to the vestry. After the concluding prayer, I asked a general question: *"Is there any comment or comments in regard to today's service?"* Unanimously, the elders voiced their gratitude to me. They then insisted that we hold an urgent Kirksession to hear more on the occultism attached to the cross symbols as I had indicated. Furthermore, the same session would come up with the way forward on how they could deal with symbols in a weeks' time. And for sure, the meeting took place. Having revealed the Satanism that was concealed for a long time and whose evil influence was visible in everyday life of the Church, one elder commented, *"It is very unfortunate that, such channels through which Church defilement takes place had never come to our attention and realization."* As I listened and surveyed the facial expression of the elders, I could note three elders who were very uncomfortable with what the other elders were saying. They were not excited at all about the whole matter. Apart from those three elders, I was amazed at the degree of excitement the other elders displayed.

It was during that meeting for Church leaders that I elaborated what each of the symbols ingrained in the Church building stood for. I singled out the symbols embedded one step before the main entrance door and others lined up all the way to the altar.

I called upon the people to note that, as one faced the embedded cross from outside, it was in an upside-down position. I then explained the **upside-down cross** position was the creation of Freemasonry aimed at distorting and demeaning the Cross of Jesus Christ. The other way to demean it was the fact that, one could not enter the Church without stepping on it. Anything that one stepped on was meant to discredit that thing because the foot is regarded as a carrier of dirt and filth through footsteps on the ground as one walks. That was why the Jews had to have a person wash his or her feet before getting into the house. The Masonic people liken this cross to a doormat that is placed at the main entrance door of a house so that people can wipe their feet on it before getting into the house.

It can as well represent the mud scraper that is placed next to the main door for people to scrap the mud jammed under the shoes before getting into the house. I told my listeners that in the occult world, the cross is known as the Southern Cross and it is intended to ridicule the **Christian Cross** and religion. Otherwise, the greatest obstacle to occultists as far as Christianity is concerned is the Cross as we have seen. The cross is the symbol Christ is likened with. That's why as we have seen, the breaking of the cross is one of the first tasks new members of Freemasonry are asked to perform as part of the oaths they take. By breaking the cross, the candidate declares that he has nothing to do with Christianity.

 As one stands at the entrance of Sigona sanctuary, what one notices is the line-up of cross symbols rooted on the floor upon which people walk on, all the way to the altar. The second symbol that follows as one enters the Church is the **lotus flower** engraved on the floor.

I explained that one of the strongest associations of the lotus flower with religion is one observed in Hinduism. The lotus flower is associated with beauty, fertility, prosperity, spirituality and eternity. Many gods and goddesses of Hinduism are linked to this flower in one way or another. Buddhists have an association with this lotus flower in their religion. The lotus fortified in the floor at Sigona Church is contained in a circle. When contained in a circle, a **Lotus symbol** is spiritually destructive with; sexual connotations, a spirit of materialism, unbelief, strife and pride among others. The Hindu goddess of learning is shown sitting on a lotus. Also, the goddess Lakshmi, the Hindu goddess of wealth, is usually depicted with lotus flower. In Hinduism, lotus also represents the concept of **primordial birth** from the cosmic waters of creation. It is no wonder the Freemasons and other occult secret societies use the lotus flower as one of their highly esteemed symbols. It is one of those symbols they like using in defiling institutions, Business premises and sanctuaries. (*The readers can Google Lotus and its spiritual implications*).

As people listened attentively, I told them how a visiting intercessor from Ngong who had joined us in one of our Saturday fellowships confessed that the night prior to her coming to Sigona Church, she had seen a vision in which she was entering into Sigona Church but with great difficulty because the floor was very slippery at the main door. As she fought to maintain balance and avoid falling, she clung to a rope hanging by the entrance. However, the rope was too weak and eventually snapped. To me, that was a real confirmation of the abomination that these symbols stood for.

The breaking of the rope that this intercessor saw was an indication of the spiritual defilement that these symbols were causing to the Church building. There is therefore nothing to anchor on spiritually. It was the first time for this intercessor to come to P.C.E.A Sigona. In fact, she had lost her way before she finally located the Church's site. Earlier on, an intercessor from PCEA Sigona had confessed to having a dream in which she found herself collecting and throwing away torn, dirty and smelly shoes that had flooded the entire Church floor. This then tells how much this Church building is held captive by the powers of darkness.

The third symbol is placed halfway between the main entrance door and the altar and also at the central part of the Church. Here was the JiteGemea cross that was fixed in the Church logo and contained in a circle.

I had told people that the cross in a circle is regarded in the occult world as the most destructive symbol. The symbol is a representation of the PCEA's old logo with a capital G at the center of the cross, which is a representation of the Freemasonry, Illuminati god or GAOTU. Wherever this symbol dwells, the environment is surrendered to **GAOTU** which then releases all kinds of occultic influence. It hinders anything to do with spiritual development in the life of the Church. The environment becomes impervious to the Holy Spirit.

The fourth symbol I pointed to was the **cross** next to the altar, which was positioned in the very place where people stood when one was presenting tithes and sacraments or other religious ceremonies such as receiving baptism, wedding solemnizations, offering special prayers to a Church member, confirmations, commissioning of Church leaders, ordinations, Sunday School children being prayed for, among others.

Again, the whole occultic idea was to demean the cross by stepping on it. This was essentially defiling what was spiritually being bestowed upon the candidate by rendering it null and void. How can one take vows affirming commitment to God's way by stepping on the cross? Yet this is what happens when sacraments and religious ceremonies are performed such as; ordination, commissioning, baptism, solemnization of weddings in seeking acceptance before the throne of God. All these become the highest level of mockery to God. And for sure, this is how the secret societies have designed it to work by totally disconnecting one from God. Yet God is always beckoning believers to His kingdom.

The fifth symbol was the **coffin shaped cross**. This symbol was placed on the upper part of the front wall facing the congregation just below where the elders sit. This cross comprises of two coffins. One represented by the vertical arm of the cross and the other by the horizontal arm of the cross. In the occultic world, a coffin is a symbol of death. While the dead body represents physical death, the coffin represents spiritual death.

Pointing at the occultic significance of the coffin; Ron G. Campbell in his book, '**Free from Masonry (***Pg111***),**' says that, "*The most obvious symbol in the Master Mason degree....is the coffin. It is the analogue of ancient mysteries and represents a covenant with the grave.*" It then turns out that those who worship in a building where a coffin or coffins are entrenched could be likened to the people Jonah talks of when he says; "*Those who cling to worthless idols forfeit the grace that could be theirs*" (Jonah 2:8).

The sixth item I pointed out were the **memorial plaques** stuck on the pews. Those were in memory of the departed people. In fact, in the occultic spiritual world, the memorial plaque turns the pews they are attached to into altars of the dead and could be likened to graves. To occultists, the people sitting on those pews could as well be sitting on graves. They get defiled.

I wonder whether the same believer would feel comfortable if seated on a dead person's grave. Would one dare spend a night in the mortuary in the presence of corpses? What makes a corpse create an environment of fear? It is because from it emanates the spirit of death which defiles the environment making it non-conducive to Godliness which then permeates to people's mind. On the same note, the presence of a coffin related symbol (*altar*) in the Church creates the spirit of fear, confusion, unbelief, turmoil, spiritual dryness, leadership wrangles, materialism and prayerlessness among others.

The seventh occultic **cross** symbol at Sigona Church that I pointed out was the symbol of the **cross** covering the **roof internally**, running west to east with the longer arm of that cross facing the altar and the shorter bar facing the main door. As one enters the sanctuary, the cross view is **upside down**. Remember the intended reason for distorting the cross in an upside-down position is to ridicule the Christian Cross and religion. Such a big cross covering the whole roof of the Church, is occultic with oppressive spiritual forces emanating from above the congregation. This cross occultly communicates with all the other occultic symbols on the floor. In the occultic world, symbols do communicate as they release the frequency of evil powers. They are aligned in the air waves and at the same time sending forces through vibrations.

There was also the eighth idol representation flooding in the **tainted glass windows** that carry the occultic colours of; **orange, blue** and **green**, with their evil representation through vibrations of; Sun-god, water spirits and the mother earth goddess.

Such tainted windows are a characteristic of many Church buildings

universally. An example of the tainted glass windows at Sigona Church is the picture shown here. To the human eyes, such windows look beautiful but to the occultists, they see the representations of the three gods. The colours get dedicated through some witchcraft including chanting evil influences upon them. Otherwise, as colours they are okay but when they get dedicated, they become carriers of evil powers.

Jeremiah lamented over what the Israelites had done by flooding the Temple with dedicated things that he referred to as idols. Hear what he says, *"The people of Judah have done evil in my eyes... They have set up their detestable idols in the house that bears my name and have defiled it"* (Jer. 7:30).

The other area I spoke against was the issue of taking dead bodies into the sanctuary during the funeral service. In fact, this was one of the other reasons the defenders of these negative altars at PCEA Sigona could not leave any stone unturned until they had forced me out of the Church because I had openly declared my stand by making it clear that *"as long as I am the parish minister, no dead bodies would be placed in the Church during the funeral services."*

In this regard, I had given them two alternatives:

1. When a family decided that a funeral service be held in the sanctuary, the body would not be brought inside the sanctuary. Instead, the service would continue and the vehicle carrying the corpse would join the procession of other vehicles heading to the grave side after the service for the burial. In this way, I had discerned that the dead body could not add further defilement to the sanctuary.

2. The funeral service would take place at the grave site where the body is also laid to rest.

These decisions caused great uproar among some of the Church leaders some of whom were promoters of the evil symbols. They used them to control people's minds. But there were those who came to my support because they had understood the spiritual implications. During the time I ministered at Sigona Church, no dead bodies were brought into the sanctuary. But no sooner had I left the parish than the having dead bodies in the Church building resumed. The incoming ministers compromised either out of fear or to sustain and maintain their material gain.

I told the Sigona Congregation that those gods entrenched in Church buildings, tainted glass windows and other parts of the building were purposely placed there by people who knew what they were doing. It was all witchcraft aimed at manipulating the minds of the congregation.

I further reminded the leaders that from the time Satan and a third of the fallen angels were cast out of heaven and fell down on earth, the devil has ever been busy planting his altars to defile peoples' minds. He thus, manipulates their minds with various deceptions. In doing so, he uses people whom he has already won over to his kingdom. Here I did refer to the book of Revelation 12:9; *"The great dragon was hurled down – that ancient serpent called the devil or Satan who leads the whole world astray."*

I organized a one-day comprehensive seminar where I taught on matters of idolatry and its impact on sanctuaries.

As a conclusion to this teaching, I quoted John Ankerberg and John Weldon in their book, '**The Secret Teachings of the Masonic Lodge'**, *Pg.76* where he brings about the revelation that: *"For almost three hundred years,' masonry has influenced the Christian Church. Today, however, such influence is perhaps greater than ever before. But most people, Christians included, have little knowledge of Masonry and little understanding of its applications or of how deeply unchristian it is. Indeed, the very reason that Masonry continues to find an influence within the Church is Christian ignorance as to its real teachings and not just its claims. Once it is understood what masonry really teaches, a great deal of the confusion over this subject will be dissipated."*

The above named two authors further remind us that the occult agenda in targeting the Church is so well calculated but disguised in a way that one can't easily notice. In fact, they remind us that, *"Freemasonry, like a pirate ship, floats with a friendly banner inscribed with Jehovah's name that the unsuspecting may become an easy prey. The end result is a classic and cunningly devised duping of both mason and non-mason alike."* (p262)

After the teachings, people asked many questions, which I answered, and a few others made comments.

Question: *How come that we have occultists in the Church yet they all claim to be Christians with some claiming to be born again?*

Answer: *The devil is a great manipulator and a recruiter. This is a group of a worldwide cartel of a secret society known by such names as Freemasons, New Age Movement and Illuminati. They use money to reach out. They greatly support the Churches financially and, in this way, manipulate the congregations to elect them in positions of power. In many Churches they hold the chairmanship of both the congregations and various committees. So, they end up being involved in Church constructions through building and even in the designs. They manage to infiltrate occultic symbols in these buildings. In 2nd Corinthians 11:14, Paul talks of such people when he says, **for such men are false apostles, deceitful workmen, masquerading as apostles of Christ.** And no wonder as Satan masquerades as an angel of light. It is not surprising, then, if his servants masquerade as servants of righteousness."*

But it is also good to say that there are many in these groups who have been caught up in this falsehood web without knowing that they have enjoined themselves to such evil groups. They are lured with money and it is not until they take the third-degree vow that they come to know about it. Unfortunately, at such stage in time they cannot go back because that would mean, being killed or sometimes being asked to surrender back all the privileges one had acquired from this group. The different ranks are numbered from number one to thirty-three- referred to as degrees.

Question: *How can one identify these evil symbols?*
Answer: *"Look for any symbols entrenched in the floor. Such are not decorations as the builders will want us to think. Those squares, triangles, diamonds, crosses, circles that encircle a given design among others are not well-meaning. Watch out for tainted glass windows of the Church buildings. I have already stated what each of these colours stands for. Look out for any other symbolic representation on the walls and on the roof. Look for any symbolic representation on the floor, at the main entrance door, or around the altar. It does not call for any psychological learning for one to know that stepping on a symbol of a Cross means being disrespectful and demeaning the Cross, which is the symbol of salvation."*

After this I opened the floor for some comments. The first comment was from an elder who said: *"Moderator, on behalf of these leaders, I take this opportunity to thank you for this great teaching and a great revelation as well. It has even taken great courage for you to expose this truth. I say this because I would think that many people with this truth cannot do what you are doing for fear of being intimidated and humiliated. But it is also within your calling because I remember you stating that when God called you, he also spoke to you through the book of Jeremiah 1:17 which says, "Get yourself ready! Stand up and say to them whatever I command you. Do not be terrified by them." Mine is to encourage you to say all this truth in whatever forum that God will give you, knowing that God is faithful and he will stand with you for he is not a man that he should lie. Meanwhile, I am calling upon my colleagues to wake up and strategize on a way to liberate this Church building from occultic bondage. From the Moderator's teachings, the whole truth is that we worship in a Satan-bound building and I concur with the speaker that, our Church is not a Church building as we have always been made to believe but it is a disguised Masonic Temple. In fact, if one looks critically at the shape of our church building, it is in designed in the shape of a coffin. In this regard, I propose*

309

we have an urgent Kirksession meeting to deliberate on the way forward preferably, this coming Saturday."

The second comment was also from an elder who said, *"I support the move that we hold an urgent Kirk session meeting this coming Saturday."*

The proposal was unanimously taken. There was a lot of excitement as people talked about all that pertained to my teaching. But there were those three elders who, in spite of the excitement among other elders, were busy talking to the elders, trying by all means to discredit my teachings. I overheard one of them saying, *"This man is teaching a lot of heresy. What we have in this building are all decorations, or you can call them artifacts."*

The Kirk session met on Saturday and deliberated on the issue of symbols entrenched in the church building. They passed a resolution to have the symbols removed. They further said that tiles would be put in place after the removal of the cross symbols on the floor. It was also resolved to remove and burn that coffin-shaped cross and replace it with one that did not have any satanic manipulation.

But in the midst of this discussion, the three elders tried in all ways to block any action to remove the symbols. They vehemently and persistently declared that the symbols were artifacts and removing them would be like demolishing the whole Church building. Nevertheless, the meeting came to an end after a prayer.

Personally, I have lived around Sigona since 1993, and I have known the Sigona congregation as one with constant strife and a strong spirit of unbelief in all kinds of turmoil.

I had always wondered what was contributing to this *"chronic"* negative spiritual lifestyle in that Church. It was not until the time I became its parish minister in 2010 that the truth surfaced. The negative influences were birthed out by the entrenched symbols flooding the Church. God cannot shower His blessings in a house meant to be a house of prayer but had ended up disregarding the Cross and were guiltlessly stepping on it.

On Tuesday of the following week, after the Kirk session meeting on Saturday, two smartly dressed people came to my office and handed me what they referred to as a Court Order. They would ask me to sign it. Upon asking what it was for, they responded, "*You have been accused in the court of law at Limuru for having interfered with the Church building.*" At first, I felt like not signing the document, but at the same time, I remembered what Jesus said when Christians are taken to court for the sake of the gospel; "*the Holy Spirit will be in charge and will speak on their behalf.*" I also recalled the words of Jesus, "*Blessed are you when people insult you, persecute you, and falsely say all kinds of evil against you because of Me. Rejoice and be glad*" (Mt. 5:11).

But I also knew that PCEA had a rule stating that when any of its pastors was taken to a court of law, the head office was supposed to appoint a lawyer to represent that pastor. Little did I know that the P.C.E.A leadership was the mastermind of plotting my being taken to court as one way of trying to get rid of me by denying me a lawyer. This was also a way of silencing me. It was one of the ways of protecting those idols in the buildings of those church denominations from being removed. It was also an action that would open a wide avenue for unblocked corruption to mushroom in the Church especially at the head office. It was meant to block me from any further aggressively addressing the evils taking place in the denomination perpetrated by some of those at the head office. Corruption had already become a well-grounded venture since the time I left the position of the GA Moderator.

At that very time, the whole congregation at Sigona was at arms advocating for the removal of those satanic symbols. That time I felt like Elijah when he was running for his life from Ahab and Jezebel. But I could at the same time associate myself with the words God consoled Elijah with, to wake up and eat for the journey was long. I was facing a very high-level spiritual warfare but I also knew that, "*In all things God works for the good of those who love him, who have been called according to His purpose*" (Rom.8:28). I was also aware that "*In all these things, we are more than conquerors through Him who loved us*" (Rom.8:37). In any case, "*I can do all things through Christ who gives me strength*" (Phil. 4:13).

I mobilized a strong and dedicated intercessory group denominationally and nationally. Armed in this way, I went to the court to face my accusers. I was all alone, apart from the intercessors who were interceding for me. All other people in PCEA, including my fellow pastors, had retreated from me, possibly for fear of being victimized if found sympathizing with me. I was now being treated like an outcast and a heretic, one worth being burnt at a stake. The good news was that the Sigona Church congregation had come to the realization that those symbols were demonically polluting the Church environment, and they were jubilant that the Kirk session had authorized their removal. Consequently, they had already learned that some elders had taken me to the court of law.

MY EXPERIENCE IN THE COURT OF LAW

My accusers had opted to take me to Limuru Court (thirty kilometers away from where I lived) because that is where they had made all the connections, possibly through bribery, to fix me up. This was and still is a common thing in Kenya. It is possible that the magistrate of their choice was part of the scheme. Otherwise, the nearest court was at Kikuyu Township (ten kilometers from where I lived and still live). Another reason why they chose Limuru could be because the magistrate could possibly be a believer in occultism. Otherwise, the magistrate at the Kikuyu Law Courts, where they should have taken me, was a staunch Christian.

When my day in court on May 26th, 2010, beckoned, I expected to find some people who had come to show their solidarity with their former GA Moderator, but I found none. Likewise, I expected to find some Church members having come to stand with me, but its only one person, David Kibiru Gathoga, a member of Sigona Church, who had come. But why did people fail to come and stand with me? The reason is that, though many of them were in support of what I was advocating for, they feared being intimidated by the head office or by some Muguga Presbytery members who had verbally circulated a message that threatened anybody who would dare show any sympathy with me. They warned people against any association with me; otherwise, such people could be excommunicated from taking the Holy Communion. The pastors would as well be dealt with, meaning one could be transferred to a remote area or to other hardship areas. Nevertheless, I mobilized intercessors for long sessions of prayers on the 22nd of May, 2010. These would meet on different days.

What would follow is a series of court appearances until judgment day. The D-day finally came-the Day of Judgment as stated earlier the 7th. of October, 2010. As usual, outside the court room I found a big crowd of people who had come for the hearing of their cases and with others having escorted their friends or relatives to give them moral support. Standing outside, the court as I waited for the court room to open, I felt like Martin Luther the renown protestant reformer when he was standing at the highest Court and in the presence of all-powerful people in Germany including the king and pope's representatives!

Like Martin Luther, rather than burn with anger and hatred, my heart was puffed up with joy. I could recall Martin Luther's words as he gave his final words in the German Court at Worms, where he said, "*My conscience is bound by the Word of God, here I stand, I cannot do no other; may God help me. Amen. I cannot and I will not yield, for it is unsafe for a Christian to speak against his conscience.*"

I was also being encouraged by the word that God had given me in my devotion that morning; the Words as found in **Psalms 37:5**: "*Commit thy ways unto the Lord; trust in him, and he will act*" I was also reminded of **Isaiah 41:10-11**: "*So do not fear, for I am with you; do not be dismayed, for I am your God. I will strengthen you and help you; I will uphold you with my righteous right hand. All who rage against you will surely be ashamed and disgraced; those who oppose you will be as nothing and perish.*" The Holy Spirit continued to minister to me through the words as found in the book of **Romans 8:31-35**, "*If God is for us, who can be against us…Who shall separate us from the love of Christ…hardship or persecution, famine or nakedness or danger or sword?*"

The words in **Isaiah 54:17,** "*No weapon that is formed against you shall prosper, and every tongue that shall rise against you in judgment you shall condemn. This is the heritage of the servants of the Lord, and their righteousness is of me, saith the Lord,*" were also echoing in my mind.

I knew that God was ministering to me this way because of the tens of intercessors who were actively praying and fasting for my deliverance. I had already received numerous text messages of encouragement, some carrying some **prophetic** utterances and scriptural passages.

I was in that mood of meditation when a smartly dressed young man approached me and said; "*I am assuming you are David Githii just because you are the only person wearing a clerical collar among these people gathered here.*" In response, I said; "*Yes that is me.*" Then, he continued to introduce himself; "*Well, my name is…from …advocates firm and I am a born-again Christian. I am not the lawyer who had this case from the beginning but that lawyer called me this morning and expressed his inability to come but instead asked me to come and represent him. I am a person who stands for the truth of the gospel and in this case, I would love to hear from you in regard to the development that led to your being brought to this court.*"

Apart from his continued nodding of his head as an indication that he was following what I was saying, the man remained silent as I narrated the whole story to him. When I finished, he said:
"*That is quite contrary to what is contained in this file that I am taking with me into the court room to argue the case on behalf of our clients. In this file, you are accused of having plotted to demolish the whole Church building, but as I now hear from you, you only pointed to what you called Satan's strongholds that are entrenched in the Church building. Let me tell you Reverend Githii, you are not here by mistake; you are under a very important agenda of God. What concerns me is that, the Church is swimming under a very strong current of idolatry. So, I am not surprised that God has raised you at such a time to be His voice in the midst of a voiceless Church. Meanwhile, I will just go ahead and do my work as I am obliged to do within my profession. I just wish I had a way to help but if God wills it, He will see you through in His own ways.*"

This Lawyer was still speaking when we saw a person coming from the direction of the court room. I told the young lawyer: "*This man should be coming to summon us to get into the court room.*"

But to our surprise, when the man reached all those assembled, he said, "*I am very sorry. I don't have good news for you. The magistrate had earlier twice confirmed his coming but the message he has now sent indicates that, he will not make it to the court today and he has asked me to tell you that your cases will be heard this coming Friday. I am sorry, but that is how things stand for now.*" Then the man left.

The young lawyer then turned to me and said, "*Let me go to court number two and see whether the magistrate there will be willing to hear our case today.* "He left me and headed to court number two. After ten minutes he came back, was all smiles. He said: *"It has worked, the magistrate in court number two has agreed to hear this case and we should then proceed there."*

When we got into the court room, it was fully packed. We got seats in the front part of the court, very close to the magistrate. After sometime, the magistrate called out our case. The young lawyer stood up and presented the case. The magistrate asked me some questions in regard to my intention to have the Church demolished. I explained what went on during my sermon and how the elders later held a Church committee meeting and how they came to a decision that those symbols be removed, the ones on the floor and the one up in the front wall of the Church.

That decision had been declared on Saturday, but when I reported to the office on Tuesday the following week, I was presented with a court order. After some further explanations from the lawyer and me, the magistrate ruled that the case be solved back in the Church. To him that was an argument touching on some ecclesiastical matters that could be amicably dealt with in the Church courts or committees for that matter.

When we got outside of the courtroom, the young lawyer said:
"David, I am amazed at your courage and I urge you not to think otherwise, continue to fight the good fight. It is a good calling that God has given to you. You can already see how He is fighting for you. You can now witness this in the way God blocked the lawyer who was assigned this case all the way from the beginning and making him fail to come in the last minute. This is the way God works, closing some doors while he opens others. And it is the same scenario with the magistrate who was supposed to handle this case failing to come at the last minute as well. These are the signs that this is a divine battle. I am sorry that I could not speak on your behalf as I had to handle the case professionally as the lawyer of your accusers. I had to totally go against you."

The young lawyer shook my hand and said: *"May the Almighty God continue to lead you into winning battles."* He then left.

I held a brief discussion with my friend David Kibiru Gathogo. He invited me for lunch and before long I was on my way home, praising

God for the victory He had given to me. I am always thankful to God for bringing David Kibiru into my life. He has been a great supporter of my Ministry. Ever since that time, he and his family have been constantly in my prayers. In fact, because his home is not far from mine, I always say a prayer over his household any time I pass – by his home in the course of my jogging.

"EXCOMMUNICATION"

Now that the Court had set me free, this was not taken lightly by my accusers. They were displeased by the court's decision because things did not go the way they had anticipated. Their agenda was to have me humiliated even if it meant being jailed. They were also concerned that my continued presence at Sigona Church would make the symbols in the Church building very vulnerable for removal. They remembered how we had the symbols at St. Andrews Church removed at night. That was the kind of scenario they feared. Remember the battle was being fueled from the Head Quarters by some leaders who forcing the Muguga Presbytery to act according their selfish will.

They therefore planned to leave no stone unturned until those symbols had all the security required. Already the congregation was very bitter about the presence of the symbols in the sanctuary. They had already realized that the entrenchment of the symbols was occultic and was meant to help the occultists in the congregation to take control of the mind of the congregation and to cause spiritual malnourishment and constant strife in the Church. The Church had never known any peace. Not one minister had not shed tears in this Church.

To make sure that the symbols had sound security, Muguga Presbytery, in conjunction with some of the head office leadership, decided to forcefully remove me from Sigona Church in an effort to safeguard the symbols. It all started with the forced 1-month leave. But I decided to go back earlier on the 10th. October 2010, on my accord for the sake of the congregation, which had no minister in my absence. I still ministered on the 17th. October defiantly since no provision had been made for a replacement, and I felt it my responsibility the flock was spiritually nourished. I continued ministering against the decision of the leadership. *'A category A'* meeting was held on 12th October at Muguga Presbytery to have me kicked out of Sigona. But my concern for the congregation, who were like sheep without a shepherd, inspired me, despite these protracted agitations, to have me out finally. True to their word and without any communication with me, I was replaced with a new minister, Rev. Kagiri, who reported to the parish in early January 2011. My last Sunday at Sigona was on the 2nd. January, 2011. As I handed over to the new minister, little did I know that the church had no plans to post me elsewhere or to give me any work. In fact, some members of the congregation wanted to hold a demonstration in my support and even asked me to join them in pulling Sigona Church out of the PCEA denomination and that I be the parish minister of that independent Church. But I calmed them down by reminding them that, for the time I was the GA Moderator, I was always cautioning the Church ministers to obey the head office officials, Church courts, and committees' decisions, and therefore, I had to abide by that.

I advised them to respect the Head Office and presbytery decision that I vacate. They also wanted to reject the new minister but I convinced them to accept the minister because he was ignorant of what had been going on. He had obeyed by reporting to the parish he found himself posted to. They listened to me but they remained bitter that I had not been posted. I was unceremoniously sidelined from PCEA with the sole aim of not only getting rid of me but also to torture me psychologically and especially in the area of finances as no salary would be forthcoming. That was great torture to me and my family more so because we had pressing issues to handle including the payment of a loan. As I bid people farewell, many of them were in tears.

The Head Office officials never talked to me. They never even told me that I had been sidelined from the Church or I was being disciplined. They never even made a phone call, a text or email. They just slammed the doors against me. They were watching me hoping that I would opt to do one of the following out of which they would defrock me by accusing me of desertion of duty.

1. To look **for a university where I could teach**. They knew that I had the necessary papers as I had been a senior lecturer at Daystar University.

2. Go overseas to look for greener pastures. Having done my post graduate studies in the USA, they would have expected me to have some contacts.

3. The third option they presumed was for me **to start my own ministry**.

Unfortunately for them, I never did any of those things. Instead, I remained at home for a whole year (2011) feeding the few cows we had. We sold the few litres of milk that the cows produced and it helped us in buying some food. In all this, I never doubted or questioned God. More than anything else, I was encouraged by Paul's words found in the book of Romans 8:28; "*And we know that in all things God works for the good of those who love him, who have been called according to His purpose.*"

In spite of the obstacles, I never lost the understanding that it was God's choice to labour with Him in His vineyard. The words of the young lawyer whom I had encountered at Limuru Law Courts that I keep on fighting the good fight also became a beacon of spiritual support in my life.

I will forever be thankful to the many intercessors both at and Sigona Church and those scattered all over the nations who lifted my spirit through their intensive prayers and a few who could go for some days in intensive prayers and fasting. Those were very difficult days for me and my family and nobody seemed to care. Can you imagine a former moderator going to cut Napier grass for the cows, cutting it into pieces and doing all the labour that zero grazing cows require? At one time I was so low as the bank was pressurizing me on the loan payment but God spoke to me the words of encouragement reminding me that, "*Though I walk in the midst of trouble, you preserve my life, you stretch your hand against the anger of my foes*" (Psalm 138: 7).

The question that kept coming in my mind was: "*How on earth could a Church that preaches Christ be so protective of idols that were defiling the Church and even put me into such deep humiliation, frustration, torture even to an extent of looking for ways to have me eliminated?*" I further wondered what was the difference between the Church's behaviour and that of Ahab and Jezebel who harassed Elijah and even plotted to have him killed or the Pope who persecuted and harassed, the reformer, Martin Luther, or King Zedekiah who had Jeremiah put into the cistern and he had to sink into the mud and left there to die as reflected in Jeremiah 38.

All these people suffered just because they had pointed out the wickedness that existed among the supposedly God's people- the Israelites and God's House, the Temple. But I also knew that the issue of symbols was only the tip of the iceberg. The whole bitterness with my persecutors was mainly the fact that I had brought changes in the church, something they were trying to undo but without any success. **Secondly**, they hated me for being so proactive in exposing the corruption that was going on, with some in the head office taking the lead.

Thirdly, the bone of contention was my endeavor in introducing praise in worship into the denomination.

Fourthly, notable is also the way they were against my accomplishment in introducing into the denomination the ministry of Elder Districts and the training of elder candidates, before the ordination among others.

Fifthly, some were bitter with my aggressiveness in fighting homosexuality and devil worship in the denomination and my persistent call on the church to form commissions to investigate the mushrooming of the wickedness in the church.

Sixth was my notable persistent call for terminating the denomination's partnership with PC (USA), which was already ordaining homosexuals and solemnizing their weddings.

Seventh, there was also the notion that I should not have changed the church logo.

Eighth was also the fact that I should not have pointed to the Scottish Culture as the foundation of the gospel the denomination received.

Ninth, decentralization was also another aspect they condemned me for having introduced in the church. By doing this, they claimed I had cut off the flow of money from **Parishes** and **Presbyteries** in the **Head Quarters** coffers.

I found it even more ironic as the incoming Moderator of the General Assembly, Rev Gathanju had already come up with a good theme with guiding words for the future in the course of the 19th. GA based on Hosea 4:6 "*My people are destroyed for lack of knowledge.*" This was an indication that there were areas in the Church's life that people were ignorant of and it was a high time, the mysteries of the gospel were exposed. Yet, there I was, undergoing persecution just because God was using me to pass the knowledge that He was giving to the Church in exposing the hidden evil schemes through which the enemy had put the Church into bondage.

Remember I had not advocated for the removal of the symbols. I had just pointed out those symbols lined up in the Church building. It was the Sigona Church leadership who advocated for their removal. The whole movement of removing symbols came from the elders and was later upheld by the congregation. I had just done what Jeremiah had done in obedience to God's command, who, in pointing out the idols in the temple, had declared, "*The people of Judah have done evil in my eyes...They have set up their detestable idols in the house that bears my name and have defiled it*" (Jer. 7:30). For this act of exposing the idols entrenched into the temple building, Jeremiah had to undergo all kinds of torture. They had lowered him in cistern without water but mud. (Jer. 38:6).

In the same manner, by putting me out of Church service for twelve months, the Church had lowered me into a rejection cistern with no '*water but mud.*' I was made to remain out of the Church service from January 2011 to January 2012. It was a time of great stress. Although this was the case, I was happy knowing that I was suffering for the cause of the truth of the gospel. But at the same time, I recalled the words that Jesus used in consoling his disciples when he said,
"*If they persecuted me, they will persecute you also... They will treat you this way because of my name... If I had not...spoken to them, they would not be guilty of sin. Now, however, they have no excuse for their sin.... If I had not done among them what no one else did, they would not be guilty of sin*" (Jn. 15:20-23).

True to these words, the Church was persecuting me because I was doing and saying things that no one else had done or said in the history of PCEA. Unfortunately, that had made the Church guilty of sin because they persecuted me rather than being doers of God's Word. They turned out to be good listeners of the **Word**, hence deceiving themselves, thinking that, by persecuting me, they were engaging in a wonderful ministry, shouting, '*away with him!*' By doing this, my persecutors failed to understand the anointing that

God had bestowed upon me to shed light and, at the same time, pave the way for PCEA's spiritual path.

Unfortunately, some of the leaders of this denomination were hooked up in greed and in the spirit of unbelief. They turned a deaf ear to God's sent messengers. They were busy looting the Church funds and properties and had totally deviated from God's original purpose in introducing this denomination in East Africa. They even drifted from the path I had set for the Church - the path that was meant to propel it into a deeper understanding of the scriptures. This was a path that created safeguards and paved the way for more economic resources for the Church.

Instead, they scooped away what my tenure of office had solidified. They even anchored their association with those who had embraced the ordination of homosexuals and same-sex marriages. These Church liberals defended the evil altars that continually defiled the Church.

As a result of denying the truth and fighting those who dared speak the truth, it is not a surprise that PCEA continues to get deeper into God's curse and Judgment. It is not until the Church leadership mobilizes the entire Church and members for repentance that God's heart could be touched, as happened with the people of Nineveh (Jonah 3). PCEA should also ask for forgiveness from the people they have persecuted over the years- people like Rev. Dr. Timothy Njoya and many others who have already gone and are undergoing very severe persecution at the hands of PCEA leadership, both spiritually and physically. Many have died as victims of depression and physical assault.

No one denomination in the world is guilty of persecuting the people who stood for the truth. The graves are full of such saints. Many tortured and killed have been proclaimed saints years after their torture to death. These atrocities can be traced from the early church:

Thomas More, an English lawyer, philosopher, and statesman during the reign of King Henry VII, is an example of a person who was made a saint after being killed as a heretic. More opposed Henry's decision to break away from the Catholic Church and establish the Church of England. As a result, he was accused of treason and heresy and was executed in 1535. Thomas More was canonized 400 years later in 1935 as a saint by the Catholic Church!

Jan Hus, a Czech priest and religious reformer who challenged the practices of the Catholic Church in the 15th. Century was burned at the stake for heresy in 1415 and was posthumously declared a martyr and saint by the Hussite Church from its establishment in 1420, five years after his death. Although the Catholic Church has not officially canonized him as a saint, he is considered a Martyr and a significant figure in the Protestant Reformation.

Here closer home, the **Ugandan Martyrs** were canonized as saints almost 80 years after being killed. The Ugandan Martyrs were a group of 23 Anglican and 22 Catholic converts to Christianity who were executed between 1885 and 1887 for refusing to renounce their faith. They were killed under the orders of King Mwanga II of Buganda, who opposed the spread of Christianity in his kingdom. In 1964, Pope Paul VI canonized the Ugandan Martyrs, recognizing their courage and steadfastness in the face of persecution. They are now celebrated as saints and their feast day is observed on June 3rd.

In general, the PCEA Church leadership is required to lead the church into deeper and deeper spiritual reawakening. Among other things, the leaders need to intensify the '*Ministry*' of intercessory that I had pioneered. The church leadership will need to lead the church into prayerfulness and humility, seeking God's face and surrendering its persistent wickedness.

It is in this regard that God says, "*If my people who are called by my name will humble themselves and pray and seek my face and turn from their wicked ways, then will I hear from heaven and will forgive their sins and will heal their land.*" PCEA, like any other Church, is God's spiritual land. PCEA has a God-given mandate to lead the redemption of Kenya in the areas of financial, political, economic, spiritual, and social liberation. This is the message I was delivering to the church through my 35-page book; '**Kenya Repent or Perish**.'

Surprisingly, the symbols at Sigona remain intact, and people consciously step on them and even continue worshipping the coffin-shaped cross in the upper part of the front wall of the church. But the fact remains that until these symbols are removed, the congregation will continue to suffocate in the spirit of unbelief; the rich oppressing the poor, hatred, jealousy, and the oppressive spirit of the pastors will also continue to increase in the form of a curse upon the congregation. The Bible clearly says, "*Whoever has ears, let him hear what the Spirit says.*" Revelation 3:22

KENYAN PARLIAMENT OCCULTIC SYMBOLS CONTROVERSY

The controversy over occultism symbolism in parliament was stirred after a special invitation to Parliament in 2005 to be part of the ceremony that marked that year's parliamentary opening session.

PRAYER IN PARLIAMENT

Since Kenya attained independence in 1963, parliamentary sessions have been held with prayers. The mainstream denominational Church leaders from the Presbyterian Church of East Africa, Anglican Church, and Roman Catholic Church, as well as Muslims, participate in the delivery of such prayers.

In 2005, and by virtue of my being the Moderator of the General Assembly, I happened to be one of those Church leaders who were participating in this kind of forum. The practice was to have a typed prayer to be read out. This is important just in case the state or the media would like to have access to that prayer for one reason or another.

The first person to pray was the Archbishop of the Roman Catholic Church. He was followed by the Anglican Archbishop. As the latter was approaching the end of his prayer, my hand was already in my pocket, fishing out the written prayer. But somehow, my mind got disconnected from the action of pulling out the prayer when my eyes were mysteriously attracted to some symbols embedded in some parts of the building, especially on the walls and grills.

The symbols in the chambers were in the form of different representations, such as frogs, snakes, charging bulls, and rhinos among others. Some were patterns grilled on the windows and staircases. As the ACK Archbishop Nzimbi was finishing his prayer, I had not pulled my prayer out of my pocket, and when my turn to pray came, rather than read my written prayers that I had with me, I verbally and prayerfully plunged into denouncing the '*Satanic altars*' in parliament. I got vigorously engaged in exposing and cursing the idolatry that was disguisedly represented in parliament.

I had felt a move of the Holy Spirit commanding me to pray over those evil altars through which Kenya existed in bondage. I knew that I was plunging myself into a fierce storm, but I had to obey God, knowing that, in a fierce storm, one must do one thing- put the ship of faith in a certain position and keep her there to anchor the ship unto the Cross, totally trusting and depending on God.

In my prayers, I called upon God to open the eyes of all those people in the building and see the idolatry and evil altars that grazed in the building's environment so that He could reveal the symbols of negative influence on the chamber's environment. As I bombarded the kingdom of Satan as well as calling for the removal of those altars, the whole House was in a continuous murmuring mood. I am sure those who knew and valued those Masonic symbols were cursing me for having let the cat out of the bag. Of course, there were those who were angered by the fact that I had exposed the gods of the Illuminati that the Freemasons and New Agers worshiped. Such were occultly dedicated through chanting upon them some witchcraft in manipulative maneuvers. It included the spirit of deception, which in turn controlled the mind of the members of parliament. In that way, the parliamentarians acted and debated in accordance with the will of the Freemasonry/ Illuminati, Humanists, and the New Age Movement agenda. In fact, these groups of people have the agenda to create a worldwide evil religion and government. God forbid! Nevertheless, I continued amidst the murmurs. I kept asking God to reveal to them these satanic representations so that they would not only repent but have them removed and instead paint or hang on the walls pictures or paintings like those of people picking coffee or tea, herds of hybrid cows, Kenyan land features like Mount Kenya and so on.

My question was and still is:

"Why flood parliament with idolatry-oriented symbols in form of drawings, images and pictures, sculptures, and the like?" At one time, I posed this question to a politician who told me that he was a born – again Christian: *"Why don't we draw pictures that reflect our everyday life experiences in parliament like children learning in a classroom, well-bred cows grazing at a farm; mountains like mount Kenya and mount Kilimanjaro; some farm vegetation like coffee, tea, or pyrethrum; some of our skyscrapers; or even renowned athletes like Kipchoge Keino, Paul Tergat, Catherine Ndereba, or historical, and vital sites like the Mombasa harbour and so on?"*

In response, the politician said:

"But you know we do not have much say over that building. We just found it the way it was originally constructed by the British authorities. I assume, one time, God will forward a leader with the spirit of the likes of Josiah, Gideon, Hezekiah, and Asa. Such were courageous enough to handle that kind of spiritual warfare. Remember, you are talking of tackling some satanic strongholds, some of which are treated as gods by some in government to the extent of worshiping them. It will take a person with God's anointing for that kind of mission."

I also pointed out to the politician the idolatry entrenched in various buildings in Nairobi, including those sculptures on the grounds of the University of Nairobi, the Attorney General Chambers, and the High Court, where some occult figures are portrayed. There is the Babylonian Lion at the Attorney General Chambers, and its representation is on the Court of Arms, which is a representation of magical powers.

WIDE MEDIA COVERAGE

Thank God, the media took pictures of many of these satanic symbols and had them exposed through the evening news in accordance with my prayers. That evening, as the media reported on the opening of parliament with some details on the president's speech, they showed the occult symbols in parliament. The reader of the news in one of the media houses said, *"It was during the session of prayers that the Moderator of Presbyterian Church of East Africa, Dr. David Githii, came up with what he referred to as, 'Satanic Altars in Parliament.' Here are some of the symbols we tapped and we are now exposing."* The media took quite some time to show what I had referred to as the real cause of defilement in the Kenyan Parliament. This, as the reader of the news put it, *"was a great revelation by Dr. David Githii, the Moderator of the PCEA Church. Unfortunately, there was a group of those in the House who were angered by such a revelation. They kept on murmuring even as Githii went on with his evil-exposing prayer."*

The following day, one of the daily newspapers carried the heading, '**Dr. Githii:** '*From St. Andrews to Parliament.*' The paper then narrated how, having exposed the symbols at St. Andrews, I had this time exposed the symbols that flooded parliament buildings. This story appeared in the Newspaper the following day. The next day, as I was walking, I met a man who, upon seeing me, warmly shook my hand and then, pulling the newspaper from his pocket, quickly pointed to the story about me. He said: *"This is great! And what courage! You have amazed us all. This is a great revelation from God. In fact, people everywhere are talking about this very timely revelation. God has a purpose for you to be born in Kenya and for a time like this when the country is bowing down to idolatry of every kind. If I were to be asked, people could elect a person of your caliber as the president to deal with idolatry in our country. We are not going anywhere so long as our country is in the bondage of idolatry, some of which was planted by the Westerners and the others by those who took over when our country attained independence."*

The person went on to further say, *"When I read about this story on how you courageously exposed Satanism that is draining the brains of our lawmakers, I recalled this word from the book of Jonah 3:8, that says: '**Those who cling to worthless idols forfeit the blessings that could be theirs.**' This then means that a country like Kenya will remain dwarfed in all sectors of its life so long as idolatry supersedes God's honour. One will only need to look at the history of the Israelites. Any time they leaned towards idolatry, their nation suffered a lot of catastrophes. But no sooner had they reverted to the true worship of God God then plugged them into prosperity. This is true with the Kingship of the likes of Hezekiah, Josiah, David, and Asa."*

The news continued: *"But then there is this PCEA Moderator of General Assembly, Dr. David Githii, who prayed against what he termed as 'Satanic Altars in Parliament.'* The news analyst then went ahead to show the kind of satanic symbols that had eternally flooded the parliament buildings. He displayed all the Masonic symbols.

They were able to show most of them as they had gone to all corners of the buildings after the parliamentary session. For the first time in the history of Kenya, people would come to know the evil powers that had formed a dark cloud in parliament, which, in fact, were controlling Kenya as a nation. That was the year 2005.

The following year, in 2006, I was likewise invited to be part of those opening parliament with prayers. I repeated the exposition of the ungodly altars through the prayers and the media did the same in exposing them. Through those expositions, Kenyans were able to witness the occultic symbolism in parliament buildings. They were even able to see the snake symbolism on the speaker's seat. In that way, they were able to relate the occultic representation in parliament with the unwelcoming behavior of the members of parliament and their obvious attachment to immorality, corruption, lies, character assassination, greed, and all kinds of manipulation.

The exposition of these evil altars became the talk of the day this time, too. People talked about them in their houses, offices, matatus, markets, and so on. In many ways, it would become a point of reference over a long time. Many people thanked God for bestowing such courage on me, for not many would have dared to be outspoken in such a way. Most people would always fear for their lives. But when God calls a person with a mission to be accomplished, He also equips and protects that person.

It's like what we read about Samson in Judges 14:5-6, "*Suddenly a young lion came roaring towards him. The spirit of the Lord came upon him in power so that he tore the lion apart with his bare hands as he would have torn a young goat.*" Without this provision of God's power, Samson could not overcome the lion. This also happened to David upon being anointed. Samuel told him, "*The spirit of the Lord will come upon you in power…and you will be a changed person…do whatever your hand finds to do, for God is with you*" (1 Sam.6-7). That is exactly what happened to me at this time of exposition of satanic altars. God also raises people who come to the aid of the person he has raised. For example, God had raised King Fredrick to come to the aid of Martin Luther, the Reformer. He hid him even as the pope had issued a bull indicating that whoever would kill him would become a saint straight away.

1.The Snake Symbol   2.The Star at Parliament   3.Lucifers Eye on the Speakers

In an article in the Daily Nation newspaper of Tuesday, February 10, 2009, the writer who refers to himself as MMK in his defense of my claims of satanic symbols in the Kenyan Parliament had this to say:

*"Let me explain by introducing my new favourite pastor, Rev. Dr. David Githii, head of the Presbyterian Church of East Africa (PCEA). He argues that Kenyan government buildings harbor many satanic symbols and that Kenya is a country reeling under '**the great influence of devil worship.**' Four years ago, he was quoted in the East African Standard saying that "the two snakes at the entrance to the Kenyan House of Parliament, the huge Masonic star at the entrance to the (parliament), the frogs and tortoise signs in the High Court must be demolished...., nor did his investigations into the insidious nature of Lucifer stop there. He constantly points to the goddess called 'Ambe,' which echoes in Harambee.*

He said, *"Elaborating on the reasons I questioned the chanting of Harambee, MMK further said the combination of 'Har' and 'Ambe' gives 'Harambee' but with an extra 'e' at the end to become 'Harambee' for better sounding in Swahili. 'Harambee' then became a slogan derived from the chanting by the Indian coolies as they hailed their Goddess 'Ambe,'"* as I explained earlier. MMK continued to explain the fact that *"rather than people attacking me, they should first carry out research to determine what I am talking about."* He said, *"Dr. Githii is right. 'Ambe' is a Hindu goddess. Unfortunately, little did Kenyans suspect that while chanting Harambee, it was something in the Gujarati language. Otherwise, the word Harambee came into usage in Kenya through the courtesy of the Indians who built the Kenya-Uganda railway and would chant the phrase as they toiled under the gaze of man-eating lions."*

In the year that followed, I was not invited as great pressure mounted from the occultists who felt their covert evil space had been inappropriately invaded. They demanded that I should not be invited to that year's session of opening the parliament. Henceforth,

I was blocked from any involvement in offering prayers at any other government-related functions. This did not bother me because the truth had come to be known by Kenyans, and that was God's agenda. It was immediately after this that I wrote the book, '**Exposing and Conquering Satanic Forces over Kenya**,' a book that was widely read both locally and internationally.

PCEA REACTION TO THE MEDIA COVERAGE

This action further fueled the PCEA liberals' anger. They now combined their efforts with some liberal members of parliament. A business Committee meeting was urgently summoned to deal with me once and for all. As the Moderator, I had to open that meeting with some devotion. I then based my devotion on Josiah, the king of Israel, as recorded in 2 Chronicles 34. This chapter is a representation of how King Josiah destroyed all the satanic altars in all of Israel. I mainly focused on verses 4 and 7, which say, "*Under his direction, the altars of the Baals were torn down; he cut into pieces the incense altars that were above them and smashed the Asherah poles, the idols, and the images....and crushed the idols to powder.*"

I also referred to Jehu in 2 Kings 9: 22 thus: "*When Joram saw Jehu he asked, "Have you come in peace, Jehu?" "How can there be peace," Jehu replied, "as long as all the idolatry and witchcraft of your mother Jezebel abound?"*

I also referred to King Asa, whose national reform is found in 2 Chronicles 15:8, which says, "*he took courage. He removed the detestable idols from the whole land of Judah and Benjamin.*" And what was the result of this courageous move? The Bible says, "*There was no more war until the thirty-fifth year of Asa's reign.*" Otherwise, as verse five indicates, before Asa dealt with this menace, the Bible says, "*In those days it was not safe to travel about, for all the inhabitants of the lands were in great turmoil.... because God was troubling them with every kind of distress.*"

Based on this scripture, I then elaborated on the negative influence of planted altars in a building or in the country, for that matter. I taught quite a lot about this, and by the time I was done, all the business committee members were on my side. In one accord, they declined to carry out any debate regarding my pointing fingers at the negative altars in parliament. This was a bomb that God defused.

They had come with one voice, to have me expelled from the Church, but God had a different agenda.

Suffice it to say that, in spite of many having come to an understanding of what I was exposing, there were many in both the Church and the secular world who did not understand, but there were also those who were the authors of the evil I was speaking about. They were bitter that I had exposed their gods. The latter attacked me in futility because rather than the battle calming down, it was gaining momentum.

The whole battle was focused on my being defrocked, as that would have snatched me from the forum from which I was speaking and, hence, rendered me voiceless. It is no wonder there were constant meetings held to come up with ways and means of expelling me from the church, as we have seen. It was either my being impeached or even being defrocked. But God's word held ground thus, "*No weapon forged against you will prevail, and you will refute every tongue that accuses you. This is the heritage of the servants of the Lord, and this is their vindication from me.*" This theme was also articulated in verses 11, 14, and 15: "*I will build you with stones of turquoise, your foundations with sapphires…In righteousness, you will be established: tyranny will be far from you; you will have nothing to fear. Terror will be far from you. If anyone does attack you, it will not be my doing; whoever attacks you will surrender to you.*"

PROTECTION OF SATANIC SYMBOLS

In my assessment of the way PCEA handled the controversies that cropped out at P.C.E.A Sigona Church and the earlier controversies at St. Andrews Church, the Church of Torch, and St. Margret's Church in Mombasa and the way they treated me was a clear indication that the denomination's leadership was reluctant in addressing the idolatry that was infiltrating the denomination including the mushrooming homosexuality, devil worship, and corruption.

Instead, the Masonic endeavors in the Church advanced the protection of idolatry. They ensured they did everything within their power to have all idols in the Church solidly secured. It can only take a very determined heart to address the idolatry. For example, the removal of some symbols from PCEA St. Andrews was not done without a strong fight and resistance from those who wanted the symbols to be protected. That is why I became the focus of attack for an accusation that I was not protecting the idols from being removed.

They argued that, by virtue of my being the Moderator of the General Assembly, I had all the powers to protect the symbols, which they referred to as "*Artifacts.*" They had even disregarded the resolutions passed by both the St. Andrews Kirksession and Milimani Presbytery authorizing the removal of the symbols for spiritually polluting the Church environment.

This controversy, especially the one over Sigona Church, and the exposure of symbols flooding parliament buildings were not only eye-openers but triggers as well. This was not only to PCEA members but also to Kenyan citizens who had come to learn the truth behind what I was advocating for. It is good to say that God used these controversies to release the new revelation to the nation and the body of Christ. The church had kept a blind eye to these pagan representations in church buildings, though somewhere in their hearts, they had come to know the truth. This came out clearly in the GA Moderator Rev Gathanju's 19th GA theme, '*My people perish for lack of knowledge.*' This exposed the mockery that the theme portrayed. Otherwise, if it were not so, then when this knowledge of the mysteries of the gospel was offered by God through my teachings, it would have been embraced rather than rejected. It is one of those aspects of knowledge that people lack.

I felt that the Church leadership deliberately kept on a defilement trail, which in the eyes of God was like embracing sin, something that the Bible has pointed to when it says, "*If we deliberately keep on sinning after we have received the knowledge of the truth, no sacrifice for sin is left, but only a fearful expectation of judgment*" (Heb.10:26). Here, we are talking of severe judgment. This is a Judgment that could see the Church derailing or dying in almost all its faculties of life.

The Bible makes this clear when it says,
"*Anyone who rejected the law of Moses died without mercy on the testimony of two or three witnesses. How much more severely do you think a man deserves to be punished who has trampled the Son of God underfoot, who has treated as an unholy thing the blood of the covenant that sanctified him, and who has insulted the spirit of grace? The Lord will judge his own*

people…. It is a dreadful thing to fall into the hands of the living God" (Heb.10 28-31). The words, *'trampled the son of God under foot'* would also point at the crosses on most of the floors of church buildings that people step on. This disqualifies the church from being a church of God. God is after a church that leads the way to righteousness.

That is why a Church that cherishes things to do with occultism is under God's curse and judgment. Otherwise, how does the Church dare trample on the cross, the symbol of one who died to redeem the world, the Son of God? How can one trample on the symbol of our salvation? The cross also symbolizes the blood that gave birth to the New Covenant, the old having failed to redeem humankind. The cross also represents the grace that Jesus Christ so willingly bestowed upon us, grace that surpasses all understanding, leading to an abundance of life.

There are many denominations whose Church buildings have tens of crosses and other negative symbols on the floor, some taking the shape of diamonds, stars, and other occultic shapes which are mistaken for decorations but are disguised occultism and remain so wherever they are positioned in the buildings as we established. This is regardless of the kind of beauty they carry with them. Most of them remain occultic symbols aimed at defiling the Church building.

There is a high likelihood that occult symbols exist in seven out of ten PCEA buildings in Kenya, and this is also true of sanctuaries in other denominations, including Roman Catholics, the Anglicans, Baptists, Methodists, and so on. In many cases, as stated earlier, there is one symbol strategically entrenched on the floor at the main entrance door, and whoever walks into the sanctuary has to step on it. Notable also is the usually small tainted- glass windows at the top of the main entrance wall above the door with the gods in the form of colours that are a presentation of orange (Sun god), green (mother earth goddess}, and blue (water spirits). This is all Illuminati and New Age occultism. These spiritually disarm the believers as they enter the sanctuary. They also pollute their minds with spirits of strife, the spirit of unbelief, meanness, and satanic mind control, which activates the spirit of immorality, hatred, greed, pride, and all kinds of spiritual manipulation.

9 THE DEFILEMENT OF CHURCHES AND INSTITUTIONS THROUGH NAMES

TAKING DEAD BODIES INTO THE SANCTUARY

While in the office of General Assembly Moderator, one of my major concerns revolved around the defilement of churches and institutions caused by bringing dead bodies into the sanctuary for funeral services. I persistently called upon the church to stop this negative practice. This was one other area that made the PCEA leadership refer to me as a radical reformer. As the Moderator, I persistently questioned this undesirable habit, arguing the church building is meant for the living but not the dead.

There is a feeling in some denominations that the final service in a person's life acts as the lift/elevator to take the person to heaven. Missing such a service, therefore, means missing the entry point to heaven. There is also a feeling that the higher the position in leadership one had in the Church, the better the mansion in heaven, hence the elevation of such a person's funeral. The question of wealth also comes in. Thus, the more well-off the person is, the more lavish the funeral. The understanding has always been the better the burial ceremony the better the crown that awaits one in heaven. It's no wonder people intensify campaigns for Church positions to the extent of bribing their way in.

In my teachings, I reminded PCEA membership of the old African culture, which was also in line with the Jewish culture, where the living was not supposed to have any association with a dead body. It was regarded as an already defiled object. This is why the two Jews could not stop to help that person who was beaten up by the robbers and therefore appeared dead. But then, the Good Samaritan, whose culture did not forbid him from touching a dead body, took care of him.

In the African culture, and especially among my fellow Agikuyu people, when it was certain that someone was nearing the end of his or her life, they abandoned the person to die either in the house or in a designated place. The house was then left to be destroyed by some undergrowth. Nobody else would occupy such a house. Another way was to take the person into the bush to die there to be eaten up by the wild animals. It was taboo to touch a dead body as it was believed that such a body was already defiled. And worse still, it was believed that the spirit of the death could pollute any living person who happened to handle the dead body. Such a defilement would call for cleansing before the person was allowed to interact with other people. I am not saying bodies shouldn't be handled, but it's important to be mindful of avoiding contamination when handling dead bodies.

Is it not true that even today many people will really refrain from viewing a dead body because of the negative lasting image that will linger in their mind? Is it not true that it would be one of those psychological tortures of the mind if one was forced to spend a night in the mortuary amidst dead bodies? This is because, one's mind interprets that, the mortuary is already saturated by the spirits of death, and therefore it creates a fearful environment. It is these spirits that would inhabit the sanctuary while the dead body resides there.

In my teachings, I reminded the PCEA leadership that the denomination founder John Calvin was totally against having dead bodies in the sanctuary. He had even given instructions that after his death, his body was not to be taken into the Church building. He had told his family and close friends never to treat his dead body with high esteem because a dead body stinks. He was to be removed from the mortuary straight to the graveside for burial. When someone passes away the spirit of death that was lurking gives way and, their soul departs from their physical body, which is left to decay and eventually return to the earth, becoming a home for worms and decaying into soil.

Calvin believed that a dead body should therefore not be given much honor. He had further given instructions that his grave should not be marked, because, *"The body itself is soil and to soil it will return, it therefore needs no ceremonies, ceremonies are held in heaven over the victorious soul."* And that is the whole truth. A dead body stinks and that is why dead bodies and the coffins are perfumed in order to defuse the smell.

Why then take smelly things in the house of God? This is what I called upon the church to embrace- the avoidance of taking dead bodies into the Church buildings at the time of a funeral service. As led by the Holy Spirit, I asked the Presbyteries and Business Committee to deliberate and come up with a resolution banning the taking of dead bodies into the sanctuary. I argued that, Jesus had categorically stated that, His house was a house of prayer and it was embracing the presence of God. A dead body in the Church building is like an idol. It is not even referred to by the dead person's name-It's a corpse, heavily sprayed with chemicals to overcome the smell.

In coming out with this proposal, I faced a lot of opposition because it is a tradition that had been so much embraced that those who resisted this move argued that the sanctuary acts as a lift/elevator in the spiritual realm to *'accelerate the lifting of the soul'* to its final destiny. Worse still was the fact that some dead bodies were being buried within the Church compound.

In emphasizing my sentiments, the People Newspaper, dated 4th Oct 2008, in a clip written by Loise Wambugu entitled: **Stop Memorial Services for The Dead**, stated:

"THE OUTSPOKEN Presbyterian Church of East Africa, PCEA Moderator David Githii, now wants Christians to stop taking dead bodies in the Church buildings at the time of conducting memorial services for the dead. Speaking at Tumutumu PCEA Church, Githii claims taking dead bodies to the Church for service was only meant to defile the Church with spirits of death, adding that burying the dead within the Church compound is not a godly act. The controversial cleric said that, for a long time there has been defiling of Church buildings through activities that the occults have been conducting. Githii said that God's blessings cannot be achieved if the Church leadership cannot change some of the ways they are doing things. The church should be observant because, as the Bible says, "And no wonder, Satan himself masquerades as an angel of light... his servants masquerade as servants of righteousness," as found in 2 Cor. 11:14.

In the same, Newspaper, the reporter Stephen Munyiri had the following to say in his article entitled: '**Keep The Dead Out Of Church Says Cleric**': "*Presbyterian Church head David Githii is at it again, pronouncing yet another controversial edict. The Reverend has asked his flock to stop holding prayers for the dead in the Church building, terming the practice as blasphemy and defilement of God's house.*"

Stephen further said, "*Githii eulogizes the fact that, when a person dies and you take the body inside the Church, are you not insulting God? When one dies, that's all and there is nothing we can do about it.*" Stephen continued; "*So, stop this nonsense of placing dead bodies in the Church building, ostensibly to pray for him or her to go to heaven. Do you mean a small part had been left behind waiting for the Church's intervention before one goes to heaven? He asked the congregation at Tumutumu PCEA Church during centennial celebrations. This is why the Church leaders look at him as a controversial and radical Church reformer. And for sure, this cleric is a reformer. He has introduced a new face into the PCEA in all its sectors.*"

The truth of the matter is that though I never had a breakthrough in this endeavour, this issue will take place not so long in the future. In any case, at the time of Corona Pandemic, the Church had no choice but to totally refrain from taking dead bodies to the sanctuaries simply because the health protocols did not allow this. The myth that PCEA and other Churches must eulogize dead bodies in the sanctuary got demystified then because the circumstances of the protocols prevented any in-person gatherings or handling bodies infected by the virus. Does this mean the diseased persons did not go to heaven because their bodies were neither taken to the mortuary nor to the sanctuary?

It was after I had finished my tenure at GA Office as Moderator and had been posted to PCEA Sigona in October, 2009, that I decided to test the waters. No sooner had I got inducted into the parish on 21st. March, 2010, then I made a declaration that for as long as I was the parish minister, no dead body would be accommodated into the sanctuary for a funeral service and that all funeral services would be held at the grave site. Some elders swore that such a move would only happen over their dead bodies.

It then happened that one of the staunch Church members, Minywe died. He was greatly respected because he was the chairman of the development committee and credited with having made the groundbreaking of PCEA Sigona sanctuary. Thus, the elders held to their guns that his body was to be taken inside the sanctuary as per the tradition of the Church. But I insisted that as long as I was the parish minister, nothing of the sort would take place. The elders called for an urgent meeting and threatened to expel me from their parish but to their surprise, I still held my ground.

It was then that they sent a delegation to the deceased's wife pleading with her to contest the decision that her husband's funeral service be held at the grave site. Again, to their surprise she said, "*I will go with what the Parish Minister is advocating for. The funeral service will be held at the gravesite.*" With this new twist, they had no alternative but to give way for the gravesite funeral service. And this became the tradition during the time I remained at PCEA Sigona Parish. Nevertheless, this trend came to an end as soon as I came out of that parish. The incoming minister could not withstand the pressure.

ENTRENCHED GRAVES IN CHURCH PREMISES

Another thing I was opposed to was having graves within the church premises or compound. A grave in the Church compound becomes an altar for the devil to destroy and defile the already dedicated sanctuary through a service conducted by the Kirksession or the Presbytery. I quoted Isaiah 42:8 which says; "*I am the LORD; that is my name! I will not yield my glory to another or my praise to idols.*" Note the exclamation mark in "*That is my name!*" in the above verse. It communicates God's seriousness in the rejection of anything that would be pushed to share His glory. When a place is dedicated in the name of God, it is not advisable to come and plant something that is not conducive to the Spirit of God. Those who practice witchcraft and want to defile the Church carry out their evil manipulation using the negative spirits whose abode is in the graves. The spirits of death dominate such an environment. Who doesn't have some kind of fear they pass alone in graveyards at night? Won't you be fearful if you were to sleep overnight in the same room with a corpse?

Another question I posed to the congregation as I drew their attention to a grave just next to the door of PCEA Tumu Church was:

"Do you notice how near the church building is to the graves? Do you also notice that they are mostly placed in front of the entrance of the Church? – The dead are believed to communicate and watch the people as they come to Church and as they come out. People unconsciously give reverence to these graves." Has not God said, *"You shall not bow down to them or worship them, for I, the Lord your God, am a jealous God, punishing the children for the sin of the fathers to the third and fourth generation of those who hate me, but showing love to... those who love me and keep my commandments?"* (Ex. 20:5-6)

In one of the GAC, I called upon the delegates to do something about the Church's defilement. I said: *"In view of the dishonor to God by burying dead bodies in the Church compound, and also by placing dead bodies into the sanctuaries at the time of funeral services, I am calling upon this GA to forthwith stop the burying of dead bodies in any of the PCEA compounds and also ban the placing of dead bodies in the sanctuary."* But in spite of my very progressive endeavour to convince the church at the times of the funerals, I never made a breakthrough in this call. I was even called names because I was blocking the easier way for dead people to get to heaven and to be buried with the greatest honour that a Christian deserves.

I argued that graves defile the Church compound. While addressing Church leaders at Nakuru I remember saying: *"It is unfortunate that dead bodies are buried in the Church compound in the name of honouring a person for the work done by him/her. Yet, the same compound was dedicated in a service, set aside to be used only to glorify God."* I reminded my listeners the fact that, it is the same God we claim to worship and whose kingdom we propagate, who at the same time says, *"I am the Lord; that is my name! I will not give my glory to another or my praise to idols"* (Isa. 42:8). God would hate to dwell in the same building where the spirit of the death is honoured by having graves around it or in it. This practice of having dead bodies in the church compounds was part of the Scottish missionary traditions. In fact, every church in Europe has its compound flooded with graves. No wonder the church has continued to progressively die.

NAMING OF CHURCHES AFTER PEOPLE

Another issue that irritated the PCEA leadership was my calling upon the Church to address the naming of Churches after people. I insisted that names have power and they can be strongholds of either blessings or curses. My argument was that the name of a Church is supposed to form a positive altar for the Lord. Where a Church building is named after a person that name of the person becomes the altar and as we well know, God will never share His glory with a person or an idol.

Naming of sanctuaries after people glorifies the person rather than God. It changes from being a habitation of God's spirit to a human altar, which then defeats the original purpose for which the Church building was meant to stand for. Holding a renowned Church person or dead body at the expense of Godliness is demeaning the name and image of God.

One will not need to carry out an extensive research work to discover that PCEA surpasses all other denominations worldwide in naming Church buildings after dead people and places. And this was my concern as I spent a lot of time to take this message to the congregations, parishes, presbyteries and various Church committees or courts. To test this, one will only need to ask a person who worships in a Church named in memory of a dead person, "*Where do you worship?*" A worshipper at PCEA Muraguri Memorial Church, for instance will obviously respond; "*I worship at Muraguri Church.*" **Muraguri** is the Agikuyu's name for a **witchdoctor**.

Here the glory of man and the accompanying spirit of witchcraft overshadow the glory of God. It will then not be surprising to find that a good number in that congregation will in one way or another be practicing some witchcraft, divination or consulting mediums, just because, the spirit overshadowing that Church is one of occultism.

The magnitude of defilement that negativity in a name cause is reflected in the fact that, God had to change the names of; Jacob to Israel (prince); Simon to Peter (Rock), Abram to (Abraham), **Sarai** to Sarah, Saul to Paul. God could not carry out His purposed destiny through these people while they bore names that were defiled. For example, Jacob means, Conman or a liar. Could God use a person with that name to establish his people, the Children of Israel? Would not the spirit of conmanship have overwhelmed them? No! On the contrary, because of the change in name, they were to be known as, Children of the Prince.

In my teachings on this subject, I did indicate that some names of places are Satan's strongholds because of their past history. Speaking to some Church leaders in Meru, I remember telling them that:

"The naming of churches either brings a blessing or curses. When the name of a church has a negative connotation, it is no wonder some Churches, parishes, and presbyteries are ever in constant strife, the spirit of unbelief is rife, financial constraints abound, and financial misappropriation is the order of the day, immorality is a common phenomenon, divisions are not new, scandals are numerous over the years. I said, the Church will need to encourage positive names of Elder Districts, Parishes, and Presbyteries."

I further said, *"I would challenge some of you to carry out some research on the names the Church you come from. You will be surprised to learn the meaning behind most of these names is negative in terms of Godliness."* While sanctuaries are supposed to carry the altar of Jesus Christ, such Churches named after people carry the altar of the person so named. Worse, some of these people were immoral, alcohol and drug addicts, oppressors, corrupt, weak in their family affiliations and family lineage. Some had attachment to occultism/witchcraft, or to murderers, rapists, homosexuals, and rebellious people.

Suffice to say that every human being is sinful in nature. Therefore, to name the church by a person's name is to infiltrate that person's weakness or sinfulness into that sanctuary. The Bible affirms this when it says: *"For all have sinned and fall short of the glory of God"* (Romans 3:23). Psalms 51:5, further confirms this when it says: *"Surely I was sinful at birth, sinful from the time my mother conceived me."*

My research had revealed that more than 70% of PCEA congregations are either named after dead people or after the names of their location. Churches named after dead people are dominant in most of the parishes and presbyteries. All said and done; names carry curses or blessings. For example, Jacob's name had to be changed from Jacob to Israel because; the name Jacob had a bad connotation meaning a liar or a conman.

Secondly, when a Church building, parish or presbytery is named after a person, the glory goes to the name but not to God and in whose name the building is set up as we have seen. For example, when a Church is named, PCEA Calvary Church or PCEA Blessing Church, there is some connection with the spiritual realm. Thus, accordingly, these Churches named after people unless after the Apostles, are adulterated by the names they bear, making the Spiritual environment very hard and impermeable to the spirit of God.

Biblically, the Holy Spirit is likened to a dove, and as much as a natural dove cannot land on a thorn-covered tree with poisonous fruits, in the same way, the Holy Spirit cannot land on a defiled sanctuary which in the spiritual realm is like a thorny tree with bitter fruits. This is, therefore, also true of the sanctuary named after an individual's name. It is for this reason that, in one of the GAC meetings, I called upon the delegates to come up with two resolutions. I said:

"In view of this, I am calling upon this GAC to formulate a way in which before a Church, Parish or Presbytery is given a name, the Kirk-session is to deliberate on the right name, a name with spiritual attachment, which will then be affirmed by the Presbytery. And for the Elder Districts-the Local Church Committee is to qualify the right name of a given Elder District- a name that glorifies God."

For resolution number two, I said; *"In view of the negative spirit that is founded on a person's name over the Lord's sanctuary, I am calling upon this GA to instruct parishes and presbyteries to stop forthwith, the naming of Churches after people. On the same note, I am calling upon this GAC to encourage the Kirk-sessions through the Presbyteries to change names of Churches bearing the names of people to more positive and biblical names. I also call for the Presbyteries to be empowered to recommend the names given to Congregations and Parishes before such come into effect."*

Unfortunately, these two views were not upheld by the delegates. Some called it crazy ideas. They argued that, a name is a name and nothing negative or positive can influence the working environment

341

through a name. But there were quite a number who understood me. One such positive person said:

"The problem we have is that, the Scottish missionaries never reviewed the way negative spirits work in resisting God's spirit. They themselves never believed in the existence of evil spirits with their continued thriving in some kind of strongholds. In fact, what the Moderator is revealing is the way the devil has cunningly held sanctuaries in bondage. We might oppose what he is saying now but before long others will buy into the idea and the naming of not only sanctuaries, parishes and presbyteries, Elder Districts but the institutions as well will be named as per biblical names. I find it unfortunate that many times, we just act emotionally having not taken time to reason out the pros or cons of a motion. Could it be a sign of spiritual dryness. It is unfortunate that our spiritual arteries are so hardened by both the Scottish culture and traditions but future generations will have spiritual softened hearts."

CHURCHES NAMED AFTER MISSIONARIES

The naming of churches after people was the creation of pioneer missionaries in keeping with their traditions back in Europe. No wonder then the first sanctuary ever built at Thogoto by these missionaries was named after the missionary Watson; hence, the name of the church became '**Watson Memorial Church.**' 'Memorial' means in memory of the person whose name it bears.

In a regional seminar held at PCEA Nyamachaki, I gave another example of the name **Nyamachaki**. This Church had its name adopted from the nickname of Marion Stephenson who was one of the pioneer missionaries and who used to talk a lot about cheques. She was the one who received donations from overseas and she was therefore involved in all sorts of financial transactions from overseas and whenever she would be asked about payments on various areas of Church life, she would have comments like: *"I am waiting for a cheque from overseas; I will issue a cheque; yesterday I signed some cheques."* She was therefore nicknamed Nyama-check or Cheque (Nyamachaki which in Gikuyu language refers to one who is accustomed to mentioning 'cheques').

The Africans were not able to pronounce the word cheque, hence, pronounced it as *'chaki'* and because money was not easily forthcoming, there was a lot of strain and workers were straining a lot. They could go for long periods without salaries and this made them feel so much oppressed. What this entails from a spiritual perspective is that PCEA Nyamachaki's foundation was based on strain and oppressiveness. There was some remarkable degree of financial greed. No wonder the constant financial strain, strife, greed and power struggle and other negative concerns in this Church over the years.

As if that was not enough, this Church has given birth to PCEA King'ong'o, (King'ong'o is a name of a prison). Hence, this Church is embraced by a spirit of captivity. Such a Church will portray a strong spirit of unbelief and inner fighting. There is also, PCEA Kimathi. As much as Dedan Kimathi did a wonderful job in leading the struggle for Kenya's liberation from the British Colonialists through Mau Movement, he was at the same time not a Christian, leave alone being a Presbyterian. By virtue of being a Mau freedom fighter Kimathi had shed a lot of blood though for a better cause. Incidentally he was born on reformation day just like me but on (31st. October, 1920). No wonder, he had the spirit of a reformer. But remember, God had restrained David from building him a temple because he had shed a lot of blood.

Remember, we disqualified the naming of churches after people. There is a category of Churches that are named after the missionaries, yet, it is a known fact that most of the missionaries had an orientation in Freemasonry/Illuminati. And even the few that had no inclination to occultism had dubious spirituality. Many of them had their focus on acquiring land and exploitation of the raw materials to feed the factories back home yet they had Churches named after them.

In a seminar held at PCEA Dr. Arthur Memorial Church, in Nakuru Town, I informed the participants that the congregation and parish were named after a missionary a Dr. Arthur who was missionary medical doctor at the Thogoto mission area. He had nothing to do with ecclesiastical missionary work.

He was the pioneer medical doctor at Kikuyu Mission Hospital located at Thogoto. Dr. Arthur only stepped in to facilitate the

343

parochial work at the Church of Scotland mission at Thogoto when the missionary branch lacked a missionary priest. He then took the dual responsibilities of priest/medical doctor. Dr. Arthur did not have any theological knowledge on the scriptures and was more of a lay person. He also sided with the colonialists to oppress the Africans as the African representative in the Legislative Council.

Yet despite all these, PCEA rewarded him by naming a Church in his memory. It therefore goes without saying that, the Church named after him carries his spirit that dictates the lifestyle of that Church. It is no wonder this Church Parish is historically marked by strife that has, in some instances, led to physical confrontations. Dr. Arthur, like the other missionaries, did not believe either in salvation or in the works of the Holy Spirit.

CHURCHES NAMED AFTER THE LOCAL ENVIRONMENT

I was persistent and very vocal in calling upon the PCEA to avoid naming Churches after the Church's location. The negative names of places act as curses over the lands. It becomes a negative territorial spirit. People with authority can curse the land. For example, Joshua had cursed Jericho by declaring, "*Cursed before the Lord is the man who undertakes to rebuild this city, Jericho: At the cost of his first born will he will lay its foundation; at the cost of his youngest will, he set up its gates*" (Joshua 6:26). We find the pronouncement of this curse fulfilled in 1st Kings 16:34 where it says, "*Hiel of Bethel rebuild Jericho. He laid its foundations at the cost of his firstborn son Abiram, and he set its gates at the cost of his youngest son Segub, in accordance with the word of the Lord spoken by Joshua son of Nun.*"

I remember a time I was speaking to a Church leadership gathering in Mount Kenya Region and in discouraging them from naming Churches after places; I highlighted some Churches that bore names glorifying the devil. There is PCEA King'ong'o Church. This place, **King'ong'o** shares the same name with King'ong'o Maximum Prison. You can imagine the negative activities that take place in this kind of infamous prison. It also creates a hostile environment through the spirits of: oppression, torture, bloodshed, meanness, hunger, thirst, lust, homosexuality, hostility, strife among others.

Then there is this other Church named, PCEA **Kiangoma** in Nyeri. '**Kiangoma**' in Gikuyu language means Lucifer. Yet, people worship in this Church 52 Sundays in a year enjoying Holy Communion and baptisms not realizing that all this is done in the worship of Lucifer. This means, all worship activities lean towards glorifying Lucifer who has legal ground as the place bears his name.

I further drew attention to my listeners in regards to the name 'PCEA **Itura-Miro** Church'. The name '**Ituramiro**' in the Gikuyu language could also refer to the female genitalia. There is also PCEA **Menengai** Church in Nakuru Presbytery. The name **Menengai** in Maasai means '*the place of skulls*.' Thank God, the leadership of Menengai Church assimilated my teaching and hence, changed the name of the church to '*Beulah*.' In the Bible Beulah is a name symbolic of the heavenly Zion.

I remember telling my listeners: "*Suffice it to say that, out of ten names of PCEA Churches, nine are either named after dead people or after localities.*" My sentiments were echoed by the Nairobian Newspaper of April 4-10, 2014 (Pg1&11) written by James Mwangi and John Muthoni (Website http://revdavidgithii.me/crev/article/2923), where the authors said: "*Githii also condemned some names that are given to Churches, terming them as demonic. He singled out PCEA* **Kiangoma** *Church, saying the name symbolizes the devil. He urged Churches to conduct research on the names that they give to their institutions so that they do not become satanic altars. He added that the past leaders laid the foundations of pride, arrogance and witchcraft, saying the vice can only be eliminated through repentance and change of names. The buildings would then undergo some cleansing through the anointing.*"

A good example of the way the bad spirits act negatively towards the kingdom of God was the Limuru Presbytery. This was the home of most resistance in presbyteries in all my six-year tenure as the GA Moderator. The leaders were persistently campaigning for my removal from the position of the GA Moderator. They spent a lot of their precious time and money in mobilizing people for a vote of no confidence in the entire six years I was in office.

All the way, I knew that it was not that the leaders were bad; rather, it was the spirit of negativity in the name of Limuru. The name Limuru comes from a Maasai name, "*Lemoro,*" meaning a thorny tree with very bitter fruits growing in a very cold place. Also important to note is the fact that this place, Limuru, is known to be very cold. Worse, Limuru had been known to have been a place of many tribal battles. Thus, Limuru is the very stronghold of **Lemoro** spirit, an evil spirit that has dominated this place.

In the midst of Limuru Presbytery is a place bearing the name '*Kamandura*'. Kamandura in the Gĩkũyũ language means to crash down. It's no wonder then the presbytery officials were constantly trying to crash whatever was Godly including the renewed praise in worship. They even looked for ways to have me eliminated. It all started when Rev. Ndegwa, who was PCEA Kamandura Parish minister, defied the Limuru Presbytery resolution that there would never be overnight prayer keshas held within its jurisdiction. It then happened that Rev. Ndegwa organized an overnight prayer in Kamandura parish. The presbytery approached me to have him transferred. I remember telling the delegation led by Kamweru, "*What is wrong with people spending time seeking God's face in an overnight fellowship if it is according to their will? Why do you want to dwarf people's spirituality rather than opening even wider doors for people to tap God's power? I will not have Ndegwa transferred.*"

Kamweru responded by saying:

"*This time round, you will know that we are true defenders of the traditions inherited from the Scottish Missionaries. We will do all we can to ensure that you are dealt with in accordance to our church traditions and constitution. You are the worst enemy of the church.*"

It was from that time that these presbytery officials declared total war on me, Rev. Ndegwa, and the entire Kamandura congregation. I am forever thankful to Kamandura parish leaders and the entire congregation. They acted bravely in spite of being harassed and being put into police cells. One dominant characteristic of negative spirits entrenched in the naming of a parish, presbytery diocese, cell group, elder district, or an institution is the spirit of strife, rebellion, arrogance, hatred, greed for money and power, immorality, demonic sacrifices, among others.

Other examples include PCEA Kamahuha, whose English translation is Abscess (a disease that occurs under the skin, forming

346

a very painful lump with pus). PCEA Kiahuko is derived from the phrase meaning a place dominated by moles. Others that we saw earlier and whose meanings I gave include PCEA King'eero. The name King'eero in the Gikuyu language means 'Place of Slaughter,' yet there exists PCEA King'eero Church. PCEA Bahati is associated with bloodshed in the struggle for independence. Those martyrs had challenged and fought against the British colonizers for their illegal occupancy in Kenya. Besides shedding a lot of blood, they rejected anything to do with Christianity. They likened Christ to a colonizer because the missionaries collaborated with the colonizers to fight Mau. There is also PCEA Kariobangi derived from Gikuyu *bangi'*, meaning opium. The place was originally famed for being a habitation of opium smokers. Suffice it to say that 80% of PCEA sanctuaries and parishes carry such negatively named places, including those named in memory of dead people, hence attracting curses, as we have seen.

CHURCHES NAMED AFTER FEATURES

There are also Churches in the PCEA and possibly in other denominations that are named after physical features like rivers, hills, mountains, and all kinds of landscapes. This has also a negative impact on the spiritual life of the churches or institutions. Have you ever wondered why witch doctors like to carry their occultic work around the waters -around rivers, lakes, and even oceans? It is in the flooded waters that most of the evil powers dwell. Waters also contain all sorts of dirt. This is one reason why in founding the original city of Babylon, Nimrod settled next to rivers, Euphrates and Tigris. Nimrod is the father of all Satanism in the world. This is why the Bible describes Babylon as '**BABYLON THE GREAT, THE MOTHER OF PROSTITUTES AND OF ABOMINATIONS OF THE EARTH**' (Rev. 17:5)

For example, we have PCEA Ngong, named after Ngong Hills, and PCEA Longonot, named after Mt. Longonot. There is also PCEA Athi River, named after Athi River and Milimani Presbytery, 'Milimani' being Kiswahili for a place with hills.

It is also good to note that there are institutions named after the local environment. A good example is a school in Nyeri County, formerly known as 'Kiangoma Secondary School.' This school had been operating under the influence of the spirit of Lucifer, thus turning it into a stronghold of the devil. The school had, over the years, experienced all kinds of turmoil with its academic performance ever declining. Remember, Kiangoma means Lucifer in Kikuyu.

The school was later named Mukurwe -ini Boys High School. Incidentally, Mukurue is the name of a huge tree that has a spreading canopy, giving shelter to wildlife and human travelers. And soon after the change of name the school was rated among the most improved schools both in the District and Provincial levels. Formerly, less than 15 candidates would have applied for admission to this school. After the change many KCPE students scrambled for admission in this school. Names carry either a curse or a blessing. Before the change, the school was known for the spirit of rebellion.

I remember in one of the seminars, I was teaching about the subject of naming the church and the participants got angry with me. One person said, *"You cannot change all church traditions as you seem to think. We are called to defend our traditions.*

In response, I said:

"You will not in any way succeed in this venture. You might resist this naming system but so long as my thinking is in alignment with God's will, it will definitely come to pass. God will use the future generation to accomplish God's will. Otherwise, God's will is the most hopeful, pleasant, and glorious thing in the world. It is the continuous working of His omnipotent power for our benefit, with nothing to prevent it, if we remain surrendered and believe that with Him, all things are possible. There is no stone He cannot roll. He rolled the one that had stressed the women who kept on wondering, "Who will roll the stone away from the entrance of the tomb.... But when they looked up, they saw that the stone, which was very large, had been rolled away" (Mark 16:3-4).

In this respect, I configured that most of the PCEA traditions could be likened to large stones blocking the advancement of God's kingdom. In reality, they represent the traditions of the elders, which were the rules that the Jewish religious leaders gave to the people and which they, in turn, passed on to their children; laws added to the Old Testament, which in themselves were very oppressive to God's kingdom. It is in this connection that the Jewish leaders confronted Jesus by asking him, *"Why do your disciples break the traditions of the elders?"* to which Jesus replied, *"And why do you break the commandment of God for the sake of your traditions."*

By following the path of the tradition of the elders, PCEA has, over the years, broken the commandments of God. It was for this purpose that God had me as the GA Moderator for six years to break up these traditions that were a real stumbling block to the spiritual life of the Church. The forces of darkness tried all the more to attack me, but God remained faithful in His purpose of having chosen me.

Otherwise, we live fascinating lives if we are living in the center of God's will. All the attacks that Satan hurls at us through the sins of others are not only powerless to harm us but are transformed into blessings along the way. Isn't it glorious to know that no matter how unjust some opposition may be, by the time it reaches us, it becomes God's will for us and ultimately works in the accomplishment of our destiny in the fulfillment of God's purposes?

REBELLION HAS CONSEQUENCES

As much as I cautioned the PCEA on the need to renounce the naming of churches and institutions, the mushrooming homosexuality, devil worship, and the predominant corruption, I at the same time cautioned on the looming wrath of God and His eminent punishment as a warning and awakening call. Unfortunately, they persistently turned a deaf ear, and instead, they fueled my harassment.

This is what I persistently voiced, calling PCEA to revert to biblical names in their naming of Church-related institutions as well as Masonic symbols found in church buildings. But instead, this call was one of the reasons that led to my being persecuted. The leaders loathed my exposition of this truth. They feared that the exposition of that kind of truth could cause a revolution, leading Church members to call for the change of names of their congregations, parishes, presbyteries, and other Church-related institutions.

Remember, there were Church leaders already initiated into Freemasonry, Illuminati, and New Age Movement. They had to defend their cause and also feared that my continued persistent calls for a change of names could make some people leave PCEA, as they were not ready to have their names changed. They also did not like my persistence in pointing out the wickedness in the Church, especially the state of corruption and the misappropriation of Church money by the top Church leaders.

They wanted all wickedness to remain covered as usual. They, therefore, pointed an accusing finger at me, referring to me as a prophet of doom. But in the real sense, they were the real representation of the prophets of doom, for they were crippling the Church by siphoning all the financial wealth of the Church. To them, the initials PCEA stood for **Please, Collect Everything Available.** They could even come up with fake Church projects in order to create avenues to collect money from the parishes and presbyteries so that they would feed their greed. I was vehemently opposed to these evil trends in the mishandling of the Church, both spiritually and physically.

I am always thankful to God, who made me sail through many trials. I've always believed that it's important not to compromise with the devil's agents in order to truly glorify God spiritually. The strength of a vessel can be demonstrated only by the hurricane, and in the same way, the power of the gospel can be fully shown only when a Christian is subjected to some fiery trial. If God would manifest the fact that "*He gives songs in the night,*" He must first make it night. God is still on His throne and He can turn defeat into victory in a matter of seconds in time, if we really trust Him.

No wonder God's wrath fell on the denomination. I had earlier predicted God's action upon the Church unless it mobilized the entire membership and leadership in an intensively focused repentance. I said that unless there was a national prayer of fasting and repentance organized, PCEA Church would travel through a very rough path in the years to come. It did not take long before things started to happen. The papers started reporting on some mysterious tragedies that hit the Church, including road accidents and other mysterious things.

Accordingly, those tragedies stirred up superstitious debates online and offline. Many people believed that those accidents that had caused the deaths of tens of PCEA members had been linked to devil worship, which I had severally pointed out in spite of persistent persecution by some of the top Church leadership. The sequences of such tragedies included:

APRIL 2012: Seven young members of PCEA from Dagoretti were killed by flash floods at Hells Gate National Park in Naivasha. The irony of the accident was that where these young people were, there wasn't a drop of rain. The floods came from far where heavy rains had occurred. A number of other students got injured. The devil enjoys human sacrifice, especially from those disconnected from God. He behaves like a lion out for a hunt, and then he encounters a cow that has gone astray. The lion will easily enjoy that cow as an easily attained meal.

AUGUST 2012: About 13 members of the Church's Woman Guild perished in a bus accident in Tanzania. They were in a group of 82 Woman's Guild members from Thika travelling for a Church mission in Dar-es-Salaam. The government dispatched military aircraft to evacuate the group. Later, there was a lot of pointing of fingers at some individuals who were exposed for having some association with witchcraft.

March 2013: A group of 62 young people belonging to PCEA were attacked by a swarm of bees while hiking on Mt. Longonot. Two fell into the crater, and one succumbed to injuries.

December 2013: PCEA Youth from Nairobi were involved in a bus–trailer collision at Mariakani, Mombasa, where three died while dozens were injured. These young men and women were coming from a conference in Kwale. The incidence was widely covered by the Nairobian Newspaper of March 28 – April 3, 2014, pg12-13. The denomination was heavily suffering in all faculties of its life - economically, spiritually, socially and politically. It seemed the denomination's turmoil would continue until there was sincere repentance before God.

The denomination will need to learn to listen to the servants of God who are sent to them with a message. It is unfortunate that rather than listen to such, some leaders stone them and even expel them from the Church. A classic example is my case. Rather than listen to the message I had for the Church, I got expelled.

Rev. Njoya was another servant who had been fought over the years. There are many clergymen, church members, intercessors and elders who ministered under very stressful situations because they were seen as deeply involved in scriptures and as people having welcomed the attributes of the Holy Spirit in their spiritual lives. This stigma still grips tightly the spiritual life of the church. But I still believe that with time and with the new church leadership, things will take a better course.

I pointed to the overseas Churches that were once mega Churches, but they were now fast dwindling. I gave the Church of Scotland as an example. This denomination was in her final death kicks. I also gave the example of the Church in America, commonly referred to as PC (USA), which in the 1950s comprised 40% of the entire American population. But this has gone so low because the church has gone so worldly that it is already advocating homosexuality and same-sex marriages as part of its Church traditions.

10 A LOOK AT CHURCH AND POLITICS

As it has always been the tradition the Moderator of the General Assembly was not supposed to be involved in matters relating to politics. Any engagement on such matters was considered unbiblical and against the church constitution and its traditions.

The fact that I was not buying into this view resulted in some PCEA leaders pointing an accusing finger at me for pointing out visible wrongs within the Kenya Government. These included its oppressive spirit, the promotion of devil worship (*for which a commission had been set up by President Moi to investigate*), and there was also what seemed like chronic corruption. As would be expected, some of the government officials were not happy with the way I exposed this wickedness. They called it radicalism.

Let me re-emphasize the fact that the basis of the argument by the PCEA was the denomination's traditions. Traditionally, it was an anathema for the Moderator of the General Assembly to speak on matters especially perceived negatively from the government's point of view. The Moderator of GA was supposed to remain politically neutral but at the same time be seen to support the government of the day. Those who advocated for this cited Romans 13:1-2;
"Everyone must submit himself to the government authorities, for there is no authority except which God has established...he who rebels against the authority is rebelling against what God has instituted." But Jesus lived in the midst of political wrestling with the Jews and the Roman Empire authorities, and His death was politically motivated.

PCEA held the view that, in matters related to politics, the Moderator is regarded as a *'Spiritual Father,'* hence speaking *'negatively'* in matters relating to government is a no-go zone. The Church is treated as a holy institution, and therefore, it should be voiceless when it comes to correcting the government's injustice or corrupt ways. That was why the top Church leadership before me and after me remained silent in spite of the many evils that were eating up the nation. These included many corruption scandals and all kinds of injustices. The

GA Moderator can hardly speak out to point an accusing finger at the government.

I tried to educate the Church that the verse in Romans 13 was used by the missionaries or imperial government to brainwash Kenyans so that they could not correct the government's wrongs and all kinds of manipulation. It was meant to block Christian converts from engaging in politics. They feared that since Christians were the educated ones, hence the enlightened ones, they would easily demand their national rights as indigenous Kenyan citizens if they were allowed to delve into the political arena. In this way, the Christians were fooled never to question British oppressive manipulations and their unconstitutional occupation of Kenya.

For example, a convert could be a milkman for the settler. The milk was taken by the white settler who schemed out the cream, and then the milkman was given the schemed milk. The milkman was not supposed to ask why he was given the schemed milk, and if he did, he was told, *"As a Christian, you are not supposed to ask such a question because that is what we call politics, and politics is not for Christians. They are supposed to wait for their reward, which is treasured for them in heaven."*

I told the Church leaders that while the Bible says that we are all equal in the eyes of God, the missionaries had obscured the image of God by demeaning the Africans to the status of monkeys. They had forgotten that God is not a respecter of human races and their locations in the world. God looks at the state of the heart.

THE LAUNCHING OF THE AGANO PARTY

While I was the PCEA Moderator of the General Assembly, I was invited by Mr. Mwaura Waihiga, the leader of a political party known as Agano, to be their guest speaker at the launching of this party. It was on a Saturday. Apparently, that day, I was engaged in some Church business in Nyeri, 150 km from Nairobi. However, my packed schedule was suddenly interrupted by a call from Mwaura.

He informed me that he was launching a political party and wanted me to be a guest of honour as a way of seeking God's blessings upon it. Despite my telling him that I was not in a position to be present since I was really tied up in Nyeri. He persisted asking me to avail myself by all means. I also persistently told him I had a very loaded Sunday service the following day that involved a gathering from PCEA Nyeri Region. But Mwaura insisted by saying,

"Dr. Githii, you are a respected national figure, well regarded by many people in Kenya. Your being the guest of honour will create some trust in this party among the people. Just remember, we are talking about claiming the restoration of this nation to Godliness, and you are known as a leading advocate on this issue. Please, do your best to avail yourself."

I made some consultations with the Church leaders who had accompanied me, and they advised me to proceed to Nairobi for that function because, as they put it, *"God was as well concerned about the lack of nationally integrated political leaders in Kenya. It is a ministry calling."* I, therefore left for Nairobi late that Saturday afternoon. The function was taking place at Lillian Towers, next to Nairobi University, where I arrived around 7 pm. No sooner had I arrived than I was sandwiched by a host of different media houses who started fielding questions wanting to know more about '*My Agano Party.*'

I immediately protested, *"I don't understand what you mean. This is not my party; I am just a guest of honour at the party's launching event."* One media man shouted at me, saying, *"Don't be a hypocrite! We know this is your party, and you want to run for the presidency."* Then I responded by telling this reporter, *"That is your own creation; I don't even know anything about this party, not even the content of their constitution. I just responded to an invitation just like other invited guests. It just happens that Mwaura is my good friend from the Christian perspective."*

The media continued bombarding me with questions to which I was responding as I moved towards the high table. As soon as I sat down, I inquired from Mwaura Waihiga what was happening because I could not understand all the talk about '*my party.*' In response, Mwaura told me:

"All this is a reflection of your personality. You are a person widely known not only because you are an outspoken Moderator of General Assembly but people also regard you as a God-fearing person and one who carries great concern for the welfare of this nation. You have conveyed your concern for this nation outwardly and courageously to the extent of putting it in writing in some of the books you have written. In which you have pointed to the satanic influence that is dwarfing the life of this nation in many ways and,

especially, those in our parliament. You talk a lot in favour of the common person. It, therefore, is not surprising that the media believe you are capable of launching a political party."

He continued to say,
*"They can visualize you in the kitchen as the chief cook- **'the president,'** ensuring that Wananchi is being fed on a good diet politically. I really admire your courage. And this being the case, there is no better person to launch this party than you. Thank you, Moderator, for accepting our invitation. Soon, you will have the floor to tell the nation what God will lead you to say. The time has come for the truth to be exposed. We will start with prayers and continue with the program and when the time comes, I will invite you to the podium to deliver your speech and then declare and decree the official launching of this party."*

Mwaura then took to the podium recognized me and the host of other guests. The master of ceremony then took over. Some individuals gave their speeches. Then Mwaura's turn came, and he delivered his speech in which he delved into the background of the party, its mission and vision. After he was done, he introduced me briefly and then invited me to the podium. As soon as I had stood up, the entire congregation gave me a standing ovation as they applauded while clapping their hands and chanting, *"Kenya belongs to the Almighty God! Kenya belongs to Jehovah Sabaoth!"* The media personnel each scrambled for vantage positions to best capture the moments.

In my speech, I thanked Mwaura for having come up with the idea of forming a party that I hoped would operate in glorifying God by dissociating itself from all that was polluting Kenyan lives, such as the ongoing evils that included corruption, impunity, political manipulation, homosexuality, abortion, devil worship among other vices. Even as I said that, I had in mind the words in the book of Hosea 4: I-3, which says;
".... the Lord has a charge to bring against you who live in the land: There is no faithfulness, no love, no knowledge of God in the land. There is only cursing, lying and murder, stealing and adultery; they break all bounds, and bloodshed follows bloodshed. Because of this, the land mourns, and all who live in it waste away."

356

I went on to explain how Kenyans were traveling on a very rough path as a result of having not-so-God-fearing political leaders and the fact that Kenyans were yearning for upright, God-fearing leaders. These are people who could not be corrupted. It is for that reason that I called upon the party officials to open their doors wide for Church people who felt called into the political arena to vie for positions without the party asking for high nomination fees like many of the parties were doing.

I also called upon them to encourage faith-based individuals to participate in politics, for that was the only way Kenya as a country could be liberated from the hands of some manipulative cartels. As my speech progressed, some images razed in my mind of the likes of William Wilberforce, through whose political influence the slave trade was abolished, and Martin Luther Junior, who also paved the way for the liberation of slavery in America. After giving a rather long speech, I declared the party launched and concluded with a prayer, but little did I know the political fire I had lit.

The following day, and to my surprise, all the Kenyan newspapers carried the news that I had launched my personal Christian-oriented political party by the name **Agano**. They labeled it 'Christian' just because the word Agano in Kiswahili language means **Covenant** and concluded that such a party, especially having involved me in its launching, should be a Christian-based party led by a person of my caliber.

The Sunday Nation newspaper of October 15, 2006, stated, "**From Pulpit to Power:** Cleric's Dream of Taking Over the Government." It went on to say, "Githii has demonstrated this by launching his party called Agano." The paper further said, "Every reasonable person must agree that starting a religious-based party in a country of many contesting faiths is an ill-advised action, even a dangerous one. At the party's launch, a grinning Rev Githii as was very much in evidence... wanted to be identified with an exclusivist, theocratic venture."

The paper went on to advocate that "fronting political parties robs the Churches of society's respect and makes them become fair game for all and sundry. Let's not beat about the bush. It is simply unfortunate that an important denomination such as the PCEA has a leader who cannot grasp this." The media got involved in talking about Agano Party which they maintained was owned by me. This propaganda venture generated quite some debate among Kenyans and led to an **Interdenominational Pastors' Conference** with over one hundred pastors in attendance.

Some pastors responded that it was not evil for Christians to be involved in politics, as the papers were implying. Pastor David Oginde of the Nairobi Pentecostal Church said the issue of plunging the Church into politics had not been *'formally discussed,'* but he indicated that there was a general feeling among faith-based persons that they had been let down by politicians who pursued their own narrow selfish interests. He said it was high time the Church got connected in the political realm in Kenya.

Speaking on behalf of her organization, The Netherlands Institute of Multiparty Democracy (NIMD), Njeri Kabeberi, who had sponsored that meeting in conjunction with the local Center for Multiparty Democracy (CMD), revealed that NIMD would encourage the participation of all faith groups in politics, not just Christians. She went on to say that her organization had helped women, the youth and the disabled to take part in politics and that the faith initiative was part of a project to encourage the participation of people from outside the political mainstream. She observed that *"Dr. Githii's more hard-line position is supported by an organization called National Conscience People's Movement whose pamphlet, 'The Voice of Conscience', states: "Real politics is for the upright."*

In that meeting, Ms. Jedidah Wanyeki, who was by then a parliamentary aspirant in Ol Kalou, said her group was *"urging Churches to raise men and women of integrity to take up leadership both at the local and national level."* She said, *"The candidacy of Pastor Mike, who lost the Nakuru by-election recently, was 'a test case'.* The paper went on to say that I had asked the faith-based persons to cooperate and ensure their agenda was promoted in local authorities and parliament, reminding them that similar unity had been *'fruitful'* at the National Constitutional Conference.

Reacting to this, Mvita MP Najib Balala, a Muslim, warned that mixing religion and politics would breed conflict, *"We should not mix religion with politics,"* he said. But as much as Balala could say that Muslims are allowed to go for politics, religion is not considered a hindrance. Another prominent politician, by then Langata MP Raila Odinga, in opposing Christians from joining politics is reported to have said, "*Such people who advocate for such a move are misguided.*" He went on to say, "*If they want to become politicians, let them come instead of hiding under the cover of religion. If I want to preach, I'll leave politics and go to preach. The two cannot be mixed.*"

But Raila was contradicting himself because his party, **CORD**, was an umbrella of many faith-based persons who had opted to go for politics, including a very prominent preacher, Margaret Wanjiru.

Those who are well versed in Kenya politics know that most politicians do not mean what they say. The truth is that they fear that if many God-fearing clergy fronted themselves for political positions, they would be a force to reckon with in paving a fruitful path for Kenyans. They would stand for the truth, and quite a number of politicians in Kenya hate the truth.

They would have hated to have me launch a personal political party, for I would be a power to reckon with. They had, therefore, to fight me from every side in the way of tarnishing my name. They wanted to take advantage of the ignorance that the pioneer missionaries planted among their converts, telling them that the Christians' focus was not on things to do with the world but those to do with heaven. Unfortunately, many faith-based persons today are held captive by this European manipulative invention.

It is this ignorance that I persistently fought for the six years I was PCEA General Assembly Moderator. It pains me to see faith-based persons complain that the government is doing enough to bring change in people's lives in terms of infrastructure, hospitals, and water, among other essential services, yet they have always voted the so-called '*non-deeply rooted God-fearing people*' because as the missionaries told Christians, '*politics is a dirty game.*' I experienced this when, in 2013, I vied for the position of Kiambu County governor. Many faith-based persons would address me in a very concerned and sympathetic manner, saying, "*Of all the people, why did you decide to get into the political arena? You are such a clean person to expose yourself to be dirtied. Many of us faith based persons are not supporting you in that adventure. We don't think that this is a good path for an admired man of God like you to follow.*"

That alone explains the extent the pioneer missionaries brainwashed the African converts into thinking of politics as a dirty game that would lead them straight to hell. During the campaigns, there were people who told me that they could not vote for me because I did not have money to dish out to them and that I could not lie or come up with propaganda in my campaigning. They said I was a man of integrity to lie. Adding that Politics is a dirty game and I am a clean person. Some even told me that I was good Presidential material, but unfortunately, I was a true and staunch Christian. After the results were announced, I met a fellow Christian at Kikuyu Town who, after greeting me, was quick to say,

"You see, I and other Christians had pleaded with you not to get involved in politics because Christians don't think that is a viable way for a Christian to take. You did not even believe us when we told you that Christians will not vote for you. It is not that they hate you. But it is because they don't believe it worthwhile for Christians being involved in that dirty game."

I told this person that I felt so good that I had taken that decision because I satisfied my conscience. It all depends on one's motive when he or she decides to venture into a new field. Mine was to look for a way that could help in uplifting people's lives, and that I had no other motive, and that is what God looks at. But if people reject me, then I cannot feel guilty. Instead, my heart is puffed up with pity for the people, especially when I see their struggles, something that reminds me of a school that I got posted to and for ten years, none of the children had qualified to join high school. But then I got there, despite stiff opposition against me to be headmaster of the school. The opposition was mostly led by the teachers, who were primarily drunkards. They messed up with school girls and made students work in their 'shambas.' They resisted me because they feared I could fight their evil ways. It was the same scenario being repeated in politics. I was being rejected for fear that I would expose and fight evil in the political arena. But in the case of the school, the students and the parents had paved the way for me to be headmaster. And the school's performance drastically changed. The school held position two out of 258 schools that comprised of Nakuru District. Many pupils could now attain very high marks. Otherwise, prior to that, the school used to be among the last 20 out of 258 schools.

I then said to my friend,

"In fact, there was a pupil who in 1977 attained 36 out of 36 points in Certificate of Primary Education (CPE) (the best performance at the time)." Then my friend asked, *"Does that mean you can venture into politics again?"* I said, *"Why not? I would go for it. Why leave the enemy to trample on people with a clique of leaders feeling that they are there for their own stomachs power and to protect their wealth? I told you it's all about the motive and the will to see people liberated from their chronic problems."* I reminded him of Elisha's prayer to God over his servant, saying, *"O Lord, open his eyes so he may see"* (2 Kings 6:17).

That is my prayer that God may open the people's eyes to see the potential of other leaders they have, yet they are enslaved by a few who have dominated power over the years. Political power is a distributive element. It cannot be held captive by a few individuals. This is the dilemma Kenya is sailing through. They are easily cheated by simple slogans and enticing manifestos and handouts.

POLLUTED KENYAN POLITICAL LEADERSHIP

In the General Assembly meeting held at St. Andrews Church in April of 2006, I took a lot of time to educate the Church delegates on the importance of allowing Christians who wished to vie for political positions to do so without strings attached. I reminded the delegates of the fact that Calvin, the founder of Presbyterian Denomination, encouraged Christians to participate in politics and never to compromise when those governments required them to stay out of politics.

Calvin called for the respect of the government, but he, at the same time, called upon the Church not to compromise with wicked politicians. As he put it, *"The Church cannot remain as a spectator when a nation is being torn up by corrupt governments."* He often quoted Psalms 11:3: *"When the foundations are being destroyed, what can the righteous do?"* Calvin, therefore, called upon faith-based persons to participate in politics because, as he said, *"the worst thing is when faith-based persons sit back, leaving the running of their country in the hands of people who do not fear God."* Building on that, I told the delegates, *"Time is gone when whoever joins politics was regarded as one who 'has gone back to the world.' Faith-based persons live in the world, and they have to lead in influencing the world to make better societies."*

No wonder, then, people used to refer to me as the cleric who was bold enough to point out the occultic attachment of politicians and their greedy pursuits to satiate their hunger for wealth. In a sermon on September 17th, 2006, I pointed out these as I was preaching at Ol Kalou in Nyandarua County, where I said that 60% of the members of parliament had some attachment to witchcraft. I gave reasons for this. And as usual, there was a heavy media presence.

The Daily Newspaper reported the highlights thus;
"On Sunday, 17th September, Dr. Githii, the Moderator of the PCEA, delivered a stunning and brave sermon in Ol Kalou, Nyandarua, accusing MPs and other leaders of practicing witchcraft...Githii said that more than 60% of Kenyan MPs are involved in witchcraft and that some carry charms and amulets to help them sort out personal problems." It seems my claim of 60 per cent of MPs being involved in Witchcraft invoked the need to verify the truth of my statement. The media people questioned the validity of this statement. The Standard Newspaper, therefore, dispatched several journalists to research this truth nationwide.

Their findings were highlighted in the same report on September 25th. In which part of the report said that my claim;
"Was supported by Mr. Akiba Bakari, a self-acclaimed ghost buster in Coast Province, and Mzee Kazungu wa Simba, a medicine man from Matuga constituency in Kwale District.... The two men confirmed that cabinet ministers and MPs in government and from the opposition frequent their homes. They said their diaries are actually full with politicians' appointments ahead of the general elections."

The interviews gave more details on this. For example, in the Standard Newspaper of September 24th. 2006, a renowned witch doctor, Simba, said, *"A session with him cost 988.80 shillings.... He says Cabinet ministers and MPs visit him often. He claims he is particularly popular with MPs."*

It was in that regard that the Standard Newspaper of Monday 25th. September 2006 called upon the church leaders to come out and be counted in the exposure of idolatry and other evils affecting the nation. The newspaper said,
"Religious leaders must emulate Githii's actions and preach against witchcraft and expose MPs and other leaders who practice witchcraft. In

doing this, we will have used our efforts and energies to reinstate modern values and sanity in our society. Any of the problems that face Africa could be resolved if witchcraft was demystified and exposed."

It is important at this juncture to say that, in the six years I was the Moderator of GA, the media e greatly boosted my efforts to expose evil and wickedness in the country and church. They were an added asset in my endeavor to speak out on various national issues, including untying the knots that had tied the church both physically and spiritually. I identified the media as my co-workers in the Lord's Vineyard.

Another area that the Media had helped expose was the occultism that flooded the Kenyan Parliament buildings. The truth was that the environment in parliament was strongly influenced by demonic altars, so much such that, in order to effectively deal with those powers, it required many God-fearing members of parliament. I quoted 2 Corinthians 10:3-5; *"For though we live in the world, we do not wage war as the world does. The weapons we fight with are not the weapons of the world. On the contrary, they have the divine power to demolish strongholds. We demolish arguments and every pretension that sets itself up against the knowledge of God, and we take captive every thought to make it obedient to Christ."*

Further, I reminded my audience that while the Speaker of Parliament is assumed to be in total control of matters taking place in Parliament buildings, the truth of the matter is that the one in total control was Lucifer, who is well entrenched in the Speaker's Chair through the '**all-seeing eye**.' I told my hearers that *"Satan himself masquerades as an angel of light,"* and likewise, *"his servants masquerade as servants of righteousness."* (2 Cor.11:14).

The orb entrenched in the chair is always the one in control or the one who has the legal power. Here, we are referring to Lucifer, who is the one entrenched in the speaker's chair. In this case, the speaker is held captive. This is true because the legs of the speaker's chair are in the form of cobras.

I told the journalists that the next time they went to parliament, they should look at the **Blazing Star** (*pentagram*) hangings at the **arch** on parliament's main gate. Through this occultic symbol, members of parliament are demonically scanned as they enter the parliament premises. It has a representation of sexual connotations. I asked them to also look at the symbol of a snake on the speaker's Chair as well as the '**All-Seeing Eye**' (*the eye of the devil or Lucifer*). The devil is, therefore in total control of the House even as the speaker is assumed to be the one in charge. Those were just a few examples among many others that I pointed out.

As already indicated earlier, I had persistently pointed out the strong Indian goddess represented through '*Harambee*' and its influence in key areas of commerce and government. I repeated that through the spirit of this goddess, corruption in Kenya is greatly promoted. The journalists were listening to me attentively but wondering what all the talk meant in the real life of the country.

Rather than focus on good leadership skills, they turn to tribal feelings and bribe their way through their occultic attachment. The good people are left out either because they have no money to give, disregard the application of tribal connections, and are not able to tell lies and give empty promises or because they are believers. The end result is spelt out by King Solomon when he says in Proverbs 29:2, "*When the righteous thrive, the people rejoice; when the wicked rule, the people groan.*" Until Kenyans look and vote for a leader whose leadership will incorporate godliness, there will always be a hue and cry. King Jehoshaphat, King Hezekiah, King David and King Josiah are good examples of godly based leadership. It is thus not surprising that their times of kingship were the most prosperous for Israel.

In my travel and speaking engagements as Moderator G A, I used to tell my listeners that spiritual manipulation had greatly and negatively affected the lives of Kenyans. The people don't necessarily like it, but they focus on the politicians' manipulative, hopeful stories and empty promises in terms of physical development. Most of these politicians pollute the national environment in all sectors through their occultic attachment. They fail to become leaders but remain politicians - people who know how to mobilize and chant slogans that are meaningless only to pull crowds. We lack leaders (*Statesmen*) who can lead people to a destination of realistic transformation, people who focus on the next generation but not the next election.

The politicians lack a tangible impact on the lives of the people who elected them. This is a real tragedy that such people end up taking offices that are meant to lift up people's lives. Voters easily become confused and get misled by these seemingly experienced mobilizers. They easily lose their reasoning power and thus end up electing the best noise makers, activists and the most skilled people in carrying out corruption. Such elected disappointments ensure all doors that would lead to prosecuting corruption are closed so that they freely carry out their heinous agenda.

They will rant about scandals which are buried as soon as they surface. No sooner do such scandals reach the courts than they evaporate, never to be heard again. It is like sending a thief to catch a thief. Instead of leaving no stone unturned until they barricade the thief, they leave no stone unturned in protecting their comrades. Such corrupt thieves have led Kenyans to believe that the only way of entry into parliament is through money. And it is only those with financial muscles that easily and corruptly bulldoze their way through. They have made the masses believe that it's only the rich people who can be voted in as national leaders, including the position of presidency.

This is because they dish out money to voters as a way of making a covenant with them, and when they get into Parliament, the Senate, the County Assembly, and in Governorship, they do three things: First, to recover all money they used in bribing the electorate to vote them in. They also look for money to bribe in the next election, and finally, they pocket some money to accumulate wealth. It is not that the electorate does not understand all this. Well, they do only that they are manipulatively carried away. They lose their conscience and are sort of hypnotized as their lives are wrecked by the corrupt politicians.

The electorate sometimes justifies corrupt politicians taking their hard-earned taxes by accepting small returns through manipulative projects as bribes. They are made to believe that a good politician is one who steals but brings back the money to them. The issue of servant leadership is thus thrown out of the window. Voters are not interested in a candidate's background-after all. The nastier the person, the better a politician. They love crooks, the arrogant and the rebellious. They prefer people whose characters scare away the good leaders who could have led them to greener pastures. Because the good people don't want their names to be muddied or, in Kiswahili, 'kupakwa matope.'

Kenyans should be aware that God made each one of us citizens in this land. This is why our National Anthem takes as the number one priority to honour God and calling upon Him to bless our nation. But we should know that God cannot bless a nation whose leadership is characterized by scandals of corruption and all kinds of manipulators who have no regard for Him. He cannot bless a nation whose leaders are greedy, who oppress the poor and misuse their power!

God has categorically stated in Jonah 2:8 that "*those who honor idols surrender the blessings that would otherwise have been theirs.*" Isaiah also affirms the same message in Isaiah 42: 8 by expressing the fact that God cannot be involved in any environment where another god or gods take the glory and praise. But with good politics, God is quick to quicken the developments, both physical and spiritual. The church has a role to play in voting for the right people. These should be people who are leaning more toward God. These should be people who bear a good track record in their life, people who have proved through their past that they can be entrusted with a nation or any other mandate for that matter.

These are people who can pave the way for economic development, creation of employment and well-meaning programs, and promote agriculture, infrastructure and medical care. Such should be able to deal harshly with anything to do with corruption which is the greatest national enemy. Such are the people who will address idolatry in the nation, including all kinds of symbolism.

Unfortunately, people were misled to believe in fake Christianity-people who come to them pretending to be Christians, but in reality, most of them are Devil Worshippers, Freemasons, Atheists, New Agers or hypocrites clothed in ship skin. But in reality, they are wolves.

To affirm this, in an article by the Sunday Standard of 26th March 2006, the writer said, "*Whatever changes we make in parliament, however good they may be, without changing the mentality of our pampered members, will amount to new wine in old wineskins."* The article went on to say: *"We are talking of people who are there to further their personal interests and to get rich quickly. Most of them do not understand the standing orders, and neither do they know their role as lawmakers. We are looking at some who.... because of some political wave, found themselves in parliament... Let us have a visionary and credible membership in the house, a team of selflessly dedicated go-getters before we even venture into the carvings and symbols."*

Another reference made by the Daily Nation Newspaper on November 6th., 2006 in part stated: *"The prosecution of perpetrators of corruption in our land has been slow. One thing is clear: many of the current crop of politicians, some of whom are seeking the highest office in the land, have been adversely mentioned in condoning corruption. We should do away with such persons. My advice to fellow Kenyans is this: Shun political parties; let us elect individuals...We need new blood. We need persons who are not tainted, persons who will purge corruption without fear or favour"* (emphasis mine).

David Schwartz, in his book, '**The Magic of Thinking Big**'(p325), where shares the same mind as Herbert Hoover thus: *"In business situations, we again find individuals patterning their thinking after that of the superior... compare what you find with the behavior of their superior and you discover that they are the same."* He adds, *"Every year, many corporations that are taken over experience a great decline in growth and performance. And How? By changing ...executives at the top. Companies (and colleges and churches and clubs and unions and all other types of organizations) are successfully rebuilt from the top down, not from the bottom up. Change the thinking at the top and you automatically change the thinking at the bottom."*

I found it fascinating and interesting that most of the time I said something touching on the nation, the media, in most cases would opt to carry out some research to verify the truth behind my utterances. One of the journalists described my utterances as, *'prophetic statements with a prophetically inspired voice.'*

RENEWAL OF THE MIND

In an effort to undo the manipulative mindset, the missionaries had polluted the African mind. I had taken a lot of time teaching in the congregations, parishes, presbyteries and even in seminars. Deviations from the Christian *'norms'* were deemed so negative that anyone involved with the government, such as being an employee in positions like chief or police officer, was seen as having *'gone back to the world or backslidden for that matter.'* That was one area of ignorance that I constantly tried to fight by educating the Church membership.

I gave them the knowledge and made them understand that such a mentality could be traced back to the times the missionaries and imperialists imparted the spirit of manipulation on Africans. These collaborated with the British colonizers to play their politics focused on taking over the African land. Hence, as the imperialists physically colonized the Africans, the missionaries colonized the minds of their converts. This blinded or brainwashed those who formed the Christian community with the constant misleading phrase that politics is a dirty game for Christians. The catch was that African faith-based persons should never attempt to venture into it.

Looking at the mess happening in Kenyan politics pained me so much that I took it as a God-given mandate to enlighten Kenyans on the whole truth. I had begun with the Presbyterians because that was where I had an open forum. Otherwise, I would be quick to say that all Churches are victims of the brainwashing. Even as I write this book, this colonial garbage is still tightly fixed in the minds of some Christians, but thank God, there is more and more infiltration of the truth among many in the Christian circles.

I thought that one thing the missionaries or imperialists had in mind was the various ways they could block the African mind from ever questioning the illegal occupation of Europeans in Kenya. They understood, as we have already seen, that if ever such a question would arise, it could be propelled by the educated Africans who were also Christians. These were well enlightened by virtue of being educated. If such a question arose, it would have been led by the Agikuyu who were the first beneficiaries of the Christian imperialist education.

That was why some missionary bodies in Kenya at first hesitated to educate Africans, fearing that such converts would later enlighten the members of their communities, leading them to question the illegal occupation of the British in Kenya.

Incidentally, the largest number of pioneer missionaries settled in what we call the Mt. Kenya region. The Anglicans settled at Kabete, where they have the 'Mother Church'; the Presbyterians settled at Thogoto; while the Roman Catholics settled at Riruta, which later got carved out of Kiambu to be part of Nairobi; and the African Inland Mission settled at Kijabe. The Methodist Church settled in Meru County. It was from these bases that all other denominational affiliations were birthed. The Seventh Day Adventists had their main settlement in the western part of Kenya.

DISTORTION OF THE AFRICAN MIND

To block the African Christians from the mentality of questioning the whites on their illegal occupancy in Kenya, both the colonialists and the missionaries collaborated in deviating the Christians' minds to focus more on faith or to be heaven-bound than on earthly bound, especially on 'their land.' They would quote such scriptures like, "Set your minds on things that are above, not on things that are on earth.... When Christ who is your life appears, then you also will appear with him in glory" (Col. 3:2, 4).

They manipulated the African mind by convincing them matters relating to their land were not important because they had a better land in heaven. They would quote scriptures that would completely tie or block their mind. One such scripture they quoted in line with the heavenly land is Hebrews 11:15, where Christians are; "longing for a better country- a heavenly one. Therefore, God is not ashamed to be called their God, for he has prepared a city for them."

They were thus drilled to believe that what mattered to them were not earthly things, including earthly wealth and politics, but the most important thing was the person's final destiny after death. They even composed hymns that Africans could sing to that effect. For example, there is this hymn that says, "Mburi na ng'ombe na mbia itiri na bata, kindu kiria kina bata no riri wa Jesu" (The worldly wealth in terms of goats and cows are useless; the real wealth is based on trusting in Jesus). By then, one's wealth was valued in terms of the number of livestock- cows, goats and sheep. Barter trade was the way of life then.

To further format this negative mentality in the African mind, they would quote such scriptures like, "*Since then you have been raised with Christ, set your hearts on things above…set your minds on things above, not on earthly things*" (Col. 3:1-2). They were told to go after the true Christening of mind which would mean a denial in going after things to do with politics or people's welfare.

The converts were told that true Christianity could not accommodate politics, which, in reality, was described by the missionaries as a dirty game. According to this mentality, when a Christian engaged in politics, it tainted their pure-heartedness. They were not even allowed to have an African representing them in the British Colonial Legislative Council (**LegCo**). Instead, the Africans were represented by the Presbyterian missionary William Arthur. The Africans were treated as third-class citizens and were even blocked from voting in matters of governance. The Indians held the second position in citizenship, and they were allowed to vote.

The truth of the matter is that, the Western Colonialists knew very well that it was the enlightened Christians that shaped the politics in their countries. As we know by now, it is through Christian people like William Wilberforce that the worldwide slave trade came to an end. People like Martin Luther King, Jr., a Baptist pastor, led the political environment that birthed Black American freedom from slavery in America. His famous prophetic words, '*I have a dream,*' created a force to reckon with. The American Constitution was formulated in the Christian spirit. In fact, all the signatories to this document were Christians in one way or another. Majority of the American and European presidents have been Christians.

I, therefore, made it my duty to call upon the Church to repent the sins of handing the national governance to non-believers in the guise of being faithful to the manipulative teachings of the Western Missionaries. I constantly reminded the believers, and especially the Church leadership that God gave Adam dominion over the land, and that included politics. In any case, the Bible itself is flooded with politics. Jesus had to wrestle with politics every day as he confronted the Pharisees and Sadducees.

For Moses to bring about the deliverance of the Israelites, he had to engage in very deep politics. And what of all the prophets and the kings who were regarded as righteous in the eyes of God? Think of such kings we mentioned earlier, like David, Hezekiah, Josiah, Asa, Manasseh and others. These Kings deeply loved God, and that was why God favoured them in their rulership. I called upon faith-based persons to come out of the cocoon of the colonial mindset to enjoy the truth of the Gospel.

Is it not for this reason that Jesus said: *"You will know the truth, and the truth will set you free."* King Solomon reveals the same when he says, *"When the righteous are in authority, the people rejoice; when the wicked rule, the people groan"* (Prov. 29:2). I further called upon faith-based persons to embrace the truth that I was exposing. Otherwise, when people refuse to embrace the truth, they remain in bondage and slowly perish. No wonder Hosea says: *"My people are destroyed from lack of knowledge"* (Hos. 4:6). When people lack the divine knowledge or the spirit of discernment, they just watch the world crumbling around them. It is for this reason that King David poses the question: *"When the foundations are being destroyed, what can the righteous do?"* (Ps. 11:3).

What the Psalmist is asking, in our life's context, is:
"What action are Christians taking when the education system is crumbling? When the health and welfare is falling apart? When the agricultural produce continue to dwindle? When the young people dying en mass due to alcoholism and drug addiction? While unemployment continues to rise? While families are breaking up? While corruption and impunity become the order of the day? While insecurity is rising up? While the destruction of the unborn through abortions thrive? When homosexuality, lesbianism and devil worship are finding an open door in the nation?"

This has always been my argument: One obvious step that the believers could take is to pave the way for fellow believers to find their way into political leadership. Christians should let go the colonial hypnotization. Neither Jesus nor Paul nor the Apostles expressly oppose the inclusion of believers into the political system. Paul defends this course when he says: *"Let every soul be subject to the governing authorities. For there is no authority except from God, and the authorities that exist are appointed by God. Therefore, whoever resists the*

371

authority resists the ordinance of God, and those who resist will bring judgment on themselves. For rulers are not a terror to good works, but to evil" (Romans 13:1-3-The Maxwell Leadership Bible).

One may be tempted to ask, can God say,
"There is no authority except from God…For rulers are not a terror to good works, but to evil" and open this door for non-Christians? Would He not block non-Christians and oper. that door for those who would imitate Him in their rulership? These are the people likely to emulate Jesus, whose mission is to redeem. His words affirm this when he says,
"The spirit of the Lord is upon me because He has anointed me to preach good news to the poor. He has sent me to proclaim freedom for the prisoners, to release the oppressed" (Luke 4:18).

It is those genuine upright faiths-based people who would strive to drive people politically into seeking God's guidance in the political leadership, which is in accordance with God's will as reflected by His words;

"If my people who are called by my name will humble themselves and pray and seek my face and turn from their wicked ways, then will I hear from heaven and will forgive their sins and will heal their land" (2 Chr. 7:14).

God places people in all kinds of leadership positions with the expectation that they would take that opportunity to glorify His name. Otherwise, the book of Jonah 2:8 shows the repercussions when people fail to honour him. They forfeit the blessings that could have been theirs, as we have already seen.

In my endeavor to reach out to the Christians and upright faith-based people, I felt that the one reason for God to put me in the Moderator's position was to use me to unearth the manipulative spirits fixated in the minds of Africans so that they could be denied their right to participate in political matters. That was one area of knowledge that Christians lacked largely. It thus came as no surprise that some of the top leadership in the PCEA and a cartel of liberals accused me of advocating for things that were not part of the traditions of the denomination.

That is part of the reason they mobilized people to strongly oppose my administration, including plotting to impeach me. They had tried severally in many meetings to pass a vote of no confidence in me without success. God denied them that opportunity as they were not for him. Nevertheless, they persisted with all kinds of persecution, both physically and psychologically. They termed my call for faith-based persons to be allowed to vie for political positions as the highest level of radicalism.

In spite of the oppressive opposition from my own church, I aggressively went around the denomination, teaching the Christians about the hypocrisy of the whites. They had come as explorers, imperialists and missionaries but with specific agendas. The early explorers like David Livingstone and Captain Lugard's agenda, for instance was to look for the best places in Africa where the British and other colonialists could come and settle to mine and produce raw materials for the industries back home in Europe and elsewhere. One of the strategies used was to arm-twist and then conquer by converting the natives to Christianity. This conversion was not so much for the sake of the gospel of Christ but was bait to colonization. After all, most of the early missionaries and imperialists were well schooled in a Freemasonry mindset.

The so called western '*saviours*' claimed to have the light to dispel the darkness that hovered over not only Kenya but Africa as a continent. They regarded Kenya as another **Canaan** full **of milk** and **honey**. It was very fertile and productive in all ways with great weather. As hinted above, the missionaries, therefore, grabbed the window of opportunity that the Gospel presented to manipulate biblical texts in certain contexts to suit their manipulative motives.

The converts were asked to be mindful of things to do with life after death but not to be concerned with what was going around them. The Africans were conditioned to look up to heaven, while the missionaries and the imperialists looked down on the land. No wonder, during the Mau uprising, the missionaries were very reluctant to condemn the massive killings of the '*natives*' that were being carried out by their counterparts. In fact, the missionaries acted as the imperialists' spies on the Africans.

In retrospect, these influences conditioned the African converts to believe that they were to live peacefully and be content with what they had. They were not to question the contemptible discrimination inflicted upon them by the European imperialists. The converts were expected not to complain about anything since God was taking care of their lives. Further, the missionaries manipulated their minds through such biblical verses like Luke 12:22-24; "*Therefore I tell you do not worry about your life what you will eat or about your body, what you will wear. Life is more than food, and the body more than clothes.*"

The Africans were expected not to be concerned about the welfare of their country and any kind of development. After all, being obedient to the whites was a reflection of being obedient to God.

WHITE SUPREMACY

The missionaries and imperialists gave the impression that they were small gods, especially because they portrayed Christ as a white person and the devil as black. Western Colonialists believed that Africans were a cursed lot through the lineage of Ham, whose bloodline was purported to have been cursed by his father Noah through his son Canaan. On their part, they claimed to have come through the lineage of Japheth, whom Noah highly blessed. It is for this reason that the Europeans generally treated Africans inhumanely. The missionaries also did this.

The whites had come to discredit the truth as presented in the scriptures, including the creation of the human being. This was more so as a result of Charles Darwin's authorship of his book, '**The Origin of Species**', published on 24th November 1859. This book introduced the scientific theory that populations evolved over generations through a process of natural selection. The book presented a body of 'false evidence' that the diversity of life arose by common descent through a branching pattern of evolution. This was said to have progressively developed into baboons where the Africans attained human status, but the Europeans got elevated to an enlightened state. This is something that denies Jehovah Elohim the attribute of being the sole creator of all human races.

As a result, the Europeans felt mandated by God to tame and '*civilize*' the cursed 'baboons.' One of the ways to tame them was to convert them from their *'primitive'* culture, including African traditional religions and initiate them into the European religion, education and culture. They also converted the land of Africa into their property and used the Africans as their laborers or **squatters** in their *'very own grabbed lands.'*

It was this ungodly spirit of prejudice that I aggressively spoke against. The more aggressive I became, the more some of the PCEA leaders and the cartel of liberals attacked me. They portrayed and upheld some sainthood in the missionaries and a whole lot of Europeans. It was therefore not unexpected when a huge number of Christians sided with the colonialists in fighting Mau Freedom Fighters who engaged in guerrilla warfare from forests, mountains and caves where many got imprisoned with thousands killed or maimed. Their demands were that the Europeans hand over back the land to the Africans. Unfortunately, many church converts had acted as colonial loyalists.

There is this affirmation that I came across in the Daily Nation Newspaper of Monday, August 25, 2020, titled, '**Season of darkness**: *Biden, Trump in a life-and-death biblical drawl'*. Biden, in his campaign for the presidency, is quoted to have said, *"The current president has cloaked America in darkness for much too long.... If you entrust me with the presidency, I will draw on the best of us, not the worst. I will be a ray of light, not the darkness."* The author of the article, Mr. Orwell, continues to say: *"But the light-and-darkness metaphor came originally from medieval chemistry, or alchemy, astrology and Gnosticism. It only acquired its current religious connotation later. In this politics of colour and light, white was angelic, while black was demonic. This contrasting imagery spread widely when it was racially applied to North Africans during the 12th-century Christian crusade against Islam. Medieval paintings show black Saracens torturing Christ during the passion, beginning the tradition of the black bugaboo. In cognitive psychology, this visualized schema of colour has been found to influence perception, understanding and memory. That's because it's not only based on generalization, but also serves to deny the complexity of imaginary concepts key to human relations. In classical rhetoric, it tends to demonize and weaken opponents. Biden was following in that tradition of tarring and feathering his opponent with demonic imagery to neutralize them."*

This was the same psychological application of white/black that the missionaries hypnotized the Africans with. Being white, they portrayed Africans as having come from the lineage of Noah but through his grandchild Canaan, whose descendants were to be slaves of both Japheth and Shem. On the same note, Africans were to be enslaved by the whites who claimed to have come from Japheth, one of Noah's children upon whom he heaped blessings. Thus, being white was a symbol of God's image and therefore, by virtue of being black, the Africans were symbolically a representative of the devil.

In brainwashing the Africans, the missionaries, through deception, used biblical verses to arm-twist the African minds. They told them that for them to make it to heaven, they had to play their role in curving their way by overlooking things to do with the world, especially the material gains. One of the verses is in Matthew 6:19; *"Do not store up for yourselves treasure on earth, where moth and rust destroy, and where thieves break in and steal. But store up for yourselves treasures in heaven where moth and rust do not destroy, and thieves do not break in and steal."*

That being the case, the Africans were not to rear hybrid livestock: cows, goats, sheep and poultry like chickens. Neither could they grow cash crops like tea, coffee, or pyrethrum, among others, which were considered 'superior' to them. Africans could only keep these low-grade animals and grow Indigenous crops which were native as their 'class' would dictate.

Hybrid animals and crops were reserved for *'whites'* who were 'considered' superior. This made it criminal for an African to indulge in raising the same. They were to accept their low status because that was one of the ways to cultivate their relationship with God and to ensure that they were in obedience to both God and the small gods-the whites as their rewards would be great in heaven.

THE RIGHT TO VOTE

The Africans were barred from voting, ideally to maintain European control. They were manipulated and convinced this was the prerogative and mandate of the Europeans and Indians. They were told that politics defiles the Christian mind, which resulted in African converts believing it was not worthwhile and godly but defiling to get into politics as believers. They were constantly reminded of Paul's words to the Colossians, that;

"As God's chosen people, holy and dearly loved, clothe yourselves with compassion, kindness, humility, gentleness and patience... let the peace of Christ rule in your hearts, since as members of one body you were called to peace" (Colossians 3:12, 15).

The Africans were, therefore, to maintain peace and loyalty to the *'whites'* who preferred being addressed as *'Bwana'* or *Lord*. This was regardless of their age. Even the *'white'* children would be addressed as *'Bwana'* by adult Africans. The European dogs were accorded more honour than Africans! They would be fed with **pure milk** whereas the **Africans** got **skimmed milk**. Unlike the *'Whiteman's dog'* which had a special place in the *'Bwana's'* car, the African could not be allowed in. Africans slept on skins and leaves!

No wonder most of the faith-based institutions in Africa are still drunk in the notion that active politics or even exercising their democratic rights is ungodly. Consequently, when a Christian decides to run for a political office, the first people to fight him or her are the fellow Christians. It is not until that time the Christians will come to the full realization that what is called politics is all about the welfare of the person, something that God is concerned with, and until such a time that God will give them David's, Josiah's and Hezekiah's, to man their governance that they will realize that politics is also for them.

The truth of the matter is that just because believers are conditioned to think that politics is a *'dirty game'* does not mean that faith-based institutions do not have God-given potential and a democratic right to actively take up leadership positions for the welfare of their God-given nations. It is high time that faith-based institutions break free from this long-standing negative and *ungodly mindset* or *narrative* and embrace political leadership. They should be concerned when their nations are falling apart.

It is in this connection that the Bible poses the question, *"When the foundations are being destroyed, what can the righteous do?"* The words of Isaiah 60:1-2 should be an awakening call to Christians when he says, *"Arise, shine, for your light has come. See, darkness covers the earth, and thick darkness is over the people, but the Lord rises upon you, and His* glory appears over you." It's time that the faith-based institutions and, more so, the church came to know the truth because it is the church that can free the people from the colonial 'mindset.' The believers will then join those who feel pained when they witness the crumbling of the nations because of greed, corruption, oppression of the common person, and mismanagement of resources, among other vices.

I pointed the PCEA church to what Robert Liardon observes in his book, '**God's Generals**', when he says that during John Calvin's stay in Geneva, "*Government and religion were tightly intertwined. In fact, rarely did any concept exist or any event take place in which both weren't deeply involved.*" This point is important to Presbyterians as John Calvin is the founder of the Presbyterian Denomination. My argument was: "*How, then, could PCEA deviate from the mindset of its founder? All world religions anchor their faith in the vision set by the founders. PCEA Church should not be an exception.*"

I also kept reminding the Church that during the missionary era in Kenya, Dr. William Arthur of the Church of Scotland Mission represented the Africans in the '**LEGCO**,' which is today's Parliament. I, therefore, called upon the Church to allow Faith-based persons, including the clergy, who felt called, to vie for Parliamentary and Civic seats to make way for the Church's participation in the liberation of the nation from the many evils suffocating it.

The only way to save a person from drowning is by jumping into the water. Similarly, the rehabilitation of our nation will require God-fearing Kenyans to jump into politics and actively participate in Kenya politics. Otherwise, to stand on the fence and be involved in a game of ever complaining and blame games without taking action is futile and meaningless. To break this colonial mentality, I highlighted some past key Church leaders who, at one time or another, became prominent in politics. Such include Bishop Beecher of the Church Missionary Society (**Anglicans**) and Rev. Dr. Arthur of the Church of Scotland Mission (**Presbyterian**), who at different times represented the interests of Africans in the colonial **LEGCO**. The latter was also actively involved in the recruitment of the African Carrier Corps, who were involved in the 1st World War (1914-1918).

Upon Kenya's independence, Bishop Lawi Imathiu of the **Methodist Church** of Kenya was nominated to parliament by the first President of Kenya, Mzee Jomo Kenyatta. Under Mzee Jomo Kenyatta, the country had enjoyed cordial relations with **Cyprus** owing to his longtime friendship with **Archbishop Makarios,** who was at the same time, the President of Cyprus.

In more recent times, we have witnessed the active participation of Church leaders in political movements that were actively involved in liberating **Zimbabwe** (then Rhodesia) from the yoke of colonial domination. Reverends Ndabaningi Sithole, Canaan Banana, and Bishop Abel Muzorewa were household names in this regard. In fact, Rev. Canaan Banana went on to become the first President of Independent Zimbabwe, while Rev. William Tubman was the President of **Liberia** for a long time.

Another example of faith-based persons involved in politics of the day in the **USA** is Rev. Dr. Martin Luther King Jr., who politically paved the way for the emancipation of black people in attaining Civil liberties. This had been previously the preserve of the white people in that Country. Again, when blacks in **South Africa** were suffering under white Supremacy in the **apartheid regime**, it took the leading role of Church leaders such as Rev. **Dr. Allan Boesack** and **Archbishop Desmond Tutu** to champion the cause of liberation and freedom.

In the **Netherlands,** we have the supreme example of Abraham **Kuyper,** one of the leading theologians and a strong **evangelical believer** who, in 1874, entered the Dutch parliament as a representative for the newly founded Anti-revolutionary Party, which opposed the principles in the French Revolution and political liberalism. He became the **Prime Minister** of the Netherlands in 1890.

In Kenya, during **President Mwai Kibaki's** regime, there were some **faith-based leaders in parliament,** some of whom held cabinet positions. These were Pastor **Akaranga,** who was the minister for human resources in the office of the president and Pastor **Dzoro,** who was the minister of tourism and natural resources. **Archbishop Ondiek** was also a member of Parliament. As I pen this book, the current President of **Malawi**, Lazarus Chakwera, is a Bishop who was once a Bible School teacher in Kenya.

In order to convince people that faith-based people can take the role of Presidents, I used to highlight here and there some of the American Presidents who were rooted in Christianity. Among these, I would talk about George W. Bush, Franklin Roosevelt, Harry Truman, John F. Kennedy, Ronald Reagan and Jimmy Carter. I also would highlight other global leaders, especially from Western countries, in the same light, such as From UK: Prime Ministers Tony Blair, David Cameron, Theresa May, Gordon Brown, Margaret Thatcher and William Gladstone. I also would point out Monarchs such as King George VI Queen Victoria, and from other countries examples like King Juan Carlos I of Spain, Queen Margrethe II of Denmark. Other world leaders from Europe I mentioned included those from Germany who served as Chancellor, like Angela Merkel, Helmut Kohl and Konrad Adenauer. While from France, I could highlight Presidents like Charles de Gaulle, François Mitterrand and Jacques Chirac, from Poland, President Lech Walesa. From Ireland-Mary McAleese. I also pointed out some Presidents from Asian countries like South Korea - Moon Jae-in, and the Philippines-Rodrigo Duterte.

To begin with, from America is President George W. Bush, whom I will give a little more space and detail as an example of a President who fully applied biblical principles in leadership:

THE AMERICAN PRESIDENTS

One of the staunch Christian presidents is George W. Bush (2001-2009). This is well illustrated in his autobiography, '**George W. Bush'**, by Paul Kengor. From this book, we can learn that Bush's Christian faith could be traced right from childhood. A case in point is when he and his dad, George H. Bush, were watching a high-school football game. It was then the young Bush, in reference to his demised sister, Robin said, "*Dad I wish I was Robin.... because Robin is in heaven.... she can probably see the game better from up there than we can from down here*" (page 4). What can you deduce from this? It is a fact that God had, at a very early age, planted a seed of spirituality in his mind. It was a mustard seed. No wonder, in the course of his early life, he was an active member of the church, including being a

Sunday school teacher, then moving on to being a church deacon, among many other positions and contributions in the church.

This being his background, from his first day as president, he always began each morning with prayer and by reading his daily devotions. He highly believed in the power of prayer and its transforming abilities. He is quoted to have said this in a Hispanic Prayer Breakfast, thus: "*The greatest gift people can give to a president or people in positions of responsibility ...is prayer*" (p160). He carried this belief in the power of prayer with him in every meeting that he chaired. He always turned to a cabinet member and requested him/her to offer an opening prayer.

Prayer was part of his presidency. One church minister in reference to Bush is quoted to have said; "*This is the first time in my life that I have really loved a president. He is the best role model for serious Christians in a long time*" (p162). In another reference to Bush, Marvin Olasky, editor-in-chief of Word Magazine, said, "*He is our first modern president who is born again not only in his heart and mind but in his actions...He shows his belief that Christianity makes a difference*" (pp163). Another who also pointed to Bush's faith said that; "*Bush was doing a very admirable, very clear and profound job of showing faith to be part of his life*" (p163).

A popular speaker in Christian conferences, Parshall, in reference to President Bush, said, "*He's so unhesitatingly unembarrassed by his faith.... He works into his verbiage, his public policy, and his comportment. He's so comfortable with his faith. And he is sincere about it. His faith so totally defines him*" (p164). Asked by the liberals why he was so much hooked to faith in God, he is quoted to have said, "*I build my life on a foundation that will not shift. My faith frees me.... Frees me to enjoy life and not to worry about what comes next. I have never plotted the various steps of my life.... I live in the moment, seize opportunities, and try to make the most of them*" (p323).

To further emphasize his point, he made a reference to Oswald Chambers' devotional book, '**My Utmost For His Highest**', by saying, "*Each morning as you wake, there is a new opportunity... God does not tell you what he is going to do next... A life of faith is not a life of one glorious mountaintop experience after another, but it is a life of day-in and day-out consistency, a life of walking without fainting. Living a life of faith* *means never knowing where you are being led. But it does mean knowing the One who is leading"* (p323). Here, when Bush talks of his steps being led by God, he is referring to the words in Jeremiah 10:23; *"I know, O Lord, that a man's life is not his own; It is not for man to direct his steps."*

David, in his Psalms, supports this when he says, *"If the Lord delights in a man's way, he makes his steps firm.... The Lord upholds him with his hand"* (Psalm 37:23). What Bush is testifying is that he looks to God for guidance on daily basis-to control his steps. Bush got his daily encouragement from Oswald's daily devotion book, as shown above. Bush would constantly say, *"My determined purpose is to be my utmost for His highest"* (p239).

Bush did not anchor his faith in God for his provision of leadership guidance. In his inaugural speech as the governor of Texas, he said, *"The duties that I assume can best be met with the guidance of One greater than ourselves. I ask for God's help"* (p31). In further emphasizing this, Bush would say, *"You know people search for something good in times of darkness, and our faith provides that.... That is a wonderful thing about Christianity. There is spiritual reassurance"* (p74).

For Bush, faith encompasses a broad range of beliefs. To him, it is rooted in genuine Christianity, which involves examining one's conscience and considering the consequences of one's actions. This being the case, the genuine Christian politician will examine the sincerity of his or her intentions and be acutely aware of the fallibility of human reason. Subjecting decisions to extra moral tests, unrelated to strict political calculations, can promote responsible leadership in any viable politician. In this anchorage, faith gives us a conscience to keep us honest. Bush believes that there are three components in faith: It provides confidence it offers guidance, yet faith does not mean that leaders can automatically think they know all God's ways. Also, faith believes that God is behind all that pertains to life and history.

Bush believed that to attempt great things for God, he had to submerge himself in prayers and surround himself with prayerful people. This was why, from the first day he integrated his faith into his presidency, he made his Inaugural Day a National Day of Prayer. He understood that he could in no way succeed in that noble task without God's support and without the prayers of the people. He called upon the Americans to wear the helmet of prayerfulness. He felt like the act of God placing him into the presidency was for him to propagate the kingdom of God.

It is for this reason that he embarked on uprooting what he thought was the evil that was defiling the country. One of the first things that he had to handle and which he thought was an abomination in the eyes of God and the nation was the rampant abortion. He authorized a ban on all U.S funding of international abortion, and next, he signed the **Born Alive Infants Protection Act**. For decades, infants who survived abortion were left to die once outside their mothers' wombs. This was the ordeal since the abortion became legal in 1973. It now became illegal to abort.

Later, when faced with the need for approval on funding embryonic stem-cell research, he signed the sanctity of life bill. The promoters of this move believed that using stem cells from human embryos for research could extensively improve lives by potentially finding cures for devastating diseases like Alzheimer's, which can cause immense suffering and ultimately lead to a fatal outcome. Contrary to this understanding, Bush felt that those embryos were, if not alive themselves, at the earliest stage of development. With this in mind, he resolved to halt federal funding for the same. In other words, he refused to sign it. He was also opposed to homosexuality, which he called *'a great evil.'*

In his governorship inaugural speech, he made it clear that the duties he assumed could best be met with the guidance of God, who is greater than all the human race. Bush said that he believed faith in God could change anybody because it had changed him. He stated that his relationship with God was through Christ, who had given him meaning and direction. In this case, his faith had made a great difference in his personal life. He firmly believed in the power of intercessory prayers. He believed he could not accomplish his job without God's zeal in it. He tapped his wisdom and courage from prayers.

On the issue of having God-fearing people join the wagon of politics, Bush is quoted to have said,

"We will welcome, and we should welcome, the presence of people of faith into the political arena. It is essential that believers enter the political arena. Just as your faith determines how you live your life, your involvement in politics helps determine how well our democracy functions" (p69). For Bush, *"True faith cannot be isolated from the rest of life, and faith without works is dead"* (p89). Quoting Martin Luther King Jr., Bush said that churches are not the servants of the state but, rather *"the conscience of the state"* (p100). His message here was anchored on Psalm 11:3, *"When the foundations are being destroyed, what can the righteous do?"*

Bush argued that, constitutionally, the church-state issue was often misinterpreted. Otherwise, the words separation of church and state are not found in the U.S Constitution. They come from a letter by Thomas Jefferson, who, though a vital founder, was neither a signatory of the Constitution nor present at the Constitutional Convention. What the Constitution says about religion is primarily in the First Amendment, where it relays two things: *"That the government has no right to; number one, establish a religion; number two, prohibit the free exercise of religion."* Bush referred to the freedom of religion as; *"one of the central freedoms"* in the Bill of Rights. Bush made it clear that what he could not do as a president was to establish theocracy. In defense of his faith, Bush said, *"The American founders never expected or intended that a president leave his faith at the front desk into the Oval Office each day"* (p166).

One of his earliest executive orders was to sign into action a White House Office of Faith-Based and Community Initiatives. This was to ensure that local community *'helpers and healers'* could receive federal money while they faced bureaucratic hindrances. Besides this, he created a Compassion Capital Fund that was aimed at marching private giving with federal money. It recommended allowing taxpayers to deduct charitable contributions. This was to ensure that faith-based groups were not denied federal contracts because they were faith-based. By doing that, he was accused by some liberals of refusing to respect the wall between the church and state.

In his response, he said, *"Faith teaches that God has a special concern for the poor...faith proves itself through actions and sacrifice, through acts of kindness and caring for those in need"* (p 100). In emphasizing this fact, he is quoted to have said, *"The order demands that faith-based organizations should not be held to a different standard denied a government grant because they are faith-based. The days of discrimination against religious groups because they are religious are coming to an end"* (p101).

In his call to come up with a compassionate movement, he talked of supporting faith-based institutions because their faith-rooted component could demonstrate compassion and inspire hope in a way that the government never should. One of the things that exposed Bush to realms of poverty was that time he accepted a full-time position with Project PULL (Professional United Leadership League), an inter-city poverty program. Through his own account, *"PULL introduced Bush to a world he had not seen: a tableau of homelessness, drug and alcohol abuse, fatherless children, single mothers, teens who could not read, boys who hid guns under their shirts. "It was tragic, heartbreaking,"* but also *"uplifting"* (p15). This was later to become the birthing of compassionate conservatism, which Bush introduced in America when he became the president.

Bush's call to the presidency was triggered by a sermon delivered by Pastor Craig, preaching at the First United Methodist Church. Craig talked about how Moses had responded to God's call to go and deliver the children of Israel from bondage in Egypt. At the end of the sermon, Bush felt the message was for him. He told some clergy he later met, *"I believe that God wants me to be president... I cannot explain it, but I sense that my country is going to need me. Something is going to happen, and at that time, my country is going to need me. I know it won't be easy, on me or my family, but God wants me to do it... my life will never be the same"* (P61,62).

In reference to the distortion of America spiritually, economically, politically and even socially, Bush learned from Evans that the upheavals going on in America could be compared with a cracked wall, which a house owner kept on plastering and applying some paint on, but the crack kept on recurring. One day, a person learnt how the crack had consumed money and time, then, addressing the house owner, he said, *"Sir, the crack on your wall is not the problem.... Your problem is that you have a shifting foundation. Fix the foundation first, and you will solve the cracks on your wall"* (P33). Bush saw this purely as a way of referring to the American society. He said, *"We have serious cracks in our culture that no amount of plaster will fix...unless we shore up our moral foundation"* (P33). He regretted that the foundation laid by the American founding fathers was full of cracks.

While aggressively campaigning for the White House, Bush was confronted by a journalist who challenged him to name his favourite philosopher. They were surprised because, in his response, he cited Jesus Christ as the greatest ever living philosopher, the leader who is admired worldwide, a philosopher-king. When asked why pick on Jesus, he said it was because no one else would have changed his heart. He is the only philosopher who can turn around the human heart.

Bush's religious adherence was so self-expressed that he opened up the White House for prayers. When they were not praying, some members of the Bush White House worshiped and studied the Bible together and, at times, including the president himself. At one time, he held *"an informal religious service in the plane. Rice led the group in hymns, and Hughes gave a short sermon. They ended up with Bush's favourite hymn, "Amazing Grace,"* .... *recalled Bush....* *"You know, I did feel the presence of God amongst my friends on Air Force One"* (P169).

No wonder some observers were eager to call Bush a *"faith-based presidency"*, claiming that he had pursued a *'religious renovation'* of government, when in fact, his religious streak marched what the American government founders envisioned: a government whose leaders were deeply grounded in faith, but also mindful of the need to separate church and state.

While Bush had always been a religious person, the turning point in deeper spiritual experience was the time he met Billy Graham, whom his father had invited to their home. Bush W. Bush spent quite some time with Graham as they walked away from home, viewing the sceneries and with Graham talking to him about spiritual matters. It was then that Bush took a large step that would make him the deeply devout Christian he remains to date.

In regard to this encounter with Billy, Bush says,
"I got to spend a weekend with the great Billy Graham. And as a result of our conversations and his inspiration, I searched my heart and recommitted my life to Jesus Christ" (P23). Graham lit a spark inside Bush that rekindled a spiritual flame that became his main drive not only in

politics but in his everyday life. Before his change of life, Bush led a rather nasty life. We can learn this from his confession. In this regard, he says, "*I had a drinking problem...There is only one reason why I am in the Oval Office and not in a bar. I found faith. I found God... I would not be president today if I hadn't stopped drinking seventeen years ago. And I could only do that with the grace of God.*" (P25)

It is because of this tight grip on his religious faith that Bush is on record as believing that the act of homosexuality is a sin and that the concept of marriage should be a preserve of opposite sexes-the union between a man and a woman, meaning, he is opposed to both homosexuality and same-sex marriage. It is for the same reason that he is opposed to the act of reckless abortion. In this regard, he is quoted to have said,
"*The right thing to do is to treat abortion as exactly what they are-a medical procedure that any doctor is free to provide and any pregnant woman free to obtain... abortions need to be moved out of the fringes of medicine and into the mainstream of medical practice*" (P303).

During his campaign to get into the White House, many tried to tarnish his name because of his faith. A journalist pointed to him the danger of not changing his tactics for the time he was the president. I can discern him say that for him true faith could be comparable to a tree and its leaves. Remove the leaves, and they wither and die. In this case, Bush would say of the Christian faith, "*It is my foundation and if it costs me votes...so be it.*" (p65). Bush would hate to let his faith weather and die because of earthly things. His call is upward, not downward.

There was this other time when Bush's faith was exposed worldwide. That was on September 11th, 2001, when commercial airliners were turned into bombs, crashing into the Twin Towers in New York. Around that time, Bush spoke to a group of clergy. Finding his comfort in the life and words of former president Lincoln, he told the clergy that Lincoln knew that his burdens were too great for any man, so he carried them to God in prayer. He had been driven many times to his knees by the conviction that he had nowhere else to go. The clergy told him that he had the same advantage because he prayed every day. And now, with this crisis, Bush began praying for forbearance and guidance from the throne of God each day while on his knees. He, at the same time, called upon the Americans to pray to a power greater than any of them.

The first thing that Bush put in place with the help of clergy, including Billy Graham, was the National Day of Prayer and Remembrance, which he described as a counterattack to the prevailing evil. The nation's elite attended this prayer meeting, including former Presidents Jimmy Carter, Gerald Ford, and the Clinton family, among others. In his speech, Bush said,

"We are here in the middle hour of our grief. So many have suffered so great a loss, and today, we express our nation's sorrow. We come to God to pray for the missing and the dead and for those who love them…. In many of our prayers this week, there is searching and honesty. God's signs are not always the ones we look for. We learn in tragedies that His purposes are not always our own. Yet the prayers of private suffering, whether in our homes or in cathedrals, are known and heard and understood. On this National Day of Prayer and Remembrance, we ask Almighty God to watch over our nation and grant patience and resolve in all that is to come. We pray that he will comfort and console those who now walk in sorrow. We thank him for each life we now must mourn and the promise of life to come" (P131).

After the service, Bush was quick to say that he did not view his speech as an opportunity to rally the nation to war but rather as a means of religious expression to help his country mourn. He said, *"I really looked at it from a spiritual perspective…. That it was important for the nation to pray."* To me, the moment was a more inspired tradition of *"The Battle Hymn of the Republic, chosen by Bush"* (P131).

In a different prayer session, he ended his speech by saying,

"We can… be confident in the ways of providence, even when they are far from our understanding. Events aren't moved by blind change and chance. Behind all life and all history, there is a dedication and purpose, set by the hand of a just and faithful God… we pray for wisdom to know and to do what is right" (P326).

Osama bin Laden and Saddam Hussein's Iraq were considered by Bush to be a representative of an evil empire on earth, and it became Bush's personal purpose to wipe out this evil out of the world. Many, and mostly within the conservatives, held a sense that God had raised Bush for a duty calling like this. On this, Bush himself; *"believes that that God charts his ultimate course, and that his duty is to accept God's calling and forge ahead. In so doing, he says that he relies on his faith for guidance and forbearance in a battle against what he views unequivocally as pure evil. This is his 'charge to keep'"* on his spiritual journey" (Page xi).

In referring to Bush's deep trust in God at this time of crisis, the Christianity Today newspaper said:
"President Bush, from the day of attacks on the World Trade Center, has led the nation with a deft spiritual presence that radiates solidarity with people of all faiths...Bush displayed great skill at expressing his spiritual and moral convictions... we are able to face the tragedy and attack...because we see a president who is calm because of his dependence on God." (P128).

Bush spent the rest of his presidency calling upon the Americans not to fear evil but to take offense against it. He called upon them to proceed with God's help, to seek to do God's will. And to ask for strength and wisdom through prayers and through being obedient to the Word and God's commands as contained in the Holy Bible, which, in fact is the breath of God. He told the Americans not to despair but to be strong and courageous. He also talked of some positive aspects that had come out of that crisis. He maintained that the prayers that had rung out across the nation since that day were part of *'the good that has come from the evil of September 11th.'*

He gave the Americans hope that something good would come from the wreckage of those attacks, given his belief that God works all things for eventual good. He reminded them of the words of the German Theologian Dietrich Bonhoeffer, who said, *"I believe that God can and wants to create good out of everything, even evil."* He asked the Americans to pray for God's protection because, in accordance with Psalm 18:2, *"God is our Rock in whose refuge we take, our Fortress, our deliverer, our Shield, our Horn of Salvation and our Stronghold."*

Please note that Bush was not the only believing President. There are many others, but I have given greater space for George W. Bush because, for me, his life has best answered the biblical question; *"When the foundation is being destroyed, what should the righteous do?"* (Psalm 11:3).

Other God-fearing presidents and American Christian personalities and leaders who greatly influenced American political life and are worth noting include;

George Washington (1789-1797): He was the first chief executive who unabashedly integrated his faith into public life. He is known to have prayed on his knees on the snow of Valley Forge asking God for his intervention in critical times in his presidency. In his inaugural speech, he is quoted to have said, *"It would be particularly improper to omit, in this first official act, my fervent supplication to that Almighty Being, who rules over the universe."* In his farewell speech, he declared, *"Of all the dispositions and habits which lead to political prosperity, Religion and morality are indispensable supports."*

Woodrow Wilson (1913-1921): The 28th. President of USA. He was a Democrat and is known for his progressive policies and leadership during World War 1. He was a Presbyterian elder who read the Bible daily. The Bible, he argued was the one supreme source of revelation of the meaning of life. He often affirmed the fact that, America was born to exemplify that devotion to the elements of righteousness from which were derived revelations of Holy Scripture. He routinely invoked God's work as his own. He was a prominent moralizer who saw things in terms of good and evil.

He is said to have had a superb command of reformed theology and drew his greatest strength from the sources of Christian faith. He never thought about public matters, as well as private ones, without first trying to decide what faith and Christian love commanded in the circumstances. There is no way one can talk of serious political issues without touching on his faith. He was the one who first came up with the proposal for the formation of a League of Nations, which he felt would advance God's will on earth. Speaking on this vision, he is quoted to have said,
"It has come about by no plan of our conceiving, but by the hand of God who led us this way... We can only go forward, with lifted eyes and freshened spirit, to follow the vision...America shall by truth show the way."

Franklin Delano Roosevelt (1933-1945): FDR was the 32nd. President of the United States. In 1935, in a radio broadcast, he declared, *"We cannot read the history of our rising and development as a nation without reckoning with the place the Bible has occupied in shaping the advances of* *the republic."* He insisted on seeking divine guidance in his endeavor to make America what God had destined it to be. In 1941, he wrote a personal prologue to a special edition of the New Testament, which was distributed to millions of U.S soldiers; *"As a Commander in chief.... I take pleasure in commending the reading of the Bible to all who serve in the armed forces of the United States."* It was his belief that soldiers should read the Bible in preparation for war. It is a source of gaining courage and self-esteem. His everyday schedules were wrapped up by faith in God, through whose empowerment he believed he could be propelled to do everything and overcome every obstacle in his leadership.

Harry S. Truman (1945-1953): Truman followed the footsteps of his predecessor, Roosevelt, on faith based on God's providence. Through his staunch faith in God, he influenced major historical events one of them being the birthing of the state of Israel. This was in spite of being opposed by his key advisers and State House staff. He was on his knees many times, praying for a breakthrough in the endeavor. He had mobilized many other believers who were in unity with him in prayer. And God made it happen. His formal announcement of America's recognition of Israel came to the United Nations eleven minutes after Israel became a state. He confessed that the creation of the state of Israel had taken God's hand. Rabi Isaac Halevi, a Jew, told Truman, *"God put you in your mother's womb so you would be the instrument to bring the rebirth of Israel after 2,000 years."*

John F. Kennedy (1961-1963): He is known as a person who feared God. At one time, he said, *"The rights of man come not from the generosity of the state but from the hand of God."* In giving a speech, he is known to have said, *"My fellow citizens of the world: Ask not what America will do for you, but what together we can do for the freedom of man,"* and he ended the speech with a forthright religious invocation, by saying; *"Let us go forth to lead the land we love, asking for God's blessing and His help, but knowing that here on earth, God's work must truly be our own"* (p178). It sounded like a forthright benediction from a clergyman.

Ronald Reagan (1981 to 1989): The 40th President of the United States was an influential American politician and actor. Reagan had a strong faith and often spoke about his belief in God. He was fearless when it came to his talking about Jesus Christ and the importance of moral values in leadership. One of his famous quotes about faith and leadership is, *"Without God, democracy will not and cannot long endure."* Reagan's charismatic leadership and optimistic vision made him a beloved figure in American history.

Jimmy Carter (1977-1981): Former American president. He is known for his strong Christian faith and actively lived out his beliefs while in office and beyond. Carter saw his faith as a guiding force in his life and leadership. One of his well-known quotes about the place of religion in leadership is, *"We must adjust to changing times and still hold to unchanging principles."* Carter believed that religious values should inform and guide political decisions, emphasizing the importance of morality and compassion in leadership. He is known worldwide as a God-fearing man.

OTHER WORLD LEADERS

Some of the UK Prime Ministers who openly professed their Christian faith and made statements about the role of their faith in leadership include:

Tony Blair: Tony Blair, who served as Prime Minister from 1997 to 2007, openly identified as a Christian. He often spoke about the influence of his faith on his political decisions and the importance of moral values in governance.

David Cameron: David Cameron, Prime Minister from 2010 to 2016, also openly acknowledged his Christian faith. He emphasized the role of his faith in shaping his values and guiding his leadership, particularly in promoting social justice and compassion.

Theresa May: Theresa May, who served as Prime Minister from 2016 to 2019, was a practicing Christian and spoke about the significance of her faith in her approach to leadership. She highlighted the importance of Christian values such as fairness, responsibility, and respect for others.

Gordon Brown: Gordon Brown, who served as Prime Minister from 2007 to 2010, is a member of the Church of Scotland and has spoken about the importance of his faith in his life and political career.

Margaret Thatcher: Margaret Thatcher, who served as Prime Minister from 1979 to 1990, was a member of the Church of England and often referenced her Christian beliefs in her speeches and public statements.

William Gladstone: William Gladstone, who served as Prime Minister multiple times in the 19th century, was a devout Christian and actively engaged in religious and philanthropic activities throughout his life.

MONARCHS

Just like some UK Prime Ministers, there have been Queens and Kings who openly professed their Christian faith. Here are a few notable examples:

King George VI: King George VI, who reigned from 1936 to 1952, was also a devout Christian. He famously delivered a Christmas broadcast during World War II, where he referenced his faith and called for unity and hope.

Queen Victoria: Queen Victoria, who reigned from 1837 to 1901, was deeply religious and identified as a devout Christian. She attended church regularly, and her faith played a significant role in her personal life and reign.

There have been many monarchs in other parts of the world who I highlighted that openly professed their Christian faith. Here are a few examples:

King Juan Carlos I of Spain: King Juan Carlos I, who reigned from 1975 to 2014, is a devout Catholic and has been open about his faith throughout his reign.

Queen Margrethe II of Denmark: Queen Margrethe II, the current reigning monarch of Denmark, is also a devout Lutheran and has spoken about the importance of her faith in her role as Queen.

There have also been many monarchs in other parts of the world who openly professed their Christian faith. Here are a few examples:

King Juan Carlos I of Spain: King Juan Carlos I, who reigned from 1975 to 2014, is a devout Catholic and has been open about his faith throughout his reign.

Queen Margrethe II of Denmark: Queen Margrethe II, the current reigning monarch of Denmark, is also a devout Lutheran and has spoken about the importance of her faith in her role as Queen.

GERMANY

German Chancellors who openly professed their Christian faith and made statements about the role of their faith in leadership include:

Angela Merkel: Angela Merkel, who served as Chancellor of Germany from 2005 to 2021, openly identified as a Christian. She often spoke about the importance of her faith in shaping her values and decision-making process, emphasizing principles such as compassion, justice, and solidarity.

Helmut Kohl: Helmut Kohl, Chancellor from 1982 to 1998, was also known for his Christian faith. He believed that his faith provided a moral compass for his leadership and played a role in promoting unity, both domestically and internationally.

Konrad Adenauer: Konrad Adenauer, the first Chancellor of post-war Germany from 1949 to 1963, was a devout Catholic. He frequently emphasized the significance of Christian values in governance, such as human dignity, freedom, and social justice.

FRANCE

French presidents who openly professed their Christian faith and made statements about the role of their faith in leadership include:

Charles de Gaulle: Charles de Gaulle, who served as the President of France from 1959 to 1969, was a devout Catholic. He often spoke about the importance of his faith in guiding his decisions and shaping his vision for France.

François Mitterrand: François Mitterrand, president from 1981 to 1995, was also a practicing Catholic. He discussed the influence of his faith on his political beliefs and emphasized values such as solidarity and social justice.

Jacques Chirac: Jacques Chirac, president from 1995 to 2007, was a Catholic who frequently spoke about his faith. He highlighted the importance of Christian values in building a just and balanced society.

THE REST OF EUROPE

Some few notable examples of European countries and their leaders who have openly professed their Christian faith:

Poland - Lech Walesa: Lech Walesa, the former President of Poland and Nobel Peace Prize laureate, is a devout Catholic. He has often discussed the role of his faith in his fight for democracy and human rights.

Ireland - Mary McAleese: Mary McAleese, the former President of Ireland, is a practicing Catholic. She has frequently spoken about the importance of her faith in her personal and public life.

ASIAN COUNTRIES

Some notable examples of Asian countries and their leaders who have openly professed their faith:

South Korea - Moon Jae-in: Moon Jae-in, the current President of South Korea, has openly identified himself as a Roman Catholic. He has spoken about the influence of his faith on his values and decision-making.

Philippines - Rodrigo Duterte: Rodrigo Duterte, the former President of the Philippines, has identified himself as a Roman Catholic. While he has made controversial statements about the Church, he has also expressed his personal beliefs, which embrace the faith.

THE MAKING OF A NEW KENYAN CONSTITUTION

The issue of making a new constitution for Kenya arose when I was in office as the GA Moderator. I championed the course of blocking the national movement of making a new Wako 2005 Draft constitution. Having gone through the draft of the constitution, I discovered that there was a lot that was leaning towards occultic practices. For example, the constitution had many grey areas that were leaning towards the legalizing of same-sex marriages, homosexuality and abortion, among other evils.

I, therefore, took the role of opposing the passing of this constitution. Thank God quite a number of other clergymen and women joined me in this endeavor, and by God's grace, we managed to block the first introduction of the new constitution. But this was not without the shedding of blood. For example, the Saturday Nation newspaper of December 10, 2005, pg. 6, reported that;

"At least eight people were killed as police battled crowds in Kisumu and in Mombasa. Politicians were accused of dividing the people. Instead of focusing on the contents of the proposed constitution, they engaged in smear campaigns against their rivals", critics said. *"Most Kenyans rejected the proposed constitution, handing the Government a humiliating defeat. While announcing the new cabinet on Wednesday, President Kibaki said his government would start talks to give Kenyans a new constitution. But the Rev Dr. Githii said embarking on a review now would only cause trouble. 'It would be unwise because it would plunge the country into more chaos,'"* he added.

The contradiction that surfaced after the government was defeated was its further zeal to call for a renewed writing of a new constitution, yet the country was under very charged strife between the government and those who were opposed to the new constitution. It was at this time that I became quite outspoken in opposing this move. One of the leading newspapers in Kenya quoted me as saying: **"Church Head Wants Review Postponed;**

"The Presbyterian Church of East Africa has asked the Government not to review the constitution right away, saying that the country is too polarized after the referendum. Before doing so, Moderator David Githii said in Nyeri on Thursday the Government should allow a "reasonable period of healing." He added: *"The country is in bad shape following the sharp divisions that emerged during the referendum campaigns, characterized by conflict and hatred."* He pointed out that the most important thing at the moment was not having a new constitution, adding:

"The most important thing is peace and tranquility. And to achieve this, we should be given enough time for reconciliation." He was presiding over the annual general meeting for the Church's boys' and girls' brigade team at Kirimara High School, Karatina."

I was known for calling upon those in power within the government hierarchy to create a reconciliatory environment. I even singled out the president, asking him to make an effort to reach out to the leaders of other political parties in trying to heal the spirit of ethnicity that had greatly caused divisions among the forty-two tribes in Kenya by then. But at the same time, I called upon other political parties to embrace the same spirit of willingness to lead their followers into the spirit of reconciliation. Otherwise, if the willingness was only from the ruling party, then the reconciliation may never be a reality.

The Nation Newspaper of December 13, 2005, reported the same saying thus;
"Rev Dr. David Githii, the Moderator of the Presbyterian Church of East Africa was speaking at Ihururu PCEA in Nyeri during a dedication service. The area MP, Prof. Wangari Maathai, was in attendance. She had, in the last week asked the President to reach out to leaders from all political parties. The Moderator said that the spirit of reconciliation among some leaders was wanting." The paper further said, *"Listening to Githi's calmness but tough address, one was left in no doubt about the kind of leadership to expect from the new PCEA boss."* The said Newspaper persistently elaborated and approved my endeavour to reach out to the political hard cores in the government for national reconciliation, calling them to the realization that the country did not belong to individuals, for; *"Everyone has a duty to ensure that peace and tranquility prevails."*

As we already said, when at first the move to change the constitution surfaced, I was at the forefront of blocking its passing through a referendum. Thank God we managed to block this first move to change the constitution. Unfortunately, the second phase of making up a new constitution surfaced, and through a referendum, it got officially published on May 6th. 2010. It was then subjected to a referendum on the 4th of August 2010 and was promulgated on the 27th of August the same year.

However, that time around, I was no longer the Moderator of the General Assembly and unlike the first referendum campaign, I had no forum to campaign against it. As it is, this constitution has remained a thorn in the flesh, especially in the government administration. No wonder many in the government and common people later called for the amendment of this very constitution. As I wrote this book, there was a call to change this very constitution after only duration of ten years through what was known as the Building Bridges Initiative (BBI).

TRIBAL CLASHES: THE RECONCILIATORY SPIRIT

Another issue that made me move widely across the country was the political violence that occurred soon after the 2007 General Elections that ignited a fire in the whole country, with over 1,200 people losing their lives. I went all over the country calling upon the warring parties and politicians to reconcile and embark on preaching love among the different ethnic groups. There was then a high spirit of antagonism among politicians from different tribes.

I traveled widely, urging Kenyans to quickly come to reconciliation while I, at the same time, called upon the Church to engage in prayers for the country and, where possible, do some fasting, asking God to hasten the reconciliation process so that peace and tranquility would be achieved. I told the various people I met that what we mostly needed as a country was how we could move forward instead of politicking and trying to outwit one another. I called upon Kenyans to forget the elections and the referendum campaigns, which had so much divided people, leading to tribal strife. I still portrayed the same zeal in correcting both the Church and government even after I had left the Moderator of General Assembly position when my tenure of office had ended.

There are those who thought that I should not look neutral as it was my tribe that was being fought, with a number of them set ablaze while taking refuge inside the Assemblies of God Church building. I emphasized the fact that the Church's mandate was to be the voice of the people. I, therefore, deviated from the PCEA's traditional way of remaining silent and maintaining that the Church should always refrain from involving itself in divisive politics. The work of the church at such times is to engage in serious prayers. The reconciliatory role is upon the government, which should ensure that security is tightened at such times.

I did all I could to call upon the government to bring to an end the shedding of blood. As already stated, this was after the general elections where the opposition rejected the results that had indicated that HE Mwai Kibaki had won and Rt. Hon Raila had lost. At one time, I was confronted by a group of people from a different tribe from mine, and they almost beat me up, but I was saved by people from that very tribe who recognized me. I heard one say, "*Leave this pastor alone. This is the controversial PCEA Moderator who is known for fighting evils in this nation. It is he who exposed the evil representations in parliament. He is a reconciler as well as a fighter for the oppressed. He is like Njoya, and in fact, he resembles him."* This group even agreed that I pray for them.

SELFLESS CALL

I have always felt that my call is not just confined to the Church environment. My call entails all aspects of life because I am called to serve the persons who are in the likeness of God's image. In doing this, I am always aware that this kind of call is just like one enlisted in a battle where one was not supposed to retreat. It is for this reason Paul talks about this kind of engagement when he says, *"Endure hardship...like a good soldier.... No one serving as a soldier gets involved in civilian affairs-he wants to please his commanding officer"* (2 Timothy 2:3-4)

That being the case, the soldier is always confined to the battle, and more so, being in the frontline for the crisis at hand. As a Christian soldier, faltering for even one moment would put God's interests at risk. Other lives would be harmed by any such hesitation and God's work would suffer if I simply fold my hands. I must not linger at this point; or even indulge with any people who are leaning to non-godly service. My service is to better the lives of all humanity.

There is this story that has always motivated me to keep on fighting for the welfare of the people for they are the component of God's image and kingdom. The story has it that a famous general once related this sorrowful story from his own wartime experience: His son was the lieutenant of an artillery unit, and an assault was in progress. As the father led his division to charge, pressing on across the battlefield, suddenly, his eyes caught sight of a dead artillery officer lying right before him. Just a glance told him it was his son.

The general's fatherly impulse was to kneel by the body of his beloved son and express his grief, but the duty of the moment demanded he press on with the charge. So, after quickly kissing his dead son, he hurried away, leading his command in the assault. What a story loaded with words and a spirit of encouragement! One thing every person is to bear in mind is that, evil never surrenders its grasp without a tremendous fight. We never arrive at any spiritual inheritance through the enjoyment of a picnic but always through fierce conflict on the battlefield. Every human with the capacity to win spiritual freedom does so at the cost of blood.

Satan is not put to flight by our courteous request. He completely blocks our way, and our progress must be recorded in blood and tears. We need to remember, or else we will be held responsible for the arrogance of misinterpretation. We actually draw our strength from the distress of the storm. This is no accident or coincidence. The Bible clearly points to this when it says, "*We must go through many hardships to enter the kingdom of God*" (Acts 14:22). Matthew 11:12 tops this up when it says, "*From the days of John the Baptist until now, the kingdom of heaven has been subjected to violence and the violent take it by force.*"

I hope this book will shed some light on what was going on behind the scenes. People belonging to the occultic world thrive through all sorts of propaganda and character assassination, whether in the Church or in politics. They frame their words in such a way that they seem to carry the whole truth and nothing but the truth: "*It is no wonder because Satan himself masquerades as an angel of light. It is not surprising, then, if his servants masquerade as his servants of righteousness. Their end will be what their actions deserve.*" (2 Cor. 11:14).

11 SOUGHT TO BE COMPROMISED

My agitation to bring changes into the church made the so called PCEA watchdogs panic. They drew their daggers concealed in their sheaths as they cunningly tried to woo me into submitting to their manipulation. They came up with some strategies on how to win me and, therefore, wreck my objectives. They organized sessions where I was persuaded to maintain the status quo- to let things remain as they had been over the years.

Let me highlight some of the occasions I was met by some highly placed Church leaders with the aim of having me drift from my course of bringing about both spiritual and physical Church reformation. Such people would cunningly lure me into meeting them. Some went to the extent of getting me into a kind of memorandum of understanding with them. Here are the highlights of some of these approaches:

1. LURED BY THE PAST MODERATOR, GATU

One of the past Moderators, Dr. John Gatu, happened to be the loudest voice in the entire PCEA. He was very uncomfortable with the speech I had delivered at the time of my installation on the 17th. GA Moderator. He could not relax when the church was being invaded by what I had described as putting '**new wine into old wineskins**.' What also shook him was my condemnation of the way the missionaries wrapped up the so-called '*gospel*' with their Scottish culture.

His discomfort stemmed further from my emphasis on the apostolic church, which deviated from the Scottish lifestyle that had been introduced. He was resistant to any changes in worship, including the inclusion of other musical instruments apart from the customary drum. He was uncomfortable with the raising of hands and personally verbalized prayer. He, therefore, decided to try exercising his unsurpassed authority and influence in the Church to manipulatively convince me to take the path of the liberals.

I was aware of the power that this past Moderator wielded for many years, but this did not dim my spirit and zeal to embark on liberating the Church. The truth of the matter was that this past Moderator was not only the spokesperson of the church but was greatly 'revered' bordering on being 'worshipped.' Whatever he rejected could not be questioned by anybody and whatever he gave a green light to, none could reverse. For your information, Rev. Gatu had been the PCEA Secretary General for 18 years and the GA Moderator for 6 years, all adding up to a quarter of a century. He was, therefore, deeply rooted in the church in all its aspects.

In fact, many people, including the first president of Kenya, H.E. Jomo Kenyatta, referred to PCEA as 'Gatu's Church.' He was the Church kingmaker. He, therefore, could not digest the fact that someone so junior in the Church leadership like me could have the courage to change the long-cherished church traditions. Having found me a hard nut to crack, he decided to summon me to his home. He did this to let me understand who he was in relation to the administrative powers in the PCEA. When I got to his home, he put me in a semi-dark room where he gave me a long lecture, commanding me to act according to his instructions on the way church meetings should be conducted. At one point he said:

"Listen! People have elected you, but I was not in favour of that because this kind of responsibility requires a very experienced clergyman. You are too green for this work compared with the other candidates you were competing with.

He continued to say: *"Remember that there were times you were completely detached from the life of the Church. Think of those more than four years you spent in America in pursuit of Theological education, and there are the other three years you were a senior lecturer at Daystar University.*

He further said: *"This is why I am concluding that you have very little experience and exposure to church life. You need to stoop low to listen to your seniors, that is, the past Moderators, the senior clergy, and the senior* lay people - the most senior and materially stable people. When you cooperate with them, you will as well climb the ladder to 'material wealth'"

He went on to say:

"While some of your competitors had spent between five to ten years in Church administration, you have never been in the Head Office administration, not even for a day. Now listen very carefully. One thing to bear in mind is that any time you are chairing a meeting and it happens that I raise up my hand and possibly there is someone else or others for that matter who happen to be raising up their hands with an aim to give some contribution, you have to understand that, there is no way you can give any other person the opportunity to speak before I speak.

He said: *"Also when I speak, you cannot give another person a chance to speak after me. Over the years, I have been qualified as the Church father and, hence, the Church consultant. For this reason, my words are taken as final. Otherwise, giving another person to speak after me is demeaning the Church fatherhood and the authority so represented."*

As if that was not enough, he went on to say:

"You are not the only new Moderator I am telling this. It is what I tell every Moderator-elect. Fortunately, they have all upheld my advice and no wonder they have always enjoyed my support during their time in office. After all, it is I who has always advised the Church on the right caliber of person to be elected as the Moderator, and it is for this reason that I feel I have been let down when the Church chose you as the Moderator without considering the candidate of my choice, something I have never witnessed over the many years I have been the consultative figure in this Church.

He further said: *"Nevertheless, and listen to this, I will help you as long as you will take the path of my instructions. It is quite vital you collaborate and toe the line with my instructions or guidance, otherwise, if not, you are doomed to fail. I cannot watch you drifting the denomination from the path established by the missionaries through your Pentecostal Spirit and its traits. This would be ignoring the laid Scottish traditions in which the church is set, which is ideally a Reformed Church Spirit."*

In my response to the long lecture, I said: "*I believe it is God who has called me, and it is him who will direct me in accordance with his word. Isaiah 30:21 says: 'Whether you turn to the right or to the left, your ears will hear a voice behind you, saying. This is the way; walk in it.'*" I could tell from his facial expression that he did not like my response. For he said, "*It is a journey; let us see what will happen.*" Rev. Gatu finally said, "*I cannot just watch the wonderful foundations being wrecked, not when I am alive.*"

He wanted the status quo of both the physical and spiritual aspects of the Church to remain. In fact, he had persistently voiced out that the Church could only change over his dead body.

As this past Moderator talked, I could sense the kind of bitterness and anger that tormented his mind. He could hardly understand why he had not been able to block my election.

Not long afterwards, we had a Business Committee Meeting and having handled the first agenda to which several people contributed, Rev. Gatu raised his hand and authoritatively expressed what was on his mind. He gave the way forward through a decision he considered best regarding the conclusion of the agenda. Afterwards, it looked like the people relaxed, seemingly assuming his decision was final and binding.

But then I said; "*We have heard the thoughts of the past Moderator, but I wonder whether there is another person with a contrary opinion.*" It took a while before there was a response. But two hands were raised, and I gave them an opportunity. These two gave their opinions, which were contrary to that of the past Moderators.

A couple of other people gave their contributions which were also contrary to Rev. Gatu's view. I then called for a vote where Rev. Gatu lost.

At this juncture, Rev. Gatu got very angry, and he said, "*Moderator, you have already mishandled your position by ignoring my wise counsel.*"

As it turned out, I had ignored all that Rev. Gatu told me. I continued to give people chances to speak after he spoke, and he became very stressed and strategized on another way of brainwashing me. This time, he used some PCEA tycoons.

2. LURED BY PCEA CHURCH TYCOONS

The people I am referring to here were three very prominent and very wealthy individuals who were sent to woo me into a meeting with them in one of the luxurious hotels in Nairobi. When we came to the core purpose of the meeting, the first person said:

"The three of us, as you can tell by the looks, are well-established people. In fact, each of us owns a coffee mill. We own big acreages of coffee farms plus other very valuable properties. Here, we are meeting you as representatives of several others like us who are PCEA members. We have called you so that we can formulate a way for us to work together with you in the advancement of the fraternity of the Presbyterian Church of East Africa. Our main concern is the way you have spelt out your role as the Moderator of General Assembly in your installation speech."

They went on to explain that they were not in favour of what I had said during my installation speech. They particularly pointed out my endeavor to pave the way for the Holy Spirit into the Church. They also hated the fact that I was to introduce keyboards and drum sets into the Church worship. Worse, they did not like the idea of introducing praise in worship teams– worship accompanied by rhythmical movements while singing. To them, this was a total distortion of the style of worship that the PCEA had practiced over many years.

To substantiate this, one of them said, *"The three of us are staunch Presbyterians. In fact, we were baptized as children, and the PCEA you want to birth is totally different from the one we know, and this is why we thought of meeting you so that we can streamline things. The three of us are long-time ordained elders, and we have served this Church in different capacities over the years. It is only recently we felt concerned about the kind of life that the so-called Moderators of the General Assembly undergo. The three of us can easily qualify as the generals of the Presbyterian Church army. It is for this reason that we want to have an agreement that will greatly benefit you."*

Another person picked up the conversation and said, "*First, you have a big title, 'The Moderator of General Assembly,' but the title does not match the salary you are earning. You are just earning peanuts. We would like a person of your caliber to get a salary that goes hand in hand with the title. We have therefore decided to design a better salary for you. We want you to be a rich man because that is what such a position entails. We are going to make a 'fat salary' for you.*"

Another of those liberals confronted me with a lot of bitterness, saying:

"*You should by now be a very rich person, but unfortunately, you are not. By virtue of your holding the GA position, you are placed in a gold mine. All the PCEA wealth is in your hands, yet you are struggling in the area of finances. Why not take the opportunity that has been bestowed upon you? If you cannot take that golden opportunity, why are you blocking us from eating while we are in these offices?*"

Yet another carried on with the conversation by saying:

"*Secondly, we don't want you to be driving a vehicle that belongs to the Church. We are going to buy you a far more decent vehicle whose log book will bear your name. In fact, we have already identified the vehicle whose make is a Prado.*"

Further, he said, "*Thirdly, we know that by virtue of being a General Assembly Moderator, you will be having a series of invitations to be a guest of honor in many fundraisings, both Church and national. We don't want you to be giving out some fifty or hundred thousand as the custom of the Church has been. We want to be giving you money in terms of several hundreds of thousands. This is a Church of economically stable people and we would hate to see the General Assembly Moderator lowering the status of the Church by dishing out small amounts of money. You need only to let us know when you expect to be involved in a fundraising, and the rest is for us to handle. And we will not make up a follow-up as to how much money you have given in any given fundraising. That money is for you to manage.*"

Another person, in conclusion, said, "*In doing all this, we are kind of getting into a memorandum of understanding with you. We want you to reciprocate by abandoning all these strategies you have advocated for in the introduction to the Church. This is a Church with well-grounded traditions which were set up by the pioneer missionaries. The main work of any*

Moderator is to safeguard these traditions. Traditionally, this Church has nothing to do with the Holy Spirit. God is the Spirit, and there is no need to bring in another so-called Holy Spirit. God Himself is Holy. This is why many in the Church are concerned about the trend you have advocated for. Let the denomination retain its status quo."

I replied: *"This is a wonderful idea but I suggest we come up with a day for the second meeting where we shall talk more. I believe there are other areas of Church life that you could put in some advice as well. For sure, you are well versed in the history of this Church, and I am willing to hear more. So, we need a time we can talk at length. Meanwhile, I have an important Church meeting that I am chairing within the next one hour."* We then checked our diaries and came up with a date for our next meeting.

But in reality, I had already disqualified the whole talk as Satan's way of blocking the move of the Holy Spirit that God had already paved the way for into the Church through me. I left the room; I had already decided that I was never to meet them again. And true to my resolve, I never agreed to meet them again in spite of their persistent calls. I knew that God was watching every move I made– yet gold and silver belong to Him. I strongly felt that I could not compromise the gospel with a good vehicle, a *'fat salary'* or good money for the fundraisings, some of which I could pocket.

All this time, the words in Matthew 6:33 echoed in my mind; *"But seek first his kingdom and his righteousness, and all these things will be given to you."*

3. LURED BY THE EAST AFRICAN REVIVAL MOVEMENT

Rev. Gatu had so far lost in this game. But he did not give up easily because he created yet another avenue through which to get me. This time round used these leaders of the East African Revival Movement to try to win me over. They met me in my office and told me not to do things in accordance with my installation speech. One of them said: *"This Church has had a harmonious life since the first missionary Watson planted it at Thogoto in 1898, and now we are in 2003. This is the main reason for us to come and see you. All other General Assembly Moderators have constantly protected the traditions of this Church over the years, and it cannot be that God has talked to you differently. Just bear in mind that our Church has nothing to do with the Pentecostal Spirit. We are a reformed Church."*

These members went on to give the reasons why I should abandon the issue of the Holy Spirit, the introduction of musical instruments, and free physical movements during worship services that included clapping or raising of hands. They categorically stated that:

"Only when you abide by our instructions can we come to your support in the leadership of this Church. We have always done it to all other seating Moderators. You don't have to distort what past Moderator Gatu and other past Moderators have for so many years worked hard to preserve. We are here because of this concern over your administration. It is also very important that you follow the Church traditions by the letter and word for word. Why should you give so much emphasis to the scriptures over the Practice and Procedure, which is the pointer on the path the Church has to walk in?"

Ironically, I expressed gratitude for their concern, but I also reminded them that if they believed my actions aligned with the Holy Spirit's work, then they were themselves responsible. By 'themselves' I meant the Church. I reminded them that it was the Church that had given the recommendation that I go for further studies. In emphasizing this, I said, *"In fact, the final words which the then GA Moderator said as he released me, which also acted as the blessings for my studies were: 'Go, study, research and bring us the new learning, it is for this reason that we are sending you.'"*

I told them that I was doing what the Church recommended my studies to be based on. My implementations were based on what I acquired in the USA at both the University of Dubuque in the state of Iowa and Fuller Theological Seminary in the State of California, both in the USA. I have also taken some leadership studies in Scotland.

When they insisted that I relax my agenda, I told them to plan another meeting someday so that we could polish out the matter in an amicable way, but in reality, I knew in my heart that I was not to have another meeting with them. In spite of their persistence, I never met them again. It was no surprise to me when they joined the

Church liberals to give me hostile resistance and opposition in my administration. Again, Rev. Gatu and the liberals lost.

4. LURED POLITICALLY

There was this time when Kenya was just about to go for a referendum. Those who were for the change of the constitution had the '**Banana**' as their symbol, while the opponents had an '**Orange**' as their symbol. Having realized that the draft of the new constitution had a fusion of things that would hurt the life of Kenyans, including the sneaking in of abortion and homosexuality, I became very aggressive in opposing the making of a new constitution.

I went around the country rallying support for people to vote '**No**' when the referendum took place. My call was supported by many, including those who were formerly for the new constitution. Some of those who still felt a new constitution was necessary were angered by the ground I was able to cover. They referred to my move as '*a radical spirit fronted by a reformist, David Githii.*' Some were even plotting to silence me in various ways. But I kept on insisting that I had no apology for that. I knew that the path I had taken was dangerous, but I felt it was a mission that God had bestowed upon me, and I had to move forward. Those who opposed me even tried to reach me through bribery.

I remember this day I put up at Stem Hotel in Nakuru because of an early Church function around there the following day, which was, in fact, a Sunday. While I was having my breakfast early the following morning, two PCEA elders approached me and said: "*Good morning, moderator; so you did put up here?*" I said, "*Yes, I have some work around here and the function starts very early for me to drive all the way here from Nairobi. So, I decided to put up here for the night so that I may be fresh and in good shape for the meeting.*"

To my surprise, they drew my attention to one of the then-prominent politicians in Nakuru seated alone. One of them said; "*Why don't you dine together with Honorable Mirugi?*" By then, they had already picked up my meal to relocate me to sit next to the politician. I had no option but to follow them, though I had no idea that this was a premeditated move. Hon. Mirugi stood up while at the same time stretching his hand to shake mine in a very jovial mood. He said, *"Welcome, my Moderator, and what a privilege to meet you this morning."* Soon, the two elders excused themselves and left the two of us alone together. It was then that the politician spoke out his agenda: *"Now, Moderator, my being here is not by coincidence. I have been sent by very concerned politicians attached to the State House. We have been trying to monitor your movements and your aggressive campaign against the 'Banana' side, which, of course, is the government side.*

He went on to say," *It is our feeling that you should not be supporting the 'Orange' side as far as the referendum is concerned. As you know, the 'Orange' symbol belongs to the opposition side, who, as you know are campaigning against the new constitution. My purpose for being here is to meet you this morning and on behalf of the Banana side. My mission is to really urge you to join our side as far as the referendum campaign is concerned.*

He further said, *"As government, we want to have a new constitution by all means, by hook or crook. And as I have already hinted to you, I have been sent by some very senior people in the government to request you to be one of our campaigners, and since we don't want you to do this for nothing, I was told to tell you that, you can suggest how much we can give you for we really want your support. It is very important that we have you on our side."*

The politician went on to say:

"By virtue of your position as the Moderator of the General Assembly and the influence and courage you portray, you are a force to reckon with as far as this referendum issue is concerned. You have a strong impact- a big voice not only in this country but internationally as well. But of more importance, PCEA, to which you are the Moderator, has a big following especially from the Gikuyu people. In fact, if you observe this campaign critically, you will note that the Agikuyu dominate the Banana side while most of the other tribes dominate Orange. And this is our concern: why is it that you, being a Mugikuyu, are clinging to the divide of other tribes?"

He went on to say,

"You should be your brother's keeper. Let me put it rightly: we want to give you a job as one of the chief campaigners on the government side, and it is you who will tell us the kind of commission you want. We have money, and I am sure, like any other person, you have needs, including those of your ministry and what an opportunity to carry out some harvesting. We have many clergymen and women, including bishops, whom we have commissioned to act as catalysts in this campaign, but the truth of the matter is that they are not of your caliber. We want to give you good money and, at the same time, connect you with the people who matter in this country. We want you to be a man of high status. We want to have a continuous working relationship even after the referendum and even after you are done with your Moderator's tenure of office."

As this politician spoke, these words kept coming into my mind; *"Seek first the kingdom of God, and other things will be added unto you"* (Matt.6:33), and my immediate response was:

"It is really good that you, who are part of the political cream of this nation, have considered me as one who can help you in delivering success in this campaign. In helping you, I would not require any payment for this is all about the nation. My only concern is that this constitution does not wholly stand for the kingdom of God. It is mixed with some ungodliness. Think of the clauses that are making way for the introduction of homosexuality and abortion, among others. God has helped me in that I am never led to do things because of money."

I went on to say: *"This is why some people in PCEA are fighting me, saying that I am behaving like a dog that lies in the lime trough meant for the goats, yet the dog itself does not eat lime, but when the goats come to eat the lime, the dog barks at them making it impossible for them to eat it. Some very corrupt and greedy leaders in PCEA blame me for not helping myself with Church money and, at the same time, say that I am so protective and not allowing others to dip their hands in it. Unfortunately, my conscience and the love I have for the Church cannot allow me to open the door for these people to mess up with Church funds. And it is the same thing when we come to this nation. I love it, I love the people of all tribes and I cannot give in when it comes to protecting the nation's morality and integrity. I cannot exchange my love for this nation with money.*

He went on to say, "*My conscience cannot allow me to help in laying the groundwork for the entrenchment of murders through the killing of children in abortion. I also cannot withstand homosexuality and all other kinds of wickedness in the nation. I would rather create opportunities for Godliness to embrace the nation. In this way, God's presence will guide the nation.*"

I could tell the politician was already disillusioned in his spirit. His face had grown pale and he never wanted to look straight in my face. Finally, he said: "*Moderator, I believe by nature of your responsibility, you are a very busy person, and this could not be the best time for us to talk, for I have already seen you twice looking at your watch. I therefore suggest we make an appointment to meet somewhere in Nairobi and I will also come with one or two other people because we really want to cooperate with you in this matter. We can even strategize how some of the clauses that you refer to as ungodly can be worked out later in the form of amendments.*"

I said, "*Okay, I agree with you. We can always make some arrangements on how we could meet.*"

I proposed a date the following week, but he said it was not convenient for him because there was a very important motion in parliament that he did not want to miss out on but because of the importance and urgency in regard to winning me over, he will skip the parliamentary debate so that we could meet. We then parted company.

Later in the week, I called Hon. Mirugi, and I informed him that some urgent work in the Church had cropped up and I would not be available for the meeting. He then proposed another date, and I told him that my diary was really congested. He then promised to call me later when I got my diary organized to create space for us to meet. True to his word, he gave me a call but I responded that my diary could not allow for a meeting with him. Somehow, he realized that I was not for the meeting, and he never called again.

After this, at times, I could see and sense suspicious vehicles tracking me, but at such times, I alerted the intercessors to intensify their prayers regarding my security, and it worked.

From a human perspective, that was not an easy deal to overlook, for it would easily make way for quick wealth and very high-status connections. But I felt that I had a call from God, which I had to protect. After all, how could I be fighting corruption and at the same time be part of it. At least, Kenyans and the Church needed some role models whom they could look at.

The good news after all this was that the results of the referendum on November 21st. 2005 indicated a resounding win by the *'orange'* side with over 1 million votes above what the *'banana'* side government had garnered. God is always looking for people who can firmly stand in the gap as far as the nation and the Church are concerned. The words of the book of Jeremiah kept echoing in my mind; *"Get yourself ready! Stand up and say to them whatever I command you. Do not be terrified by them, or I will terrify you before them."* Jeremiah 1:17

I was also encouraged by the lives of others who, when they upheld what they believed was a God-given mission, never looked back in spite of the financial gain and promises of power they received. They could not sell out their God-given mandate. In this case, I had in mind Jesus himself, his disciples, prophets like Jeremiah, Isaiah, and Ezekiel and other modern heroes like Nelson Mandela, Kwame Nkrumah, Jomo Kenyatta; Martin Luther the reformer; John Wesley; Martin Luther King Junior; Mother Teresa; William Wilberforce and John Calvin including some archbishops and popes, among others.

All these people qualified to be called reformists because they were after making a better life for the people who were under the oppression of evil cartels, most of which held prime positions in governments and the Church. The said heroes lived their lives focusing on correcting the evil that was taking place both locally and internationally among the people at the time they lived. They were imitators of Jesus Christ who called upon his would-be followers to take up the cross and follow him. No wonder the Presbyterian Church of East Africa leadership would refer to me as a radical reformist. Therefore, they looked for any opening to expel me from the Church.

12 THE AGITATIONS FOR IMPEACHMENT

Unfortunately for me, when the liberals found that I was a tough cookie and that they could not melt out my stand, they sought ways to get rid of me and initiated my impeachment as the GA Moderator. Here, I will highlight some of these moves against me.

1. ATTEMPTED IMPEACHMENT AT GAC HELD AT KIHUMBU-INI.

The first attempt to have me impeached was through a GAC that met at Kihumbu-ini in April 2004. As we stated earlier, this was my first Church Court to chair since the time of my election and consecration a year earlier.

For the reader who is not well versed with PCEA administrative protocol, there are three of the so called PCEA courts. These are The Kirk session, General Administrative Committee(GAC) and the General Assembly (GA).

Kirksession operates at the parish level. The GAC brings together the cream of the leadership of presbyteries in an annual meeting. This court meets twice a year preceding the GA. Its venue is rotated within the presbyteries. The GA meets every three years and usually takes five to six days for its deliberations. The dockets on both GAC and GA are distributed to the delegates a week before the meeting takes place. The delegates had, therefore, already read or gone through all the materials and were privy to my intentions, so they were prepared to counter this raft of transformative measures that I outlined earlier in my report to that GAC, which briefly included the following;

- Changes in worship include more musical instruments, key-boards, drum-sets and the use of public address systems and the removal of a one-man drummer.
- Prohibiting non-converts from holding offices or any leadership positions in the Church, including eldership or deaconship.

Prior to that meeting, I had carried some teachings in presbyteries and regions that had made the liberals feel that I should not be allowed to continue educating the denomination members on what had been kept secret over the years. The cartel of the liberals included the clergy, elders and some of the East African Revival Movement leaders.

There had also been pressure from some church leaders from the Church of Scotland who felt that I was invading their space in the treasured traditions of the PCEA Church. These people had combined forces with some PCEA church leaders to wage war against me. They were always looking for an opportunity to have me impeached by the key Church committees or courts. Many times, they had tried to raise a vote of no confidence against me, but they could not wrestle me out of God's grip. His Word kept on affirming to me, *"You are my servant; I have chosen you… Do not fear, for I am with you; do not be dismayed, for I am your God; I will uphold you with my righteous right hand. All who rage against you will surely be ashamed and disgraced; those who oppose you will be as nothing… Though you search for your enemies, you will not find them"* (Isa 41:10 -12).

The liberals had smelt a rat upon reading my report and had begun to work out various strategies through which they could impeach me and have me voted out of the GA seat and replaced by someone they had already identified. Lawyers had drawn scandalous documents which were to be circulated to the delegates on arrival to the venue against me. One of those documents called upon the delegates to take note of the: *"Alarming distortion of PCEA by the unschooled into Presbyterianism, Moderator David Githii. The Church traditions are heading for total distortion. What will you tell the future generations? Where were you? It is now or never!"*

Late arrivals had their documents placed on top of their bed pillows. I did not know of such a move until very late at night when one of the clergymen came to me like Gamaliel while most of the delegates were asleep. He let the cat out of the bag by whispering to me what was going on amongst the delegates. As he moved away, he said, *"Things are really serious. They claim to have an established formula to have you impeached tomorrow, and as much as some of us will spend the night praying for you, it seems your opponents have already won the battle. They are already celebrating. Anyway, shalom."* Even as that clergyman left me on a negative note and with a fearful message, I was already experiencing a lot of peace. I had a nice and restful sleep.

Early in the morning, someone knocked at my door and said, *"I hope you have known the fact that a high-level campaign to replace you has been going on all night."* I responded:

"Well, someone hinted to me late last night." The man went on to say, *"It seems they have already carried the day; not many people are on your side. People love you, but their mind is already poisoned not only verbally but there has been an exchange of money in the form of bribery."*

I then said: *"You know, right from the word go, I had no ambition of becoming a GA Moderator. I was even surprised that, like David, God chose me among other very influential candidates. So, it is the same God who has an answer. I am fully convinced that these people will not overcome the will of God. Let us wait and see the course things will take. Otherwise, in all these things, we are more than conquerors. I stand with God's word through which he commissioned me into this work: Like Jeremiah, when God called me, he at the same time mandated me; 'to uproot and tear down; to destroy and overthrow; to build and to plant.'"* (Jer. 1:10). In doing this, God has assured me that; *"They will fight against you but will not overcome you, for I am with you and will rescue you."* (Jer. 1:19). That was April 2004.

THE MEETING

The meeting opened with a prayer followed by a song. Then, there followed some announcements, the roll call and a short speech to welcome the delegates. Then came time to deliver the sermon, which was the prerogative of the GA Moderator. It was around Easter; therefore, I took the scriptural passage from Mark 16:3 about the women who went to the tomb and wondered, *"Who will roll the stone for us?"*

Basing my sermon on that and as guided by the Holy Spirit, I called the delegates to the realization that there were many 'stones' that were blocking the life of PCEA both physically and spiritually. I uncovered such 'stones' as the blockage of the Holy Spirit in the life of the PCEA Church and the *'worship'* style in Scottish traditions rather than having its centrality as spelt out in scriptures.

I also pointed to the delegates that PCEA Church had, over the years, operated in the hands of some liberal cartels who operated in the spirit of New Agers, Illuminati and Freemasonry, which also happened to be the foundation of PCEA. I told the delegates that Freemasonry started in Scotland in the year 1307, and it was after almost 600 years that the so-called missionaries brought the half-baked gospel to us.

By then, Freemasonry had penetrated into the Church of Scotland to such an extent that the majority of the clergy had been initiated into Freemasonry who worshipped the Great Architect of the Universe, whose representation is a capital **G**. The Masonic constitution launched in 1723 had been authored by a Presbyterian minister, Anderson. Thus, the missionaries who claimed to bring the gospel were at the same time establishing pathways for the propagation of Freemasonry into the *'Third World Countries,'* thus presenting a distorted gospel.

I had mentioned the symbols of their gods that they also placed into the sanctuaries they built. I said, *"God has given you an opportunity to liberate the Church; this is the best time to roll out the Scottish stone. Give me a chance; let us go for it! Like David of the Bible, I will lead you to knock down this Goliath who has been entrenched in the Church in the form of a foreign culture and false gods."* There was then a big shout of *'Amen!'* I heard a section of delegates shouting *"comrades, let us go for it. It is now or never!"* I then called one of the past Moderators, who seemed deeply touched by my devotion, to lead the delegates in a prayer of repentance.

After the devotion, the delegates went for a tea-break before getting into the real business of the day. As delegates enjoyed a cup of tea, there was an ongoing discussion, some in small groups. From what I could hear, it was all based on my devotion. Some were aggressively analyzing the stones that had blocked the advancement of the Church over many years and the light that had come that morning.

But there were those who were even opposed to *'such theories'*, including the claim that some missionaries were Freemasons. I heard one say, *"How can he come up with that blasphemous statement? It is for this reason that we will leave no stone unturned until we get him not only* from the position of Moderator but also kick him out of the Church. Otherwise, if allowed to continue occupying that seat, he will totally distort the Church traditions, beliefs and partnerships."

The more the small groups of people continued to talk, the more the emotions ran high. I heard another one shout, "*I am personally amazed by the Moderator's courage, an affirmation that he is a divine calling. There is no way I will support his impeachment.*" Another one said, "*You go ahead and support him, but understand that you stand with the minority. I had initially advocated by all means that we avoid having him elected, but I was opposed by many. Now, you can see the bitter confusion he is creating in the Church.* "Then he shouted very loudly for everyone to hear, "*Comrades, let us vote this man out. If not, our good Church as we know it will no longer be the same.*"

At that juncture, the bell rang, and people were now busy walking back to the hall. When we went back to the hall, I asked for some feedback on my devotion. There were several hands raised. I gave them an opportunity to speak, whereupon a debate ensued, and I could tell that those who were pro-impeachment had declined in numbers. Many had been convinced through my sermon that much of what had been referred to as PCEA traditions were, in fact, Scottish culture, which was not conducive to church development both spiritually and physically.

It is no wonder, then, that when I asked for a vote, those who had aggressively campaigned for my impeachment lost, though not by a big margin. We then proceeded with the agenda for the day which included the reading of my report. It was out of reading the report that many more delegates yielded to my ideas.

The whole issue reminded me of God's words found in Jeremiah 15 21; "*I will save you from the hands of the wicked and redeem you from the grasp of the cruel.*" And again, in the words of **Isaiah 41 11**, "*All who rage against you will surely be ashamed and be disgraced; those who oppose you will be as nothing and perish.*"

2. IMPEACHMENT ATTEMPT THROUGH BUSINESS COMMITTEE

The pressure here came as a result of three incidents that is, the removal of the symbols from St. Andrews Church and my call to the church to detach from PC (USA) because they were ordaining gays and even solemnizing their marriages. There was also my call to form a commission to investigate the reasons behind the continued growth of homosexuals in PCEA. But there was also the issue of my call to the government to remove the occultic symbols that were flooding the Kenyan Parliament Buildings. I was also exposing and fighting corruption that had formed layers in the life of the church.

The Business Committee always met at the Head Office in South C in Nairobi and its membership comprised two people from each presbytery, a minister and the pairing elder. It also included the past Moderators.

The liberals felt oppressed by my constant call against things that they had thrived on- especially corruption. They could no longer sit down and watch me continue exposing the evils in the church, including the mysteries of their religion's inclination towards devil worship. They manipulated their way to collude with some of my colleagues at the General Assembly offices and in some presbyteries. One key head office official had even been promised the position of GA Moderator after the impeachment and eventual defrocking.

Another one had been promised a future position as the Secretary-General. Those officials had tricked me into agreeing to summon a Business Committee to deal with what they called; *Teething issues in the Church.'* A Business Committee was therefore summoned with one hidden agenda - to have me kicked out of office, something that I had no idea about. I came to know about the agenda just as I was heading to the meeting.

As I closed my office door, my driver came and, in great panic, said to me, *"Moderator, do you know that this meeting has been purposely set to have you impeached and, where possible, even defrocked?"*

He went on, *"Three of your very supportive members of the Business committee have just approached me and told me that the meeting is set to impeach you, and they are the prime movers of that motion. They are no longer supporting you to continue being the Moderator."*

Then I asked him, *"What are the accusations?"* He replied, *"You are being accused of having deliberately exposed the symbolisms, some wickedness in the church, and your call for the church to form a commission to unearth the ongoing homosexuality and devil worship."* He added, *"You are being accused of your claim to change the worship style, which would call for the introduction of the keyboard, clapping of hands, individualized prayers, i.e. Praise in Worship. They are also against commissioned intercessors."*

He then said, *"It is argued that, while some of these issues could be traceable, you should not expose the nakedness of the church. The church is like the body that one has to be very careful not to be exposed to cold weather. In other words, you are being accused of having championed the controversial removal of the Masonic symbols in St. Andrews Church, an issue that has become international."*

He also said, *"You are also being accused of calling upon the removal of similar symbols in the Kenyan Parliament when you prayed during the opening of the parliamentary session. They say these controversies, which were not only aired locally but internationally as well, have greatly tainted the name of the Church not only locally but internationally. BBC had also taken on the issue as they accused you of having formed a demolition squad to demolish all the Churches that were built by the pioneer missionaries from Europe."*

He further said, *"They have told me that the strategy is so well planned in such a way that this time round, you have no way of escape. They tell me the Church is collaborating with the Freemasons and their agents in parliament."*

I responded: *"You don't have to worry. These people are fighting a losing battle. What has greatly stirred their anger the most is what I have done in not supporting them in the protection of the symbols removed at St. Andrews Church and the exposition of the negative symbols in parliament and the one on 'Harambee.' This stirred the anger of the liberals into declaring that enough is enough."*

I further said, "*They think they can manipulate God as they are doing with the people. God is not a man that they can close the door He has opened. There is no way they can do this.*"

I went on to say: "*It is God's agenda that this Satanism that is eating both the Church and nation be unearthed.*" I reminded him, "*The words that God affirmed when he called me remain fresh and active. For this is what he told me when he opened this GA seat to me, 'They will fight against you but shall not prevail against you, for I am with you (Jer. 1:19). I, therefore, have no apology for exposing these evil powers of darkness, including those in the Church buildings. But you know what? This battle belongs to God, and there is no way they will be able to impeach or defrock me. Has not God promised me, saying, 'Have I not commanded you? Be strong and courageous. Do not be terrified, do not be discouraged for the Lord your God will be with you wherever you go.'*" I gave him counsel; "*Just be interceding even as I face these people. Don't see Goliath; instead, see David.*"

I then proceeded to the meeting. As I walked, I kept on thinking and wondering why my colleagues in the Head Office would stoop too low to betray me in this manner. Why this greed for power? Why on earth did they arm-twist me to agree to summon the Business committee only to come and pass a vote of no confidence in me as the Moderator? Why did they disguise their real agenda? That was only self-talk.

But one thing that I so vividly remember was that, I felt a lot of peace even as I continued in faster strides to get into the board room for the meeting. Finally, I got there and took my seat, and for sure, the environment was very hostile. There was a lot of deep breathing. Every eye in that room gazed at me with visible and obvious hostility.

Before the meeting began, I had to first give the devotion as that was the Moderator's prerogative. This time around, I focused on the book of Judges 6, where the whole community rose against Gideon for having smashed Baal, the god they worshiped. They had called out in unison against Gideon's father, saying, "*Bring out your son. He must die because he has broken down Baal's altar and cut down the Asherah pole beside it.*"

Now, listen to what Gideon's father told them; "*Are you going to plead Baal's cause...If Baal is really a god, he can defend himself when someone breaks down his altar.*" I continued to address the Committee members by saying: "*From a psychological point of view, I can tell you are all very upset, and this is not without a reason. I even feel that you are not as angry as you ought to be. I have followed all that has been said about the Church through social media, the radio, TV and the newspapers. It is really disgusting and if I were you, I would have been angrier than you. But why the anger? It is because your attitude is like that upheld by Gideon's community. You are angry because I have led the way to smash the occultic symbols in St. Andrews and in Parliament.*

I asserted:

But I know your main anger and bitterness is more focused on the removal of symbols from St. Andrews Church." I queried them: "*Why are you defending these evil representations visibly manifest in both national and Church life? And for your information, I have no apology to offer. This is a battle that God has enrolled me into, and I will fight on, no retreat from my side. But, know this one thing; this is a battle you can hardly win.*"

I then called upon the Secretary-General to move the motion. He made it known to the Committee that the agenda for the meeting was triggered by the on-going controversies based on the removal of symbols from St. Andrews Church that had really tainted the name of the Church. He then said, "*Moderator, you can lead the members in deliberating this agenda.*" I stood up and said: "*We all know that according to our Church's constitution, when a Church leader is under scrutiny by a certain committee or court, one has to abdicate the seat, and another person takes the seat as the chairman. Therefore, now that I am under your scrutiny, I beg you to elect a person, in this case, a past Moderator, to take the seat, and then I will leave you to deliberate upon my fate as the Practice and Procedure bestows that power upon you, otherwise, as things stand, I have no apology. In fact, it is you who owes me an apology.*"

They elected my predecessor, the Very Reverend Dr. Jesse Kamau, to take over the seat. As Jesse was preparing to stand and proceed to come and take the seat, I said, "*It is good that you have chosen Dr. Jesse, but before I vacate the chair, I have a question that, as soon as you answer it, I will leave immediately.*"

I explained that:

"The root cause of the removal of St. Andrews symbols was as a result of five people (including Rev. Kibicho) who in 1994 had left for Scotland on an exchange program. It was while they were there that they noticed some ungodly symbols entrenched on the windows, walls, floors and even the roofs of many of the Scottish Sanctuaries. These, in most cases, were in the form of images, tainted glass, sculptures, pictures, and statues, among others. "I went on to say, *"The tainted window glasses were loaded with many of such images and pictures, including those of serpents. One could easily tell the fact that those were not godly symbols, for some were in the form of pictures of people holding serpents. They likened such symbols to those Ezekiel saw entrenched in the Jerusalem Temple. Ezekiel testified, "I saw it portrayed all over the walls all kinds of crawling things and detestable animals and all the idols of the house of Israel"* (Ezekiel 8:10).

One thing the St. Andrews visiting group realized was that the same kinds of symbols were familiar at St. Andrews Church, where they had come from. They inquired as to why such ungodly symbols could be installed in the architectural structure of the church. They were told that some of those symbols could be traced prior to AD 637, when Christianity found its way to Scotland. Otherwise, prior to that, the Scottish people worshipped all kinds of idols, which had really flooded the pagan temples.

When the Churches were constructed, some of the pagan gods that were formerly installed in those temples were transferred to the Christian sanctuaries as a way of preserving and honouring them. The people feared being persecuted by those gods for ignoring them. The Scottish Church was then saturated with the dominance of gods in the form of idols. This was especially true since the time of Emperor Constantine in AD 312 after Constantine had defeated Maxentius, his rival to the throne. He claimed to have seen a Christian cross in the sky with the words, *'by this you will conquer.'* And true to the words he had seen on the cross, he won the battle. He, therefore, credited the Christian God whom the Christians worshipped as one who had enabled him to win the battle. Before this, Christians knew only the life of persecution. He consequently gave Christians the liberty to live without persecution.

Further, he had embarked on a widespread construction of Cathedrals. He even gave some of the pagan temples to be owned by Christians by converting these formerly pagan temples for Christian use. Such temples were still flooded by pagan gods which were never removed. On further inquiry, the guests were told that the other source of the pagan symbols entrenched in the Church buildings were installed by the Freemasons. Incidentally, they were mandated by the Church and state to be the sole builders and designers of the Church buildings, not only in Scotland but in the whole of Europe, as well as they had lived in Palestine/ in the Holy Land during the time of crusades. They, therefore, claimed to have the Holy Land anointing.

I further explained that when the St Andrews team came back from Scotland in 1994, they informed the leadership in St. Andrews about the history behind the symbols that flooded that sanctuary. It was then that the Kirk session decided through a minute to have those symbols removed. However, according to the PCEA constitution, the Kirk Session had no mandate to remove them without a nod from the Milimani Presbytery.

The Kirksession, therefore, wrote to the Mililani presbytery under which jurisdiction St. Andrews Church was. The presbytery likewise, through minutes, gave the green light to have the symbols removed. Then came my question to the Business Committee; *"Now tell me, with St. Andrews Kirk session having recommended the removal of the symbol and with the presbytery having allowed the same, does the Moderator of General Assembly have powers to veto what a presbytery had decided, noting that, constitutionally, the presbytery is autonomous in its decisions and no other powers can reverse any of the decisions carried out by that court?"*

This question put the whole committee in a dilemma. The truth of the matter is that the moderator has no power to veto a decision made by a presbytery. The members of the committee remained silent for a while, and then one of the members raised his hand to speak, *"Moderator, you are taking this committee for a ride. All that you said is geared at confusing us. I find myself confused in all these matters. The fact is that whatever you come up with to manipulate our minds will not hinder us from achieving our motive for calling this meeting."* Another person took to the floor and said, *"Moderator, to substantiate what you* have said, can we have the delegate from Milimani Presbytery add some meat to what you have already said?"

I then called upon the Milimani Presbytery member to speak out, and he said, "All that the Moderator has said is the whole truth and nothing but the truth. I am both a member of St. Andrews Kirksession and also a member of Milimani presbytery." He then went on to elaborate on the fact that, just as I had said, the two courts, the Kirk Session and the Presbytery, had passed the resolutions that the symbols be removed, and that went back to 1994. The only unfortunate thing, he explained, was that when St. Andrews members attempted to remove the symbols, some wealthy and well-established members in the congregation aggressively resisted this.

At that juncture, the speaker took a deep breath and said, "As a result of the pressure that these defenders of the symbols exerted, it made me personally come to believe that there was a hidden connection between those people and the symbols because they were ready to use all their resources and power for the protection of those symbols which they termed as; '**The preservation of History**.' They were even ready to engage in a physical fight if need be."

He further explained that the only unfortunate thing with those who craved the removal of the symbols was that the former Moderator of the General Assembly by then came to the support of the other group. He claimed that those symbols had a historical significance and, hence, could not be touched.

That being the case, he further added:

"The proponents of the removal of the symbols gave up until the year 2003 when Rev. Githii became the Moderator, and during his installation speech, he had hinted that he would, by all means, pave the way for the acceptance of the Holy Spirit in the Church. He also informed the GA that he was to indulge himself in fighting all kinds of idolatry, including corruption in the Church."

That Business Committee member continued to elaborate that after my speech, part of St. Andrews Church members and a section of the leadership felt that their eight -year prayers to have the idols removed had at last come. They felt that this was an opportunity that

425

could be put into action without further delay. But before fully executing the move, a number of intercessors comprising some members, elders and deacons went for a number of days in prayer and fasting, after which, on one Saturday night, they removed almost all the symbols in the sanctuary.

He further said: *"In fact, these same people had earlier threatened to take those who had removed the symbols to a court of law, but when they realized that the Church constitution stated that if a Christian took another Christian to court, such a person should first surrender any position of leadership, that they retreated. This was because some of those people were elders, deacons and even members of various Church committees like the Development Committee. They dropped that idea and reverted to attacking Dr. Githii, treating him as the scapegoat. I believe that controversy was triggered by what appeared in one of the most widely read newspapers in Kenya that carried a headline stating that Dr. Githii had formed 'a squad to demolition' all pioneer missionaries Scottish built Churches."*

At that juncture, I could tell the members of the Business Committee were in a confused state. After another long silence, one delegate stood up and apologetically said:

"Moderator, I will first ask for forgiveness. I did not know this issue had had some history behind it, and that history, as demonstrated by the Business Committee Member from Milimani Presbytery leaves no doubt that the Moderator was not involved because it can be traced to around 10 years ago. And since this case has been handled and qualified by both the Kirk Session and Presbytery, then, by virtue of our Church Constitution, the Moderator has no power to veto a resolution passed by the Presbytery. This makes him innocent."

He went on to say:

"My emotions towards all this controversy were stirred by all that I heard from the media portraying our Church as a cult centred on devil worship. I now sympathize with you, Moderator, because your name has been so much tarnished to the extent of making the PCEA fraternity come to hate you, something that has led to this committee being summoned purposely to have a vote of no confidence against you and, therefore defrock you out of this Church."

Another member raised his hand, and I permitted him to speak; he went on to say, "*Fellow members of this esteemed committee, having heard from the horses' mouth and having been made aware of the controversy behind it, I am calling upon you to have this agenda withdrawn immediately and never to have it surface again because why should we punish our so hardworking and innocent Moderator.*" He sat down. I then said, "*The speaker has asked this committee to stop deliberating on this matter. Is that the feeling of the committee members, or is there another opinion?*"

One other person stood up to speak. He said, "*We might seem to be walking on a path of injustice, being unconstitutional and unbiblical if we pursue this agenda. My understanding is that both the member from Milimani Presbytery and the Moderator have let the cat out of the bag. We all now understand what transpired over the St. Andrews symbolism controversy, which is the bone of contention that led to the calling of this Business Committee Meeting. It would be a waste of time to advance this agenda any further. I am therefore asking the Moderator to call for a vote over this agenda. Let us see how many people want us to further dwell on this agenda and those who are against it. The constitution is so clear on such a matter, and it is in line with the Moderator's question.*"

I stood up and said, "*Let us vote as a way to point to the direction this committee will take*", but someone else chipped in; "*Rather than waste time in voting, Moderator, just ask whether there are people opposed to what the previous speakers have said.*" I then put the question, "*Do we have people or a person who thinks contrary to what the speaker has stated that we call off this agenda? If there is such a person or people, please let me see by a show of hands?*" Surprisingly there was not a single hand raised up.

I continued, "*Do I then take it that all are of the opinion that we bring this agenda to an end?*" There was a unanimous shout; "*Yes! Yes! Yes!*" I then said, "*Can you confirm the position by raising of hands.*" To my surprise, there was a forest of hands raised up, with some even raising both hands. I then said, "*Case concluded.*"

I called upon the delegates to join me in singing the hymn, '*Guide Me O the Great Jehovah.*' The singing could be heard from far away as people shook hands in joy. After singing, I called on two people to pray. It was also agreed that since the sole agenda for summoning the committee had now been resoundingly trounced, there was to be no more debating after all what had been put on paper as other agenda items were non-issues meant to sugarcoat the real agenda.

I adjourned the meeting and was surrounded by many members congratulating me for the wise way of handling the meeting. At the same time, they promised their great support to my leadership as they had realized that, indeed, God was totally on my side. One of the members said, *"In fact, all the media houses in this country and even BBC, were eagerly awaiting the outcome of this meeting to announce that you have been defrocked. Unfortunately for them, they have no news to broadcast. We have all ended up in great shame."*

In fact, this reminded me of Isaiah's words in Isaiah 41:11, which say, *"All who rage against you will surely be ashamed and disgraced; Those who oppose you will be as nothing and perish."* It also reminds me of Isaiah 54:17, that says, *"No weapon fashioned against me shall prosper."*

We shook hands and I was congratulated by the members. The defeat of that agenda meant that God had again fought for me. What again came to my mind were the words that God's messenger, Jahaziel, had told King Jehoshaphat when he was confronted by a huge army. Jahaziel came with very encouraging words, as stated in 2nd Chronicles 20:15; *"Do not be afraid or discouraged because of this vast army. For the battle is not yours, but the Lord's.... You will not have to fight this battle; take up your positions; stand firm and see the deliverance the LORD will give you."*

3. IMPEACHMENT ATTEMPT THROUGH GAC AT MOI ACADEMY

Having failed to impeach me through the Business Committee, the cartel of liberals who had vowed to leave no stone unturned until I got impeached strategized on a GAC Meeting that was to take place in Nakuru. Their aim was to continue inciting the Church members and other Church leaders against my leadership so that they could mobilize them to emotionally have me expelled from the church. It is no wonder, therefore, that the spirit of arrogance persisted.

I likened those people to '**Judaizers**' who, in Acts 15, are reported to have tried all they could to dilute Paul's' message by preaching a contrary message to the very people Paul had led to the Lord. They preached to them from one region to another that in order to be recognized in the kingdom of God, they had to undergo physical circumcision. Likewise, the PCEA cartel was campaigning from one presbytery to another, stirring people to vote me out in the forthcoming GAC in a month's time. This was after the Business committee had thrown away the issue of my being voted out by the Business Committee.

The so-called '**Judaizers**' had really covered the ground so much so that it was clear that come the day of the meeting, they would have me voted out of the seat of the Moderator. A lot of money had been used to bribe some of the key delegates and GAC members. This included the Presbytery Moderators and their clerks. Unfortunately, some officials from the head office were also compromised.

One of the strategies that the liberals had formulated was to hire street boys commonly known as '*chokora*' who spend their time loitering and scavenging the streets of Nakuru town.

Instead of the church strategizing on how to feed or settle those children, they instead schemed on how to use them to fulfill their evil plans. The other group targeted for recruitment was the '*Matatu and Bus Stage (Terminus) idlers and, to some extent, the Matatu operators*".

The people they referred to as idlers were the people who hung around those localities looking for means to meet their needs. These are good people, but the '*Judaizers*' wanted to manipulate them to accomplish their evil plans. But what they did not realize was that '*matatu*' operators are very mature people. They could not enter into any memorandum of understanding with them. That was an abuse to '*matatu*' operators whom I really respect, and so do many other people.

The strategy was to hire those groups and transport them to the venue. They would then be instructed to cause chaos by long sustained chants of, '*Githii must go! Githii must go!*'

This they did while raising placards with all sorts of abusive names against me to provoke the masses to join the mob in creating hell and chaos. The '*Judaizers*' called themselves '*PCEA Watchdogs*', and for sure, they could bark! But as they engaged in all manner of shenanigans, God was at work in other ways.

CHANGE OF VENUE

Initially, this GAC meeting had been planned to be held at Nakuru High School, just next to Nakuru town. However, God, in his divine ways, changed this venue that could have easily been accessed by the idlers that the liberals had planned to transport to cause mayhem in line with their evil schemes. This is what actually happened, just one week prior to the meeting, God made the place to run out of water and a few other necessities that were vital for the sustainability of the delegates.

A new venue had thus to be looked for. It turned out to be a school known as Moi Forces Academy, which was adjacent and within the same locality of the Lanet Army Barracks-the training ground of the Kenya Army. There was also a school for the trainees' children. In other words, the venue's proximity to the barracks threw the dynamics of the evil plans in disarray. This was an environment where the *'watchdogs/liberals'* could not attempt any chaotic move. But most importantly, the idlers or any other hired groups could not dare venture there. Otherwise, it would be at their peril.

MESSAGE FROM INTERCESSORS

One week before the GAC meeting, I received a call from some intercessors from a Pentecostal Church in Kirugoya. The caller said: *"Moderator, I am calling you on behalf of a group of intercessors with whom we fellowship together. We are not PCEA members, but God connected us with you when you were praying in parliament and exposed the idols that are entrenched there. Since then, God put in us the burden to be praying for you. Recently, as we were praying, God showed one of us a big storm coming our way. We, therefore, took it to mean that there is a big spiritual warfare that will soon confront you very forcefully. We, therefore, decided to engage ourselves in prayer and fasting. So, as I talk to you, we are intensively praying. Are you aware of any impending danger to your life or ministry? What do you think is happening?"*

I responded:

*"Thank you for obeying God's voice to stand with me. It is true. There is a storm brewing within the PCEA. A crucial meeting is coming up soon, and there is a move to pass a vote of no confidence against me and have me defrocked from the Church. This is all coming out as a result of my persistent call for the removal of **Satanic symbols entrenched in St. Andrews Church** in Nairobi.*

I further said:

"The Freemasons and other devil worship-oriented people have ganged together to have me out of the church because of the removal of those symbols. I am also being accused of fighting corruption in the Church and other wickedness. But most of the anger is in my consistency in exposing the idols in some of our Church buildings, like St. Andrews Church, the Church of the Torch and others. This also includes the exposition of those idols entrenched in our Kenyan Parliament, including the All-Seeing Eye and the snake-shaped armchair of the Speaker."

Then the caller said:

"Okay, God has shown us the scheme of the devil over your life and now that we have known the scheme that the devil has already laid down, we will continue to seek God's face and direction. You should also be always in a prayerful mood, including fasting. It is the best weapon you have to penetrate through such a very forceful cloud of darkness. Meanwhile, please read 2 Corinthians 10:5 onwards."

I took this intercessor's advice very seriously, and I went to the Bible Translation Literature (BTL) Retreat Centre, located in Ruiru, for a three-day quiet Time. The same intercessory team called me three days prior to the meeting and said:

"Moderator, as I had told you, we have been in intensive prayers and fasting, and God has directed us to tell you to be very obedient and do as He directs; otherwise, if you miss one step, the battle will take a very high turn. Secondly, the Lord says that, you be the first person to step into that hall where the meeting will take place."

The intercessor went on to say:

"When you get into that hall, we advise you to do the following: You will first have to silence all the negative tongues that will enter into that room, that those tongues will be imprisoned so that they will not spit any demonic poison. In doing this, you will quote Isaiah 41:11, that says, 'All who rage against you will surely be ashamed and disgraced; those who oppose you will be as nothing and perish.'"

Also, thank God in accordance with His words in Isaiah 42:6: *"Thank God for having called you in righteousness, taking hold of your hand and for choosing you to be a covenant for the people and a light to those still grooming in darkness. Thank Him for making you into a threshing sledge, new and sharp, with many teeth, as found in Isaiah 41:15. Thank God for His promises, quoting Isaiah 43: 1-3, where He has promised to be with you even as you pass through waters, rivers and through fires."*

The intercessor added, *"After this, you can make decrees and declarations through other quotations like in Luke 10:19 and 2 Corinthians 10:3-5. We have declared that the peace of God that surpasses all understanding be with you. Amen."*

The intercessor went on:

"Please, Moderator, note that, for the prayers to be effective, you have to be the first person to get into that hall. Understand that the prayers I am talking of here are aimed at scattering and diffusing all the negative tongues that would find their way into the meeting. It is also necessary that you anoint that hall and claim and declare its possession. Such prayers will spiritually destroy any occultic rituals that could have been brought into the hall. It will even paralyze any occultic objects that might have been planted there or those that would be brought in by the delegates, including the non-tangible ones like anger, hatred, curses thrown at you and all other kinds of manipulations."

THE SERVING OF HOLY COMMUNION

Two days before the meeting, I received a call from another person who described herself as a prayer warrior, speaking on behalf of a bigger prayer warriors' group, and whom God had commanded to

432

stand with me after my prayers in parliament through which much of the idolatry in parliament was exposed. The caller continued to tell me that since that time, they had come to know me as one anointed by God to face the strongholds of the devil; hence, they had been standing with me. She gave the reason behind calling me being the rumors of people planning to defrock me through a forthcoming meeting to be held in Nakuru.

She said:

"As I speak to you, we have been in prayer and fasting on your behalf, praying that God would see you through. One of us was shown the picture of Gideon and was told that that is the spirit that God has given unto you. Meaning, you will win this battle under the support of some intercessors/prayer warriors. Gideon had only three hundred. In our intercession and listening to God, the outcome is that, among other things, God wants you to do all you can to make a way to serve the delegates with Holy Communion. The Holy Spirit indicates that when you do this and any other thing God will reveal to you or through others, you will be in a position to dismantle all the schemes of the devil, and you will be an overcomer. But obedience is paramount in this spiritual battle."

I responded, *"You know what? I will not strain in making the arrangements in the serving of Holy Communion. That is automatic. Otherwise, procedurally, the Holy Communion is served the evening before the beginning of the GAC business the following day."* The caller then said, *"Oh, praise the Lord! We are happy to hear that. All the best. We are your foot soldiers."*

THE VISION

While going to Nakuru, my starting point is at Zambezi, which is the location of my home. Between Nakuru and Zambezi is a distance of over 100 miles. Due to the poor state of the road, I needed at least two hours to cover the distance and be at the venue by 7.00 am. I had slept early as I needed to get a good sleep. But something happened 15 minutes before waking up. I had a vision in which I found myself standing somewhere where there were white and rather short people who were building a wall around me very fast.

They were moving as fast as a cassette player when it was set to rewind up either in reverse or fast forward. Soon, the wall was completed, and then, at that very time, I woke up. Looking at the watch, it was exactly the time I had wanted to wake up. What came into my mind were words in Jeremiah 1:18; "*Today I have made you a fortified city, an iron pillar and a bronze wall to stand against the whole land-its officials, its priests... They will fight against you but will not overcome you, for I am with you and will rescue you. Declares the Lord.*"

I had alerted my driver, Muruthi to report at my home by 5.00 am for departure to Nakuru '*for I needed to visit my farm located in Njoro*' prior to the starting of the meeting at around 3 pm. I told him that because I did not want him to know what I was planning, but in reality, I did visit the farm, but only after spending sometime at the meeting's venue. Otherwise, my going early was in accordance with the advice from the intercessors who had alerted me to be the first person to step into the meeting hall where the one-week meeting was to take place.

Muruthi came in time, and we embarked on the two-hour journey. We finally arrived at the meeting venue around 7.00 am. I found about five women at the meeting's venue in the process of lighting up the fire to start the one-week duty of cooking for the delegates – of course, there were many others to join them in the course of the day. I inquired from them about the location of the hall where the GAC meeting was to take place. This was from the 5th - 10th April, 2005. One woman pointed to the hall, but I requested them to accompany me for some prayers in that hall. When we got inside, I asked one of them to lead in a chorus – it was after this that I embarked on the utterance of the prayers as previously guided by the intercessors and prayer warriors.

I also made further prophetic utterances using my own words. I thanked God for having chosen me right from the time I was in my mother's womb. I even thanked him for making it possible for me to overcome so many challenges not only in the time that I had been the Moderator of GA but right from my childhood. I gave Him gratitude as a God of yesterday, today and in the future. I thanked him for being so protective, something that affirmed him as my **Ebenezer**. I then asked two of the women who had introduced themselves as intercessors to pray for the journey mercies of the delegates and all those who would be participating in one way or the other in the meeting. After that, the women headed back to continue with their cooking business. The assembly of the delegates was scheduled to start at 3.00 pm.

Meanwhile, my driver and I headed 30 miles away for Njoro where I wanted to visit friends as well as see my farm. Otherwise, if it were not for the spiritual warfare prayers early that morning, I would have left Zambezi at around noon. We came back from Njoro at around 3:00 pm as the serving of the Holy Communion was to take place at 5:00 pm. At that time, it was expected that, all the delegates would have arrived.

One of the things I immediately noticed upon arrival was the various groupings of the delegates, with each group engaging in conversations in hushed tones! The people looked so worried and engulfed in panic. I began visiting each of these groups and asking each of them, "*Why do you look so unhappy and somehow worried? Are you not aware that this will be one of the best GAC meetings you have ever experienced?*" I could notice people looking at each other, and my assumption was that they were communicating that I did not know what was going on. This is because I had not shared with anybody what I was undergoing. People loved me but were being overpowered by the PCEA watchdog group, which was also a composition of Freemasonry that was using a lot of money to bribe their way through. It was already time to go and pick the Holy Communion.

ST. ANDREWS' CHURCH MAGAZINE (The Spark)

In the course of St. Andrew's symbols controversy, a group of youth from that Church had come up with an idea of compiling and publishing all the Masonic symbols that had been removed in a magazine they called, '**The Spark.**' A picture of each symbol that had been removed from St. Andrew's Church building was placed there. Each symbol had its accompanying Masonic meaning. They had purposely printed them in order to sell them in the GAC meeting.

They thought that as a result of the magnitude of the controversy, they could sell this like hot cake.

Unfortunately, they came to realize that the opponents of the removal of the symbols were busy looking for those magazines to confiscate and have them burnt. They therefore stopped the idea of having them sold and approached me and explained the whole scenario and then said, *"We have therefore thought it wise to hand over these magazines for your use in whatever way you think can reach the people to expose the truth."* I then had these magazines secretly placed in my vehicle.

THE MEETING

I left the groupings and proceeded to the room where the Holy Communion preparation was taking place. Before long, we were in procession heading to the hall where I was to celebrate the Holy Communion. As I received the Holy Communion elements, I was surprised to see the PCEA watchdog group sitting quietly in the front row. They looked composed and emotionless. I then started to deliver the devotion. I used two items: One was The Spark Magazine. The other item I used was a Newspaper cutting. As I did this, I picked one of the 'Spark' magazines and said:

"I am aware that all of you have been following the controversy over the radio, TV and Newspapers, but you hardly know what those evil-related symbols at St. Andrews Church were. I have all that was removed from St. Andrews Church contained in this magazine called 'Spark.' I now challenge each one of you to take this magazine, peruse it and then you will understand why the controversy over the symbols has gone overboard. I am sure after you have seen what we are calling evil symbols, your stand will never be the same again."

I then said:

"I have stationed people at every door of this hall; as you move out, you will be given a copy of this magazine. Remember what Apostle John advises us when he says, 'Do not believe every spirit but test the spirits to see whether they are from God, because many false prophets have gone out into the world... but every spirit that does not acknowledge Jesus is not from God....

This is the spirit of antichrist which you have heard is coming and even now is already in the world.'" (1st John 4:1-3). I reminded the delegates of what John further says; *"You will know the truth, and the truth will set you free"* (John 8:32).

THE NEWSPAPER CUTTINGS

As the controversies raged, the media kept on highlighting the developments every day. I kept on cutting those highlights from the newspapers, and I had quite several. Thus, as I was developing my sermon at the opening of the GAC, I picked one of the newspaper cuttings whose title was, **'Twenty-six presbyteries have rejected the PCEA Moderator Dr. Githii.'** I also noticed that the article appeared on Fool's Day, April 1st. The Holy Spirit led me to focus on this article. In order to get into the matter, I first praised the delegates and said,

"What concerns me at this point and time is the presence of a cartel in the Church who are promoting hatred and division in this denomination. These are the people who have caused all the controversy that is currently permeating into the Church. They are misleading people not to accept the truth that the symbols entrenched at St. Andrews were the work of Freemasonry."

I continued: *"It is quite unfortunate that this cartel is portraying you (delegates) as fools. And what a better illustration on this than the content of an article that appeared in the Daily Nation Newspaper of April 1st.?"* Of course, the newspaper article appeared on April 1st, which is considered the Fools Day worldwide. I took the opportunity to make use of that newspaper cutting to completely expose the cartel to the delegates.

I went on to say,

"It reflects the fact that this cartel considers you as fools, and it is for that reason that they had made the article appear on a 'Fools Day,' giving a distorted impression that the top church leadership is composed of fools who cannot understand the manipulation formulated to divide up the Church. All I know is that you are not a bunch of fools but a spiritual and dedicated group of people who have the PCEA at heart and who would do anything

that would bring about the development of this Church in all its faculties; people who are ready to undergo all kinds of hardships, if need be to glorify God."

As I spoke, I was psychologically studying the delegates' body language and I could tell that my speech at that point was agitating them. I could tell that I had won the battle by 50 percent. At that juncture, I said, *"This is why I am urging you to take time to scrutinize the symbols that were removed from St. Andrews' as contained in the Spark Magazine. As I had earlier said, the magazine will be given to each one of you as you get out of this hall after we are done with the Holy Communion."*

I also took the opportunity to remind the delegates of Hosea's words; *"My people are destroyed for lack of knowledge"* (Hosea 4:6). I further reminded the delegates that what the Church was facing was a very strong negative wave of evil powers, in the form of spiritual warfare.

I then said,

"In connection to spiritual warfare, the Bible says, "For though we live in the world, we do not wage war as the world does. The weapons we fight with are not weapons of this world. On the contrary, the weapons of our warfare are not carnal but mighty through God to the pulling down of strongholds. Casting down imaginations, and every high thing that exalts itself against the knowledge of God, they have divine power to demolish strongholds" (2 Cor. 10:3-4).

I then went ahead and celebrated the Holy Communion. As I concluded the service, I reminded people to take copies of the magazine and take time to look at the pictures of the symbols that had been removed from the St. Andrews Church. Then I said, *"And some of these are just similar to those others that are entrenched in our parliament building."* I then gave the final benediction.

After this, people went out of the hall even as the *'Spark'* magazines were being handed out to them. Suffice it to say that within the next fifteen minutes, the whole atmosphere had changed. I heard one person say to the other, *"You mean these snake-shaped symbols on the window grills were entrenched into the sanctuary?"* The other person responded: *"Don't you see these distorted biblical figures and crosses?"* another one shouted as if he wanted me to hear him saying, *"The*

438

Moderator and some of the St. Andrews Church leadership had a divine revelation to see these evil altars. We should now rally behind the Moderator."

One of the statements that appeared in Spark Magazine read: "*Many of the colonialists who came as missionaries in the late 1800s and early 1900s doubled as missionaries and Freemasons irrespective of their names and denominations. As these missionaries-cum-Freemasons acquired plots for building churches, they incorporated the Masonic Altars of sacrifice. Later while they built the Masonic lodges, they replicated in them these same altars. And as a result, the sacrifices, which they would perform on the altars in lodges, would result in psychic spiritual energy, which the Freemasons could and still use to control and manipulate legitimate worship in churches and through witchcraft.*"

To verify such a strong statement, one would only need to carefully scrutinize those churches that were built by the missionaries (and, in fact, some modern ones) and critically examine some of the symbols portrayed in them in the form of decorations, whether on the window panes, the grills, the walls, the seats, the hinges, the floors and accompanying interior and exterior decorations and shapes or patterns.

In a follow-up to what I was advocating, the Sunday Standard Newspaper of January 25th. 2004, had this to say: "*Church leaders who were members of the Freemason society include Dr. James Anderson, a Church of Scotland minister accredited with the writing the Masonic Constitution. Dr. Steel, a former Moderator of the Church of Scotland and Geoffrey Fisher, a former Archbishop of Canterbury, was also a confessed Freemason.*"

Eventually, the one-week GAC meeting turned into a historical meeting of fellowship. In my mind I felt that God had abruptly stopped a big storm that I felt had been somehow, '*capsizing my boat.*' It was at that moment that I recalled the time the boat in which the disciples were with Jesus was almost capsizing. The disciples went and woke him (Jesus), crying out, "*Master, Master, don't you care that we are drowning.*" Jesus then got up and rebuked the wind and the raging waters. The storm subsided, and all was calm. (Lk.8: 24). I also recalled Paul's words in Roman 8:28; "*And we know that in all things God works for the good of those who love him, who have been called according to his purpose"* and that; *"In all these things we are more than conquerors through him who loved us"* (Roman. 8:37) and in any case; *"I can do everything through him who gives me strength"* (Phil. 4:13). I felt so much encouraged by these scriptures.

OTHER DEVELOPMENTS ON THIS GAC MEETING

In the GAC at Moi Forces Academy, I had also taken the opportunity to educate the delegates on the things we as leaders needed to focus on as the way forward for the Church. The focus should be on reviving the spiritual life of the Church. We are to seek ways and means of developing the Church physically and, by so doing, create some channels of income generating projects rather than depending on foreign donors.

The theme that I had developed as a pointer to the way forward for the Church was, *"Leave it alone for one more year, and I will dig around it and fertilize it"* from Luke 13:8b. I was pointing the Church to my endeavours in uplifting the PCEA Church which was already at the lowest ebb in matters relating to spirituality, financially, politically and socially.

The pastors were living in abject poverty and under the oppressive hands of the elders and those in key positions in the Church hierarchy. This forced most of the pastors to yield to the elder's manipulation in order to survive. The elders, in most cases, took advantage of the poor conditions the pastors lived in to dictate to them the pattern of life the parish had to take. This, in most cases was designed to drift the members from worshiping in Spirit and truth.

By then, very few pastors owned personal vehicles or homes. Most of the pastors lived from hand to mouth. Thank God because, between the time I became the Moderator of GA in 2003 and 2005, I had already made some accomplishments. It was these achievements that I highlighted in that GAC in my report that was already in the GAC Docket, reference- 2nd. GAC, 2005.

The report indicated that Many Parishes had been sub-divided. From 28 Presbyteries at the beginning of the 17th GA, we now had 42

Presbyteries. The Elders' District had greatly gained activation, with elders now rotating within their Elder Districts. Congregations had embarked on breaking up on some Sundays and engaging in worshipping in their respective Elder Districts (Cell Groups). That was already proving to be potentially positive spiritually, socially and financially. This was the Apostolic Church principle. The early Church had no sanctuaries for the first 300 years. The Church existed as pockets of House Churches, which were found in different locations in some regions, cities and towns.

At the time of the meeting in Nakuru, many New Church dedications had taken place. Most of the Churches were well-constructed and well-designed. While that was a good move, I cautioned the leaders not to put a lot of emphasis on putting up magnificent Church buildings while neglecting good budgets for missions, evangelism, training and equipping the disciples. I reminded the delegates that big Cathedrals in Western countries were being turned into museums and apartments just because the Church leaders concentrated more on wonderful Church buildings and their maintenance and neglected the souls, which were the best temples of God.

A flow back to the Church by members who had earlier left, especially the youth, had also been witnessed in the said period. There were other new members who had embraced our church by joining to become members. This was a result of peeling off the Scottish cultural attachment to worship and the introduction of modern musical instruments. There was improved spiritual warmth in welcoming new members. The improved Elder Districts fellowships had also acted as catalysts to attract new neighborhood members. The Church institutions such as hospitals and schools reflected a great deal of improvement.

I turned the delegates' attention to the fact that, in many cases, when a minister got transferred, they lost part of their salary, especially the unpaid salaries some of which had been in several months' arrears. It seemed like when one got transferred, they never received their unpaid money. This had left many families straining. That issue was debated, and my views were greatly supported. The presbyteries were asked to revisit the issue and make the parishes that had not

441

paid pastors' arrears to do so with immediate effect. Otherwise, that was described as robbery without violence.

Addressing the issue of financial flow in both parishes and presbyteries, I proposed the following:

- In order to come out of financial constraints, the Parishes and Presbyteries needed to strategize ways and means of coming up with **income-generating projects** in the form of bookshops, guest houses, rental houses, large-scale farming, and beekeeping, among others.
- The place of Church groups needed to be addressed as far as the **collection of Church finances** was concerned. PCEA is like a mother pig that is vigorously sucked by twenty piglets. The mother is left skinny and with little to feed on, yet the piglets continue enjoying the sucking. The fundraising organized by those groups through printed cards had really tarnished the image of the Church. To outsiders, the PCEA was a shameless beggar. As I put it, *"Why can't the congregations do these fundraisings silently without flooding fundraising cards all over?"* I even suggested that we discard all those fundraising-oriented groups and have at least three fundraisings in a given congregation in a year, and out of the proceeds, the groups be given support in accordance with their needs.
- The presbyteries and parishes should carry out thorough **teaching on tithing**. Otherwise, if tithing were honoured in the congregations, there would be no need to carry out fundraisings. The groups would only table their annual budget and be funded by the parish funds.
- While I cautioned the ministers to **anchor their faith in God** and not to be tempted by the spirit of materialism.
- I also reminded believers of the importance of **the Church laity to take good care of the ministers** assigned to them by the Appointment Committee. That was because a minister well-kept gave dignity to the Church, glorified God, and motivated the minister to work. It also brought blessings to the congregation, parish and the individuals who gave the material and spiritual support to their shepherd. Their support brings blessings, while curses abide when the minister is left to undergo harsh conditions. I was insisting on that because many parishes had

neglected their ministers, making many of them live a very-stressful life.

- I also reminded the delegates that I had made it my personal campaign to go through the presbyteries conducting seminars to motivate the Church members and, especially, the elders to give support to pastors to own vehicles. I encouraged them to help pastors organize fundraisings for that purpose. Looking back at the time of writing this book, I am grateful to God that only one out of a hundred do not own a vehicle. In fact, more than anything else, the pastors are in competition over the make of the car one is driving. It is not even surprising to see more than one vehicle in some families.

- I also alerted the delegates on the need to **progressively improve Church worship** through the further introduction of musical instruments and by creating a better environment conducive to the presence of the Holy Spirit. I reminded the delegates that Praise is an act of faith that affirms the character and redemptive power of God in all circumstances. If God truly dwells in the praises of His people, the regular practice of praise must be built into the lifestyle of the spiritual warrior. God waits for the congregation to praise him so He can pour out His power into the sanctuary.

I further told the delegates that praise releases divine power to transform our perspective and our response to problems. A good example of this is found in 2Chr.20:21, 24, where Jehoshaphat involved praise as he was heading to face a big army, thus:

"After consulting the people, Josephat appointed men to sing to the Lord and to praise him for the splendor of his holiness as they went out at the head of the army, saying, 'Give thanks to the Lord, for His love endures forever...When men of Judah came to the place that overlooks the desert and looked toward the vast army, they saw only dead bodies lying on the ground; no one had escaped."

Here, we note that instead of further mobilization of the army and its weapons, the procession engaged in praising God, the impact being the death of all their enemies.

2006 GENERAL ASSEMBLY AGITATION

In the year 2006, a GA election was to take place. I had already done the three years which is usually referred to as the first term. Constitutionally, the Moderator is in office for three years, after which an election takes place. Thus, the same moderator can be re-elected, or he/she can lose, meaning the elected person takes over as the GA Moderator. When a Moderator is re-elected, he/she will be in office for the next non-renewable three-year term in office.

In the history of the church, every Moderator elected had served for two terms. The elections for the second term were just carried out as a formality. But this was not so with me. In my case, the re-election was quite dramatic. Swords had been drawn to make it impossible for me to be re-elected. It was seen as a good time to finally get me out of the office. Now that the liberals had failed in all their previous strategies to impeach me for the last three years. They now wanted to use this opportunity to block my re-election.

They, therefore, poured out their resources to block me from being re-elected. They campaigned day and night, including using aircraft to fly to far flung places like Pwani Presbytery in Mombasa, as well as to Tanzania which was treated as a Mission Presbytery.

In many places around Kenya, the convoy of vehicles engaged in strategized campaign trails which could be seen. But the worst of their maneuvers was experienced on the day of the elections. Constitutionally, on Election Day, every presbytery is expected to hold the elections in their presbytery headquarters. They are also supposed to begin their meeting at 10 am with no other agenda apart from that of elections. The whole process is supposed to be harmonious.

It should open with a devotion led by the presbytery Moderator and then follow the reading of the candidate's curriculum vitae. Delegates are then given voting cards in which each person is expected to write the name of the person he or she chooses to elect. These votes are then presented to the Moderator, who then ensures the votes are counted one at a time with the delegates as witnesses. Whoever of the candidates acquires more votes than the others, no matter the difference even if it is by one vote, is considered as the choice of that presbytery. The results are tabulated and sealed in an envelope as the delegate's watch. The following day, all the presbyteries then forward the candidates of their choice to the Office of the General Assembly.

On the third day, the Business Committee meets to have the envelopes containing the names of each of the presbytery's candidates of choice opened, and then the votes are counted. But one thing is critical: the winning candidate has to acquire two-thirds of the total presbytery's votes. If not, then there is a runoff, and if after this, none of the candidates gets the two-thirds, then the General Administrative Committee meets to take a vote where whoever wins with a simple majority becomes the Moderator-elect.

If the losing party feels dissatisfied, they can call for further re-election during the forthcoming GA Meeting just before the Moderator-elect is installed in office. This means the Moderator-elect is not yet the Moderator until he wins in the GA forum by a simple majority.

However, it is important to state that the latter two stages in elections have never happened in the history of the PCEA Church. If anything, the elections had always ended at the first stage of voting.

The D-Day of my re-election was the time the PCEA watchdog group focused on. Exactly ten minutes before the beginning of the meetings, a text message was released to all presbyteries' delegates, relaying the following message; "*This is urgent but not so good news. The Moderator of GA, Rev. Dr. David Githii, has just been involved in a fatal road accident, and as this message gets to you, he is in a comma. It is also unfortunate that his driver has lost both of his legs. Please pray for the Moderator, his driver and their families. It is unfortunate that being in that condition, Githii does not qualify for candidature in these ongoing elections.*"

Immediately, I received calls from three people from different presbyteries. The first two did not say anything about the accident. They only enquired about my whereabouts and how I was doing, to which I responded that I was fine. It was the third person, Mr. Kibathi from Kirimara Presbytery, who, after enquiring how I was doing and having heard that I was fine, then posed the question,

"Then why this text message indicating that you have been involved in a fatal road accident and you are in a comma and that your driver has lost both legs." I said; *"For sure, I could not be speaking to you if I was in a comma. It is all the manipulation of the PCEA watchdog group."* Then Kibathi said, *"This is a very high degree of spiritual dryness and portrayal of people who can easily kill for power. Thank you, Moderator; you just relax because this is not your battle; it is the Lord's battle."*

Nevertheless, this second term, Moderators elections were held on this day, the 13th. December, 2005. The Business Committee met as expected to receive the election results. Surprisingly, I was leading with 24 votes, Rukenya was second with 16 votes, and Kibicho had 3 votes. The number of presbyteries dictated that the winner had to garner 29 presbyteries, which were two-thirds of the existing number of presbyteries. This means I fell short by 5 presbyteries to win the election. Thus, constitutionally, there was to be a runoff. Rukenya's name and my name were floated again in the presbyteries for re-election.

The Presbyteries had the Moderator elections on the 27th December 2005, and which were received by the Business Committee, which met to receive them on the 30th. December, 2005. This time, I got 27 votes, while Rukenya retained his 16 votes. Again, I fell short by 2 votes to make 29 presbyteries. Constitutionally, the GAC had to meet and vote to decide on the winner, this time with a simple majority.

On January 10th. 2006, the GAC met to finalize the Moderators election with a nomination of the candidate. I opened the meeting with a devotion in which I gave a general message that had nothing to do with the election. I always felt in my spirit that there was no way I could fight for myself or take the opportunity to campaign for myself. After the devotion, I asked the delegates to appoint one of the past Moderators to preside over the elections. The watchdog group was quick to appoint Dr. Jesse Kamau.

The people who were on my side smelt a rat. To drift the tight grip that the watchdog group seemed to have taken, one person said, *"A point of order! I feel we cannot have Dr. Jesse take that seat because he is already the chairman of the panel that is overseeing the whole process of the current Moderator's re-election. This means he is the one to receive the outcome of the results from this seating. It is, therefore, not procedural to have him conduct this present election. In view of this, I am, therefore, proposing Rev. Dr. George Wanjau to take the seat."*

The watchdog group aggressively defended Dr. Kamau to remain in the chair, but they were overwhelmed by the logic behind the constitution. At that point I left the meeting for constitutionally; the election debate could not go on in my presence. Dr. Wanjau had a hard time, for each side was determined to convert as many people to their side. The debating went on from 11 am to around 4 pm when they all agreed on voting. When the voting finally ended, I emerged as the winner. But the watchdog group was so annoyed that they categorically indicated they would front a candidate for election on the day the GA meets. This meant that, instead of having me consecrated as the Moderator-elect, there was first to have an election where if I got defeated, the GA would have installed the winner as the moderator-elect.

The GA took place at PCEA St. Andrews Church in Nairobi from the 17th to the 22nd. April, 2006. But before getting into the main GA meeting, the watchdog group had placed another stumbling block. Through the Secretary-General, they had initiated an early morning Business Committee meeting with the aim of having all the previous written petitions to the Business Committee aimed at impeaching me revisited but which the Business Committee had earlier disqualified. They had argued that such were beyond the scope of the committee and only qualified to be deliberated by the GA delegates before the Moderator's election took place. Their expectation was that if the petitions carried the day, there could be no need for the Moderator's election as the petitions would have led to my impeachment. This is why the Secretary General had been advised to call for a Business meeting.

The group had accused the Business Committee of having not critically looked at the petitions. The Secretary-General had called a Business Committee meeting that was to meet before the main General Assembly meeting would start. This meeting took place at 7. am with all members of the Business committee present. I never resisted this meeting because I believed the battle was not mine but Yahweh's. In fact, I opened the meeting with a short devotion, after which I called upon the Secretary-General to table the agenda.

447

The Secretary-General said:

"A group of Church leaders, both clergy and elders, have a great concern over the way the previous petitions forwarded to the Business Committee have been mishandled, yet the petitions are pointing to the wrong direction the Church was heading. They are therefore calling upon the Business Committee to release those petitions so that they can be deliberated in the General Assembly forum. That is why we are gathered here, and now the Moderator can open the floor for discussion on this very sensitive matter."

I declared the floor open for discussion. The first three people talked in favour of not fronting these petitions on the GA floor. I then gave the opportunity to past Moderator Rev. Muindi, who in the past was very agitated with me and had been breathing fire and brimstone. Everybody expected him to speak with fury as he called for the petitions to be released to the General Assembly for discussion. But to the amazement of everyone present, he said:

"I am not sure whether we are using our time wisely. Why did we wake all these people so early? I have personally come to the conclusion that I will no longer follow an individual. We are experiencing all this upheaval just because past Moderator Gatu is opposed to the current Moderator's occupation of the GA seat. There are times we need to think and reason and not be led by the flesh but by the Holy Spirit of God. I, therefore, feel that we should no longer go around the mountain; let us support Dr. Githii. I have been all the way opposed to his administration, not because it is bad but because he does not regularly consult me as a past Moderator. I have come to realize that, it is me who is detached from God's mysterious ways of doing things. The whole truth is that, so far, Githii has done more than any of us accomplished within the two terms we were in office, including me."

None in the room could believe his or her ears. We had all expected a bomb from past Moderator Rev. Muindi. In the past, he had been one of the most critical people as far as my leadership was concerned. He had now dissociated himself from past Moderator Rev. Gatu, who was the author of all the turbulence my administration was experiencing. It seemed Rev. Muindi was also a leader of a group of people in the meeting who had been very supportive of the petitions that were to be tabled in the GA. I say this because, when he declined to support the motion, a big group of people also turned to the support of non-submission of the petitions.

It also seemed that when Rev. Muindi spoke, Rev. Gatu lost the aggressive moral authority he had. He spoke with a less forceful voice. But he insisted that the petition should be brought up in the General Assembly. Unfortunately for him, when I called for the voting, he was almost alone because the people behind him also realized that they were fighting a losing battle as far as the recalling of the previous petitions was concerned. They now anchored on creating a way to cause a repeat of the election in the General Assembly. And now that we were done with the petition issue, we all proceeded to the main General Assembly meeting.

THE GENERAL ASSEMBLY DEBATE

After the early morning meeting, we headed to the hall where the GA was meeting. The 17th. GA, in which I had been the moderator for three years, was now over. We were now starting the 18th. GA. The theme of the GA was, '**Bear Fruit, fruit that will last,**' as recorded in the gospel according to St. John 15:16. As we got into the hall, I could sense the spirit of hostility in the air. There were people still standing outside the hall because, like many others, they had anticipated turmoil to emerge in the early part of the meeting.

A lot of campaigning was still going on with the watchdog group mobilizing people to vote for their candidate when the time for the election came. There were even notes that were being circulated informing delegates to aggressively send me home. One such note was passed to me. It read, '*He has ruined the ever-treasured traditions of our Church. Rev. Githii must, therefore, go home. This opportunity has to be utilized to the maximum to cut short his leadership. Another three years with him would leave this denomination without its cultural foundations as inherited from the Scottish people. We would have lost this heritage. Comrades, it is now or never.*'

As the procession moved slowly towards the front part of the hall, I could see a lot of people glued to their mobile phones. I then realized there were a lot of campaign text messages exchanging hands. When the Secretary-General called the house to order, his first statement was, "*Welcome to the 18th GA. I kindly ask everyone to turn off their phones and observe silence as we are now getting into the GA Business.*" He said, then proceeded thus, "*I now call upon the 17th. GA Moderator to come and declare the 18th. General Assembly officially opened.*"

I stood up and declared the GA officially opened. Then, the Secretary-General made the roll call to ensure all the delegates had arrived. Soon, the time came for me to give my speech. Dr. Wanjau was elected the acting Moderator as I had to vacate my seat in order to read the speech and leave the GA floor to pave the way for the Moderator's election.

I thanked the delegates for the wonderful support I had received during my three years tenure in office. I highlighted some of my accomplishments, including the **subdivision** of many parishes and even presbyteries. I pointed to some **projects** we had started and had some of them finished and were already proving to be great assets to the entire Church. I also pointed to the **spiritual growth** that was already very noticeable in all sectors of the Church. In particular, was the **praise in worship,** including the drum sets, public address systems, the keyboards; and all that entailed the renewed and well-polished **Elder District** activities. There was a noticeable great **increase in giving** among the Church members, which also paved the way for the Church to initiate **new projects** from congregations, parishes, presbyteries and the General Assembly.

In conclusion, I said, "*And in doing all these brethren, I did it to the glory of God and in liberating the church from the bondage of the Scottish traditions and culture. And in this case, I have no apologies.*"

Constitutionally, when a Moderator has finished reading his or her speech, he removes the Moderator's ecclesiastical robes and then leaves the GA floor. As soon as I finished my speech, I took off the robes, placed them on the table where the acting Moderator was seated and then proceeded to a room in isolation. But one thing was clear in my mind- there were so many intercessors who had been praying and fasting for some time, specifically for this moment I had now entered.

In addition to this, together with a number of intercessors, we had taken quite some time the previous evening praying in that hall, anointing every seat and all the premises surrounding the hall, including the ground. The intercessors had also strategically taken positions in the hall. They could be found in every corner of the hall and every roll of chairs. Even as the lobbying was taking place in the hall prior to the opening of the GA, the intercessors were busy renouncing the evil lobbying and canceling all the text messages being sent.

I knew there were many prayer warriors behind me, but I could not at the same time ignore the fact that the PCEA watchdog group had spent sleepless nights with finances going all over presbyteries and parishes, reaching out to the delegates, bribing and brainwashing them to vote me out. I realized it was a great satanic power, but then I comforted myself through Paul's words to the Romans that assure thus; "*And we know that in all things God works for the good of those who love him, who have been called according to his purpose*" (Rom. 8:28).

This was the time everybody had been waiting for. It was a time for curving out the next phase in my ministry. As I remained alone in that room, God reminded me of the words which I always look to as His commission to me when I became Moderator; "*Get yourself ready! Stand up and say to them whatever I command you. Do not be terrified by them, or I will terrify you before them....Stand against the...priests and the people of the land. They will fight against you but will not overcome you, for I am with you and will rescue you, declares the Lord*" (Jer. 1:17-19).

I also remembered the other words that God popped up in my mind as I took the vows of office during my time of consecration as the 17th. GA Moderator; "*You must go to everyone I send you to and say whatever I command you. Do not be afraid of them, for I am with you and will rescue you...I have put my words in your mouth. See today I appoint you over nations and kingdoms to uproot and tear down, to destroy and overthrow, to build and to plant.*" -Jeremiah 1:9-10. The other thing I remembered was being involved in an intensive prayer asking God to stand in the GA and let the people know that I was not in that seat by accident or coincidence; I was there because it was His will, and that should stand.

I was still praying when somebody knocked on the door, and a minister came in. He said, "*You cannot believe it. After you left, the acting Moderator said: 'This is a very crucial moment in the life of this Church. It is time we have an election to determine whom God wants to be the 18th GA Moderator. Not what people want but what God wants. And before we venture into the elections, let one person lead us with a word of prayer.'* He continued, *"After the prayers, the Moderator said, 'In front of me is the name of Rev. Dr. David Githii, whom the GAC elected as the 18th GAC Moderator, but constitutionally, where an aggrieved party calls for another election, we have no choice but to go ahead with elections. Now I am calling for the name or names of other candidates who are vying for this position.'"*

The moderator remained quiet as he gazed his eyes over the GA delegates for any hand. Two minutes went by, and there was no hand. Then he said, *"That was the first call and now I make the second call. Is there a name or names of people who are being fronted to run for the position of 18th GA? If so, show by lifting up your hand."* Again, three minutes went by, and there was no hand. The Moderator then said, *"This is the third and final call. Is there a candidate to be fronted by this GA body to run for the position of 18th? GA. If so, please indicate so by raising your hand."*

Again, two and half minutes went by, and there was no show of any hand. By then, it was so silent that one could hear the sound of his neighbor's heartbeat. Some people were breathing heavily, but there were also many who were submerged in silent prayers and a few who were shedding tears. Finally, the Moderator stood up and made this pronouncement;

"Seeing there is no name being fronted to challenge the election of Rev. Dr. Githii as the 18th. Moderator of GA. I now call upon all those in favour of his being re-elected to stand and, by a show of raising your hands, declare your choice of David Githii as the 18th. GA Moderator." The speaker went on to tell me, *"David, I could not believe my eyes, for in the air was a forest of hands. Truly, you are God's choice. Fear came upon the opponents, and they froze. And now that you are the Moderator of 18th. GA, let me take you for the consecration."*

When we got to the floor, there was deafening clapping of hands that went together with the East African Revival chorus, *"Tukutendereza."* Looking into the congregation, I could see many people crying with joy. So many people were waving their hands to me in a celebratory and congratulatory mood. Dr. Wanjau embraced me and I could feel the warmth and joy in his heart. He whispered to me, *"Brother, God has spoken. Who can thwart what He has planned? Congratulations! That is the real hand and voice of God. Like King David, you are God's choice, and you are after His heart. Be assured of my continued support."* Meanwhile, some of the presbytery Moderators and clerks came forward and shook my hand, each whispering some words of encouragement.

The next thing was for Dr. Wanjau and Dr. Jesse to dress me into the very ecclesiastical robes I had removed. This was followed by prayers by Dr. Wanjau and then a number of praise songs. After this, it was my turn to give an acceptance speech. I first thanked the delegates for re-electing me indicating that they have faith in my leadership. But I also reminded them that for any progressive Church development, both physically and spiritually, I would need their unwavering support.

I reminded them that united we stand, divided we fall. I also called upon the PCEA watchdog group to support but not fight me for the sake of it. I said, *"If I were not leading the Church in the right direction, then there was no way I could be giving this acceptance speech to you, for the GA had an opportunity to elect another person. Just bear in mind that you are not supporting me per se; in reality, you are supporting the body of Christ. I love you and it is my wish to work with all people for the welfare of this denomination."*

I then thanked the government for having made it possible for us to have a government official present to grace the occasion. I took that opportunity to ask the government to declare total war on corruption, the entrenchment of tribalism nationally and idolatry in the nation of Kenya. I also warned against allowing wickedness like homosexuality and devil worship to infiltrate into the nation as it was already happening in some of the Western countries.

In his speech, the guest of honour, the late Vice-President Michael Wamalwa Kijana, thanked me for having been re-elected for a second term that would take the next three years. Among other things, he said, he praised me for the good work I had already accomplished. Saying;

"In reading your report to this GA, I can see that there is a lot you have accomplished within the last three years. I now can understand why some people refer to you as a controversial Moderator. Such accomplishments

cannot be achieved without some opposition for many people always want to maintain the status quo. Any introduction of changes, whether in the Church, government or institutions, will always encounter some resistance, with the opposition calling the proponent of such change 'Controversial' because of refusing to be compromised. I would encourage you to keep on keeping on. Please remain assured that, where need be, the government will assist."

After the morning session, we had lunch with a group of church leaders. It was while taking lunch that Vice President Wamalwa addressed us and, with his focus on me, said,

"We are ever proud of PCEA. The history of Kenya as a nation cannot be written without the mention of PCEA. This is because much of the Kenyan foundations were laid down by the Presbyterians, including, the education and agricultural sectors. We cannot forget the Scottish Missionaries for the good work they did to lay down these foundations. It is true, as you have indicated, about the various scourges in government. As a government, we are doing all we can to fight tribalism, corruption and other types of wickedness. But of most importance, we will need the Church to partner with us in this battle. The Church should stand out and be counted as the voice of the nation. And this is why they refer to you, as controversial because you speak out the truth. Unfortunately, not many, even among the pastors, want to expose the truth. Many fear for their lives, but one thing I know is that if one fights for the kingdom of God, God will always be on that person's side. He will offer total protection."

He further said:

"Moderator Githii, there are many who admire your courage and take you as a good role model especially among the young people. You are one of the very few people who point out the ills of this nation and, at the same time, point out how such ills could be eliminated. You are very concerned about the idolatry in this nation, something many people do not understand. I encourage you to pursue that subject but at the same time teach them a lot on the same. People need to understand the truth behind it. And with these few remarks, I thank you all and wish you a successful 18th. General Assembly."

After lunch and after the departure of the guest of honour, many people around wanted to shake my hand and, at the same time, express their joy and offer words of encouragement. Many explained

454

their amazement in the way things turned out that no name was presented to oppose me, yet the talk was all over that there was no way I could be installed as the 18th. GA Moderator.

Many expressed the fact that I was indeed God's choice. It remained a mystery how the very wealthy and widely outspoken opponents would be silenced in a twinkle of an eye. Yet they had used so much of their resources and time to block my being elected. None of them could master the courage to utter a word against me from the entire gathering that had jam-packed St. Andrews Presbytery Church Hall. This was despite the acting Moderator deliberately giving them quite ample time before he could make the next call for a proposed candidate to oppose me.

Within the five days duration of the proceedings, I contributed a lot in educating the Church on the best ways to make it shine both spiritually and physically. Among other things, I called upon the delegates to battle homosexuality, corruption and other wickedness that were dwarfing the denomination. I pledged to continue with the reformist agenda that had placed me on a collision path with traditionalists and the Freemasons in the Church. I had even revisited the issue of the church logo, which had a crucifix with the G in JiteGemea (*Self-reliance*).

I revisited this issue because there were some who had threatened to raise a motion on the non-acceptance of the new logo. Accordingly, I informed the delegates that the word '*self-reliance*' entrenched in the **logo** was not meant to be what it reflected in the minds of the people.

It was a way formulated to disguise the infringement of the capital **G,** which is a representation of the Masonic and Illuminati gods. This was also the god worshipped by the New Age Movement. (*The reader can Google these for a better understanding of what these occultic groups stand for – New Age Movement, Freemasonry and Illuminati*).

I also took the opportunity to defend my rightful contributions to the Church within the past three years. I highlighted the fact that, for those three years, I had traversed East Africa, visiting presbyteries, Parishes, Church groups and even congregations. I found wide doors open in all those places apart from the Limuru Presbytery whose leaders had blocked me from carrying out any activity in that

Presbytery. It is worth noting that God blessed my second term in office. I accomplished many things that became pillars of growth, both spiritually and physically. However, this was not without many further attempts to impeach me. There was a feeling that even after my exit, ways and means should be devised to kick me out of the church.

THE SPIRIT OF AGITATION AT WORK

1. SIGONA PARISH

Having finished my six years in office, I was posted to PCEA Sigona Church in October 2009. This was a one-congregation parish comprising slightly over 200 members and located next to Sigona Golf Club and Wida Highway Motel.

In posting me to Sigona Parish, Rev. Gathanju and his team deliberately decided to overlook the historical procedure of posting a past moderator who had completed his tenure of office. The customary way and the church position is that after the end of the term or terms of any Moderator of the General Assembly, the outgoing Moderator has a session with the incoming officials, that is, the Moderator, the Secretary-General and his deputy to map out and agree on the location of posting the outgoing Moderator.

In fact, in most cases, the officials would have the outgoing Moderator indicate his choice because he was in a better position to identify one that suits his skills. In my case, I was never consulted, whether verbally or through a phone call, a text message or email. I only found a letter delivered to my home indicating that I had been posted to PCEA Sigona Church. I had not anticipated that because I could remember that in our time when my predecessor vacated the office back in 2003, as the incoming officials, we did talk with him, and we agreed that he be posted to Lay Training and Conference Center as the director.

Nevertheless, I was aware that there were many avenues that were being created through which to '*finish*' me. The liberals were not happy with the changes that had occurred in the Church within the six years I was the GA Moderator. They were also uncomfortable with the changes I made in the quality of worship. God had used me through the Business Committee to peel off most of the Scottish traditions that had dwarfed the Church spiritually over the years. This, therefore, necessitated many changes in worship, which, as we have seen, included the introduction of praise in worship, drum sets and keyboards. The demonic PCEA logo was also reworked and restructured. As a result, I had already rubbed shoulders the wrong way with many who felt that the Church's status quo should have been maintained. They had all the way vowed to kick me out of the church at one given time.

They accused me of aggressively exposing the Church's wickedness, including corruption, that was being practiced in many areas within the Church. They also accused me of having defrocked six pastors for practicing homosexuality and devil worship. They also accused me of having aggressively carried out some teachings that exposed the Satanism that the missionaries had secretly embedded in the Church. These included; the Masonic symbols, divide and rule, referring to anything African as evil, resistance to the Holy Spirit, among others. They, therefore, described my ways of exposing the hidden mysteries as; 'exposing the Church's nakedness.' It was for that reason that they had vowed to ensure that they would undress me by expelling me from the Church or altogether do something worse to me.

Whatever the case and without bitterness, I decided not to ask why I was being treated differently from other past Moderators. Some of the Head Office Officials through the presbytery had intimidated members of the Sigona congregation to sign a document to express their displeasure and disregard for my coming to be their parish minister. This document was in two copies, the original and photocopied one. The original copy with signatories was taken to the Head Office Officials on October 21st. 2010, while the presbytery had remained with the copy.

It is the practice of the Church that when a minister is transferred to a new parish, the presbytery has to invite that person and receive him or her through written minutes. That being the case, the Muguga presbytery invited me in spite of knowing that there was already a major move to reject me through the umbrella of a wide range of cartels under the direction of some of the past Moderators and the Head Office officials.

Let me re-emphasize that some of the Head Office Officials had directed the presbytery to incite Sigona Church members to stage a demonstration that would bar me from getting to the presbytery meeting. The good news was that, there were a few but influential members of both the presbytery and Sigona Kirksession who were on my side but who had to work very secretly. Among them was the Moderator of the presbytery, Rev. Stephen Wainaina. By then, I had alerted some key intercessors in various presbyteries since I had commissioned quite a number of them when I was an active GA Moderator. There were a lot of prayers going on with many already dry fasting.

The date designated for my reporting was October 21st. 2010. That morning, Rev. Wainaina called to tell me that the meeting was still on as scheduled and that I could attend the meeting right from the beginning. He also told me that he and a few others, both in the presbytery and Kirk session, were monitoring the situation on the ground and hoped that with all the prayers people were pouring out, God would intervene and save the situation.

He added;

"Moderator, you have really fought for God in uplifting both the spiritual and physical life in this Church during your time as GA Moderator and I don't see how God can abandon you at this time of need. Be encouraged and stand with Paul's words to the Romans in Romans 8:37, that states, 'In all these things we are more than conquerors through him who first loved us.' He further went on to say, *".. and also, in Romans 8:31, Paul further says, 'If God is for us, who can be against us?"*

He also went on to tell me that the Head Office Officials had called intimidating him as well as instructing him to block me from getting into the presbytery meeting: *"They are talking like worldly people. They think that finishing you, as they like to call it would be one of their greatest accomplishments in their time in office."*

In response, I said,

"Let me not come to the meeting at the beginning. I suggest that as you get to the agenda prior to the item on me, call me at that time. It will take me less than ten minutes to get to the venue of your meeting. In this way, we will not create any tension within the meeting." Wainaina then agreed with my suggestion.

Meanwhile, after dressing for the meeting, I laid on the bed as I waited for the hint from the moderator to get to the meeting. In the process, I fell asleep, and God gave me a dream. I saw myself teaching a group of PCEA leaders on; **'The lack of spiritual nutrition in PCEA.'** I was teaching on a subject which likened PCEA to a plateful of food that was not nutritious, meaning that in spite of PCEA's size that covered East Africa, it lacked spiritual nutrition. At one point in the course of my teaching, I noticed that rather than people looking at me, they were all looking fearfully beside my right hand. I turned and looked in the same direction and saw a very big bull that had already positioned itself to hit me with its long horns. I hit it with the Bible I held in my hands. The bull immediately became paralyzed. I immediately then woke up.

No sooner had I woken up than Rev. Wainaina called me. I immediately got into the car, and after six minutes, I was already approaching the main gate where the presbytery office was located. But alas! There was a big trailer (truck) parked next to the gate, hence blocking the gate. The trailer's front part was in the shape of a bull. I immediately realized that symbolically, that was the very bull I had seen in the dream, indicating that the spirit that I was at war with was one of Baal, also known as Apis. According to Ankerberg and Weldon in their book; **The Secret Teachings of the Masonic Lodge'**, *"...is a sacred Egyptian bull to whom divine honors were paid because of its close association with the leading Egyptian deity Ptar, the Egyptian creator of the universe. The bull was held up to be special because it was believed to be the mediator between Ptar and the people"* (p206).

This is the very god worshipped by the Freemasonry, the Illuminati and the New Agers, whom they refer to as The Great Architect of the Universe. It is Albert Churchward, in his book; **'Arcana of Freemasonry**: *A History of Mason's Signs and Symbols,'* says that;

"Freemasonry, taken as a whole, i.e., in all its degrees from first to thirty-third, is the ritual of Ancient Egypt" (p117).

I stopped my vehicle behind the truck, and I was preparing to come out and request them to give way when the trailer driver came out and said, *"I have seen you through the side mirror. Let me clear the way for you."* And with this statement, I felt convinced by the Holy Spirit that I had already overcome the rebellious Baal spirit in accordance with the dream. I drove into the presbytery offices compound, hoping to see some demonstrators, but it was all quiet.

I proceeded to the room where the presbytery was holding the meeting. I got into the presbytery office and I requested the secretary to inform the moderator that I was around. Before long, the Moderator called the secretary and asked her to let me into the meeting. Immediately I got in, all the eyes were gazing upon my face. Some with positive reflective faces while others, I could tell, were throwing curses upon me.

The Moderator said, *"Very Revered, Dr. Githii, we are happy to have you."* Then he addressed the presbytery members, saying, *"We all know that the past Moderator has been posted to Sigona Parish in our presbytery, and I think our main responsibility is to welcome him through a presbytery minute and communicate the same to the Head Office..."* but even before he had finished, there were already five hands raised up. The Moderator asked one of them to speak.

The speaker said,

"With all due respect to you, Moderator, we all know that Sigona Parish has rejected the past Moderator, and we have the Sigona membership signatories appended to the same in a letter copied to the Head Office. I then don't understand when you say that our main obligation is to accept him."

The Moderator then pointed to another speaker who said, *"Mr. Moderator, you are misleading this presbytery; how can you welcome the past Moderator, yet the parish he has been posted to has already rejected him? Do we have the power to enforce a minister to a congregation? The answer is no! We cannot, as a presbytery do this injustice not only to the presbytery but also to Sigona Parish as well. I move we close this motion with a minute stating that this presbytery cannot accept Githii because he* has nowhere to land as the parish he was posted to has slammed the door against him."

Another person shouted, "That is all; let not the Moderator place us in a situation of beating about the bush. Githii has no place in this presbytery. After all, he has caused a lot of damage to this noble denomination. He will go to the archives of the Church as the most destructive GA Moderator that the denomination has ever had. No wonder the Head Office is giving us a hand in rejecting him, and if the Head Office Officials have rejected him, who are we to go against their wishes?"

At that juncture, the Moderator decided to bring about the bomb that he had shelved. He said:

"We are all well versed with our Church constitution, and in no way do we argue with its articles and bylaws. The constitution says that no Church court or committee can act upon matters whose only source or evidence they have is a copy of the matters in question. Now, considering that the said Sigona Parish gave the presbytery the copy of the signatories and gave the original to the Head Office, what mandate do we then have to deliberate on this issue of whether to receive him or not? Sigona Parish should have given the Presbytery the original copy with signatories but not the copy."

He went on to say:

"The presbytery has no option but to go by the only original letter we have, which is this one indicating that the past Moderator has been posted to Muguga Presbytery and of which, I am the Moderator, and I say it again, the Parish deviated from the constitutional procedure they should follow. They should have given the presbytery the original letter with the signatures and given the copy to the Head Office and not vice versa. How can we discuss the contents in a copy when we should be discussing the contents in the original document? This is out of order- unconstitutional, and way off the traditions of the church. Can someone respond to this constitutional matter?"

Someone said:

"Moderator, you have explained the situation quite well, and I don't think there is any member here who can argue on this case. Yes, what we have is a copy. The truth of the matter is that Sigona Parish Kirksession did not follow the right procedure. They should have given the presbytery the original collective signatories and passed the copy to the Head Office if it were necessary to do that. I, therefore, agree with you, Moderator, that we now have no option but to accept the past Moderator. After all, the parish itself does not even tell us why they are rejecting him. What we have is a copy of signatures with the heading, 'As a parish, we reject Githii to be our parish minister.' This then is followed by a long list of signatures. I therefore move that a minute be written stating that; "Muguga Presbytery has unanimously accepted Githii as Sigona parish minister. But then the presbytery will come up with modalities based on how to educate Sigona Congregation on how to work with Dr. Githii."

The Moderator said: "Is there any objection to what that member has said?" The next speaker said,

"I concur with what that member has said; otherwise, going in any other way will betray us as people who are not well versed with our constitution, which is quite dangerous as far as presbytery membership is concerned." The Moderator chipped in, "Then all those in favour of moving by the constitutional guidelines that the presbytery has accepted the past Moderator as henceforth being the parish minister in Sigona Parish, just show by raising up your hands."

To my surprise, all the members raised their hands. None wanted to betray his or her ignorance in regard to the Church constitution, for such a person could even be questioned by the Moderator as to his or her integrity in matters to do with the Church constitution, something that can easily lead to one being disqualified as a member of the presbytery.

There was this other man who, having raised up his hand, said,

"Now that we have accepted Dr. Githii as Sigona Parish minister, I have a feeling that he should not report immediately. Already, tension is very high, and who knows whether the congregation would defy a presbytery's decision and come out with some demonstrations. I therefore strongly feel that we give the past Moderator a month's leave so that during that time, the presbytery will have time to heal the congregation through some education in the form of counseling. I strongly feel that this is the only way we can help the past Moderator to have a safe landing."

After two other people had affirmed the same, it was decided that I keep off from the parish until the end of one month. When asked whether I was comfortable with that, I said,

"I am trusting God in all this transformation, and I will keep my spiritual ears open for His guidance. I have always anchored my faith in what His Word says in Isaiah 30:21; "Whether you turn to the right or to your left, your ears will hear a voice behind you saying, 'This is the way walk in it.'" After this, the Moderator said a closing prayer, and we headed for a cup of tea.

I remained at home for the first week. But come the following week, God spoke to me through his Word in Jeremiah 15:20-21 which says;

"I will make you a wall to these people, a fortified wall of bronze; they will fight against you but will not overcome you, for I am with you, to rescue and save you…I will save you from the hands of the wicked and redeem you from the grasp of the cruel." Further encouragement came from Jeremiah 45:5 that says, *"wherever you go I will let you escape with your life."* Further, Jeremiah 1:19 says; *"They will fight against you but will not overcome you, for I am with you and will rescue you."*

Armed with these words of encouragement, I resolved to activate my duty of taking over Sigona Parish. I decided to go ahead and report to the parish before the one month was over. This was on 25th. October, 2009, and as the day's preacher! That meant, overlooking the decision of the presbytery that I stay away for one month. I had woken up on that Sunday in time, prepared myself and off I headed for Sigona Church's first service which was mainly dominated by the youth. I headed for the vestry where the service leaders were gathered. They had all the service program worked out and were almost leaving for the service.

I greeted them, and I proceeded to open my bag, took out my robe and dressed myself. Then I said,

"I am sure by now you know that I am the current minister to this parish and I have come this morning as the preacher. Let me have the name of the person leading the service and the two scripture readers." At that juncture, one of them said, *"But we have been instructed not to have you in this parish."* In response, I said, *"That is okay, but as you know, the presbytery*

has already accepted me and in the PCEA. In accordance with the church traditions, the minister is always in charge as long as one has been received by the presbytery, and without any more waste of time, let me know as to who is leading the service and those who are supposed to read the scriptures."

Realizing that they could not resist any more, they gave me the names I had asked for and then we were on our way for that morning's service. I had already prayed a lot for God to give me the Word for the day's services. As a result, the Spirit of the Lord had led me to the book of Genesis 39 where we find the story of Joseph and Potiphar's wife, but I focused on Genesis 39:11 as the key verse. It says; *"One day (Joseph) went into the house to attend to his duties, and none of the household servants was inside. She (Potiphar's wife) caught him by his cloak and said, come to bed with me! But he left his cloak in her hand and ran out of the house."*

In my sermon, I emphasized the fact that, in spite of Joseph being accused by Potiphar's wife to her husband and even being imprisoned, the whole truth was known by only two people-Joseph and Potiphar's wife! If only the husband had taken trouble to find out the truth, he would have found Joseph innocent and at the same time discovered the unfaithfulness of his wife. He never gave Joseph an opportunity to defend himself. He acted under the evidence of Joseph's cloak.

I then said:

"I find the same scenario existing between this congregation and myself. Of course, you have all signed a document indicating that you don't want me to minister to you. But for what reason? I guess your answer could be, 'We signed because we were led to do so by our elders,'

I went on to say:

"But the truth is, how much of that truth, if any, do you know? Like the case of Joseph and the wife of Potiphar, in the present scenario where you are resisting receiving me, the real truth is known by me and the Head Office officials. It is the Head Office that forced the Presbytery to ensure that I am not accepted in this Presbytery. Likewise, the Presbytery has forced the Sigona Kirksession to ensure that I don't land in this Parish. Hence, the Kirksession has somehow forced the congregation to resist receiving me.

464

These are the people who have incited the presbytery to reject me, and then the presbytery has incited Sigona Kirksession who then have incited you. But none of these bodies has the truth. In fact, there are a lot of emotions involved. And it is the same with some of you."

I went on to say:

"I am sure at one time, some of you have been accused falsely by people who wanted to tarnish your name. They then spread some false propaganda. If not you, then you may know of someone who was falsely accused of some negative things and false judgments. Remember, if only Potiphar had tried to dig out the real truth behind Joseph and his wife, he would not have Joseph, the manager he loved imprisoned.

I further said:

You have been misled and made to believe in falsehood. You were not made even to pray for God to reveal the truth to you. You are following a few people who also don't know the truth behind the struggle between me and the head Office Officials. The question you need to ask yourself is: Have I really prayed about this issue? What if the issue has been falsified like that one of Joseph, and then I become a partaker of what I have no clue about? That is food for thought for you."

After the sermon, we sang the final hymn and the procession headed back to the vestry. It is the procedure that when the leaders of the first service get back to the vestry, one person says a concluding prayer. That is exactly what happened. After the person had prayed, I greeted the elders who were already gathered in the vestry, and I could hardly hear their response. The environment was somehow cold and lacked excitement. It seemed they had already prepared the service. From their facial expression, I could tell that there was great anger and rejection among those elders. I then addressed them:

"I am sure by virtue of being elders, you are all aware that I was posted to this parish and the presbytery has affirmed this by accepting me. It is for this reason that I am here. Where possible, we can talk more after the service. Meanwhile, you can give me the name of the person to lead the service and those who are going to read the scriptures."

One elder said, *"Well, what we know is that the presbytery one week ago gave you a kind of leave for one month and asked you not to come to this* congregation until that period is over. In this regard, you are not supposed to come and interfere with the running of this parish."

Another very respectable elder responded:

"I think at this juncture, we should also learn to discern the ways of the Holy Spirit. I was in that presbytery meeting and Dr. Githii said that he would move according to how the Holy Spirit directs him. In this case, if this is the way the Holy Spirit has directed him, we should be mindful not to be seen as if we are at war with that power. I am therefore requesting that we let Dr. Githii handle the service, for if this is from God, there is no way we will overcome him. After all, he is a past Moderator and we should give that position its due respect."

Another elder burning with anger said: *"This is totally unacceptable. If we let things go the way you are putting it, we will find ourselves being disciplined by the presbytery for allowing this to happen, yet we are the custodians of presbytery powers. We reject this move and…"* I interjected, *"This is not something we can debate; I am the parish minister, and I am calling an end to this debate. Now I am calling upon three people to volunteer themselves, one to lead the service and the other two to read the scriptures."*

Immediately, three people volunteered. I then said a prayer and called upon the elders to move as a procession. All joined the procession apart from three who resisted in protest and remained back. As we moved from the vestry towards the sanctuary, I noticed a number of groups of people who were engaged in some discussions in low tones. I just assumed that those were people interacting before getting into the sanctuary for the service.

They could also be people who had attended the first service and were among those standing outside as they interacted among themselves and those coming to the second service. But I later learnt that the moment I got into the premises for the first service that morning, the message that I had already reported to the parish had spread like wild fire. The presbytery clerk had already received the message, and he had immediately informed one of the key Head Office Officials, they had immediately collaborated with some of the Sigona Parish elders, who immediately coordinated themselves and had already organized with some of the congregation members to carry out a demonstration to force me out of the Church premises. But it also happened that, there was a very prominent elder among the Sigona Parish Kirksession who had a very solid contact with the State Security Department. This elder was on my side. He did not see the reason why the Head Office was inciting people to reject me.

This elder had some very reliable contact with the Interior Security in the country. Having contacted them, they had then dispatched some plain-clothed police officers. The groups of people that I had seen as we moved in a procession towards the sanctuary were meant to cause uproar and block me from entering the sanctuary, but the security officers were there in time, even before the procession had left the vestry. News of the presence of police had quickly circulated among the Church members; thus, people were talking in low tones because they were held captive, as any attempt to disrupt the service could lead to being arrested.

There was also the other side of the story. Those who had attended the first service were already at loggerheads with those who were coming for the second service. Many of those who were part of the first service in the procession argued that what I had said in the first service had shed light upon their original thinking. Many were already in support of me. I was not aware of all this even as I continued with the procession into the sanctuary.

In the sanctuary, the service progressed well and when it came to the time of sermon delivery, I repeated word for word what I had preached in the morning service. At the end of the service, the procession went back to the vestry. It was there in the vestry that I asked whether there was any comment about the service.

One person said:

"Moderator, your sermon was an eye-opener to many, including myself. Personally, and I think it is the same case with many of us here, I had no idea that this fight was being fueled by some in Head Office and some Muguga Presbytery Officials. Personally, I will have nothing to do with this controversy and also, having briefly talked with some of these elders, many of them have embraced you, and I would now request you to be at peace. And on behalf of some of these elders who were involved in mobilizing people for the demonstration, I apologize. Keep on praying for us. Also, please allow

me to thank this elder (pointing to him) for making that arrangement for the Policemen to come. It would have been chaotic, and the media would have greatly damaged the name of this Church."

I then thanked the elders for having finally embraced me and I also promised to do my best towards the promotion of the parish both physically and spiritually. We concluded with a word of prayer and then had a cup of tea and some sweet potatoes. We had a very productive ministry for the first six months until that Sunday. I pointed to the crosses entrenched on the church building floor and cautioned the congregation on the negativity of stepping on the symbol of the cross because it is the symbol of our salvation. That time, hell broke loose. The consequences are covered in the chapter dealing with controversies over symbolisms under the topic, *'Controversies over Masonic symbols at PCEA Sigona.'*

2. LIMURU PRESBYTERY AGITATION

One of the most opposed presbyteries to my Church restoration process was Limuru Presbytery. The leaders persistently engaged in rebellion and resistance to anything that I set in motion. This presbytery had continued over the years to be a source of destructive spirits. Some years back, a minister had committed suicide in that presbytery after being psychologically tortured by some of the presbytery leaders. At one time, this presbytery was at the point of defrocking Rev. Waihenya (PCEA Secretary General 23rd./24th. GA), who was a parish minister in that Presbytery for refusing to toe the line in their evil activities. Thank God, as GA Moderator, I came to his rescue. The former South Kiambu Presbytery had to be sub-divided into three because of the fighting spirits after which the other two Presbyteries, the former Kikuyu and Githunguri, had always enjoyed peace – yet Limuru Presbytery inherited that spirit of rebellion.

My differences with the Limuru Presbytery started when Rev. Chrispinus Ndegwa failed to comply with the Presbytery's minutes that had banned overnight prayers (Kesha) and anything to do with praise in worship or any musical instruments like, key boards, drum sets or anything to do with intercessory prayers. Rev. Ndegwa had defied this order and held an overnight prayer meeting at

Kamandura Parish where he was the parish minister, and I stood by him despite Presbytery officials demanding disciplinary action against him.

I had told them Rev. Ndegwa had been led by the Holy Spirit in carrying on the kesha while the Presbytery officials were acting in the flesh in trying to restrain him. I did not see what was wrong with overnight prayers, praise and worship or the use of musical instruments to warrant his being transferred. I told them to be careful lest they be fighting God in their intentions. I am reminded of the account of Necho, king of Egypt and what Josiah told him in 2 Chr. 35:21 in case they fell into the same trap by their intents against Rev. Ndegwa.

One of those officials had then angrily responded, *"We knew that you would support him because you bear the same spirit. Meanwhile, remain assured that we have declared war on you as well. We have nothing to do with you in the ministry. You will never minister in our presbytery."* And with that, they left my office, led by the then presbytery clerk, Mr. Kamweru.

By God's grace, I managed to escape three attempted assassinations. In one such attempt, I had to stop a police road block, meanwhile, my pursuers escaped. In another, I had to stop at a matatu stage as they were in hot pursuit, and they feared the mob and therefore abandoned their mission.

My confrontation with Limuru Presbytery was mainly their heavy resistance to anything to do with Church revival. They were against my call to eliminate the imported Scottish culture, which they took as the total scriptural truth. Limuru Presbytery rejected any decisions or otherwise, from the Head Office. They had refused to comply with the Church rule requiring leaders to be in office for a maximum of three years, after which one would step down to pave the way for new leadership. Those in leadership on my taking over as Moderator of GA remained in their seats even after their three-year term's tenure had expired. It is no wonder, then, that for a long time, Limuru Presbytery lagged behind in matters of spirituality and physical growth. They had even for long refused to remit any money to the Church ministers who were against their rebellion.

The presbytery further refused to release any minister transferred by the Church unless such ministers were loyal to the Church courts. They refused to accept the ministers posted in this presbytery by the said **Appointment Committee**. They even withheld funds that the Head Office had accessed them. They also encouraged non-payment of the presbytery and parishes to access money. The presbytery leaders were always busy inciting parishes and presbyteries to join them.

One day, I called for a meeting of the whole presbytery with the aim of convincing them not to carry on the decision they had made to defrock Rev. Ndegwa. My aim was to bring about a spirit of reconciliation. The truth of the matter was that although they came, they did all they could to humiliate me. They called me names; they didn't even give me a glass of water to quench my thirst. I remember one of them, vibrating in anger, saying to me, "In *your administration, you are as dormant as Mt. Longonot.*"

Due to their spiritual dryness, they could not realize how such negative behaviour towards a Church father could negatively affect not only their lives but the lives of their families as well. I am sure that by the time of writing this book, some of them have already paid the prize. The Word of God says, "*If anyone destroys God's temple, God will destroy him*" (1 Cor. 3:17). Many faced calamities in their lives. The ring leader had his family disoriented and even lost some of his family members.

Unfortunately, the said presbytery leaders did not get any support from the entire **Kamandura** congregation. Many times, there were confrontations on Sundays as the presbytery tried to bring the congregation into submission. Those wars were at times so intense that the police had to intervene with Kamandura Church leaders getting locked in police custody.

There were those who even went into fasting for several days, crying or call it pleading to God to bring down the seemingly evil leadership. As a result of the believers' prayers, this arrogant spirit was brought down. And likewise, the power fueling that negativity- the spirit of rebellion fell down. The previous spiritual awakening that had been resisted began sprouting immediately. In order to bring lasting peace, the presbytery later got divided into three presbyteries.

3. RUNGIRI PRESBYTERY AGITATION

The other presbytery leaders who resisted my administration were those from Rungiri Presbytery. The animosity between them and I cropped up after I had declared that I would go with some intercessors to pray over the ground where the pioneer Scottish missionaries first settled in 1898, a place that later acquired the name **Kihumo**. This was the place where the missionaries put a temporary Church structure before they later moved to Thogoto. Kihumo in Kikuyu language means, '*the original.*' Kihumo was, therefore, the original location of what later became a large denomination bearing the name Presbyterian Church of East Africa (PCEA).

At the time, the church was referred to as the **Church of Scotland Mission** (CSM). Currently, there exists a Church bearing the name PCEA Kihumo Church. It was around that time that the Rungiri presbytery decided to rename the Church after the late Rev. **Githieya**, hence, PCEA Githieya Memorial Church. I was to be the guest of honour to bless this occasion, and I felt the Spirit of God leading me to take that opportunity to lead prayers aimed at:

1. Thanking God for the safe landing of the missionaries and for their endeavor to bring some **gospel light to the Africans**.

2. Confessing on behalf of the missionaries any sins they might have committed, such as:

a) The introduction of Scottish culture as part of Christianity where one could not be recognized as a true Christian unless they had been assimilated into the Scottish ways of life. These included; walking, laughing, eating, and a conformed mannerism in singing, among others.

b) They also indirectly introduced African Christians to smoking cigarettes and drinking beer. They themselves did those things.

c) They carried out nepotism and family divisions. This happened when a person decided to be a Christian convert, but the family resisted, and the missionaries took that person by force. This left the family disoriented and hateful. They also treated the convert as a civilized person and the others as uncivilized.

471

3. Those missionaries also had a broad hatred. The body of missionaries was at loggerheads with each other, mainly Anglicans, Roman Catholics, Presbyterians, Methodists and African Inland Mission. They had what I would describe as a *'traditional hatred.'* They came to Kenya with the same garbage of hatred that they had in their countries of origin. This had developed deep roots over the centuries.

To say the least, those missionaries were rivals back home in many ways. Therefore, the missionaries taught their Church members to perpetuate such hatred against their fellow Christians from other denominations to the extent that one could only marry from his or her own denomination. They, therefore, created boundaries in their efforts to evangelize beyond which each denomination could not cross. In simple words, the missionaries introduced the spirit of hatred rather than that of love.

It was out of that concern that I decided to go to **Kihumo** and renounce the negativity which had been planted by the missionaries among the African Christians. I was concerned that some of the things the missionaries did to their converts, whom they described as *'primitive'* and *'uncivilized,'* included the introduction of their trust in Darwinism. This placed the *'White'* as more superior to the African. These could have become generational curses in their families. Hence, the need for confessing such sins on behalf of their families.

4. That area was the very place where the first British Explorer, Captain Fredrick Lugard, made a blood covenant with the Gikuyu chief, Waiyaki wa Hinga. It was also the place where the first blood was shed when the porters whom the British colonialists used as workers clashed with the Agikuyu. It is where the porters started stealing from the Agikuyu not only crops from their farms but also animals like goats and rams. When Chief Waiyaki intervened, the colonialists had him arrested and got him locked in their camp at Fort Smith, which is in the neighbourhood of PCEA Kihumo Church. They later decided to deport Waiyaki to Kismayu but had him buried alive at Kibwezi as a way of sacrificing to the Mother Earth goddess. They believed that such a ritual could enhance their possession of Kenyan soil in totality.

5. It was for those reasons that I felt the need to include a prayer of confession over the atrocities caused by both the missionaries and the colonialists. It was also important to confess the sins of the early converts because they treated the unconverted as outcasts (*Gentiles, uncivilized pagans*). When Rungiri Presbytery leadership approached me to conduct the renaming ceremony of that sanctuary, I found a wonderful opportunity to include a prayer of confession on behalf of the missionaries, the colonialists and even the early converts.

6. The Colonialists later shed a lot of blood within the eight years of Mau Freedom Fighters' resistance (**1952-1960**).

Unfortunately, Rungiri Presbytery officials were not for my idea. They were so spiritually blind that they could not comprehend what I was talking about. But it was not their fault; it was the missionaries who knew nothing to do with spiritual warfare and passed that ignorance to their converts. But as for me, I learned all about what involves spiritual warfare during my deep studies in this field at Fuller Theological Seminary in California, USA. Among others, I came to learn about the generational curses, ancestral curses, and territorial spirits, among others.

As a result of ignorance in spiritual warfare, Rungiri Presbytery officials stirred up the other members of the presbytery who then conspired to totally block me from not only carrying out that sanctuary renaming ceremony but also never to ever perform any function in that presbytery, including preaching there. They argued that they were the custodians and protectors of Scottish Church traditions, and they could not give leeway for them to be diluted. After all, the issues to do with the settlement of both the missionaries and colonialists around Kihumo had nothing to do with the dwarfed spiritualism and physical development within PCEA Church.

They called me names and ensured nothing of the sort would ever take place. That function was called off and, indeed, never took place. Like Limuru Presbytery, Rungiri Presbytery officials were therefore at arms against any call that the Church courts like the GA, GAC or the Business Committee would come out with. They really resisted my endeavour towards **spiritualizing** the worship by liberating it from the Scottish cultural ties and to give it an African taste. After all, not everything African is evil, as the missionaries had made people believe.

By spiritualizing, I mean letting in the praise in worship, which was one of those ways the Bible calls; '**Worshiping in Spirit and truth.**' Unfortunately, Rungiri presbytery leaders referred to me as; '*The destroyer of the true Scottish foundations of Presbyterianism as set up by John Knox.*' I argued that, the Church of Scotland lost much of what John Knox believed in and especially the line of Church prayerfulness. John Knox was so prayerful that the Queen feared him for his intensive and deep prayerfulness, which made her unable to overcome him. Regarding this, the queen is reported as having said, "*I fear the prayers of John Knox more than all the assembled armies of Europe.*"

For many years, PCEA leaders had failed to inspire the flock into earnest prayerfulness. Instead, they craved to financial milking of the Church members. There existed a very strong spirit of demanding money from the congregations and not so much mindful about spiritually equipping the Church members. This was another spirit that the missionaries planted in PCEA.

Rungiri Presbytery was sailing in this boat even as the leaders fought my administration. The leaders carried in their own ways all the '*Moderator's Duties.*' While the work of dedicating newly built Churches is fully assigned to the GA Moderator, Rungiri Presbytery leaders blocked me from carrying this sort of work in their Presbytery. For example, instead of inviting me to dedicate PCEA Gaitumbi Church, they gave that honour to one of their Presbytery leaders to dedicate it. Dr. Njoya was a member of that Presbytery. I called upon the presbytery to avoid that kind of rebellion because it not only defiled the Church but the leaders and their families as well. Church fatherhood should be honoured for God to bless the believers.

MINISTERS' FRATERNAL MEETING HELD AT MOMBASA

This minister's fraternal meeting had taken place in Mombasa. In my address to the ministers, I focused on the theme: '**Bear Fruit, Fruit**

that will last' (John 15:16). I had already noted that some ministers were still reluctant in embracing the changes that the GAC held at Kihumbui-ini had initiated. I therefore found it important to take that opportunity, as the Moderator of the General Assembly, to persistently wish for a change of heart in such reluctant ministers who wanted to stick to the traditions held over the years that could be very destructive to the Church. I had also noticed that such ministers were not fully implementing the resolutions of Kihumbuini GAC and were still leaning towards Scottish traditions.

I reminded them that this was why Jesus outrightly disregarded the Jewish traditions that did not have any basis on the Word of God as practiced by the Pharisees and Sadducees. These they referred to as; **'The Traditions of the Elders.'** Jesus was calling upon the Pharisees and Sadducees, elders and priests to discard those traditions that were proving to be a hindrance to the grace of God. Jesus was seeing them as playing the role of idolatry, and to which the Word of God says, *"Those who cling to worthless idols forfeit the grace that could be theirs"* (Jonah 2:8).

I reminded the ministers that what I had referred to as the Tradition of the Elders was the disguised Scottish culture that got fused with the gospel. I further told ministers that *"...it was the Scottish cultural traditions that the missionaries asked the African Church elders to always protect from any 'distortion' and that is why constitutionally, their role of leadership was referred to as"; 'Ruling Elders.'"* Their ruling superseded that of one of the pastors.

When, as the Moderator of the General Assembly, I had come in with full force to change those deep-rooted Scottish Traditions to a Bible-based cultural set-up, most of the elders and clergy were at arms to block me. I told the ministers that the church leaders who were opposed to the new move were forgetting that the Church is a living organism, a body that derives her life from Jesus, who is the head of that body and from whom; *"the whole body, is joined and held together by every supporting ligament, grows and builds itself up in love, as each part does its work."* (Eph. 4:16).

I also told the ministers that the church was like a big engine which needed a lot of mechanical power to keep every segment of it functioning. The same was true of the church. The leaders must laboriously work to keep the wheels of organizational life spinning. But they must depend on Jesus Christ who is the founder and therefore gives the church its spiritual life. It is he who bought it at a great price through the shedding of His blood. It is this Jesus who gave the testimony by saying, "*I will build my Church, and the gates of hell shall not prevail against it*" (Matt. 16:18). Like on many other occasions I spoke to church leaders, I still echoed Michael Brown's argument in his book, '**Revolution in the Church,**' where he says; "*If the Church traditions will not change or go away by themselves. If your structure stands in the way of the spirit, why remain loyal to the structure? If your spiritual or political alliances keep you from fulfilling your calling, why maintain the carnal bond?*" I further highlighted what Robert Raines says in his book, '**New Life in the Church**'; "*The old and rigid order of the Church traditions, sometimes become so stiff and conditioned such that there is no room for new life… Churches suffer from the hardening of institutional arteries. New blood is sometimes blocked, and the church suffers from the lack of spiritual nourishment leading to spiritual malnutrition.*"

I told the ministers that the old arteries represented by the old Scottish traditions had to open up for new blood that will rejuvenate God's kingdom according to the truth in the scriptures. The unfortunate thing is that even when the Holy Spirit wants this stiffness in the arteries to be removed, there will always be those who, according to Michael Brown, will shout loudly saying, "*Who wants that kind revolution in the Church – revolution that challenges our traditional styles and structures, questions our traditional methods and models, and confronts our traditional forms and fetishes.*"

I further told the ministers that my main focus was to soften the old arteries so that, both in the present and in the future, the youth would find youthful arteries carrying spiritual youthful blood so that the denomination could be saved. As things had been before my taking over as the GA Moderator, many young people were already moving out of the denomination because of the spiritual cholesterol that had blocked them from worshiping God in Spirit and in truth. They were restricted from dancing for the Lord as David did. They could not raise their hands in praise, and they could not say "*Amen or Hallelujah or even utter a verbal prayer.*" They were supposed to stand like soldiers on a Guard of honour being paraded and inspected.

I told the ministers:

"This is nonsense and a disgrace to the kingdom of God. Like Gideon and his soldiers, we have to break the pots, letting the fire of the Holy Spirit to dominate in worship and also blow the trumpets through praises, using key boards and drum-sets and any other kinds of musical instruments, with shouts of joy. This is a battle that God will not let me lose. And I hear his soft voice as written in Joshua 1:9, telling me: 'Have I not commanded you? Be strong and courageous. Do not be terrified; do not be discouraged, for the Lord your God will be with you wherever you go" (Joshua 1:9).

My agitation was contrary to what the elders and senior clergy, including some of the past moderators advocated for. According to the missionaries' indoctrination, the ordained church leaders, both elders and the clergy, were supposed to be very protective over the traditional style of worship. Praise in worship was to be static with no rhythmical movements. It was a well-known fact that the devil hates Christian vibrancy because such praise causes him to flee. It also creates a way for the Holy Spirit to enjoin the congregation.

The missionaries knew this secret, as revealed by Jesus when He said, *"Unless I go away, the Counselor will not come… when he comes, he will guide you into all truth."* It is this truth that the missionaries did not want the African converts to attain, for they could no longer be brainwashed. The Holy Spirit could lead the Africans into winning spiritual warfare's. Hence the missionaries' strategy to resist not only praise in worship but the works of the Holy Spirit as well. Thomas B. White, in his book; **'The Believer's Guide to Spiritual Warfare,'** tells what worship contributes to the spiritual warfare when he says, *"Praise in Worship is an act of faith that affirms the character and redemptive power of God in all circumstances. If God truly dwells in the praises of his people, the regular practice of praise must be built into the lifestyle of the spiritual warrior… God waits for us to praise him so He can pour his strength into us. Praise releases divine power to transform our perspective and our response to problems."*

As much as I suffered in my endeavor to have praise in worship fortified into the Church, one thing that encouraged me to keep on paddling the canoe was that I knew that if the vessel had to be enlarged for spiritual undertaking, then I should never be frightened by the plotting and threats. I had to look to Him, who fetched me out of the world and counted me to be one of the chosen ones to run in the farthest lane, a lane many hate to encounter. Every runner prays to get the ballot on lane one. They dislike any lane after number two, especially the outermost lane. But God had given me this last lane. I kept the race knowing that when the call and the Spirit of God drove me, then I was always under the guard of angels protecting me from feeble tolerance of others: From their narrow-mindedness, their harsh vindictiveness, and everything else that would damage my testimony for Him who came not to destroy lives but to save them. I believe in angelic support as per Psalms 91:11, "*For he will command his angels concerning you to guard you in all your ways,*" and Psalms 34:7, "*The angel of the Lord encamps around those who fear him, and he delivers them.*"

I always felt that I was a co-worker with Him in His vineyard. Not that there was no anguish and the feeling of being pressured, but I felt, I had to take my stand like a stoic person. A stoic person despises the shedding of tears. He feels pain but restrains from shedding tears which then would expose him as a coward and then becomes a laughing stock: One without restraint of spirit! Thus, although my soul grieved, I was fully convinced that nearly all of God's jewels were crystallized tears. And no matter how overwhelming, any burden God has lovingly placed with His own hands on our shoulders is a blessing. Another area I touched on in this fraternal meeting was regarding talents in church members.

I pointed out that every opportunity was to be used in tapping Church members' talents or gifts. I was led to point out this because the Church had even failed to tap the talents of the people whose gifts could facilitate the Church's life, including running projects.

I called upon the clergy to safeguard the talented members because some of these talents were suppressed by some church leaders who thought that if people were given an opportunity to use their talents, they would overshadow the existing leaders, especially the elders.

There existed a presumption among the clergy and other Church leaders that if people with talents were given an opportunity, such could overshadow the existing leaders and, especially, elders. The fear of the elders was that they would end up losing their positions as a result of this.

Therefore, it follows that we had people who could suggest a variety of quality development in the Church, yet, the seasoned church leaders would hate to have such talented people given an opportunity. Incidentally, many of such active leaders had not been ordained on the basis of their talents or gifts, but as a result of their connections with those ordained before them. It was a corrupted chain of creating church leadership.

As I have already indicated, it was unfortunate because many of the so-called Church leaders were handpicked either because they were ordained as elders after their father or mother had retired from eldership; or because one was a good tither or was a financially able person who gave generously to the cause of the Church. Or worse still, such a person was a relative of one of the Church leaders or a key friend to one of the Church leaders, among others. In other cases, the parish minister would force the way for a person to be elected because such a person fully supported that minister in matters of finances or protected him or her from some wickedness he or she had committed.

In such a case, the minister created some influence in the Kirk session for that person to be elected. Unfortunately, most of those people are spiritually dry. They have nothing to offer to the body of Christ. Instead, they form controlling cartels in the circles of leadership. But it is important also to note that, there are numerous other very good people in the positions of leadership. The only dilemma is that, in most cases, they are in the minority, and their endeavor to have the church to the right way has always been buried under the noise of the cartels.

They always lost in their agenda. And that is true in many other churches. There are even cases where, instead of praying for the Holy Spirit to lead the way in the elections, money exchanges hands. One of the elements that breed in such situations is jealousy and suspicion among many Church leaders, especially among the elders, ministers and Church group leaders. This is something that has always spiritually suffocated the Church.

To emphasize my point in my teachings, I advocated that a non-Godly way of carrying out the elections is a sin, and it should be avoided by all means. The Church leadership should aim at tapping the Church members' talents so that such talents can be utilized in promoting the kingdom of God.

I drew the attention of my audience to what Franklin Covey advocates for in his book, '**The 7 Habits of Highly Effective People**,' in this book, he points out that people with a '*Scarcity Mentality*' find it very difficult to share recognition and credit, power or profit even with those who help in the production. They also have a very hard time being genuinely happy for the success of other people. In such a case, I told them that the Church would need to promote the category of people that Franklin calls; '*The Abundance Mentality*' – these people take the personal joy, satisfaction, and fulfillment in the success of others.

They have repented and have, therefore, overcome the sin of selfishness. In fact, that was the way the early Church functioned. They trained and tapped every talent or gift in every Church member (Eph.4:11-12,1Cor. 12, Rom.12:6-8). They were totally dependent on the Holy Spirit to inspire and give directions as to what each member should be doing. The Bible says, "*And the Lord added to their number daily those who were being saved*" (Acts 2:42). To complement this, I referred to Robert Raines, who, in his book; '**New Life in The Church**', emphasized the necessity of some old structures dying for newer ones to spring up in the spirit. I also stressed the importance of teaching and training in the Church to equip the unequipped for ministry. If this path is not followed, the outcome is that of limping leaders. In this case, it is blind people leading blind people! To stress this point again, I referred to what William Beckham says in his book; '**The Second Reformation**':

"*A large number of Church members are consumers, not producers. They are consumer Christians because the traditional Church has no viable context in which to make them producers or use them in a productive way. Consumer Christians present 80% of Church members who are supported and ministered to by the other 20% who produce.*"

I also referred to what Rick Warren highlights in his book, '**The Purpose Driven Church**', as to what should be the goal of any serious Church when it comes to teaching and training. He does this with reference to his own Church when he says, "*Our goal is to help develop a lifestyle of evangelism, worship, fellowship, discipleship, and*

480

ministry. *We want to produce doers of the Word, not hearers only – to transform, not merely inform. One of our slogans is 'You only believe the part of the Bible that you DO.'"*

Roberts Raines tops this up when he says, *"Trained, spiritual leaders will have the vision and courage under God to engage in the mission of the Church. There is the possibility that we shall recover our mission to the world."*

In pointing the ministers towards this direction, I could feel resistance from some of the clergy. Such were used to plot my downfall, especially after such emphasis in meetings and seminars.

I therefore called for the restoration of the New Testament characteristics of the Apostolic Church. That remained my goal and target. But I would admit that this was always a tough cookie. It took the hand of God. I had to move with a lot of patience, which should always be the case with one trying to put new wine into old wineskins. One thing I understood was that every bit of sorrow was yet another note from God's guitar or keyboard. And that every deliverance was another theme represented for His praise. Further, I inwardly understood that waiting on God and abiding in His way was to know him in; *"the fellowship of sharing in His suffering"* (Phil. 3:10) and *"to be conformed to the likeness of his Son"* (Rom. 8:29).

I also understood that if God's desire was to enlarge one's capacity for spiritual understanding, I then should not be frightened by the greater realm of suffering that constantly threatened not only my faith but my health as well. Otherwise, the Lord's capacity for sympathy is greater at all times. For me, one stinging sorrow missed would have been one blessing missed and unclaimed. And not so much for me but for the church membership and especially the youth, who so much thirsted for God's spiritual enrichment but were like a panting deer in a waterless wilderness.

The bottom line is that if I never suffered the humiliation, frustration and torture, the flock in PCEA who are now enjoying the praise in worship and other spiritual benefits would have remained buried underneath the traditions. The clergy who were treated like slaves by the senior clergy and the elders would have remained impoverished and as a condemned lot for many years. I felt a sense of purpose, like; Mandela, William Wilberforce, Martin Luther King and Martin Luther the reformer, whom God had brought into this world with a mission to be accomplished.

If ever they failed to pursue their calling, then it is likely that South Africans would still be swimming under apartheid; slavery of Africans would have continued to cause havoc, Afro-Americans would have been consumed in oppression, and Protestantism would not have been born. Any of these accomplishments would have taken far, much longer if they had never been rescued at the time of these heroes.

13 THE TRUTH OF THE MATTER

In many circles within the Presbyterian community, including the media, I was commonly referred to as, Githii, the *'reformist.'* Others who looked at me with a negative eye referred to me as Githii, the controversial Moderator. But why would people consider me as a reformist? It is because I had the spirit of wanting to set things right in an aggressive way. This is the same spirit that was dominant in the life of Martin Luther, the reformer. It was not until God revealed to me that it was from him that I found rest. He revealed to me that he had delayed the day of my accepting him as Lord and Savior till October 31st. 1976, on a Sunday. No wonder, then, on 31st. October is the date and month that is globally known as '**Reformation Day.'**

That was the day Martin Luther the Reformer nailed the 95 Theses on the door of the Wittenberg Church in Germany. That action generated a debate that finally gave birth to the Protestant Movement. (It had taken me three weeks looking for an opportunity to make a confession that led to my being saved.) On this day of my conversion, I realized that God had instilled in me the spirit of reformation even before I was born. It is, therefore, not unexpected that some close friends have jokingly referred to me as *'Githii the Reformer.'* It does not surprise me that even during the period I was at St. Paul's United Theological College, people had nicknamed me *'Moderator.'* I excelled in the Presbyterian Community leadership and also as the school's student body treasurer.

THE RESTORATION SPIRIT

Restoration refers to bringing back something to its original state or condition, such as something that was malnourished. It calls for some revitalization through repair, rebuilding or renovation. It could be something seemingly deformed but that needs activation through restoration or reformation. My spirit of reformation can be traced back to the time I was a headmaster. I had brought restoration to many run-down schools and had their life rejuvenated. A good example we had given was Chetptoroi Primary School in Njoro, which had, in ten years, never sent a child to high school due to poor academic performance. In 1977, when I became headmaster, 7 children performed so well and were admitted to various government-sponsored secondary schools, with one of them joining the famous Starehe Boys Centre in Nairobi. The following year, 1978, 24 students got admitted to national, provincial and district schools, with one, Lucy Wairimu, acquiring 36 points, which were the highest CPE points one could score in primary school examinations. In this case, she got 36/36. The school itself was number 2 out of 258 schools in Nakuru District unlike the previous years where it was ranked among the last. The excelling of this school triggered the building of a secondary school.

During a parent's day meeting, I invited the Provincial Primary Schools Inspector, Mr. Muriu, as a guest of honour. The children had various presentations, including athletics. Mr. Muriu challenged the parents to start a secondary school that could absorb other pupils from the surrounding schools who missed admission to the other secondary schools in Kenya.

The challenge was taken by the Director of Beeston Saw Mills. He had his board take up the burden. They produced all the building materials while the parents offered labour. To the surprise of many people, four classes were completed within one month. The District Education Officer in Nakuru came to inspect and he expressed surprise at the way the school buildings had come up. I was given the green light to admit new students. Twenty-four of them were thus admitted. Consequently, I became the headmaster of both primary and secondary schools. None else had this kind of responsibility out of 258 schools that comprised the Nakuru District.

In all the schools I had led before, the same high academic standards and excellent performance continued to be evident. These schools include Olmanyatta Primary School and Baruti Primary School, both in Nakuru County. These two schools were at their lowest, but after taking up as the head, they were uplifted and got a new lease on life.

I was taken to Baruti School as a result of the then Nakuru Mayor, Mburu Gichua, who demanded the then-District Education Officer, Mr. Murani, to take one of his very able headmasters to this school.

This was in a land the mayor had assisted certain individuals in purchasing and settling there. They had complained to him about the poor academic standards of the school. After being identified as one of the most able headmasters, I was transferred from Ol Manyatta Primary School to Baruti Primary School. The authorities asked me to restore the school's academic performance...I remember the DEO telling me,

"By transferring you to Baruti School, we are responding to the mayor's rather firm request that we take one of our very able headmasters there. We picked you as you have demonstrated to be such a hard-working person and one who can be trusted with any kind of leadership. I am sure the way I have come to know you, you will excel. All the best."

I responded, *"I would not boast, but I am thankful to God who has bestowed upon me such a talent. My leadership ability is a gift from God."* And true to his word, in my second year in that school, it was among the best four schools out of the district's 258 schools.

I am always thankful to God, who, in spite of the tribulation I went through with the PCEA leadership, never faltered in fighting the good fight. One of the scriptures that kept on strengthening me is Psalm 37:23; *"If the Lord delights in a man's way, he makes his steps firm, though he stumbles he will not fall for the Lord upholds him with his hand."* Though the struggle continued, the more it heightened, the more God paved the way for more fruitfulness in the life of PCEA.

Many doors were opened, paving the way for lasting fruitfulness. Unfortunately, much of this fruitfulness fell into the pockets of some leaders, almost drifting its life back to the wilderness physically and spiritually. But thanks to God for a lot of this fruitfulness, especially in the spiritual aspect, it is still so visible. This fruitfulness is still propelling the church despite the human obstacles continually being created by human beings. Has not God chosen us to bear fruit- fruit that will last as stipulated in John 15:16? I have no way to boast about all this, for it all took place through what Zechariah declares; *"Not by might nor by power, but by my spirit, says the Lord Almighty"* (Zechariah 4:6). All glory belongs to God, and this is our main call - to glorify Him whenever He places us in a position of power. Whether in the Business arena or Political arena.

By the time I became the Moderator of the General Assembly, the Church was in a very depressed situation. Everything was crumbling in terms of spirituality and finances. They lacked sound administration. Church institutions were dismal. Integrated Church groups were at their lowest ebb, among other things. In many ways, the clergy was a depressed lot, and the Church was tied up in corrupt activities. There is a general feeling among many in the PCEA, both in leadership and members, that if I never became a GA Moderator, PCEA would have continued marching downhill towards the cliff and never recovered.

I say that because since the end of my tenure, I have met many people who commended me for having come out as the most able Moderator of the General Assembly, especially when it came to general administration and also in boldness and courage. I had to face the mighty in the church, both clergy and lay people, who thrived through corruption from both the Head Office kitty and the financial flow from institutions like the hospitals. There were all kinds of wickedness.

Suffice it to say that much of what is positively taking place in the life of PCEA is, by God's grace, my creation. Talk of decentralization; paving the way for numerous subdivisions of parishes, presbyteries, Elder Districts; numerous church buildings, the vibrant Elder Districts ministry; vibrant praise in worship; the awakening of ministers' welfare; the launching of **PUEA**, the lifting face of **WOGET** project in Mombasa; the liberation of institutions like hospitals and schools; the training of the would-be elders; the initiation of many income generating projects from parishes to General Assembly, among others.

For sure, they referred to me as one possessed by the reformation spirit. And for sure, God used me to bring some lasting reformation into the church or call it a great and visible transformation.

MOCK RESIGNATION

At one time, in order to provoke the church leadership to have dialogue with me, I thought of writing a letter threatening the Church that I was to resign unless the matter I was raising was discussed. I went ahead and wrote a letter addressing it to the Head Office Officials. I knew such a letter could lead to some dialogue with those in leadership. The tradition is that when those in Head Office receive such a letter, they refer it to the presbytery one hails from. The presbytery would then meet and select a few people and send them to the author of the letter in order to have a sitting with him or her. Those people would then listen to the complaints or concerns of the person and then take the report back to Category A of the presbytery.

The author of such a letter would then be summoned by the presbytery to present his or her case and reasons for resigning. Further, the presbytery would seek advice from the head office and then the letter would be tabled in a Business Committee. The Business Committee would send two to three people to further have dialogue with the complainant and would then report back to the Business Committee. In some cases, the Church would involve a counselor to find out the root cause of the idea of one's resignation-with a view to finding out if the person was depressed, stressed or acting emotionally.

But for my case, in view of my being a past Moderator, the Head Office and the Business Committee would wholly handle my case.

Unfortunately, my letter was ignored, and nobody even contacted me, not even through a phone call, email or verbally. I failed in my theory of wooing the Head Office Officials and the Business Committee to listen to my concerns in regard to the mushrooming corruption and wickedness in the Church. Otherwise, there was no way I could resign from the Church that I had known all my life, a Church I really loved and cherished, and that was why I had accepted the suffering in my endeavor to redeem it from the entanglement of many knots.

It is no wonder that some of the PCEA leadership had set up all sorts of mechanisms to frustrate me and possibly expel me. They had symbolically positioned themselves like attentive cats eagerly waiting for a rat to come out of the hole, aiming to pounce on the rat as soon as it showed up. They were eagerly waiting for any opportunity to expel me from the PCEA. The fact that the Head office leaders did not act on my letter is an indication that they ignored my letter. Then one wonders how it is that when they came to declare that I was no longer a member of PCEA because of what they called "Church defamation," why then did they write to all congregations stating that I was no longer a member of PCEA because I had resigned? This is absurd and hypocritical!

INTERVIEW BY THE MEDIA

Following one of the incidences of the common occurrence of demonic attacks on school children by what was termed as evil spirits, Nairobian, a sister newspaper of the Standard Newspapers, invited me for an interview.

The attacks had led to many pupils becoming unconscious, and pastors were involved in carrying out the deliverance.

It was then that the Standard Newspaper, through its sister paper, The Nairobian Newspaper, decided to carry out some research on these spiritual attacks. In doing this, they had identified some clergymen and women whom they would interview individually in regard to that negative spiritual occurrence.

I happened to be one of those selected clergy. They visited me at home for the interview. I answered their concerns from my spiritual understanding of the spiritual warfare point of view, theological perspective and according to my understanding of demonology. But then, there was this question my interviewer, Mwangi, fielded me;

"Now that there is all this going on in schools, including abortions, homosexuality, devil worship, lesbianism, and we also hear that there is a lot of corruption going on, do you think such things are taking place in the churches as well?" ...., these things are also going on in churches. You can't believe it, but during my six years in office as the GA Moderator, I defrocked six pastors for being homosexuals and devil worshipers. And even after I finished my six years tenure as the GA Moderator, I am also constantly

calling upon the church to address these wicked and evil ways of life and the Godly way.

But then Mwangi conclusively asked me, *"Now that you have said that there are some occultists who target schools with the aim of spiritually manipulating the pupils and some of them are traffickers of drugs to students and even brainwashing them into homosexuality and lesbianism including devil worship, are these things traceable in the Churches?"*

I said, *"That is obvious."* Mwangi then insisted, *"What prove do you have on this?"* Hitting the nail on the head, I said,

"It will surprise you to learn that each of the clergy I defrocked for being both devil worshipers and homosexuals had each a common statement; 'Now that you have defrocked me, what are you to do with all the others who are doing the same, for we are several?'"

I told the reporter that I had raised a motion in the General Assembly held in April of 2012, where I pleaded with the church to form a commission to investigate the penetration of devil worship and homosexuality in the church, but the leaders turned a deaf ear.

A week after the interview, news surfaced in that week's issue of **'The Nairobian'**, a sister paper of the Standard Newspaper. They analyzed what each of the interviewed people had said as the possible spiritual causes of the presence of evil spirits in schools. But in my report, they also highlighted that I had said that during my tenure of office as the Moderator of the General Assembly, I had defrocked six clergymen for being homosexuals and devil worshipers. To the PCEA leadership, the rat had finally come out of the hole. It is this last highlight that rattled the PCEA leadership, who then accused me of defaming the church. They had found a rope to tighten around my neck.

THE UNCONSTITUTIONAL SO-CALLED DEFROCKING

As a result of the interview with the Newspapers, the PCEA Head Office officials led by the Moderator General Assembly Rev. Gathanju had summoned the officials of Kajiado Presbytery and instructed them to urgently call for a presbytery meeting under whose jurisdiction I served on 1st April 2014 and to sign minutes stating that the Presbytery had 'defrocked' or expelled me and to forward the same to the PCEA Head Office the following day, 2nd April.

Meanwhile, the PCEA Head Office, like the Sanhedrin that had quickly assembled at night to put Jesus on trial, urgently summoned the Business Committee (which is the PCEA executive body) to meet on 3rd April to affirm and take action as per the Kajiado Presbytery minutes of having 'defrocked' me. They would then be required to come out with a resolution advocating for my being 'defrocked'.

The said church officials had summoned the Business Committee to come and affirm the Kajiado Presbytery resolution on my being 'defrocked.' Why? The Nairobian Newspaper reported that: "*Rev. Githii, the former Moderator of PCEA Church, affirmed that such wickedness was also taking place in Churches, PCEA being one of them. He substantiated this statement by declaring that, in his six-year tenure in office as the GA Moderator, he had defrocked six pastors for being involved in homosexuality and devil worship. But he was quick to add that, this is a common phenomenon in most of the churches in Kenya and worldwide. This spells a tragedy for the church and the nation, for the nation depends on the church for spiritual guidance. In his interview with us, Githii further said, "I have noted with great concern the rapid recruitment of homosexuality and devil worship globally."*

The paper went on to say: "*Further, Githii claimed homosexuality was fast mushrooming in the church because of PCEA's close partnership with PC (USA) denomination in the USA. A church that is already ordaining gay church leaders and even practicing same-sex marriages.*"

The GA Moderator and other liberals, therefore, grabbed this opportunity to now accuse me of having taken a defamatory path to tarnish the name of PCEA through the Nairobian newspaper. My testimony to the media was with claims that there was already rampant corruption and ongoing homosexuality and devil worship among some pastors and elders, and, to some extent, the members became the prime gear to have me expelled from PCEA Church. They insisted that nothing of that nature ever existed in the denomination - no homosexuality, no corruption, no lesbianism, and there was nothing like a partnership with PC (USA) because they

490

always prayed over all the donations they received as well as for the church regarding the same. As such, there was no spiritual pollution. At one time, Rev. Gathanju, the GA Moderator, said, *"Our church is the model for the cleanest church in Africa, if not in the world."*

As instructed by the head office, Kajiado's presbytery had met on April 1st. (*Fool's Day*) and as dictated to them to meet and pass the resolution on my being 'defrocked'. The minutes were then delivered to the Head Office on April 2nd. With the Business Committee meeting the following day, April 3rd. At the PCEA Head Office in the presence of media houses. At around 11 am, Rev.David Riitho Gathanju, the then PCEA Moderator in the midst of a big group of media people, delivered the message that the Church had 'defrocked' me from being not only a PCEA Clergyman but also from being a member of PCEA Church. The invitation of all Kenyan and some international media to that meeting was so that the message of my 'defrocking' would be both national and international news. That was to make sure that all the world would know of my being 'defrocked', especially their good friends and best donors, the PC (USA) and Church of Scotland. Of course, such kind of news would attract more donations from global partners. And for sure, things worked according to their plan. Faced with a multitude of media houses, the Moderator read the verdict to the media, conclusively declaring that the church had '*defrocked*' me and that I am no longer an ordained minister and no longer a member of the PCEA Church.

In doing so, Gathanju and his Business Committee acted in the spirit of the Jewish Court, Sanhedrin, who, in condemning Jesus, did not follow the procedure as laid down to guide the honorable Jewish Court. That was a council composed of Elders, the chief Priests and the Teachers of the Law, as indicated in Luke 22 66.

In the same way, PCEA leadership did not follow the laid down Church administrative protocol. For an ordinary pastor, the procedure of expelling or defrocking him or her would include the Kajiado Presbytery leadership sending the presbytery officials, including a retired minister, to the pastor under discipline for some dialogue. After such a meeting, they would report their findings to the presbytery.

After this, the Secretary-General is authorized to write a letter to that person communicating the final findings. Such a letter is given to at least two members of the Business Committee, a church minister and an elder to take it to the person and then have time to pray with him, and it becomes a case concluded. These people would, at the same time, take back all the church's ecclesiastical property.

In regard to my case, the Business Committee was supposed to send three to four of its members, including a past Moderator, to come to me for some dialogue then they would take their findings back to the Business Committee. Later, the Business Committee would then summon me and interrogate me, after which they would come up with a final decision. Afterwards, a letter to that effect would be written, and three Business Committee members, including a past Moderator, would have been selected to deliver the letter, but most important, was to talk and pray with me and my family. The issue of 'expulsion' or 'defrocking' would not surface because the whole thing was not a disciplinary case.

This is the only procedure any GA Moderator's expulsion or defrocking should follow. Therefore, any so-called **'defrocking'** that did not follow the laid down constitutional protocols is administratively considered **fake, null** and **void**. That being the case, I am staunchly entrenched in the books of PCEA even as my impact on the PCEA body outshines any other GA Moderator's work over the centuries. That being the case, PCEA leadership never **'expelled'** or **'defrocked'** me. The Business Committee and Kajiado Presbytery were only used as rubber stamps. And the said Presbytery meeting was another Sanhedrin. There is no way a minister can be defrocked through the media. Instead, any defrocking should be shielded from the media because any minuted matter remains confidential.

Nobody had even informed me of the forthcoming 'expulsion' or 'defrocking'. I only learned of the 'expulsion' or 'defrocking' when the media people called me for the interview. The decency of PCEA is that it follows the protocols on defrocking a minister to the letter because it is equal to dealing with the life of a person, and any condemnation by mistake is regarded as a sinful drifting from the churches' spiritual path and even the constitution or Practice and Procedure. The Use of the Media was out rightly wrong and out of the long-cherished protocol spirit of PCEA. The Practice and procedure of PCEA require the use of the appropriate Committees or courts whose deliberations, discussions and outcomes are minuted for execution, and this remains confidential. In fact, the church leaders acting in such an unprocedural way, that they could be accused of church defamation. The accusing finger was on them, not me.

I can be physically out of sight but never out of mind, for my work speaks loudly about my presence. My name is highlighted everywhere in the life of PCEA. The 19th/20th GA removed my portrait from the GA Moderator's Office wall where the portraits of past moderatos are hung, but the pressure from the church clergy forced the Moderator to return it. One of the clergymen who agitated for my photo to be placed back was Rev. Dr. Timothy Njoya. He even confronted the Moderator about the issue.

Attempts were made to return the original status of the church (*Gucokia rui mukaro*), including doing away with praise in worship, but it became a hard cookie. Even the attempt to remove all the plaques entrenched in the buildings that I had dedicated became impossible. The roots had so much deepened. Any attempt to reverse such things as the training of elders before ordination or doing away with **decentralization became impossible**. It was the work of the Holy Spirit and not the work of man. What of the various Ministers I had ordained!

ANOTHER INTERVIEW BY MEDIA PERSONNEL

No sooner had the media finished with the Business Committee than they engaged in a campaign to trace my whereabouts. The first caller from K24 Media House asked, "*Dr. Githii, where are you? I am in the company of a host of Kenyan media houses, and we cannot wait to speak to you. It is very important that we meet you within the next few minutes. The PCEA Business Committee has just met, and they have told the world that you have been defrocked. We have covered this declaration, and we have to hear from your side; otherwise, this will be a crucial part of today's evening news broadcast and the same will also be published in tomorrow's dailies. Unfortunately, we cannot do this without having heard from you. Are you, by chance, within or near Nairobi?" We have just finished with the PCEA Business Committee, who have declared that you are, with immediate effect, defrocked, and you are no longer a member of PCEA Church. We want to hear the version of your story. How can we meet you the soonest possible?"*

In response, I said,

"I am at home located in Zambezi on the way to Limuru. I am just hearing of my being defrocked for the first time from you. What I know is that I have for a long time differed with PCEA leaders over some issues in the Church, but it had never occurred to me that they would ever 'expel' me. How can they so unconstitutionally do that? They have terribly overlooked the laid down procedure in carrying out an 'expulsion' or 'defrocking' especially one of a past Moderator. There is a laid down procedure to follow within the Church's practice and procedure. This clearly defines the protocol that should have been followed. Anyway, I am in Zambezi, not far from Westland. What of meeting at ABC Place which is located in Westland's?"

Media: *"Let us then meet there shortly."*

It took me fifteen minutes to get to ABC Place. On my arrival, there was a crowd of journalists, and as soon as they saw me, they hurriedly started setting up their equipment, ready for the interview.

Media: *"David, what has led to all this?"* I gave the version of my predicament, which was a result of my persistence in pointing out the already prevailing corruption, homosexuality, and devil worship in the Church and also my persistent call upon the denomination to terminate its partnership with the American denomination. But, they argued that there was no way they could terminate the partnership as the American based denomination was their best donor.

It was easier for them to have me kicked out of the church than disown the PC (USA) denomination. These leaders acted as the prosecutors and judges. I even told the media of an instance in which I had gone to represent PCEA Church at the PC (USA) General Assembly and upon refusing to the part of the leaders lobbying for the motion to open the door to ordain homosexuals and solemnize their marriages, they ended up denying me everything pertaining to the all 'invited delegates package' including food.

My story excited the media people. I overheard one of them say, *"This man is being tortured for speaking the truth. There is no better way to indicate the rottenness of the Church when it comes to wickedness and financial greed. I just wish we had a couple of Church ministers of his caliber. These are the kind of people we need even in the national governance, including the presidency, for transparency and justice over governments."*

When we came to the end of the interview, K24 TV boarded me in their vehicle to host a recording of a one-on-one interview for that evening news forum. What followed was a constant invitation by various media houses including local radio broadcasting houses like Coro and Inooro. This generated a lot of anger from PCEA leaders because of my outspokenness in the media, especially on Sundays. I also felt bad because I have a deep love for PCEA, but I was in a dilemma. It was important that I defend myself by letting the truth be known.

TAKEN TO THE HIGH COURT

At that juncture, the Church leadership decided to have me completely torn apart. They decided to take me to the High Court, where they accused me of continued church defamation in connection with the interview that had been carried out by Mr. Mwangi of **The Nairobian.** And how another interview with media houses after being defrocked. Media houses had also persistently called me to express my feelings based on my being expelled from the church. Such included Inooro Radio/TV, Coro Radio/TV, and Citizen TV among others. But more so, this time round, through other media stations, including Radio and TV stations and through social media. This was just because I had said that during my tenure in office as GA Moderator, I had defrocked six ministers. This was framed as having defamed the church.

All this was geared towards my psychological torture. This was why they had acted very fast on my being '*defrocked*', making it happen within three days- from 1st to 3rd April. They were also talking about finishing me economically. But what they did not know was that my spirit was equated to that of John Calvin, who, while under much pressure from those who opposed him in the formation of

Presbyterian Denomination in the 16th. century had said, *"I am one who has the law of my Heavenly master so much at heart that I will not be moved from asserting it with a good conscience for the sake of any living man."* Yes, like John Calvin, there is no way I could compromise the Godly with ungodliness.

The aim of taking me to the Kenyan High Court PCEA leadership was to ultimately have me imprisoned or have my property confiscated, rendering me into deep poverty and, thus, emotionally tortured. What bothered the Church leaders was my uncompromising spirit. Contrary to their thinking, I could not yield because my conscience kept on telling me that, He who called me to His service remained on the throne and He is ever faithful. It is Him who sent ravens with meat and bread to feed Elijah. I had witnessed this when I had been forced to remain for one year at home over the Sigona symbols controversy. The Church leadership had denied me everything, including what would have been my salary.

In the High Court, the PCEA leadership filed under a certificate of urgency an order to restrain or block me from mentioning the words PECA, Homosexuality, Lesbianism, Devil Worship, Illuminati, corruption, nepotism, greed, oppression, symbols at Watson Memorial Church and so on. But the court declined their request, arguing that; *'Considering that the plaintiff in this case, PCEA Church, did not take any action against the more serious utterances made by the defendant, the court, therefore, declines the request to restrain the defendant from making those less serious and weighty utterances. The previous inaction is thus a significant factor in this ruling.'*

Noting all that was going on around my life, my only concern here was: *"Why should some of the Church leaders claiming to be servants of the Living God behave so unjustly mistreating me beyond even the people, Christian's call, 'The people of the world?'"*- people who have little knowledge about God, regarded as anti-Christ. That also reminded me about April 2006 when I was undergoing re-election for my second term in office as the Moderator of the General Assembly. This was the day of the election, when timely text messages were sent to members of all the presbyteries participating in the elections, purporting I was in a comma after being involved in *'a fatal road accident'* so that I could be disqualified from the race!

I am sure the reader will agree with me that, even in political campaigns, one cannot hear or witness such a high degree of manipulation of the truth, the highest degree in the spirit of deception. This only explains the extent to which PCEA leadership was enslaved by the spirit of greed for power and money. It is a sign of spiritual decay; even atheists would think twice before daring to act that way. Their conscience cannot allow it.

UNEXPECTED BACKUP

In a surprise twist of events, I had unexpected support from outsiders rather than the PCEA church, which is expected to stand with the truth at all times, especially on matters spiritual and religious.

The Shepherd Magazine of May 2014 (pg. 5) by Samuel Ochieng stated that;

"When David Githii recently accused PCEA, alleging rampant corruption, homosexuality and devil worship in the denomination, many were shocked, and they were even more shocked when the Church's top brass quickly denied the allegations and accused Githii, a former Presbyterian Church of East Africa (PCEA) moderator for six years, of insincerity. They later defrocked him."

The Standard Newspaper of Friday, April 4, 2014, p10 by James Mwangi and John Muthoni also reported on this matter, saying:

"The Presbyterian Church of East Africa Moderator, David Gathanju, has refuted claims by the former Moderator, David Githii, that the Church condones acts of homosexuality and devil worship. In their defense, the top Church leadership argued that while in office, Githii informally raised issues that were deemed to be his personal opinion but could not become Church policy because the issue had to be deliberated over by the necessary courts of the Church with justifications raised and relevant resolutions made for them to pass as policies. He added that there has never been any formal discussion generated by Githii in any committee on devil worship in the Church and the purported homosexuality. But Githii said he has all the way pointed the Church to these issues, but they have always turned a deaf ear."

The Shepherd Magazine went on to indicate that as much as PCEA leaders denied the fact that there were no homosexuals and devil worshipers, there were many pastors who agreed with Rev. Githii the fact that homosexuality and devil worship were fast seeping into the denomination. A number of them acknowledged the existence of the problem and were agonizing over how to deal with it.

This notion was acknowledged by some Kenyan Church leaders who believed there was already a prevalent understanding among many Pentecostal and Mainstream Churches whom The Shepherd Magazine has interviewed believed that the Church universal had in many ways been infiltrated by devil worshipers and homosexuals, yet it is a known fact that one actually cannot be gay or a devil worshiper and be a Christian at the same time.

For example, at a press conference called by the Kenya Christian Professional Forum (KCPF) in Nairobi, two pastors, including Rev. Wainaina, outspokenly said that they could no longer bury their heads in the sand over the matter. They spoke of *"the struggle they faced when dealing with the increasing number of homosexuals in their congregations, most of whom were already coming in the open, thanks to increased media reporting and a 'more enlightened society.'"*

Rev Wainaina castigated PCEA for 'defrocking' me, saying, *"Churches must learn to accept leaders with divergent opinions. "Rev. Githii was not just a mere member of the Church, he was a leader and knew what he was saying,"* he said.

Paul Habwe, the senior pastor of Pentecostal Evangelism Fellowship of Africa (PEFA) in Donholm, also admitted that homosexuals were indeed in Churches. He lamented that *"homosexuality is increasing because most people have shunned moral family values and opted to follow negative Western influence."* He pointed out that procreation was under threat because homosexuals cannot reproduce by themselves.

The Shepherd Magazine of May 2014 went on to say that, while there were no clear statistics on the number of homosexuals in Kenya, concern was rife that the number of homosexuals in Kenya was fast growing, especially among young people. However, according to the 2007 Pew Global Attitudes Project – a non-partisan American think-tank based in Washington DC, it was observed that *"96 percent of*

Kenyans believe that homosexuality is a way of life that society should not accept, which was the fifth-highest rate of non-acceptance in the 45 countries surveyed."

In a further development on my defrocking, the Shepherd Magazine stated that; *"Many in the KCPF conference felt that PCEA jumped the gun, which is a hypocritical way of covering the Church. But the truth of the matter is that PCEA and many other Churches worldwide are only letting their Churches continue rotting within. It would be better to apply medicine to the wound, though painful, rather than allow the gradual decaying of the Church. One would wonder, for how long would the Church continue to bury its neck in the sand? It is this hypocritical attitude that has almost killed the Western Church."*

The Nairobian Newspaper of March 28th. -April reviewed the fact that; *"Many people commend Githii for his fearless and non-compromising stand. Such is the caliber of people that the present Church wants. Githii had blasted the denomination over 'evil symbols and alleged association with gays and lesbians in its congregations and said his appeal for change had been ignored by the Church's leadership for long, a claim the current Moderator, Rev. David Gathanju, seemed to contradict himself when he admitted that there had been cases regarding homosexuality in PCEA. He said: "We have another case, that of the 1990s and the said pastor was expelled. This case involved a parish minister who manned a parish in Nyeri."*

Many attempts have been made to have the said pastor restored to the priesthood, but by the time of writing this book, the door had not yet opened. But the truth of the matter is that when this same pastor got defrocked in 1990, the statement he made revealed the populous condition of homosexuals in the PCEA, for he asked, *"Now that you have defrocked me, what are you to do with those other colleagues and lay people in the Church who are sailing in the same boat?"* This then supports my endeavor to awaken the Church to the realization of this poisonous virus to the Church's spirituality.

By this pastor and others making such a statement, God was summoning the Church to come to the realization that there were already pastors who were homosexuals and devil worshipers who were at the same time actively carrying out the recruitment in the entire Church. Unfortunately, the Church was not ready to act on them because some of them were in the top Church leadership, like presbytery clerks and Moderators plus Session Clerks. Such leaders act as a cover to those other homosexuals in the parishes and Presbyteries.

In fact, they joined hands in campaigning for their colleagues to be elected in the various key top leadership positions. It is due to this patronage that the Church officials wanted the status quo to remain as a way of safeguarding their votes. Each leader aspires to be re-elected not only to the same positions after their time in office expires but to be placed in other prime positions in the Church even after their time in office expires. They have to be careful not to lose members in the church leadership to assist during election times as voters as well as campaign agents. Such members would also assist in furthering their wicked agenda of recruiting more to homosexuality and occultism. In other words, this is a cartel behaving like a mole in the church. They are protectors of their own. Leaders will protect evil-doers so long as they deliver votes. They protect their positions; then, they protect the spiritual welfare of the church. It is all about money and power, a very secularized spirit.

During my tenure of office as the Moderator of the General Assembly, as I said earlier, six ministers had been defrocked, but thereafter, no single homosexual minister has been defrocked from 2009 to the time of this book's publication, that is over fifteen years later. This is despite the continued increase in devil worship, homosexuality, idolatry and immorality. Corruption involving a high-level misappropriation of Church money, among others, still thrives, yet these evils are condoned. But get me right, this trend of homosexuality and devil worship is not wholly confined to the PCEA. It is an evil that has penetrated the entire body of Christ. It is for that reason that Shepherd Magazine is quoted to have said, "*The good news is that Githii does not accuse PCEA alone; he also sees the same trend of clergy and lay people being involved in homosexuality and devil worshipping in other Churches. He warned Americans and other Churches practicing homosexuality that they were 'doomed to hell'. The Rev. Dr. Githii warned that just as God refused to spare Sodom and Gomorrah from fire, He would not spare homosexuals and those defending that act.*"

This magazine goes on to remind the reader about my psychological torture in the hands of PC (USA), the American Presbyterian Church. The paper says: "*Githii had stood in the American Presbyterian Church General Assembly and denounced homosexuality and same-sex practices. This was not taken easily by this denomination that even went ahead and denied him everything including food. The main core and bone of contention was David's refusal to support an agenda the American General Assembly had regarding the ordination of homosexuals and the consent to embracing same-sex marriage. Githii did express this same view to the PCEA, the view that all the pollution that has blurred the Church is a product of Western Churches. This was a very bold step that Githii took.*"

Several times, I had cautioned PCEA, warning them that unless they repented and towed God's path of spiritual life, God's wrath would catch up with them. One way to repent was the termination of their partnership with their foreign donors, who were already submerged into unethical biblical principles. True to my prophecy, within a span of two years, the Church lost members in unexplained mysterious circumstances, as indicated elsewhere in this book.

That is what happens to those who disconnect themselves from God's covenant. This is exactly what happened to the children of Israel who, after disconnecting themselves from their covenant with God, turned to worshiping idols. These idols were also being worshiped by other foreign nations, like the Moabites. It is, therefore, in this connection that God said, "*I will...forsake them, I will hide my face from them, and they will be destroyed. Many disasters and destruction will come upon them, and on that day, they will ask, '**Have not these disasters come upon us because our God is not with us?**... I will certainly hide my face on that day because of all their wickedness in turning to other gods.*"

I am sure, in one way or another, the PCEA fraternity has witnessed many things going wrong in the denomination, yet no serious step has been taken to lead the Church to a more pronounced repentance movement. The truth of the matter is that God loves PCEA, and He is counting on it to accomplish much of His agenda, including being one of the churches he could use as a springboard for End Time Revival. But they will need to put their house in order spiritually. They will need to weed out those traits of wickedness that hamper God's spiritual penetration into the denomination. And that was why God was using me to expose the altars and teach about the church's lack of knowledge about it. Why torture me, then?

Globally, there are many pastors who have been totally derailed from the truth of the gospel, and they have turned into con pastors. A modern classic example is Shakahola, where Pst. Mckenzie, though not proven guilty at the time of writing this book, is said to have led many members to a death trap. The Shakahola story dominated the public domain because the pastor of a church misled many to die by being promised that by fasting to death, they would meet with Jesus. Many churches are 'Shakahola' in disguise, spiritually killing millions of souls in exchange for the offertory, tithes, first fruits, oppressive constitutions, traditions, by-laws, 'founder's visions and missions', cultural set up, doctrines and all kinds of manipulation in falsified miracles of deliverance.

Another shocker is the recent proclamation that caused a stir in the church following Pope Francis' same-sex blessings policy, which received worldwide press coverage in late 2023. NBC News (nbcnews.com/news), for instance, carried the following sub-heading in its OUT News on its Website: "*Pope's same-sex blessings policy triggers both healing and pain for gay Catholics.*" In the same feature a pertinent question was raised as heading; "**How to deal with same-sex unions? It's a question fracturing major Christian denominations**: *Divisions over marriage, sexuality and inclusion of gays and lesbians are proving insurmountable for the foreseeable future in many sectors of Christianity.*"

A January 8th. 2024 by the Associated Press reported the following; "*Catholics around the world are sharply divided by the Vatican's recent declaration giving priests more leeway to bless same-sex couples. Supporters of LGBTQ inclusion welcome the move; some conservative bishops assail the new policy as a betrayal of the church's condemnation of sexual relations between gay or lesbian partners. Strikingly, the flare-up debate in Catholic ranks coincides with developments in two other international Christian denominations- the global Anglican Communion and the United Methodist Church- that are fracturing other differences in LGBTQ- related policies*" NBC News.

REASONS BEHIND MY BEING MOCKINGLY DEFROCKED

I trust this book answers one question that has persisted in peoples' minds for quite some time: *"Why was Githii really 'defrocked' under the leadership of the General Assembly Moderator, David Gathanju?"* There could be several reasons, all of which rotate around my pointing fingers at some ills that contaminated the Church. But top on the list was my call for the Church to be detached from the PC (USA), which was already ordaining and solemnizing same-sex marriages and my call for the formation of a commission to investigate the already proliferating homosexuality, lesbianism and devil worship into the PCEA denomination. But it is also important to say this virus is mushrooming in all denominations.

But another notable reason was my persistent exposure to the rampant corruption in the Church spearheaded by some of the Head Office leadership. I warned them about the consequences of corruption. One time, when I was speaking to some top church leaders from presbyteries, one of the leaders was daring enough to ask me why I should bother to talk about Church corruption while the virus was all over the world. I should first take the message to the world. To drive my argument home, I quoted the book of Ecclesiastes 7:7, where it states; *"Extortion turns a wise man into a fool, and a bribe corrupts the heart."*

I further told him that it is the devil that creates this mentality through the deception he uses to corrupt the heart, only to later expose the same person. This truth surfaced nine years after I had been expelled when the Sunday Nation Newspaper of October 19, 2017, reported that,

"Former Moderator of the General Assembly of the Presbyterian Church of East Africa David Gathanju...has been charged with stealing close to Ksh.40 million. Rev Gathanju, who served as the Moderator between 2009 and 2015.... has been charged with another felony against the Church...Ms. Atambo ordered that the accused be detained...."

This did not take me by surprise. I always knew the pregnancy of corruption would one day be birthed out, for there is nothing hidden that will not surface someday. This was just one way that God wanted to show the PCEA fraternity that what I had echoed some years past that made me get blacklisted by the PCEA was nothing but the truth. This then explains why some of the top Church leaders conspired to have me expelled from the Church because they had identified me as the only voice that could lead to their being exposed to their corrupt practices in the church. I was indeed the voice of conscience. Here I am not talking of Rev. Gathanju. I am talking about the rampant corruption mushrooming in the denominations.

There were even those who looked for a broader door to the recruitment of more homosexuals and devil worshipers. They knew that when it came to defending the cause of God's people, I acted very aggressively. There is no way I could leave any stone unturned until I had exposed that which was bringing deception in the body of Christ.

The cartel understood that without me, the church could be invaded by more corruption, devil worship, immorality and homosexuality. They, therefore, found the action of getting me out of the way as the best to clear the pathway for them to distort and *"eat up"* the Church like underground rodents. They surely did it, such that by the time they left the office, the Church was tilted towards financial bankruptcy, creating an outcry in the whole denomination.

Most of the assets that were bought during my tenure were already sold out in the spirit of dishonesty. The homosexuals found even deeper roots in the Church. As you read this, things are not getting any better. Anybody from PCEA that I meet talks of negative things taking place, meaning the Church is degenerating down towards the cliff. Some of them have regrettably said, *"We wish we had listened to you. Our Church would have not gone haywire."*

Unfortunately, that trend will prevail until the Church acts in accordance with Peter's words; *"Repent…every one of you, in the name of Jesus Christ for the forgiveness of your sins. And you will receive the gift of the Holy Spirit. The promise is for you and your children"* (Acts 2 verse 38). This will not happen until they get liberalized from the grip of both idolatry and Freemasons in showing that there cannot be more of God while idolatry prevails. Jehu asked, *"How can there be peace… as long as all idolatry and witchcraft… abounds"* (2 Kings 9:22)

For sure, the Church will need leaders possessed by the either the spirit of Biblical Jehu or David in order to redeem it. The Church will need to declare total spiritual warfare by building up a strong Intercessory Ministry with coordination from the Elder Districts to the presbyteries. Unfortunately, this kind of ministry is always blocked by the liberals. As stated elsewhere, in my tenure, I had commissioned many intercessors, but no sooner had I left my office than those intercessors were fought from every side, and the intercessory spirit I had initiated got diluted.

The liberals know the secret that no Church can survive without intercessors. They are the Church's gatekeepers. Therefore, all they do is block these gatekeepers. Without intercessors, I would not have moved PCEA from one glory to another. This included the destruction of the former occultic JiteGemea logo, which had enslaved the denomination over the years. There was no way we would have managed to remove those occultic symbols from St. Andrews Church and elsewhere without intercessors.

It is unfortunate that the church members and even leaders are not aware of the presence of Freemasons among the church members. These are people who can act like moles as they eat up the church occultly.

REFLECTION ON MODERATORS'

A reflection on the past Moderators' themes seemingly supports the fact that the church is on the wrong path. Therefore, my role in the PCEA church is evident. Let us look at each of these themes.

Rev. Dr. Jesse Kamau 1997-2003

Rev Jesse gave a prophetic message that things were wrong in the PCEA Church, and it called for **a renewal of the church**. This indicated that there were many wrong things in the church system. Hence his theme from Revelation 21:5," *Behold I am making all things New*". He was my forerunner because when I came in, my work was restoration. And to show the urgency of this theme, he stuck with it for his two terms in office.

This was a futuristic message implying that new things would come after him. And indeed, in tune with the Spirit, it ushered me in as I came in with fundamental changes that greatly reformed PCEA Church together with its institutions, as has been elaborated in this book. For sure, new things occurred in the church during my tenure in office. Dr. Jesse obeyed the prophetic voice of God.

My themes 2003-2009

My first theme's message when I took over the reins of the PCEA church was anchored in Luke 13:8; "*Leave it alone. and I will dig around it and fertilize it.*" In saying so, I had taken responsibility as one called to build his kingdom and true to the word, I lived this word despite many obstacles placed along my reformation path. The roots grew deeper. My second term's theme, on the other hand, was based on John 15:16: '*You did not choose me, but I chose you and appointed you so that you might go and bear fruit that will last.*' which was a call to the church to come and fulfill the purpose of God by bearing fruits that would last. This became evident in the restoration of the spiritual and physical life of the church and its institutions.

Rev. David Ritho Gathanju 2009- 2015

Then followed my successor, Moderator of General Assembly, Rev. David Gathanju Ritho's theme derived from Hosea 4:6, which says, "*My people are destroyed for lack of knowledge.*" This is a contradiction of what I had already done. It is that knowledge that the church lacked that I had taken the time to impart by calling upon the church to do away with idolatry, corruption and wickedness. But instead of building upon this knowledge, he decided to overlook it and even persecute me for the same. His other theme for the second term was from James 1:22; "*Be doers and not only listeners.*" It was a pointer as to how much the church had lacked knowledge of the schemes of the devil such that they became hearers of the word but were not doing what they heard in the word. This further implied that the word was not penetrating the hearts of the people in the church because of allowing idolatry, wickedness and other evils in their midst. This was indeed the result of rejection of the knowledge I had exposed the church to.

Rev. Dr. Julius Mwamba 2015- 2021

The worrisome situation in the church was affirmed by one of the themes of the subsequent Moderator of General Assembly, Dr. Mwamba, divinely derived from 1Kings 18.30 which talks of repairing the altars; "*Then Elijah said to all the people, 'Come near me'. So, all the people came near to him. And he repaired the altar of the Lord that was broken down.*" Symbolically, the church as an altar was broken. Many things had gone wrong, and the altar needed to be repaired. That means what I had done to raise a good altar had been destroyed. The church needed restoration after Rev. Gathanju, during whose tenure the church still needed some knowledge, which was not forthcoming. And therefore, the altar which is the church, continues to deteriorate. The second theme, *'Be Vessels of Honour,'* from 2 Tim 2:21, indicates that the church had lost the mark in honouring God as a vessel. The fear of the Lord had continued to grow dim.

Moderator of GA Rev. Thegu Mutahi 2021-2027

The theme Moderator of GA, Mutahi Thegu, further confirmed the endeavours to undo what I did for PCEA Church, her institutions and the nation that greatly compromises godliness. The theme derived from Haggai 1:5b, "*Consider your ways,*" hit the nail on the head and further called the PCEA Church to a reawakening. The church seemingly is not walking in obedience to the scriptures again because of idolatry and all sorts of evil. They thus need to give careful thought to their ways. Ways that continually demean the kingdom of God. The difference between me and the other Moderators is that they pointed to the problem but gave no solution. This is unlike my theme from Luke 13:8; "*Leave it alone. and I will dig around it and fertilize it."* In this case I referred to PCEA as the fruitless tree where the servant had refused to work for its production. I therefore gave the solution that I would dig it and fertilize it, and I did it, and all PCEA members and the world as my witness in this. In my 2018 GA Theme, I called upon the church to leave no stone unturned in our continued endeavor to bear fruit, fruit that will last, as recorded in John 15:16.

The Theme was chosen for the 24th. GA portrays the PCEA church as being persistently rebellious. The source of the theme is Joshua 24:15, where Joshua declares, *"As for me and my household, we will serve the Lord."* Joshua says this after accusing Israelites of idolatry and urging them to *"throw away the gods of your forefathers worshipped beyond the River and in Egypt, and serve the Lord."* Joshua warned Israelites that unless they repented, the Lord *"will turn and bring disaster"* upon them. The theme comes with a warning to PCEA, that is, to *"throw away the foreign gods that are among you and yield your hearts to the Lord"* (Joshua 24:23). Among the foreign gods that the PCEA is being accused of include Their partnership with PC(USA) who are well anchored into gayism, and where they are ordaining homosexuals and lesbians. Both the dollars and materialistic greed are idols. Corruption and nepotism are idols. There is also embracing wickedness, including giving work to people riddled with scandals, corruption, power struggles, adherence to some Scottish traditions, and evil symbols entrenched into the sanctuaries, institutions and other church affiliations which has been sanctioned. The classic example is the belittlement of the church logo, which is totally overshadowed by an occultic cross, as shown on the cover of the

PCEA Desk Diary for the year 2024, sanctioned by the committees concerned.

This indicates the depth under which the church is consumed in idolatry. It is the logo on the cover of the desk diary that should outshine in prominence without any occultic representation around it. Just as it is reflected on the PCEA pocket diary. But the occultists know that the pocked diary carries very little information. It just hints at what the desk diary has widely elaborated. It is called a *"cover"* because it has given cover to all that is sandwiched between the page's hard covers. The cover carries authority over all that is written in the desk diary. The work of the occultic cover on the Desk Diary is to distort and defuse all that is represented on the various dates in the year.

The distorted cross on the Desk Diary's front cover is the same distorted cross common in Ecclesiastical robes of Ministers especially scarfs.

In this case, the denomination, like the Israelites, has turned to wickedness and this is manifest in the state of the denomination. Another good example is what transpired in the General Assembly that began in early April this year, which reflected confusion. This seems to have caught the attention of His Excellency the President when he attended part of the GA. On the day he graced the occasion, he could be seen referring to *"Mtu ya keyboard"* when he requested for a song to be played, apparently wondering whether the keyboardist was ready or able to play the song. Earlier, the keyboardist seemed to be struggling to find the right notes to play during congregational worship.

As if that was not enough, there was an induction of a person riddled with scandals as the PCEA Financial Controller, something that irked Rev Dr. Timothy Njoya to storm out of the meeting in protest. One then wonders whether the church has any power or moral authority to question the government on nepotism, corruption and all kinds of manipulation. No wonder then the moderator's selection of the theme of the year calls on the people to take a stand on whom they will serve.

And like Joshua, this is what I was calling the church to throw away and be anchored into the Holy Spirit, scriptures and intercession-only in this way can the numerous Freemasons/Devil Worshippers in the church be overcome.

14 CHARTING A NEW PATH

END OF MY TENURE IN THE GA OFFICE

Having been appointed Moderator GA in 2003, my tenure had come to an end in the year 2009. It was time to hand over the leadership to another Moderator, who, in this case, was Rev. Gathanju. In my handing over at the General Assembly held at St Andrew's Church in April 2009, the GA qualified me as the first-ever Moderator to have attained such a clean bill of health when it came to the defense of denomination from misappropriation of finances and a clear conscience in the welfare of the denomination. This was also reflected in defense of the spirituality of the church.

This is how one newspaper summarized my achievement in the Presbyterian Church of East Africa:

"In 2003, Rev Dr. David Githii, a born-again Christian, was unanimously elected by the majority of the presbyteries to head the Presbyterian Church of East Africa (PCEA) as the Moderator of the General Assembly, a position he held for six years, the maximum duration in that position. It was while he was the Moderator of the entire PCEA Church that David embarked on bringing drastic changes to the Church.

The paper went on to say:

"These changes were worthwhile because, in its history, this Church had rejected the role of the Holy Spirit in the Church, a negative spirit that the Church inherited from its pioneer founding Scottish Missionaries. They had as well rejected any use of musical instruments in the Church, something that was upheld in the African cultural set up. In fact, they labeled anything African as pagan in nature. What they called Christianity was, in reality, the Scottish culture. The African leaders had been well brainwashed and drilled to accept the Scottish cultural aspect to stand for Christianity. You can then imagine the kind of opposition that David had to encounter when he came up with the changes. By the time David left the office, the Church had experienced a total revival and many beneficial changes, both physical and spiritual."

The paper went on to elaborate;

"These changes were not taken positively by the so-called status quo Church liberal leadership. It caused a lot of conflict between David and these leaders who were not focused on the scriptures but rather focused on the westernized Church traditions and the greed for power and money." In saying this, the paper hit the nail on the head.

Thank God I overcame every hindrance that was raised by the liberals. This was not a surprise to me, for the Bible affirms its truth when it says, *"In all these things, we are more than conqueror"* (Romans 8:37). In any case, and as Paul says, *"I can do all things through him who gives me strength"* (Phil.13:4).

THE WAY FORWARD

Now that I was no longer in PCEA or in any other church for that matter, after having been mockingly expelled, I decided to still wait upon the Lord to give me the direction on my next move. But it is worthwhile confessing that I felt very lonely. I was already used to being in the midst of clergy and among the people as we served God's kingdom, and there, I was with nobody to turn to. I had suddenly become an outcast. Nobody in PCEA could associate with me. But I remembered words I had read in a book that highlighted the fact that the person who will ultimately soar like an eagle to the heights of a cloudless day and live in the sunshine of God must be content to live a relatively lonely life: A life that is dedicated to God.

The Holy Spirit had, at the same time, revealed to me that no one ever comes into full realization of the best things of God in his spiritual life without learning to walk alone with Him. I thought of Abraham. He stayed a long time in the wilderness waiting for the promised son. Moses was in the wilderness for a long time when he saw the burning bush where God spoke to Him. I also thought of John, who had to write the book of Revelation while lonely on the Island of Patmos. Jacob was alone when he wrestled with an Angel of the Lord who then whispered in his ear; *"Your name will no longer be Jacob, but Israel"* (Gen. 32:28).

I was also reminded of Dr. Moon of Brighton, England, who was suddenly struck with blindness. It was through this wilderness of blindness that God enabled him to invent the Moon Alphabet for the blind, through which thousands of blind people have been able to read the Word of God and, therefore, come to the glorious saving knowledge of God. All these people went through experiences with God, and one thing remains true: He stamped their cause. God knew why I had to undergo such an unexpected and rather painful experience. But I decided never to compromise my conscience as far as fighting against corruption, homosexuality, evil-founded partnerships and devil worship were concerned in the church.

I decided to have a period of six months to pray and discern the direction God could whisper to me in accordance with His word in Isaiah 30:21, where God says, *"Whether you turn to the right or to the left, you will hear a voice behind you, saying, 'This is the way, walk in it.'"*

I prayed to God for discernment on which of the **three options** available I would pursue:

The first of these options was to venture **back into education** by looking for a teaching position at a university. Remember, at one time, I was a senior lecturer at Daystar University, and the Vice Chancellor did not want to part with me, but because the church had recalled me, I had to leave. So, there was an open door for me to go back to Daystar or even look for another university because my credentials are good.

Secondly, like many people, I would have opted to look for ways to go overseas, and it would not have been difficult for me to **go to the USA**, a country I really love. It is there I spent much time as I took my post graduate studies. The people there are very receptive and full of kindness and understanding. America is a very accommodating country. It is a country that promotes the needy worldwide.

Thirdly, there was the option to **continue in the ministry**. In this case, I could register a ministry with the Kenyan Government as the law stipulates.

That being the case, I opted first to wait but **wait in prayer**. Through tough times of experience over the years, I have learned valuable lessons: Waiting may seem an easy thing to do, but it is **a discipline that a Christian soldier does not learn without years of training**. It calls for the fulfillment of God's words in Psalm 46:10; *"Be still and know that I am God."* While this is the crucial thing to do, marching and drills are much easier for God's warriors than standing still, For being still are **times of indecisions and confusion**, when even the most willing person, who eagerly desires to serve the Lord, does not know which direction to take.

So, what should you do when you find yourself in this situation? Should you allow yourself to be overcome with despair? Should you turn back or compromise in cowardice or in fear or rush ahead in ignorance?

The answer is No! You should simply wait- but wait and pray. Call upon God and plead your case before Him, telling Him of your difficulty and reminding Him of His promise to help. But you have to wait in faith for this is where faith is most applicable. It is an opportunity to express your unwavering confidence in God and to believe that even if He keeps you waiting until midnight, He will still come at the right time to fulfill His vision for you.

This means waiting in tested patience and never complaining about what you believe to be the cause of your problem, as the children of Israel did against Moses. Accept your situation as it is, and with your whole heart, place the problem into the hands of your covenant God. While removing any self-will, say to him, *"Lord, not my will, but yours be done."* (Luke 22:42). At such time, one says, I do not know what to do, but I am in great need. I will wait until you divide the floods before me or drive back the enemies. I will wait even if you keep me here many days, for my heart is fixed on you alone.

My spirit will wait for you with full confidence that you will be my joy and my salvation, *"for you have been my refuges, a strong tower against my foe"* (Psalm 61:3). These revelational thoughts became my shield. I further anchored my confidence in the words found in Psalm 18:2; *"The Lord is my rock, my fortress and my deliverer...in whom I take refuge. He is my shield and the horn of my salvation, my stronghold."*

In my prayers, I used to thank God by saying, *"Though I walk in the midst of trouble, you preserve my life; you stretch out your hand against the anger of my foes, with your right hand you save me... will fulfill his purpose for me"* (Psalm 138:7). I always felt great breakthroughs in my prayers for my conscience was quite clear. I had no regret in what I was doing. I also felt God's word constantly telling me that; *"I can do all things through Christ, who strengthens me"*, as Philippians 4:13 points out.

THE ESTABLISHMENT OF THE MINISTRY

After waiting for six months and fervently praying with intercessors from various locations, both within and outside of Kenya, it became clear that it was the opportune moment to resume and embark on a ministry journey. The intensity of our prayers played a pivotal role in this realization. My initial dilemma was deciding whether to align the ministry with the term '**church**' or '**altar**.' Through my studies, I have come to realize that the word church is not in the Bible. This may take most of the readers by surprise, but the truth of the matter is that what is referred to as the Greek word for the church, "Ecclesia" or 'Ekklisia' does not mean church in Greek.

The word church comes from the old German word '**Kirche**', which in Scotland and parts of England was written as Kirk and which in older Greek was pronounced 'ku-ri-a-kos' or 'kyriakon,' which means pertaining to. For example, 1st Corinthian 11:20 has "...the Lord's (kuriokos) Supper (deipnon).' This is because the word 'kuriakon' comes from the word 'kurios,' which means '**Lord**.' It was this word 'Kuriokos' that got translated as **CHURCH**, yet the word itself means pertaining to the Lord.

In the Oxford English Dictionary, the word *'ecclesia'* means, *'**summoned**."* This is the same as *'**called out**.'* Simply put, the word *'**Ecclesia**'* means *'**to call out**.'* This word was never used to refer to a group of religious people. *'Ecclesia'* is only used correctly in only three biblical verses found in Acts 19:32: *"Now some cried one thing, some another, for the '**assembly**' was in confusion and most of them did not know why they had come together.... but if you seek anything further, it*

514

shall be settled in the regular 'assembly'...he dismissed the 'assembly'" (emphasis is mine) (Acts 19: 39, 41).

The right Greek word for the bolded word *'assembly'* is *'ecclesia',* which, as it indicates, does not stand for church. Then the question comes: How did the word church come to be represented by the word *'ecclesia'* and not *'kurakkan?'* The accusing finger points at King James of England, who in 1611 embarked on the translation of the Bible.

He set up a group of people to carry out the translation but had them bound to adhere to the work in line with 15 rules, one of them being to strictly use the word *'ecclesia'* (*To Call Out*) for the word *'church.'*

King James knew that the word *'ecclesia'* was not even a synonym of the word church, and that was why he dictated the use of the word *'ecclesia.'* Henceforth, people have come to believe that *'ecclesia'* means church, which in reality is not true. The final product of the so-written Bible was King James Version (KJV) which was so widely used and was treated as almost sacred. Nobody dared to point to the misuse of the Greek word *'ecclesia'*, not even the **Puritans,** who were so critical of church doctrines.

Another perspective that I took in looking at the use of the word church is the way people have come to associate it with a building. Surprisingly, the **115** times the New Testament uses the word *'ecclesia'* it always refers to a *'called-out assembly'* and never to a building, yet it is common to hear a Christian going to a Sunday Service saying, **"I am going to the church,"** meaning, the person is going to a building whose identification is the name church.

The speaker here is referring to the church building, as the church. Another will say, *"I live two miles from our church."* In other words, the speaker here is telling us that he or she lives two miles from the building they call church. It is all about the church building. This revelation put me in a dilemma because I felt some reluctance in registering a ministry bearing the word church. It is for those reasons that in choosing the name of my ministry, I opted to adopt the word; **'Altar.'** But why the word Altar?

THE ALTAR

I picked this name, altar, as the pointer to the spiritual perspective of my ministry. The word altar bears a different perspective from the word church. But then one will ask: what is the difference between the word **Altar** and the word **Church**? My research showed me that an altar has far more spiritual authority in the spiritual realm than the word church. To begin with, the word altar appears **378** times in King James Version in **321** verses. Secondly, this word is spread all over the Bible from Genesis to Revelation.

This is not true of the word **church**. This word is not found in the Old Testament. In the gospels, it appears only once in Matthew 16:18, out of **3,779** verses in the synoptic gospels. The word church is found more in the Pauline letters and also in the book of Revelation. In total, this word appears **115** times in the Bible as compared to **378** times on the word **altar**. This means the word altar appears **263** times over the word church. This then shows the significance of the word altar over the word church. Altar carries far much anointing over the word church. After all, **the word church exists in a distorted fashion**. With this conviction, I decided on a ministry in the spirit of an altar.

The Christian altar is dedicated to speaking blessings upon it and through the application of the anointing oil and other elements like salt, plus some prophetic utterances. There is no altar worth its name that can be raised without anointing it, and all that pertains to the acts involved in the dedication. Jesus himself was anointed by Mary prior to his being killed by the Roman government. No king was consecrated without the use of oil, including David and Saul. God's altar carries heavenly anointing.

EL GIBBOR EVANGELISM AND INTERCESSORY ALTAR

Having prayed for six months in seeking God's direction, I decided to register a ministry called, **El Gibbor Evangelism and Intercessory Altar. El** is the Hebrew word for Lord God Almighty, and **Gibbor** stands for Almighty. This combination is found in **Isaiah 9:7**, that states, *"The zeal of the Lord Almighty will accomplish this."* El Gibbor has the same meaning as **El-Shaddai,** only that El-Shaddai has an additional meaning, that is, **Our All-Sufficient God**. In running this ministry, I wanted to highlight its main focus. I placed emphasis on two key aspects: **Evangelism** and **Intercessory**. That's why the ministry is called **El Gibbor Evangelism** and **Intercessory Altar**.

EVANGELISM

I included Evangelism because many modern churches have lost focus on it. They have become self-centered and neglected this vital power of the church. The Apostolic spirit of going out for Evangelism has become so much condensed to such an extent that most of the churches have a very squeezed budget for mission work. After witnessing this over the years in ministry, I decided to prioritize evangelicalism in my own ministry.

I see Evangelism as the primary way Jesus recommended for spreading the gospel. It was His final mandate to His disciples through the Great Commission; *"Therefore go and make disciples of all nations."* (Mt. 28:19). This is why, in registering El Gibbor Altar, I made evangelism one of the important arms of the ministry. This fact is supported by Emil Brunner (1931) and Thomas Schumacher, who are in agreement; thus, *"The church exists by mission just as a fire exists by burning. Where there is no church, there is no mission, and where there is neither church nor mission, there is no faith."* These scholars are affirmatively telling us that, without the enthusiasm for Evangelism, the church leaves a lot to be desired.

INTERCESSORY

This is another arm of the El Gibbor Altar. Prayerfulness is our focus. The importance of prayer in church life is indicated in Luke 11:1-4. The disciples could have asked for many other things, but they only asked Jesus this; *"Lord teaches us how to pray."* Praying is interceding. One of the main works of the Holy Spirit is the engagement in prayer. The Bible tells us that the Holy Spirit is an intercessor, *"but the Spirit Himself intercedes for us with groaning too deep for words"* (Rom. 8:26-ESV). Jesus had a ministry of intercession while He was here on Earth, showing us the importance of prayer.

THE TENETS OF FAITH AND BELIEFS OF EL GIBBOR ALTAR

Elgibbor Altar believes:

1. That the **Bible remains and will ever be the Authority** of God's Word. It is a breath of God.

2. That the **Church is the tool of God's Evangelism** and **Mission** as initiated by Jesus Christ, who came on earth as the first ever missionary of the New Testament Church, as Jesus himself stated in Luke 4:18-19.

3. That **Jesus Christ is the Way,** the Truth, and the Life. He is the bridge to reaching the Father and His Eternal Kingdom.

4. That the **Holy Spirit is the power** that comes from God to make things happen in the Body of Christ and has to be embraced.

5. That there is an **urgent need for the world revival** as the world continues to slide into decay. And that the birthing of End Time Revival will be midwifed through in-depth prayers, repentance and unity in the body of Christ.

6. That **Jesus died and was resurrected** so that believers *"might have life and have it abundantly,"* and he co-exists with the Father and the Holy Spirit.

7. That there is an **existence of evil powers and Godly powers**. The evil powers act against God's Kingdom. There exist two types of altars, just as there are two types of powers.

DO I HAVE ANY REGRETS ABOUT THIS TURBULENCE-MARKED PATH?

Even as you now approach towards the end of this book, one question that is likely to surface in the reader's mind is: Has the author ever regretted having plunged himself on this path of life? The answer to this is a big NO! Regret only comes from looking back. When I reflect on my ministry, I see abundant physical and spiritual fruits. In the Church work, I greatly brought restoration to the parishes when I became the chief administrator.

For example, before my being posted to Rongai parish which had 14 congregations, the parish was struggling both economically and spiritually. The denominations Business Committee proposed demolishing it and merging a section with Molo Parish to the north, another part being enjoined with Njoro Parish to the south and the rest with Nakuru Parish to the East. But the Appointment Committee recommended that I be posted there before conclusively dismantling it. Thus, in January 1986, I was posted to Rongai Parish.

They were not wrong. I had the life of the parish totally restored. The spiritual uplifting of the people greatly contributed to the economic life of the parish. The parish improved so much to the extent that it was recognized in a General Assembly as the most improved parish in the whole PCEA Church. It was among the best performers in the denomination. The same scenario was noticeable in the other parishes that I was posted to. It even turned out that I was henceforth being posted to the parishes that were experiencing both spiritual and physical constraints.

We find a similar positive restoration in Loresho Parish and Mathare Parishes which by then were both in Nairobi Presbytery. These two parishes were to extremes. While Loresho was comprised of extremely rich people but very low spiritually, Mathare Parish, on the other hand, was located in the Nairobi slums and was therefore comprised of very poor and spiritually low people. I revolutionized the spiritual life in Loresho and at Mathare Parishes. I greatly raised the standards both physically and spiritually. I finally subdivided Mathare Parish into two able parishes.

Prior to my becoming the Moderator, the Church was at a very low ebb, both spiritually and economically. The Moderator, by then, had written a letter to all congregations asking them to urgently double their giving as the Church was on the verge of bankruptcy. One of the renowned tele-evangelist Bishops in one of the Pentecostal Churches somehow saw that letter and boasted through the media that she could easily buy the PCEA Church, yet hers was a congregation Church.

When I became the Moderator, I had the whole life of the Church changed. The Church went into high gear spiritually, and it became so financially stable that we came up with many income-generating projects, including Milele Beach Hotel (formerly Giriama Hotel) in Mombasa, completed Milele Hotel located in South B in Nairobi. We also came up with the Milele Hotel in Nakuru Town. We even made a purchase of a building that had previously belonged to a famous politician's school, the late Arthur Magugu. I also started the Presbyterian University, where I became the first Chancellor. It did quite well during my tenure of office as Chancellor.

I restored many PCEA-owned institutions, which had become a laughing stock as their conditions had become pathetic over the years. I helped in the restoration of institutions like Kikuyu Hospital, Chogoria Hospital, Tumu Hospital and a number of schools. I also came up with ideas that will have a lasting impact for generations, including changes in worship styles for the PCEA. This truth is confirmed through one of the popular newspapers in Kenya, the Daily Nation, on Monday, February 20th. 2006, in which the reporter Mburu Mwangi, in his article titled: **A Reformist Unfazed By 100 Years of Church Tradition**, stated that:

"The Rt. Rev David Githii ascended to the leadership of the PCEA Church in a radical reform in the way members conducted themselves during prayers, breaking away from traditional methods of worship since the Church's inception by Scottish missionaries more than 110 years ago. Conservative methods of prayer soon gave way to more liberal worship to counter the growing threat of the more charismatic evangelical Churches. However, this was not without fierce resistance from the elderly members of the Church, who viewed Dr. Githii's changes suspiciously. Nevertheless, the new Moderator went ahead with this and other reforms. When they confronted him on the issue of 'satanic symbols', Dr. Githii led the anti-symbols crusade with gusto. He helped in the destruction of occult symbols estimated by retired cleric Timothy Njcya to be worth millions."

I am always thankful to God whose zeal, as stated in Isaiah 37:32, accomplished all this. He gave me the spirit of courage and non-compromising. The Bible refers to non- compromisers as those who; *"wash their robes that they may have the right to the tree of life so that they may go through the gates into the city"* (Rev. 21:14).

I am always grateful to God for blessing the work of my hands and expanding my boundaries in laboring in His vineyard. David's words in Psalm 4:1, *"Thou hast enlarged me when I was in distress,"* served as the foundation for this belief.

This verse explains my attitude towards the fiery life that I have been through. It is one of the greatest testimonies ever written regarding the effectiveness of God's work on our behalf during times of crisis. It is a statement of thanksgiving for having been set free not from suffering but rather through suffering. In stating, *"Thou hast enlarged me when I was in distress,"* the psalmist is declaring that the sorrows of life have themselves been the source of life's enlargement.

CALLED TO FIGHT THE GOOD FIGHT

In 1st Timothy 6:12, Paul calls upon Timothy to; *"Fight the good fight of faith."* Oh, if only we could see the powerful armies supporting us when we turn away from darkness towards God, we wouldn't be bothered by the enemy's attempts to distress or discourage us. Even the weakest believer, when they yield themselves to the Godhead in the name of Christ with childlike trust, receives the full support of God's miraculous attributes for help and guidance.

This is what this autobiographical book stands for. The book clearly gives a reflection of the good fight that I have fought and will continue to fight spiritually, politically, socially and economically. A fight aimed at the redemption of the oppressed, the disabled, men and women and the youth. It signifies a life well lived, free from compromise despite tempting influences. I've made it a habit to always look for the silver lining in stormy clouds. And once I find it, I continue to focus on it rather than on the dark gray in the center.

I always avoid getting discouraged, no matter how tough the opposition may seem. I strongly believe this is what God desires of each of His servants. He wants us to be; *'more than conquerors,'* turning stormy clouds into chariots of victory. An army *'becomes more than conquerors'* when it drives its enemies from the battlefield and confiscates their food and supplies. This is not true of a discouraged army because it enters the battlefield with the certainty of defeat. They easily compromise with the enemy and, therefore, become the enemy's plunder.

I find great inspiration in the words that describe the next phase of life for those who overcome. Revelation 12:11 says, "*They overcame by the word of their testimony, and they did not love their lives so much as to shrink from death.*"

My word to the reader is that: "*If you want your sympathy for others to be enlarged so that they can experience freedom, redemption and love, then you must have your life narrowed to certain degrees of suffering. For Joseph's dungeon was the very road to the throne. He would have been unable to lift the iron load placed on him by his brothers had he not experienced the iron in his own life. Your life will be enlarged in proportion to the amount of iron you have endured, for it is in the shadows of your life that you will find the actual fulfillment of your dreams of glory.*"

So do not complain about the shadows of darkness - *in reality, they are better than what your dreams could ever be.* Do not say the darkness of prison has shackled you, for your shackles are the wings - *wings of flight into the heart and soul of humanity.* And the gate of your prison is the gate into the heart of the universe. God has enlarged you through the suffering of sorrow's chain.

My reader, just think of this; **If Joseph never became a prisoner in Egypt, he would never have become Egypt's governor**. The iron chain that bound his feet brought about the golden chain around his neck. Every flower, even the most beautiful, has its own shadow beneath it as it basks in the sunlight. Also, *'where there is much light, there is also much shade.'* It's fascinating how certain flowers not only thrive in the shade but actually prefer dark corners, where they beautifully flourish without direct sunlight. It is true to say that if God has called one to His highest and best, then such a person will inevitably experience times of crisis. When faced with the failure of resources, one can either face ruin or discover something better than ever imagined or dreamed of.

When we have **a strong sense of determination** and *stay true to the path we believe is meant for us, incredible things can unfold in our lives.* It's about embracing the journey and trusting in our own unique path. But it is all safe if only we **rely on God's infinite help.** We must be willing to let go, surrender completely to Him, and cease from our own wisdom, strength and righteousness. We must be '*crucified with Christ*' (Gal. 2:20) and yet alive with Him. Only God knows how to lead His called ones to the point of crisis, and He knows how to lead them through it.

But this also calls for both obedience and a lot of patience in waiting upon him. This is why the psalmist says, *"I waited patiently for the Lord; he turned to me and heard my cry. He lifted me out of the slimy pit, out of the mud and mire; he set my feet on a rock and gave me a firm place to stand"* (Psalm 40:1-2). In 1 Samuel 15:23, when Saul lost patience in waiting for Samuel and went on with the sacrifice, Samuel told him, *"Because you have rejected the word of the Lord, He has rejected you as king."* Haven't each of us experienced this a thousand times and found it to be true?

In the course of this rough journey, I had always felt like Joseph. Someone had said of Joseph when he was in the dungeon, *'Iron entered his soul.'* And the strength of iron is exactly what he needed, for earlier, he had only experienced the **glitter of gold**. He had been rejoicing in youthful dreams, and dreaming actually hardens the heart. Otherwise, **someone who sheds great tears over simple romance or heartbreak** will not be of much help in a real crisis because true sorrow will be too deep for such a person. *We will need iron in life to enlarge our character.*

The gold is simply a passing vision, whereas the iron is the true experience of life. The chain that is the common bond uniting us to others must be one of iron. The common touch of humanity that gives the world true kingship is not joy, but sorrow-*gold is partial to only a few, but iron is universal.* The heavier the load of iron, the better the crown or robe in heaven. They are dressed in white robes.

No wonder an elder asked John:

"WHO ARE THESE ARRAYED IN WHITE ROBES, AND WHERE DID THEY COME FROM?"

" THESE ARE THE ONES WHO COME OUT OF GREAT AFFLICTION AND WASHED THEIR ROBES AND MADE THEM WHITE IN THE BLOOD OF THE LAMB. THEREFORE, THEY ARE BEFORE THE THRONE OF GOD AND SERVE HIM DAY AND NIGHT IN HIS TEMPLE..... THEY NEITHER HUNGER ANYMORE...THE LAMB...WILL SHEPHERD THEM AND...WILL WIPE AWAY EVERY TEAR FROM THEIR EYES" (Rev. 7:13-17: The Maxwell Leadership Bible).

SPEAKING ENGAGEMENTS

After my exit from PCEA, I was invited to speak in a church gathering based on *'overcoming leadership obstacles,'* they wanted me to focus my deliberations on how I managed to infiltrate into the so much spiritually hardened PCEA ground prior to my becoming the GA Moderator. Below, then, is the ground I covered in my deliberation.

In my opening remarks, I said,

"I had always expressed the fact that when God sent me to head PCEA, He was placing in me the same call He had placed in some biblical leaders like Jeremiah, Moses, Gideon; Josiah, Hezekiah; the Apostles, and even Kenyan Freedom Fighters like: Jomo Kenyatta, Dedan Kimathi, Jaramogi Oginga Odinga including my own father who was jailed for seven years with hard labour for being a prominent Mau Mau leader."

Each of these people were responding to a call they believed was from God to bring liberation in one way or another. Like them, I was obeying God's call when He spoke to me through these words; *"See, today I appoint you…. to uproot and tear down, to destroy and overthrow, to build and to plant"* (Jer. 1:10). God further said to me through his Word; *"Stand in the court of the Lord's house, and speak to all the people who come to worship in the Lord's house, tell them all the words that I command you to speak to them. Do not diminish a word. Perhaps everyone will listen and turn from his evil way, that I may relent concerning the calamity which I purpose to bring on them"* (Jer. 26:2-3, New King James Version).

To further show the seriousness of the call, again, God, through his Word, said, *"Get yourself ready! Stand up and say to them whatever I command you. Do not be terrified by them…. they will fight against you but will not overcome you, for I am with you and will rescue you."* (Jer. 1:17, 19). That is why I had that strong drive to uproot, destroy, tear down and overthrow the Scottish traditions, the Traditions of the Elders, and expose all kinds of occultism, especially those relating to Freemasonry, the New Age Movement and the Illuminati.

This also included exposing the hidden mysteries through which occultism operated in distorting and destroying PCEA as a denomination. That is a special anointing that God has bestowed upon me just as he does to those; *"who love him, who have been called according to His purpose"* (Rom. 8:28). The empowerment by God for a given cause was a common occurrence in the Bible. Think of David, when; *"Samuel took the horn of oil and anointed him…. from that day on the Spirit of the Lord came upon David with power"* (1 Sam. 16:13). In Psalms 89:20-2, God affirms his choice on David, saying, *"I have found David my servant, with my sacred oil I have anointed him. My hand will sustain him…"* In empowering his servants, God instills the power of the Holy Spirit. This is true in the life of Samson and Saul.

When a lion came roaring towards Samson, *"The Spirit of the Lord came upon him in power so that he tore the lion apart with his bare hands as he might have torn a young goat"* (Judges 14:6). When Samuel anointed Saul, he told him; *"The Spirit of the Lord will come upon you in power….do whatever your hand finds to do, for God is with you"* (1 Sam.10:6-7).

But that kind of empowerment does not occur to those who are chosen by people but God. If Samuel chose any of David's brothers, such as Eliab or Abinadab or any other of Jesse's sons, then God would not have provided that person with the power of His Spirit, for it would not be His choice. Samuel almost failed by considering his choice based on the human criteria of physical or external appearance. But God was quick to tell him, *"Do not consider his appearance or his height…The Lord does not look at the things man looks at. Man looks at the outside appearance, but the Lord looks at the heart"* (1 Sam.16:7).

Man's choice would not have killed Goliath nor brought any victory to the Israelites. Paul supports this argument when he says, *"And we know that in all things God works for the good of those who love him, who have been called according to his purpose…. And those he predestined, he also called, those he called, he also justified; those he justified, he also glorified"* Romans 8:28, 30).

These kinds of biblical references motivated my spirit and gave me great confidence and trust in God and, more so, the fact that God could not leave or forsake me. It was with this understanding that I stuck on the door of my office these words; '**When God sends us on a stony path, He provides strong shoes.**' God cannot send any of His ambassadors without equipping him or her well. But it is as long as that person is closely attached to God, like David and as long as that person has the heart of Christ and strives to move along in sync with the spirit of the Ten Commandments. I use the word; **'strive'** because the path is slippery.

The other encouragement that God gave me was the words He spoke through the prophet Isaiah; *"No weapon fashioned against you will prevail, and you will refute every tongue that accuses you"* (Isa. 54:17). The Lord also encouraged me further through his words of promise; *"If anyone attacks you, it will not be my doing; whoever attacks you will surrender to you"* (Isa. 54:15.).

It was with that confident assurance of God's support that I took the theme based on Luke 13:8b; *'Leave it alone… and I will dig around it and fertilize it.'* God revealed to me that PCEA could be likened to the tree referred to in this verse. The gardener had neglected it and that was why the owner proposed it be cut down.

In the same vein, I realized that PCEA had a lot of spiritual potentiality which had been dwarfed by the Scottish traditions. These are the so-called Traditions of the Elders and other occultic-related pollution which rendered infertile the spiritual soil from which the Church *'tree'* fed. The traditions were like bushes that had malnourished the PCEA spiritual tree over many years. To make it worse, new bitter roots in the form of homosexuality, lesbianism and corruption had crept in.

Quite often I kept wondering why the church leadership could not comprehend the simple concept in my teachings. It had great and relevant ways to handle church affairs. But then, the Holy Spirit reminded me of the negative attitude of Jewish leaders towards Jesus when he expected them to respond positively and embrace His teachings. This is because they perceived Jesus as one bent on breaking their traditions. They even questioned whose authority he did what he did.

But Jesus told them, *"If you hold to my teaching, you are really my disciples. Then you will know the truth, and the truth will set you free"* (Jn. 8:31-33). They quickly came into the defense of their traditions by saying, *"We are Abraham's descendants and have never been slaves of anyone. How can you say that we shall be set free?"* (Jn. 8:33). And from that time, Jews started plotting and strategizing how to derail Jesus' Ministry- but Jesus knew something that the Jews didn't know, that, as far as His ministry was concerned, not even; *"The gates of hell will overcome it"* (Mt. 16:18).

I was thus viciously confronted by the Liberals because of the same mentality that existed in the times of Jesus. I was seen as one bent on breaking traditions. The liberals claimed sole ownership of the PCEA and, hence, the custodians of its Scottish heritage. Their main role is always to derail the Church from the spiritual path as outlined in the word of God and to plunge it more and more into paganism under the guise of *'preservation of Scottish heritage.'* This was why they were angered by my calling upon the Church to cleanse all the wickedness that was creeping in to cripple the denomination.

Unfortunately, not many people, even among the church members, could easily buy into my revelation. Those things were so foreign to them. The Church lacked the medium of the Holy Spirit that could lead them to gain some understanding. In the absence of the Holy Spirit, there was no room left to discern the revelation God had bestowed upon me. Paul makes this clear when he says, *"The man without the Spirit does not accept the things that come from the Spirit of God, for they are foolishness to him, and he cannot understand them, because **they are spiritually discerned**"* (1 Cor.2:14).

I carried out a lot of teachings through sermons, writings, seminars, congregations and even in Church meetings. It is for that reason that I wrote the book; **'Phases of The Church'**, in which I traced the history of the Church universally and emphasized more on the history of the Presbyterian Church. In my expositions, I pointed out why Paul had to caution his opponents that the reason why they could not comprehend his message was that; *"We speak of God's secret wisdom, a wisdom that has been hidden and that God destined for our glory before time began. None of the rulers of this age understood it, for if they had, they would not have crucified the Lord of glory"* (1 Cor. 2:7- 8).

In 1Cor.2:13-14, Paul refers to *'deep things'* that he calls **'God's mysteries.'** On the same note, like Paul, I told my opponents that God has bestowed upon me a special revelation accompanied by a very strong sense of discernment.

I explained that God had favoured me in that He had removed all kinds of fear in my ministry. The devil uses fear to intimidate God's ambassadors, especially those who tend to expose his hidden mysteries, schemes and all kinds of manipulations. That was why Apostle Paul was quick to admit that the exposing of those mysteries was greatly resisted by the devil, who even created so much fear so that the truth would not be exposed. Hence, Paul called upon the Ephesian Christians to support him in his ministry. He said, "*Pray also for me, that whenever I open my mouth, words may be given to me so that I will **fearlessly** make known the mystery of the gospel.... pray that I may declare it fearlessly, as I should*" (Eph. 6:19-20-emphasis mine).

How did Paul attain that knowledge of God's mysteries? Well, it was not only through the Holy Spirit but also through his '**Great learning**' under such knowledgeable teachers like Gamaliel. It was in this same way that God revealed to me those mysteries through the power of the Holy Spirit but also through my learning under knowledgeable professors especially at the University of Dubuque in Iowa and Fuller Theological Seminary in California, USA. The research of my doctoral dissertation has taken me to the archives of Edinburgh University and The National Library, both in Scotland, and other research centers like Kenya National Archives, located in Nairobi.

My dissertation was based on tracing the role played by the PCEA in the development of Education in Kenya. Education was originally initiated by the pioneer missionaries from Scotland and later picked up by PCEA. I had, therefore, to go to Scotland for the research. It was through that research that I unearthed a lot of hidden mysteries of the Scottish traditions that, in their endeavor to plant the Gospel, the missionaries disguised as '**Christianity.**' I came to discover that those traditions had, over the years continued to hold PCEA hostage in both their spiritual and physical developments.

As stated above, it is unfortunate because when the missionaries brought the gospel into Africa, they never taught their converts how to overcome the schemes of the devil, including all kinds of his manipulations. They themselves did not know how to wage spiritual warfare since they had refused to embrace the power of the Holy Spirit, who is the source of such power. In fact, almost all of these missionaries even struggled in verbalizing a prayer in a Church service or any such place where one was to offer a prayer in public.

All such prayers were written down and read aloud as people listened quietly, meaning such a prayer did not come from the heart. The only Scottish missionary who was known to be a prayerful man of God was Dr. Irvine. As an intercessor, Irvine tried to create a prayerful Church at Chogoria, but he was greatly frustrated by other Scottish missionaries who insisted that the Church of Scotland did not believe in a Church that would embrace both the Holy Spirit and salvation among other Christian doctrines.

Knaap was another Spirit-filled missionary. He hailed from America, and his missionary work was supported by the Gospel Missionary Society (**GMS**). He established his mission work at Kambui, presently in Kiambu County. He believed in the Church's empowerment through the power of the Holy Spirit. He even baptized through immersion unlike the Scottish missionaries who baptized through sprinkling.

Unfortunately, he never trained leaders who could take over on the eve of his departure. He, therefore, handed over his well-established ministry to the Scottish missionaries whose headquarters was located at Thogoto. The latter discarded all the good Gospel traits that GMS had been anchored on, among them the influence of the Holy Spirit and baptism through immersion. The GMS Mission work was then swallowed up by the Church of Scotland Mission (CMS). Everything turned into Scottish culture.

Suffice it to say that many of the European missionaries were connected to the Masonic or Illuminati spirit – hence, they never pointed to their converts such biblical truths like: "*..our struggle is not against flesh and blood, but against rulers, against the authorities, against the powers of this dark world and against the spiritual forces of evil in the heavenly realms*" (Eph. 6: 12). It was a taste of Christianity but not the whole doze. In other words, it was a half-baked gospel.

In fact, the Holy Spirit was closed out, and anybody suspected of accommodating the Holy Spirit in any way in his or her Church life got excommunicated, yet the Bible says, "*cursed is the one who blasphemes the Holy Spirit.*" In this case, PCEA had been operating under this sort of a curse until that time I became the GA Moderator, and by God's help, I streamlined the way for the Church to accept the role of the Holy Spirit in the Church, including the creation of a new logo.

It was not until then that the Church embraced musical instruments and joyfully engaged in worshipping the living God as it should be. The church, over the years had been in spiritual imprisonment. They were not exposed to the spiritual armor with which they were to confront Satan. I even commissioned intercessors in every denominational Presbytery and Parishes.

The African music was rhythmical in style, while the missionaries' one was static and motionless- it was seen as the civilized way of worshiping God. On the other hand, as they put it, the African way was a symbol of paganism portraying evil. That was why I had to fight hard to have praise in worship to be incorporated into church music. The book of Psalms is all about praise. Paul also called Christians into praise when he told the Colossians, "*Let the word of God dwell in you richly as you teach and admonish one another with all wisdom, and as you sing Psalms, hymns and spiritual songs with gratitude in your hearts to God*" (Col. 3:16). Gratitude in your hearts, here means, with hearts puffed up with joy, the joy that is self-expressed externally. Psalms 47:1 affirms joyful praise when it says, "*Praise God, clap your hands for joy, all peoples with loud songs.*"

That move faced a lot of persecution from the liberals. There was even continuous scheming to have me impeached, as we have seen, but God stood with me. The words of Isaiah 41:10-11 kept on echoing in my mind; "*You are my servant; I have chosen you…. So do not fear, for I am your God. I will strengthen you and help you; I will uphold you with my righteous right hand. All who rage against you will surely be ashamed and disgraced; those who oppose you will be as nothing and perish.*" And true to these words, I have seen many fall by the wayside. Some of those were key Church leaders who plunged into total disgrace and shame. Some had their wicked ways exposed nationally, especially on issues of corruption.

As stated elsewhere, one of the main areas in which I came face to face with my opponents was when I embarked on changing the denomination's **JiteGemea** logo, which had a representation of the

Masonic god whose symbol is capital 'G.' This is affirmed by Yvonne in his book; **'Freemason: Death in the Family'** (Page 160), whereby he points to the fact the capital **G** is a representation of the Masonic deity known as the Great Architect of the Universe (**GAOTU**). Yvonne further reveals that 'G' also represents the '**Grand Geometrician**,' the generative principle and **Gnosticism**. The latter was one early Church cult that emphasized salvation through secret knowledge of the mysteries of the spiritual realm rather than the uniqueness of Jesus Christ. The capital G had cunningly been engraved in the Church logo through the word JiteGemea.

That's why when a new logo was created with the capital 'G' removed, PCEA had a spiritual breakthrough, and members started witnessing God's blessings. Things started happening in this Church hitherto not witnessed before. Such included rehabilitation of hospitals and academic institutions, the inflow of Christians who had left PCEA, the construction of new Churches, various subdivisions of Elder Districts, Parishes and Presbyteries and the birthing of many income-generating projects.

There was even an awakening in the life of PCEA's overseas influence, especially in England and the USA. I even tried to bring about the creation of an Overseas Presbytery, but this was greatly opposed by some leaders in the Church. In fact, I defended the pastors operating overseas by then because the liberals wanted to have them defrocked or expelled, claiming that they had deserted their duties by settling in America. This was a tough battle on my side. I thank God that I succeeded and the Diaspora Ministers were accepted by the Church through the Business Committee and even those who settled in America after them.

I have in mind such ministers who have tirelessly established PCEA-oriented Churches in America. In the past, I have personally participated in some of the services in these churches. There is also Rev. Kibathi, who has worked tirelessly to propagate God's kingdom in the United Kingdom. What makes me even more proud of these ministers is the fact that most of them happen to be my former students in theological schools in Kenya.

Whenever I have gone to America and witnessed the wonderful ministries and the spiritual influence the Diaspora Church ministers are imparting in this rapidly spiritually declining society, I am always thankful to God for using them to support the sustainability of the mission work in the Western countries, which were at one time, the prime movers of mission work in the world but have themselves turned into mission fields.

I have a dream that the universal Diaspora churches in Western countries will be the catalyst for the revival of the old churches. The Diaspora churches will act as yeast to cause the spiritual reawakening in those once vibrant denominations.

Joseph Parker, an English Congregationalist preacher of the nineteenth century, once said, "If we, as the Church, do not get back to spiritual visions, glimpses of heaven, and an awareness of a greater glory and life, we will lose our faith. Our altar will become nothing but a cold, empty stone, never blessed with a visit from heaven."

This, I think, is what befell the Western denominations. They lost their faith, and their altar became cold, empty cathedrals with empty pews and, hence, stopped experiencing visits from heaven. Ezekiel had the same observation over the Jerusalem Temple, where he says, "The glory of the Lord departed over the threshold of the temple" (Ezek. 10:18).

These are the denominations that once had spiritual wings spread out globally, spreading the good fragrance of the gospel, but unfortunately, they became faithless, and prayerlessness crept in. They looked at the Bible as an old write-up, not much different from the Greek and Roman writers like Aristotle, Socrates and Cicero, among others. They got disconnected from the heavenly antennae whose wiring is faith. It is that connection that brings about the beauty of heaven. Otherwise, brightly coloured sunsets and starry heavens, majestic mountains and shining seas, and fragrant fields and fresh-cut flowers are not even half as beautiful as a soul who is serving God out of love. This is despite the wear and tear of a believer's inner life of holiness, having carried his or her sweet bouquets like a fresh lily in a secluded valley on the edge of a crystal stream.

In the present world, God is looking for people who have seen their Lord but not the doubting Thomas. He is looking for those well-wired with heavenly power, people who are not looking for some external signs of confirmation that it is all possible to remain attached to the Tree of Life, and people who will not drift from the central part of faith.

As of now, God is looking for servants on whom He can place the weight of his entire love, power, and faithful promises. His engines are strong enough to pull any weight we may attach to them. In many instances, the cable we fasten to the engine is often too weak to handle the weight of our prayers. God, therefore, continues to train us in His refining school of faith as a way of getting rid of the dross of fear and untrustworthiness.

Such people, who are called, have to bear the spirit of the likes of Jomo Kenyatta, who, in wrestling for independence out of the colonial hands, asked the Kenyans, "*If I take hold of the mouth of the beast, will you withstand the back kicks?*" And the people unanimously agreed to this. With this unified resolve flooded under persecution, the colonialists were finally sent packing. This is the kind of spirit that God had bestowed upon me, as well. I called upon congregations and the spiritually untarnished clergy and elders to rally behind me.

SPOKEN WORDS OF WISDOM

1. C.S. Lewis

"You can't go back and change the beginning, but you can start where you are and change the ending." -C.S. Lewis is a famous writer and theologian.

2. L.B. Cowman (Statements from: "Streams in the Desert" by L.B. Cowman 1st. Published in 1925)

a. "Tribulations imprint is on every great achievement. It is the door to triumph."

"No one wins the greatest victory until he has walked the winepress of woe."

"The footprints are visible everywhere; the steps that lead to the thrones are stained with spattered blood and scars. And scars are the prize for scepters."

"We will wrestle our crowns from the giants we conquer. It is no secret that grief has always marked the trail of the reformer."

b. *Every great book has been written with the author's blood.*

c. "The strength of a hurricane can be demonstrated only by the hurricane. On the same note, the power of the gospel can be fully shone only when the believer is subjected to some fiery trials. For God to give songs in the night, the day has to fade away, and then God brings in the night."

3. Martin Luther King Jr.,

"The ultimate measure of a man is not where he stands in moments of comfort and convenience, but where he stands at times of challenge and controversy."-

4. Nelson Mandela

a."*Leadership is not about the size of your office or the title on your business card. It's about the depth of your commitment and the quality of your character.*"

b."A winner is a dreamer who never gives up."

c."*Difficulties break some men but make others.*"

d."Courageous people do not fear forgiving for the sake of peace."

e."*It is in your hands to create a better world for all who live in it.*"

f."*It always seems impossible until it's done.*"

5. Mahatma Gandhi

a."In a gentle way, you can shake the world."

b."*The best way to find yourself is to lose yourself in the service of others.*"

c."Strength does not come from physical capacity. It comes from an indomitable will."

d."*The future depends on what you do today.*"

e."An eye for an eye only ends up making the whole world blind."

f."*The best way to find yourself is to lose yourself in the service of others.*"

"THE ZEAL OF THE LORD GOD ALMIGHTY HAS ACCOMPLISHED THIS" (Isaiah 9:7)

A long journey begins with one step, and so with this book:

IT (book) IS FINISHED!

This book is part of the books that cover Dr. David M. Githii's autobiography. The others include; 'Life through the Burning Bush' and 'Called to serve relentlessly.'

Other books written by the author include; 'Progressive Infiltration of Idolatry into the Universal Church and Nations: A Chronological Perspective,' 'Kenya Repent or Perish,' 'How to Grow a Healthy' and 'Vibrant Church Through Small Church Groups,' 'Tithing: Principles and Practices,' 'Phases of The Church,' 'Exposing and Conquering Satanic Forces over Kenya." Unfortunately, apart from the 'Progressive Infiltration of Idolatry in the Universal Church and Nations' (a must-read book), all others are out of print.

Remarks by Githii's children on him:

1. **Nicholas muhia**

   I grew up knowing no other Hero, but my father. He has been a great father to us, bringing us in fear of God, in Christian life. He is a role model to me, to whom I admire many of his characteristics. He is a man of courage, God fearing, charismatic speaker, a leader, a teacher, full of wisdom, giver of the needy, and a man of the people. His heart is in the ministry, where he has served God truthfully. May God bless you father; may he give you strength and good health. May he give you many more years. May you be loved by your grandchildren and great grandchildren.

2. **Ben Muhia**

   Tribute by His Firstborn — Benson Githii Muhia
   They say a father is a mirror through which a son glimpses his future.
   If that's true, then I've been blessed to watch a lion walk through fire — unburned, unbowed, and unbought.
   Dr. David M. Githii is not just my father. He is a spiritual force. A reformer.
   A living sermon wrapped in courage.
   In a world drowned in noise, he dared to thunder truth.
   In the midst of storms, he danced with Scripture.
   And me? Well, as his firstborn, I once tried to argue with him using logic —
   I lost faster than Pharaoh's army in the Red Sea!
   Lesson learned: never debate a man who reads Greek, Hebrew, and Revelation for fun.
   I've watched him plant seeds in dry seasons — seeds that bloomed by faith alone.
   Scripture says, "The righteous man walks in integrity; his children are blessed after him."
   I am that blessing. I am that witness.
   Dad, you didn't just write books.
   You wrote legacy — into the world, and deep into our hearts.
   — Benson Githii Muhia

3. **Mary muhia**

   A lot can be said about my dad, but I will keep it brief. He is a giant of faith — steadfast, unwavering, and unafraid to stand alone. He has often said that he is at peace even when others oppose him, because as long as God is on his side, nothing else matters. His strength and conviction have been one greatest lessons in my life.

   Dad, I am the woman I am today because of you. Your faith has been my foundation, your wisdom my guide, and your courage my inspiration. Thank you for introducing me to faith — it has shaped my life as a wife, a mother, and the very essence of who I am. I am forever grateful to you
   Wangari

4. **A. Muhia**

   My father, Dr. David M. Githii, walks in integrity like few I've ever known. He doesn't just preach truth — he lives it. Transparent in his dealings, unwavering in his convictions, and unshakable in his faith, he has been a pillar in both the church and the community.

   As a former Moderator of the PCEA Church, his leadership was marked by bold decisions and servant-hearted reforms. He helped launch church partnerships, invested in people, and gave generously — not just in sermons but in substance. From establishing a secondary school to founding El Gibbor Ministries, his impact is still unfolding.

   "Mūndū mūnene ti ūrī indo, nī ūrī wendo." — A great person is not measured by possessions, but by love.

   Dad, your legacy isn't just in books or buildings — it's in people who now stand taller because you lifted them.
   — Amos Muhia